GALATIANS

VOLUME 33A

THE ANCHOR BIBLE is a fresh approach to the world's greatest classic. Its object is to make the Bible accessible to the modern reader; its method is to arrive at the meaning of biblical literature through exact translation and extended exposition, and to reconstruct the ancient setting of the biblical story, as well as the circumstances of its transcription and the characteristics of its transcribers.

THE ANCHOR BIBLE is a project of international and interfaith scope: Protestant, Catholic, and Jewish scholars from many countries contribute individual volumes. The project is not sponsored by any ecclesiastical organization and is not intended to reflect any particular theological doctrine. Prepared under our joint supervision, THE ANCHOR BIBLE is an effort to make available all the significant historical and linguistic knowledge which bears on the interpretation of the biblical record.

THE ANCHOR BIBLE is aimed at the general reader with no special formal training in biblical studies; yet it is written with the most exacting standards of scholarship, reflecting the highest technical accomplishment.

This project marks the beginning of a new era of cooperation among scholars in biblical research, thus forming a common body of knowledge to be shared by all.

William Foxwell Albright
David Noel Freedman
GENERAL EDITORS

THE ANCHOR BIBLE

GALATIANS

◆

A New Translation
with Introduction and Commentary

J. LOUIS MARTYN

THE ANCHOR BIBLE
Doubleday
New York   London   Toronto   Sydney   Auckland

THE ANCHOR BIBLE
PUBLISHED BY DOUBLEDAY
a division of Bantam Doubleday Dell Publishing Group, Inc.
1540 Broadway, New York, New York 10036

THE ANCHOR BIBLE, DOUBLEDAY, and the portrayal of an anchor with
the letters A and B are trademarks of Doubleday, a division
of Bantam Doubleday Dell Publishing Group, Inc.

Library of Congress Cataloging-in-Publication Data

Bible. N.T. Galatians. English. Martyn. 1997.
    Galatians: a new translation with introduction and commentary /
by J. Louis Martyn. — 1st ed.
    p.   cm. — (The Anchor Bible ; 33A)
    Includes bibliographical references and indexes.
    1. Bible. N.T. Galatians—Commentaries.   I. Martyn, J. Louis
(James Louis), 1925–   . II. Title.   III. Series: Bible. English.
Anchor Bible.   1964 : v. 33A.
BS192.2.A1   1964.G3   vol.33A
[BS2683]
227'.4077—dc21   96-37760
                                                         CIP

ISBN 0-385-08838-8
Copyright © 1997 by Doubleday, a division of Bantam
Doubleday Dell Publishing Group, Inc.

10 9 8 7 6 5 4 3 2 1

For
Ernst Käsemann

CONTENTS

◆

Contents

Contents

PREFACE

◆

During the years in which this volume has been in preparation, I have happily incurred numerous debts to earlier commentators — especially H. Schlier, F. Mussner, and H. D. Betz — to seminar students, to graduate assistants, to several colleagues and friends, and to the learned and generous-spirited editor, Noel Freedman. I thank them all. Near the close of the work, almost the whole of the manuscript received the detailed and perceptive critique of Paul W. Meyer. Former students of this scholar will be able to imagine the profound nature of his notes, many of which, being essays in themselves, formed the basis of unhurried discussions in which I was without exception instructed in matters of import for the understanding of Paul's Galatian letter. Together with those who use this commentary, I am greatly indebted to this true confrere for sharing his remarkable gifts.

The volume is dedicated to the interpreter whose reading of Paul's letters has fundamentally influenced my own, and whose enthusiastic friendship has been for almost half a century a gracious source of encouragement. Comrades for a few days within the Day of God.

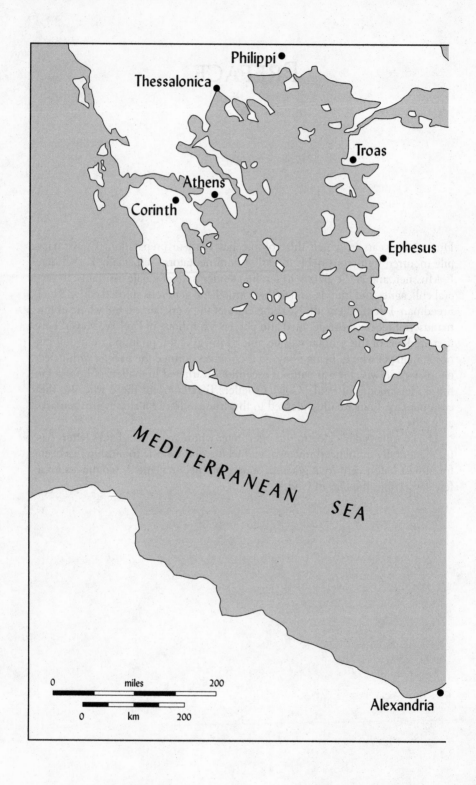

Philippi

Thessalonica

Troas

Athens

Corinth

Ephesus

MEDITERRANEAN SEA

0   miles   200

0   km   200

Alexandria

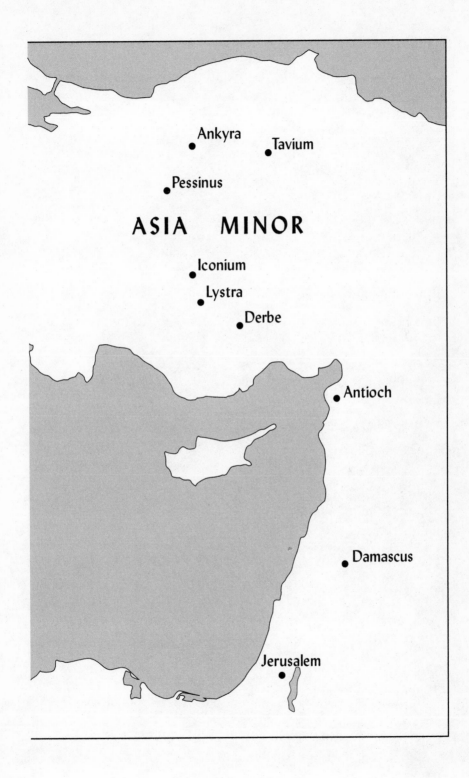

ABBREVIATIONS

◆

BIBLICAL BOOKS (WITH THE APOCRYPHA)

ABBREVIATIONS are those used by the Society of Biblical Literature. Quotations are sometimes drawn from RSV and NRSV; where there is no notation, the translations are those of the author.

PSEUDEPIGRAPHA OF THE OLD TESTAMENT

ABBREVIATIONS are those used by the SBL (plus *JosAs* for *Joseph and Asenath*). Quotations are drawn from *OTP*, occasionally with minor changes made from the original texts.

THE WRITINGS OF PHILO

TEXTS: *LCL*, from which English quotations are drawn, sometimes altered slightly on the basis of the Greek.

ABBREVIATIONS

de Abr.	On Abraham
de Conf. Ling.	On the Confusion of Tongues
de Cong.	On the Preliminary Studies
de Dec.	On the Decalogue
de Deo	(see in Bibliography F. Siegert, *Philon*)
de Mut.	On the Change of Names
de Op. Mundi	On the Creation
de Post. Caini	On the Posterity and Exile of Cain
de Praem.	On Rewards and Punishments
de Sac.	On the Sacrifices of Abel and Cain
de Somn.	On Dreams
de Spec. Leg.	On the Special Laws
de Virt.	On the Virtues
de Vita Cont.	On the Contemplative Life
de Vita Mos.	On Moses
Heres	Who Is the Heir

Leg. ad Gai.	Embassy to Gaius
Leg. Alleg.	Allegorical Interpretation
Quest. Gen.	Questions and Answers on Genesis
Quod Det.	The Worse Attacks the Better
Quod Deus Imm.	On the Unchangeableness of God
Quod Omn.	Every Good Man Is Free

THE WRITINGS OF JOSEPHUS

TEXTS: *LCL*, from which English quotations are drawn, sometimes altered slightly on the basis of the Greek.

ABBREVIATIONS

Ant.	*Jewish Antiquities*
Ap.	*Against Apion*
J.W.	*Jewish War*

DEAD SEA SCROLLS

TEXTS: Usually E. Lohse (ed.), *Die Texte aus Qumran* (Darmstadt: Wissenschaftliche Buchgesellschaft, 1971); English quotations are drawn sometimes from G. Vermes, *The Dead Sea Scrolls in English* (3rd ed.; London: Penguin, 1987) and sometimes from F. G. Martinez, *The Dead Sea Scrolls Translated* (Leiden: Brill, 1994), occasionally altered slightly.

ABBREVIATIONS

CD	*Covenant of Damascus*
1QM	*War Rule*
1QS	*Rule of the Community*
1QSa	*Appendix to 1QS*
1QH	*Thanksgiving Hymns*
1QpHab	*Pesher on Habakkuk*
11QMelch	*Melchizedek*
11QTemple	*Temple Scroll*
4QFlor	*Florilegium (Midrash on the Last Days)*
4QMMT	*Miqsat Ma'aseh ha-Torah; Halakhic Letter*
4QpsDan Aa	*Pseudo-Daniel (4Q246)*
4QpNah	*Pesher on Nahum*

RABBINIC LITERATURE

TEXTS used by Elizabeth Shanks to make a final check of the rabbinic references:

Mishna: Shisha Sidrei Mishna (6 vols.; ed. C. Albeck; Jerusalem: Mossad Bialik, 1952–1958).

Tosepta: Tosepta 'al pi Ketav Yad Erfurt veVienna (ed. M. S. Zukermandel; supp. S. Lieberman; Jerusalem: Defus Merkaz, 1937).

Mekilta: Mekilta deRabbi Yishmael (ed. H. S. Horowitz; comp. Y. A. Rabin; Jerusalem: Sifre Wahrman, 1970).

Sipra: Sipra ha-Nikra Torat ha-Kohanim (ed. Y. Meir; Jerusalem: Defus Oren, 1983).

Babylonian Talmud: Vilna edition

Palestinian Talmud: Krotoshin edition

Genesis Rabba: Midrash Bereshit Rabba (3 vols.; ed. J. Theodor and C. Albeck; Jerusalem: Sifre Wahrman, 1865).

Lamentations Rabba: Midrash Ekhah Rabba (ed. S. Buber; Tel Aviv, 1963).

Canticles Rabba: Midrash Rabba Shir ha-Shirim (ed. S. Dunsky; Jerusalem: Devir, 1980).

Tanhuma: Midrash Tanhuma (ed. S. Buber; New York: Sefer Publications, 1946).

Midrash Psalms: Midrash Tehillim (ed. S. Buber; Jerusalem: Vogshel, 1966).

'Abot de Rabbi Nathan: 'Abot de Rabbi Natan (ed. S. Schechter; New York: Feldheim, 1967).

Pesiqta Rabbati: Pesiqta Rabbati: deRav Kahana im Arba Perushim (ed. S. A. Rubin; Jerusalem: HaVa ad leHotza at Kitvei ha-Garsha Rubin, 1968).

Pesiqta de Rab Kahana: Pesiqta deRav Kahana al pi Ketav Yad Oxford (2 vols.; ed. D. Mandelbaum; New York: JTS Publications, 1962).

Targums:

Fragment Targum: The Fragment Targums According to Their Extant Sources (2 vols.; ed. and trans. M. L. Klein; Rome: Biblical Institute Press, 1980).

Targum Onqelos: The Bible in Aramaic, Vol. I: The Pentateuch According to Targum Onkelos (ed. A. Sperber; Leiden: Brill, 1959).

Targum Pseudo-Jonathan: Targum Pseudo-Jonathan of the Pentateuch: Text and Concordance (ed. E. G. Clark; consult. W. E. Aufrecht, J. C. Hurd, and F. Spitzer; Hoboken: Ktav, 1984).

Targum Canticles: Hamesh Megillot (ed. D. Kafakh; Jerusalem: Ha-agudah le-hatsalat ginze Teman, 1962).

Targum of Isaiah: The Targum of Isaiah (ed. and trans. J. F. Stenning; Oxford: Clarendon, 1949).

ABBREVIATIONS

Mishna:

   m. 'Abot

m. B. Bat.	*Baba Batra*
m. Ber.	*Berakot*
m. Bik.	*Bikkurim*
m. Ned.	*Nedarim*
m. Rosh Hash.	*Rosh Hashana*
m. Sanh.	*Sanhedrin*
m. Sota	

Tosepta:

t. Shabb.	Shabbat
t. Sota	
Mek.	Mekilta

Sipra

Babylonian Talmud:

b. B. Mes.	Baba Mesia
b. B. Qam.	Baba Qamma
b. Ber.	Berakot
b. Mak.	Makkot
b. Ned.	Nedarim
b. Qidd.	Qiddushin
b. Sanh.	Sanhedrin
b. Shabb.	Shabbat
b. Sukk.	Sukka
b. Yebam.	Yebamot
b. Yoma	

Palestinian Talmud:

p. Bik.	Bikkurim
p. Ned.	Nedarim
Gen. Rab.	Genesis Rabba
Exod Rab.	Exodus Rabba
Lam. Rab.	Lamentations Rabba
Cant. Rab.	Canticles Rabba
Tanh.	Tanhuma
Midr. Pss.	Midrash Psalms
'Abot. Nat.	'Abot de Rabbi Nathan
Pesiq. R.	Pesiqta Rabbati
Pesiq. Rab Kah.	Pesiqta de Rab Kahana

Targums:

Fragment Targum	
Tg. Onq.	Targum Onqelos
Tg. Ps.-J.	Targum Pseudo-Jonathan
Tg. Cant.	Targum of Canticles
Tg. Isa	Targum of Isaiah

NONCANONICAL EARLY
CHRISTIAN LITERATURE

Ascents of James	*The Ascents of James* (cited by book, chapter, and verse in Clementine *Recognitions* and by page numbers in R. E. Van Voorst, *Ascents*, and F. S. Jones, *Source* [see Bibliography]).
Clementine *Hom.*; Clementine *Recog.*	Pseudo-Clementine *Homilies* and *Recognitions* (see B. Rehm in Bibliography)

Ep. Pet. Jas.	*The Epistle of Peter to James* (cited by chapter and verse, and by page numbers in HS)
Eusebius *EH*	Eusebius *Ecclesiastical History*
Herm. Man.	*Hermas Mandates*
Herm. Vis.	*Hermas Visions*
Ign. *Magn.*	Ignatius *Letter to the Magnesians*
Ign. *Smyr.*	Ignatius *Letter to the Smyrnaeans*
Irenaeus *Haer.*	Irenaeus *Against Heresies*
Justin *1 Apol.*	Justin *First Apology*
Justin *Dial.*	Justin *Dialogue with Trypho*
Testim. Truth	*Testimony of Truth*

GREEK AND LATIN LITERATURE

(Neither Jewish nor Christian. The works are sometimes abbreviated in obvious ways.)

Achilles Tatius
Aristides *Orationes*
Aristophanes *Lysistrata*
Aristotle
  Metaphysics
  Rhetoric
Artemidorus Daldianus
Cicero *Topica*
Demosthenes *Epistolae*
Diodorus Siculus
Diogenes Laertius *Lives*
Empedocles
Epictetus
  Discourses
  Enchiridion
Epicurus *Sententiae*
Euripides *Iphigenia Taurica*
Galen
Heraclitus
Hesiod *Works and Days*
Homer
  Iliad
  Odyssey
Lysias
Petronius *Satyricon*
Philostratus *Apollonius*
Plato
  Apology
  Gorgias

  Laws
  Phaedrus
  Philebus
  Theages
Plutarch
  Demosthenes
  Moralia
Polybius
Quintilian *Institutio Oratoria*
Seneca *Epistolae*
Sophocles *Trachiniae*
Thucydides

COMMENTARIES ON GALATIANS

The name of an author either standing alone or followed by a page number refers to a commentary on Galatians (included is B. M. Metzger, *A Textual Commentary on the Greek New Testament*).

Amiot, F., *Saint Paul: Epître aux Galates. Epîtres aux Thessaloniciens* (Paris: Beauchesne, 1946).

Aquinas, T., *Commentary on St. Paul's Epistle to the Galatians* (trans. F. R. Larcher; Albany: Magi, 1966).

Becker, J., *Der Brief an die Galater* (Göttingen: Vandenhoeck & Ruprecht, 1976).

Betz, H. D., *Galatians* (Philadelphia: Fortress, 1979).

Bligh, J., *Galatians: A Discussion of St. Paul's Epistle* (London: St. Paul, 1969).

Bonnard, P., *L'Epître de Saint Paul aux Galates* (Neuchâtel: Delachaux & Niestle, 1972).

Borse, U., *Der Brief an die Galater* (Regensburg: Pustet, 1984).

Bring, R., *Commentary on Galatians* (Philadelphia: Muhlenberg, 1961).

Bruce, F. F., *Commentary on Galatians* (Grand Rapids: Eerdmans, 1982).

Burton, E. D., *The Epistle to the Galatians* (Edinburgh: T. & T. Clark, 1921).

Calvin, J., *The Epistles of Paul the Apostle to the Galatians, Ephesians, Philippians and Colossians* (Grand Rapids: Eerdmans, 1965).

Cole, R. A., *Galatians* (Grand Rapids: Eerdmans, 1989).

Cousar, C. B., *Galatians* (Atlanta: Knox, 1982).

Duncan, G. S., *The Epistle of Paul to the Galatians* (London: Hodder & Stoughton, 1934).

Dunn, J. D. G., *The Epistle to the Galatians* (London: Black, 1993).

Erasmus, D., *Paraphrases on Romans and Galatians* in *The Collected Works of Erasmus*, vol. 42 (ed. R. D. Sider; Toronto: Univ. of Toronto Press, 1984).

Fitzmyer, J. A., "Galatians," *NJBC*.

Fung, R. Y. K., *Galatians* (Grand Rapids: Eerdmans, 1988).

Getty, M. A., *A Commentary on Galatians and Romans* (Garden City: Image Books, 1982).

Hansen, G. W., *Galatians* (Downers Grove: InterVarsity, 1994).

Lagrange, M.-J., *Saint Paul Epître aux Galates* (Paris: Gabalda, 1950).

Lietzmann, H., *An die Galater* (4th ed., with a postscript by P. Vielhauer; Tübingen: Mohr/Siebeck, 1971).

Lightfoot, J. B., *The Epistle of St. Paul to the Galatians* (original, 1865; Grand Rapids: Zondervan, 1957).

Longenecker, R. N., *Galatians* (Dallas: Word, 1990).

Lührmann, D., *Der Brief an die Galater* (Zürich: Theologischer Verlag, 1978); *Galatians* (Minneapolis: Fortress, 1992); in general, page numbers refer to the German edition.

Luther, M., *Lectures on Galatians — 1535 — Chapters 1–4* and *Lectures on Galatians — 1535 — Chapters 5–6; 1519–Chapters 1–6* (*Luther's Works*; 55 vols.; ed. J. Pelikan; Saint Louis: Concordia, 1955–1976) vols. 26 and 27.

Lyonnet, S., *Les Epîtres de Saint Paul aux Galates, aux Romains* (Paris: Cerf, 1966).

Matera, F. J., *Galatians* (Collegeville: Glazier, 1992).

Metzger, B. M., *A Textual Commentary on the Greek New Testament* (London: United Bible Societies, 1971).

Mussner, F., *Der Galaterbrief* (Freiburg: Herder & Herder, 1974).

Neil, W., *The Letter of Paul to the Galatians* (Cambridge: Cambridge Univ. Press, 1967).

Oepke, A., *Der Brief des Paulus an die Galater* (rev. by J. Rohde; Berlin: Evangelische Verlagsanstalt, 1973).

Osiek, C., *Galatians* (Wilmington: Glazier, 1980).

Rohde, J., *Der Brief des Paulus an die Galater* (Berlin: Evangelische Verlagsanstalt, 1989).

Schlier, H., *Der Brief an die Galater* (Göttingen: Vandenhoeck & Ruprecht, 1961).

Sieffert, F., *Der Brief an die Galater* (Göttingen: Vandenhoeck & Ruprecht, 1899).

Zahn, T., *Der Brief des Paulus an die Galater* (Leipzig: Deichert, 1905).

GENERAL ABBREVIATIONS

AB	Anchor Bible
ABD	*Anchor Bible Dictionary* (ed. D. N. Freedman; New York: Doubleday, 1992)
AJBI	*Annual of the Japanese Biblical Institute*
ANRW	*Aufstieg und Niedergang der Römischen Welt* (ed. H. Temporini and W. Haase; Berlin: de Gruyter, 1971–)
ATR	*Anglican Theological Review*
BAGD	W. Bauer, W. F. Arndt, F. W. Gingrich, and F. W. Danker, *A Greek-English Lexicon of the New Testament and Other Early Christian Literature* (Chicago: Univ. of Chicago Press, 1979)

BDF	F. Blass and A. Debrunner, *A Greek Grammar of the New Testament and Other Early Christian Literature* (trans. and rev. R. W. Funk; Chicago: Univ. of Chicago Press, 1961)
BETL	Bibliotheca Ephemeridum Theologicarum Lovaniensium
Bib	*Biblica*
BibInt	*Biblical Interpretation*
Billerbeck	H. Strack and P. Billerbeck, *Kommentar zum Neuen Testament aus Talmud und Midrash* (6 vols.; Munich: Beck, 1926–63)
BJRL	*Bulletin of the John Rylands Library*
CBQ	*Catholic Biblical Quarterly*
CR	*Critical Review of Books in Religion*
DK	H. Diels and W. Kranz, *Die Fragmenta der Vorsokratiker* (3 vols.; Berlin: Weidmann, 1951–1952)
EA	*Ex Auditu*
EDNT	*Exegetical Dictionary of the New Testament* (ed. H. Balz and G. Schneider; Grand Rapids: Eerdmans, 1990–)
EJ	*Encyclopedia Judaica*
EvT	*Evangelische Theologie*
ExpTim	*Expository Times*
FBK	P. Feine, J. Behm, and W. G. Kümmel, *Introduction to the New Testament* (Nashville: Abingdon, 1966)
FV	*Foi et Vie*
HeyJ	*Heythrop Journal*
HR	*History of Religion*
HS	E. Hennecke, *New Testament Apocrypha* (2 vols.; ed. W. Schneemelcher; Philadelphia: Westminster, 1963–65)
HTR	*Harvard Theological Review*
IBS	*Irish Biblical Studies*
IDB	*Interpreter's Dictionary of the Bible*
IDBS	*Interpreter's Dictionary of the Bible Supplement*
IEJ	*Israel Exploration Journal*
Int	*Interpretation*
JBC	*Jerome Biblical Commentary* (ed. R. E. Brown et al.; Englewood Cliffs: Prentice-Hall, 1968)
JBL	*Journal of Biblical Literature*
JJS	*Journal of Jewish Studies*
JR	*Journal of Religion*
JRH	*Journal of Religious History*
JSHRZ	*Jüdische Schriften aus hellenistisch-römischer Zeit* (ed. W. G. Kümmel; Gütersloh: Mohn, 1973)
JSNT	*Journal for the Study of the New Testament*
JSS	*Journal of Semitic Studies*
JTC	*Journal for Theology and Church*
JTS	*Journal of Theological Studies*
Judaica	*Judaica: Beiträge zum Verständnis . . .*

KB	L. Koehler and W. Baumgartner, *Lexicon in Veteris Testamenti Libros* (Leiden: Brill, 1958)
LCL	*Loeb Classical Library*
lit.	literally
LSJ	H. G. Liddell and R. Scott, *A Greek-English Lexicon* (2 vols.; rev. and aug. H. S. Jones; Oxford: Clarendon, 1951)
LuthW	*Luther's Works* (ed. J. Pelican and H. Lehman; Philadelphia: Fortress, 1958–1986)
LXX	Septuagint
MH	J. H. Moulton and W. F. Howard, *A Grammar of New Testament Greek*, vol. 2 (Edinburgh: T. & T. Clark, 1928)
MM	J. H. Moulton and G. Milligan, *The Vocabulary of the Greek Testament Illustrated from the Papyri* (London: Hodder & Stoughton, 1930)
MT	J. H. Moulton and N. Turner, *A Grammar of New Testament Greek*, vol. 3 (Edinburgh: T. & T. Clark, 1963)
MTZ	*Münchener theologische Zeitschrift*
Neot	*Neotestamentica*
NJBC	*The New Jerome Biblical Commentary* (ed. R. E. Brown et al.; London: Chapman, 1995)
NovT	*Novum Testamentum*
NTS	*New Testament Studies*
OHCW	*The Oxford History of the Classical World* (ed. J. Boardman, J. Griffon, and O. Morray; Oxford: Oxford Univ. Press, 1986)
OTP	*The Old Testament Pseudepigrapha* (2 vols.; ed. J. H. Charlesworth; New York: Doubleday, 1985)
PSB	*Princeton Seminary Bulletin*
RAC	*Reallexicon für Antike und Christentum* (ed. T. Klausner; Stuttgart: Hiersmann, 1950–)
RB	*Revue Biblique*
RGG	*Die Religion in Geschichte und Gegenwart* (ed. K. Galling; Tübingen: Mohr/Siebeck, 1957–1965)
RSR	*Religious Studies Review*
SBL	Society of Biblical Literature
SJT	*Scottish Journal of Theology*
ST	*Studia theologica*
TAPA	*Transactions of the American Philological Association*
TDNT	*Theological Dictionary of the New Testament* (10 vols.; ed. G. Kittel and G. Friedrich; Grand Rapids: Eerdmans, 1964–1976 [German volumes began in 1933])
TEH	*Theologische Existenz Heute*
TLZ	*Theologische Literaturzeitung*
TRE	*Theologische Realenzyklopädie*
TrinJ	*Trinity Journal*
TS	*Theological Studies*

TTZ	*Trierer theologische Zeitschrift*
TU	*Texte und Untersuchungen*
TZ	*Theologische Zeitschrift*
USQR	*Union Seminary Quarterly Review*
VF	*Verkündigung und Forschung*
WD	*Wort und Dienst*
WF	*Wege der Forschung*
WW	*Word and World*
ZBG	M. Zerwick, *Biblical Greek* (Rome: Biblical Institute, 1963)
ZNW	*Zeitschrift für die neutestamentliche Wissenschraft*
ZTK	*Zeitschrift für Theologie und Kirche*

TRANSLATIONS OF THE BIBLE

JB	*Jerusalem Bible*
NAB	*New American Bible*
NEB	*New English Bible*
NJB	*New Jerusalem Bible*
NRSV	*New Revised Standard Version*
REB	*Revised New English Bible*
RSV	*Revised Standard Version*

TO THE GALATIANS: A TRANSLATION

◆

Chapter 1 1:1. Paul, an apostle — that is to say a person who has been sent on a mission; sent, however, not by a group of other human beings, nor even by an individual human being, but rather by Jesus Christ and God the Father, who raised him from the realm of those who have died — 2. and all of the brothers and sisters who are with me; to the churches of Galatia: 3. May grace and peace come to you from God our Father and from the Lord Jesus Christ, 4. "who gave up his very life for our sins," so that he might snatch us out of the grasp of the present evil age, thus acting in accordance with the intention of God our Father. 5. To God be glory throughout the whole of eternity. Amen!

6. I am amazed that you are so rapidly defecting from the God who called you in his grace, and are turning your allegiance to a different gospel. 7. Not that there really is another gospel; but the point is that there are now among you some persons who are frightening you and whose preaching shows that they wish to change the gospel of Christ into its opposite. 8. Regardless of who might preach it — whether I myself or an angel from heaven — if someone should preach to you a gospel contrary to the gospel I preached to you, let him stand under God's curse. 9. As I have said before, I say now once again, if someone is preaching to you a gospel contrary to the one you originally received, let him stand under God's curse.

10. Am I now engaged in rhetorical arguments designed to sway the crowds; or am I intent on pleasing God? Do I seek merely to please human beings? If I were still doing that, I would not be a slave of Christ.

11. For, concerning the gospel preached by me, I want you to know, my brothers and sisters, that it is not what human beings normally have in mind when they speak of "good news." 12. For I did not receive it from another human being, nor was I taught it; it came to me by God's apocalyptic revelation of Jesus Christ.

13. I can give the grounds for that assertion by tracing God's way with me. You have already heard some things about my past, the course and nature of my life when I lived in the religion of Judaism. You know that for some time I persecuted the church of God to an extreme degree; I even had it as my goal to destroy it entirely. 14. And my doing that sprang from the fact that in regard to matters of

the Jewish religion I outstripped many of my fellows, being far more zealous than they for the traditions handed down from my forefathers. 15. But all of that came to an end. God had in fact singled me out even before I was born, and had called me in his grace. So when it pleased him 16. apocalyptically to reveal his Son to me, in order that I might preach him among the Gentiles, I immediately kept to myself, not asking advice from anyone.

17. Nor did I make a trip up to Jerusalem to see those who were already apostles before I became one. On the contrary, I went away to Arabia, and later I returned to Damascus.

18. Then, after three years had passed, I did go up to Jerusalem in order to visit Cephas, and I stayed with him two weeks. 19. I saw none of the other apostles, except James, the brother of the Lord. 20. What I am writing to you now is no lie, God being my witness! 21. Then, I went to the regions of Syria and Cilicia. 22. And through the whole of this time, I was still unknown by sight to the churches of Judea which are in Christ. 23. They only heard it said about me that "the man who formerly persecuted us is now preaching the faith that he had earlier tried to destroy"; 24. time and again they ascribed glory to God because of me.

Chapter 2 2:1. Then, after fourteen years, I went up to Jerusalem again, accompanied by Barnabas; and I also took along Titus. 2. I went up as a result of revelation. And I communicated to them the gospel that I preach among the Gentiles; then I did the same thing in a private setting with those who were the acknowledged leaders, lest it should somehow turn out that in my work I was running or had run in vain. 3. But my anxiety proved baseless, for Titus, who was with me, was not compelled to be circumcised, even though he was a Greek. 4. Yet, because of the False Brothers, secretly smuggled in, who indeed came in stealthily in order to spy out our freedom that we have in Christ Jesus, their purpose being to enslave us, 5. to whom we did not give in even momentarily, so that the truth of the gospel might remain, coming eventually to you. 6. Moreover, from the acknowledged leaders of the Jerusalem church — what sort of persons they were is to me a matter of no consequence; God does not play favorites — those leaders did not add anything to my gospel. 7. On the contrary, they saw clearly that I had been entrusted by God with the gospel as it is directed to those who are not circumcised, just as Peter had been entrusted with the gospel to those who are circumcised. 8. For he who was at work in Peter, creating an apostolate to those who are circumcised, was also at work in me, sending me to the Gentiles. 9. Coming to see that fact, and thus coming to perceive the grace given to me by God, James and Cephas and John — those held by the Jerusalem church to be "the pillars" — shook hands with me and Barnabas, signifying that, in fellowship with one another, we were to go to the Gentiles and they to those who are circumcised. 10. The only other move on their part was a request that we remember "the poor," and this was a request which I was eager to carry out.

11. But when Cephas came to Antioch, I opposed him to his face, because in fact he stood condemned. 12. It happened in this way: Before the arrival of some

messengers from James, Cephas ate regularly with the Gentile members of the Antioch church. But when those men came, he drew back and separated himself from the Gentile members, because he was afraid of the circumcision party. 13. The other Jewish members of the Antioch church joined him in playing the hypocrite, so that even Barnabas was carried away by their hypocrisy. 14. But when I saw that they were not living out the truth of the gospel in a single-minded fashion, I said to Cephas, in front of the whole church, "You, a Jew by birth, are living like a Gentile, not like a Jew. How can you then compel the Gentile members of the church to live in the Jewish manner? . . ."

15. We are by nature Jews, not "Gentile sinners." 16. Even we ourselves know, however, that a person is not rectified by observance of the Law, but rather by the faith of Christ Jesus. Thus, even we have placed our trust in Christ Jesus, in order that the source of our rectification might be the faith of Christ and not observance of the Law; for not a single person will be rectified by observance of the Law. 17. If, however, seeking to be rectified in Christ, we ourselves have been perceived to be sinners, then is it true that Christ has become a servant of sin? Absolutely not! 18. For, as the incident in Antioch reveals, the way in which I would show myself to be a transgressor would be to rebuild the walls of the Law that I have torn down. 19. For, I have died to the Law, through the Law, in order that I might live to God. I have been crucified with Christ. 20. It is no longer I who live, but rather Christ lives in me, and the life I now live in the flesh I live in faith, that is to say in the faith of the Son of God, who loved me and gave himself up to death for me. 21. I do not nullify God's grace! For if it were true that rectification comes through the Law, then Christ would have died for no purpose at all.

Chapter 3 3:1. You foolish Galatians! Who has cast a spell on you, doing so in spite of the fact that in my sermons a picture of Jesus Christ marked by crucifixion was painted before your eyes? 2. Tell me just one thing! Did you receive the Spirit because you observed the Law, or as a result of the proclamation that has the power to elicit faith? 3. Are you really so foolish as to think that, having begun in the Spirit, you are now being perfected by means of the flesh? 4. Have you experienced such remarkable things in vain, if, indeed, that is conceivable? 5. When God even now supplies the Spirit to you, and when he works wonders in the midst of your communities, is he doing those things because you observe the Law, or is he doing them through the proclamation that elicits your faith?

6. Things were the same with Abraham: "He trusted God, and, as the final act in the drama by which God set Abraham fully right, God recognized Abraham's faithful trust." 7. You know, therefore, that those whose identity is derived from faith, these are the children of Abraham. 8. And the scripture, foreseeing what is now happening—namely that God is rectifying the Gentiles on the basis of faith—preached the gospel ahead of time to Abraham, saying, "In you all the Gentiles will be blessed." 9. So then, it is those whose identity is derived from faith who are blessed with faithful Abraham.

10. For those whose identity is derived from observance of the Law are under

the power of a curse, because it stands written: "Cursed is everyone who is not steadfast in observing all of the things written in the book of the Law, so as to do them." 11. That before God no one is being rectified by the Law is clear from the fact that, "The one who is rectified by faith will live." 12. Moreover, the Law does not have its origin in faith; if it did have its origin there, it would not say, "The one who does the commandments will live by them."

13. Christ redeemed us from the Law's curse, becoming a curse in our behalf; for it stands written: "Cursed is everyone who is hanged on a tree." 14. He did this in order that the blessing of Abraham might come to the Gentiles in Jesus Christ; in order, that is, that we might receive the promise, which is the Spirit, through faith.

15. Brothers and sisters, drawing an illustration from everyday life among human beings, let me say that once a person has ratified his will, no one annuls it or adds a codicil to it. 16. Now the promises were spoken to Abraham "and to his seed." The text does not say, "and to the seeds," as though it were speaking about many people, but rather, speaking about one, it reads, "and to your seed," and that seed is Christ. 17. What I am saying is this: The covenant, validated by God when he gave it, is something that the Law, coming into the picture 430 years later, does not invalidate, as though the Law were designed to nullify the promise. 18. For if the inheritance came from the Law, then it would not spring from the promise. And we know that is not the case, for God graciously gave the inheritance to Abraham by the promise.

19. Why, then, the Law at all? It was added in order to provoke transgressions, until the seed should come to whom the promise had been made. The Law was instituted by angels through a mediator. 20. Now a mediator does not represent one person (a singular party), but God is the one. 21. Is the Law, then, effectively opposed to the promises [of God]? Absolutely not! For if a Law had been given that was strong enough to make people alive, then things would have been made right by the Law. 22. But in actuality, the scripture imprisoned everything under the power of Sin, in order that the promise might be given via the faith of Jesus Christ to those who believe. 23. Before faith came, we were confined under the Law's power, imprisoned during the period that lasted until, as God intended, faith was invasively revealed. 24. So then, the Law was our confining custodian until the advent of Christ, in order that we should be rectified by faith. 25. But now that faith has come, we are no longer under the power of that confining custodian.

26. For you are — all of you — sons of God through the faith that is in Christ Jesus. 27. For when all of you were baptized into Christ, you put on Christ as though he were your clothing. 28. There is neither Jew nor Greek; there is neither slave nor free; there is no "male and female"; for all of you are One in Christ Jesus. 29. And, if you are Christ's, then as a result of that, you are seed of Abraham, heirs in accordance with the promise.

Chapter 4 4:1. What I mean can be made yet clearer by a picture: So long as the heir is a child, he is no different from a slave, even though, in prospect, he is lord of the entire household. 2. He is under the authority of guardians and managers until the arrival of the time set by the father for his passage to the status of an adult.

3. Something very like this is true of us. When we were children, we were held in a state of slavery under the power of the elements of the cosmos. 4. But when the fullness of time came, God sent his Son, born of a woman, born under the power of the Law, 5. in order that he might redeem those held under the power of the Law, in order, that is, that we might receive adoption as sons. 6. And because you are sons, God sent the Spirit of his Son into our hearts, crying, "Abba, Father!"

7. So then, you are no longer a slave, but rather a son; and if you are a son, you are also an heir by God's act of adoption.

8. It is true that formerly, not knowing God, you were enslaved to things that in nature are not gods. 9. But now, knowing God — or rather, being known by God — how is it that you are turning back to the weak and impotent elements, wishing once again to be their slaves? 10. You observe days and months and seasons and years. 11. I am anxious about you, worrying that the labor I have spent on you might prove to be labor lost!

12. Brothers and sisters, I beg you to become as I am, because I have become as you are. You did not wrong me in any way. 13. You know that it was due to an illness of mine that I preached the gospel to you in the first place; 14. and, although you were tempted to be offended at my sickness, you neither despised me nor regarded me with contempt. On the contrary, you welcomed me as an angel of God, indeed as Christ Jesus. 15. What has happened to the intense elation you felt? For I can give you evidence of that earlier feeling: Had it been possible, you would have plucked out your eyes and given them to me! 16. So then, has it turned out that I am now your enemy, rather than your friend, for having spoken the truth to you? 17. The people who have come into your churches with their false gospel are courting you, saying that they are deeply concerned about you, but they do not really have in mind what is good for you. On the contrary, their threat that you will be excluded springs in truth from their desire that you will make them the object of your affection. 18. To be courted by someone who is concerned for your welfare is in every instance a good thing; and not only when I am present with you. 19. My children, I am going through the pain of giving birth to you all over again, until Christ is formed in your congregations. 20. Would that I could be there with you now, and that I could change my tone of voice; for I am quite uncertain about you.

21. Tell me, you who wish to live under the power of the Law! Do you really hear what the Law says? 22. For, while it does stand written in scripture that Abraham had two sons, one from the slave girl and one from the free woman, 23. the crucial point is that the son from the slave girl was begotten by the power of the flesh, whereas the son from the free woman was begotten by the power of the promise. 24. These are allegorical matters; for these women are two cove-

nants. One of these covenants is from Mount Sinai; it is bearing children into the state of slavery; it is Hagar. 25. Now this Hagar represents Mount Sinai in Arabia. Hagar also stands in the same oppositional column with the present Jerusalem, for like Hagar the present Jerusalem is in slavery together with her children. 26. But the Jerusalem that is above is free; she is our mother. 27. For it stands written in scripture:

Rejoice, you barren woman, you who are not giving birth to children! Scream and cry aloud, you who are not in birth pains! For the children of the woman who is in lonely desolation are more numerous than the children of the woman who has a husband.

28. And you, brothers and sisters, are children of the promise in the pattern of Isaac. 29. Moreover, just as, at that time, the son begotten by the power of the flesh persecuted the son begotten by the power of the Spirit, so the same thing is true today. 30. But what does the scripture say? It says:

Throw out the slave girl and her son. For the son of the slave girl will certainly not come into the inheritance along with the son of the free woman.

31. Therefore, brothers and sisters, we are not children of the slave girl. On the contrary, we are children of the free woman. **Chapter 5** 5:1. It was to bring us into the realm of freedom that Christ set us free. Stand your ground, therefore, and do not ever again take up the yoke of slavery!

2. Look here! I, Paul, say to you that if you undergo circumcision, Christ will be of no help to you. 3. I testify once more to everyone who gets himself circumcised, that he is obligated to observe the whole of the Law. 4. Speaking to those of you who think you are being rectified by the Law, I say: You have nothing more to do with Christ; you have fallen out of the realm of grace!
5. With us things are entirely different: having the Spirit in our hearts, and having the confidence that comes from faith, we eagerly await the hope of rectification. 6. For in Christ Jesus neither circumcision nor uncircumcision accomplishes anything at all. The real power is faith actively working through love.
7. For some time you ran a good footrace. Who has hindered you from staying on course, so that you are no longer obediently committed to the truth? 8. The persuasion that is proving effective among you is not coming from the God who calls you. 9. It is like a little bit of yeast working its leavening power throughout the whole lump of dough.
10. In the realm ruled over by the Lord, I have confidence in you, believing that, as the future unfolds, you will not really follow these alien paths of thought. The man who is disturbing your minds will suffer his judgment, no matter who he is. 11. As for me, brothers and sisters, if, on occasion, I am preaching, as part of the gospel message, that one should be circumcised — as some wrongly report to you — why am I being persecuted to this day? My preaching circumcision

would amount to wiping out the scandalous character of the cross. 12. I wish that the people who are troubling your minds would castrate themselves!

13. For you were called to freedom, brothers and sisters; only do not allow freedom to be turned into a military base of operations for the Flesh, active as a cosmic power. On the contrary, through love be genuine servants of one another. 14. For the whole of the Law has been brought to completion in one sentence: "You shall love your neighbor as yourself!" 15. But if you snap at one another, each threatening to devour the other, take care that you are not eaten up by one another!

16. In contradistinction to the Teachers, I, Paul, say to you: Lead your daily life guided by the Spirit, and, in this way, you will not end up carrying out the Impulsive Desire of the Flesh. 17. For the Flesh is actively inclined against the Spirit, and the Spirit against the Flesh. Indeed these two powers constitute a pair of opposites at war with one another, the result being that you do not actually do the very things you wish to do. 18. If, however, in the daily life of your communities you are being consistently led by the Spirit, then you are not under the authority of the Law.

19. The effects of the Flesh are clear, and those effects are: fornication, vicious immorality, uncontrolled debauchery, 20. the worship of idols, belief in magic, instances of irreconcilable hatred, strife, resentment, outbursts of rage, mercenary ambition, dissensions, separation into divisive cliques, 21. grudging envy of the neighbor's success, bouts of drunkenness, nights of carousing, and other things of the same sort. In this regard, I warn you now, just as I warned you before: those who practice things of this sort will not inherit the Kingdom of God.

22. By contrast, the fruit borne by the Spirit is love, joy, peace, patience, kindness, generosity, faith, 23. gentleness, self-control. The Law does not forbid things of this kind! 24. And those who belong to Christ Jesus have crucified the Flesh, together with its passions and desires.

25. If, then, we live in the Spirit — and we do — let us carry out our daily lives under the guidance of the Spirit.

26. Do not think of yourself as better than others, provoking one another, envying one another.   **Chapter 6**   6:1. Brothers and sisters, if someone should be caught committing a transgression of some sort, you who are spiritual are to restore that person to his former condition in the community, doing so in a spirit of gentleness, taking care, lest you yourself be tempted. 2. Bear one another's burdens, and in this way you will bring to completion the Law of Christ. 3. For if someone thinks he is somebody, when in fact he is nothing of the sort, he deceives himself. 4. In place of such self-deception, let each one of you consider his own work; then you will keep your boasting to yourself, not directing it to your neighbor. 5. For each one will bear his own burden.

6. The one who is being taught the word is to share his goods with the teacher. 7. Do not be deceived, pretending that it is possible to thumb your nose at God. For whatever a person sows is exactly what he will reap. 8. One who sows to his

own flesh will reap corruption from the Flesh; but one who sows to the Spirit will reap eternal life from the Spirit.

9. Do what is right, without growing weary of it; for at the appropriate time we will reap a harvest, if we do not give up. 10. Every time we have an opportunity, then, let us work for the good of all, and especially for the good of those who make up the household of faith.

11. Notice the large letters I am using, as I now seize the pen to write to you with my own hand. 12. Those who wish to put on a good show in the flesh, they are the ones who are trying to compel you to undergo circumcision. Indeed, they are doing that only in order that they themselves might escape the persecution that awaits those who preach the cross of Christ. 13. For these circumcised people do not even keep the Law themselves! Their insistence on circumcising you springs, then, from their desire to boast in regard to your flesh.

14. As for me, God forbid that I should boast in anything except the cross of our Lord Jesus Christ, by which the cosmos has been crucified to me and I to the cosmos. 15. For neither is circumcision anything nor is uncircumcision anything. What is something is the new creation. 16. As to all those who will follow this standard in their lives, let peace and mercy be upon them, that is to say upon the Israel of God.

17. Let no one make trouble for me anymore. For I bear in my own body scars that are the marks of Jesus.

18. Brothers and sisters, the grace of our Lord Jesus Christ be with your spirit. Amen!

INTRODUCTION

◆

GALATIANS AS DRAMA

Reading Paul's letter to his Galatian churches is like coming in on a play as the curtain is rising on the third or fourth act. The opening lines of the letter tell us three things. First, to read this letter is to be involved in high drama, for one senses between Paul and the Galatians both deep affection and angry tension. Second, Paul and the Galatians have a rich history with one another. Important developments antedate the writing and the reception of the letter. Third, what has already occurred has involved a number of persons in addition to Paul and the Galatians. Genuine understanding of the letter involves discerning the roles played by these other actors, as well as the roles played by Paul and the Galatians. Somewhat as though we were witnessing a play in a theater, then, we pay attention. And as the drama of the letter unfolds, we start to put the pieces together, beginning with a brief sketch of the players.

§1 THE DRAMATIS PERSONAE

Messenger. If the letter were literally presented to us today in dramatic form, we would see an actor seated and reading aloud from an epistolary scroll he holds in his hands. Not himself the author of the letter, he is a messenger, sent to Galatia by the author, Paul, with instructions to assemble the church in first one Galatian city and then another, in order to read the letter to them.

Paul. In the settings in which the letter was actually read aloud, Paul was made present in a significant sense by that reading, not least because, in passage after passage, the Galatians heard the locutions and cadences of the man with whom they had had a very impressive and fascinating history, beginning with their birth as churches. At several points the letter provides us with glimpses of earlier scenes in that history, enticing us to imagine and reconstruct them.

The Galatian Churches. In three passages, for example, Paul speaks explicitly of the birth and early life of the Galatian churches (3:1–4; 4:13–14; 5:7a). To the Galatian Gentiles he — a Jew — had preached the good news of the redeeming power with which God had invaded the world by sending his Son (1:16). Moreover, Paul preached this good news without laying on the Galatians any cultic requirements, such as the rite of circumcision. In those early days there was obviously nothing but the deepest affection between the apostolic evangelist and his newborn congregations.

The Catechetical Instructors. That affection continued for some time after Paul left Galatia (5:7a), in part because, before his departure, he trained a number of catechetical instructors, who then continued to teach the Pauline gospel in the churches (6:6). It is possible that the messenger who read the letter to the Galatians was one of these instructors, who, having carried news of the Galatian churches to Paul, returned to Galatia with Paul's letter.

The Teachers and Their Followers. The major item in the news carried to Paul was the arrival in his Galatian churches of a group of traveling evangelists, who had brought a gospel emphasizing circumcision, and thus fundamentally different from his. Partly because these evangelists soon acquired numerous followers in the churches, shoving aside the Pauline catechetical instructors, we will call them the Teachers (§6 below; Comment #6).[1]

As we read the letter, we sense that, in addition to the actors mentioned thus far, there were others whose voices one can hear from offstage, so to speak.[2]

The Jerusalem Church. We do not know how much information Paul gave the Galatians about the church in Jerusalem when he was with them. We can be confident, however, that, from the Teachers, they heard a great deal about the "mother church" (4:26).[3] And as the Galatians listened to Paul's letter, they heard still more, probably sensing for the first time that Paul's feelings about that church ranged from respect to ambivalence to outright anger (Comment #46).

Peter, James, and John. In the period prior to Paul's coming to Galatia, a meeting was convened involving the Jerusalem congregation and the one in Antioch, the latter being represented by Barnabas and Paul (2:1–10). At that meeting Paul had cordial and mutually respectful relations with Peter, James, and John, the dominant leaders of the church in Jerusalem. Later his confidence was severely shaken, as — from his point of view — a shadow fell over the scene of the Jerusalem church.

The False Brothers. In the Jerusalem meeting Paul had had to do battle with a party in the Jerusalem church whose leaders were trying to halt the circumcision-free Gentile mission of the Antioch church. In the conference Paul and Barnabas had been victorious over these Jerusalem opponents. Later, however, these persons — dubbed by Paul "the False Brothers" — acquired a new level of power in the church of Jerusalem, influencing James to support, at least in part, their point of view (2:12). Still later these False Brothers may even have offered support to the Teachers, thus seeming to Paul to dog his tracks. Developments of this sort cast an increasingly dark shadow over Paul's picture of the Jerusalem congregation.

The Church in Antioch. Paul's history with this church can be divided into two periods. For a significant part of Paul's early years as an evangelist, the Antioch

[1] J. L. Martyn, *Issues,* 7–24.
[2] The roles played by these offstage actors have been recently and provocatively interpreted by Vouga, "Der Galaterbrief."
[3] Regarding the Teachers' relation to the Jerusalem church, and the possibility of comparing them, in this regard, to the "pseudo-apostles" of 2 Cor 11:13, see Comment #46.

church served as a completely supportive home base. Later there was a painful break, after which Paul worked without ecclesiastical support (2:1–14).

Bearing in mind this brief sketch of the (human) players in the Galatian drama, we can turn to other matters that will be of further help in our reading of the letter.

THE BIRTH AND EARLY LIFE OF THE GALATIAN CHURCHES

§2 THE GOOD NEWS ARRIVES IN GALATIA

As Paul was passing through Galatia on his way to evangelistic labors in the metropolitan centers around the Aegean Sea, an illness of some kind compelled him to pause (4:13–14).[4] There the sickness that could have been an obstacle to his work became instead the occasion on which he preached to the Galatians the good news: God's Christ had faithfully suffered the ignominious death of crucifixion in their behalf, indeed in behalf of all human beings (3:1; 1:4). In this message God acted to kindle the Galatians' faith (3:2). Freed now from the anxious fears of superstition (4:8–9a), they received the Spirit of Christ, being thus born as vibrantly alive members of the church of the true God (1:13). Led by the Spirit, they learned confidently to cry out to God as their Father (4:6).

The birth of these churches gave great joy both to Paul and to the Galatians themselves. Indeed, in those early days the Galatians were not only enthusiastically thankful to God for their common life of mutual affection in Christ (5:22–23a). They were also in love, as it were, with Paul, finding him to be the true messenger of the true God (4:14–15). To use Paul's own language, we can say that the Galatian churches were located "in Christ" (cf. 1:22). Literally, they existed in some geographical locale.

§3 THE LOCATION OF THE GALATIAN CHURCHES

In Gal 1:2 Paul says that he is writing to "the churches *of Galatia,*" using the geographical term to identify his addressees by their location. With this expression he could be referring to churches situated anywhere in the Roman province of Galatia, an area that, in Paul's time, included south-central Asia Minor, as well as the region from which the province took its name, that of the old Celtic kingdom in the north (see map).[5] If we had only Gal 1:2 and Acts 13:14–14:23, we might conclude that the churches of Galatia were founded by Paul and Barnabas — as daughter churches of the church in Antioch — in some of the cities in the southern part of the province, such as Derbe, Lystra, Iconium, and Pisidian Antioch.[6]

In Gal 3:1, however, Paul uses an ethnic term, addressing the recipients of the

---

[4]Regarding the urban nature of Paul's churches, see Meeks, *Urban.*
[5]A basic study on Galatia and the Galatians is still that of Stähelin, *Galater;* see also Mitchell, "Population"; idem, *Anatolia;* Magie, *Roman Rule;* Chevallier, *Roman Roads;* A. H. M. Jones, *Cities;* Sherk, "Roman Galatia"; and a forthcoming book by C. Breytenbach.
[6]So Mitchell, *Anatolia,* 3–4.

letter as *Galatai*, "Galatians," "Celts."[7] It is a very unlikely way of speaking to persons living in the southern part of the Roman province, where there were few if any Celts. It is, however, a natural way of addressing a group of ethnic Galatians living in the northern part of the province, descendants of the Celts who had made up the old Galatian kingdom centered in Ankyra and Pessinus (with perhaps an admixture of some Greek and a few oriental immigrants). The manner of Paul's address in 3:1 suffices by itself to show with a high degree of probability that the churches were located in those Hellenized, Celtic cities in the north (note also the references to Celtic Galatia in Acts 16:6 and 18:23).[8] And that conclusion is confirmed by a second intersection of geography and ethnicity.

At numerous points Paul tells the Galatians that they are by no means to submit to the Teachers' demand that they be circumcised. At none of these junctures does he differentiate one group from another, saying in effect, "Those of you who are of Jewish descent may retain your circumcised state. Those, however, of Gentile descent must not submit to circumcision" (cf. 1 Cor 7:18). On the contrary, Paul speaks throughout the letter to former Gentiles, uncircumcised persons with some degree of Hellenistic culture, who previously worshiped pagan gods (4:8–9).[9] There were no Jews in Paul's Galatian churches.[10] That is precisely what we should expect of Christian congregations in the northern cities of the old Celtic kingdom, in which, as far as we know, there were no Jewish communities in the middle of the first century.[11] The Galatian churches, perhaps only two in number, were almost certainly located in the Hellenized Celtic cities

---

[7]"The Greek word *Galatai* is a variant form of *Keltai* or *Keltoi*, 'Celts' (Latin *Galli*)" (Bruce 3). From the Danube basin in central Europe, the Celts spread not only westward, to Gaul and Britain, but also eastward, to Macedonia and eventually to the center of northern Asia Minor, giving their name to that region, as their kinsmen gave essentially the same name to Gaul.

[8]See Haenchen, *Apostelgeschichte*, 423 n2 (Ramsay versus Lake); Conzelmann, *Acts*, ad loc. The argument of W. Michaelis for the province hypothesis — a relative late-comer in the history of the interpretation of Galatians — is comprehensively and fairly presented by Mussner (6–7), before he rejects it. See also Schweizer, *Einleitung*, 70.

[9]The level of the Galatians' Greek culture cannot be fixed with great accuracy. The letter itself shows us that these urbanites knew and used the Greek language (only persons in the Galatian countryside were limited to Celtic). Note also the Marcionite prologues, where, by identifying the Galatians as Greeks, the author may have meant only that they were Greek speaking (Souter, *Text*, 188–191). At numerous points in the commentary we will see that Paul presupposes some knowledge of popular philosophy on the part of the Galatians, the ancient theory of opposites, for example. See §10 below and Comment #41.

[10]*Pace* Davies, Review of H. D. Betz; Wessels, "Call"; Mitchell, *Anatolia*, 5; cf. J. L. Martyn, *Issues*, 4 n3.

[11]There are a few inscriptions that may indicate the presence of some Jews in ethnic Galatia in the second or third century C.E. (Trebilco, *Communities*, 137, 243 n49). We have, however, no literary, archaeological, and epigraphic evidence — synagogue remains, inscriptions, etc. — reflecting the existence of Jewish communities in Ankyra and Pessinus in the middle of the first century (private letter from Helmut Koester, May 6, 1992). See further Mitchell, "Population"; idem, *Ankara*, nos. 133, 141, 209b, 418, 509–512; Bittel, "Grabsteine," 110–113, nos. 6–9; Feldman, *Jew and Gentile*.

of Ankyra and Pessinus (with possibly a third church in the trading center of Tavium).[12]

§4 THE DATE OF THEIR BIRTH

Convincing attempts to present a chronology of Paul's travels and labors are based on a simple rule: Our first and decisive attempt to discern the chronology of Paul's work is to be made on the basis of the letters alone. As a second and separable step, we may turn to Acts. Even in that second step, however, one accepts from Acts only points of confirmation and supportive elucidation.[13] Observing this rule in the course of our exegesis of Galatians, we will find that Paul's labors fall into two clearly distinguishable periods.

Not long after his call to preach the gospel of Christ, Paul spent about a decade (perhaps A.D. 38–48) serving as an evangelist of the Antioch church. In this early period he worked shoulder-to-shoulder with his trusted coworker Barnabas, preaching Christ both in the area surrounding Antioch (Syria) and in the region somewhat further to the west (Cilicia; Gal 1:21–24; 2:11).[14] This period came to its end, however, when — not long after the conference in Jerusalem — Paul experienced a traumatic estrangement from the church in Antioch and a painful break with Barnabas himself (2:11–14). Indeed, this estrangement from Antioch was accompanied by the development of mutual mistrust between Paul and the church of Jerusalem (Comment #46).

It was at the beginning of this second period — ca. A.D. 48 or 49 — that Paul came to Galatia. No longer working in the company of Barnabas (Comment #17), Paul knew himself now to be something of a lone-wolf evangelist.[15] The

---

[12]Pessinus was the locus of a major sanctuary dedicated to Cybele, the Great Mother of Life and the lover of Attis. See Nock, *Essays*, 2.893; Vermaseren, *Cybele*, 13–31; H. Koester, *Hellenistic Age*, 191.

[13]Some of the basic lines of research in this matter were laid down in two studies published in the late 1930s by John Knox: "Fourteen" and "The Pauline Chronology." Cf. also the pertinent works of Ernst Barnikol, the first of which was published in 1929 (see Jewett, *Chronology*, 80–81). The comprehensive attempt of Knox was given in *Chapters*. See also Buck, "Collection"; idem, "Date"; Hurd, *Origin*; Buck and Taylor, *Paul*. Three astonishingly detailed and impressive attempts have appeared more recently: Jewett, *Chronology* (the research was included in the author's dissertation of 1964); Suhl, *Chronologie*; Luedemann, *Chronology* (German original 1980). In many regards these are very helpful studies. See further Hurd, "Chronology"; Corley, *Colloquy*; a postscript Luedemann provided for the English translation of his chronology with responses to reviewers; Murphy-O'Connor, "Missions"; Suhl, "Chronologie"; idem, "Beginn"; Knox, "Chronology"; Georgi, *Remembering*; Slingerland, "Acts 18:1–18"; Hyldahl, *Chronologie*.

[14]The place-names "Syria" and "Cilicia" are twice linked in the book of Acts, namely at 15:23 (the churches addressed in the "apostolic decree") and at 15:41 (Paul's itinerary immediately *after* the Jerusalem conference portrayed in Acts 15). Neither reference is of much significance for understanding Gal 1:21.

[15]Crucial is Paul's silence about Galatia in 1:21, where he is referring to his work — with Barnabas — as an evangelist of the Antioch church. To be sure, his references in 2:1, 9, 13 indicate that the Galatians knew of Barnabas, but it seems probable that that knowledge came from the Teachers. Paul may have had coworkers other than Barnabas when he

shocking divorce from the Antioch church — and the mutual suspicion between himself and the Jerusalem church — deepened Paul's major theological conviction: God was making things right in the world by the faithful death of Christ, rather than by the observance of the Sinaitic Law (2:11–21). Extremely confident now of his own call directly from God, quite apart from ecclesiastical sponsorship (1:1; 4:27), Paul was also convinced that God was creating his worldwide church both from Jews — assuming their continuance of Law observance, so long as it did not hinder fellowship with Gentile Christians — and from uncircumcised Gentiles (2:7, 9).

The Galatian churches, drawn wholly from Gentiles, were not founded, then, as daughter churches either of the Jerusalem church or of the church in Antioch. They understood themselves to be the children of God himself, born by the power of the Pauline gospel.

§5 THE STATE OF THEIR HEALTH AT THE TIME OF PAUL'S DEPARTURE

Everything in the letter indicates that on the day of Paul's departure, and for some time thereafter, the Galatian churches were in a state of good health, continuing the Spirit-filled and enthusiastic life that had characterized the days immediately after their birth (1:6; 4:14–15; note the imperfect-tense verb in 5:7a). By the time he left them, Paul had equipped these churches with catechetical instructors who continued to teach the gospel in the Pauline form (6:6). We may imagine that these instructors were the people who sent (or carried) a message to Paul about the arrival and work of the incursive Teachers.

§6 THE ARRIVAL AND WORK OF THE TEACHERS

Not very long after Paul's departure, a group of Christian-Jewish evangelists — the Teachers — came into Galatia, preaching with considerable effect a gospel quite different from the one the Galatians had received from Paul. Since at later junctures we will be concerned to offer a profile of the Teachers and an account of their message (Comments #6, #7, and #33; see also §7 below), it will suffice here to mention two matters. First, the Teachers claimed to be connected in a significant way with the church in Jerusalem. To some degree at least, this claim must have been not only legitimate but also a major reason for their success among the members of Paul's Galatian churches.[16] Second, they centered their message in the covenantal, Sinaitic Law, identifying it as the venerable and permanent word of God, confirmed to eternity by God's Messiah/Christ. Telling the Galatians that, apart from this divinely ordained anchor, they were cast adrift on the stormy sea of life, the Teachers offered them a security that appeared to many an absolute Godsend.

---

came to Galatia (cf. 1:2), but he refers only to his own labor when he speaks of the birth of the Galatian churches (4:12–20).

[16] Cf. Käsemann, "Only the authority of the church in Jerusalem could shake the authority Paul had in his own churches" ("Legitimität," 490).

§7 Bad News Is Carried to Paul

We can easily imagine the depth of Paul's consternation and anger on the day when — extremely busy in the early part of his work in Macedonia and Achaia — he looked up to see the sad faces of his Galatian catechetical instructors, as they arrived with bad news. They may have said something like the following:

> Very persuasive evangelists have arrived in our Galatian churches, saying that they have the true, Lawful gospel as it is preached and preserved in what they call "the mother church of Jerusalem." They say that you left us with a Lawless gospel, so deficient for the strains and stresses of everyday life as to be worse than none. Not surprisingly, then, their own message is utterly different from the one we received from you. Worse still, with their message they are convincing a number of our members that, in order to be included among God's people, Israel, we must commence observance of the Law with the rite of circumcision. Indeed, in their attempt to undermine your influence, these new evangelists are not only maligning you. They are also attacking us, persuading our brothers and sisters to terminate our work (cf. 6:6).[17] It is imperative that you come back to us immediately (cf. 4:20)!

THE WRITING OF THE LETTER

§8 Place

We do not know precisely where Paul was when he received such bad news. We can assume only that he was in Macedonia or Achaia, having recently come there from Galatia, determined to commence his labors in the area surrounding the Aegean Sea.[18] Fully occupied with his work in this new region, Paul could not bring himself to travel back to Galatia (4:20). He therefore composed the highly emotional letter (3:1), sending it by a trusted messenger — probably one of those who had brought the bad news to him — with instructions to assemble the Galatian churches one by one, in order to read the letter to them in the context of a service of worship (1:5; 6:18).

§9 Date

Regarding the letter itself, the truly important chronological issue is not its absolute date, but rather its place in the chronological order of Paul's letters. Here we are fortunate to be able to reach reasonably firm conclusions, by tracing the history of collections assembled for the Jerusalem church, first among the members of the church in Antioch, and later among the members of Paul's own churches, almost totally Gentile in background (Comment #24). To some degree, the order of the letters can be determined on the basis of the presence and character of

---

[17]Eckert, *Streit,* 147.

[18]The major clue to Paul's location when he wrote Galatians is the absence of a reference in the letter to his own collection for the Jerusalem church (Comment #24). Not yet having conceived of that collection, he was probably in Philippi or Thessalonica, on his first trip outside of Asia Minor (and years before making preparations for his final trip to Jerusalem, *pace* Borse, *Standort;* Vouga, "Der Galaterbrief").

references to Paul's own collection in certain ones of them, and by noting the absence of such references in others. Prior to conceiving the plan for his own collection, Paul wrote 1 Thessalonians, Galatians, and Philippians.[19] After he conceived that plan, he communicated it to his church in Corinth (perhaps in the letter he mentions in 1 Cor 5:9); he spoke of it in a second letter to the Galatians, no longer preserved (1 Cor 16:1–2); he reemphasized it several times in writing to the Corinthians (1 Cor 16:1–4; 2 Corinthians 8 and 9), and finally he referred to it with some anxiety in writing to the church of Rome (Rom 15:25–33). Galatians thus antedates all of the Corinthian letters, and Romans comes after them.[20]

At a number of points in the present commentary we will see that this chronological order is important for the reading of Galatians itself. And one hardly needs to add that it is a matter of considerable consequence for our efforts to understand the unfolding of Paul's theology, in the midst of the strains and stresses in his various churches. It is especially important for our attempts to understand Paul's view of Israel, for there was some development in this view between Galatians and Romans (Comments #37 and #52, and §13 below).

§10 LITERARY STRUCTURE AND SYNOPSIS

We may doubt that Paul would have fully recognized as his own any of the modern structural analyses of Galatians, but, if we begin with his use of epistolary formulas, we can arrive at a structure that warrants some degree of confidence.[21] Not confined to the prescript and the subscript, these formulas are found in the body of the letter (see italicized expressions in the left column below), indicating that the document is a letter from beginning to end, not merely a speech enclosed between epistolary prescript and subscript.[22]

Epistolary analysis can be supplemented, however, by observing signs of rhetorical form. The document is a letter, but it is also a substitute for the oral communication that would have taken place had Paul been able to travel again to Galatia; and, as a substitute for oral communication, the letter does in fact reflect

---

[19]The character of Paul's letter to Philemon precludes our dating it by reference to Paul's collection. Moreover, the order of 1 Thessalonians, Galatians, and Philippians with respect to one another has to be discerned on grounds other than the Pauline collection, for the attempts to find in these letters indirect references to that matter are more ingenious than convincing.

[20]One notes that, working on grounds other than the history of the collections for Jerusalem, Jewett arrives at the same relative order: Galatians, the Corinthian correspondence, Romans (chart at the end of *Chronology*). Coming not long after Paul's departure from Galatia and shortly before the inauguration of his collection, Galatians is probably to be dated about A.D. 50, after 1 Thessalonians and before Philippians.

[21]See especially White, *Greek Letter*; Doty, *Letters*; Dahl, "Galatians"; Stirewalt, *Epistolography*.

[22]Kennedy is correct to say of many Greco-Roman letters that their structure "resembles a speech, framed by a salutation and complimentary closure" (*Interpretation*, 141). Cf. Seneca: ". . . my letters should be just what my conversation would be if you and I were sitting in one another's company or taking walks together . . ." (*Epistolae* 75.1–2; Malherbe, *Theorists*, 28). Epistolary formulas are often found, however, in the body of a letter, and they are helpful guides to the author's intentions.

Paul's training in rhetoric. In 3:11–12, for example, Paul shapes to his own purpose the form in which a rhetorician deals with a contradiction between two specific laws, both of which are found in the grand structure of the law (Comment #35).[23] Even taken by itself, this example suffices to show that there is some pertinence to the current concern among scholars to take into account the rhetorical elements in the body of this letter.[24] If we assume, however, that Galatians must conform essentially to the recommendations of the ancient rhetoricians, we will put the letter into a straitjacket, concluding that it is either forensic, deliberative, or epideictic, whereas strong arguments have been advanced that it is none of these.[25]

As we will see in the Notes and Comments, then, there are definite limits to the pertinence of rhetorical analysis.[26] The oral communication for which the letter is a substitute would have been an argumentative sermon preached in the context of a service of worship—and thus in the acknowledged presence of God—not a speech made by a rhetorician in a courtroom. Specifically, Paul's sermon would certainly not have been a defensive speech delivered in a metaphorical court of law with the Galatians sitting as judges, considered by Paul competent to decide the case.[27] It follows that, taken as a whole, the letter is not an instance of judicial rhetoric. But neither does Paul write in order to persuade the Galatians to cleave to him and his gospel and to reject his opponents and their gospel (see Note on Gal 1:6).[28] The letter is also not an instance of deliberative rhetoric.

[23]See also 3:15, where Paul employs the rhetorical *topos* of dissociation (Comment #37).
[24]The current debate about the rhetorical form of Galatians was creatively opened by H. D. Betz—who takes the body of the letter to have the form of judicial rhetoric—and it has grown into a subject of its own. See, for example, Hester, "Structure"; Hübner, "Galaterbrief"; Lyons, *Autobiography*, 96–105; Suhl, "Galaterbrief"; Barclay, "Mirror-Reading"; R. G. Hall, "Inference"; Pitta, *Disposizione*; D. F. Watson and A. J. Hauser, *Rhetorical Criticism*. Among the treatments in the commentaries, that of Longenecker is noteworthy. Arguments for finding an instance of deliberative rhetoric are put forward, to name a few, by Kennedy, *Interpretation*; R. G. Hall, "Outline"; Smit, "Speech"; and Vouga, "Gattung" (critique: Schrage, "Probleme," 11 n52). Regarding the thesis that Galatians is an instance of judicial rhetoric, see further the reviews of H. D. Betz's commentary by Meeks, Meyer, and Aune; also Siegert, *Argumentation*, 1 n2; Boers, *Gentiles*, 45; Jegher-Bucher, *Galaterbrief*.
[25]See again the reviews of H. D. Betz by Meeks and Aune. Recently, Vos has argued that, to judge from Galatians 1–2, Melanchthon had good reason to call the letter didactic: "Argumentation." See also Schrage, *Korinther*, 1.77.
[26]Recently, T. Martin ("Stasis") has advanced a rhetorical thesis that is so fanciful as to have the effect of suggesting a moratorium of some length in this branch of research.
[27]As noted above, this is the thesis of H. D. Betz: The situation of Galatians is that of "a court of law with jury, accuser, and defendant . . . the addressees [the Galatians] are identical with the jury, with Paul being the defendant, and his opponents the accusers" (24). To one degree or another, H. D. Betz's analysis has been adopted by a number of other interpreters.
[28]This is the thesis of Kennedy and R. G. Hall. Note Hall's statements: "The major purpose of Galatians is not to defend some past action (judicial) or to praise some and blame others (epideictic) but to persuade the Galatians to cleave to Paul and his gospel and to reject his opponents and their gospel (Gal 1:6–9, cf. 6:12–16) . . . Galatians as a whole is

Paul's oral sermon would have been a reproclamation of the gospel in the form of an evangelistic argument (Comment #9). At several junctures that argument proves to be very peculiar, however, because of Paul's conviction that he can proclaim the gospel only in the presence of the God who makes the gospel occur, being its always-contemporary author. Rhetoric, then, can serve the gospel, but the gospel itself is not fundamentally a matter of rhetorical persuasion (1:10–12). For the gospel has the effect of placing at issue the nature of argument itself. That is to say, since the gospel is God's own utterance, it is not and can never be subject to ratiocinative criteria that have been developed apart from it.[29]

These limitations on rhetorical analysis converge when one considers the matter of rhetoric and cosmos. All instructors in legal rhetoric, for example, take for granted the basic integrity of the law, and for that reason these instructors make two assumptions. They assume that, in a debate, both speakers are working in the same cosmos, each calling in his own way on the commonly held structure of that cosmos, as that structure exists in the intact body of law. Thus, instructors in rhetoric assume that the winner of a debate is the one who calls most consistently and most persuasively on the commonly held body of law, that body of law being one of the elements of the cosmos.

These assumptions do not hold true for Paul. He takes his bearings from the good news that in Christ — and thus in the act of *new* creation — God has invaded the cosmos. Paul does not argue, then, on the basis of a cosmos that remains undisturbed, a cosmos that he shares with the Teachers. A basic part of his message, in fact, is the announcement of the death of that shared cosmos with its legal elements, and the emergence of the new cosmos with its new elements (Gal 4:3; 6:14–15; Comments #41 and #51). What requires emphasis is the fact that the newness of this cosmic good news brings about a newness of rhetoric. A sterling example has been mentioned above: Paul's use in 3:11–12 of the rhetorical form of the Textual Contradiction (see Comment #35).[30] This one example suffices to show that Paul cannot and does not argue on the basis of the assumed integrity of the cosmos to which the Teachers point when they speak of "the Law."

It follows that, in composing the body of the letter (1:6–6:10), Paul shows rela-

---

an exhortation, as every deliberative speech is" ("Outline," 279, 284). If H. D. Betz gave too little attention to Galatians 5 and 6 (see Kraftchick, "Ethos"), does not R. G. Hall give too much weight to his own reading of those chapters? See now, however, Hall's quite suggestive "Arguing."

[29] Cf. 1 Cor 1:18 and the comments on this verse in J. L. Martyn, *Issues*, 217–221. At issue here is what might be called the communicability of the gospel. On the one hand, in his oral preaching, as in his epistolary repreaching, Paul does not speak "in tongues" (1 Cor 14:2). In his communication he employs the everyday Greek of the city streets, observing, for the most part, the normal rules of grammar, and using some of the argumentative forms we know to have been taught by the rhetoricians of his day. On the other hand, however, Paul does not and cannot take as the foundation of his rhetoric substantive presuppositions he knows to be already present in the minds of his hearers. See Comments #8 and #9.

[30] Cf. especially Vos, "Antinomie."

tively little concern with observing certain rules set out in the standard teaching of rhetoric. Rather, he concentrates his attention on reproclaiming the gospel in light of the Teachers' message, taking into account the ways in which their attacks on him distort the gospel, and considering as well the ways in which their exegetical treatments of Abrahamic traditions are misleading the Galatians.

To be yet more specific, we can see that, for Paul, the relation between rhetoric and the human situation is highly significant. In Galatians we find repeatedly the linguistic pattern *hypo tina einai*, "to be under the power of something" (see Comment #39). This pattern reflects Paul's belief that all human beings are subject to powers beyond their control. And the corresponding apocalyptic motif of divine invasion indicates his certainty that that universal state of enslavement has been broken only by God's movement into the human scene from beyond it. Fundamentally, what the Galatians need from Paul, therefore, is not a persuasive and basically hortatory argument as to what they are to do to remedy their situation. They need to be taught by God (cf. 1 Thess 4:9), so that they *see* the cosmos that God is bringing into existence as his new creation (Comment #49). Their need of that real vision is what basically determines the nature of Paul's rhetoric.

Thus, because Paul's rhetoric presupposes God's action through Paul's words, this rhetoric proves to be more revelatory and performative than hortatory and persuasive, although it is both. Here the distinction between *antithesis* and *antinomy* is crucial (see Comment #51 and Glossary). It is a distinction closely related to that between an *argument* and an *announcement*.[31] To take an example, in writing this letter Paul is not at all formulating an argument designed to persuade the Galatians that faith is better than observance of the Law.[32] He is constructing an announcement designed to wake the Galatians up to the real cosmos, made what it is by the fact that faith has now *arrived* with the advent of Christ (Gal 3:23–25).

In short, Paul is concerned in letter form to repreach the gospel in place of its counterfeit. Rhetorically, the body of the letter is a sermon centered on factual and thus indicative answers to two questions, "What time is it?" and "In what cosmos do we actually live?"

The better part of wisdom lies, then, in the thesis that, although it contains passages that partially support both of the major rhetorical analyses (judicial to some degree are 1:17–24 and 2:17–21; deliberative to some degree is 5:13–6:10), the body of the letter as a whole is a rhetorical genre without true analogy in the ancient rhetorical handbooks of Quintilian and others.[33] Fundamentally, as said above, it is a highly situational sermon.

[31] Cf. Siegert, *Argumentation*; N. Schneider, *Antithese.*
[32] So Wuellner, "Toposforschung."
[33] Quintilian would have begun teaching rhetoric about the time of Paul's death. See especially the assertion of Malherbe that, in the writing of 1 Thessalonians, Paul created a new, Christian, literary product (*the Thessalonians*, 69). Cf. Luz's comments on the genre of Matthew (*Matthew*, 44–46), and the recent and suggestive investigation of apocalyptic rhetoric in R. G. Hall, "Arguing."

These observations reveal the simplicity of the grand structure:

Prescript	1:1–5
Theme	1:6–9
A Series of Explicating Theses and Supporting Arguments	1:10–6:10
Subscript	6:11–18[34]

PRESCRIPT. 1:1–5

1:1–5. *Epistolary Prescript*　As an apostle sent into his work not by human beings of whatever ecclesiastical authority, but rather by Jesus Christ and God the Father, Paul addresses his Galatian churches, climactically bringing them into God's presence by leading them to say "Amen!" when he ascribes glory to God (unique in Paul's prescripts). The form of Paul's rhetoric is fundamentally influenced by his conviction that both his speaking and the Galatians' hearing occur in God's presence.

INITIAL REBUKE STATING THE THEME OF THE ENTIRE LETTER. 1:6–9

1:6–9. *First Rebuke Paragraph*: "I am amazed that you are so rapidly defecting . . ."　Instead of striking the letter's major theme in a thanksgiving paragraph, Paul does that by rebuking the Galatians for defecting from the God who called their churches into existence. Theme: There is only one true gospel, and the Galatians are turning from it to a false one conveyed to them by the Teachers. At the climax of his rebuke, Paul delivers the Teachers to God, so that God can curse them (cf. 4:30).

TRANSITION. 1:10

1:10. Rhetorical Transition　Before stating the initial thesis regarding his gospel, Paul recapitulates the letter's first sentence, contrasting the rhetorical persuasion of the crowd with the apostolic pleasing of God.

---

[34]Cf. R. G. Hall, "Outline," 287.

INITIAL EXPLICATING
THESIS AND ITS
DEMONSTRATION.
1:11–2:21

THESIS 1:11–12

1:11–12. *Disclosure Formula,* "I want you to know."

Paul states the letter's *initial thesis:* His message is the gospel of Christ apocalyptically revealed to him by God, not taught him by another human being.

DEMONSTRATION.
1:13–2:21

1:13–2:14. *Disclosure Formula,* "You have already heard . . ."

Here Paul commences a narrative designed to demonstrate the initial thesis (a) by contrasting his apocalyptic vocation with religious tradition (1:13–16), (b) by refuting the Teachers' charges that he is an unfaithful student of the Jerusalem apostles (1:17–24), and (c) by tracing the history created by the march of the apocalyptic gospel into the world, in spite of opposition in the church itself (2:1–14).

2:15–21. Climax of the narrative in the form of a gospel-based ratiocinative argument introducing the second thesis

Addressing the Teachers themselves — for the first and only time — Paul concludes the narrative with his *second thesis* and with a supporting argument: The content of the gospel can be drawn from Jewish-Christian tradition itself: In the faith of Jesus Christ, God has acted to make things right.

SECOND REBUKE. 3:1–5

3:1–5. *Second Rebuke Paragraph* — "You foolish Galatians!" — with the third thesis, and with its demonstration from the birth of the Galatian churches

Resuming the mood of rebuke evident in 1:6–9, Paul extends the narrative still further, contrasting the march of the gospel into Galatia with the defection occurring at the present time. *Third thesis:* The message that has the power to evoke faith is the opposite of observance of the Law.

FIRST EXEGETICAL
ARGUMENT. 3:6–4:7

3:6–4:7. Exegetical Argument signaled by

Continuing motifs from his initial argument about the content of the gospel and from the

25

catena of quotations from scripture and leading to the fourth thesis

preceding rebuke, Paul composes an exegetical section designed to modulate the Teachers' theme of descent from Abraham into the gospel theme of descent from God, the *fourth thesis*.

DISTRESS. 4:8–11

4:8–11. *Distress Paragraph*: "How is it that you are turning back . . . ?"

Paul speaks a third time about the Galatians' defection (1:6–9; 3:1–5; cf. 4:12–20; 5:7–10; 6:12–13), accenting their reenslavement to the elements of the cosmos, again expressing his distress, and again identifying their defection as a defection from God (1:6).

REQUEST AND DISTRESS. 4:12–20

4:12–20. *Request Formula*, "I beg you to become as I am," introducing yet another paragraph expressing the pathos of *distress*, "Would that I could change my tone of voice . . ."

Requesting the Galatians to become as he is, just as he has become as they are, Paul again contrasts the Galatians' joy at the initial advent of the gospel with their present seduction at the hands of the Teachers (cf. 3:1–5). It is a development that places him in the anxious distress of a mother whose birth pangs have not fully produced the child. For Christ has not yet been formed in the common life of the Galatian communities.

SECOND EXEGETICAL ARGUMENT. 4:21–5:1

4:21–5:1. *Exegetical Argument* based on Genesis 16–21 and Isaiah 54, and introducing the fifth thesis

Having expressed his distress via the metaphor of a woman experiencing birth pangs of uncertain outcome, Paul composes a second exegetical section, focusing it on the birth of the Galatian churches. In this way he finds his *fifth thesis* in scriptures cited by the Teachers: Rightly heard, the Law itself contains (a) a witness to the birth of the Galatian churches into freedom, and (b) a command that they evict the Teachers from their midst, thus sealing the freedom given them by Christ.

TRANSITION TO PASTORAL SECTION. 5:2–12

5:2–12. *Writer's Reference to Writing*: "I say to you . . ."

Continuing to speak in the indicative mood, Paul expresses his care for the Galatians by placing before them a warning prediction

(a) regarding the consequences of their defection if they should carry it through completely, and (b) regarding the future judgment of the Teachers' leader.

PASTORAL GUIDANCE.
5:13–6:10[35]

5:13–24. Pastoral guidance, first part: Daily life in wartime. Sixth thesis	Paul completes the body of the letter by speaking as a pastor, answering the Teachers' charge of ethical chaos by showing that his gospel does provide guidance for daily life. There is indeed a positive relationship between the Law and daily life in the church. Even here, however, Paul places the major accent not on exhortation, but rather on an indicative portrait of the effects of two powers: the Impulsive Desire of the Flesh and the Spirit of Christ. Thus the *sixth thesis:* Continue to lead your daily life guided by the Spirit, and, doing so, you will not carry out the Impulsive Desire of the Flesh.
5:25–6:10. Pastoral guidance, second part: Exhortation	Transforming a series of aphorisms into apocalyptic exhortations, Paul composes the final part of his pastoral section, focusing his attention on specific needs of the Galatian churches.

AUTOGRAPHIC SUBSCRIPT.
6:11–18

6:11–18. *Autographic subscript:* "Notice the large letters I am using, as I now seize the pen to write to you with my own hand." The major theme restated and developed.	Summarizing the letter, Paul returns to the major theme of 1:6–9, thus closing with yet another attack on the Teachers, and with a final witness to the new creation that God is bringing into being by the gospel, namely the church that leaves behind all marks of religious distinction.

HISTORY OF INTERPRETATION

The earliest interpretation of the letter was carried out by the Galatians themselves. We have no sources by which in the proper sense to reconstruct that

---

[35] Regarding the use of the term "pastoral" in the analysis of 1 Thessalonians, see Malherbe, *the Thessalonians*, 69–94; for its pertinence to the study of Galatians, see Literary Structure and Synopsis of 5:13–24 in the present volume.

interpretation, but we are not wholly in the dark. From the letter itself we can surmise that in the Galatian churches, there will have been two major interpretations.

§11 INTERPRETATION BY THE TEACHERS AND THEIR FOLLOWERS

As Paul wrote his letter, he assumed that the Teachers, being still active in his Galatian churches, would be present when the letter was read aloud (see especially the Notes on 2:15–21). There is no reason to think that his assumption was incorrect. Indeed, we can match it with one of our own: The Teachers will have assured the Galatians that they were more than competent to offer their help in the interpretation of the volatile letter. We can first imagine, then, certain aspects of the interpretation of the document by the Teachers and their enthusiastic followers. Three matters in particular will have seized their attention: Paul's sharply critical reference to the Jerusalem church (4:25–27), his outrageous comments about the Law (notably 3:19–20), and his less-than-satisfactory reference to Israel (6:16).[36]

Jerusalem. The Teachers will not have failed to note Paul's references to the Jerusalem church in 4:25. For there, as we will see, Paul says that, insofar as the Jerusalem congregation is lending its sponsorship to the Teachers' Law-observant Gentile mission, it is in slavery and is begetting children into slavery (spawning Law-observant churches, that is, among the Gentiles; Comment #46). If the Teachers themselves considered the Jerusalem church to be their "mother," as seems very likely, we can easily imagine the depth of their anger at Paul's words.

The Law. Even the followers of the Teachers may have been momentarily inclined to applaud some elements in Paul's exegetical demonstration that the Law bears witness to the birth of their own churches (4:21–5:1). And they will surely have been pleased — on the first reading — to hear his positive reference to the Law in 5:14. The picture he draws of the Law's genesis, however — it was instituted by angels acting in God's absence (Comment #38) — must have struck followers of the Teachers as altogether unacceptable. And his charge that the Law is one of the cosmic powers that enslave human beings (3:23; 4:3–5; Comment #41) will certainly have been considered monstrous.

Israel. Similarly, both the Teachers and their followers will have been offended by the way in which Paul refers in closing to "the Israel of God" (6:16; Comment #52). For with that expression he says that the God of Israel is first of all the Father of Jesus Christ, and thus that Israel is the people whom God is calling into existence in Christ (1:6, 13). The Teachers' followers will also have noticed that, although Paul refers to Abraham, to Sarah (the "free woman" of 4:22), and to Isaac, he nowhere mentions the long history of God's dealings with the people of Israel.[37] Indeed, whereas the Teachers are inviting all of the Galatians to enter

---

[36]The Teachers may also have shown the Galatians that Paul's interpretation of Gen 17:8 as a reference to a singular seed is contradicted by the whole of Genesis 17 itself. See Note on Gal 3:16.

[37]Paul's use of the prophetic call traditions in 1:15 is as punctiliar as are his references to Abraham in 3:6–29.

the company of Law-observant Israel, referring to this holy and elect people of God as "the (plural) seed of Abraham," Paul speaks of Christ as the singular seed of Abraham, thus seeming to eclipse the sacred history of Israel (Comment #37).

We cannot be greatly surprised, then, to find in Paul's later letter to the Romans evidence suggesting that, under the influence of the Teachers, the Galatian churches refused to participate in the collection Paul proposed to assemble from his churches for delivery to the church in Jerusalem (Rom 15:26; Comment #24). Politically, the interpretation of Galatians by the Teachers and their followers seems to have won the day. Greatly offended by the letter, these persons apparently persuaded almost all of their colleagues in the Galatian churches to distance themselves from Paul, taking care, in fact, not to be perceived in Jerusalem as belonging to the orb of Paul's circumcision-free mission.[38] In the end, that is, the Teachers were probably as successful in their hostile interpretation of Paul's letter as they were in their initial mission among the Galatians. Had they brought to their side *every* member of the Galatian churches, however, we could very well lack the letter itself.

§12 INTERPRETATION BY THE PAULINE CATECHETICAL INSTRUCTORS
The preservation of the letter strongly suggests that the Teachers' success was less than total. It is easy to imagine that at least some of the Pauline catechetical instructors heard the letter as Paul intended (and it is their reading of the text to which we will most often refer in the commentary; see also §18 below). They may well have had to leave their Galatian cities in order to find themselves in a truly Pauline congregation, perhaps moving as far as Ephesus or another of the Aegean cities. In that case they would have taken at least one copy of the letter with them, and their doing that would be one explanation of the document's being preserved and eventually placed in a collection of Paul's letters.[39]

§13 INTERPRETATION BY PAUL HIMSELF
It is virtually inconceivable that the readings given his letter in Galatia — especially its interpretation by the followers of the Teachers — remained unknown to Paul. We are to imagine the apostle receiving a discouraging report from the messenger whom he had trusted to deliver the letter.[40] Indeed, there is reason to think not only that Paul learned of the hostile interpretation but also that, after learning of it, he took measures to correct it, with regard to all three of the matters so offensive to the Teachers: the linking of the Jerusalem church to slavery (4:25), the absence of God in the portrait of the Law's genesis (3:19–20), and the apparently un-Jewish reference to the Israel of God (6:16).

(1) *A second letter to the Galatian churches.* The messenger may have told Paul that, after hearing his highly critical reference to the Jerusalem church, the Teachers intensified their efforts to portray him as a man who has no genuine

---

[38]See J. L. Martyn, *Issues*, 39.
[39]On Marcion's collection, see §15 below. For the thesis that Paul himself is responsible for the initial collection of his letters, see Trobisch, *Letter Collection*.
[40]Contrast *1 Clem.* 65.

respect for that oldest of the congregations, and who thinks unimportant the relation of his own Gentile churches to that Jewish church in Palestine.[41] That would have been a view that required fundamental correction. At the conference in Jerusalem (2:1–10) Paul had been the participant most energized by the vision of one worldwide church drawn both from Jews and from Gentiles (Comments #18 and #19).[42] Even after the nefarious activity of the False Brothers and the Teachers, to contemplate a genuine divorce between his churches and the church in Jerusalem would have seemed to Paul the same as suggesting that the word of God had failed (cf. Rom 9:6). His first interpretive step seems, then, to have been a corrective supplement to the letter, in part a guide to its interpretation. That interpretive supplement lay in the conception of a plan to assemble a collection from his Gentile churches for delivery to the church in Jerusalem, thus clearly expressing his own concern for the unity of God's church throughout the whole of the world. He wrote a second letter to the Galatians (subsequently lost), placing before them his determination to collect funds for the Jerusalem church, and even suggesting a way by which they could assemble the money that would represent them (1 Cor 16:1–2).

(2) *A letter to the church in Rome.* Later he wrote to the church in the capital of the empire. Here he made use of his letter to the Galatians, and part of his reason for doing so may have been to guard that earlier letter from interpretations he considered misleading.

Why would it be in a letter to the Roman church that Paul should be concerned to correct misinterpretations of his earlier letter to the Galatians? The reason is complex: As he wrote the Roman letter, Paul was surely thinking of several weighty matters. He was contemplating the Spanish mission he planned to launch from that church. With that mission in mind he was determined that the Roman church have a fully accurate grasp of his gospel, being thereby able enthusiastically to support his work in Spain. He was thus concerned that his Spanish mission not be seen as an attempt to make the worldwide church a purely Gentile affair.[43]

For that reason alone his thoughts also went to the east, to the Jewish-Christian church in Jerusalem, and specifically to the trip he had momentarily to make to that church, in order to deliver to it his collection. For the collection was Paul's crucial witness to the grand unity of the church of God in the whole of the world.

As we have already noted, there was in the Jerusalem church a group of persons who did not at all share Paul's conviction that the unified church included circumcision-free Gentile congregations. These persons were the False Brothers, leaders by now of the circumcision party that had caused Paul great difficulties

---

[41] In Gal 2:10 Paul had already begun to correct an earlier form of the Teachers' charge that he cared nothing for the Jerusalem church.

[42] Cf. Achtemeier, *Quest.*

[43] So Keck, "Judgments." The literature on the purpose of Romans is extensive. Beyond the commentaries (recently Fitzmyer and Stowers), see especially Donfried, *Debate* (notably, with minor reservations, the chapter by Jervell); Jewett, "Mission"; Sampley, "Different Light."

in Jerusalem itself (2:4–5), in Antioch (2:12), and in Galatia (Comment #46).[44] Paul's plan to journey to Jerusalem thus brought to him the prospect of a renewed confrontation with a group that was both hostile to him and influential in Judea and beyond. This prospect created in Paul a considerable amount of anxiety (Rom 15:30–33).

There is, moreover, reason to think that Paul's anxiety was related both to the Galatians and to the letter he had written to them. The False Brothers' circumcision party in the Jerusalem church was almost certainly in touch with the Teachers, both before and after the latter's work in Paul's Galatian congregations. We have already noted the probability that, under the influence of the Teachers, the Galatian churches had refused to participate in Paul's collection. We must add that this step had very serious consequences for Paul's trip to Jerusalem. The apostle had now to consider the possibility that, when the Jerusalem church debated within its own ranks whether to accept his collection, some of those in the circumcision party — already knowing the answer — would ask him whether any of the funds were coming from the Galatian churches. Should that question be posed, he would have to admit that the Galatians had withdrawn from the circle of his churches. Paul may even have had to consider the possibility that Jewish Christians in the Jerusalem church who knew enough to ask that embarrassing question might also know something of his Galatian letter, such as the three crucial matters mentioned earlier (the Jerusalem church; the Law; Israel; cf. Acts 21:21).

We have no indication, to be sure, that Paul ever regretted writing the Galatian letter, but one can easily imagine that, on the eve of his last trip to Jerusalem, he regretted the harsh interpretation that had been placed upon the letter by the Teachers' followers. Such regret, in any case, is consonant with the fact that, in writing to the Romans, Paul clarified, supplemented — perhaps one should even say modified — some of the things he had said to the Galatians about the Law and about Israel.

Seen in this way, parts of Romans constitute an interpretation of Galatians made by Paul himself. Because Galatians has sometimes seemed to give the Christian church permission to adopt an anti-Judaic stance (see §17 below), Paul's own interpretation of that letter is truly important. By attending briefly to the ways in which Paul spoke in Romans about the Law and about Israel, we may be able to see more clearly what he intended when he referred to the Law and to Israel in the earlier letter to the Galatians.[45]

The Law. Writing to the Gentile Christians in Galatia and being concerned about their incipient adherence to the Law as the means of salvation, Paul portrayed the Law itself as an enslaving tyrant, thus expressing a view of the Law

---

[44] Perhaps one should add references to difficulties in Philippi and Corinth. See Gnilka, *Philipperbrief*; Georgi, *Remembering*; Käsemann, "Legitimität"; Barrett, "Opponents"; Furnish, *II Corinthians*.

[45] Elsewhere in this volume I have cautioned against an unsophisticated interpretation of Galatians on the basis of Romans. With care, however, and within definite limits, that route can be helpful, as we will see in the Appendix to Comment #49.

foreign to all strains of Jewish and (first-century) Jewish-Christian thought known to us.[46]

When he writes to the Romans, Paul does not reverse himself as regards there being a connection between the Sinaitic Law and tyranny; but his concern that he be accurately understood by Law-observant Jewish Christians (both in Rome and in Jerusalem) does lead him to a carefully nuanced formulation of that connection. Thus, in Romans he says that the Law itself is holy and even spiritual (Rom 7:12, 14), an affirmation that would surely have been misunderstood had he said it to the Gentile Christians in Galatia. He still insists, however, that when this holy and spiritual Law is faced with the overwhelming and malignant power of Sin, it proves to be impotent to bring Sin under control (Gal 3:21; 5:16; Rom 8:3). That controlling task is accomplished by God's sending of his Son, not by the Law. In the light, then, of God's act in Christ, Paul sees that the Law, being impotent, has fallen into the hands of Sin, and Sin has been able to use the Law to kill human beings (Rom 7:7–11). From Galatians to Romans, therefore, Paul is fundamentally consistent in drawing a connection between the Law and tyranny, but in Romans he clarifies — to some extent modifies — what he had said in Galatians. The Law is connected with tyranny, but only by way of Sin. For the tyrant itself is Sin, even the holy and spiritual Law being the instrument in Sin's hands, and, in that sense, Sin's effective power (cf. 1 Cor 15:56).[47]

Israel. Focusing his Galatian letter tightly on the difference between two *Gentile missions* — the Teachers' and his own — and thus referring nowhere to non-Christian Jews, Paul had spoken of the churches born in his mission as "the Israel of God" (6:16). It was a locution subject to possible misunderstanding, not least if reported to the Jerusalem church. In Romans, then, Paul clarifies and supplements his use of the word "Israel," composing three long and complex chapters on the subject of God's faithful relationship to Israel (Romans 9–11). He is aware that some have charged him with a callous apostasy from this special people of God, the people to whom the proper mission of the Jerusalem church was directed.

Significantly, he does not defend himself by speaking immediately of his high regard for Israel's lengthy history. He begins, rather, with the history of the gospel, referring to his deep pain and profound grief at one aspect of that history: most of Israel is now rejecting the gospel. As a world traveler, Paul is well acquainted with universal human disobedience to God (Rom 1:18–32). The disobedience of Israel, however, has about it something special. It is the great contradiction: the very people specially blessed by God is now largely disobeying God's gospel. This development is necessarily the great contradiction, because Paul can deny neither God's ancient election of Israel nor God's present, elective utterance of the gospel. Squarely facing this paradox, Paul necessarily sees that Israel is now standing "between God and God" (cf. Rom 11:28).[48] In the final analysis, the great

---

[46]Both gnostic and orthodox Christians of later centuries drew distinctions between enslaving and liberating parts of the Law. See footnote 108 in Comment #48.

[47]See Meyer, "Worm."

[48]This is a perceptive expression coined by Gerhard Ebeling and quoted by Luz, *Geschichtsverständnis*, 296.

contradiction, incomprehensible to human reason, points, then, to God's own mystery, about which Paul has to speak in parables (Rom 11:16–24) and in the mysterious language of apocalyptic (Rom 11:25–36), in order to affirm God's sovereign election, God's faithfulness to Israel, and God's invincible power.

There are elements of this discussion that clarify and explicate what Paul had said about Israel in Galatians. The author of Galatians had said explicitly that Christ was the seed of Abraham (Gal 3:16), but he had also denied a line of physical descent in the many generations between the patriarch and Christ (Comment #37). Now, preparing for his trip to the Jewish-Christian church in Jerusalem, Paul speaks explicitly of Abraham, Sarah, Isaac, Rebecca, and Jacob. He also makes clear that the patriarchs, being the first embodiment of God's gracious election, form the first fruits (Rom 11:16). Thus, by considering the patriarchal history, he demonstrates that God is true to his word of elective grace (Rom 9:6–13).[49] Indeed, because God's word is both invincible and indelible, the ancient election of Israel remains a paradigm for God's dealing with all of humanity.

However different these affirmations may seem from those in Galatians, the basis on which Paul states them is precisely the basis of everything he had said in Galatians: the gospel of Christ. That God is true to his gospel-word of elective grace means, as Paul had said in Galatians, that the true Israel is the Israel *of God*. Far from rescinding this earlier reference, Paul now explicates it by speaking of a division within Israel: "not all who are descended from Israel belong to Israel" (Rom 9:6b; RSV). Genuine descent happens solely by God's election. That is true today, Paul claims, as one sees in the history of the gospel; it was also true in every patriarchal generation (Rom 9:6–13).

In this elective gospel Paul also sees, however, the invincibility of God's graceful word. This word tells Paul that Israel stands not between God and Satan—the dualistic motifs of Rom 8:38–39 are not continued in Romans 9–11—but, as we have already said, between God and God. Thus, it is both true and of crucial importance that Paul now makes explicit the salvation of "all Israel" (Rom 11:26). It is equally important to notice the grounds for that eschatological confidence. All Israel will be saved because, being the God who rectifies the ungodly, God is also the one whose capacity to show mercy is more powerful than the capacity of human beings to be disobedient (Rom 11:30–31). Paul was surely familiar with the classic view of Israel's eschatological relation to all other human beings: at the End the Gentiles will flow up to Jerusalem, being saved by absorption into Israel (as the Teachers in Galatia had probably claimed; e.g., Isa 2:2–3; *Pss. Sol.* 17:30–32). In Romans Paul reverses that view, affirming *Israel's* ultimate salvation because he knows of God's ultimate purpose for *all* human beings: "God has shut up all into disobedience, in order that he might have mercy on all" (Rom 11:32; an interpretation of Gal 3:22).[50]

Surprisingly, in this climactic sentence of his discussion of Israel, Paul does not mention Israel! He speaks rather of God's powerful mercy being shown to all

[49] Cf. Walter, "Römer 9–11"; Meeks, "Trusting."
[50] See Bassler, *Impartiality*.

human beings, and he bases his argument on that comprehensive mercy. It is clear, therefore, that in Romans Paul basically derives his theology of Israel from the universality of the gospel, about which he had already spoken in Galatians. Far from laying a foundation for the view that the church has replaced Israel, this theology is free of anti-Judaic cant. It is a theology drawn from the gospel, and fundamentally, it is Paul's theology both in Galatians and in Romans.

§14 SECOND-CENTURY JEWISH CHRISTIANS

Jewish-Christian groups of the second century — in some instances one should say Christian-Jewish groups — were as hostile to Paul's theology, and especially to his Galatian letter, as were the followers of the Teachers in Galatia and the circumcision party in Jerusalem.[51] Here the primary sources are the *Epistle of Peter to James* (where Paul is said to have preached a Law-less and therefore false gospel) and the *Ascents of James* (where Paul's work is charged with having greatly hindered the growth of the church among Jews). Both of these documents are pseudonymous.[52]

§15 MARCION

More than compensating for the hostility of Jewish-Christian groups, Marcion held Galatians in extremely high regard. One can even say that Marcion developed the kernel of his theology from Paul's tendency to think in terms of pairs of opposites; and that tendency is nowhere more clearly and strongly in evidence than in Galatians. Marcion therefore placed Galatians at the head of his collection of Paul's letters, in order to display what he characterized as a series of ontological antitheses between the old and the new.[53]

In the process he showed a keen sensitivity for Pauline passages that speak of polarity, but he failed utterly to note that for Paul these polar opposites were not wooden, ontological antitheses, but rather dynamic, apocalyptic antinomies (Comments #41 and #51). The difference is monumental. Marcion's concern for inflexible, antithetical consistency led him finally to posit a distinctly un-Pauline antithesis between a creator God and a redeemer God. In this way Marcion's ontological antitheses, altogether unlike Paul's apocalyptic antinomies, became anti-Judaic, with disastrous results, extending into the anti-Judaism that is yet present in some corners of the Christian church (cf. §17 below). Franz Overbeck put the matter in a memorable sentence: "Paul had only one student who understood him, Marcion, and this student misunderstood him."[54]

[51] On the use of the expressions "Jewish-Christian" and "Christian-Jewish," see footnote 96 for chapter 1 (Comment #6) and the Glossary.
[52] On the *Epistle of Peter to James*, see HS 2.111–112 (Strecker); Klijn and Reinink, *Evidence*, 31–32, 37, 69; H. D. Betz 9 and 331–332. On the *Ascents of James*, see J. L. Martyn, "Clementine Recognitions"; Van Voorst, *Ascents*; F. S. Jones, *Source*. See further Comments #6 and #33.
[53] Marcion's order was Galatians, 1 Corinthians, 2 Corinthians, Romans, Ephesians (designated as the letter to the Laodiceans), Colossians, Philippians, Philemon. The study of Harnack, *Marcion*, remains a classic. More recently, see especially Hoffmann, *Marcion*; Clabeaux, "Marcion."
[54] Overbeck, *Christentum*, 218–219.

§16 LUTHER

A few modern exegetes would be tempted to say something similar about the sixteenth-century reformer Martin Luther, not least because of his pejorative and indefensible references to "Jews, Turks, papists, and sectarians."[55] Luther is one of a number of interpreters, for example, who, over the centuries, have given a distinctly anti-Judaic reading to Gal 4:21–5:1, finding the synagogue in the enslaving covenant of Hagar and the church in the liberating covenant of Sarah.[56] Numerous students, however, both Roman Catholic and Protestant, find help in Luther's passionate love affair with Galatians, the letter he dubbed his "Katie von Bora," the name of his betrothed, who later became his wife. For, both in his Roman Catholic period and after he became the unwilling founder of the Lutheran Church, Luther was captivated by the message of God's free and powerful grace that he heard in Galatians.[57] With some notable reservations, not least ones related to Luther's portrait of Judaism,[58] the reformer's interpretation has happily influenced — to one degree or another — most readings of the letter since his time. Moreover, Luther's interpretation reminds us of a truly important fact of early Christian history: Like Luther, the author of Galatians was considered by numerous Christians of his time to be, in a significant sense, a heretic.[59]

§17 GALATIANS AS READ BY JEWS AND CHRISTIANS TODAY

Significant advances have been made in the reading of Paul's letters — not least the one to the Galatians — as the result of an ecumenical development: Since the middle of the nineteenth century a number of Jewish scholars have added their own learning and talents to the common attempt to understand the apostle. Begun in the work of the historian Heinrich Graetz (1817–1891), modern Jewish study of Paul includes the labors of Leo Baeck, Joseph Klausner, H. J. Schoeps, David Daube, Samuel Sandmel, Shalom Ben Chorin, Pinchas Lapide, H. Maccoby, Alan Segal, Jacob Taubes, and, recently, Daniel Boyarin.[60] The most theo-

---

[55] See, for example, Luther, *Lectures on Galatians — 1535*, 9.

[56] See J. L. Martyn, *Issues*, 191–208.

[57] Luther's first lectures on Galatians, given from October 27, 1516, to March 13, 1517, when he was still a Catholic (we have a student's notebook), were expanded and published by him in 1519 (second edition 1523). He offered Galatians lectures again in 1531, and these were prepared for publication in 1535 by G. Rörer. See *Luther's Works* (55 vols.; ed. J. Pelikan; Saint Louis: Concordia, 1955–1976) vol. 26, *Lectures on Galatians — 1535 — Chapters 1–4*, and vol. 27, *Lectures on Galatians — 1535 — Chapters 5–6; Lectures on Galatians — 1519 — Chapters 1–6*. Luther's two readings — the differences became in time a matter of interest to the reformer himself — are sensitively analyzed and compared with one another in K. Bornkamm, *Auslegungen*.

[58] Cf. Hillerbrand, "Luther"; Boyarin, *Politics*, 41–42.

[59] For the sake of brevity, I use the term "heretic" simply to reflect the fact that to the Teachers — indeed, to a powerful segment of the Jerusalem church — Paul's theology was *fundamentally* erroneous and therefore unacceptable. See H. D. Betz, "Heresy."

[60] Baeck, "Romantic Religion"; Klausner, *Paul*; Schoeps, *Paul*; Daube, *New Testament*; Sandmel, *Genius*; Ben Chorin, *Paulus*; Lapide and Stuhlmacher, *Paul*; Maccoby, *Mythmaker*; Segal, *Convert*; Taubes, *Paulus*; Boyarin, *Politics*.

logically profound contribution is that of Baeck; the most directly pertinent to the study of Galatians, that of Boyarin.[61]

From this welcome development, both Christians and Jews find it easier to distinguish peripheral issues from ones that are of true import. One of the latter — certainly more important since the Holocaust — is the question whether at least some of the anti-Judaic accents in the interpretations of Paul by Marcion, Luther, and others are justified. Specifically, has Paul's Galatian letter received anti-Judaic interpretations because it is itself — at least in part — an anti-Judaic document, in the sense that, in writing it, Paul intended to pit himself against the religion of Judaism as such? Maccoby, for example, is almost certainly correct in his interpretation of Gal 3:19–20: In that passage Paul portrays the genesis of the Sinaitic Law as an event in which God played no role (Comment #38).[62] What more could one need in order to conclude that the document reflects an anti-Judaic intention?

Several other passages could also be cited as anti-Judaic, not least because, beginning with Marcion and Tertullian in the second century, some of these texts have seemed to be nothing other than Pauline attacks on the synagogue.[63] Moreover, Boyarin is right to point out that, after the political and cultural ascendancy of Christianity in the West, numerous Christians have used these Galatian texts in forming systems designed to coerce non-Christians into a nominally Christian, religious universality.[64] In addition to Gal 3:19–20, one could list especially 1:13–16 (note *Ioudaïsmos*, "Judaism," in 1:14), 2:13–16 (note *Ioudaioi*, "Jews," in 2:13 and the expressions *Ioudaïkôs zên* and *Ioudaïzein*, "to live in the Jewish manner," in 2:14), 3:16, 3:28, and 4:21–5:1.[65]

As we come to each of these passages in the course of reading the letter as a whole, we will consider the possibility of an anti-Judaic intention on Paul's part, only to discover that it is not present in the text, a conclusion that now finds

[61] On Leo Baeck as a theological interpreter of Christianity, see Mayer, *Christentum und Judentum*, especially 58–75; the critique of Mayer in Jacob, *Christianity Through Jewish Eyes*; J. L. Martyn, *Issues*, 47–69; Klappert, "Brücken."

[62] Maccoby, *Mythmaker*, 188–189. See also, however, the cautionary review by J. L. Martyn, *Issues*, 70–75.

[63] As hinted above, the *locus classicus* for this reading of Galatians is 4:21–5:1, a passage in connection with which a major modern interpreter of Galatians says, "According to Galatians, Judaism is excluded from salvation altogether . . ." (H. D. Betz 251). Glimpses into the history of the interpretation of this passage are provided in J. L. Martyn, *Issues*, 197 n11.

[64] Boyarin's justified charge against the history of Christian coercion runs throughout his fascinating book *Politics*. When he says, however, that Paul's universalism "seems to *conduce* to coercive politico-cultural systems that engage in more or less violent projects of the *absorption* of cultural specificities into the dominant one" (228; emphasis added), he fails to reckon adequately with the difference between Paul's intentions and those of later interpreters. Note, for example, the *way* in which Paul reverses the ancient Israelite hope of absorbing the Gentiles into herself (§13 above).

[65] Contemplating the standard reading of Gal 4:21–5:1, one can scarcely avoid recalling the statues of church and synagogue that flank the south portal of the Strasbourg cathedral, even though the thirteenth-century architect was consciously thinking of the then-current interpretation of 2 Corinthians 3. Cf. Zinn, "History."

agreement in the study of Boyarin.[66] For without exception, in the passages listed, as in others, the ruling polarity is not that of Christianity versus Judaism, church versus synagogue. As we will see repeatedly, that ruling polarity is rather the cosmic antinomy of God's apocalyptic act in Christ versus religion, and thus the gospel versus religious tradition (cf. Comments #10, #13, #43, and #48).[67] Even before we come to detailed exegesis of these passages, then, four brief comments related to the cosmic antinomy between apocalypse and religion may prove helpful.[68]

[66]Boyarin, *Politics*, 136–157. One must note, however, that we have here an instance in which a common conclusion is reached by different, partially contradictory routes. Boyarin's discussion is somewhat complex: "I argue that while Galatians is not an anti-Judaic text, its theory of the Jews nevertheless is one that is inimical to Jewish difference, indeed to all difference as such" (*Politics*, 156). As we will see below, one of the clearest indications that Galatians is not an anti-Judaic text lies in the fact that the letter contains no theory of the Jews, properly speaking.

[67]Here and elsewhere, I use the term "religion" to speak of the various communal, cultic means — always involving the distinction of sacred from profane — by which human beings seek to know and to be happily related to the gods or God (e.g., *eusebeia*; Epictetus *Ench.* 31:1; Paris Papyri 29:10; *religio* as respect for what is sacred: *religio, id est, cultus deorum* [Cicero]). In the sense in which I employ the word, religion is a human enterprise. Thus, in Paul's view, religion is the polar opposite of God's apocalyptic act in Christ. It is patriarchal (i.e., human) tradition, by which one knows what is sacred and what is profane, instead of the apocalypse of God that effects the end of that distinction (*patrikê paradosis* instead of *apokalypsis*; Gal 1:13–16; cf. Gal 5:6; Rom 14:14). In Galatians religion is Gentile observance of the Law as though Christ had not differentiated its promissory and guiding voice from its cursing voice, causing the former alone to be pertinent to the church's daily life (Comment #48). Religion, therefore, provides the human being "with his most thorough-going possibility of confusing an illusion with God" (Käsemann, *Questions*, 184; cf. 191 and idem, *Essays*, 78: religion involves the setting aside of sacred space, sacred time, sacred persons). The polarity between religion and apocalypse is also evident in the difference between superstition and faith. For Paul religion is the human being's superstitious effort to come to know and to influence God, rather than the faith that is elicited by God's invasive grace and that is active in the love of neighbor (Gal 4:8–10; 5:6, 13–14; Rom 1:25). To be sure, the new community created by God's act in Christ engages in the thankful worship of God, indeed worship in everyday life (Romans 12). This community even has rites, such as baptism (Gal 3:26–28) and the eucharist (Gal 2:12; 1 Cor 11:23–26), and it knows that it is distinct from the world at large (see Gal 6:10, and note Paul's use of the term *hagioi* in other letters, e.g. Phil 1:1; 1 Cor 5:9–13). The formula of Gal 3:28 shows, however, that, in the life of the church, worship of God is the corporate act in which the religious distinction of sacred from profane is confessed to have been abolished precisely by God's redemptive deed in Christ. The Christ who is confessed in the formula *solus Christus* is the Christ in whom there is neither Jew nor Gentile. Instead of being the holy community that stands apart from the profane orb of the world, then, the church is the beachhead God is planting in his war of liberation from all religious differentiations. The distinction between church and world is in nature apocalyptic rather than religious. In short, it is in the birth and life of the church that Paul perceives the polarity between human religion and God's apocalypse; and for that reason a significant commentary on Paul's letters can be found in the remark of Dietrich Bonhoeffer that "God has founded his church beyond religion . . ." (*Swords*, 118; cf. idem, *Letters*, 168). See Morse, "Dialogue."

[68]Cf. Käsemann, *Questions*, 188–195; Walter, "Religiosität," 436–441.

The Practice of Judaism by Jews
Although that antinomy plays a highly important role in the whole of Galatians, Paul never presents it as an attack on the practice of Judaism by Jews. On the contrary, the issue he poses is without exception internal to the church. When Paul uses the term *Ioudaios*, "Jew," in 2:13, 14, 15; 3:28, he refers to Jewish Christians, not to non-Christian Jews. And when he speaks of living in the Jewish manner (*Ioudaïkôs zên* and *Ioudaïzein* in 2:14) he refers to a specific turn of events within the life of the church, Jewish Christians compelling Gentile Christians to accept the Jewish food laws (cf. 2:3 and 6:12). None of these references suggests a critique of the synagogue.

Characteristic of Galatians is the sequence of four vignettes Paul provides of the church in Jerusalem (Comment #46). Not one of these vignettes has to do with the Temple cultus. All reveal the polarity between divine acts and religious acts *within* the church.

Are things not different, however, in Paul's reference to Judaism itself (*Ioudaïsmos*) in 1:13–14? There, preparing to speak of the point at which God called him to preach Christ to the Gentiles, Paul refers to his earlier life as a zealously observant Jew (cf. Phil 3:5–6). And if we read that reference together with the affirmations of 4:3–5, we must conclude that the letter does contain an *implication* with regard to Judaism: Paul's zealous observance of the Law failed to liberate him from enslavement to the elements of the old cosmos. That liberation came through God's apocalypse of Jesus Christ, not through any religion, including that of Judaism.

Two qualifications are crucial, however. First, in referring to God's apocalypse of Jesus Christ, Paul is speaking of a deed of the God of Abraham, Isaiah, and Jeremiah. Second, he is offering the personal testimony of one Christian to other Christians who are tempted to commence observance of the Law *as* the means of salvation. He is not formulating an attack on Jews who worship in the synagogue. It is true that, to a great extent, the cosmic antinomy between religion and apocalypse is *the* issue of Galatians. It is also true that, in the final analysis, this cosmic antinomy cannot be anything less than comprehensive (note both Gal 3:22a and its rewording in Rom 11:32). The fact remains, however, that Paul always focuses this antinomy on issues that are internal to the church.

Opposition Among Religions
In Galatians the polarity between apocalypse and religion spells the end of all forms of opposition among religions. The apocalyptic, baptismal formula of Gal 3:28 — "There is neither Jew nor Greek . . . in Christ Jesus" — expresses Paul's certainty that Christ is precisely not a religious figure at all, in the sense of playing a role in the distinction of sacred from profane. Of equal import is the resulting portrait of the patriarch who finds in Christ his singular seed (3:16). From the two exegetical sections of the letter (3:6–4:7; 4:21–5:1), we sense that Paul understands Abraham in the light of Christ, Abraham's nonreligious seed. True enough, the Teachers are presenting the patriarch as the quintessential religious

figure, the paradigmatic proselyte who observed the Law even before Sinai. Seeing Abraham in the light of God's act in the Christ in whom there is neither Jew nor Gentile, Paul, however, finds in the patriarch himself a figure as far removed from the world of religion as is his seed.[69] Like Christ, that is, Abraham plays no role in the distinction of sacred from profane. Just as the covenant God made with him did not consist of commandments, so it involves neither sacred rites such as circumcision, nor sacred times, nor special foods. That covenant is God's promise, and nothing other than the promise (Comments #37 and #48). Abraham is located prior to the distinction of sacred from profane — Sinai — and the advent of Abraham's seed, Christ, far from being a sacred event in a religious history that includes Sinai, involves the termination of the sacred/profane distinction that was introduced (by angels) at Sinai.

With the advent of Christ, then, the antinomy between apocalypse and religion has been enacted by God once for all. Moreover, this antinomy is central to the way in which Paul does theology in Galatians, not least in connection with one of its major themes, rectification. As the antidote to what is wrong in the world does not lie in religion — religion being one of the major components of the wrong — so the point of departure from which there can be movement to set things right cannot be found in religion; as though, provided with a good religious foundation for a good religious ladder, one could ascend from the wrong to the right. Things are the other way around. God has elected to invade the realm of the wrong — "the present evil age" (1:4) — by sending his Son and the Spirit of his Son into it from outside it. This apocalyptic invasion thus shows that to take the Sinaitic Law to the Gentiles — as the Teachers are doing — is to engage in a mission that is marked at its center by the impotence of religion.

We sense, then, the reason for Paul's certainty that neither Christ nor Abraham is a religious figure, but we also see that, in Paul's view, the antinomy between apocalypse and religion militates against the emergence of religion *within* the church. And for that reason the church is not a new religion set over against the old religion, Judaism (see footnote 168 in Comment #45).

Turning to Religion After the Apocalypse of Christ
The picture of religion in Galatians does not portray the service of worship in the synagogue. On the contrary, that picture is specifically focused on the issue that has been posed by the Teachers' work in the Galatian churches. When Gentiles turn to the observance of the Sinaitic Law after having been baptized into Christ, Paul says that they embrace a form of religion that is for them indistinguishable from the pagan religion into which they were born! For this step removes them from Christ (4:8–11; 5:4). Quite specifically, then, for Gentiles Law observance is nothing other than a religion — as opposed to God's apocalypse in Christ — and therefore enslaving.

[69] Similarly, the prophetic figures of Isaiah and Jeremiah, whose shadows we sense behind 1:15, bear their own witness, so to speak, to Paul's being called by God out of the realm of traditional religion.

The Letter's Horizon: Two Gentile Missions

Finally, there is the closely related matter of the letter's horizon. Just as there were no Jewish communities in the Galatian cities, and no former Jews in the Galatian churches, so no Jews are addressed in the Galatian letter, and no Jews are being spoken about in the letter.[70] Paul had, in fact, no reason to think that the members of his Galatian churches would ever come into contact with non-Christian Jews.[71] Thus, the subject of church and synagogue lies beyond the letter's horizon.[72] We can return to the way in which the term "Jew" is used in the formula of Gal 3:28, for it indicates what we might call the letter's theological topography:

> There is neither Jew nor Greek; there is neither slave nor free; there is no "male and female"; for all of you are One in Christ Jesus.

With this formula Paul speaks specifically and exclusively to those who are *in Christ Jesus*.[73]

Moreover, and of great importance, Paul's use of the formula has specifically to do with the difference between the Teachers' mission to the Gentiles and his own. Here his focus is entirely clear. Wherever the Gentile mission is empowered *by God*, it does not continue the distinction between Jew and Gentile.[74] But this focus tells us that Paul is concerned with these two Gentile missions, not with two institutions, church and synagogue (Comment #45). The difference is

[70]Anti-Judaic writings always speak *about* Jews (Gager, *Origins*, 35–112). Except for his testimony about his own past life, however, Paul includes among the dramatis personae of Galatians (§1 above) no non-Christian Jews, either in Judea or in the Diaspora. We have already noted that we find no Jewish institutions, such as the Temple and the synagogue. A Christian interpreter can be challenged — even moved — by the willingness of a Jewish colleague to try the experiment of reading Galatians as a letter addressed to himself (Boyarin, *Politics*, 228–260). It is certainly not for me to say how that reading should proceed. I can only warn of its danger. For, removed from its original setting, Galatians can be made to say many things, as the history of its interpretation in the hands of the imperial church attests. See J. L. Martyn, *Issues*, 191–208.

[71]Given this factor, it did not occur to Paul to include in his Galatian letter warnings against Gentile-Christian pride comparable to the warnings of Rom 11:13–36. Nor did he think to caution his readers against saying to Jews that God played no part in the genesis of their Law. In Galatians Paul reveals a genuine horror at the spectacle of a Gentile church cut off from the Jewish *churches* of Judea (Gal 2:2, 10).

[72]Paul was well acquainted with the institution of the synagogue, not only because of the role it played in his youth but also because it was the setting in which, as an apostle, he was several times subjected to severe discipline for preaching the gospel to Gentiles without requiring their circumcision (1 Thess 2:15–16a; 2 Cor 11:24; cf. Fitzgerald, *Hardships*). We can also assume that before his call to be an apostle, he was accustomed to speaking in the synagogue setting (Gal 1:14; Phil 3:4–5). Everything in Galatians, however, shows that this letter is in no degree comparable to a sermon Paul might have conceived for a synagogue service.

[73]It is apparently Boyarin's tendency to omit this final phrase that leads him to find in Galatians a theory of the Jews (*Politics*, 156).

[74]According to Gal 3:26–29, Gentiles become children of Abraham only by incorporation into the Christ who is beyond all religious differentiation.

monumental. For the letter's consumptive focus on the evangelization of Gentiles means that there is no Jewish horizon in Galatians.[75] For that we must go to Romans 9–11 (§13 above).

To be sure, taken out of its setting, placed, for example, in the hands of the imperial church that—leaving the message of Galatians far behind—came to see itself as the true religion, while viewing the synagogue as a false religion, Galatians can be made to say many things, some of them hideous. Read in its own setting, it is not an anti-Judaic text.[76]

THE PRESENT VOLUME

§18 LISTENING WITH GALATIAN EARS

Like other volumes in the Anchor Bible, the present translation and commentary is designed "to make available all the significant historical and linguistic knowledge which bears on the interpretation" of the document that is its subject.[77] In this case that knowledge is employed with a specific goal in mind.

---

[75] As we have noted above, Paul's reference to his early life in 1:13–14 causes Judaism to lie *just beyond* the letter's horizon. And the Teachers, not to mention their supporters in the Jerusalem church, will have sensed as much. Thus, later, anticipating his final trip to the Jerusalem church, Paul extends his horizon so as to include all of Israel (Romans 9–11), although, as we have seen in §13 above, even in Romans the redemption of all Israel is said to be the result of *God's faithfulness* to Israel, not to Israel's observance of the Law. The expanded picture in Romans serves only to emphasize by contrast, then, that Galatians itself does not contain a "theory of the Jews" (*contra* Boyarin, *Politics*, 156). And the absence of such a theory is reason enough to say, *with* Boyarin, that Galatians is not an anti-Judaic text (ibid.).

[76] In light of the later emergence of the imperial church as the "true religion," we can pose the issue in a slightly different way, church and world: When Paul quotes the baptismal formula of 3:28, with its accent on the newly created unity in Christ—"for all of you are One in Christ Jesus"—does he himself employ the motif of unity in order to substitute a new form of anthropological polarity for an old one, the church *versus* the world? In short, in Paul's view is the church nothing other than yet another pattern of "us" versus "them," no longer Jew versus Gentile, but rather Christian versus non-Christian? And, if so, did Paul play a role in laying the foundation on the basis of which a politically powerful church (certainly not existent in Paul's time) could coerce non-Christians into a nominally Christian, religious universality (cf. again Boyarin, *Politics*, 228)? For one major reason these questions must be answered in the negative. For Paul God's good news is marching into the whole of the world under the banner of the Christ who was crucified by the powers of the world (Gal 3:13; 1 Cor 2:8). True enough, in the cross power met power, God's power vanquishing the powers of the world (see J. L. Martyn, *Issues*, 279–297; Cousar, *Cross*). But God's victorious power is evident not in the political might of an imperial church, but rather in the foolishness of this cross-centered gospel that brings its proclaimers into solidarity with those who are weak and stumbling (2 Cor 11:29). As God's new creation, the church lives under this cross, and for that reason the church is called to serve the world, not to stand aloof as a new "us." See Comment #40 and Note on 6:10.

[77] See the statement of the General Editors, W. F. Albright and D. N. Freedman. The text interpreted in this volume is that of Galatians in K. Aland et al., *Novum Testamentum Graece* (27th ed.; Stuttgart: Deutsche Bibelgesellschaft, 1993). See Aland for text-critical sigla.

According to an oral tradition, the Greek lexicographer Walter Bauer formulated the following interpretive rule:

On the way toward ascertaining the intention of an early Christian author, the interpreter is to ask how the author's document was understood by those who first read or heard it.[78]

Working at the present volume over a period of years has convinced me that Bauer's rule is more than an interesting suggestion. I have not applied it rigidly or even with total consistency. Bearing in mind, however, (a) that all actors in the Galatian drama are to us moderns very strange characters indeed — not least Paul himself[79] — and (b) that Paul's text will have been heard differently by different segments of the Galatian churches (see §11 and especially §12 above), I have found that to ask about their understandings of Paul's text is to gain a surprising entrance into Paul's intentions. The document is a letter, crafted in order to speak to a circle of listeners who were well known to Paul, and whom he considered to be in a life-and-death crisis.[80] Paul knew, in fact, that the Galatians would hear his letter with the sermons of the Teachers still ringing in their ears, and with the Teachers themselves still in their midst, more than ready to continue their sermons, forming them largely as interpretive refutations of Paul's letter (§11 above).

In this situation Paul gave considerable thought to the way in which his words would strike the ears of the original listeners, one of his major concerns being to draw unmistakable distinctions between his own theology and that of the Teachers. We have hinted above (and see Comment #37) that, in the history of the letter's interpretation, Paul has been credited more than once with theological views that seem in fact to have been held not by him, but rather by the Teachers! We can be certain that the Teachers themselves did not make this mistake, and the same can be said of virtually all members of the Galatian churches. It becomes doubly important, then, for the modern interpreter to take a seat in one of the Galatian congregations, in order — as far as possible — to listen to the letter with Galatian ears. That attempt is obviously complex, for to hear the letter as the Galatians heard it requires that we listen to the voice of Paul with one ear, while listening to the voices of the Teachers with the other. Complex and demanding as it may be, however, that attempt defines the major route along which I have tried to honor the dynamics of this ancient document, thus hoping to arrive at an interpretation that is — to some extent — both scientific and empathetic.

---

[78]Having heard this Bauer tradition from theological students in Göttingen in 1957, I later encountered it in conversations with E. Käsemann. See J. L. Martyn, *Issues*, 209–229.

[79]To speak only of the world of art, can anyone imagine Paul sitting quietly and listening to a Beethoven symphony, or standing for the better part of an hour before Vermeer's *Young Woman with a Water Pitcher*?

[80]Cf. Howard, *Crisis*.

BIBLIOGRAPHY

◆

Bibliographical items are abbreviated in the footnotes, articles by using a word or words here italicized, books by using a word or words here in boldface. Reference works and commentaries on Galatians are listed under "Abbreviations." In text and footnote citations, when the name of a scholar is not followed by a title, the reference is to a commentary on Galatians.

Aageson, J. W., **Written** Also for Our Sake: Paul and the Art of Biblical Interpretation (Louisville: Westminster/John Knox, 1993).

Achtemeier, P. J., "An *Elusive Unity*: Paul, Acts, and the Early Church," *CBQ* 48 (1986) 1–26.

———, The **Quest** for Unity in the New Testament Church (Philadelphia: Fortress, 1987).

Agus, A. E., The **Binding** of Isaac and Messiah (Albany: SUNY Press, 1988).

Allison, D. C., "*Peter* and Cephas: One and the Same," *JBL* 111 (1992) 489–495.

Amir, Y., "*Die messianische Idee* im hellenistischen Judentum," *Freiburger Rundbrief* 25 (1973) 195–203.

Anderson, A. A., "*The Use of 'ruaḥ'* in 1QS, 1QH, and 1QM," *JSS* 7 (1962) 293–303.

Applebaum, S., "Judaism (North Africa)," *ABD*.

Ashton, J., **Understanding** the Fourth Gospel (Oxford: Oxford Univ. Press, 1991).

Attridge, H. W., The Epistle to the **Hebrews** (Philadelphia: Fortress, 1989).

Aune, D. E., The New Testament in Its **Literary** Environment (Philadelphia: Westminster, 1987).

———, Review of H. D. Betz, *Galatians, RSR* 7 (1981) 323–328.

Aus, R. D. "Three *Pillars* and Three Patriarchs: A Proposal Concerning Gal 2:9," *ZNW* 70 (1979) 252–61.

Baarda, T., "*Openbaring* — Traditie en Didache," *Zelfstandig geloven* (ed. F. H. Kuiper et al.; Kampen: Kok, 1987) 152–167.

———, et al., **Paulus** en de andere joden (Delft: Meinema, 1984).

Babcock, W. S. (ed.), Paul and the **Legacies** of Paul (Dallas: SMU Press, 1990).

Badenas, R., **Romans** 10:4 in Pauline Perspective (Sheffield: JSOT, 1985).

Baeck, L., "Romantic Religion," *Judaism and Christianity: Essays by Leo Baeck* (ed. W. Kaufmann; New York: Atheneum, 1981) 189–292.

Baird, W., "'*One* Against the Other,'" *The Conversation Continues: Studies in*

Paul and John in Honor of J. Louis Martyn (ed. R. T. Fortna and B. R. Gaventa; Nashville: Abingdon, 1990) 116–136.

Bamberger, B. J., *Proselytism in the Talmudic Period* (New York, 1939, 1968).

Bammel, E., "*Galater* 1,23," ZNW 59 (1968) 108–112.

_____, "*Gottes DIATHEKE* (Gal III 15–17) und das jüdische Rechtsdenken," NTS 6 (1959/60) 313–319.

Banks, R. J., "The Eschatological *Role* of the Law in Pre- and Post-Christian Jewish Thought," *Reconciliation and Hope* (ed. R. J. Banks; Grand Rapids: Eerdmans, 1974) 173–185.

Barclay, J. M. G., "'Do we undermine the Law?' A Study of *Romans 14.1–15.6*," *Paul and the Mosaic Law* (ed. J. D. G. Dunn; Tübingen: Mohr/Siebeck, 1996) 287–308.

_____, *Jews in the Mediterranean Diaspora from Alexander to Trajan (323 BCE–117 CE)* (Edinburgh: T & T Clark, 1996).

_____, "*Mirror-Reading* a Polemical Letter: Galatians as a Test Case," JSNT 31 (1987) 73–93.

_____, *Obeying the Truth: A Study of Paul's Ethics in Galatians* (Edinburgh: T & T Clark, 1988).

_____, "Paul Among *Diaspora Jews*," JSNT 60 (1995) 89–120.

_____, "Paul, *Philemon*, and the Dilemma of Christian Slave-Ownership," NTS 37 (1991) 161–186.

_____, "Thessalonica and Corinth: Social Contrasts in Pauline Christianity," JSNT 47 (1992) 49–72.

_____, and J. Sweet (eds.), *Early Christian Thought in Its Jewish Context* (Cambridge: Cambridge Univ. Press, 1996).

Barnard, L. W., "*Hadrian* and Judaism," JRH 5 (1969) 285–298.

Barnikol, E., *Die Drei Jerusalem Reisen des Paulus* (Kiel: Mühlau, 1929).

Barrett, C. K., "Acts and the *Pauline Corpus*," ExpTim 88 (1966) 2–5.

_____, "The *Allegory* of Abraham, Sarah, and Hagar in the Argument of Galatians," *Rechtfertigung: Festschrift für Ernst Käsemann zum 70. Geburtstag* (ed. J. Friedrich et al.; Tübingen: Mohr/Siebeck, 1976) 1–16.

_____, "*Cephas* and Corinth," *Abraham Unser Vater: Festschrift O. Michel* (ed. O. Betz et al.; Leiden: Brill, 1963) 1–12.

_____, *The Epistle to the Romans* (New York: Harper & Row, 1957).

_____, *Freedom and Obligation* (Philadelphia: Westminster, 1985).

_____, "Paul and the 'Pillar' Apostles," *Studia Paulina in honorem Johannis de Zwaan septuagenarii* (ed. J. N. Sevenster and W. C. van Unnik; Haarlem: Bohn, 1953) 1–19.

_____, *Paul: An Introduction to His Thought* (Louisville: Westminster/Knox, 1995).

_____, "Pauline *Controversies* in the Post-Pauline Period," NTS 20 (1973) 229–245.

_____, "Paul's *Opponents* in II Corinthians," NTS 17 (1971) 233–254.

_____, *The Second Epistle to the Corinthians* (New York: Harper & Row, 1973).

_____, *The Signs of an Apostle* (London: Epworth, 1970).

_____, "What *Minorities?*" *Mighty Minorities?* (ed. D. Hellholm et al.; Oslo: Scandinavian Univ. Press, 1995) 1–10.

Barth, K., *Church Dogmatics* (4 vols.; Edinburgh: T & T Clark, 1936–1970).

Barth, M., *Ephesians* (AB; 2 vols.; Garden City: Doubleday, 1974).

_____, *Israel and the Church* (Richmond: Knox, 1969).

_____ "The Kerygma of Galatians," *Int* 21 (1967) 131–146.

_____, *The People of God* (Sheffield: JSOT, 1983).

Bassler, J. M., *Divine Impartiality* (Atlanta: Scholars, 1982).

_____, "Divine *Impartiality* in Paul's Letter to the Romans," *NovT* 26 (1984) 43–58.

_____, "God (NT)," *ABD.*

_____, *God and Mammon*: *Asking for Money in the New Testament* (Nashville: Abingdon, 1991).

_____ (ed.), *Pauline Theology, Volume I* (Minneapolis: Fortress, 1991).

Batiffol, P., *Studia Patristica* (2 vols; Paris: Leroux, 1889–1890) "Le Livre de la Prière d'Aseneth," 1.1–87.

Baumgarten, A. I., "The Pharisaic *Paradosis*," *HTR* 80 (1987) 63–77.

Baumgarten, J., *Paulus und die Apokalyptik* (Neukirchen: Neukirchener, 1975).

Baumgarten, J. M., "Does *tlh* in the Temple Scroll Refer to *Crucifixion?*" *JBL* 91 (1972) 472–481.

Beck, N. A., *Mature Christianity in the 21st Century: The Recognition and Repudiation of the Anti-Jewish Polemic in the New Testament* (New York: Crossroad, 1994).

Becker, J., *Das Heil Gottes* (Göttingen: Vandenhoeck & Ruprecht, 1964).

_____, *Paul: Apostle to the Gentiles* (Louisville: Westminster/Knox, 1993).

Beker, J. C., "The *Faithfulness* of God and the Priority of Israel," *HTR* 79 (1986) 10–16.

_____, *Paul the Apostle* (Philadelphia: Fortress, 1980).

Belleville, L. L., "'*Under Law*': Structural Analysis and the Pauline Concept of Law in Galatians 3.21–4.11," *JSNT* 26 (1986) 53–78.

Ben Chorin, S., *Paulus der Völkerapostel in jüdischer Sicht* (München: Paul List, 1970).

Berger, K., "*Abraham* in den paulinischen Hauptbriefen," *MTZ* 17 (1966) 47–89.

_____, *Die Gesetzesauslegung Jesu* (Neukirchen: Neukirchener, 1972).

_____, "Die sog. '*Sätze* heiligen Rechts' im N.T.," *TZ* 28 (1972) 305–330.

Bertram, G., "*ôdin*," *TDNT* 9.667–674.

Betz, H. D., "Apostle," *ABD.*

_____, "*Heresy* and Orthodoxy in the NT," *ABD.*

_____, *2 Corinthians 8 and 9* (Philadelphia: Fortress, 1985).

Betz, O., "Rechtfertigung in *Qumran*," *Rechtfertigung: Festschrift für Ernst Käsemann* (ed. J. Friedrich et al.; Tübingen: Mohr/Siebeck, 1976) 17–36.

_____, "*stigma*," *TDNT* 7.657–664.

Beyer, H. W., "*katêcheô*," *TDNT* 3.638–640.

Beyer, K., *Semitische Syntax im Neuen Testament* (Göttingen: Vandenhoeck & Ruprecht, 1962).

Birdsall, J. N., "Problems of the *Clementine Literature*," *Jews and Christians: The Partings of the Ways A.D. 70–135* (ed. J. D. G. Dunn; Tübingen: Mohr, 1992) 347–361.

Bittel, K., "Christliche und jüdische *Grabsteine*," *Bogazkoy V* (Abh. der Deutschen Orientalgesellschaft 18; Berlin, 1975) 110–113, nos. 6–9.

Blank, J., *Paulus und Jesus* (Munich: Kösel, 1968).

Blinzler, J., "*Lexikalisches* zu dem Terminus *ta stoicheia tou kosmou* bei Paulus," *Studiorum Paulinorum Congressus Internationalis Catholicus 1961* (Rome: Pontifical Biblical Institute, 1963) 2.429–443.

Bloch, R., "Quelques aspects de *la Figure de Moïse* dans la Tradition Rabbinique," *Moïse, l'homme de l'Alliance* (ed. H. Cazelles et al.; Paris: Desclee, 1955) 93–167.

Boers, H., *The Justification of the Gentiles: Paul's Letters to the Romans and the Galatians* (Peabody: Hendrickson, 1994).

Bonhoeffer, D., *Letters and Papers from Prison* (New York: Macmillan, 1953).

———, *No Rusty Swords: Letters, Lectures and Notes 1928–1936* (ed. E. H. Robertson; New York: Harper & Row, 1965).

Borgen, P., *Bread from Heaven* (Leiden: Brill, 1965).

———, "Judaism (Egypt)," *ABD.*

———, "*Paul Preaches Circumcision* and Pleases Men," *Paul and Paulinism* (ed. M. D. Hooker and S. G. Wilson; London: SPCK, 1982) 37–46.

———, "Philo," *ABD.*

———, "Some Hebrew and Pagan Features in Philo's and Paul's Interpretation of *Hagar and Ishmael*," *The New Testament and Hellenistic Judaism* (ed. P. Borgen and S. Giversen; Aarhus: Aarhus Univ. Press, 1995) 151–164.

Bormann, L., et al. (eds.), *Religious Propaganda and Missionary Competition in the New Testament World: Essays Honoring Dieter Georgi* (Leiden: Brill, 1994).

Bornkamm, G., *Paul* (New York: Harper & Row, 1971).

Bornkamm, K., *Luthers Auslegungen des Galaterbriefs von 1519 und 1531: Ein Vergleich* (Berlin: de Gruyter, 1963).

Borse, U., *Der Standort des Galaterbriefes* (Köln: Hanstein, 1972).

Bousset, W., *Kyrios Christos* (Nashville: Abingdon, 1970).

Bouwman, G., "Die Hagar- und Sara-Perikope (Gal 4,21–31); Exemplarische Interpretation zum *Schriftbeweis* bei Paulus," *ANRW* 2.25.4, 3135–3155.

Bovon, F., "*Une formal prépaulinienne* dans l'Epître aux Galates (Gal 1.4–5)," *Paganisme, Judaïsme, Christianisme* (ed. A. Benoit et al.; Paris: de Boccard, 1978) 91–107.

Boyarin, D., *A Radical Jew: Paul and the Politics of Identity* (Berkeley: Univ. of California Press, 1994).

———, "Was Paul an 'Anti-Semite'? A *Reading* of Galatians 3–4," *USQR* 47 (1993) 47–80.

Brandenburger, E., *Fleisch und Geist* (Neukirchen: Neukirchener, 1968).

Braude, W. G., *Jewish Proselytizing in the First Two Centuries of the Common Era* (Providence: Brown Univ. Press, 1940).

———, *The Midrash on Psalms* (New Haven: Yale Univ. Press, 1959).

Braumann, G., *Vorpaulinische christliche Taufverkündigung bei Paulus* (Stuttgart: Kohlhammer, 1962).

Breytenbach, C., "Versöhnung, Stellvertretung und Sühne," *NTS* 39 (1993) 59–79.

_____, et al. (eds.), *Anfänge der Christologie: Festschrift F. Hahn* (Göttingen: Vandenhoeck & Ruprecht, 1991).

Brinsmead, B. H., *Galatians — Dialogical Response to Opponents* (Chico: Scholars, 1982).

Brocke, E., and J. Seim (eds.), *Gottes Augapfel* (Neukirchen: Neukirchener, 1986).

Broer, I., "'Vertreibe die Magd und ihren Sohn!' Gal 4,21–31 im Horizont der Debatte über den Antijudaismus im Neuen Testament," *Der bezwingende Vorsprung des Guten; Festschrift Wolfgang Harnisch* (ed. U. Schoenhorn and S. Pfürtner; Münster: LIT, 1994) 167–198.

Brown, A. R., *The Cross and Human Transformation* (Minneapolis: Fortress, 1995).

Brown, R. E., *The Birth of the Messiah* (rev. ed.; New York: Doubleday, 1993).

_____, "The Burial of Jesus (Mark 15:42–27)," *CBQ* 50 (1988) 233–245.

_____, *The Churches the Apostles Left Behind* (New York: Paulist, 1984).

_____, *The Death of the Messiah* (2 vols.; New York: Doubleday, 1994).

_____, "Not Jewish Christianity and Gentile Christianity but *Types* of Jewish/Gentile Christianity," *CBQ* 45 (1983) 74–79.

_____, and J. P. Meier, *Antioch and Rome* (New York: Paulist, 1983).

_____, et al., *Mary in the New Testament* (Minneapolis: Fortress, 1978).

_____, et al., *Peter in the New Testament* (Minneapolis: Augsburg, 1973).

Büchsel, F., "allêgoreô," *TDNT* 1.260–263.

Buck, C. H., "The Collection for the Saints," *HTR* 43 (1950).

_____, "The Date of Galatians," *JBL* 70 (1951) 113–122.

_____, and G. Taylor, *Saint Paul: A Study in the Development of His Thought* (New York: Scribner's, 1969).

Bultmann, R., "ginôskô," *TDNT* 1.689–719.

_____, "kauchaomai," *TDNT* 3.645–654.

_____, "pisteuô," *TDNT* 6.174–228.

_____, *Stil der paulinischen Predigt und die kynisch-stoische Diatribe* (Göttingen: Vandenhoeck & Ruprecht, 1910).

_____, *Theology of the New Testament* (New York: Scribner's, 1951–1955).

_____, "Zur Auslegung von Galater 2,15–18," *Exegetica* (Tübingen: Mohr/Siebeck, 1967) 394–399.

Burchard, C., "Das doppelte Liebesgebot in der frühen christlichen Überlieferung," *Der Ruf Jesu* (ed. E. Lohse et al.; Göttingen: Vandenhoeck & Ruprecht, 1970) 39–62.

_____, "The Importance of Joseph and Asenath for the Study of the New Testament," *NTS* 33 (1987) 102–134.

_____, "Joseph and Asenath," *OTP*.

Bussmann, C., *Themen der paulinischen Missionspredigt auf dem Hintergrund der spätjüdisch-hellenistischen Missionsliteratur* (Bern: Lang, 1975).

Caird, G. B., A *Commentary on the **Revelation** of St. John the Divine* (New York: Harper, 1966).

Calder, W. M., "*Adoption* and Inheritance in Galatia," *JTS* 31 (1930) 372–374.

Callan, T., "The Background of the Apostolic *Decree* (Acts 15:20, 29; 21:25)," *CBQ* 55 (1993) 284–297.

———, "Pauline *Midrash*: The Exegetical Background of Gal 3:19b," *JBL* 99 (1980) 549–567.

Callaway, M. C., "The Mistress and the Maid: *Midrashic Traditions* Behind Galatians 4:21–31," *Radical Religion* 2 (1975) 94–101.

Campbell, D. A., "*Romans 1:17* — a *Crux Interpretum* for the *Pistis Christou* Debate," *JBL* 113 (1994) 265–285.

Campbell, W. S., ***Paul's Gospel** in an Intercultural Context: Jew and Gentile in the Letter to the Romans* (Frankfurt: Lang, 1991).

Catchpole, D. R., "Paul, James, and the *Apostolic Decree*," *NTS* 23 (1977) 428–444.

Cerfaux, L., "La *tradition* selon Saint Paul," *Recueil Lucien Cerfaux* (2 vols.; Gembloux: Duculot, 1954) 2.253–263.

Chesnutt, R. D., "Joseph and Asenath," *ABD*.

Chevallier, R., *Roman Roads* (Berkeley: Univ. of California Press, 1976).

Christiansen, E. J., *The Covenant in Judaism and Paul* (Leiden: Brill, 1995).

Clabeaux, J. J., A *Lost **Edition** of the Letters of Paul* (Washington, D.C.: Catholic Biblical Association, 1989).

———, "Marcion," *ABD*.

Clark, K. W., "The *Meaning* of *energeo* and *katargeo* in the New Testament," *JBL* 54 (1935) 93–101.

Cohen, S. J. D., "*Crossing* the Boundary and Becoming a Jew," *HTR* 82 (1989) 13–33.

———, "The Rabbinic *Conversion* Ceremony," *JJS* 41 (1990) 177–203.

———, "Was *Timothy* Jewish (Acts 16:1–3)? Patristic Exegesis, Rabbinic Law, and Matrilineal Descent," *JBL* 105 (1986) 251–268.

Cohen Stewart, G. H., *The **Struggle** in Man Between Good and Evil: An Inquiry into the Origin of the Concept of Yeser Hara* (Kampen: Kok, 1984).

Collins, A. Y., *The Apocalypse* (Wilmington: Glazier, 1979).

———, "Early Christian *Apocalypses*," *IDB*.

Collins, J. J., *The Apocalyptic **Imagination*** (New York: Crossroad, 1984).

———, "Early Jewish *Apocalypticism*," *IDB*.

———, "Sybilline Oracles," *OTP* 1.317–472.

Colpe, C., *Das **Siegel** der Propheten: Historische Beziehungen zwischen Judentum, Judenchristentum und Islam* (Berlin: Institute Kirche und Judentum, 1990).

Connolly, R. H., ***Didascalia** Apostolorum* (Oxford: Clarendon, 1929).

Conzelmann, H., ***Acts** of the Apostles* (Philadelphia: Fortress, 1987).

———, ***History** of Primitive Christianity* (Nashville: Abingdon, 1973).

Corley, B. (ed.), ***Colloquy** on New Testament Studies* (Macon: Mercer, 1980).

Cosgrove, C. H., "*Arguing* Like a Mere Human Being: Galatians 3.15–18 in Rhetorical Perspective," *NTS* 34 (1988) 536–549.

————, *The Cross and the Spirit* (Macon: Mercer, 1988).

————, "Justification in Paul: A Linguistic and Theological Reflection," *JBL* 106 (1987) 653–670.

————, "The Law and the Spirit" (Dissertation, Princeton Theological Seminary, 1985).

Cousar, C. B., "Continuity and Discontinuity: Reflections on *Romans 5–8* (In Conversation with Frank Thielman)," *Pauline Theology, Volume III: Romans* (ed. D. M. Hay and E. E. Johnson; Minneapolis: Fortress, 1995) 196–210.

————, *The Letters of Paul* (Nashville: Abingdon, 1996).

————, Review of Hamerton-Kelly, *Sacred Violence*, CR 1994, 196–199.

————, A *Theology of the Cross: The Death of Jesus in the Pauline Letters* (Minneapolis: Fortress, 1990).

Cranfield, C. E. B., "St. Paul and the *Law*," *SJT* 17 (1964) 43–68.

————, "'The *Works* of the Law' in the Epistle to the Romans," *JSNT* 43 (1991) 89–101.

Cruz, H., *Christological Motives and Motivated Actions in Pauline Paraenesis* (Frankfurt: Lang, 1990).

Cullmann, O., *Christ and Time* (London: SCM, 1949).

Dahl, N. A., "The *Atonement*—an Adequate Reward for the Akedah? (Rom 8:32)," *Neotestamentica et Semitica: Studies in Honor of Matthew Black* (ed. E. E. Ellis and M. Wilcox; Edinburgh: T & T Clark, 1969) 15–29. Also in Dahl, *Jesus the Christ* (Minneapolis: Fortress, 1991) 137–151.

————, "*Contradictions* in Scripture," *Studies in Paul* (Minneapolis: Augsburg, 1977) 159–177.

————, *The Crucified Messiah* (Minneapolis: Augsburg, 1974).

————, "Form-Critical *Observations* on Early Christian Preaching," *Jesus in the Memory of the Early Church: Essays by Nils Alstrup Dahl* (Minneapolis: Augsburg, 1976).

————, "Formgeschichtliche *Beobachtungen* zur Christusverkündigung in der Gemeindepredigt," *Neutestamentliche Studien für Rudolph Bultmann* (ed. W. Eltester; Berlin: Töpelmann, 1957) 1–9.

————, "Der *Name* Israel: I. Zur Auslegung von Gal 6.16," *Judaica* 6 (1950) 151–170.

————, "Paul's Letter to the *Galatians*, Epistolary Genre, Content, and Structure," *SBL Seminar Papers* (Atlanta: Scholars, 1973).

————, *Studies in Paul* (Minneapolis: Augsburg, 1977).

————, *Das Volk Gottes* (Darmstadt: Wissenschaftliche Buchgesellschaft, 1963).

Dalbert, P., *Die Theologie der hellenistisch-jüduschen Missionsliteratur unter Ausschluss von Philo und Josephus* (Hamburg: Reich, 1954).

Daniels, J. B., "Barnabas," *ABD*.

Daube, D., *The New Testament and Rabbinic Judaism* (London: Athlone, 1956).

Davies, W. D., *The Gospel and the Land* (Berkeley: Univ. of California Press, 1972).

BIBLIOGRAPHY

———, "A Note on *Josephus, Antiquities* 15.136," *HTR* 47 (1954) 135–140.

———, *Paul and Rabbinic Judaism* (London: SPCK, 1955).

———, "Paul and the *People* of Israel," *NTS* 24 (1977) 4–39.

———, Review of H. D. Betz, *Galatians*, *RSR* 7 (1981) 314–318.

———, *Torah in the Messianic Age and/or Age to Come* (Philadelphia: Society of Biblical Literature, 1952).

———, and D. C. Allison, *A Critical and Exegetical Commentary on the Gospel of Saint Matthew* (2 vols.; Edinburgh: T & T Clark, 1988–1991).

de Boer, M. C., *The Defeat of Death* (Sheffield: JSOT, 1988).

———, "*Images* of Paul in the Post-Apostolic Period," *CBQ* 42 (1980) 359–380.

———, *Johannine Perspectives on the Death of Jesus* (Kampen: Kok Pharos, 1996).

———, "Paul and Jewish *Apocalyptic Eschatology*," *Apocalyptic and the New Testament: Essays in Honor of J. Louis Martyn* (ed. J. Marcus and M. L. Soards; Sheffield: JSOT, 1989) 169–190.

———, "Which Paul?" *Paul and the Legacies of Paul* (ed. W. S. Babcock; Dallas: SMU Press, 1990) 45–54.

Deichgräber, R., *Gotteshymnus und Christushymnus in der frühen Christenheit* (Göttingen: Vandenhoeck & Ruprecht, 1967).

Deidun, T. J., *New Covenant Morality* (Rome: Biblical Institute Press, 1981).

Delling, G., "*baskainô*," *TDNT* 1.594–595.

———, "*stoicheô*," *TDNT* 7.666–687.

DeMaris, R. E., *The Colossian Controversy* (Sheffield: Sheffield Academic Press, 1993).

Dibelius, M., *James* (Philadelphia: Fortress, 1976).

Dietrich, E. L., "Shmone Esre," *RGG* 5.1462–1463.

Dinkler, E., "Der Brief an die Galater. Zum Kommentar von Heinrich *Schlier*," *VF* 7 (1953) 175–183 (= Dinkler, *Signum Crucis*, 270–282).

———, *Signum Crucis: Aufsätze zum Neuen Testament und zur christlichen Archäologie* (Tübingen: Mohr/Siebeck, 1967).

Dion, P. E., "Letters (Aramaic)," *ABD*.

Dittenberger, W., *Orientis Graeci Inscriptiones Selectae* (2 vols.; Hildesheim: Olms, 1970).

Dodd, B. J., "*Christ's Slave*, People Pleasers and Galatians 1.10," *NTS* 42 (1996) 90–104.

Dodd, C. H., "*ENNOMOS CHRISTOU*," *Studia Paulina in honorem J. de Zwaan* (ed. J. N. Sevenster and W. C. van Unnik; Haarlem: Bohn, 1953) 96–110.

Donaldson, T. L., "The '*Curse of the Law*' and the Inclusion of the Gentiles: Galatians 3.13–14," *NTS* 32 (1986) 94–112.

———, "*The Law That Hangs* (Matthew 22:40): Rabbinic Formulation and Matthean Social World," *CBQ* 57 (1995) 689–709.

Donfried, K. P., "Justification and Last *Judgment* in Paul," *ZNW* 67 (1976) 90–110.

——— (ed.), *The Romans Debate* (rev. ed.; Peabody: Hendrickson, 1991).

———, *The Setting of Second Clement* (Leiden: Brill, 1974).

Doty, W. G., *Letters in Primitive Christianity* (Philadelphia: Scholars, 1973).

Drane, J. W., *Paul Libertine or Legalist* (London: SPCK, 1975).

Duff, N. J., *Humanization and the Politics of God: The koinonia Ethics of Paul Lehmann* (Grand Rapids: Eerdmans, 1992).

———, "The *Significance* of Paul's Apocalyptic for Theological Ethics," *Apocalyptic and the New Testament: Essays in Honor of J. Louis Martyn* (ed. J. Marcus and M. L. Soards; Sheffield: JSOT, 1989) 279–296.

Duling, D. C., "The *Promises* to David and Their Entry into Christianity," *NTS* 20 (1973) 55–77.

Dunn, J. D. G., "*Echoes* of Intra-Jewish Polemic in Paul's Letter to the Galatians," *JBL* 112 (1993) 459–477.

———, "4QMMT and Galatians," *NTS* 43 (1997) 147–153.

——— "The Incident at Antioch (Gal. ii.11–18)," in Dunn, *Jesus*.

———, *Jesus, Paul and the Law: Studies in Mark and Galatians* (Atlanta: Westminster, 1990).

———, "The *New Perspective* on Paul," *BJRL* 65 (1983) 95–122.

———, "*Once More, Pistis Christou*," *SBL Seminar Papers #30* (Atlanta: Scholars, 1991) 730–744.

———, *The Partings of the Ways Between Christianity and Judaism and Their Significance for the Character of Christianity* (Philadelphia: Trinity, 1991).

——— (ed.), *Paul and the Mosaic Law* (Tübingen: Mohr/Siebeck, 1996).

———, "The *Relationship* Between Paul and Jerusalem According to Galatians 1 and 2," *NTS* 28 (1982) 461–478.

———, *Romans* (2 vols.; Dallas: Word, 1988).

———, "The *Theology* of Galatians," *Pauline Theology, Volume I* (ed. J. Bassler; Minneapolis: Fortress, 1991) 125–146.

———, *The Theology of Paul's Letter to the Galatians* (Cambridge: Cambridge Univ. Press, 1993).

———, *Unity and Diversity in the New Testament* (Philadelphia: Westminster, 1977).

———, "*Works* of the Law and the Curse of the Law (Galatians 3:10–14)," *NTS* 31 (1985) 523–542.

Ebeling, G., *The Truth of the Gospel* (Philadelphia: Fortress, 1985).

Eckert, J., *Die urchristliche Verkündigung im Streit zwischen Paulus und seinen Gegnern nach dem Galaterbrief* (Regensburg: Pustet, 1971).

Eckstein, H. J., *Verhiessung und Gesetz: Eine exegetische Untersuchung zu Galater 2,15–4,7* (Tübingen: Mohr, 1996).

Egee, O., "*Rechtswörter* und Rechtsbilder in den paulinischen Briefen," *ZNW* 18 (1917/18) 84–108.

Ehler, B., *Die Herrschaft des Gekreuzigten: Ernst Käsemanns Frage nach der Mitte der Schrift* (Berlin: de Gruyter, 1986).

Ehrman, B. D., "*Cephas* and Peter," *JBL* 109 (1990) 463–474.

Eissfeldt, O., *The Old Testament: An Introduction* (New York: Harper & Row, 1965).

BIBLIOGRAPHY

Ellis, E. E., "The Circumcision Party and the Early Christian *Mission*," *TU* 102 (1968) 390–399.

———, *The Old Testament in Early Christianity* (Tübingen: Mohr/Siebeck, 1991).

———, "Paul and His Co-*Workers*," *NTS* 17 (1971) 437–453.

———, "Paul and His *Opponents*: Trends in the Research," *Christianity, Judaism, and Other Greco-Roman Cults* (4 vols.; ed. J. Neusner; Leiden: Brill, 1975) 1.264–298.

———, "Traditions in 1 Corinthians," *NTS* 32 (1986) 481–502.

Engberg-Pedersen, T. (ed.), *Paul in His Hellenistic Context* (Minneapolis: Fortress, 1995).

Esler, P. F., "Making and *Breaking* an Agreement Mediterranean Style: A New Reading of Galatians 2:1–14," *BibInt* 3 (1995) 285–314.

Fee, G. D., *God's Empowering Presence: The Holy Spirit in the Letters of Paul* (Peabody: Hendrickson, 1995).

Feldman, L. H., "*Abraham* the Greek Philosopher in Josephus," *TAPA* 99 (1968) 143–156.

———, *Jew and Gentile in the Ancient World* (Princeton: Princeton Univ. Press, 1993).

———, "Josephus," *ABD*.

Ferguson, E., *Backgrounds of Early Christianity* (2nd ed.; Grand Rapids: Eerdmans, 1993).

Fishbane, M., *Biblical Interpretation in Ancient Israel* (Oxford: Clarendon, 1985).

Fitzgerald, J. T., "The *Catalogue* in Ancient Greek Literature," *The Rhetorical Analysis of Scripture: Essays from the 1995 London Conference* (ed. S. E. Porter and T. H. Olbricht; Sheffield: Sheffield Academic Press, 1996).

———, *Cracks in an Earthen Vessel: An Examination of the Catalogues of Hardships in the Corinthian Correspondence* (Atlanta: Scholars, 1988).

——— (ed.), *Friendship, Flattery, and Frankness of Speech* (Leiden: Brill, 1996).

———, "Virtue/Vice *Lists*," *ABD*.

Fitzmyer, J. A., "The Contribution of *Qumran Aramaic* to the Study of the New Testament," *NTS* 20 (1974) 382–407.

———, "*Crucifixion* in Ancient Palestine. Qumran Literature and the New Testament," *CBQ* 40 (1979) 493–513 (= Fitzmyer, *Advance*, 125–146).

———, *The Gospel According to Luke* (AB; 2 vols.; Garden City: Doubleday, 1981, 1985).

———, "*Jewish Christianity* in Acts in Light of the Qumran Scrolls," *Studies in Luke-Acts* (ed. L. E. Keck and J. L. Martyn; Philadelphia: Fortress, 1980) 233–257.

———, "Paul and the *Law*," in Fitzmyer, *Advance*, 186–201.

———, Review of Luedemann, *Chronology*, *TS* 48 (1987) 162–164.

———, *Romans* (AB; New York: Doubleday, 1993).

———, *To Advance the Gospel* (New York: Crossroad, 1981).

Flusser, D., "The *Dead Sea Sect* and Pre-Pauline Christianity," *Aspects of the Dead Sea Scrolls* (ed. C. Rabin and Y. Yadin; Scripta Hierosolymitana 4; Jerusalem: Magnes, 1958) 215–266.

Foerster, W., *Gnosis* (Oxford: Clarendon, 1972).

Franklin, E., *Luke: Interpreter of Paul, Critic of Matthew* (Sheffield: JSOT, 1994).

Fredriksen, P., "Judaism, the Circumcision of Gentiles, and Apocalyptic Hope: Another Look at *Galatians 1 and 2*," *JTS* 42 (1991) 533–564.

Freeman, K., *Ancilla to the Presocratic Philosophers* (Cambridge: Harvard Univ. Press, 1948).

Friedrich, G., "*euaggelizomai*," TDNT 2.707–737.

_____, "Ein *Tauflied* hellenistischer Judenchristen," *TZ* 21 (1965) 502–516.

Friedrich, J., et al. (eds.), *Rechtfertigung: Festschrift für Ernst Käsemann* (Tübingen: Mohr/Siebeck, 1976).

Froelich, K., "*Fallibility* Instead of Infallibility? A Brief History of the Interpretation of Galatians 2:11–14," *Teaching Authority and Infallibility* (ed. P. Empie et al.; Minneapolis: Augsburg, 1980) 259–269.

Furnish, V. P., "'He *Gave Himself* [Was Given] Up . . .': Paul's Use of a Christological Assertion," *The Future of Christology: Essays in Honor of Leander E. Keck* (ed. A. J. Malherbe and W. A. Meeks; Minneapolis: Fortress, 1993) 109–121.

_____, *The Love Command in the New Testament* (Nashville: Abingdon, 1972).

_____, *The Moral Teaching of Paul* (rev. ed.; Nashville: Abingdon, 1985).

_____, "On Putting Paul in His *Place*," *JBL* 113 (1994) 3–17.

_____, "Paul the Theologian," *The Conversation Continues: Studies in Paul and John in Honor of J. Louis Martyn* (ed. R. T. Fortna and B. R. Gaventa; Nashville: Abingdon, 1990) 19–34.

_____, *II Corinthians* (AB; Garden City: Doubleday, 1984).

_____, *Theology and Ethics in Paul* (Nashville: Abingdon, 1968).

Gager, J., *The Origins of Anti-Semitism* (Oxford: Oxford Univ. Press, 1985).

Gale, H. M., *The Use of Analogy in the Letters of Paul* (Philadelphia: Westminster, 1964).

Gallas, S., "Fünfmal vierzig weniger einen . . . Die an Paulus vollzogenen *Synagogalstrafen* nach 2Kor 11,24," *ZNW* 81 (1990) 178–191.

Gasparro, G. S., *Soteriological and Mystical Aspects in the Cults of Cybele and Attis* (Leiden: Brill, 1985).

Gaston, L., "Israel's *Enemies* in Pauline Theology," *NTS* 28 (1982) 400–423.

_____, *Paul and the Torah* (Vancouver: Univ. of British Columbia Press, 1987).

Gaventa, B. R., "*Apostles* as Babes and Nurses in 1 Thessalonians 2:7," *Faith and History: Essays in Honor of Paul W. Meyer* (ed. John T. Carroll et al.; Atlanta: Scholars, 1990) 193–207.

_____, *From Darkness to Light: Aspects of Conversion in the New Testament* (Philadelphia: Fortress, 1986).

_____, "Galatians 1 and 2: *Autobiography* as Paradigm," *NovT* 28 (1986) 309–326.

————, "The *Maternity* of Paul: An Exegetical Study of Gal 4:19," *The Conversation Continues: Studies in Paul and John in Honor of J. Louis Martyn* (ed. R. T. Fortna and B. R. Gaventa; Nashville: Abingdon, 1990) 189–201.

————, "*Mother's Milk* and Ministry in 1 Corinthians 3," *Theology and Ethics in Paul and His Interpreters* (ed. E. H. Lovering and J. L. Sumney; Nashville: Abingdon, 1996) 101–113.

————, "*Our Mother St. Paul*: Toward the Recovery of a Neglected Theme," *PSB* 17 (1996) 29–44.

————, "The *Purpose* of the Law: Paul and Rabbinic Judaism" (M.Div. Thesis, Union Theological Seminary, 1973).

————, "The *Singularity* of the Gospel," *Pauline Theology, Volume I* (ed. J. Bassler; Minneapolis: Fortress, 1991) 147–159.

Georgi, D., "Corinthians, Second Letter to the," *IDBS*.

————, "Exegetische *Anmerkungen* zur Auseinandersetzung mit den Einwänden gegen die Thesen der Bruderschaften," *Christusbekenntnis im Atomzeitalter? TEH* 70 (1959) 111–114.

————, *Die Geschichte der Kollekte des Paulus für Jerusalem* (Hamburg: Reich, 1965).

————, *The Opponents of Paul in Second Corinthians* (Philadelphia: Fortress, 1986).

————, *Remembering the Poor: The History of Paul's Collection for Jerusalem* (Nashville: Abingdon, 1991).

————, *Theocracy in Paul's Praxis and Theology* (Minneapolis: Fortress, 1991).

————, "Weisheit Salomos," *JSHRZ*.

Gerhardsson, B., *The Shema in the New Testament* (Lund: Novapress, 1996).

Gese, H., *Vom Sinai zum Sion: Alttestamentliche Beiträge zur biblischen Theologie* (Munich: Kaiser, 1974).

Ginzberg, L., *The Legends of the Jews* (7 vols.; Philadelphia: Jewish Publication Society, 1909–1938).

Gnilka, J., *Das Evangelium nach Markus* (2 vols.; Zürich: Benziger, 1978–1979).

————, *Der Philipperbrief* (Freiburg: Herder, 1976).

Goldin, J., *The Fathers According to Rabbi Nathan* (New Haven: Yale Univ. Press, 1955).

Goodenough, E. R., *By Light Light* (New Haven: Yale Univ. Press, 1935).

Goodman, M., "*Jewish Proselytizing* in the First Century," *The Jews Among Pagans and Christians in the Roman Empire* (ed. J. Lieu, J. North, and T. Rajak; London: Routledge, 1992) 53–78.

Goodman, M., "*Proselytizing* in Rabbinic Judaism," *JJS* 40 (1989) 175–185.

Graf, D. F., "Nabateans," *ABD*.

Grässer, E., *Der Alte Bund im Neuen: Exegetische Studien zur Israelfrage im Neuen Testament* (Tübingen: Mohr/Siebeck, 1985).

————, "Das eine *Evangelium*. Hermeneutische Erwägungen zu Gal 1,6–10," *ZTK* 66 (1969) 306–344.

Green, M. J., *Dictionary of Celtic Myth and Legend* (London: Thames & Hudson, 1992).

————, and A. Sutton, *The Gods of the Celts* (Gloucester: A. Sutton, 1986).

Green, W. S., "*Messiah* in Judaism: Rethinking the Question," *Judaisms and Their Messiahs at the Turn of the Christian Era* (ed. J. Neusner, W. S. Green, and E. S. Frerichs; Cambridge: Cambridge Univ. Press, 1987) 1–13.

Greenberg, M., *Ezekiel 1–20* (AB; Garden City: Doubleday, 1983).

————, "Three *Conceptions* of the Torah in Hebrew Scriptures," *Die Hebräische Bibel* (ed. E. Blum; Neukirchen: Neukirchener, 1990) 365–378.

Gunther, J. J., *Paul: Messenger and Exile: A Study in the Chronology of His Life and Letters* (Valley Forge: Judson, 1972).

Gutbrod, W., "*Israel*," *TDNT* 3.357–390.

Güttgemanns, E., *Der leidende Apostel und sein Herr: Studien zur paulinischen Christologie* (Göttingen: Vandenhoeck & Ruprecht, 1966).

Haacker, K., "Die *Geschichtstheologie* von Röm 9–11 in Lichte philonischer Schriftauslegung," *NTS* 43 (1997) 209–222.

————, "*Glaube* II," *TRE* 13.277–304.

Haenchen, E., *Die Apostelgeschichte* (Göttingen: Vandenhoeck & Ruprecht, 1956); *The Acts of the Apostles* (Philadelphia: Westminster, 1971).

Hafemann, S., *Paul, Moses and the History of Israel* (Tübingen: Mohr/Siebeck, 1995).

Hahn, F., *Mission in the New Testament* (London: SCM, 1965).

————, "*Taufe* und Rechtfertigung," *Rechtfertigung: Festschrift für Ernst Käsemann* (ed. J. Friedrich et al.; Tübingen: Mohr/Siebeck, 1976) 95–124.

Hainz, J., "Koinônia bei Paulus," *Religious Propaganda and Missionary Competition in the New Testament World: Essays Honoring Dieter Georgi* (ed. L. Bormann et al.; Leiden: Brill, 1994) 375–392.

————, *Koinônia. "Kirche" als Gemeinschaft bei Paulus* (Regensburg: Pustet, 1982).

Halivni, D., *Midrash, Mishnah, and Gemara* (Cambridge: Harvard Univ. Press, 1986).

Hall, B. B., "Battle *Imagery* in Paul's Letters" (Dissertation, Union Theological Seminary, 1973).

Hall, R. G., "*Arguing* Like an Apocalypse: Galatians and an Ancient *Topos* Outside the Greco-Roman Rhetorical Tradition," *NTS* 42 (1996) 434–453.

————, "Historical *Inference* and Rhetorical Effect," *Persuasive Artistry: Studies in New Testament Rhetoric in Honor of G. A. Kennedy* (ed. D. F. Watson; Sheffield: JSOT, 1991) 308–320.

————, "The Rhetorical *Outline* for Galatians: A Reconsideration," *JBL* 106 (1987) 277–287.

Hall, S. G., *Christian Anti-Semitism and Paul's Theology* (Minneapolis: Fortress, 1993).

Hamerton-Kelly, R. G., *Sacred Violence: Paul's Hermeneutic of the Cross* (Minneapolis: Fortress, 1992).

Hanks, T. D., "Poor, Poverty (NT)," *ABD*.

Hansen, G. W., *Abraham in Galatians: Epistolary and Rhetorical Contexts* (Sheffield: JSOT, 1989).

BIBLIOGRAPHY

Hanson, P. D., "*Apocalypse* (Genre)" and "Apocalypticism," *IDBS* 27–34.

———, "*Apocalypses* and Apocalypticism," *ABD*.

———, The *Dawn* of Apocalyptic (Philadelphia: Fortress, 1975).

Harnack, A., The *Constitution* and Law of the Church in the First Two Centuries (New York: Putnam, 1910).

———, *Marcion*: Das Evangelium vom fremden Gott (2nd ed.; Leipzig: Hinrichs, 1924).

Harnisch, W. "*Einübung* des neuen Seins. Paulinische Paränese am Beispiel des Galaterbriefs," *ZTK* 84 (1987) 279–296.

Haussleiter, J., Der *Glaube* Jesu Christ und der christliche Glaube (Erlangen: Deichert, 1891).

Hawkins, J. G., "The *Opponents* of Paul in Galatia" (Dissertation, Yale Univ., 1971).

Hay, D. M., "Pistis as 'Ground of Faith' in Hellenized Judaism and Paul," *JBL* 108 (1989) 461–476.

———, and E. E. Johnson (eds.), *Pauline Theology, Volume III: Romans* (Minneapolis: Fortress, 1995).

Hays, R. B., "Christology and Ethics in Galatians: *The Law of Christ*," *CBQ* 49 (1987) 268–290.

———, *Echoes* of Scripture in the Letters of Paul (New Haven: Yale Univ. Press, 1989).

———, The *Faith* of Jesus Christ: An Investigation of the Narrative Substructure of Galatians 3:1–4:11 (Chico: Scholars, 1983).

———, "Justification," *ABD*.

———, The Moral Vision of the New Testament: *Community*, Cross, New Creation (San Francisco: HarperSanFrancisco, 1996).

———, "Pistis and Pauline Christology: *What Is at Stake?*" *SBL Seminar Papers* #30 (Atlanta: Scholars, 1991) 714–729.

———, "*Psalm 143* and the Logic of Romans 3," *JBL* (1980) 107–115.

———, "'The *Righteous One*' as Eschatological Deliverer: A Case Study in Paul's Apocalyptic Hermeneutics," *Apocalyptic and the New Testament: Essays in Honor of J. Louis Martyn* (ed. J. Marcus and M. Soards; Sheffield: JSOT, 1988) 191–215.

———, "The Role of *Scripture* in Paul's Ethics," *Theology and Ethics in Paul and His Modern Interpreters: Essays in Honor of Victor Paul Furnish* (ed. E. H. Lovering, Jr. and J. L. Sumney; Nashville: Abingdon, 1996) 30–47.

Heiligenthal, R., "Soziologische *Implikationen* der paulinischen Rechtfertigungslehre im Galaterbrief am Beispiel der 'Werke des Gesetzes,'" *Kairos* 26 (1984) 38–53.

Hempel, J., "Amen," *IDB*.

Hengel, M., *Acts* and the History of Earliest Christianity (Philadelphia: Fortress, 1980).

———, The *Atonement*. A Study of the Origins of the Doctrine in the New Testament (London: SCM, 1981).

———, *Crucifixion* (Philadelphia: Fortress, 1977).

_____, *The Johannine Question* (London: SCM, 1989).

_____, *The Pre-Christian Paul* (Philadelphia: Trinity, 1991).

_____, *Son of God* (Philadelphia: Fortress, 1976).

_____, "Die *Stellung* des Apostels Paulus zum Gesetz in den unbekannten Jahren zwischen Damaskus und Antiochien," *Paul and the Mosaic Law* (ed. J. D. G. Dunn; Tübingen: Mohr/Siebeck, 1996) 25–52.

_____, "Die *Ursprünge* der christlichen Mission," *NTS* 18 (1971) 15–38.

Hester, J. D., "The Rhetorical *Structure* of Galatians 1:11–2:14," *JBL* 103 (1984) 223–233.

Hill, C. C., *Hellenists and Hebrews: Reappraising Division in the Earliest Church* (Minneapolis: Fortress, 1991).

Hillerbrand, H. J., "Martin *Luther* and the Jews," *Jews and Christians: Exploring the Past, Present, and Future* (ed. J. H. Charlesworth; New York: Crossroad, 1990) 127–150.

Hock, R. F., *The Social Context of Paul's Ministry: Tentmaking and Apostleship* (Philadelphia: Fortress, 1980).

Hoffmann, R. J., *Marcion: On the Restitution of Christianity* (Chico: Scholars, 1984).

Hofius, O., "'*All Israel* Will Be Saved': Divine Salvation and Israel's Deliverance in Romans 9–11," *PSB*, Supplementary Issue #1 (1990) 19–39.

_____, "Das Gesetz Mose und das *Gesetz Christi*," *ZTK* 80 (1983) 262–286.

Holladay, C. R., "Aristobulos (OT Pseudepigrapha)," *ABD*.

_____, *Fragments from Hellenistic Jewish Authors: Volume 3, Aristobulos* (Atlanta: Scholars, 1995).

Hollander, H. W., and M. de Jonge, *The Testaments of the Twelve Patriarchs: A Commentary* (Leiden: Brill, 1985).

Holmberg, B., *Paul and Power: The Structure of Authority in the Primitive Church As Reflected in the Pauline Epistles* (Philadelphia: Fortress, 1980).

Holtz, T., *Der erste Brief an die Thessalonicher* (Zürich: Benzinger, 1986).

Holtzmann, H. J., *Lehrbuch der historisch-kritischen Einleitung in das Neue Testament* (2nd ed.; Freiburg: Mohr/Siebeck, 1886).

Hong, I. G., *The Law in Galatians* (Sheffield: JSOT, 1993).

Hooker, M. D., *From Adam to Christ: Essays on Paul* (Cambridge: Cambridge Univ. Press, 1990).

_____, "*Pistis Christou*," *NTS* 35 (1989) 321–342.

Howard, G., *Crisis in Galatia* (Cambridge: Cambridge Univ. Press, 1979).

_____, "The *Faith* of Christ," *ExpTim* 85 (1974) 212–215.

_____, "*Notes* and Observations on the 'Faith of Christ,'" *HTR* 60 (1967) 459–465.

_____, *Paul: Crisis in Galatia* (2nd ed.; Cambridge: Cambridge Univ. Press, 1990).

Hübner, H., "Der *Galaterbrief* und das Verhältnis von der antiker Rhetorik und Epistolographie," *TLZ* 109 (1984) 241–250.

_____, *Law in Paul's Thought* (Edinburgh: T & T Clark, 1984).

Hultgren, A. J., "On *Translating* and Interpreting Galatians 1:13," *Bible Translator* 26 (1975), 146–148.

———, "Paul's Pre-Christian *Persecutions* of the Church: Their Purpose, Locale, and Nature," *JBL* 95 (1976), 97–111.

———, "The *Pistis Christou Formulations* in Paul," *NovT* 22 (1980) 248–263.

Hurd, J. C., "*Chronology*, Pauline," *IDBS* (1976) 167.

———, *The Origin of I Corinthians* (New York: Seabury, 1965; Macon: Mercer, 1983).

Hurtado, L. W., "The Jerusalem *Collection* and the Book of Galatians," *JSNT* 5 (1979) 46–62.

———, *One God, One Lord: Early Christian Devotion and Ancient Jewish Monotheism* (London: SCM, 1988).

Hyldahl, N., *Die Paulinische Chronologie* (Leiden: Brill, 1986).

Jacob, W., *Christianity Through Jewish Eyes* (New York: Hebrew Union College Press, 1974).

Jaubert, A., *La notion d'alliance dans le Judaïsme aux abords de l'ere chrétienne* (Paris: PatSor, 1963).

Jegher-Bucher, V., *Der Galaterbrief auf dem Hintergrund antiker Epistolographie und Rhetorik. Ein anderes Paulusbild* (Zürich: Theologischer Verlag, 1991).

Jeremias, G., *Der Lehrer der Gerechtigkeit* (Göttingen: Vandenhoeck & Ruprecht, 1963).

Jeremias, J., *Jesus' Promise* (Naperville: Allenson, 1958).

Jervell, J., *The Unknown Paul: Essays on Luke-Acts and Early Christian History* (Minneapolis: Augsburg, 1984).

Jewett, R., "The *Agitators* and the Galatian Congregation," *NTS* 17 (1971) 198–212.

———, *A Chronology of Paul's Life* (Philadelphia: Fortress, 1979).

———, "Ecumenical Theology for the Sake of *Mission*: Romans 1:1–17+15:14–16:24," *Pauline Theology, Volume III: Romans* (ed. D. M. Hay and E. E. Johnson; Minneapolis: Fortress, 1995) 89–108.

———, *Paul's Anthropological Terms* (Leiden: Brill, 1971).

Johnson, E. E., *The Function of Apocalyptic and Wisdom Traditions in Romans 9–11* (Atlanta: Scholars, 1989).

Johnson, L. T., *The Letter of James* (AB; New York: Doubleday, 1995).

———, "Rom 3:21–26 and the *Faith* of Jesus," *CBQ* 44 (1982) 77–90.

Johnson, W., "The Paradigm of *Abraham* in Galatians 3:6–9," *TrinJ* 8 NS (1987) 179–199.

Jones, A. H. M., *The Cities of the Eastern Roman Provinces* (rev. ed. M. Avi-Yonah et al.; Oxford: Clarendon, 1971).

Jones, F. S., *An Ancient Jewish Christian Source on the History of Christianity: Pseudo Clementine "Recognitions" 1.27–71* (Atlanta: Scholars, 1995).

Juel, D., "*The Lord's Prayer* in the Gospels of Matthew and Luke," *PSB*, Supplementary Issue #2 (1992) 56–70.

———, *Messianic Exegesis* (Philadelphia: Fortress, 1988).

Kamlah, E., *Die Form der katalogischen Paränese im Neuen Testament* (Tübingen: Mohr/Siebeck, 1964).

Kampen, J., and M. J. Bernstein (eds.), *Reading 4QMMT* (Atlanta: Scholars, 1996).

Käsemann, E., "A Critical Analysis of *Philippians* 2:5–11," *JTC* 5 (1968) 45–88.

_____, *Essays on New Testament Themes* (London: SCM, 1964).

_____, *Jesus Means Freedom* (Philadelphia: Fortress, 1970).

_____, "Die *Legitimität* des Apostels," *ZNW* 41 (1942) 33–71 (= *Das Paulusbild in der neueren deutschen Forschung* [ed. K. H. Rnengstorf; Darmstadt: Wissenschaftliche Buchgesellschaft, 1964] 475–521; references are to these pages).

_____, "*Liebe*, die sich der Wahrheit freut," *Kirchliche Konflikte* (Göttingen: Vanderhoeck & Ruprecht, 1982) 157–167; "*Love* That Rejoices in the Truth," *Religion and the Humanizing of Man* (ed. J. M. Robinson; Waterloo: Council on the Study of Religion, 1972) 55–65.

_____, "Das Motiv der *Leiblichkeit* bei Paulus" (unpublished paper).

_____, *New Testament Questions of Today* (London: SCM, 1969).

_____, *Perspectives on Paul* (London: SCM, 1969).

_____, *Romans* (Grand Rapids: Eerdmans, 1980).

Kay, J. F., *Christus Praesens* (Grand Rapids: Eerdmans, 1994).

Keck, L. E., "The *Function* of Rom 3:10–18 — Observations and Suggestions," *God's Christ and His People: Studies in Honor of Nils Alstrup Dahl* (ed. J. Jervell and W. A. Meeks; Oslo: Universitetsforlaget, 1977) 141–157.

_____, "The *Introduction* to Mark's Gospel," *NTS* 12 (1966) 352–370.

_____, "'*Jesus*' in Romans," *JBL* 108 (1989) 443–460.

_____, "Paul and *Apocalyptic Theology*," *Int* 38 (1984).

_____, *Paul and His Letters* (rev. ed.; Minneapolis: Fortress, 1988).

_____, "Paul as *Thinker*," *Int* 47 (1993) 27–38.

_____, "Poor," *IDBS*.

_____, "*The Poor* Among the Saints in Jewish Christianity and Qumran," *ZNW* 57 (1966) 54–78.

_____, "The Poor Among the *Saints* in the New Testament," *ZNW* 56 (1965) 100–129.

_____, "*Rethinking* 'New Testament Ethics,'" *JBL* 115 (1996) 3–16.

_____, "Searchable *Judgments* and Scrutable Ways," *Pauline Theology, Volume IV* (ed. D. M. Hay and E. E. Johnson; Atlanta: Scholars, 1997).

_____, "Toward the *Renewal* of New Testament Christology," *NTS* 32 (1986) 362–377.

_____, "What Makes Romans *Tick*?" *Pauline Theology, Volume III: Romans* (ed. D. M. Hay and E. E. Johnson; Minneapolis: Fortress, 1995) 3–29.

Kennedy, G. A., *New Testament Interpretation Through Rhetorical Criticism* (Chapel Hill: Univ. of North Carolina Press, 1984).

Kertelge, K., "*Apokalypsis* Jesou Christou (Gal 1,12)," *Neues Testament und Kirche: Festschrift R. Schnackenburg* (ed. H. Merklein; Freiburg: Herder, 1974) 266–281.

_____ (ed.), *Das Gesetz im Neuen Testament* (Freiburg: Herder, 1986).

_____, *"Rechtfertigung" bei Paulus* (Münster: Aschendorff, 1966).

Kirk, G. S., and J. E. Raven, *The Presocratic Philosophers* (Cambridge: Cambridge Univ. Press, 1960).

Klappert, B., "*Brücken* zwischen Judentum und Christentum: L. Baecks kritische Fragen an das Christentum. Nachwort zur 3. Auflage des Leo-Baeck-Buches von A. H. Friedlander, " A. H. Friedlander, *Leo Baeck: Leben und Lehre* (Munich: Kaiser, 1990) 285–328.

_____, *Israel und die Kirche: Erwägungen zur Israellehre Karl Barths* (Munich: Kaiser, 1980).

Klausner, J., *From Jesus to Paul* (Boston: Beacon, 1939).

Klein, G., "*Galater* 2,6–9 und die Geschichte der Jerusalemer Urgemeinde," *ZTK* 57 (1960) 275–295.

_____, *Rekonstruktion und Interpretation* (Munich: Kaiser, 1969).

_____, "*Sündenverständnis* und theologia crucis bei Paulus," *Theologia Crucis — Signum Crucis* (ed. C. Andresen and G. Klein; Tübingen: Mohr/Siebeck, 1979) 249–282.

Klijn, A. F. J., "Paul's *Opponents* in Philippians iii," *NovT* 7 (1965) 278–284.

Klijn, A. F. J., and G. J. Reinink, *Patristic Evidence for Jewish-Christian Sects* (Leiden: Brill, 1973).

Klumbies, P. G., "Der Eine Gott des Paulus: Röm 1,21–31 als Brenpunkt paulinischen Theologie," *ZNW* 85 (1994) 192–206.

_____, "*Zwischen Pneuma* und *Nomos*: Neuorientierung in den galatischen Gemeinden," *WD* 19 (1987) 109–135.

Knibb, M. A., *The Ethiopic Book of Enoch* (Oxford: Oxford Univ. Press, 1978).

_____, *The Qumran Community* (Cambridge: Cambridge Univ. Press, 1987).

Knox, J., *Chapters in a Life of Paul* (rev. ed.; Macon: Mercer, 1987).

_____, "'*Fourteen* Years Later': A Note on the Pauline Chronology," *JR* 16 (1936) 341–349.

_____, "Galatians," *IDB*.

_____, "On the Pauline *Chronology*: Buck-Taylor-Hurd Revisited," *The Conversation Continues: Studies in Paul and John in Honor of J. Louis Martyn* (ed. R. T. Fortna and B. R. Gaventa; Nashville: Abingdon, 1990) 258–274.

_____, "The Pauline Chronology," *JBL* 58 (1939) 15–29.

Knox, W. L., "*Abraham* and the Quest for God," *HTR* 28 (1935) 55–60.

Koch, D. A., *Die Schrift als Zeuge des Evangeliums: Untersuchungen zur Verwendung und zum Verständnis der Schrift bei Paulus* (Tübingen: Mohr/Siebeck, 1986).

_____, "Der Text von *Hab 2.4b* in der Septuaginta und im Neuen Testament," *ZNW* 76 (1985) 68–85.

Koenig, J., *Jews and Christians in Dialogue* (Philadelphia: Westminster, 1979).

_____, "The Motif of *Transformation* in the Pauline Epistles" (Dissertation, Union Theological Seminary, 1970).

Koester, C., "The Origin and Significance of the Flight to *Pella* Tradition," *CBQ* 51 (1989) 90–106.

Koester, H., *History, Culture, and Religion in the **Hellenistic** Age* (Philadelphia: Fortress, 1980).

———, *"physis,"* *TDNT* 9.266.

Koschorke, K., *"Paulus* in den Nag-Hammadi Texten," *ZTK* 78 (1981) 177–205.

Koskennieme, H., ***Studien** zur Idee und Phraseologie des griechischen Briefes bis 400 n. Chr.* (Helsinki: AASF, 1956).

Kraabel, A. T., "The Roman Diaspora: Six Questionable Assumptions," *JJS* 33 (1982) 445–464.

Kraftchick, S., *"Ethos* and Pathos. Arguments in Galatians 5 and 6: A Rhetorical Approach" (Dissertation, Emory Univ., 1985).

Kraus, H. J., "Schöpfung und Weltvollendung," *EvT* 24 (1964) 462–485.

Krauss, S., *Griechische und Lateinische **Lehnwörter** im Talmud, Midrash und Targum* (ed. I. Löw; Berlin: Calvary, 1898–1899).

Kuck, D. W., "'Each Will Bear His Own Burden': Paul's Creative Use of an *Apocalyptic Motif,"* *NTS* 40 (1994) 289–297.

Kuhn, K. G., *"prosêlytos,"* *TDNT* 6.727–744.

Kühner, R., and B. Gerth, *Ausführliche **Grammatik** der griechischen Sprache. Satzlehre I* (Leverkusen: Gottschalksche Verlag, 1955).

Lambrecht, J., *Pauline Studies* (Leuven: Leuven Univ. Press, 1994).

———, "Rhetorical *Criticism* and the New Testament," *Bijdragen, tijdschrift voor filosofie en theologie* 50 (1989) 239–253.

———, *"Transgressor* by Nullifying God's Grace. A Study of Gal 2,18–21," *Bib* 72 (1991) 217–236.

———, *The **Truth** of the Gospel. Galatians 1:1–4:11* (Rome: St. Paul's Abbey, 1993).

———, *"Unity* and Diversity in Gal 1–2," *Unite et Diversite dans L'Eglise* (Vaticano: Libreria Editrice Vaticana, 1989) 127–142.

———, *"Vloek* en Zegen. Een Studie van Galaten 3,10–14," *Collationes* 21 (1991) 133–157.

Lapide, P., and P. Stuhlmacher, ***Paul.** Rabbi and Apostle* (Minneapolis: Augsburg, 1984).

Le Déaut, R., *"Traditions targumique* dans le corpus paulinien," *Bib* 42 (1961) 28–48.

Lehmann, P., *The **Decalogue** and a Human Future* (Grand Rapids: Eerdmans, 1995).

———, *The **Transfiguration** of Politics* (New York: Harper & Row, 1975).

Lichtenberger, H., "Alter *Bund* und Neuer Bund," *NTS* 41 (1995) 400–414.

———, "'Im Lande Israel zu wohnen, wiegt alle Gebote der Tora auf.' Die Heiligkeit des Landes und die Heiligung des Lebens," *Die Heiden: Juden, Christen und das Problem des Fremden* (ed. R. Feldmeier and U. Heckel; Tübingen: Mohr/Siebeck, 1994) 92–107.

Lieu, J. M., *"Circumcision,* Women and Salvation," *NTS* 40 (1994) 358–370.

Lindemann, A., "Die biblischen *Toragebote* und die paulinische Ethik," *Studien zum Text und zur Ethik des Neuen Testaments: Festschrift Greeven* (ed. W. Schrage; Berlin: de Gruyter, 1986) 242–265.

_____, "Die *Gerechtigkeit* aus dem Gesetz. Erwägungen zur Auslegung und zur Textgeschichte von Röm 10:5," *ZNW* 73 (1982) 231–250.

_____, "Paul in the Writings of the Apostolic Fathers," *Paul and the Legacies of Paul* (ed. W. S. Babcock; Dallas: SMU Press, 1990) 25–44.

_____, *Paulus im ältesten Christentum* (Tübingen: Mohr/Siebeck, 1979).

Linton, O., "The Third *Aspect*. A Neglected Point of View. A Study of Gal. i–ii and Acts ix and xv," *ST* 3 (1949) 79–95.

Lloyd, G. E. R., *Polarity and Analogy* (Cambridge: Cambridge Univ. Press, 1966).

Lohmeyer, E., *Diatheke*. *Ein Beitrag zur Erklärung des neutestamentlichen Begriffs* (Leipzig: Hinrichs, 1913).

_____, *Die Offenbarung des Johannes* (Tübingen: Mohr/Siebeck, 1953).

Lohse, E. (ed.), *Die Texte aus Qumran* (Darmstadt: Wissenschaftliche Buchgesellschaft, 1971).

Longenecker, B. W., "*Pistis* in Rom 3:25: Neglected Evidence for the Faithfulness of Christ," *NTS* 39 (1993) 478–480.

Luedemann, G., *Paul, Apostle to the Gentiles: Studies in Chronology* (Philadelphia: Fortress, 1984).

_____, *Paulus, der Heidenapostel*, vol. 2 (Göttingen: Vandenhoeck & Ruprecht, 1983).

_____, "Zum *Antipaulinismus* im Frühen Christentum," *EvT* 40 (1980) 437–455.

Lührmann, D., "*Christologie* und Rechtfertigung," *Rechtfertigung: Festschrift für Ernst Käsemann* (ed. J. Friedrich et al.; Tübingen: Mohr/Siebeck, 1976) 351–363.

_____, "*Gal* 2,9 und die katholischen Briefe. Bemerkungen zum Kanon und zur regula fidei," *ZNW* 72 (1981) 65–87.

_____, *Glaube im frühen Christentum* (Gütersloh: Gütersloher, 1976).

_____, *Das Offenbarungsverständnis bei Paulus und in Paulinischen Gemeinden* (Neukirchen: Neukirchener, 1965).

_____, "*Pistis* im Judentum," *ZNW* 64 (1973) 19–38.

_____, "*Tage*, Monate, Jahreszeiten, Jahre (Gal 4,10)," *Werden und Wirken des Alten Testaments* (ed. R. Albertz et al.; Göttingen: Vandenhoeck & Ruprecht, 1980) 428–445.

_____, "Die *430 Jahre* zwischen den Verheisungen und dem Gesetz (Gal 3,17)," *ZNW* 100 (1988) 420–423.

Lull, D. J., "'The Law Was Our *Pedagogue*': A Study of Gal 3:19–25," *JBL* 105 (1986) 481–498.

_____, *The Spirit in Galatia* (Chico: Scholars, 1980).

Luz, U., "Der alte und der neue *Bund* bei Paulus und im Hebräerbrief," *EvT* 27 (1967) 318–336.

_____, *Das Geschichtsverständnis des Paulus* (Munich: Kaiser, 1968).

_____, *Matthew 1–7: A Commentary* (Edinburgh: T & T Clark, 1989).

_____, *The Theology of the Gospel of Matthew* (Cambridge: Cambridge Univ. Press, 1995).

Lyall, F., "Roman Law in the Writings of Paul—*Adoption*," *JBL* 88 (1969) 458–466.

Lyons, G., *Pauline Autobiography: Toward a New Understanding* (Atlanta: Scholars, 1985).

Maccoby, H., *The Mythmaker. Paul and the Invention of Christianity* (New York: Harper & Row, 1986).

Magie, D., *Roman Rule in Asia Minor to the End of the Third Century After Christ* (2 vols.; reprinted, New York: Arno, 1975).

Maier, G., *Mensch und freier Wille* (Tübingen: Mohr/Siebeck, 1971).

Maier, J., *Jüdische Auseinandersetzung mit dem Christentum in der Antike* (Darmstadt: Wissenschaftliche Buchgesellschaft, 1982).

_____, *The Temple Scroll. An Introduction, Translation & Commentary* (Sheffield: JSOT, 1985).

Malherbe, A. J., *Ancient Epistolary Theorists* (Atlanta: Scholars, 1988).

_____, *The Cynic Epistles* (Missoula: Scholars, 1977).

_____, "*Determinism* and Free Will in Paul: The Argument of 1 Corinthians 8 and 9," *Paul in His Hellenistic Context* (ed. T. Engberg-Pedersen; Minneapolis: Fortress, 1994) 231–255.

_____, "'*Gentle* as a Nurse': The Cynic Background to 1 Thess ii," *NovT* 12 (1970) 203–217.

_____, "God's New *Family* in Thessalonica," *The Social World of the First Christians: Essays in Honor of Wayne A. Meeks* (ed. L. M. White and O. L. Yarbrough; Minneapolis: Fortress, 1995) 116–125.

_____, "*Mê genoito* in Diatribe and Paul," *HTR* 73 (1980) 231–240.

_____, *Moral Exhortation: A Greco-Roman Sourcebook* (Philadelphia: Westminster, 1986).

_____, *Paul and the Popular Philosophers* (Philadelphia: Fortress, 1989).

_____, *Paul and the Thessalonians* (Philadelphia: Fortress, 1987).

_____, "'*Seneca*' on Paul as Letter Writer," *The Future of Early Christianity: Essays in Honor of Helmut Koester* (ed. B. Pearson; Minneapolis: Fortress, 1991) 414–421.

Mamood, C. K., and S. L. Armstrong, "Do *Ethnic Groups* Exist? A Cognitive Perspective on the Concept of Cultures," *Ethnology* 31 (1992) 1–14.

Marcus, J., "*Authority* to Forgive Sins upon Earth: The Shema in the Gospel of Mark," *The Gospels and the Scriptures of Israel* (ed. C. A. Evans and W. R. Stegner; Sheffield: Sheffield Academic Press, 1994) 196–211.

_____, "*The Circumcision* and the Uncircumcision in Rome," *NTS* 35 (1989) 67–81.

_____, "The Evil Inclination in the Epistle of *James*," *CBQ* 44 (1982) 606–621.

_____, "The Evil Inclination in the Letters of *Paul*," *IBS* 8 (1986) 8–21.

_____, "Modern and Ancient Jewish *Apocalypticism*," *JR* 76 (1996) 1–27.

_____, "Scripture and Tradition in Mark 7" (forthcoming in BETL).

_____, *The Way of the Lord: Christological Exegesis of the Old Testament in the Gospel of Mark* (Louisville: Westminster/Knox, 1992).

Martin, B. L., *Christ and the Law in Paul* (Leiden: Brill, 1989).

Martin, D. B., *Slavery* as Salvation. *The Metaphor of Slavery in Pauline Christianity* (New Haven: Yale Univ. Press, 1990).

Martin, E. D., *Studies in the Life and Ministry of the Early Paul and Related Issues* (Lewiston: Mellen, 1993).

Martin, T., "Apostasy to Paganism: The Rhetorical *Stasis* of the Galatian Controversy," *JBL* 114 (1995) 437–461.

———, "Pagan and Judeo-Christian Time-Keeping *Schemes* in Gal 4.10 and Col 2.16," *NTS* 42 (1996) 105–119.

Martinez, F. G., *The Dead Sea Scrolls Translated* (Leiden: Brill, 1994).

———, *Qumran and Apocalyptic* (Leiden: Brill, 1992).

Martyn, David, "Sade's *Ethical Economies*," *Romanic Review* 86 (1995) 45–63.

———, "*Writing Ethics*: Sublime Failures of Totalization in Kant and Sade" (Dissertation, Cornell Univ., 1991).

Martyn, Dorothy, "A Child and Adam: A Parable of the Two Ages," *Apocalyptic and the New Testament: Essays in Honor of J. Louis Martyn* (ed. J. Marcus and M. L. Soards; Sheffield: JSOT, 1989) 317–333.

———, *The Man in the Yellow Hat* (Atlanta: Scholars, 1992).

Martyn, J. L., "*Apocalyptic Antinomies* in Paul's Letter to the Galatians," *NTS* 31 (1985) 410–424; also in *Issues*.

———, "Christ, the *Elements* of the Cosmos, and the Law in Galatians," *The Social World of the First Christians: Essays in Honor of Wayne A. Meeks* (ed. L. M. White and O. L. Yarbrough; Minneapolis: Fortress, 1995) 16–39; also in *Issues*.

———, "*Clementine Recognitions* 1,33–71, Jewish Christianity, and the Fourth Gospel," *God's Christ and His People: Studies in Honor of Nils Alstrup Dahl* (ed. J. Jervell and W. A. Meeks; Oslo: Universitetsforlaget, 1977) 265–295; cf. Martyn, *The Gospel of John in Christian History*, 55–89.

———, "*Covenant*, Christ, and Church in Galatians," *The Future of Christology: Essays in Honor of Leander E. Keck* (ed. A. J. Malherbe and W. A. Meeks; Minneapolis: Fortress, 1993) 137–151; also in *Issues*.

———, "The Covenants of *Hagar and Sarah*," *Faith and History: Essays in Honor of Paul W. Meyer* (ed. J. T. Carroll et al.; Atlanta: Scholars, 1990) 160–192; also in *Issues*.

———, "The *Crucial Event* in the History of the Law (Gal 5:14)," *Theology and Ethics in Paul and His Modern Interpreters: Essays in Honor of Victor Paul Furnish* (ed. E. H. Lovering, Jr., and J. L. Sumney; Nashville: Abingdon, 1996) 48–61; also in *Issues*.

———, "*Epistemology* at the Turn of the Ages: 2 Corinthians 5:16," *Christian History and Interpretation: Studies Presented to John Knox* (ed. W. R. Farmer et al.; Cambridge: Cambridge Univ. Press, 1967) 269–287; see especially the revised form in *Issues*.

———, "*Events* in Galatia," *Pauline Theology, Volume I* (ed. J. Bassler; Minneapolis: Fortress, 1991) 160–179.

———, "From Paul to *Flannery O'Connor* with the Power of Grace," *Katallagete* (Winter 1981) 10–17; also in *Issues*.

————, "Galatians," *The Books of the Bible* (2 vols.; ed. B. W. Anderson; New York: Scribner's, 1989) 2.271–284; also in *Issues*.

————, *The Gospel of John in Christian History* (New York: Paulist, 1978).

————, "On *Hearing* the Gospel Both in the Silence of the Tradition and in Its Eloquence," *From Jesus to John: New Testament Christologies in Current Perspective* (ed. M. C. de Boer; Sheffield: Sheffield Academic Press, 1993) 129–147; also in *Issues* under the title "God's Way of Making Right What Is Wrong."

————, *History and Theology in the Fourth Gospel* (rev. ed.; Nashville: Abingdon, 1978).

————, "Introduction to *Leo Baeck*," *Jewish Perspectives on Christianity* (ed. F. A. Rothschild; New York: Continuum, 1996) 21–41; also in *Issues* as "Leo Baeck's Reading of Paul." For the German edition of Rothschild's book (Neukirchen: Neukirchener, 1997) some footnotes are added.

————, "A Law-Observant *Mission* to Gentiles: The Background of Galatians," *SJT* 38 (1985) 307–324; also in *Issues*.

————, "*Listening* to John and Paul on the Subject of Gospel and Scripture" (with B. R. Gaventa and P. W. Meyer) *WW* 12 (1992) 68–81; also in *Issues*.

————, "Paul and His *Jewish-Christian Interpreters*," *USQR* 42 (1988) 1–15; also forms part of chapter 13 in *Issues*.

————, "Paul's Understanding of the *Textual Contradiction* Between Habakkuk 2:4 and Leviticus 18:5," *From Tradition to Interpretation: Studies in Biblical Intertextuality in Honor of James A. Sanders* (ed. C. A. Evans and S. Talmon; Leiden: Brill, 1997); also in *Issues*.

————, Review of J. C. Beker, *Paul the Apostle*, *WW* 2 (1982) 194–198; also in *Issues*.

————, Review of H. Maccoby, *The Mythmaker: Paul and the Invention of Christianity*, *New York Times*, July 20, 1986; also in *Issues*.

————, *Theological Issues in the Letters of Paul* (Edinburgh: T & T Clark, 1997; Nashville: Abingdon, 1997).

Matera, F. J., "The *Culmination* of Paul's Argument to the Galatians: Gal 5:1–6:17," *JSNT* 32 (1988) 79–91.

Mayer, R., *Christentum und Judentum in der Schau Leo Baecks* (Stuttgart: Kohlhammer, 1961).

Mayes, A. D. H., *Deuteronomy* (London: Oliphants, 1979).

Mayser, E., *Grammatik der griechischen Papyri aus der Ptolemäerzeit* (2 vols.; Leipzig/Berlin: Teubner, 1906–1938).

McKenzie, J. J., *Second Isaiah* (AB; Garden City: Doubleday, 1968).

McKnight, S., *A Light Among the Gentiles: Jewish Missionary Activity in the Second Temple Period* (Minneapolis: Fortress, 1991).

Meecham, H. G., "The *Present Participle* of Antecedent Action. Some N.T. Instances," *ExpTim* 64 (1953) 285–286.

Meeks, W. A., "The *Divine Agent* and His Counterfeit in Philo and the Fourth Gospel," *Aspects of Religious Propaganda in Judaism and Early Christianity* (ed. E. Schüssler Fiorenza; Notre Dame: Univ. of Notre Dame Press, 1976) 43–67.

——, *The First **Urban** Christians* (New Haven: Yale Univ. Press, 1983).

——, "The Image of the *Androgyne*: Some Uses of a Symbol in Earliest Christianity," *HR* 13 (1973/74) 165–208.

——, *The **Moral World** of the First Christians* (Philadelphia: Westminster, 1986).

——, "On *Trusting* an Unpredictable God: A Hermeneutical Meditation on Romans 9–11," *Faith and History: Essays in Honor of Paul W. Meyer* (ed. J. T. Carroll et al.; Atlanta: Scholars, 1990) 105–124.

——, *The **Origins** of Christian Morality* (New Haven: Yale Univ. Press, 1993).

——, *The Prophet-King* (Leiden: Brill, 1967).

——, Review of H. D. Betz, *Galatians*, *JBL* 100 (1981) 304–307.

——, Review of R. E. Brown and J. P. Meier, *Antioch and Rome*, *HeyJ* 27 (1986) 455–457.

——, and R. L. Wilken, *Jews and Christians in **Antioch*** (Missoula: Scholars, 1978).

Merk, O., "Der *Beginn* der Paränese im Galaterbrief," *ZNW* 60 (1969) 83–104.

——, ***Handeln** aus Glauben. Die Motivierungen der paulinischen Ethik* (Marburg: Elwert, 1968).

Meyer, P. W., "Augustine's 'The Spirit and the *Letter*' as a Reading of Paul's Romans," *The First Christians and Their Social World: Studies in Honor of Wayne A. Meeks* (ed. L. M. White and O. L. Yarbrough; Minneapolis: Fortress, 1995) 366–381.

——, "The *Holy Spirit* in the Pauline Letters," *Int* 33 (1979) 3–18.

——, Review of H. D. Betz, *Galatians*, *RSR* 7 (1981) 318–323.

——, "Romans," *Harper's Bible Commentary* (ed. J. L. Mays; San Francisco: Harper & Row, 1988) 1130–1167.

——, "Romans 10:4 and the 'End' of the Law," *The Divine Helmsman: Studies on God's Control of Human Events, Presented to Lou H. Silberman* (ed. J. L. Crenshaw and S. Sandmel; New York: KTAV, 1980) 59–78.

——, "The '*This-Worldliness*' of the New Testament," *PSB* 2 n.s. (1979) 219–231.

——, "The *Worm* at the Core of the Apple," *The Conversation Continues: Studies in Paul and John in Honor of J. Louis Martyn* (ed. R. T. Fortna and B. R. Gaventa; Nashville: Abingdon, 1990) 62–84.

Michel, O., *Der Brief an die **Hebräer*** (Göttingen: Vandenhoeck & Ruprecht, 1966).

——, "*oikos*," *TDNT* 5.142.

Minear, P. S., "The Crucified World: The *Enigma* of Galatians 6,14," *Theologia Crucis — Signum Crucis* (ed. C. Andersen and G. Klein; Tübingen: Mohr, 1979) 395–407.

Mitchell, S., ***Anatolia**: Land, Men, and Gods in Asia Minor* (2 vols.; Oxford: Clarendon, 1993).

——, "*Population* and the Land in Roman Galatia," *ANRW* 2.7.2, 1053–1081.

——, *Regional Epigraphic Catalogues of Asia Minor II. The **Ankara** District. The Inscriptions of North Galatia*, British Institute of Archaeology at Ankara, Monograph no. 4, B.A.R. International Series 135 (Oxford: Clarendon, 1982).

Moltmann, J., *Theology of Hope* (New York: Harper & Row, 1967).

Moore, G. F., *Judaism in the First Centuries of the Christian Era: The Age of the Tannaim* (3 vols.; Cambridge: Harvard Univ. Press, 1927–1930).

Moore-Crispin, D. R., "Galatians 4:1–9: The Use and Abuse of Parallels," *Evangelical Quarterly* 60 (1989) 203–223.

Morgan, R. (ed.), *The Nature of New Testament Theology* (Naperville: Allenson, 1973).

Morland, K. A., *The Rhetoric of Curse in Galatians* (Atlanta: Scholars, 1996).

Morse, C. L., "Bonhoeffer's *Dialogue* with America," paper presented at AAR, November 1995.

———, *The Logic of Promise in Moltmann's Theology* (Philadelphia: Fortress, 1979).

———, *Not Every Spirit: A Dogmatics of Christian Disbelief* (Valley Forge: Trinity, 1994).

———, "Raising God's Eyebrows: Some Further Thoughts on the *Analogia Fidei*," *USQR* 37 (1981–82) 39–49.

Moscati, S. (ed.), *The Celts* (New York: Rizzoli, 1991).

Moule, C. F. D., "*Fulfillment Words* in the New Testament: Use and Abuse," *NTS* 14 (1967) 293–320.

———, *An Idiom-Book of New Testament Greek* (Cambridge: Cambridge Univ. Press, 1959).

Müller, U. B., *Die Menschwerdung des Gottessohnes* (Stuttgart: Katholisches Bibelwerk, 1990).

Munck, J., *Paul and the Salvation of Mankind* (Richmond: Knox, 1959).

Murphy-O'Connor, J., "An Essene *Missionary* Document? CD II.14–VI.1," *RB* 77 (1970) 201–209.

———, "Paul in *Arabia*," *CBQ* 55 (1993) 732–737.

———, "Pauline *Missions* Before the Jerusalem Conference," *RB* 89 (1982) 71–91.

———, Review of H. D. Betz, *Galatians*, *RB* 89 (1982) 257–260.

Nägeli, T., *Der Wortschatz des Apostels Paulus* (Göttingen: Vandenhoeck & Ruprecht, 1905).

Neusner, J., *The Rabbinic Traditions about the Pharisees Before 70* (3 vols.; Leiden: Brill, 1971).

———, "Was Rabbinic Judaism *Really 'Ethnic'?*" *CBQ* 57 (1995) 281–305.

———, et al. (eds.), *Religion, Science and Magic* (New York: Oxford, 1989).

Newman, C. C., *Paul's Glory-Christology* (Leiden: Brill, 1991).

Nickle, K. F., *Collection: A Study in Paul's Strategy* (Naperville: Allenson, 1966).

Nock, A. D., *Conversion: The Old and New in Religion from Alexander the Great to Augustine of Hippo* (London: Oxford Univ. Press, 1933).

———, *Essays on Religion and the Ancient World* (2 vols.; Cambridge: Harvard Univ. Press, 1972).

Norris, F. W., "*Antioch* of Syria," *ABD*.

O'Neill, J. C., *The Recovery of Paul's Letter to the Galatians* (London: SPCK, 1972).

Odeberg, H., *The Fourth Gospel* (Amsterdam: Grüner, 1929).

Oepke, A., "*mesitês*," TDNT 4.598–624.

Ogg, G., *The Chronology of the Life of Paul* (London: Epworth, 1968).

Olson, S. N., "Pauline Expressions of *Confidence* in His Addressees," *CBQ* 47 (1985) 282–295.

Overbeck, F., *Christentum und Kultur. Gedanken und Anmerkungen zur modernen Theologie* (ed. C. A. Bernoulli; Darmstadt: Wissenschaftliche Buchgesellschaft, 1963 [original, Basel, 1919]).

Overfield, P. D., "*Plêroma*: A Study in Content and Context," *NTS* 25 (1979) 384–396.

Pak, J. Y. S., *Paul as Missionary: A Comparative Study of Missionary Discourse in Paul's Epistles and Selected Contemporary Jewish Texts* (Frankfurt: Lang, 1991).

Pancaro, S., *The Law in the Fourth Gospel* (Leiden: Brill, 1975).

Perelman, C., and L. Olbrechts-Tyteca, *The New Rhetoric: A Treatise on Argumentation* (Notre Dame: Univ. of Notre Dame Press, 1971).

Perkins, P., *Peter: Apostle for the Whole Church* (Columbia: Univ. of South Carolina Press, 1994).

Pesch, R., *Das Markusevangelium* (2 vols.; Freiburg: Herder, 1980).

Peterman, G. W., "*Romans 15.26*: Make a Contribution or Establish Fellowship?" *NTS* 40 (1994) 457–463.

Pitta, A., *Disposizione e Messaggio della Lettera ai Galatti: Analasi retorico letteraria* (Rome: Pontifical Biblical Institute, 1992).

Pluta, A., *Gottes Bundestreue: Ein Schlüsselbegriff in Röm 3,25a* (Stuttgart: Katholisches Bibelwerk, 1969).

Porter, F. C., "The *Yecer hara*: A Study in the Jewish Doctrine of Sin," *Biblical and Semitic Studies* (Yale Bicentennial Publications; New York: Scribner's, 1901) 88–186.

Potter, D. S., *Prophecy and History in the Crisis of the Roman Empire: A Historical Commentary on the Thirteenth Sybilline Oracle* (Oxford: Clarendon, 1990).

Preisigke, F., and F. Bilabel, *Sammelbuch griechischen Urkunden aus Ägypten* (5 vols.; Strasbourg: Trubner, 1915–1950).

Preisker, H., "*myktêrizô*," TDNT 4.796.

Qimron, E., *The Hebrew of the Dead Sea Scrolls* (Atlanta: Scholars, 1986).

Räisänen, H., "*Galatians 2:16* and Paul's Break with Judaism," *NTS* 31 (1985) 543–553.

———, *Jesus, Paul and Torah: Collected Essays* (Sheffield: Sheffield Academic Press, 1992).

———, "*Legalism* and Salvation by the Law: Paul's Portrayal of the Jewish Religion as a Historical and Theological Theme," *Die Paulinische Literatur und Theologie* (ed. S. Pedersen; Arhus: Forlaget Aros, 1980) 63–83.

———, *Paul and the Law* (Tübingen: Mohr, 1983).

Rehm, B. (ed.), *Die Pseudoklementinen: I Homilien* (Berlin: Akademie Verlag, 1969).

——— (ed.), *Die Pseudoklementinen: II Rekognitionen* (Berlin: Akademie Verlag, 1994).

Reicke, B., "Der geschichtliche *Hintergrund* des Apostelkonzils und der Antiochia-Episode, Gal 2,1–14," *Studia Paulina in honorem Johannis de Zwaan septuagenarii* (ed. J. N. Sevenster and W. C. van Unnik; Haarlem: Bohn, 1953) 172–187.

———, "The *Law* and This World According to Paul," *JBL* 70 (1951) 259–276.

Reif, S. C., *Judaism and Hebrew Prayer*: New Perspectives on Jewish Liturgical History (Cambridge: Cambridge Univ. Press, 1993).

Rengstorf, K. H., "*apostellô*," *TDNT* 1.398–447.

———, "*gennaô*," *TDNT* 1.665–668.

Reumann, J., *Righteousness in the New Testament* (Philadelphia: Fortress, 1982).

Richards, E. R., *The Secretary in the Letters of Paul* (Tübingen: Mohr/Siebeck, 1991).

Richardson, P., *Israel in the Apostolic Church* (Cambridge: Cambridge Univ. Press, 1969).

Ridderbos, H., *Paul. An Outline of His Theology* (Grand Rapids: Eerdmans, 1975).

Riesner, R., *Die Frühzeit des Apostels Paulus* (Tübingen: Mohr/Siebeck, 1994).

Robinson, D. W. B., "*Distinction* Between Jewish and Gentile Believers in Galatians," *Australian Biblical Review* 13 (1965) 29–48.

Roloff, J., "*Anfänge* der soteriologischen Deutung des Todes Jesu (Mk. x.45 und Lk. xxii.27)," *NTS* 19 (1972) 38–64.

———, "Apostel," *TRE* 3.430–445.

Rusam, D., "Neue *Belege* zu dem *stoicheia tou kosmou* (Gal 4,3.9; Kol 2,8.20)," *ZNW* 83 (1992) 119–125.

Sampley, J. P., *Pauline Partnership in Christ* (Philadelphia: Fortress, 1980).

———, "Romans in a *Different Light*," *Pauline Theology, Volume III: Romans* (ed. D. M. Hay and E. E. Johnson; Minneapolis: Fortress, 1995) 109–129.

———, *Walking Between the Times: Paul's Moral Reasoning* (Minneapolis: Fortress, 1991).

Sanders, E. P., *Jesus and Judaism* (Philadelphia: Fortress, 1985).

———, "Jewish Association with Gentiles and *Gal 2:11–14*," *The Conversation Continues: Studies in Paul and John in Honor of J. Louis Martyn* (ed. R. T. Fortna and B. R. Gaventa; Nashville: Abingdon, 1990) 170–188.

———, *Jewish Law from Jesus to the Mishnah* (Philadelphia: Trinity, 1990).

———, *Paul and Palestinian Judaism* (Philadelphia: Fortress, 1977).

———, *Paul, the Law and the Jewish People* (Philadelphia: Fortress, 1983).

Sanders, J. T., "Paul's 'Autobiographical' Statements in *Galatians 1–2*," *JBL* 85 (1966) 335–343.

———, *Schismatics, Sectarians, Dissidents, Deviants. The First One Hundred Years of Jewish-Christian Relations* (London: SCM, 1993).

Sandmel, S., *The Genius of Paul* (New York: Schocken, 1970).

Satake, A., "*1Kr 15,3* und das Verhalten von Paulus den Jerusalemern gegenüber," *AJBI* 16 (1990) 100–111.

Schäfer, P., "Die *Torah* der messianischen Zeit," *ZNW* 65 (1974) 27–42.

_____, *Die Vorstellung vom heiligen* **Geist** *in der rabbinischen Literatur* (Munich: Kösel, 1972).

Schlier, H., *"kephalê,"* TDNT 3.673–682.

Schlueter, C. J., *Filling Up the* **Measure**: *Polemical Hyperbole in 1 Thessalonians 2.14–16* (Sheffield: JSOT, 1994).

Schmidt, A., "Das *Missionsdekret* in Galater 2.7–8 als Vereinbarung vom ersten Besuch Pauli in Jerusalem," NTS 38 (1992) 149–152.

Schmidt, K. L., *"kaleô,"* TDNT 3.487–536.

Schmithals, W., *The Office of Apostle in the Early Church* (Nashville: Abingdon, 1969).

_____, *Paul and the Gnostics* (Nashville: Abingdon, 1972).

Schneider, G., "Die Idee der *Neuschöpfung* beim Apostel Paulus und ihr religionsgeschichtlicher Hintergrund," TTZ 68 (1959) 257–270.

Schneider, J., *"parabasis,"* TDNT 5.739–740.

Schneider, N., *Die rhetorische Eigenart der paulinischen* **Antithese** (Tübingen: Mohr/Siebeck, 1970).

Schnelle, U., **Gerechtigkeit** *und Christusgegenwart* (Göttingen: Vandenhoeck & Ruprecht, 1983).

Schoeps, H. J., **Paul**: *The Theology of the Apostle in the Light of Jewish Religious History* (London: Lutterworth, 1961).

Scholem, G., *The Messianic Idea in Judaism and Other Essays on Jewish Spirituality* (London: Allen & Unwin, 1962).

Schoon-Janssen, J., *Umstrittene* **"Apologien"** *in den Paulusbriefen: Studien zur rhetorischen Situation des 1. Thessalonicherbriefes, des Galaterbriefes, und des Philipperbriefes* (Göttingen: Vandenhoeck & Ruprecht, 1991).

Schrage, W., *Der erste Brief an die* **Korinther** (3 vols.; Zürich: Benziger, 1991–).

_____, *The* **Ethics** *of the New Testament* (Philadelphia: Fortress, 1988).

_____, "*Israel* nach dem Fleische," *Wenn nicht jetzt, wann dann?* (Festschrift H. J. Kraus; ed. H. G. Gewyer et al.; Neukirchen: Neukirchener, 1983) 143–151.

_____, "' . . . den Juden ein Skandalon'? Der *Anstoss* des Kreuzes nach 1Kor 1,23," *Gottes Augapfel* (ed. E. Brocke and J. Seim; Neukirchen: Neukirchener, 1986) 59–76.

_____, *Die knokreten* **Einzelgebote** *in der paulinischen Paränese* (Gütersloh: Mohn, 1961).

_____, "**Probleme** paulinischer Ethik anhand von Gal 3,25–6,10," paper for Colloquium Paulinum in Rome, 1995 (to be edited by A. Vanhoye).

Schreiner, T. R., *The* **Law** *and Its Fulfillment. A Pauline Theology of Law* (Grand Rapids: Baker, 1993).

Schrenk, G., "Der *Segenswunsch* nach der Kampfepistel," *Judaica* 6 (1950) 170–190.

_____, "Was bedeutet '*Israel Gottes*'?" *Judaica* 5 (1949) 81–94.

Schubert, P., *Form and Function of the* **Pauline Thanksgivings** (Berlin: Töpelmann, 1939).

Schüssler-Fiorenza, E., *The Book of* **Revelation** (Philadelphia: Fortress, 1985).

Schütz, J. H., *Paul and the Anatomy of Apostolic Authority* (Cambridge: Cambridge Univ. Press, 1975).

Schwank, B., "Neue *Funde* in Nabatäerstädten und ihre Bedeutung für die neutestamentliche Exegese," *NTS* 29 (1983) 429–435.

Schweitzer, A., *The Mysticism of Paul the Apostle* (New York: Seabury, 1968).

Schweizer, E., "Gottesgerechtigkeit und *Lasterkataloge* bei Paulus (inkl. Kol und Eph)," *Rechtfertigung: Festschrift für Ernst Käsemann* (ed. J. Friedrich et al.; Tübingen: Mohr/Siebeck, 1974) 461–477.

————, *The Letter to the Colossians* (Minneapolis: Augsburg, 1982).

————, "*pneuma*," *TDNT* 6.389–455.

————, "*sarx*," *TDNT* 7.98–151.

————, "Slaves of the *Elements* and Worshipers of Angels: Gal 4:3, 9 and Col 2:8, 18, 20," *JBL* 107 (1988) 455–468.

————, "*sôma*," *TDNT* 1024–1094.

————, *Theologische Einleitung in das Neue Testament* (Göttingen: Vandenhoeck & Ruprecht, 1989); *A Theological Introduction to the New Testament* (Nashville: Abingdon, 1991).

————, "Was meinen wir eigentlich, wenn wir sagen 'Gott sandte seinen Sohn . . .'?" *NTS* 37 (1991) 204–224; "What Do We Really Mean When We Say, 'God Sent His Son'?" *Faith and History: Essays in Honor of Paul W. Meyer* (ed. John T. Carroll et al.; Atlanta: Scholars, 1990) 298–312.

Scott, J. M., *Adoption as Sons of God. An Exegetical Investigation into the Background of huiothesia in the Pauline Corpus* (Tübingen: Mohr-Siebeck, 1992).

————, "'For as many as are of works of the Law are under a *curse*' (Galatians 3.10)," *Paul and the Scriptures of Israel* (ed. J. A. Sanders and C. A. Evans; Sheffield: JSOT, 1993) 187–221.

————, *Paul and the Nations: The Old Testament and Jewish Background of Paul's Mission to the Nations with Special Reference to the Destination of Galatians* (Tübingen: Mohr/Siebeck, 1995).

————, "Paul's Use of *Deuteronomic Tradition*," *JBL* 112 (1993) 645–665.

————, "Philo and the Restoration of Israel," *SBL Seminar Papers* (Atlanta: Scholars, 1995) 553–575.

Scroggs, R., *Christology in Paul and John* (Philadelphia: Fortress, 1988).

————, *Paul for a New Day* (Philadelphia: Fortress, 1977).

Segal, A. F., *Paul the Convert: The Apostolate and Apostasy of Saul the Pharisee* (New Haven: Yale Univ. Press, 1990).

————, *Two Powers in Heaven* (Leiden: Brill, 1977).

Sheppard, A. R. R., "Pagan *Cults of Angels* in Roman Asia Minor," *Talanta* 12–13 (1980/81) 77–101.

Sheppard, G. T. (ed.), *William Perkins' Commentary on Galatians* (Boston: Pilgrim, 1989).

Sherk, R. K., "*Roman Galatia:* The Governors from 25 B.C. to A.D. 114," *ANRW* 2.7.2 (1980), 954–1052.

Shimada, K., *A Concordance to Galatians* (Japan: Private Circulation, 1994).

Siber, P., *Mit Christus Leben* (Zürich: Theologischer Verlag, 1971).

Sider, R. D. (ed.), *Collected Works of Erasmus: Paraphrases on Romans and Galatians*, vol. 42 (Toronto: Univ. of Toronto Press, 1984).

Siegert, F., *Argumentation bei Paulus* (Tübingen: Mohr/Siebeck, 1985).

———, *Drei hellenistisch-jüdische Predigten* (2 vols.; Tübingen: Mohr/Siebeck, 1980, 1992).

———, *Philon von Alexandrien: Uber die Gottesbezeichnung "wohltätig verzehrendes Feuer" (De Deo)* (Tübingen: Mohr/Siebeck, 1988).

———, Review of W. C. Van Unnik, *Das Selbstverständnis der jüdischen Diaspora in der hellenistisch-römischen Zeit, Studia Philonica Annual* 6 (1994) 192–199.

Siker, J. S., *Disinheriting the Jews: Abraham in Early Christian Literature* (Louisville: Knox, 1990).

Simon, M., *Verus Israel* (Paris: de Boccard, 1964); *Verus Israel* (Oxford: Oxford Univ. Press, 1986).

Sjöberg, E., "Neuschöpfung in den Toten-Meer Rollen," *ST* 9 (1955) 131–136.

Skeehan, T., "*Heidegger's Introduction* to the Phenomenology of Religion, 1920–1921," *Personalist* 60 (1979) 312–324.

Slingerland, D., "*Acts 18:1–18*, the Gallio Inscription, and Absolute Pauline Chronology," *JBL* 110 (1991) 439–449.

Smiga, G. M., "*Language*, Experience, and Theology: The Argumentation of Galatians 3:6–4:7 in Light of the Literary Form of the Letter" (Dissertation, Pontificia Universitas Gregoriana, Rome, 1985).

Smit, J., "The Letter of Paul to the Galatians: A Deliberative *Speech*," *NTS* 35 (1989) 1–26.

Smith, C. C., "*Ekkleisai* in Galatians 4:17: The Motif of the Excluded Lover as a Metaphor of Manipulation," *CBQ* 58 (1996) 480–499.

Smith, D. M., "*Ho de dikaios ek pisteôs zêsetai*," *Studies in the History of the New Testament in Honor of Kenneth Willis Clark, Ph.D.* (ed. Boyd L. Daniels and M. Jack Suggs; Salt Lake City: Univ. of Utah Press, 1967) 13–25.

———, *The Theology of the Gospel of John* (Cambridge: Cambridge Univ. Press, 1995).

Smyth, H. W., *Greek Grammar* (Cambridge: Harvard Univ. Press, 1956).

Snyman, A. H., "Modes of Persuasion in Galatians 6:7–10," *Neot* 26 (1992) 475–484.

Soards, M. L., *The Apostle Paul* (New York: Paulist, 1987).

———, "Seeking (*zêtein*) and Sinning (*hamartôlos & hamartia*) According to Galatians 2:17," *Apocalyptic and the New Testament: Essays in Honor of J. Louis Martyn* (ed. J. Marcus and M. L. Soards; Sheffield: JSOT, 1989) 237–254.

Souter, A., *The Earliest Latin Commentaries on the Epistles of St. Paul. A Study* (Oxford: Clarendon, 1927).

———, *Text and Canon of the New Testament* (2nd ed.; London: Duckworth, 1954).

Speiser, E. A., *Genesis* (AB; Garden City: Doubleday, 1964).

Stähelin, F., *Geschichte der kleinasiatischen Galater bis zur Errichtung der röm-*

ischen Provinz Asia (Basel: Allgem. Schweizer Zeitung, 1897. 2nd ed.; Leipzig: Hinrichs, 1907).

Standaert, B., "La rhétorique antique et l'épître aux Galates," *FV* 84 (1985) 33–40.

Standhartinger, A., *Das Frauenbild im Judentum der hellenistischen Zeit: Ein Beitrag anhand von Joseph und Asenath* (Leiden: Brill, 1995).

Stanley, C. D., *Paul and the Language of Scripture* (Cambridge: Cambridge Univ. Press, 1992).

_____, "'Under a *Curse*': A Fresh Reading of Galatians 3.10–14," *NTS* 36 (1990) 481–511.

Stanton, G., "The Law of Moses and the *Law of Christ*: Galatians 3.1–6.2," *Paul and the Mosaic Law* (ed. J. D. G. Dunn; Tübingen: Mohr/Siebeck, 1996) 99–116.

Steen, H. A., "Les *clichés* épistolaires dans les lettres sur papyrus grecques," *Classica et Mediaevalia* 1 (1938) 119–176.

Stendahl, K., *Final Account: Paul's Letter to the Romans* (Minneapolis: Fortress, 1995).

_____, *Paul Among Jews and Gentiles* (Philadelphia: Fortress, 1976).

Stenger, W., and F. Schneider, *Studien zum neutestamentlichen Briefformular* (Leiden: Brill, 1987).

Stirewalt, M. L., *Studies in Ancient Greek Epistolography* (Atlanta: Scholars, 1993).

Stone, M. E., *Fourth Ezra* (Philadelphia: Fortress, 1990).

Stowers, S. K., *The Diatribe and Paul's Letter to the Romans* (Chico: Scholars, 1981).

_____, "Letters (Greek and Latin)," *ABD*.

_____, *Letter Writing in Greco-Roman Antiquity* (Philadelphia: Westminster, 1986).

_____, *A Reading of Romans: Justice, Jews, and Gentiles* (New Haven: Yale Univ. Press, 1994).

Strecker, G., "*Befreiung* und Rechtfertigung," *Rechtfertigung: Festschrift E. Käsemann* (ed. J. Friedrich et al.; Tübingen: Mohr/Siebeck, 1976) 479–508.

_____, "Das *Evangelium* Jesu Christi," *Eschaton und Historie. Aufsätze* (Göttingen: Vandenhoeck & Ruprecht, 1979) 183–228.

_____, *Das Judenchristentum in den Pseudoklementinen* (2nd ed.; Berlin: Akademie, 1981).

_____, "The Kerygmata Petrou," *HS* 2.102–127.

_____, *Literaturgeschichte des Neuen Testaments* (Göttingen: Vandenhoeck & Ruprecht, 1992).

Strelan, J., "*Burden-Bearing* and the Law of Christ," *JBL* 94 (1975) 266–276.

Strobel, A., "Apokalyptik IV," *TRE* 3.251–257.

_____, *Untersuchungen zum eschatologischen Verzögerungsproblem* (Leiden: Brill, 1961).

Strotmann, A., "*Mein Vater Bist Du*" (Sir 51,10). *Zur Bedeutung der "Vaterschaft Gottes" in Kanonischen und Nichtkanonischen Früjüdischen Schriften* (Frankfurt: Knecht, 1991).

Stuhlmacher, P., *Der Brief an Philemon* (Zürich: Benziger, 1975).

_____, *"Erwägungen* zum ontologischen Charakter der *kaine ktisis* bei Paulus," *EvT* 27 (1967) 1–35.

_____, *Gerechtigkeit Gottes bei Paulus* (Göttingen: Vandenhoeck & Ruprecht, 1965).

_____, "Das *Gesetz* als Thema biblischer Theologie," *ZTK* 75 (1978) 251–280.

_____, *Historical Criticism and Theological Interpretation of Scripture* (Philadelphia: Fortress, 1977).

_____, "The Pauline *Gospel," The Gospel and the Gospels* (ed. P. Stuhlmacher; Grand Rapids: Eerdmans, 1991) 149–172.

_____, *Das paulinische Evangelium I* (Göttingen: Vandenhoeck & Ruprecht, 1968).

Sturm, R. E., "Defining the Word *'Apocalyptic':* A Problem in Biblical Criticism," *Apocalyptic and the New Testament: Essays in Honor of J. Louis Martyn* (ed. J. Marcus and M. L. Soards; Sheffield: JSOT, 1989) 17–48.

Suggs, M. J., "Concerning the *Date* of Paul's Macedonian Ministry," *NovT* 4 (1960) 60–68.

Suhl, A., "Der *Beginn* der Selbständigen Mission des Paulus," *NTS* 38 (1992) 430–447.

_____, "Der *Galaterbrief*—Situation und Argumentation," *ANRW* 2.25.4, 3067–3134.

_____, "Die Galater und der *Geist.* Kritische Erwägungen zur Situation in Galatien," *Jesu Rede von Gott und ihre Nachgeschichte im frühen Christentum* (ed. D.-A. Koch et al.; Gütersloh: Mohn, 1989) 267–296.

_____, "Paulinische *Chronologie* im Streit der Meinungen," *ANRW* 2.26.2, 939–1188.

_____, *Paulus und seine Briefe. Ein Beitrag zur paulinischen Chronologie* (Gütersloh: Mohn, 1975).

Sumney, J. L., *Identifying Paul's Opponents: The Question of Method in 2 Corinthians* (Sheffield: JSOT, 1990).

Synofzik, E., *Die Gerichts- und Vergeltungsaussagen bei Paulus* (Göttingen: Vandenhoeck & Ruprecht, 1977).

Taatz, I., *Früjüdische Briefe. Die Paulinischen Briefe im Rahmen der Offiziellen Religiösen Briefe des Früjudentums* (Fribourg: Editions Universitaires, 1991).

Tachau, P., *"Einst" und "Jetzt" im Neuen Testament* (Göttingen: Vandenhoeck & Ruprecht, 1972).

Talbert, C. H., "Again: Paul's *Visits* to Jerusalem," *NovT* 9 (1967) 26–40.

_____, "Freedom and Law in Galatians," *EA* 2 (1995) 17–28.

Tannehill, R., *Dying and Rising with Christ* (Berlin: Töpelmann, 1967).

Taubenschlag, R., *The Law of Greco-Roman Egypt in Light of the Papyri* (New York: Herald Square, 1948).

Taubes, J., *Die politische Theologie des Paulus* (Munich: Fink, 1993).

Taylor, G. M., "The Function of *Pistis Christou* in Galatians," *JBL* 85 (1966) 58–76.

Taylor, N., *Paul, Antioch and Jerusalem. A Study in Relationships and Authority in Earliest Christianity* (Sheffield: JSOT, 1992).

Terrien, S. L., *The Elusive Presence* (San Francisco: Harper & Row, 1978).

Theissen, G., *The Social Setting of Pauline Christianity* (Philadelphia: Fortress, 1982).

Thielman, F., *From Plight to Solution*: A Jewish Framework for Understanding Paul's View of the Law in Galatians and Romans (Leiden: Brill, 1989).

———, *Paul and the Law*: A Contextual Approach (Downers Grove: Inter-Varsity, 1994).

Thrall, M. E., *A Critical and Exegetical Commentary on the Second Epistle to the Corinthians*, vol. 1 (Edinburgh: T & T Clark, 1994).

Thyen, H., *Studien zur Sündenvergebung im Neuen Testament* (Göttingen: Vandenhoeck & Ruprecht, 1970).

Tobin, T. H., "Controversy and Continuity in *Romans 1:18–3.20*," *CBQ* 55 (1993) 298–318.

Tomson, P. J., *Paul and the Jewish Law*: *Halakha* in the Letters of the Apostle to the Gentiles (Minneapolis: Fortress, 1991).

Trebilco, P., *Jewish Communities in Asia Minor* (Cambridge: Cambridge Univ. Press, 1991).

Trible, P., "God, Nature of, in the OT," *IDBS*.

Trobisch, D., *Die Entstehung der Paulusbriefsammlung. Studien zu den Anfängen christlicher Publizistik* (Göttingen: Vandenhoeck & Ruprecht, 1989).

———, *Paul's Letter Collection* (Minneapolis: Fortress, 1994).

———, *Die Paulusbriefe und die Anfänge der christlichen Publizistik* (Gütersloh: Mohn, 1994).

Tyson, J. B., "'Works of the Law' in Galatians," *JBL* 92 (1973) 423–431.

Urbach, E. E., *The Sages* (2 vols.; Jerusalem: Magnes, 1979).

van Oort, J., *Jerusalem and Babylon: A Study into Augustine's "City of God" and the Sources of His Doctrine of the Two Cities* (Leiden: Brill, 1991).

Van Voorst, R. E., *The Ascents of James* (Atlanta: Scholars, 1989).

Vanhoye, A. (ed.), *L'Apôtre Paul* (Leuven: Leuven Univ. Press, 1986).

Verhoef, E., *Er Staat Geschreven . . . De Oud-Testamentische Citaten in de Brief aan de Galaten* (Meppel: Krips Repro, 1979).

Vermaseren, M. J., *Cybele and Attis: The Myth and the Cult* (London: Thames & Hudson, 1977).

Vermes, G., *The Dead Sea Scrolls in English* (3rd ed.; London: Penguin, 1987).

———, *Scripture and Tradition in Judaism* (Leiden: Brill, 1961).

Verseput, D. J., "Paul's Gentile *Mission* and the Jewish Christian Community," *NTS* 39 (1993) 36–58.

Vielhauer, P., *Geschichte der urchristlichen Literatur* (Berlin: de Gruyter, 1975).

———, "Gesetzesdienst und *Stoicheiadienst* im Galaterbrief," *Rechtfertigung: Festschrift für Ernst Käsemann* (ed. J. Friedrich et al.; Tübingen: Mohr/Siebeck, 1976) 543–555.

Von der Osten-Sacken, P., *Christian-Jewish Dialogue* (Philadelphia: Fortress, 1986).

———, P., *Die Heiligkeit der Tora* (Munich: Kaiser, 1989).

Vos, J. S., "Die hermeneutische *Antinomie* bei Paulus (Gal 3.11–12; Röm 10.5–10," *NTS* 38 (1992) 254–270.

———, "*Legem statuimus*; Rhetorische Aspekte der Gesetzesdebatte zwischen Juden und Christen," *Juden und Christen in der Antike* (ed. J. van Amersfoort and J. van Oort; Kampen: Kok, 1990), 44–60.

———, "Paul's *Argumentation* in Galatians 1–2," *HTR* 87 (1994) 1–16 (somewhat more detailed German version in *The Truth of the Gospel* [ed. J. Lambrecht; Rome: Benedictina Publishing, 1993] 11–43).

———, *Traditionsgeschichtliche Untersuchungen zur Paulinischen Pneumatologie* (Assen: van Gorcum, 1973).

Vouga, F., "*Der Galaterbrief*: kein Brief an die Galater? Essay über den literarischen Charakter des letzten grossen Paulusbriefes," *Schrift und Tradition: Festschrift Josef Ernst* (ed. K. Backhaus and G. Untergassmair; Paderborn: Schöningh, 1996) 243–258.

———, "Zur Rhetorischen *Gattung* des Galaterbriefes," *ZNW* 79 (1988) 291–292.

Walter, N., "Christusglaube und Heidnische *Religiosität* in Paulinischen Gemeinden," *NTS* 25 (1979) 422–442.

———, "Hellenistische *Diaspora-Juden* an der Wiege des Urchristentums," *The New Testament and Hellenistic Judaism* (ed. P. Borgen and S. Giversen; Aarhus: Aarhus Univ. Press, 1995) 37–58.

———, "Paulus und die *Gegner* des Christusevangeliums in Galatien," *L'Apôtre Paul* (ed. A. Vanhoye; Leuven: Leuven Univ. Press, 1986) 351–356.

———, *Der Thoraausleger Aristobulos* (Berlin: Akademie, 1964).

———, "Zur Interpretation von *Römer 9–11*," *ZTK* 81 (1984) 172–195.

———, "Zur theologischen *Problematik* des christologischen 'Schriftbeweises' im Neuen Testament," *NTS* 41 (1995) 338–357.

Watson, D. F. (ed.), *Persuasive Artistry. Studies in New Testament Rhetoric in Honor of G. A. Kennedy* (Sheffield: JSOT, 1991).

———, and A. J. Hauser, *Rhetorical Criticism of the Bible*: A Contemporary Bibliography with Notes on History and Method (Leiden: Brill, 1994).

Watson, F., *Paul, Judaism and the Gentiles* (Cambridge: Cambridge Univ. Press, 1986).

Watson, N. M., "*Justified* by Faith, Judged by Works — an Antinomy?" *NTS* 29 (1983) 209–221.

Way, D., *The Lordship of Christ: Ernst Käsemann's Interpretation of Paul's Theology* (Oxford: Clarendon, 1991).

Wechsler, A., *Geschichtsbild und Apostelstreit. Eine forschungsgeschichtliche und exegetische Studie über den antiochenischen Zwischenfall (Gal 2,11–14)* (Berlin: de Gruyter, 1991).

Wegenast, K., *Das Verständnis der Tradition bei Paulus und in den Deuteropaulinen* (Neukirchen: Neukirchener, 1962).

Weima, J. A. D., *Neglected Endings: The Significance of the Pauline Letter Closings* (Sheffield: Sheffield Academic Press, 1994).

Weiss, J., *Earliest Christianity* (2 vols.; New York: Harper, 1959).

Werblowsky, R. J. Z., "*Torah* als Gnade," *Kairos* 15 (1973) 156–163.

Wessels, G. F., "The *Call* to Responsible Freedom in Paul's Persuasive Strategy. Gal 5:13–6:10," *Neot* 26 (1992) 475–484.

Westerholm, S., *Israel's Law and the Church's Faith* (Grand Rapids: Eerdmans, 1988).

White, J. L., *The Form and Function of the Body of the Greek Letter: A Study of the Letter-Body in the Non-Literary Papyri and in Paul the Apostle* (Missoula: Scholars, 1972).

_____, "Introductory Formulae in the Body of the Pauline Letter," *JBL* 90 (1971) 91–97.

Whitman, J., "From the *Textual* to the Temporal: Early Christian 'Allegory' and Early Romantic 'Symbol,'" *New Literary History* 22 (1991) 161–176.

Wibbing, S., *Die Tugend- und Lasterkataloge im Neuen Testament* (Berlin: Töpelmann, 1959).

Widengren, G., "Leitende *Ideen* und Quellen der iranischen Apokalyptik," *Apocalypticism in the Mediterranean World and the Near East* (ed. David Hellholm; Tübingen: Mohr/Siebeck, 1983) 77–162.

Wilckens, U., *Der Brief an die Römer* (3 vols.; Zürich: Benziger, 1978–1982).

_____, "hypokrinomai," *TDNT* 8.559–571.

_____, *Die Missionsreden der Apostelgeschichte* (Neukirchen: Neukirchener, 1961).

Wilcox, M., "'Upon a *Tree*'—Deut 21:23 in the New Testament," *JBL* 96 (1977) 85–99.

Wildberger, H., "'*Glauben*.' Erwägungen zu *h'myn*," *Hebräische Wortforschung: Festschrift W. Baumgartner* (Leiden: Brill, 1967) 372–386.

_____, "'Glauben' im Alten Testament," *ZTK* 65 (1968) 129–159.

Wiles, M., *The Divine Apostle: The Interpretation of St. Paul's Epistles in the Early Church* (Cambridge: Cambridge Univ. Press, 1967).

Williams, S. K., "Again *Pistis Christou*," *CBQ* 49 (1987) 431–447.

_____, "The *Hearing* of Faith: *AKOE PISTEOS* in Gal 3," *NTS* 35 (1989) 82–93.

_____, *Jesus' Death as Saving Event* (Missoula: Scholars, 1975).

_____, "*Justification* and the Spirit in Galatians," *JSNT* 29 (1987) 91–100.

_____, "*Promise* in Galatians: A Reading of Paul's Reading of Scripture," *JBL* 107 (1988) 709–720.

_____, "The *Righteousness of God* in Romans," *JBL* 99 (1980) 241–290.

Wimbush, V., *Ascetic Behavior* (Minneapolis: Fortress, 1990).

Winger, M., *By What Law? The Meaning of Nomos in the Letters of Paul* (Atlanta: Scholars, 1992).

_____, "*Tradition*, Revelation and the Gospel," *JSNT* 53 (1994) 65–86.

_____, "*Unreal Conditions* in the Letters of Paul," *JBL* 105 (1986) 110–112.

Wink, W., *Engaging the Powers* (Minneapolis: Fortress, 1992).

_____, *Naming the Powers* (Philadelphia: Fortress, 1984).

_____, *Unmasking the Powers* (Philadelphia: Fortress, 1986).

Winston, D., "Solomon, Wisdom of," *ABD*.

Wolff, C., "Thanksgiving," *ABD*.

Wolfson, H., *Philo* (2 vols.; Cambridge: Harvard Univ. Press, 1945).

Wright, B. G., *No Small Difference: Sirach's Relationship to Its Parent Hebrew Text* (Atlanta: Scholars, 1986).

Wright, N. T., *The Climax of the Covenant: Christ and the Law in Pauline Theology* (Edinburgh: T & T Clark, 1991).

Wuellner, W., "*Toposforschung* und Torahinterpretation bei Paulus und Jesus," *NTS* 24 (1978) 463–483.

Yadin, Y., "*Pesher* Nahum," *IEJ* 21 (1971) 1–12.

Zahl, P. F. M., *Rechtfertigungslehre Ernst Käsemanns* (Stuttgart: Calwer, 1996).

Zeller, D., "Christus, *Skandal* und Hoffnung; Die Juden in den Briefen des Paulus," *Gottesverächter und Menschenfeinde? Juden zwischen Jesus und frühchristlicher Kirche* (ed. H. Goldstein; Düsseldorf: Patmos, 1979) 256–278.

Zenger, E. (ed.), *Der Neue Bund im Alten: Studien zur Bundestheologie der beiden Testamente* (Freiburg: Herder, 1993).

Zerwick, M., *Biblical Greek* (Rome: Biblical Institute Press, 1963).

Ziesler, J. A., *The Meaning of Righteousness in Paul* (Cambridge: Cambridge Univ. Press, 1972).

———, *Pauline Christology* (Oxford: Oxford Univ. Press, 1991).

Zinn, G. A., "*History* and Interpretation: 'Hebrew Truth,' Judaism, and the Victorine Exegetical Tradition," *Jews and Christians: Exploring the Past, Present, and Future* (ed. J. H. Charlesworth; New York: Crossroad, 1990) 100–126, plus plates.

Zuntz, G., *The Text of the Epistles: A Disquisition on the Corpus Paulinum* (London: Oxford Univ. Press, 1953).

TRANSLATION, NOTES, AND COMMENTS

◆

1:1–5 PRESCRIPT

TRANSLATION

1:1. Paul, an apostle — that is to say a person who has been sent on a mission; sent, however, not by a group of other human beings, nor even by an individual human being, but rather by Jesus Christ and God the Father, who raised him from the realm of those who have died — 2. and all of the brothers and sisters who are with me; to the churches of Galatia: 3. May grace and peace come to you from God our Father and from the Lord Jesus Christ, 4. "who gave up his very life for our sins," so that he might snatch us out of the grasp of the present evil age, thus acting in accordance with the intention of God our Father. 5. To God be glory throughout the whole of eternity. Amen!

LITERARY STRUCTURE AND SYNOPSIS

Letters of several sorts have come down to us from a number of ancient cultures, notably oriental, Greek, and Roman.[1] As one would expect, there are variations in literary structure, but there is also a great amount of common ground, not least in the prescript, which almost always consists of three elements:

(a) the author's name
(b) the name of the addressee(s)
(c) greetings.

All of the letters of Paul follow this structure for the prescript, with the possible exception of Galatians. Here, while vv 3–5 can be read as the greeting, they seem to constitute in Paul's mind a prayer, made up of a blessing (vv 3–4) and a doxology (v 5). Thus:

[1] See Dion, "Letters (Aramaic)"; Stowers, "Letters (Greek and Latin)."

(a) the author: Paul (vv 1–2a)
(b) the addressees: the Galatian churches (v 2b)
(c) a prayer consisting of a blessing (vv 3–4) and a doxology (v 5)

NOTES

1:1. *Paul.* Following the standard form of the ancient letter, both oriental and Greek, Paul begins the prescript by naming himself as author. It is probable that the Galatians know Paul only by this Latin name, but we can be confident that he did not have it from birth. Taking into account statements he makes about his earliest years in this letter (1:13–14) and in others (2 Cor 11:22; Phil 3:5–6), we can deduce that he was born in an observant Jewish home and given a Hebrew name at birth. There is no good reason to doubt that it was the ancient and honorable name "Saul," mentioned repeatedly in Acts (7:58; 9:4; etc.). When did he take the Latin name "Paul"? As a boy or young man, and very much the enthusiastic Jew, he, or his parents for him, probably followed a custom common among Diaspora Jews of adopting a Greek or Latin name which had a sound similar to that of the Hebrew name given at birth (note Jesus Justus, Col 4:11).

Manuscript editors are divided as to whether a comma is to be provided after "Paul" or after "apostle." Because of the close relationship between the word "apostle" and the prepositional phrases that follow it (see below), the comma is best placed after "Paul."

apostle. Strictly speaking, this word is a verbal adjective referring to the effect of the action denoted by the compound verb *apostellô*, "to send (*stellô*) from (*apo*)." In Greek society it was employed to refer, for example, to a naval force sent out on a mission by a city-state.[2] Members of the earliest church used the term in several ways. One usage referred to a person who, having been given a specific task by God, had been sent by God through a church to carry out that task.[3] According to this usage, the sent person carries to a significant degree not only the message but also the authority of the sender.[4]

Paul himself can use the term to refer to messengers (*apostoloi*) of local churches, trusted with the task of carrying moneys collected in those churches. These *apostoloi* doubtless understood themselves to be envoys both of the sponsoring churches and of God (2 Cor 8:23; cf. Phil 2:25). Thus, there could be a simple understanding of the relationship between the sense in which a person was sent by God and the sense in which that same person was sent by a group of human beings making up a church. One recalls the untroubled picture Luke

---

[2] Rengstorf, "*apostellô*," 407.
[3] There were several other uses — for example, to refer to Jesus' disciples — but putting them in chronological order and reconstructing the relationships among them is a complicated matter, the investigation of which is unnecessary for understanding Gal 1:1, 17, 19. See especially H. D. Betz, "Apostle."
[4] A later rabbinic formula states that "the one sent by a man is as the man himself" (e.g., *m. Ber.* 5:5). Cf. 1 Thess 2:13.

paints of the Antioch church as it deputized Paul and Barnabas, in accordance with a directive from the Holy Spirit:

> While they were worshiping the Lord and fasting, the Holy Spirit said, "Set apart for me Barnabas and Saul for the work to which I have called them." Then after fasting and praying they laid their hands on them and sent them off. So, being sent out by the Holy Spirit, they went down to Seleucia . . . (Acts 13:2–4; NRSV; cf. 1 Cor 9:5; 12:28–29; Rom 16:7).

At a date earlier than Luke's — and especially in connection with Paul himself — the relationship between divine and human commissions could also become a sharply polemical matter, as in the present instance. See the three coordinate prepositional phrases below.

that is to say a person who has been sent on a mission. These words are added in the translation, because, as Greek-speaking persons, the Galatians will have sensed from the following prepositional phrases Paul's emphasis on the verbal nature of the word "apostle."

sent, however, not by a group of other human beings. This is the first of three coordinate prepositional phrases, all of which modify the verbal adjective *apostolos,* "a person who has been sent." What is the picture that Paul here rejects in such a polemical and emphatic manner? It is that of his having been sent from a group of human beings in the sense that they *originated the action.*[5] Paul's major concern in this pointed denial is to say that he has not been sent on his apostolic mission by the members of the church in Antioch (Comments #25 and #26).

nor even by an individual human being. When we compare this second prepositional phrase with the first one, we see that the major difference is the change in prepositions. Instead of *apo,* "by," Paul now uses *dia,* which can mean either "through" (instrumental) or "by" (causal). Regarding this construction, the evidence both from the papyri and from early Christian literature is divided: in the Hellenistic period *dia* with the genitive and with a passive verb (here it is a passive verbal adjective, "a sent person") can mean either "through" (mediating agent) or "by" (originating actor).[6]

A passage in 1 Corinthians tips the balance in favor of "by":

> Faithful is the God by (*dia*) whom you were called into the fellowship of his son (1 Cor 1:9).

Both instances of *dia* in Gal 1:1 are best rendered with the word "by." In the whole of this verse Paul is concerned not with misunderstandings as to who may have mediated his sending, but rather with misconceptions as to who sent him.

human beings . . . human being. The word, once plural, once singular, is *anthrôpos,* the generic term for human being, regardless of gender. Paul is referring primarily to the church in Antioch (a group of other human beings) and to one

[5]See BAGD, "*apo,*" iv.4.
[6]Mayser, *Grammatik,* 2.2.421–423; BDF §223.

of the leading men of the Jerusalem church (an individual human being): "I was sent out on my mission neither by the church of Antioch nor by any leading member of the church of Jerusalem, such as James or Peter." Paul uses the term *anthrôpos* to point to the human orb, as that orb is to be distinguished from the realm of God. The distinction is essential to the whole of the letter (e.g., 1:12–13).[7]

Jesus Christ. As is usual in his letters, Paul employs here what had become for the Hellenistic churches of his time a compound name, "Jesus Christ," in which the order of the two words is a matter of relative indifference. Paul himself is sure to have known that "Christ" is the Greek word for "messiah," but we can discern little of the meaning that Hebrew title may have had for him when he was a Pharisee. We cannot even be sure that it was for him a well-defined term.[8] What we can say is (a) that no line of messianic expectation in Judaism looked forward to a messiah who would be subjected to execution as a criminal, and (b) that after Paul was called by God to be a Christian missioner to the Gentiles, the collocation of the two words "Jesus Christ" caused the meaning of the word "Christ" to be derived primarily from the story of Jesus, and centrally from Jesus' death "for us."

and God the Father. As H. D. Betz points out, Paul gives special emphasis to this expression in Galatians (1:1, 3, 4; 4:2, 6), and no doubt the reason is his concern to develop the notion that the Galatians are the liberated children of the God who is the gracious Father.[9] That concern may have arisen in his mind partly because he has learned that the Teachers are preaching sermons about father Abraham and about the need of Gentiles to become genuine children of Abraham.[10] We will see later that Paul himself employs Abrahamic traditions, by giving to them a distinctly secondary place (see Comment #33). For Paul God alone is the Father.[11] Within the brief span of the prescript, Paul three times refers to God as Father. In vv 3 and 4 he is the Father of Christians. In v 1 he is the Father of Jesus Christ, having shown himself to be such by performing the essential act of a father, the giving of life.

who raised him from the realm of those who have died. This clause or its equivalent is found several times in others of Paul's letters (e.g., Rom 4:24–25; 8:11; 10:9), suggesting that it is a fixed expression. Add to that fact its "ring" and its content, and one has a case for considering it to be a liturgical formula, very probably composed by Jewish Christians who drew on elements in the Jewish liturgy, such as one of the lines in what is now the second benediction in the Amidah:

---

[7]Indeed, the distinction between the human orb and the realm of God is essential to all strands of biblical tradition. See, for example, Isa 31:3.

[8]See W. S. Green, "Messiah"; E. P. Sanders, *Jesus and Judaism*, 308.

[9]H. D. Betz 39 n27. See further Bassler, "God (NT)"; Malherbe, "Family," 118–119.

[10]On the use of the expression "the Teachers" to refer to the Jewish-Christian evangelists who entered Paul's Galatian churches in his absence, see Introduction §6 and Comments #6 and #33.

[11]Juel, "The Lord's Prayer," 63.

You are mighty . . .
the one who lives forever,
the one who raises the dead.[12]

Paul's identity is given in the fact that God has sent him, and God's identity is here given by his having raised Jesus from the dead. Especially in writing to the Galatians, Paul will make clear that, like the Teachers, he knows there is only one God (see 3:20; 1 Cor 8:4–6). Equally important, however: this one God has now identified himself by his act in Jesus Christ, making that act, indeed, the primal mark of his identity.[13]

It is striking that in writing to the Galatians Paul speaks only this once of Jesus' resurrection. In Galatia that part of early Christian theology has been left intact by the Teachers. Is the singularity of this reference also an indication that Galatians lacks the apocalyptic perspective so prominent in others of Paul's letters (1 Thessalonians 4–5; 1 Corinthians 15; Romans 8)? Or is one to say that, in Galatians, Paul shifts the center of his apocalyptic perspective almost totally to the cross? See Comment #3.

2. *and all of the brothers and sisters who are with me.* In identifying himself as author of a letter, Paul sometimes mentions others also, naming them explicitly (Timothy three times — Phil 1:1; 2 Cor 1:1; Col 1:1 — Silvanus and Sosthenes once each — 1 Thess 1:1; 1 Cor 1:1). In some instances one can see that he wants to remind a given church of its having been founded by himself and others, acting as coworkers. Here he may be unable to strike that note, having been essentially alone when he came into Galatia (1:8–9; 4:13–15). But if the Teachers are telling the Galatians that he still stands virtually alone in his perception of the gospel, Paul will emphasize that, as he writes the letter, the Pauline circle of preachers is a group of some size. He intends the Galatians to know at the outset that in regard to the subject of the letter, "the truth of the gospel" (2:5, 14), he has a number of fellow workers, including both men and women (Rom 16:3–16), all working in harmony.[14]

to the churches of Galatia. As we have noted, the naming of the addressees is the second of the three standard elements comprising the epistolary prescript. As Galatians is the only Pauline letter we have that was sent to congregations in several cities, so only here does Paul identify the addressees by the plural

[12] For discussion of the Amidah, including the dating problem, see Ferguson, *Backgrounds,* and the literature cited there (554 n315).

[13] Cf. Walter, "Römer 9–11."

[14] Was Paul accompanied in Galatia by a distinctly junior partner, Silvanus (cf. Acts 15:36–16:3a)? It is impossible to know, but Gal 4:13–15 scarcely suggests such a picture. If Paul was essentially alone at the outset of his work in the west, that state of affairs seems to have been partially repeated at a later juncture. If Colossians was written by Timothy at Paul's general direction (Schweizer, *Colossians*), it shows that near the end of his life Paul had been almost completely ostracized by Jewish-Christian missionaries, presumably because of his stand on the relationship between "the truth of the gospel" and the Law (Col 4:10–11).

"churches" (in 2 Cor 1:1 Paul adds "all the saints throughout Achaia"). Nowhere in the letter, however, does he differentiate one of the Galatian churches from the others. Apparently, the virus that has spread among them is evenly distributed.[15] Doubtless Paul's messenger went to each Galatian city, assembling the church in that place, so that in the context of worship the members could hear Paul's letter as though it were one of his sermons.

The genitive *tês Galatias*, "of Galatia," is probably to be read as are the genitives in 1:21 ("the regions [not the provinces] *of Syria and Cilicia*"). The churches are in Ankyra and Pessinus (perhaps also Tavium), Celtic cities in northern Asia Minor (see Introduction §3).

Regarding the word *ekklêsia*, "church," see Note on 1:13. Having others of Paul's letters, we know that, in addition to giving the geographical location of the church to which he is writing, he often provides a significant and altogether positive characterization of that church:

to the church of the Thessalonians *in God the Father and the Lord Jesus Christ* (1 Thess 1:1)

to the church *of God* which is at Corinth, to those *sanctified in Christ Jesus called to be saints* (1 Cor 1:2)

to all God's *beloved* in Rome, *who are called to be saints* (Rom 1:7).

In the present prescript Paul provides no such characterization (the term "saints" occurs nowhere in Galatians). Why? He will give a striking portrait of the Galatian churches at 1:6, and that portrait does not present a pleasant picture. Therefore, in this prescript Paul gives a lean identification of the recipients, resulting in a tone of formality. For a brief moment, having warmly embraced the coworkers who are present with him as he writes the letter, he holds the Galatians at arm's length.

3. *May grace and peace come to you.* Precisely at this point—that is, as the third element in the prescript—Paul almost always uses the formula "grace and peace to you from God the Father and the Lord Jesus Christ" (no verb; the exception is 1 Thessalonians). It sounds very much like a salutation or greeting, and one is encouraged to view it as such by the fact that a salutation is the third element in the prescript of a huge number of ancient letters, both oriental and Greek. On the Greek side the standard salutation is *chairein*, "greetings," a word with a sound similar to that of Paul's *charis*, "grace." And in many oriental letters the key term of the greeting is *šālôm* (Hebrew) or *šelām* (Aramaic), "peace," as one can see, for example, in Dan 4:1 (Theodotion; 3:31 in the Aramaic text):

(a) King Nebuchadnezzar
(b) to all peoples . . .
(c) Peace be multiplied to you!

---

[15] As indicated in the Introduction (§18), I generally take Paul's point of view in interpreting his letter; hence the word "virus."

Thus, the hypothesis virtually suggests itself that Paul has drawn upon both Greek and oriental epistolary traditions in order to compose his own form of salutation.

As a suggestion pertinent to the Pauline letters in general, this hypothesis is probably correct. It is worth noting that in all of the letters except Galatians this formula, "grace and peace to you . . . ," comprises in itself an entire sentence which would thus be sensed by Paul's addressees in Corinth, Rome, etc., as the expected greeting. In Galatians, however, Paul does not place a stop after this formula. He pauses only after he has developed a fairly long and complex sentence which reaches through vv 4 and 5. The weighty elements that make up the latter part of this sentence are nowhere else found as parts of an epistolary greeting. We have to ask, therefore, whether in hearing them, the Galatians will have sensed that Paul has changed the expected salutation into something else.

Two related observations suggest an affirmative answer: First, there is the fact that most of the standard forms of epistolary salutation used in Paul's time were initially in vogue as oral greetings, subsequently making their way into written communication (letters). It follows that the force sensed by readers of such a written greeting would depend on the nature of the oral counterpart it evoked in their minds. One can see, for example, that in numerous Aramaic letters the term *šĕlām* meant no more and no less than its counterpart on the street, "greetings!" In other instances a blessing was pronounced, so as to relate the addressee to God. When, in Galatians, Paul departs from his standard form by expanding his usual greeting at some length, is he influenced to do so by an association with a setting of oral communication; and if so, what might that setting be?

The nature of the added clauses gives us an answer, thus leading to a second observation. In v 4 (see below) Paul probably draws on an early Christian *confession*. He then pronounces a solemn *doxology* (v 5), and he closes the sentence with the word *amên*, an exclamation by which worshipers are invited to participate in a blessing, a prayer, or a doxology. Taken as a whole, then, vv 3–5 do not merely extend Paul's greetings. They have the effect of evoking the setting of worship. Instead of following the expected form of the epistolary prescript— speaking *a greeting to the Galatian churches:* "I, Paul, salute you" — the apostle is voicing a confession and a doxology, inviting the Galatians to join him in *praise addressed to God.*

grace. As an extraordinarily weighty term, the word "grace" will doubtless have first come to the Galatians' attention in Paul's sermons. And we can assume that there, as in his letters, he often used the word to sum up the whole of God's good news in Jesus Christ (see Gal 1:6; 2:9, 21; 5:4; 6:18). The gospel is God's grace because it is the good news that, quite apart from human activity, and specifically in spite of the development of religion, God has acted in Christ to bring all people into the "space" (Rom 5:2) of the new creation in which he is making things right (Introduction §17). That Paul should allow the word "grace" to stand at the beginning of his standard greeting—in Galatians at the beginning of his prayerful blessing—is thus symbolic of the fact that the event of God's grace stands at the beginning of his new creation. When things "go wrong," as is now happening among the Galatian congregations, Paul does not first of all reach for a word of exhortation. He simply takes the congregations back to their birth. He takes them back, that is, to God's graceful election. Brought back to that point, the churches can see once again that not a single thing which human beings can do could possibly serve as the fountainhead of their redemption. God the gracious one, and he alone, shows himself to be the new creator in Jesus Christ, the one whose grace is more powerful than is evil.[16]

peace. This is a word which, in its Greek dress, the Galatians will have heard rather frequently long before they listened to Paul. To them, as to other Greek-speaking peoples of their day, it meant in the first instance the repose which comes with the absence of war. It is from Paul's preaching that the Galatians will have learned to speak of God's peace with the nuances attached to the Hebrew term *šālôm*, a word which points to health, wholeness, relational integrity, and indeed, like "grace," to God's salvation itself.

In his use of the term "peace" Paul speaks of the well-being of the *world* (beginning in the church, to be sure), and thus only *secondarily* of an inner state of mind (Rom 15:13). This well-being of the world lies in its being regrasped from the power of evil by God's deed in Jesus Christ.[17] And because God's act of regrasping the world for himself happens in his apocalyptic battle against the forces of evil and sin, peace — as Paul speaks of it — is won in a war and only then becomes true wholeness, well-being, and relational integrity.[18] Given Paul's apocalyptic frame of reference, his bold pronouncement of peace is to be understood as a confident cry of victory in the midst of God's battle of liberation (see Comments #3 and #49).

and from the Lord Jesus Christ. The literature on the title "Lord" as it is applied to Jesus Christ is immense. In Galatians two important emphases emerge. First, drawing on traditions circulating in the Christian communities in Palestine, Paul calls Jesus Christ by the title "Lord" in order to say that his cosmic rulership is on a par with that of God, although even as Lord he remains the Son of God the Father.[19] Second, speaking in this way to Gentiles, Paul both poses and answers a question that permeated the Gentile world into which he has been sent: Who is your Lord, your ruler? The answer: Neither Isis nor Caesar, but rather Jesus Christ. With this pregnant meaning the title "Lord" reemerges at the end of the letter: 6:14, 18.

4. *"who gave up his very life for our sins."* As the quotation marks suggest, there are reasons for thinking that Paul draws these words from an early Christian hymn or (eucharistic?) confession, and that his doing so will have been even more obvious to the Galatians than it is to us.[20] From the use of similar formulas

---

[16] See Käsemann, *Romans*, 96; J. L. Martyn, *Issues*, 279–297.

[17] The equivalent of this sentence is found numerous times in the Pauline writings of Käsemann; see, for example, *Questions*, 180.

[18] Recalling that the term *šālôm* is intimately related to the word family of *šqṭ* ("to be at rest"; see, e.g., Isa 32:17), it is pertinent to note that the ancient victory song of Deborah is followed by the declaration that "the land had rest (*wattišqōṭ*) for forty years" (Judg 5:31).

[19] See Fitzmyer, *Advance*, 218–235.

[20] Cf. Bovon, "Une formal prépaulinienne"; Hengel, *Atonement*; Breytenbach, "Versöhnung" (especially 67–73); Furnish, "Gave Himself."

by Paul (twice in the present letter, 1:4; 2:20; twice in Romans, 4:25; 8:32) and by the author of Ephesians (5:2, 25; cf. 1 Tim 2:6; Titus 2:14), we can see that the confession has two basic elements: an affirmation of Christ's death and a prepositional phrase pointing to the significance of that death or to the persons for whom it was enacted. In the present case the first element is expressed by the reflexive "he gave himself," indicating that Christ's life was not taken from him against his will; he gave it freely.[21] The second element is in this instance *hyper tôn hamartiôn hêmôn*, literally "for our sins," meaning "in order to remove the deadly effects of our sins."[22] From its inception the church made various efforts to interpret Jesus' death, and the present formula arose in the course of these efforts.

our sins. These words provide yet another reason for thinking we are dealing with a quotation. While Paul uses the word "sin" in the singular rather frequently, the plural form emerges only four times in the genuine letters. Of these four instances one is in a sentence Paul explicitly identifies as an early Christian confession (1 Cor 15:3); a second stands in the broad context of that confession (1 Cor 15:17); the third functions in effect as a plural adjective modifying a plural noun (Rom 7:5, "sinful passions"); and the fourth emerges in the present verse. Only when he is quoting traditional formulas does Paul speak of Jesus as having died for our *sins* (Gal 1:4; 1 Cor 15:3).

I have said above that the Galatians will have sensed the quotation marks, so to speak, even more readily than do we who are able to draw comparisons from the other Pauline letters. From whose lips will they have previously heard the formula? No certain answer can be given. Perhaps Paul himself cited the confession in his preaching to the Galatians. Could it also be that the Galatians are even now hearing this formula in the sermons of the Teachers?

The possibility of an affirmative answer emerges from Rom 3:25, for there we find a formula worded by a Jewish Christian for use among Jewish Christians:

> . . . Christ Jesus, whom God put forward as a sacrifice of atonement by his blood. God did this to demonstrate the power of his rectitude; in his divine forbearance, that is to say, he has forgiven the sins previously committed . . .[23]

The Teachers will certainly have had to interpret Jesus' death, even though — as the letter shows — they were far from taking their theological bearings from the cross as such. Toward Jesus' death they may have had a view similar to the one encapsulated in Rom 3:25. We may even ponder the possibility that, like the Jewish Christians responsible for that formula, the Teachers may have drawn on the martyrological tradition represented in 4 Maccabees, in order to see Jesus as the Law-observant, Law-confirming Messiah whose death as a *martyr* was the event in which God set things right by forgiving all sins previously committed by

[21] The expression *heauton didonai* is at home in Greek at least as early as the second century B.C. (Nägeli, *Wortschatz*, 56); but here it probably renders the Hebrew "give one's self (one's *nepeš*)." Cf. Mark 10:45.

[22] Breytenbach, "Versöhnung," 68.

[23] This tradition is discussed in Comment #28.

God's people Israel.[24] They could then invite Gentiles to enter this forgiven people, trusting that their future forgiveness would ensue from their faith in Jesus, the Messiah, and from their observance of the Law as ratified by him. It is an hypothesis worthy of consideration (see Comment #28).

However that may be, one point is certain: The formula is to a significant degree foreign to Paul's own theology; for it identifies discrete sins as humanity's (in the first instance Israel's) fundamental liability; and it sees forgiveness of sins as the remedy provided by God (see Comment #28). As we have noted, Paul, when he is formulating his own view, consistently speaks not of sins, but rather of Sin, identifying it as a power that holds human beings in a state of slavery. And he sees liberation rather than forgiveness as the fundamental remedy enacted by God. We have therefore to ask why Paul, intent on turning his customary epistolary greeting into a prayer, should do so by quoting a confessional formula, the origin and theological dimensions of which are partially alien to him. The next clause suggests an answer. Paul quotes the Jewish-Christian formula in order affirmatively to correct it by means of an additional clause.

so that he might snatch us out of the grasp of. In the main clause of the sentence Paul has followed the atonement formula in speaking of an event lying in the past: Christ gave up his life for our sins. In Comment #3 we will see compelling reasons for thinking that he is now himself the author of the final clause, ". . . so that he might snatch us out of the grasp of the present evil age." He uses the verb "to snatch out of the grasp of" (*exaireô* in the middle voice) with the meaning "to deliver, to rescue," and he employs a clause form (*hopôs* with the aorist subjunctive) that takes its temporal import from the verb of the main clause. The result is a sentence in which Christ's death is interpreted as the past event that in itself accomplished not only the forgiveness of our sins but also and climactically our deliverance from a foreign power (the present evil age). In two regards, then, this daring and dramatic affirmation serves as one of the topic sentences for the whole of the letter.

First, in it Paul speaks of our redemption as an accomplished fact, giving no indication that any aspect of it is as yet incomplete. With minor modification that proves to be the perspective permeating the letter from beginning to end. A large part of the letter's message could be encapsulated in an exclamation: "Wake up to the real world, you Galatians! God's redemptive act has been carried out!"

Second, with its final clause the sentence also voices a presupposition to which Paul returns at point after point in the letter: Human beings are held under the thumb of powers foreign to themselves.[25] In his use of the expression *exaireô ek*, "to deliver from, to rescue from," Paul may have been influenced by the LXX, where the verb *exaireô* frequently occurs with the preposition *ek* in the idiom "to rescue one out of the hand of [one's enemy]." He may also have known the use

---

[24] Cf. 4 Macc 1:8, 10; 6:27; 9:6; 13:9; 16:25; 18:3.
[25] It is thus a note one would expect Paul to strike in his statement of the letter's theme (1:6–9) rather than in the prescript (Introduction §10). See the discussions in H. D. Betz and in R. G. Hall, "Outline," 283.

of the verb in the expression *exaireô eis eleuthêrian,* "to claim as a freeman."[26] In any case, his presupposition is clear: Human beings are slaves; and the fundamental enslaving power is not a flesh-and-blood enemy, but rather:

the present evil age. These words provide a strong indication that Paul is now turning to a distinctly apocalyptic frame of reference. See Comment #3.

thus acting in accordance with the intention of God our Father. Lit. "according to the will of God and our Father." The expression "the will of God" is one Paul uses in his letters in order to point to God's sovereign intention. Jesus' giving up of his own life for our deliverance was not simply a deed of his own, but rather an act carried out in faithful obedience to God (Comment #28). It was, in fact, an act intended by God. Noting the parallels in 1 Cor 11:23 and Rom 5:8, we can say that Christ's act was God's act.[27]

The death of the Son is therefore a sacrifice enacted both by him and by God; and as such it breaks the mold of the old sacrificial pattern. The cross, that is to say, is not a sacrifice human beings make to God; it is fundamentally God's act, and as such the inversion of the sacrificial system.[28]

5. *To God be glory.* Having pronounced an extended and highly situational blessing over the Galatian congregations (vv 3–4), Paul ends the prescript with a doxology, something he does in none of his other letters. The doxology, brought into Christian worship from long usage in the synagogue, serves as the climactic exclamation at the end of a hymn or prayer in which the magnitude of God's deliverance has been celebrated, *doxa* ("glory") being God's power in action (1 Tim 1:17; 6:15–16).[29] We may assume that Paul brings the doxology from its usual liturgical setting into this epistolary introduction in order to make clear that the reading of his letter belongs properly to the context of worship (cf. Rev 1:4–6 and 10). It is there, Paul thinks, that God will cause Paul's epistolary words to become the word of God (see Comments #4 and #9).

throughout the whole of eternity. Lit. "to the ages of the ages." In Comment #3 we will see that the framework of eschatological dualism in which there are *two* ages is fundamental to Paul's theology. Here he simply uses the liturgical reference to many ages (employed a dozen times in Revelation) as a way of speaking of nontemporal eternity.

Amen! This is a Hebrew word which is rendered in the LXX by transliteration (as here in Galatians) by the word "truly," *alêthôs,* and by the expression "let it

---

[26]Lysias 23.9; Demosthenes *Ep.* 8.42, 10.14. Note also that MM 221 cite a papyrus with a reference to deliverance from *anagkê,* "Necessity."

[27]Cf. Keck, *Paul and His Letters,* 36.

[28]The complexity and mystery of Christ's death on a cross is evident in the fact that no one sentence suffices to speak of it. Paul can refer to it as God's act; he can also attribute it to other actors. In 1 Thess 2:15 he mentions "the Jews who killed . . . the Lord Jesus," whereas in 1 Cor 2:8 he says that "the rulers of this age" crucified the Lord of glory. See Cousar, *Cross;* R. E. Brown, *Death.* In the analysis of Hamerton-Kelly Jesus' crucifixion is the act in which, rather than taking vengeance by demanding a sacrifice, God himself suffers vengeance (*Violence,* 79; see also Review of Hamerton-Kelly by Cousar).

[29]Cf. Newman, *Paul's Glory-Christology.*

be so," *genoito*. It is "an exclamation . . . by which listeners join in an oath, a blessing, a curse, a prayer, or a doxology they have [just] heard, and affirm their readiness to bear the consequences of this acknowledgment."[30] By this exclamation members of the congregation confess that they are more than observers; they are participants.

COMMENT #1
THE NATURE OF PAUL'S APOSTOLATE[31]

In the letter's prescript Paul employs and embroiders elements of his customary epistolary salutation in order to accent four points at which he expects the Galatians to prick up their ears: his own apostolate, the human plight, apocalyptic theology, and the relationship between his word and the word of God. All four — the subjects of Comments #1–#4 — are directly related to developments currently transpiring in the Galatian churches, and all four prove to be fundamental to the whole of the letter.[32]

We can reconstruct in part the three-stage background against which the Galatians will have heard Paul's reference to his being an apostle (1:1).

THE GALATIANS' PERCEPTION OF PAUL WHEN HE FIRST CAME AMONG THEM

We can be confident that, in presenting his glad tiding (Comment #7), Paul identified himself as an apostle (*apostolos*), sent into his work by Christ (see 1 Thess 2:6; Gal 1:16–17). Here, however, it is the verb *apostellô*, "to send out," that is of importance. For the Galatians may well have known some form of the tradition in which that verb is used to speak of the Cynic, identifying him as a sort of apostle, even though the verbal adjective itself is not used:[33]

> The true Cynic . . . must know that he is a messenger (*aggelos*) sent by Zeus (*apo tou Dios apestaltai*) to human beings, both to show them that . . . they are seeking the true nature of the good and the evil where it is not . . . and to function as a scout (*kataskopos*) . . . [who will] find out what things are friendly to human beings and what things are hostile . . . (Epictetus *Diss.* 3.22.22–23).

This scout must also have the capacity to address human beings in a dramatically effective way, conveying to them what he has discovered:

> He must . . . be able to lift up his voice [saying] . . . What are you doing wretched people? Like blind men you go tottering about. You have left the true path and are going off on another . . . (Epictetus *Diss.* 3.22.26).

[30]Hempel, "Amen."
[31]See especially Schütz, *Anatomy*; H. D. Betz, "Apostle."
[32]The relation of the prescript to the body of the letter is analyzed by Kennedy, *Interpretation*, 147–148.
[33]Cf. Malherbe, *Philosophers*, 13 n10.

Sent by Zeus as a friendly spy, the Cynic observes how things are among human beings; and, perceiving what is truly wrong (cf. Note on 1:4b and Comment #28), he seeks to be of help.

When Paul came to the Galatians, preaching Christ to them, and identifying himself as an apostle sent to them by God, they may very well have perceived him to be similar to the genuine Cynic.[34] But their understanding of Paul's apostleship was also affected by the specificity of his glad tiding as the gospel of Christ, the Son whom God had sent into their world to redeem them from the powers of darkness. Paul's being sent into the Galatians' territory — unplanned by himself (4:13) — was itself an enactment of God's redemptive invasion of the cosmos in the sending of his Son (cf. Comment #3). With unbridled enthusiasm, then, the Galatians saw in Paul God's own messenger, an apostle in whose message and person Christ himself had come to them (4:14).

THE TEACHERS' USE OF THE TERM "APOSTLE"

Not long after Paul's departure, the Teachers arrived with their message, and here again the Galatians will have heard the term "apostle" being employed with a specific emphasis.[35] For an important part of the Teachers' sermons consists of charges they are laying against Paul and specifically against both his gospel and his apostleship.[36] We cannot know precisely what the term "apostle" meant to them, but we are not wholly in the dark.

Sometime after A.D. 70 Jewish authorities in Palestine used their own language — šālûaḥ (Hebrew), šālîaḥ (Aramaic) — to refer to an apostle (an agent) sent out to the Jewish Diaspora with an official message.[37] That development is too late to have served as the model for the early Christian apostolate, either in Jerusalem or in Antioch (see Note on 1:17).[38] The Jewish šālîaḥ and the Christian *apostolos* may, however, have common roots in the figure of the servants sent by the king of Israel to carry out a task he and he alone defines (e.g., 1 Kgdms 25:40; 2 Kgdms 10:2).[39] What is made explicit, then, in the Jewish tradition of

---

[34]The date of the founding of the Galatian churches may have a bearing on their initial understanding of Paul's apostolate. If, as is argued in Comment #17, Paul came to Galatia only after his break with the Antioch church, he will have identified himself from the beginning as one sent to them by God, not by a church.

[35]On the use of the expression "the Teachers" to refer to the Jewish-Christian evangelists who invaded Paul's Galatian churches, see Introduction §6 and Comments #6 and #33.

[36]The two negative phrases of 1:1 (technically the double *correctio*; see below) are unlikely to be a mere rhetorical stratagem designed to accentuate the positive clauses that follow, *pace* Vos, "Argumentation," 3.

[37]Rengstorf, "*apostellô*."

[38]See Schütz, *Anatomy*, 27–28.

[39]At only one point in the LXX is the Hebrew term šālûaḥ rendered by the word *apostolos*, the prophet Abijah using it to identify himself as a man sent by God to bring a message to the king's wife (3 Kgdms 14:6). In following the minds of the ancients, however, one cannot narrow the linguistic focus to a single word. As we have taken into account the role of the verb *apostellô* in Epictetus's portrait of the Cynic as a messenger sent by Zeus, so, in imagining how the Teachers read the scripture, we must consider the use of the verbs šālah and *apostellô* to identify the king's servants when he sends them on a mission. For Paul's own understanding of his apostolate, it may be pertinent to note that, in some Jew-

the *šālîaḥ* is very likely to have been true also of the Christian apostle, not least as the Teachers understood the matter: Being dispatched by God *through a church*, an apostle is obligated to subordinate his own will to the will of God, *as* God's will is perceived in that church.

The Teachers themselves do not claim to be apostles (contrast Paul's opponents in 2 Cor 11:13), but they do claim to represent the apostles in the Jerusalem church (see Comment #46). About Paul, then, they are saying in essence:

> He was at one time an apostle sent out by the church in Antioch (cf. Acts 12:25–13:3; 14:4, 14). At a meeting in the church of Jerusalem he was indeed one of those who came in good standing from the Antioch church.[40] Subsequently, however, he began to preach a Law-less gospel, and that fact shows clearly that he is not subordinating his will to God's plan, as that plan is known by the Antioch church and by the apostles in Jerusalem. In short, Paul is a renegade, an unfaithful apostle, and thus one to whom that term does not apply.[41]

THE TERM "APOSTLE" IN THE LETTER

Finally, listening to the reading of Paul's letter, the Galatians will have noticed that Paul uses the term "apostle" as his second word. Recalling both their initial impression of Paul and the charges now being leveled against him by the Teachers, the Galatians will not have been surprised to find Paul emphasizing the verbal force of the noun by means of three prepositional phrases, "sent, however, not by . . . nor even by . . . but rather by . . ." In this way Paul insists that, although he is indeed a person sent on a mission, he has been sent "by Jesus Christ and God the Father," not by a group of other human beings, such as the churches in Antioch and Jerusalem. A few sentences later he says similarly that his gospel was not taught him by another human being; it came from the apocalypse of Jesus Christ (1:12). As an apostle, then, Paul comes to his work from beyond, not from entities in this world.

In striking this contrast Paul formulates what we will call an antinomy between the action of God and the action of human beings.[42] And by formulating that antinomy, Paul sets a tone that is fundamental to his gospel, and that runs through the whole of the letter. What is making things right in the human scene does not have its origin there. What is potent to set things straight is the message

---

ish traditions, Moses and other Israelite worthies are identified as apostles of God himself. See Meeks, *The Prophet-King*; idem, "Divine Agent."

[40] Whether or not the Jerusalem apostles formally acknowledged Paul as an apostle (see Notes on 2:7, 8, and 9), they will certainly have assumed Paul's obligation to subordinate his individual will to the will of the Antioch church, if not to that of the Jerusalem church. And the Teachers must know that this was the assumption of the Jerusalem apostles. See Schütz, *Anatomy*, 22–34; Holmberg, *Power*, 15–56.

[41] Concerning the later attack on Paul's apostolate launched by the opponents who invaded his Corinthian church, see Käsemann, "Legitimität"; Barrett, "Opponents."

[42] Regarding the use of the term "antinomy," see the Glossary and Comments #41 and #51. After Galatians, Paul regularly used the term "apostle" in his epistolary prescripts, thus maintaining this fundamental antinomy (1 Cor 1:1; 2 Cor 1:1; Rom 1:1).

that is coming from God. Even the messenger himself comes from God. Neither he nor his message can be measured, therefore, by human norms (see Notes on 1:11–12, Comment #9, and J. L. Martyn, *Issues*, 89–110).

In listening to Gal 1:1, then, one senses that Paul is a truly strange person who is sure that even before his birth God determined that he would carry the gospel of Christ to the Gentiles (1:15). There were, he acknowledges, apostles before him (1:17; see 1 Cor 15:7; 9:5; Rom 16:7), but he did not receive his call from them any more than he received it from the church in Antioch. Bearing the ultimate message *from God* to human beings, he is a man whose identity is determined by the God who sent him and by the message God gave him to preach. To other human beings (sometimes including ones in the church — 2:4, 14), he is himself a stranger, a person who, in a profound sense, "comes from somewhere else." See especially 1 Cor 4:8–13 and 2 Cor 11:21–29.

COMMENT #2
THE HUMAN PLIGHT AND GOD'S REDEMPTIVE ACT IN CHRIST[43]

In the Notes we have seen reasons for taking 1:4a to be a quotation from an early Christian liturgy, a fragment of a confession in which the human plight is identified as "our sins," and Christ's death is seen as the sacrificial atonement by which God has addressed that plight. It is quite possible that the Galatians are already acquainted with this confession, using it, in fact, in the worship services now being conducted in their churches by the Teachers. Presumably, the leader of worship ended a sentence with "the Lord Jesus Christ," and the congregation responded "who gave up his very life for our sins." It is a confession affirming the salvific effect of Christ's death.

The second half of v 4 continues by giving greater specificity to the purpose for which Christ died:

> . . . so that (*hopôs*) he might snatch us out of the grasp of the present evil age, thus acting in accordance with the intention of God our Father.

In these clauses does Paul continue to quote, or does he provide his own interpretation of the liturgical fragment, tailored to developments in his Galatian churches? It is a debated point.

[43] It was from the event of Christ's crucifixion — perceived to be God's redeeming deed — that Paul came to know the true nature of the human plight. Karl Barth was right to emphasize that Paul saw Adam in the light of Christ, sin in the light of grace, and so on. See, for example, *Church Dogmatics*, 2.2: ". . . it is only by grace that the lack of grace can be recognized as such" (92); ". . . the doctrine of election . . . defines grace as the starting-point for all reflection and utterance . . ." (93). In recent decades Barth's point has been emphasized in a certain way by E. P. Sanders, *Palestinian Judaism*, 442–447. The argument of Thielman that Paul proceeds from an analysis of the human plight to its solution contains numerous insights, but the major thesis is unconvincing *for Paul* (*From Plight to Solution*). Just as Paul the Pharisee could say — knowing God's Law to be God's grace — that the knowledge of sin comes *from* the Law (Rom 3:20), so Paul the apostle insists that whatever does not flow *from* faith is sin (Rom 14:23). See further Comment #28.

For three reasons one might think that Paul continues to quote from the liturgical formula:

(1) Dahl has collected from the New Testament and from the Apostolic Fathers texts in which he finds fragments of early Christian sermons and hymns showing in most cases a teleological interpretation in which the purpose of Christ's death is accented: "Christ died . . . in order that (*hina*); Christ died . . . so that (*hopôs*)."[44] The fact, then, that the second clause of Gal 1:4 is purposive does not prove that it is secondary to the quotation in the first clause. Indeed, some of Dahl's examples — notably 1 Pet 3:18 — provide an argument for seeing the whole of Gal 1:4 as a quotation.

(2) The final phrase of v 4 runs literally "according to the will of God and our Father." Some have heard a liturgical ring in the syntax.[45]

(3) Finally, three of the expressions in v 4b occur nowhere else in the Pauline corpus and seem, therefore, to lie outside Paul's usual vocabulary: "to snatch out of the grasp of," *exaireô*; "the present age," *aiôn enestôs* (Paul speaks elsewhere of "this age," *ho aiôn houtos*); and "according to the will," *kata to thelêma*.

Weighty as these observations may be, they are more than overcome by indications that in v 4b Paul is composing relatively freely, in a style, to be sure, that is somewhat liturgical.

None of the formulations cited by Dahl (and by others) shows the distinctly apocalyptic vocabulary and thought of the second clause of v 4.[46] We are left, then, without significant formulaic parallels to that apocalyptic vocabulary.[47]

In the final phrase of v 4 Paul may have elected to use a somewhat liturgical style because of the liturgical context set by vv 3, 4a, and 5.

Most important are the expressions "to snatch out of the grasp of" and "the present age." They do not occur, as we have noted, in the creedal and hymnic fragments collected by Dahl. These particular expressions also do not occur elsewhere in Paul's letters. Two factors, however, indicate that they are very probably elements of Paul's exegesis of the formula in v 4a.

First, the verb "to snatch out of the grasp of," *exaireô*, corresponds in meaning to another verb, "to buy out of enslavement to," *exagorazô*, a term that Paul uses at two key points in Galatians (3:13; 4:5) and that, in the NT, is found with that pregnant meaning only in Galatians. We can be confident that Paul is responsible for the use of this highly situational verb in 3:13 and 4:5, even though we cannot prove that it belonged to his usual vocabulary. The Galatian situation doubtless causes Paul to reach into special corners of his stock of words. Paul has

---

[44] Dahl, "Observations."

[45] For example, Deichgräber, *Gotteshymnus*, 113 n2.

[46] For a passage showing some similarities one might turn to Heb 2:14–15, ". . . that through death he might destroy him who has the power of death . . . and deliver all those who through fear of death were subject to lifelong bondage" (cf. also Rom 6:27–28; 8:21; Col 2:15). Heb 2:14–15 may be in part a quotation from a liturgical formula, but that formula is quite unlikely to antedate Paul (Michel, *Hebräer*, 85).

[47] Here and elsewhere in the present volume (see especially Comment #3), I use the term "apocalyptic" to refer to a theological pattern of thought, not to a literary genre. See Hanson, "Apocalypse"; Sturm, "Apocalyptic."

selected "to snatch out of the grasp of" in order here in the prescript to express a major motif of the whole of the letter: In Christ God has acted to liberate human beings from enslaving forces (e.g., 5:1).[48]

Second, while it is true that Paul normally uses the expression "this age" to refer to the entity later called by the rabbis *hā'ôlām hazzeh*, one will scarcely argue that the expression "the present evil age" is linguistically foreign to him. In the NT the verb *enistêmi* (here an adjectival participle rendered "present") is virtually Paul's verb.[49] Moreover, Paul consistently employs this verb in the participial form, and in 1 Cor 7:26 he uses the participle in an apocalyptic expression similar to the one in Gal 1:4b: *hê enestôsa anagkê*, "the present (or impending) distress."

From these observations we conclude that in v 4b Paul gives his own interpretation of the Jewish-Christian atonement formula of v 4a, tailoring it to the Galatian situation.[50] The human plight consists fundamentally of enslavement to supra-human powers; and God's redemptive act is his deed of liberation.

Important, however, is the fact that Paul does not reject the Jewish-Christian formula. As we will see in 6:1, he knows very well that individuals commit discrete transgressions that can be called sins. The root antidote to an individual sin, however, is not an individual instance of forgiveness. That antidote lies in the fact that, in vanquishing the enslaving *power of Sin* (the present evil age), God has called the church into being as his new creation, and part of its task as the new creation is to deal with *discrete instances of sin*. When, then, a member of the church makes a misstep (6:1; 1:4a), he is to be brought back into the company of God's new creation. For it is *in* that newly created company that a sin is not only forgiven but also and fundamentally overpowered by God's mighty victory over Sin.

COMMENT #3
APOCALYPTIC THEOLOGY IN GALATIANS

What does Paul intend to accomplish with the interpretation he offers in 1:4b? The major key lies in his use of the distinctly apocalyptic expression "the present evil age," for it proves, in fact, to be the first of numerous apocalyptic expressions in the letter. We are thus led to consider a matter that provides an essential clue both to Paul's understanding of the human plight and to his perception of God's act in Christ.[51]

---

[48] For linguistic parallels in the orators Lysias and Demosthenes, see the Note on 1:4.
[49] Of the seven occurrences in the NT, one is in Hebrews, two in the Deutero-Paulines, and four in the genuine Pauline letters.
[50] Since the gospel Paul preached to the Galatians in the first place was doubtless fundamentally apocalyptic, it is just possible that he previously interpreted the formula of 1:4a in the way he does in 1:4b.
[51] We will shortly see that the distinction between two "tracks" of Jewish apocalyptic is essential to the reading of Galatians. On this matter, consult the extraordinarily perceptive essay of de Boer, "Apocalyptic Eschatology." In *cosmological apocalyptic eschatology*, evil, anti-God powers have managed to commence their own rule over the world, leading human beings into idolatry and thus into slavery, producing a wrong situation that was not

(1) *the present evil age* (1:4b). To speak of the present age is obviously to imply that there is another age (or something like another age), and indeed, from writings and traditions of Paul's time we know that there was a conceptual frame of reference positing *two ages*. It is a scheme fundamental to apocalyptic thought. We can be even more specific, for we know that, drawing on earlier apocalyptic patterns, the rabbis of a slightly later time spoke explicitly of "this age" (*hāʿôlām hazzeh* = *ho aiôn houtos*) and of "the coming age" (*hāʿôlām habbāʾ* = *ho aiôn ho mellôn*).[52]

Although Paul himself never speaks literally of "the coming age," his numerous references to "the present age" (in addition to Gal 1:4, see Rom 12:2; 1 Cor 1:2; 2:6; 2:8; 3:18; 2 Cor 4:4) reflect his assumption of eschatological dualism. In Paul's vocabulary the expression that stands opposite "the present evil age" is "the new creation" (Gal 6:15), yet another indication of apocalyptic thought, for it is a formulation reflecting the development of Jewish apocalyptic dualism in the time of the exile (Isa 43:18–19).[53] As we will see at numerous points in this commentary, Paul's distinction between the present evil age and the new creation is not at all a distinction between the profane and the sacred. It is in fact the end of that latter distinction. See Comment #41.

(2) . . . *God's apocalyptic revelation of Jesus Christ* (1:12); . . . *when it pleased him apocalyptically to reveal his Son to me* (1:15–16); . . . *I went up [to the Jerusalem church] as a result of revelation* (*apokalypsis*; 2:2); . . . *we were confined . . .*

---

intended by God and that will not be long tolerated by him. For in his own time God will inaugurate a victorious and liberating apocalyptic war against these evil powers, delivering his elect from their grasp and thus making right that which has gone wrong because of the powers' malignant machinations. In *forensic apocalyptic eschatology*, things have gone wrong because human beings have willfully rejected God, thereby bringing about death and the corruption and perversion of the world. Given this self-caused plight, God has graciously provided the cursing and blessing Law as the remedy, thus placing before human beings the Two Ways, the Way of death *and* the Way of life. Human beings are individually accountable before the bar of the Judge. But, by one's own decision, one can repent of one's sins, receive nomistic forgiveness, and be assured of eternal life. For at the last judgment the deserved sentence of death will be reversed for those who choose the path of Law observance, whereas that sentence will be permanently confirmed for those who do not. A crucial issue is that of determining which of these two "tracks" is dominant in a given source. In the course of the present commentary we will see that, whereas forensic apocalyptic eschatology is characteristic of the Teachers' theology, Paul's Galatian letter is fundamentally marked by cosmological apocalyptic eschatology.

[52]Both of these expressions, moreover, are to be found in the synoptic tradition, for example in Matt 12:32. We can speak of a form of eschatological dualism because of the focus on the duality of the two ages. In Galatians note, for example, 3:19–25: the arrangement of the Law was made "*until* the seed should come to whom the promise had been made . . . *Before* faith came, we were confined under the Law's power, imprisoned during the period that lasted *until*, as God intended, faith was invasively revealed. So then, the Law was our confining custodian *until* the advent of Christ, in order that we should be rectified by faith. But *now* that faith has come, we are no longer under the power of that confining custodian."

[53]See Kraus, "Schöpfung," especially 470–472 and 481; G. Schneider, "Neuschöpfung"; Stuhlmacher, "Erwägungen"; Hanson, *Dawn*, 127.

imprisoned during the period that lasted until, as God intended, faith was inva-sively revealed (apokalyphthênai; 3:23). It is striking that at these four important junctures in Galatians Paul uses the noun *apokalypsis* and the verb *apokalyptô*. In 1:12 and 16 he says that his gospel came into being when God apocalypsed Christ to him. That event was the genesis of Paul's christological apocalyptic, for it was there that God opened his eyes to the presence of the risen Lord Jesus Christ in the church.[54] Similarly, taking 1:16 in its context, we can see that for Paul the cosmos in which he had been previously living met its end in God's apocalypse of Jesus Christ (cf. 6:14). And that disjunctive apocalypse was the birth of his gospel mission. Even his subsequent travels and the inner-church battles he has to wage for the truth of the gospel are events he understands under the banner of apocalypse (2:2, 5, 14). Finally, and crucially, there is the reference to apocalypse in 3:23. There Paul speaks of "the apocalypse of faith," using that expression interchangeably with "the coming of faith" (3:25) and with the com-ing of Christ (3:24). Paul thus explicates the verb *apokalyptô* with the verbs *erchomai*, "to come [on the scene]," and *exapostellô*, "to send [into the scene]" (4:4, 6).

That is a linguistic turn inadequately represented by the usual translation of *apokalyptô* as "to reveal," "to unveil"; for it shows that in Galatians Paul's apoca-lyptic is not focused on God's unveiling something that was previously hidden, as though it had been eternally standing behind a curtain (contrast 1 Cor 2:9–10). The genesis of Paul's apocalyptic—as we see it in Galatians—lies in the apostle's certainty that God has *invaded* the present evil age by sending Christ and his Spirit into it. There was a "before," the time when we were confined, imprisoned; and there is an "after," the time of our deliverance. And the differ-ence between the two is caused not by an unveiling, but rather by the coming of Christ and his Spirit.

(3) *. . . when the fullness of time came, God sent his Son . . . God sent the Spirit of his Son into our hearts* (3:23, 24, 25; 4:4, 6). Paul's reference to God's sending of Christ in "the fullness of time" is a clear apocalyptic motif, corresponding to his speaking earlier of the present evil age. In a significant sense, the time of cosmic enslavement is now past, and its being past is a central motif of the entire letter. One might suppose, then, that the "before" has come to a clean end, being replaced by the "after." The picture, however, is not so simple. The linguistic pattern in which Paul moves easily from the verb *apokalyptô* to the verbs *erchomai*, "to come [on the scene]" and *exapostellô*, "to send [into the scene]," shows that for him the present evil age has not been simply followed by the new cre-ation. Nor do the two exist in isolation or, let us say, at some distance from one another. On the contrary, the evil age and the new creation are dynamically inter-related, as we have noted above, by the motif of invasion.

(4) *For the Flesh is actively inclined against the Spirit, and the Spirit against*

---

[54]Cf. Strobel, "In Paul's letters, apocalyptic themes are shaped in the framework of a spe-cific Kyrios christology that has its basis in the presence of the exalted Lord in the congre-gation ("Apokalyptic IV," 252). Strobel's compressed comments on Pauline apocalyptic are both complementary and corrective of the work of Beker.

the Flesh. Indeed these two powers constitute a pair of opposites at war with one another . . . (5:17). God's invasion of the present evil age involves warfare.[55] And — noting again the verbs "to come [on the scene]" and "to send [into the scene]" — we see that this warfare has been commenced not by the evil powers of the present age, but rather by the redemptive powers of the new creation.[56] The battle is thus characterized by a belligerent and liberating line of movement *from* the new creation *into* the present evil age, God's forces being the ones on the march:

Salvation is nearer to us now than when we first believed (Rom 13:11).[57]

For Paul, therefore, as for all thoroughly apocalyptic thinkers, this liberating redemption does not at all grow out of the present scene.[58] Redemption is a matter of God's invasive movement into that scene.[59]

It is this redemptive battle between two groups of forces that is reflected in Paul's numerous references to pairs of opposites.[60] One thinks again of the way in which Paul uses the expression "new creation," noting that what he intends by it is greatly clarified in his references to pairs of opposites. Ancient speculation about the world's basic elements often involved the theory that from the beginning there were pairs of opposites such as heat and cold (see Comment #41). In Paul's thought some of the creational pairs of opposites (male and female, e.g.; 3:28) have been obliterated by the coming of Christ. With that same event, however, new pairs of opposites have come into being. The Spirit and its opposite, the Flesh, for example, are not timeless first principles inhering in the cosmos from the beginning.[61] Since the Spirit is the Spirit of Christ (4:6), it is obvious that the Spirit and the Flesh — as opponents — are a pair of opposites born not of God's creative act, but of his new-creative act in the sending of his Son and the Spirit of his Son.

The dynamism of this apocalyptic pair of opposites is given not only in its being born of an invasive event but also in its being fundamental to the matter

---

[55]Cf. now J. J. Collins, *Imagination*, 126–141. The picture of a cosmic, dualistic struggle between good and evil is ancient and widespread, going as far back as Iranian traditions in which one finds mythological lists of personified spirits of good and evil (under Ahuramazda and Angra Mainyu) that are opposed to each other. See Kamlah, *Paränese*; Fitzgerald, "Lists" (with bibliography).

[56]Paul thus reverses the picture in which a state of war is precipitated by chaos breaking into the stable city-state.

[57]At numerous points the line of movement shows clearly the basic differences between the theology of Paul and that of the Teachers. See Comment #37.

[58]Cf. Keck, "Apocalyptic Theology," 234 n17.

[59]Flannery O'Connor says somewhere that "man is not condemned to be his own project."

[60]Apocalyptic bifurcation is also reflected in the rhetorical form of dissociation, evident, for example, in the exegetical argument of 3:6–4:7. There Paul dissociates both "the promise" and "the covenant" from "the Law," and he exemplifies this dissociation by means of the contradiction between Hab 2:4 and Lev 18:5. See Comments #35 and #37.

[61]On the basic meaning of the expression "the Flesh" in Galatians, see Comments #32 and #49. See further, Schweizer, "*sarx*"; Jewett, *Terms*, 49–166, 453–456.

of warfare begun with that event.[62] The motif of warfare between pairs of opposites could remind one of the philosophy of Heraclitus ("War is both king of all and father of all . . . ," Frag. 53). Or, closer in time to Paul, one could think of the theology of Qumran, in which there is strife (*rîb*) between the two Spirits (e.g., 1QS 3:13–4:26). But in both of these views the struggle is thought to inhere in the cosmos. Indeed, in the perspective of the Qumran sect the warring antinomy of the Spirit of Truth versus the Spirit of Falsehood — stemming as it does from God's original creation — will find in the new creation not its birth, but rather its termination (1QS 4:16, 25).[63] For Paul the picture is quite different; the Spirit and the Flesh constitute an apocalyptic antinomy in the sense that they are two opposed powers, actively at war with one another *since* the advent of the Christ and of his Spirit. They form a militant antinomy born of apocalypse.

(5) . . . *"who gave up his very life for our sins," so that he might snatch us out of the grasp of the present evil age . . . Christ redeemed us from the Law's curse, becoming a curse in our behalf; for it stands written: "Cursed is everyone who is hanged on a tree"* (1:4; 3:13). The various ways in which Paul speaks of Christ's death (and resurrection; 1:1) show that for him the motif of cosmic warfare is focused first of all on the cross, and it is from the cross that one perceives the contours of that warfare. There, in the thoroughly real event of Christ's crucifixion, God's war of liberation was commenced and decisively settled, making the cross the foundation of Paul's apocalyptic theology.[64] In our reading of Galatians we will find two facets of this foundation to be of great import.

First, Paul's use of apocalyptic language in connection with the death of Jesus clearly means that the turn of the ages is no longer to be thought of solely as an event in the future. Employing his own form of enthusiastic language, Paul speaks of a deliverance that has already been accomplished.

Second, Jesus' death was a vicarious act "for our sins," as the Teachers are very probably affirming, and as the Galatians certainly know already. Paul can and does affirm this interpretation himself. As we have seen in Comment #2, however, he is concerned to offer an interpretation of Jesus' death that is oriented not toward personal guilt and forgiveness, but rather toward corporate enslavement and liberation. Jesus' death was the powerful deed in God's apocalyptic war, the deed by which God has already freed us from the malevolent grasp of the present age. This is one of the major things the Galatians are not currently hearing from the Teachers. It is one of the major things Paul thinks they sorely need to hear.

(6) *I have been crucified with Christ . . . those who belong to Christ Jesus have crucified the Flesh, together with its passions and desires . . . the cross of our Lord Jesus Christ, by which the cosmos has been crucified to me and I to the cosmos* (2:19; 5:24; 6:14). Even in Galatians Paul speaks, as we have noted, of the continuation of God's apocalyptic war, but he does not thereby leave aside the cross in

---

[62] Note that Widengren identifies as the two main motifs of apocalyptic thought (a) cosmic changes and catastrophes and (b) the war-like final struggle in the cosmos ("Ideen," 150).
[63] Regarding the use of the term "antinomy," see the Glossary and Comments #41 and #51.
[64] Käsemann, *Perspectives*, 32–59; Cousar, *Cross*.

order to speak of the hope for the parousia. The war is continued under the banner of cocrucifixion. When Paul speaks of his having been crucified with Christ, he does not refer to a private and mystical event, experienced by him alone. He refers, to be sure, to his participation in the death of Christ, but just as Christ died in a head-on conflict with the Law's power to pronounce a curse on the whole of humanity (3:10, 13), so Paul's participation in Christ's crucifixion is paradigmatic for all Christians. In his case that participation involves his own death to the Law that previously formed his cosmos (2:19; 6:14). It is the death of a soldier on the battlefield.

By the same token, God's dispatch of the Spirit of Christ into the believers' hearts turns them all into soldiers active on the Spirit's field of battle. The martial, cosmic dimension of Paul's apocalyptic applies, then, to the church; and for that reason Paul can speak of the church itself both as God's new creation and as the apocalyptic community called to the front trenches in God's apocalyptic war against the powers of the present evil age (Comment #49). There, and only there, are the churches living in the real world, for it is there that the creation is being made what it now is by God's liberating invasion, an invasion that, in making things right, brings about a fatal separation from — a death to — the old cosmos (5:24).

The basic characteristic of the present time is given, then, in the fact that it is the juncture of the new creation and the evil age. The area in which human beings actually find themselves is now hotly contested territory, a place of jungle warfare in which battles precipitated by the powers of the new creation are sometimes won (Gal 2:9; 5:10; cf. 2 Cor 2:14; 1 Thess 3:6) and sometimes lost (Gal 2:13; 5:7–8; cf. 2 Cor 2:11; Gal 2:2; 1 Thess 2:16, 18).[65]

(7) . . . *having the Spirit in our hearts, and having the confidence that comes from faith, we eagerly await the hope of rectification . . . In the realm ruled over by the Lord, I have confidence in you, believing that, as the future unfolds, you will not really follow these alien paths of thought* (5:5, 10). Battles are won, and battles are lost. Other letters of Paul make clear, however, that he holds as a matter of certain hope the final victory of the powers of God's new creation (see notably 1 Cor 15:20–28). Is that note absent from Galatians? The answer is that it is not, but this answer has to be carefully phrased.

(a) In the first three-quarters of the letter — and to no small degree in the last quarter as well — Paul announces with unwavering certainty that God has already won *the* victory. In dying for us, Christ *has* snatched us out of the grasp of the present evil age; and — to combine the military and the medical metaphors —

---

[65]Thus, Christians who think themselves to be living in an uninvaded world are not living in the real world; Paul's apocalyptic task is to wake them up, and that task is cosmic. Just as all human beings exist in the grasp of "the present evil age," so the whole of the old creation has been imprisoned under Sin's power (3:22). One is reminded of the fact that in Paul's vocabulary — as in that of apocalyptic traditions of his time — the terms "age" and "cosmos" overlap to a significant degree, reflecting the cosmic scope of true apocalyptic. Paul speaks several times of "*this* cosmos" (1 Cor 3:19; 5:10; 7:31). Moreover, the ultimate event in God's establishment of his New Age is his subjection of "all things" to himself (1 Cor 15:26, 28). On all of these motifs, see Käsemann, *Perspectives*.

the message of that victorious deed is the antidote to the virus rapidly spreading among the Galatian soldiers.

(b) There are clear indications, however, that Paul is a thoroughgoing realist about the spread of that virus. At points in the composition of the letter he is driven almost to despair (e.g., 4:11, 20). One cannot be entirely surprised, then, to see that he closes the letter with an extended section of a pastoral sort (5:13–6:10). Up to that point the message is "In Christ God has done it!" Now one learns that there is something for the Galatians themselves to do: "Do not allow the freedom Christ has won for you to become a military base of operations for the Flesh!" (5:13).

(c) The note of pastoral exhortation obviously has to do with the future. Paul is telling the Galatians what to do as the future unfolds (see especially 6:7–10). One notes also that he prepares the way for such exhortation by an arresting reference to God's future, and the striking of this note is what binds the two major parts of the letter together, fundamentally affecting the nature of Paul's exhortation. Distinguishing himself and his coworkers from the members of the Galatian churches who are commencing observance of the Law, Paul says,

> With *us* things are entirely different: having the Spirit in our hearts, and having the confidence that comes from faith, we eagerly await the hope of rectification. For in Christ Jesus neither circumcision nor uncircumcision accomplishes anything at all. The real power is faith actively working through love (5:5–6).

Three messages are combined: "God has done it!" and "You are to live it out!" and "You are to live it out *because* God has done it *and* because God will do it!" What lies exposed here is the bifocal vision of apocalyptic.[66] Calling for emphasis is the fact that this vision has not robbed Paul of true realism. Exactly the contrary; it has given to him the ability to see simultaneously the continuing virus in Galatia and the antidote to that virus provided by God. *And* it has shown him which of these is the stronger. With realistic confidence, therefore, he can speak of freedom in the present: "It was to bring us into the realm of freedom that Christ set us free" (5:1).

But this freedom is itself apocalyptic freedom. One finds the marks of Paul's bifocal vision in his assertion that the church is free because it is *realistically* descended from the free woman who is *in heaven*, the heavenly Jerusalem (4:26). And in the same bifocal vision Paul sees that the future, no less than the present, belongs to God's Christ (5:5, 10), the future deed of God being as much the parent of Paul's apostolic confidence as is God's past deed. What binds all of these variegated pictures together is the victorious march of God's gospel into the world (1:13–3:5). For that victorious march is the sure expansion of the beachhead God has already won in Christ.[67]

---

[66] See J. L. Martyn, *Issues*, 279–297.

[67] In terms used in 1 Corinthians 15 and Rom 5:12–21, one could say that the dawn of God's new creation makes absolutely certain that the future of the world is the future of Christ as the corporate man (*anthrôpos*) of the new creation.

(8) . . . *the gospel preached by me . . . is not what human beings normally have in mind when they speak of "good news." For I did not receive it from another human being, nor was I taught it; it came to me by God's apocalyptic revelation of Jesus Christ* (1:11–12). This certain hope, grounded in God's invasive action in the advent of Christ, is the apocalyptic good news Paul calls "the gospel." But its being apocalyptic is underlined by the fact that it is not visible, demonstrable, or provable in the categories and with the means of perception native to "everyday" existence, native, that is to say, to existence determined solely by the present evil age. The inbreak of the new creation is itself revelation, apocalypse. The dawn of this new creation, causing the death of the old enslaving cosmos, brings about an epistemological crisis.[68] One who knows himself to be grasped by it cannot continue to perceive and to know in the old way. On the contrary, he now sees bifocally; he sees, that is to say, both the evil age and the new creation simultaneously. This bifocal, simultaneous vision is distinctly unbalanced, however, in that, just as God's power is "much more" than the power of Sin, so God causes the apocalyptic seer to see the powers of the new creation "much more" than he sees those of the Old Age (Rom 5:12–21). It is this bifocal vision that enables Paul to make confident statements about the future of the Galatian churches (5:10).

(9) *Everything* is newly perceived by the one who knows himself to be redemptively grasped by God at the juncture of the evil age and the new creation: God himself (Gal 4:8–9), God's Christ as a crucified — and victorious — criminal (3:13), Christ's crucifixion as an incorporative event (2:19–20; 5:24), Sin (3:22), the Law (2:19, 21; 4:21; 5:14; 6:2), rectification (2:16), grace (5:4), the neighbor (5:13–24), the cosmos itself (6:14). The absence of what are sometimes called the grotesque characteristics of apocalyptic must not be allowed to mislead us in our reading of Galatians. The motif of an earthquake lies at the heart of this letter without being literally mentioned. For, as we have seen above, the fundamental pairs of opposites one had assumed to be the primal and immutable elements of the whole of existence have been wiped from the face of the cosmos as though being carried away in a landslide (Comment #41). It follows that all of the key terms by which Paul bears witness to God's activity are *redefined* at the juncture *and* on the basis of the juncture.

(10) . . . *when the fullness of time came, God sent his Son* (4:4). If God's apocalyptic invasion of the cosmos in Christ creates a radically new perception of God himself, of God's Christ as a crucified criminal, of Christ's crucifixion as an incorporative event, of Sin, of the Law, and so on, it also creates a radically new perception of time (3:25; 4:4). All of the preceding motifs flow together in the question Paul causes to be the crucial issue of the entire letter: What time is it? One recalls that the matter of discerning the time lies at the heart of apocalyptic. And as the preceding analysis demonstrates, in writing to the Galatians Paul addresses the issue of time in terms clearly apocalyptic. What time is it? It is the time after the apocalypse of the faith of Christ, the time, therefore, of God's making things right by Christ's faith, the time of the presence of the Spirit of Christ, and thus

[68]J. L. Martyn, *Issues*, 89–110.

the time in which the invading Spirit has decisively commenced the war of liberation from the powers of the present evil age.[69]

Result. Finally, we can say again that there are strong reasons for holding Galatians to be a stranger to apocalyptic. It contains no reference to the future coming of Christ, to the archangel's cry, to the blowing of the last trumpet, to the general resurrection of the dead, and so on (1 Thess 4:13–5:11; 1 Cor 15:20–28, 51–58; Rom 8:18–25).[70]

The preceding observations, however — not least the one focused on the four crucial junctures at which Paul uses the noun *apokalypsis* and the verb *apokalyptô* — suggest that Paul's apocalyptic perspective is richer than one would think simply on the basis of 1 Thessalonians, 1 Corinthians, and Romans. His view has, in fact, three foci: Christ's future coming, Christ's past advent (his death and resurrection), and the present war against the powers of evil, inaugurated by his Spirit and taking place between these two events. If Paul is sure that Christ's parousia will bring the final victory of God over all his enemies (1 Corinthians 15), he is no less sure that Christ's advent has commenced the war that will lead to that victory. Thus, in an anticipatory but altogether real sense, Christ's advent is that victory, even if its victorious character can be seen only in the bifocal vision of apocalyptic. Christ's advent has already changed the world, commencing God's war of liberation in a way that can be celebrated in "enthusiastic" terms, without forgetting the future of Christ (Gal 5:5). Specifically, both God's sending of Christ to suffer death in behalf of humanity (the cross) and Christ's future coming (the parousia) are *invasive* acts of God. And their being invasive acts — into a space that has temporarily fallen out of God's hands — points to the liberating war that is crucial to Paul's apocalyptic theology.

It is this apocalyptic vision, then, that has given Paul his perception of the nature of the human plight. God has invaded the world in order to bring it under his liberating control. From that deed of God a conclusion is to be drawn, and the conclusion is decidedly apocalyptic: God would not have to carry out an invasion in order merely to forgive erring human beings. The root trouble lies deeper than human guilt, and it is more sinister. The whole of humanity — indeed, the whole of creation (3:22) — is, in fact, trapped, enslaved under the power of the present evil age. That is the background of God's invasive action in his sending of Christ, in his declaration of war, and in his striking the decisive and liberating blow against the power of the present evil age (see further Comment #39).

COMMENT #4
PAUL'S EPISTOLARY WORD AND GOD'S WORD

In three important regards the opening of Galatians (1:1–9) is unique in the Pauline letter corpus. The prescript (1:1–5) is the only one that ends with a doxology:

---

[69]On the expression "the faith of Christ," see Comment #28.
[70]Note the paucity of references to Galatians in J. Baumgarten, *Apokalyptik*. Cf. the first edition of Beker, *Paul*, but note also the preface to the first paperback edition (1984).

"To God be glory throughout the whole of eternity." The prescript is alone in ending with the participatory word "amen," repeated at the close of the entire letter. As 1:6–9 shows, Galatians is the only letter that lacks a thanksgiving paragraph.

Paul's inclusion of the doxology and his omission of the thanksgiving paragraph are interrelated. Unable as things presently stand to thank God for the Galatian churches, Paul can cause them to thank God for their deliverance in Jesus Christ. Having quoted and interpreted a confession the Galatians may be using in their current worship (1:4), and having pronounced a doxology to God (1:5a), Paul brings the Galatians climactically into God's presence by inviting them to utter the word "Amen!" It is a signal of his conviction that his own words can and will become the active word of God, because God will be present as the letter is read to the Galatians in their services of worship. One might even say that by using the word "amen," Paul intends to rob the Galatians of the lethal luxury of considering themselves observers. With him, they stand in God's presence. Fundamentally, then, they are dealing with God, not merely with Paul (1:6).

1:6–9 THE LETTER'S THEME

TRANSLATION

1:6. I am amazed that you are so rapidly defecting from the God who called you in his grace, and are turning your allegiance to a different gospel. 7. Not that there really is another gospel; but the point is that there are now among you some persons who are frightening you and whose preaching shows that they wish to change the gospel of Christ into its opposite. 8. Regardless of who might preach it — whether I myself or an angel from heaven — if someone should preach to you a gospel contrary to the gospel I preached to you, let him stand under God's curse. 9. As I have said before, I say now once again, if someone is preaching to you a gospel contrary to the one you originally received, let him stand under God's curse.

LITERARY STRUCTURE AND SYNOPSIS

The doxology of 1:5 makes the terminus of the prescript obvious. At 1:6 Paul is clearly beginning the first section of the letter's body. In letters between close friends one normally expected at this juncture a paragraph in which the writer gave thanks for the addressee.[71] Instead, having ended the prescript by looking,

---

[71] Schubert, *Pauline Thanksgivings*; Wolff, "Thanksgiving."

as it were, to heaven, speaking to God in prayer, Paul turns abruptly earthward, speaking candidly to the Galatians about the odious developments in their churches that have prompted him to write to them.[72] The result is a brief paragraph commenced with an epistolary formula of rebuke: "I am surprised at you . . ." Paul is concerned immediately to accent the absolute difference between the gospel of Christ and its counterfeit.

He thus employs this rebuke paragraph to lay out the theme of the epistle, giving a forecast of the whole. And having done that, he provides in 1:10–6:10 supporting theses, arguments, and conclusions, explicating what he has said about the term "gospel" and about its counterfeit in 1:6–9.[73]

Paul ends this paragraph on a note that is in one regard similar to the one with which he closed the prescript. In that earlier case Paul carried the Galatians into God's presence, causing them to utter the participatory "Amen!" In vv 8–9, still certain that God will be present as the letter is read aloud, he solemnly delivers the Teachers to God, so that God will place them under a curse.[74]

Notes

1:6. *I am amazed.* Paul employs here a rhetorical stratagem for which there are epistolary examples. Rather than turning at this point to the expected thanksgiving paragraph, he begins the body of the letter with a rebuke, saying with irritation, "I am astonished at you!"[75]

so rapidly. The expression (*tacheôs*) points to brevity of time measured from some juncture. Here, since Paul does not identify the juncture, two possibilities arise.

(a) Paul may mean that he is amazed to find the Galatians deserting so soon after the arrival of the Teachers. There was a period of some duration after Paul's departure during which the Galatians remained true to the gospel they received from him (so the verb in the imperfect tense in 5:7). Moreover, Greek literature provides us with instances in which *tacheôs* refers to the quickness with which a certain *process* has developed.[76] Paul may be referring, then, to the great rapidity with which the Galatians' defection is progressing since the arrival of the Teachers: "I am amazed that you have so little resistance to this virus. In a short time it is spreading among you like a plague."

(b) Linguistically, it is equally possible to find Paul expressing his amazement that the Galatians' desertion is happening so soon after his departure from them. On this reading, one would conclude that Paul wrote the letter shortly after his founding visit (or if 4:13 indicates two visits, then shortly after the second of

---

[72] The expected thanksgiving paragraph is also absent in 2 Corinthians; see Furnish, *II Corinthians*, 43.
[73] Cf. Kennedy, *Interpretation*, 148; R. G. Hall, "Outline," 287; Vos, "Argumentation," 8.
[74] As Kennedy has shown (*pace* H. D. Betz), nothing in vv 6–9 is truly comparable to the rhetoricians' comments about the stratagem of frightening the judges; *Interpretation*, 148.
[75] Vos, "Argumentation," 7.
[76] Examples are cited by Mussner 53 n54.

them). In the framework of the chronological analysis given in Comment #24, this second interpretation seems the more likely.

defecting from. For the precise meaning of this verb, *metatithesthai* in the middle voice, we have little to go on from early Christian texts. Paul uses it only this once, and other early Christian authors seldom use it in the middle voice (*Mart. Pol.* 11:1). If, however, we first ask not what Paul intended, but rather how the Galatians are likely to have understood it, we have an excellent guide in its use among popular philosophical schools: When one moved one's allegiance from one school of thought to another, one was said to have "defected from" the first.[77] Used in this way, the term reflects what we may call "conversion consciousness" in the Hellenistic world (cf. *epistrephô* in Gal 4:9).[78] A person who converted to a new philosophy/religion was said to have defected from the earlier one.

Paul, however, may think of foot soldiers defecting from the ranks of an apocalyptic army (see Comments #3 and #49). In any case, he places this verb in the present tense, indicating that the defection is in process as he dictates the letter. Yet, taking into account the whole of the letter, we see that Paul is significantly inconsistent as to the exact state of affairs. Here he says the Galatians are defecting. In 4:11 (cf. 4:20) he fears that they are falling away and that his labor on them is wasted. But in 5:10 he strikes the confident note "in the Lord" that they will not be led astray by the Teachers' message. Moreover, someone has carried to Paul the disturbing news of the Galatian developments. That person (or persons) must represent those in the churches who are resistant to the Teachers' message (cf. 6:6).

the God who called you. The text has only the substantive participle, "the one who called" (past tense), so that a reader could be tempted to see it as Paul's reference to himself: "You are defecting from allegiance to me and are going over to the religion of the Teachers." This understanding is harmonious with some of the current readings in which the letter's argument is analyzed on the basis of certain norms of classical rhetoric (see Introduction §10).

By the substantive participle "the one who called," however, Paul clearly refers not to himself, but rather to God, and the Galatians will have known as much. Elsewhere in the letter he twice refers to God by using this simple participle (1:15; 5:8), and if we turn to his other letters, we gain the impression that in Paul's preaching the Greek participle *ho kalôn*, "he who calls," virtually functions as a name for God (1 Thess 2:12; 5:24; Rom 9:12).[79] Paul never uses the verb "to

---

[77] For example, Diogenes Laertius *Lives* 7.166; cf. 2 Macc 7:24. The Galatians will have known nothing about the Jewish use of the expression *sārê dārek*, "those who depart from the way," but for Paul's thought one may also compare CD 1:13; cf. Von der Osten-Sacken, *Heiligkeit*, 142.

[78] Cf. Nock, *Conversion*; Gaventa, *Darkness*.

[79] Rom 9:12 is often undertranslated; even NRSV keeps the rendering of RSV, placing in contrast with one another "works" and "his [God's] call." The participle *ho kalôn* is not to be rendered, however, by an English gerund. It is an active substantive, referring not to God's call, but rather to God himself as the one who calls. In Romans 9 the issue Paul

call" with himself or any other person as the subject. Neither he nor any other human being can "call." Why not? Because in Paul's vocabulary the word does not mean "to speak to someone directly, so as to summon him." It refers consistently to God's creative act of summoning into existence things that have previously not existed. With this verb Paul speaks of God's elective act of calling into being the new creation, the eschatological community of the church (Rom 4:17; Gal 6:15). Regarding the relationship between God's creative election of the church and God's creative election of ancient Israel, see Comments #37 and #52.

in his grace. There are two major textual traditions: Very early witnesses, p46 and Marcion, read simply "in grace";[80] other witnesses add "of Christ," "of Jesus Christ," "of Christ Jesus," or "of God." Transcriptional probability is strongly on the side of the shorter reading (meaning "in his [God's] grace"). For Paul, grace flows both from God and from Christ (cf. 1:3, 15; 2:21; 5:4; 6:18). What is significant here, however, is the fact that Paul places side by side a reference to God as the one who "calls" and a reference to God as the one who "graces." In his grace God elects to call into being something that was not there before. The preposition "in" is local rather than instrumental. God's grace is the space into which he has called the Galatians (cf. Rom 5:2). See the Note on 1:15, a point at which Paul, again, and with significant emphasis, links the terms "call" and "grace."

a different gospel. 7. *another gospel . . . the gospel of Christ.* With these references Paul identifies the central issue of the letter. As he will clearly imply twice in the second chapter, what is now at stake in the Galatian churches is what was earlier at stake in the Jerusalem conference and in the incident in the Antioch church: "the truth of the gospel" (2:5, 14).

We know that the term "gospel" was one of the weightiest words in early Christian parlance. Numerous thorny and complex questions arise in connection with it.[81] Our concern, however, is tightly focused and relatively modest. What did the Galatians hear in Paul's use of the term? Most important, what did they hear in his distinction between the gospel he preached to them and what he identifies as its false counterpart? As these questions are discussed in Comment #7, we can confine ourselves here to the major results of that discussion:

Noting Paul's reference to "a different gospel," the Galatians will have known immediately that he is referring to the gospel they are currently hearing from the Teachers. As the term is extraordinarily dear to Paul, we can be confident he would not have employed it in referring to the Teachers' message had they not been using it themselves. We can imagine that the Teachers are saying something like this:

---

poses is the identity of the source that causes God's elective purpose to continue through the generations. And the answer is: the source is not deeds performed by human beings, but rather *God himself* in his identity as the one who *calls into existence*. Thus, Rom 9:12 can be rendered ". . . in order that God's purpose of election might continue, not because of deeds done by human beings, but because of the God who calls."

[80] See Clabeaux, *Edition*, 83–84.

[81] See notably Stuhlmacher, *Evangelium*; Strecker, "Evangelium."

The gospel is the tradition faithfully preserved in the Jerusalem church about the Law that was spoken by a glorious angel to Moses, that was observed even earlier by Abraham our father, and that is now both confirmed by the Messiah, Jesus, and, by his authority, extended as God's good news to the Gentiles.

Moreover, being greatly impressed with the Teachers' message, a sizable number of the Galatians will have had a single-minded reaction to Paul's reference: "The proclamation we are receiving from the Teachers is indeed a different gospel, and we are transferring our allegiance to it because it is far superior to the one we heard from you!"

7. *Not that there really is another gospel.* The terms *heteros*, "different" (v 6), and *allos*, "another" (v 7), are virtual synonyms in Paul's vocabulary (cf. 1 Cor 12:10; Burton 420–422; BDF §306.4). Since Paul cannot deny that the Teachers call their message "the gospel," he initially speaks of it as "a different gospel." But he can and does deny that there is really another gospel. A significant problem emerges when he seems at a later point to speak in fact of two gospels (2:7). For the moment, however, it will suffice to note his categorical denial that the Teachers' message is truly "the good news." In certain regards, the situation Paul later faces, as he writes 2 Corinthians 11, is remarkably similar. Some evangelists who call themselves "descendants of Abraham," and who are certainly Jewish Christians, have come into the Corinthian church preaching a "different gospel" (2 Cor 11:4, 22).

but the point is. Paul dictates *ei mê*, which usually means something like "except," whereas from the context one would expect *alla*, "but rather." In some documents from the Hellenistic period the two expressions seem to be interchangeable.[82] Here, at any rate, Paul's intention is transparent: he wishes to come to the root of the issue.

some persons. Recalling 1 Cor 1:11, we might expect Paul to indicate at this point how he has come to know about the recent developments among the Galatian churches. The passage in 1 Corinthians reads,

For it has been reported to me by Chloe's people that there is quarreling among you (cf. 1 Cor 16:17).

In Galatians Paul could easily have said,

But the point is, it has been reported to me that some people have come among you, frightening you with their preaching . . .

The Galatians themselves may be wondering who among them has tattled (see Note on 6:6). But neither here nor elsewhere does Paul give even a hint as to the source of his knowledge. Perhaps he thinks that to do so would be to exacerbate tensions already raging within the Galatian churches (5:15).

[82]Is this a development reflecting Aramaic influence? See BDF §443.8; K. Beyer, *Semitische Syntax*, 104 n4, 105, 138 n2.

In any case, he now refers somewhat abruptly to the Teachers, and in a way that limits their visibility. He uses, that is, the colorless expression *tines*, "some persons" (in 1:9b he uses the singular *tis*). If he knows the Teachers' names, he avoids mentioning them in order to indicate disdain. When we come to his account of the meeting in Jerusalem, we will note similarly that he does not mention the names of any of the "False Brothers" (2:4), while readily naming James, Cephas, and John (2:9). In the present verse he does not even refer to the Teachers by any of their own epithets, such as "descendants of Abraham" (contrast 2 Cor 11:22–23). Nor does he explicitly quote from them (contrast Col 2:21), although at certain junctures he may do so without acknowledging the fact (see below on 3:6–29, 4:21–5:1, and 5:16).

who are frightening you. Two matters demand attention: First, Paul uses the present tense of the verb *eimi*, "there *are* some persons who frighten and intimidate you." As he says essentially the same in 4:17 and 6:12 (note also the present participles in 5:10, 12), we can conclude that the Teachers are still among the Galatians as Paul writes. He must take that fact into account, recognizing that their presence gives them a rhetorical advantage.

Second, the participle, *hoi tarassontes*, here rendered "who are frightening," has also been interpreted to indicate that the Teachers are *confusing* the Galatians, using means perhaps analogous to those employed by political agitators of the Hellenistic period intent on misleading the crowd (cf. NAB, "some . . . must have confused you"). Here, translation is an important issue; for with the selection of this word, Paul reveals a considerable amount of his understanding of the Teachers' mode of operation and perhaps of their gospel as well. Within the Pauline corpus the term *tarassô* emerges twice in Galatians, and only there (1:7; 5:10). It seems, then, to be a term Paul carefully selects in order to say something specific about the Teachers in Galatia: they *do* something *to* the Galatian Christians. Exactly what do they do?

Attention to the early Christian use of the word suggests that "to confuse" is an inadequate translation. In the synoptic tradition the verb is passive, and it consistently means "to be troubled in one's mind as a result of entertaining thoughts that make one profoundly anxious" (Matt 2:3; 14:26; Mark 6:50; Luke 1:12; 24:38; cf. John 14:1, 27). The Lucan passages are revealing, for in them Luke allows the verb to be interpreted by *parallelismus membrorum:*

Luke 1:12. When Zechariah saw the angel, *he was troubled*, and *fear fell upon him.*

Luke 24:37–38. The disciples were startled and frightened, supposing they had seen a spirit. And he said to them, *"Why are you troubled*, and *why do such anxious thoughts arise in your minds?"*

Still more important is the use of the verb in Luke's account of the meeting in the Jerusalem church (Acts 15). There, in order to encapsulate the results of the meeting, the authorities in the Jerusalem church compose a letter to be sent to the church in Antioch. Immediately after the expected greeting, they say:

Since we have heard that certain persons (*tines*) who have gone out from us ... have said things to disturb you (*etaraxan*), unsettling your minds (*anaskeuazontes tas pseuchas hymôn*) ... (15:24).

Earlier in the chapter the same development had been directly narrated:

Some men (*tines*) came down [to Antioch] from Judea and were teaching the brethren, "Unless you are circumcised according to the custom of Moses, you cannot be saved" (15:1).

The persons coming from Jerusalem to Antioch are here portrayed as doing far more than confusing Christians there. They are creating mental anguish among the Gentile members of the Antioch church by threatening them with exclusion from salvation unless they undergo circumcision.

Returning to Galatians, we note 4:17, where, paraphrastically rendered, Paul identifies the Teachers as persons who "threaten to shut you out of salvation if you do not submit to circumcision." Noting the similarity to the references in Acts 15, one concludes that with the locution *hoi tarassontes* in Gal 1:7 Paul is not identifying the Teachers as persons who confuse the Galatians. He is saying that they are frightening the Galatians out of their wits, intimidating them with the threat of damnation if they do not follow the path prescribed in the Teachers' message![83]

they wish. In his references to the Teachers Paul does not limit himself to what might be called descriptions of their activities. He has no hesitation to speak repeatedly of what he believes to be their motives. At the present juncture he concludes from their preaching that they *intend* to alter the gospel of Christ (1:7). Later he will say that they enjoy standing in the door to life, threatening to shut the Galatians out, so that the latter will fawn over them (4:17). They wish to receive accolades and to avoid persecution from persons who would harm them if they centered their preaching on Christ's cross (6:12). Finally, they wish to have a basis for boasting (6:13).

to change the gospel of Christ into its opposite. Paul does not elsewhere use the verb *metastrephô*, but we know from other sources that it often meant not only "to alter something" but also "to change something into its opposite" (e.g., Acts 2:20; LXX of Joel 3:4 [2:31]). That usage may have a certain pertinence here, since the Galatians will have sensed that Paul does not intend to say the Teachers are making moderate changes in the gospel. He means they are turning it around 180 degrees, changing it into the not-gospel. Paul has no intention of seeking a compromise formulation which might lie somewhere between what he calls "gospel" and that to which the Teachers give the same name. The Teachers preach what they call "the gospel," but in Paul's judgment it is not the gospel *of*

---

[83] For the character of Paul's own threat, see 5:21.

Christ, an expression by which Paul means the good news that is centered in Christ's liberating death and resurrection.[84]

8. *whether I myself.* The pronoun is literally "we," a locution that could reflect Paul's intention to include his fellow workers (v 2 above). More likely, it is an editorial plural.

an angel from heaven. In the present paragraph Paul has thus far spoken of four actors: God, the Galatians, himself, and the Teachers. Now, with an abruptness that calls for explanation, he suddenly expands the dramatis personae to include an angel. Where does this angel come from? From heaven, one supposes; but to speak historically, from the Teachers' sermons, for that is the best explanation of Paul's assumption that the Galatians will understand his reference. Apparently, the Teachers are telling the Galatians that their gospel is uttered to the whole of the world by an angel who speaks through them.

This reading of Gal 1:8 is strengthened by the probability that in Jewish-Christian circles the end-time proclamation of the gospel to all nations would be carried out by an angel:

> Then I saw another angel flying in midheaven, with an eternal gospel to proclaim to those who live on the earth — to every nation and tribe and language and people (Rev 14:6; NRSV).[85]

The Teachers know, of course, that their work falls in the period prior to the parousia. One assumes that, identifying their gospel in its essence with the Law of Moses, and holding the Law to have been gloriously mediated to Moses by angels (cf. Gal 3:19), they see in the Jewish-Christian tradition cited above an indication that an angel is even now preaching the gospel to Gentiles through them. See Comment #7 and the Notes on 3:19 and 4:14.

if someone should preach. The conditional sentences that constitute v 8 and v 9 differ from one another in a significant regard. In v 8 Paul uses *ean* with the subjunctive, whereas in v 9 he dictates *ei* with the indicative. The form of the sentence in v 8, therefore, shows Paul considering for a moment—in a rather distant and theoretical fashion—the possibility that at some juncture in the future he himself or that vaunted angel of the Teachers might preach a gospel contrary to the one he originally preached to the Galatians. The distant note struck in this conditional clause is thus a way of hinting that, just as the "different gospel" is not coming from him, so in reality it is not coming from an angel either. Yet the note is only one of distance, not of impossibility. It follows that

---

[84]Paul refers to the true good news as "the gospel" (e.g., 1 Thess 2:4; Rom 1:16), "the Gospel of God" (e.g., 1 Thess 2:2; Rom 1:1), and "the gospel of Christ" (e.g., 1 Thess 3:2; Rom 15:19). With the exception of Mark 1:1, the expression "the gospel of Christ" is distinctly Pauline (about eight times). In the present instance the genitive ("of Christ") is objective: "the gospel in which Christ is preached." Note a comment of Lührmann, "*Iêsous Christos* means Jesus has died and been raised" ("Christologie," 358).

[85]Cf. Caird, *Revelation*, 182; A. Y. Collins, *The Apocalypse*, 102; Schüssler-Fiorenza, *Revelation*, 103.

one or the other of these developments is conceivable, however remote it may be. And Paul's inclusion of himself in the conditional clause is thus significant. Contemplating at considerable remove the possibility that he should lose his bearings and preach a different gospel, he insists that everyone, including himself, is subordinate to the gospel of Christ and subject to God's judgment.[86]

By contrast, Paul formulates the sentence of v 9 in such a way as to suggest that the condition laid down may very well already exist. "If it should be the case, as it apparently is, that some person (*tis*) is even now preaching to you a gospel . . ."

contrary to. Both here and at the corresponding point in v 9 Paul uses the preposition *para*, which might seem to call for the translation "at variance with" (so NEB). But in the context, as we have seen, Paul speaks of a so-called gospel that is diametrically opposed to his own, and the preposition *para* is easily capable of carrying this sharply adversative meaning.[87] The NEB translation does have, however, the virtue of accenting Paul's conviction that the gospel he preaches is the absolute norm. Whatever is at variance with it *is* diametrically opposed to it and thus at variance with the truth (2:5, 14).

stand under God's curse. The Greek word is *anathêma*, a term which has passed into other languages, English included. Paul does not need literally to identify it as *God's* curse, for in the world of Greek religions the term *anathêma* denotes something "set up" (*anatetheimenon*) in the holy precincts, and therefore set apart from the profane orb, so that the god can either receive and bless it or — more often — curse and destroy it. Thus, the term is well suited to translate the Hebrew word *ḥērem*. Both the Greek and the Israelite know that a human being does not truly have the power to curse something. The most one can do is to deliver it to God, so that, in accordance with his own purposes, God can curse it.

In the present passage Paul thinks not of some thing, but rather of some person or persons, even of an alleged angel. The resulting point is similar to that of 1 Cor 5:3–5. Paul means to say: "If some person is preaching a false gospel to you, he is to be removed from your community and delivered (along with his alleged angel!) to God, who will curse him." Later (4:30) Paul will quote a passage in which he hears scripture explicitly commanding the Galatians to remove the Teachers from their midst.

9. *As I have said before, I say now once again.* Lit. "As we have said before, I say now once again." In the first clause the verb is in the perfect tense, first person plural. Both of these factors are puzzling. The plural may be editorial (cf. the "we" of v 8), but why, then, does Paul shift to the singular in the next clause? More important, how are we to understand the past tense of the verb in the first clause? Several answers have been suggested. The past tense is (a) an indication that Paul knows he is nearly repeating the previous sentence (v 8), or (b) a way of referring to an utterance of his when he was with the Galatians, or (c) an acknowledgment that he has said this same thing in an earlier letter. The last is

---

[86] Schütz, *Anatomy*, 128.
[87] H. D. Betz cites Rom 16:17.

very unlikely; virtually everything in the letter indicates that it is the first written communication Paul has had with the Galatians. Perhaps the other two answers are not altogether mutually exclusive. When Paul was with the Galatians, he may have anticipated as a general possibility their being somehow exposed to false teaching. He may then have employed a "sentence of holy law" in order to protect them (cf. 5:21).[88] Now in v 8 he first shapes that earlier sentence in a way which takes cognizance of the Teachers' vaunted angel; then in v 9 he further sharpens the teeth of the holy law by employing the real conditional clause: "If, as seems to be the case . . ."

the one you originally received. The verb *paralambanô*, in the meaning "to receive," is half of a formula by which one normally refers to the process of handing on a tradition. Paul uses the whole of the formula in 1 Cor 15:3,

For I handed on to you . . . what I in turn had received.

He also draws on the formula in Gal 1:12. In the present verse Paul says plainly that the Galatians received the true gospel, the absolute norm enabling one to identify a different gospel as false.[89] From whom did the Galatians receive this true gospel?

The answer seems so obvious as to make the question superfluous. The parallelism between vv 8 and 9 indicates that Paul is referring to the Galatians' having received the gospel from him:

. . . if someone should preach to you a gospel contrary to the gospel I *preached to you* . . .

. . . if someone is preaching to you a gospel contrary to the one *you originally received* [from me] . . .

One recalls, however, that in v 6 Paul identifies the Galatians' tendency to accept the message of the Teachers as a defection not from him, but rather "from the God who called you [into existence as his church] in his grace [that is to say, in his gospel]." Just below the surface of Paul's words, then, lies a complexity of significance.

On the one hand, Paul can and does speak of the gospel as a tradition, as words that assume in their proclamation a certain fixity (cf. Gal 3:1; 1 Cor 15:3–5). Viewed in this way, the gospel is indeed a tradition (*paradosis*). Paul handed it to the Galatians; they received it from him.

On the other hand, however, Paul also speaks of the gospel as something that can and must be distinguished from tradition. Indeed, in this sense the gospel is not an object, but rather a divine event, a happening of which God is both the ultimate and the immediate author (*apokalypsis*). It is God's being the *immediate* author of the gospel-event that creates the distinction of gospel from tradition, a

---

[88] See Käsemann, *Questions*, 66–81; see also the critique by Berger, "Sätze."
[89] Schütz, *Anatomy*, 128.

matter to which Paul will give concerted attention in v 12. The event character of the gospel is reflected, for example, in Gal 3:1. Paul preached the *event* of Christ's crucifixion, not merely a theory about it, and he was confident that in this preaching God was himself immediately active, eliciting the hearers' faith and sending the Spirit of Christ into their hearts. Thus, in the terms of 1:6, God's immediate authorship causes the Galatians' defection from the gospel to be far more than departure from a definable tradition. It is defection from God himself, and specifically from the event of God's call. That defection is also, however, departure from the gospel-tradition delivered to the Galatians by Paul. The gospel, then, is both God's apocalyptic deed and the apostle's tradition, doubtless the former before the latter, but also the former *in* the latter. See Comment #10.

COMMENT #5
DEFECTION FROM THE GOD WHO CALLS INTO EXISTENCE

In place of the expected thanksgiving paragraph, Paul commences the body of the letter with a rebuke: "I am surprised at you Galatians!" (1:6). What precisely have the Galatians done to warrant such a sharp and immediate criticism? They have defected, Paul says, not from him, but from God himself. To make this point, Paul employs the verb *metatithêmi* ("to change one's mind," "to defect"), allowing it two important implications, one religious and one rhetorical.

Paul says that under the influence of the Teachers (Comment #6), the Galatians are experiencing a religious conversion. Gal 1:6 is the first of numerous junctures at which Paul indicates that a move into the realm of religion is a move away from the realm of Christ, a retrogression to the enslaving state of affairs regnant before Christ's coming (cf. 5:4; 4:9; Introduction §17; Comments #40 and #41). It is as though Paul had said explicitly, "You think you are in the locus of religious options, able to decide for this religion or that. Christ, however, did not found a new religion. The church of God (1:13) is not one religious option among others. What you consider a religious conversion is an abandonment of Christ."

Paul's use of the verb *metatithêmi* also proves to be revealing as regards the rhetorical nature of the entire letter. In the Introduction (§10) we mentioned recent rhetorical analyses in which it is said that the structure of the letter shows it to be Paul's part in a forensic debate: The Teachers have brought charges against him in the presence of the Galatians. With the Galatians functioning, then, as a panel of judges competent to reach a decision in a court of law, Paul formulates his defense, hoping by the power of his argument to win the Galatians over to his side. H. D. Betz, for example, finds in 1:6 the preliminary statement of the *causa*: the Galatians are "in the process of shifting their allegiance away from *Paul* . . . to his Jewish-Christian competitors and enemies."[90] Accordingly, Betz identifies Paul's epistolary intention as that of giving the Galatians "another

[90]H. D. Betz 46 (emphasis added).

chance to think over the whole question of their faith, and perhaps to reverse their decision, if indeed they have already made it."[91]

As we have seen, however, Paul does not use the verb *metatithêmi* in 1:6 to refer to the Galatians' defection from *him*. He says they are defecting from *the God who called them into existence as part of his new creation, the church*. As Paul structures his letter, then, what he finds to be at stake is not a decision the Galatians are to make, as though they were judges competent to decide a case after hearing two attorneys engage in a forensic debate. At stake is the Galatians' relation to God, and that is a matter to which they can attend only in God's presence (1:5; 6:16, 18) and only in relation to the power of the gospel-word that proceeds from God himself (1:12, 16). At numerous points in the letter Paul does employ rhetorical stratagems (see Comments #8, #9, and #35), thus formulating an argument. But he understands that argument to be a repreaching of the gospel, of which God himself is the author (cf. Rom 1:1). In Paul's own perspective, then, one might speak of the letter as an instance of rhetoric in the presence of God (Comment #9).[92]

COMMENT #6
THE TEACHERS

In specifying the Galatians' defection from God, Paul refers at several junctures to persons who are active among the congregations, and whose activity is the source of that defection.[93] Modern scholars customarily refer to these people as Paul's "opponents," and that usage is readily understandable.[94] Paul makes it clear that he views them as opponents, and there are indications that to a considerable extent they view him in the same manner. There are, however, two reasons for considering that nomenclature somewhat reductionistic. First, as we have seen in the preceding Comment, Paul is sure that, in their basic identity, these persons are opponents of God, not merely of himself. Second, as we proceed, we will see grounds for thinking that these persons pursue their own Gentile mission, independent of Paul, the conflict in Galatia having arisen because in that area they are dealing with Gentiles who have already heard Paul's message. For these reasons, then, we will refer to these persons neutrally as "the Teachers," taking care not to identify them solely on the basis of their relationship with Paul.[95]

---

[91] H. D. Betz 45; cf. 47.

[92] Cf. Terrien, *Presence*.

[93] Although, as we have seen in Comment #3, Galatians is a thoroughly apocalyptic letter, Paul does not here attribute the Galatians' defection to "the God of this world" (2 Cor 4:4) or to Satan (2 Cor 2:11; 11:14; 12:7).

[94] For example, Luedemann, *Paulus*, 2.144–152.

[95] We will deal below with the probability that the Teachers were in touch with the False Brothers and their circumcision party in the Jerusalem church, even being to some degree sponsored by that wing of the "mother" congregation (Comments #25, #45, and #46). Thus, we can assume that the Teachers were well acquainted with stories about Paul's activities, both at the Jerusalem meeting and in the Antioch incident (2:1–14). It is therefore possible that, in part, they came to Galatia in order to counter Paul's work. They seem

As Paul shapes his letter, he is constantly thinking about the ongoing activity and influence of the Teachers. Specifically, Paul knows that the Galatians will listen to his letter with the Teachers' sermons still ringing in their ears, and almost certainly with the Teachers themselves at their elbows. It follows that, in order to make an entrance into this highly charged atmosphere, we must have a reasonably reliable picture of these people and of their teaching.

Do the data available to us offer clues sufficient in number and clarity to enable us to draw a picture that elicits confidence? There are solid grounds for answering that question in the affirmative, even though we have nothing from the hands of the Teachers themselves. Anticipating some of the observations that will emerge below, we can mention the sources that are of essential help in our attempt to reconstruct a portrait of the Teachers and to suggest an outline of their message.

DATA IN THE LETTER ITSELF

Most important is the fact that there are highly revealing data in the letter itself. Paul refers explicitly to the Teachers in five passages, 1:6–9; 3:1–2, 5; 4:17; 5:7–12; 6:12–14. In the Notes on these passages, in several of the later Comments, and especially in the present Comment, we will seek to coordinate the data in these passages, so as to produce a sensible portrait.

Moreover, since in composing every sentence Paul has one part of his mind on the Teachers, his explicit references to them are accompanied by numerous allusions to them and to their work (see, e.g., 3:5). Carefully interpreted, these allusions fill out in important ways Paul's explicit references to the Teachers and their message.

PERTINENT JEWISH AND CHRISTIAN-JEWISH TRADITIONS[96]

Data in the letter show the Teachers to have connections both with Diaspora Judaism and with Palestinian, Christian Judaism. Whatever their birthplace and locale of education, the Teachers are messianic Jews, at home among Gentiles, in the sense of being able not only to live among them but also to make effective, apologetic contact with them. Several motifs that Paul connects with the Teachers — the view that Gentiles worship the elements of the cosmos, for example — find significant parallels in the apologetic literature of Diaspora Judaism (Comment #41). We can enrich our portrait of the Teachers, therefore, by relating some aspects of their message, as reflected in Galatians, to passages in some of

---

also, however, to have had their own Law-observant mission to Gentiles, apart from their concern to correct what they took to be Paul's errors. See especially Comment #33 and J. L. Martyn, *Issues*, 7–24.

[96]Here and elsewhere I intend some degree of distinction between the adjectival expressions "Jewish-Christian" and "Christian-Jewish" (and their corresponding nouns), the second word being the dominant one. Churches, for example, that were essentially Jewish sects would be groups of Christian Jews, rather than groups of Jewish Christians. See also the Glossary.

the literature of Diaspora Judaism, such as Wisdom, the writings of Philo and Josephus, *Aristobulus*, and *Joseph and Asenath*.[97]

From Galatians itself, we can also see that the Teachers are in touch with — indeed, understand themselves to represent — a powerful circle of Christian Jews in the Jerusalem church, a group utterly zealous for the observance of the Law (Comments #25, #45, and #46). Seeking to reconstruct the Teachers' message, then, we will find pertinent data in such Palestinian Jewish traditions as those preserved in Sirach and the Dead Sea Scrolls. There are even good reasons for thinking that certain traditions current in the Jerusalem church of the first cen-

[97] On Wisdom, Philo, Josephus, *Aristobulus*, and *Joseph and Asenath*, see the articles, with bibliographies, of Winston, Borgen, Feldman, Holladay, and Chesnutt in *ABD*. On the literature of Diaspora Judaism, as it is important for our understanding of early Christian theology and history, one can still learn by reading with care such older works as those of Dalbert, *Theologie*, Bussmann, *Missionspredigt*, and Georgi, *Opponents*. But see notably the corrective and enriching dimensions of more recent contributions: Borgen, "Judaism (Egypt)," *ABD*; Applebaum, "Judaism (North Africa)," *ABD*; Walter, "Diaspora-Juden"; Barclay, "Diaspora Jews"; idem, *Diaspora*. Older theories about a unified and organized Jewish *mission* to Gentiles in the first century — sometimes formulated in part by taking at face value Matt 23:15 — cannot be sustained. See, for example, Walter, "Diaspora-Juden," 50–51; McKnight, *Jewish Missionary Activity* (but also the tempering review by Westerholm, *JBL* 113 [1994] 330–332); Goodman, "Jewish Proselytizing"; Feldman, *Jew and Gentile*. But the rejection of the theory of an organized Jewish mission to Gentiles does not tell us that the motif of hoped-for conversions is wholly absent from the literature of Diaspora Judaism. We can take *Joseph and Asenath* as an example. Burchard is right both to reject the characterization of *JosAs* as a missionary tract — a document having no theme other than the conversion of a Gentile — and to affirm that it was written for Jews, born and converted (*OTP* 2.194–195). He is also right, however, (a) to identify Gentile conversion to Judaism as the author's main focus ("Importance," 104), (b) to speak of Asenath's re-creative transformation as "a pattern which conversion often followed" (*OTP* 2.192; note especially Joseph's prayer for Asenath; *JosAs* 8:9), and thus (c) to characterize conversion as the subject by which the author can remind converts "of what they, or their forefathers, gained by crossing over to Judaism" (*OTP* 2.195; cf. Barclay, *Diaspora*, 204–216). Thus, as regards our attempts to portray the Teachers in Paul's Galatian churches, *JosAs* — and other Diaspora literature as well — is helpful in a role secondary to data in Galatians itself (in spite of the fact that most of this literature is Alexandrian). In the study of Diaspora literature it is important to note two apologetic stances, and to note also their combination. *First*, there is the apologetic stance that reflects an enormous cultural and religious distance from Gentiles (see notably Barclay, "Diaspora Jews"). Jewish authors express horror, for example, at their Gentile neighbors' idolatry and sexual practices, insisting on what one might call the absolute superiority of Judaism (e.g., *JosAs* 8:5). *Second*, there is also the apologetic stance that can express a loathing for polytheism and insist on the superiority of Judaism, precisely in order to extol Gentile conversion. In *JosAs* insistence on the maintenance of an absolute religious distance from Gentiles serves the climactic presentation of Asenath as the prototypical proselyte, whose conversion is dramatized — indeed, celebrated — in fine detail, and who leads her entire family to embrace Judaism (*JosAs* 20:7–8; cf. Asenath as a City of Refuge for all Gentiles who repent, 15:7; 16:16; 19:5). As we will see, an analogous combination of these two apologetic stances proves to be characteristic of the Teachers who invaded Paul's Galatian churches. Their horror at the Godless life of Gentiles does nothing other than serve their major motif: that of recommending the path of conversion to the God of Abraham.

tury were in fact preserved and shaped in two second-century communities of Christian Jews, known to us from the *Epistle of Peter to James* and the *Ascents of James*, not to mention Christian-Jewish traditions in the canonical epistle of James and in the gospel of Matthew.[98] With caution, then, we can further enrich our portrait of the Teachers by noting certain passages in these Christian-Jewish sources.[99]

In short, then, the picture that emerges from Paul's own references to the Teachers' work shows considerable internal coherence *and* a number of motifs for which there are significant parallels in traditions connected with Diaspora Jews, Palestinian Jews, and Christian Jews of various locales. We have reason, then, to think that a trustworthy picture can be drawn.[100]

A SKETCH OF THE TEACHERS AND THEIR MESSAGE

(1) *Outsiders.* Paul consistently differentiates the Teachers from the members of his Galatian congregations. He addresses the Galatians quite directly as "you," whereas he always refers to the Teachers by such terms as "some persons," "they," "these people." The Teachers are outsiders who have only recently come into the Galatian churches.[101]

(2) *Jews.* Paul almost certainly knows the Teachers' names, or at least some

---

[98] The fact that the author of *Ep. Pet. Jas.* knew and drew on Paul's letter to the Galatians does not necessarily tell us that he had no other access to traditions of the first-century Jerusalem church (*pace* Barclay, *Obeying,* 44 n19). The history of the study of *Ep. Pet. Jas.* and of *Ascents* is complex and the critical literature extensive. See notably F. S. Jones, who has recently expressed doubt about the theory of a source called *The Preachings of Peter,* of which *Ep. Pet. Jas.* has been thought to be the first element (*Source,* xii). The source-critical issues will never be altogether settled. See Strecker, "The Kerygmata Petrou"; Klijn and Reinink, *Evidence,* 31–32, 37, 69; J. L. Martyn, "Clementine Recognitions"; H. D. Betz 9, 331–332. On James, see L. T. Johnson, *James;* on Matthew, Davies and Allison, *Matthew,* and Luz, *Matthew* (especially 79–95); idem, *Theology.*

[99] On occasion I will even cite late rabbinic traditions, but only to amplify a point secured by other sources, or to suggest a possibility not essential to the exegetical argument.

[100] The integrity of the picture that will emerge below — added to the points of similarity with certain motifs in Jewish and Christian-Jewish traditions (see especially Comment #33) — suggests that Paul was himself well informed about the Teachers and their labors. In our own effort to reconstruct a picture of the Teachers, two extremes are to be avoided. On the one side lies the temptation to be overly bold in our detective work, falling unawares into massive speculation, reconstructing an entire face, so to speak, on the basis of the cut of the mustache. Some of Paul's polemical statements were doubtless formulated by him solely for the sake of rhetorical emphasis. On the other side lies the temptation to be too modest, limiting ourselves to points which can be scientifically demonstrated beyond doubt. Exegesis is more an art than a science, although it partakes of both. It is by asking at crucial points how the Galatians are likely to have understood the text in front of us that we shall acquire both the scientific control and the poetic imagination needed for our own understanding of the text. Note the cautions offered by Barclay, "Mirror-Reading."

[101] *Pace,* for example, Munck, *Paul,* 87–90. See Hawkins, "Opponents." As we will see, the Teachers are outsiders to the Gentile communities of the Galatians, somewhat as Joseph is an outsider to the Egyptian family of Asenath in *JosAs.*

of the epithets by which they identify themselves (cf. 2 Cor 11:22–23). We can conclude, then, that, instead of using their names and epithets, he employs such colorless expressions as "some persons" in order to indicate disdain. We also note, however, that he does employ three descriptive terms in his direct references:

(a) those who are frightening you (1:7, cf. 5:10)
(b) those who are troubling your minds (5:12)
(c) those who are circumcised (6:13; see Note there).

We shall return to the first two of these below. The third almost certainly tells us that the Teachers are Jews. We thus have a group of Jews who have come into the Galatian churches from somewhere else.[102]

(3) *Christian-Jewish evangelists.* What, precisely, are they doing in these congregations? In his initial reference to the Teachers (1:6–9) Paul says that, under their influence, the Galatians are turning their allegiance to "another *gospel.*" Then, having said that, he corrects himself by insisting that in reality there is no "other gospel." Does Paul take the route that requires self-correction only for the sake of rhetorical emphasis? Probably not. It would have been easier to avoid associating the Teachers with the term "gospel" by saying that, under their influence, the Galatians are turning *away from* the gospel, in that they are giving their allegiance to a *false teaching* (cf. "the teaching of Balaam" in Rev 2:14) or to an *impotent philosophy* (cf. "philosophy . . . according to human tradition" in Col 2:8). It seems highly probable that Paul takes the path requiring self-correction because he knows that the Teachers are in fact referring to their message as "the gospel." It follows that, no less than the apostle himself, the Teachers are in the proper sense of the term evangelists, probably finding their basic identity not as persons who struggle against Paul, but rather as those who preach "the good news of God's Messiah." They are, then, Jews who have come into Galatia proclaiming what they call the gospel, God's good news. And what do they consider that good news to be?

(4) *The Law as the good news.* Although they themselves speak of the good news as the gospel of Christ, Paul repeatedly portrays them as those who find in the Law the absolute point of departure for their theology (e.g., 5:3–4). Whatever they may be saying about Christ (see below), the Law is itself both the foundation and the essence of their good news.

---

[102] Both in "Gegner" and in "Diaspora-Juden" Walter argues that the Teachers were some of the *non-Christian* Jews who, like the pre-Christian Paul himself, persecuted the church (for Walter they were intent on abolishing the circumcision-free Christian mission). Before making the case for his hypothesis by analyzing data in Galatians, Walter refers to Acts 20:3; 21:27–29; 22:22; 23:12–15 and Matt 23:15 ("Gegner," 351). The final result is a reading of the data that is at once provocative and productive. Had one asked the Teachers whether they were Jews, the response would almost certainly have been in the affirmative. As I will argue below, however, they were surely Christian Jews, in the sense that, employing the term "gospel" in their own mission, they confessed Jesus to have been the Messiah, whose death atoned for the sins of all peoples, thus opening the way for the taking of the Law to the Gentiles.

(5) *The Law as the good news for Gentiles*. For whom is the Law good news? In the Teachers' view the Law is good news for the whole of the world, and specifically for Gentiles.[103] For that reason the Teachers' evangelistic vision is, in its scope, no less universalistic than that of Paul (3:8).[104] One does well, then, to avoid referring to the Teachers as "Judaizers," as has so frequently been done. For in modern parlance the term "Judaizer" usually refers to someone who wishes to hem in Gentile Christians by requiring them to live according to "narrow" Jewish practices.[105] In their own time and place the Teachers are embarked on an ecumenical mission. They are Christian Jews active in the Diaspora, who preach their nomistic gospel in Greek, quote the Law in Greek, and interpret the Law in ways understandable to persons of Greek culture.[106] Moreover, the Teachers carry out their mission under the genuine conviction — shared, for example, by the author of Wisdom — that the Law of Moses is the cosmic Law, in the sense that it is the divine wisdom for *all* human beings.[107] From the vocabulary employed by Paul in Gal 4:24–25, we can surmise that, in issuing their evangelistic invitation, the Teachers spoke explicitly of "the covenantal Law of Sinai."

(6) *The motivation for a Law-observant mission to Gentiles*. Beyond indicating that the Teachers are greatly concerned to correct what they see as the Law-less evangelism of Paul, the letter shows that they are carrying out their Law-observant mission to Gentiles in order to keep on good terms with some persons of considerable power (6:12). But their concentration on the expression "descendants of Abraham" (see below) raises the additional possibility that they see their mission in thoroughly positive terms, perhaps understanding it to be the means by which God is filling out the infinite number of progeny he had promised to the patriarch. One notes the motivation for the Law-observant mission to Gentiles portrayed in the *Ascents of James*:

---

[103]Cf. Acts 21:20–21; *Ep. Pet. Jas*. 2:3 (HS 2.112). The Teachers are thus first cousins, so to speak, of various Diaspora Jews who dramatically portrayed and even facilitated Gentile conversions to Judaism. See, for example, *JosAs* and Wisdom, and note that in *JosAs* nomistic salvation "is a 'necessity' appropriate only for non-Jews" (Burchard, *OTP* 2.192).

[104]On the motif of universalism in some Jewish traditions, cf., for example, Urbach, "The hope for conversion did not cease as long as the belief in Israel's election and in the power of the Torah was a living and dynamic faith that deemed its purpose to be the perfection and renewal *of the world*" (*Sages*, 552; emphasis added).

[105]See Note on 2:14; Ign. *Magn*. 10:3; Burton liii–lxv.

[106]Note especially the Teachers' Pythagorean-like, columnar interpretation of Genesis 15–21 (Comment #45). As noted above, the Teachers, Christian Jews of the Diaspora, almost certainly had a close and altogether positive relationship with the circumcision party in the Jerusalem church, probably traveling to Jerusalem from time to time, perhaps even taking there a copy of Paul's intemperate Galatian letter (cf. Rom 15:30–33; J. L. Martyn, "Jewish-Christian Interpreters"). What sort of relationship would the Teachers have had on those occasions with the various types of Diaspora synagogues in Jerusalem itself (Acts 6:9)?

[107]Cf. Georgi, "Weisheit Salomos"; Walter, "Diaspora-Juden," 49. Note the claim, widespread in Diaspora Judaism, that the whole of Greek philosophy is dependent on Moses; see, for example, Walter, *Aristobulos*, 43–51; Philo *de Vita Mos*. 2.12–44.

It was necessary, then, that the Gentiles be called . . . so that the number [of descendants] which was shown to Abraham would be satisfied; thus the preaching of the kingdom of God has been sent into all the world.[108]

(7) *The Law as the source of the Spirit.* God's readiness to invite Gentiles into his own people is marked by the fact that he bestows his Spirit even on communities of Gentiles, if their communal life is ordered by correct exegesis of scripture and thus by true observance of his Law.[109] In Gal 3:1–5 there are several hints that Paul is contrasting the type of worship service the Galatians first knew under his direction with the type of worship service they are now experiencing at the hands of the Teachers. Both services have about them certain aspects of the theater. In his preaching Paul clearly portrayed before the Galatians' eyes the dramatic picture of Christ, as he suffered crucifixion (3:1). Presented with this theater, the Galatians found that the message of the cross elicited their faith and that the Spirit fell upon them.

Now a new acting company has arrived on the scene, presenting a novel and highly effective drama.[110] In the services of worship conducted by the Teachers, the Galatians see extraordinarily masterful exegetes who quote and interpret the Scriptures with the firm conviction that out of true exegesis will flow mighty manifestations of the Spirit (3:5).[111] And, indeed, developments in Galatia seem to confirm this conviction. In their dramatic services the Teachers somehow manage to demonstrate to the Galatians the impressive connection between their interpretation of the Law and the miraculous dispensation of the Spirit.[112] It follows that God is to be known as the one who supplies the Spirit to those who are both true exegetes of his Law and faithful observers of it.

(8) *The threat of exclusion.* This laying down of a strict condition for the dependable granting of the Spirit is a token for the conditional nature of the whole

---

[108]The Latin text of Clementine *Recognitions* 1.42.1 (for both Latin and Syriac, see Van Voorst, *Ascents*, 57; F. S. Jones, *Source*, 72). Here and elsewhere, I cite the *Ascents of James* both by the numbering in the Clementine *Recognitions* and by the pages in Van Voorst, *Ascents*, and F. S. Jones, *Source*. Cf. Philo *de Somn.* 1.173–176. Abrahamic traditions that may aid us in our attempt to reconstruct the Teachers' message are analyzed more fully in Comment #33.

[109]Note several of the motifs in Joseph's prayer for Asenath prior to her conversion to Judaism: "Lord God of my father Israel . . . renew her by your spirit . . . and number her among your people that you have chosen . . ." (*JosAs* 8:9); and cf. Joseph's later giving to the new convert "spirit of life," "spirit of wisdom," and "spirit of truth" (*JosAs* 19:11).

[110]Cf. the *Exagoge* of Ezekiel the Tragedian (*OTP* 2.803–819).

[111]See Note on 3:2; Sir 39:1–8; Philo *de Spec. Leg.* 1.8, 3.178 (exegetes who are more than human [*thespesioi andres*]). Cf. Georgi, *Opponents*, 112–117, 258–271; according to some Jewish traditions, "the spirit portrayed and communicated itself essentially in the interpretation of the scriptures" (114); Fishbane on mantic oracles (*Biblical Interpretation*, 268–269). Note also that the dirge of *m. Sota* 9:15 — "When ben Zoma died, there were no more interpreters" etc. — reflects the assumption of an earlier connection between exegesis and the glory of the Law (*kĕbôd hattôrâ*).

[112]The Teachers' success may have been similar to that achieved somewhat later in the Corinthian church by the pseudo-apostles. See Georgi, *Opponents*; the portrait of Abraham in Philo *de Virt.* 217; and J. L. Martyn, *Issues*, 89–110.

of the Teachers' good news. We return, then, to the fact that Paul twice character-izes the Teachers as persons who frighten the Galatians (1:7; 5:10). How are we to understand these two references? Help comes from Paul's comment in 4:17, where, employing the image of a gate, he says that the Teachers threaten to shut the Galatians out of salvation. Encountering Gentiles they consider to have been badly misled by Paul, the Teachers feel they must issue a sharp warning: "*Only if* you pass through the gate of repentance into the genuine observance of God's Law will you be included in God's people Israel, thus being saved on the day of judgment."[113]

(9) *The necessity of circumcision as the commencement of Law observance.* How is a Gentile to pass through the gate to salvation? One of the major foci of the Teachers' preaching is the subject of circumcision (e.g., 6:12). It is a subject that properly belongs to proselytizing, for, in most cases, a Gentile passes into the people of the Law by belonging to a family the males of which submit to circum-cision.[114] Circumcision is the commandment *par excellence*, the commandment which signifies full participation in the people of God. The Teachers, then, are circumcised, Christian Jews who preach circumcision to Gentiles as the act ap-propriate to the universal good news of God's Law, the observance of which is the condition for God's pouring out his Holy Spirit. They also preach the necessity of the observance of holy times (4:10) and the keeping of dietary regulations (2:11–14).

(10) *The Christ of the Law.* We may further summarize the motifs we have mentioned thus far by asking what the Teachers say about Christ, the Messiah. However difficult it may be to answer this question with the detail we would desire, and however uncertain we remain as to how the Teachers are successfully communicating their christology to the Galatian Gentiles, five points can be stated with some degree of confidence.[115] (a) The Teachers view Christ much as do the members of the strictly observant circumcision party in the Jerusalem church, perhaps seeing him as the savior who brought to completion the ministry of Moses.[116] (b) In any case, they view God's Christ in the light of God's Law, rather than the Law in the light of Christ. This means that, in their christology, Christ is secondary to the Law. (c) Paul is emphatic when he says that the Teach-ers avoid taking their theological bearings from the cross (e.g., 6:12). They must be including references to Christ's death, however, presumably understanding it

---

[113]Like the other pictures Paul paints of the Teachers, this one is decidedly negative. But the Teachers' own view of their threat was probably analogous to the harshly strict words of Joseph to Asenath (*JosAs* 8:5). When the Teachers were not dealing with Gentiles they considered to have been misled by Paul, they may have employed the image of the gate in an essentially positive way, understanding themselves to be gatekeepers intent on ushering Gentiles through the gate into full participation in the people of God, Israel. See Joseph's prayer for Asenath (*JosAs* 8:9), and cf. Comment #33.

[114]Cohen, "Crossing"; Lieu, "Circumcision."

[115]Absent from these five points is the suggestion that the Teachers' christology included dimensions of the this-worldly, political, anti-Gentile messianism we find in some of the traditions of Diaspora Judaism. See, for example, *Sybilline Oracles* 3, and cf. Amir, "Die messianische Idee"; J. J. Collins, "Sybilline Oracles."

[116]Cf. Van Voorst, *Ascents*, 163; F. S. Jones, *Source*, 160.

to have been a sacrifice for sins, perhaps emphatically for the sins of Gentiles. In short, the Teachers must see Christ's death as a redemptive sacrifice enacted in harmony with God's Law (Comment #28). (d) We can be sure, above all, that they consistently avoid every suggestion that God's Law and God's Christ could be even partially in conflict with one another.[117] (e) In their own terms, they are presumably certain that Christ came in order to fulfill the Law and the prophets (cf. Matt 5:17–18), perhaps even to complete Moses' ministry by bringing the Law to the Gentiles.[118] For them the Messiah is the Messiah of the Law, deriving his identity from the fact that he confirms — and perhaps normatively interprets — the Law.[119] If Christ is explicitly involved in the Teachers' commission to preach to the Gentiles, that must be so because he has deepened their passion to take to the nations God's gift of gifts, the Spirit-dispensing Law that will guide them in their daily life.

These ten points would seem to encapsulate most of what Paul reveals about the Teachers and their gospel in his direct references. As noted earlier, however, there are other data quite revealing of the Teachers' gospel, allusions which, carefully interpreted, fill out in important ways the picture we receive of these evangelists, and especially of their gospel.

(11) *The descendants of Abraham; the blessing of Abraham.* In our detailed consideration of 3:6–29 we will find grounds for thinking that Paul refers to "the descendants of Abraham" because the Teachers are already doing that in their own way. Specifically, the Teachers are designating themselves as Abraham's descendants, and they are telling the Galatians that they can claim that identity for themselves if they submit to circumcision.[120] Indeed, the Teachers seem also to be speaking at some length about "the blessing of Abraham," indicating that when God blessed the patriarch, he did so in such a way as eventually to bless those Gentiles who, by circumcision and Law observance, become "Abraham's true descendants."[121] We thus find solid confirmation of the suggestion of Holtzmann that "descendants of Abraham" is one of the Teachers' favorite catchwords.[122]

---

[117]Cf. Jas 1:22–25; *Ep. Pet. Jas.* 2:3 (HS 2.112).

[118]On the expectation that the Messiah will bring the Law to the Gentiles, see later rabbinic references, such as *Gen. Rab.* 98:9.

[119]For the Christian-Jewish conviction that Christ permanently confirmed the Law, see Matt 5:17–19; *Ep. Pet. Jas.* 2:5 (HS 2.112).

[120]We know that the expression "descendants of Abraham" was a significant self-designation among Christian Jews of the first century (2 Cor 11:22; John 8:33, 37). Jewish references to the proselyte as a descendant of Abraham are very numerous; see, for example, *Tanh.*, Lekh Lekha 32a; cf. Philo *de Virt.* 219.

[121]It is worth noting that the Christian Jew who authored the second-century *Ascents of James* portrayed true religion as the line extending from Abraham to his descendants. Similarly, as noted above, in the *Ascents* God's blessing of Abraham provides the motivation for the Law-observant mission to Gentiles (1.42.1; Van Voorst, *Ascents*, 57; F. S. Jones, *Source*, 72).

[122]Holtzmann, *Einleitung*, 243. See now Brinsmead, *Dialogical Response*, 107–114, and cf. Comment #45. With regard to the history of early Christian missions, it is important that, concerning the link between Abraham and the impulse to evangelize the Gentiles, it is the author of Galatians who is doing the reacting, not the Teachers. There is no good

(12) *"Jerusalem is our mother."* In Comments #45 and #46 we will see good reason to think that, in addition to identifying themselves and their Law-observant Gentile converts as "descendants of Abraham," the Teachers speak of Jerusalem as their "mother," referring thereby to the Jerusalem church.[123] We cannot say with great confidence that the Teachers have come to Galatia from Jerusalem, but there are grounds for thinking that they claim to be the true representatives of the Jerusalem church, and that, in making that claim, they are confident of the support of a powerful group in that church.[124]

(13) *Israel.* Similarly, in Comments #37 and #52, we will find that, in inviting the Galatians to claim Abraham as their father and the Jerusalem church as their mother, the Teachers promise the Galatians that they will thereby enter the company of God's people Israel. It is conceivable that the Teachers are emphasizing the antique superiority of Israel by noting — at least in effect — that Plato and Pythagoras imitated the Law of Moses.[125]

(14) *Victory over the Impulsive Desire of the Flesh.* Finally, horrified at the continuation of various Gentile patterns of life among the Galatian churches (cf. 5:20–21a), the Teachers are taking up the matter of the Galatians' daily behavior. Here, in addition to attacking Paul for leaving the Galatians without potent ethical guidance, they voice a crucial promise: "If you Galatians will become observant of the Law, we can promise you that you will not fall prey to the Impulsive Desire of the Flesh" (cf. 5:16; Comment #49; 4 Maccabees 1). In this regard, as in others, the Teachers are likely to have portrayed Abraham as the model to be emulated. For, by keeping God's commandments, the patriarch was said to have avoided walking in the path of the Impulsive Desire of the Flesh.[126]

Most of these motifs can be effectively brought together if, attempting to sense the reasons for the Teachers' remarkable success among the Galatians, we allow ourselves the disciplined freedom to imagine a sermon they might have preached on the subject of the identity and blessedness of Abraham's true descendants. See Comment #33.

---

evidence that they have developed their interpretations of the Abraham texts simply in order to counter the effects of Paul's circumcision-free mission. On the contrary, Paul takes up the traditions about Abraham — and especially the expression "descendants of Abraham" — in his argument against the use the Teachers are already making of those traditions in their Law-observant mission. One may recall a statement made by Georgi about the pseudo-apostles who came into Paul's Corinthian church: "Since there is no doubt that Paul's understanding of mission and missionaries was largely peculiar to himself, the question could arise whether the opponents of Paul did not represent the early church's general understanding of mission, which therefore could be seen entirely in the context of Jewish apologetics" (*Opponents*, 164; translation slightly altered). See also J. L. Martyn, *Issues*, 7–24.

[123] Cf. again Holtzmann, who advanced the thesis that the agitators spoke of Jerusalem (presumably H. meant the city) as their mother (*Einleitung*, 243).

[124] See Comment #46, and cf. the image of the Jerusalem church in the *Ascents of James*, Van Voorst, *Ascents*, 174–180. Note the argument of F. S. Jones for locating the *Ascents* in Judea or Jerusalem (*Source*, 157–167).

[125] See, for example, *Aristobulus* Frag. 3.

[126] CD 3:1–3; 16:4–6.

COMMENT #7
THE GOSPEL OF CHRIST AND ITS COUNTERFEIT

Although we will be moving into an area in which some points remain uncertain, an attempt to reconstruct the history of the Galatians' linguistic experience with the term "gospel" will prove to be helpful.[127]

THE TERM *"GLAD TIDINGS"* IN THE GALATIANS' VOCABULARY PRIOR TO PAUL'S ARRIVAL

The remains of Greco-Roman culture include a significant number of instances of this neuter noun in the plural (*ta euaggelia*, "glad tidings"), referring to that which is proper to an *euaggelos*, a messenger who brings good news.[128] So used, it could mean the news themselves (an inscription from the fourth century B.C. and Cicero onward),[129] or the reward gratefully given to a messenger for bringing the good news (already in Homer), or the sacrifice offered to the god held to have caused the news to be good (Aristophanes onward). We might grasp the major dimension of the first of these meanings by rendering the word as "glad tidings," bearing in mind the plural form of that expression. Basically, two uses of this plural noun may very well have been known to the Galatians: its employment in everyday parlance and its use in connection with the cult of the Roman emperor.

(1) *The popular sense of "glad tidings."* The plural noun was used fairly frequently to refer to the report of a military victory.[130] Indeed, so used, it could be linked with the word "salvation" (*sôtêria*), since a military victory often meant salvation to the residents of a city-state. In this use the noun clearly had a corporate dimension: all citizens heard the glad tidings, and all were salvifically af-

---

[127] Harnack proposed a five-stage history of the term "gospel" in its Christian usage, from Jesus into the second century (*Constitution*). Cf. Stuhlmacher, *Evangelium*; Strecker, "Evangelium"; Stuhlmacher, "Gospel." The points of disagreement between Strecker and Stuhlmacher remind one that numerous riddles remain. At what point did the noun enter early Christian thought and life as a technical term? From what source or sources did it make its entrance? If Jesus himself used it (very unlikely), or if it made its entrance in the Palestinian, Jewish-Christian church, was it drawn from the scriptures via its verbal form in 2 Isaiah? Or did the Hellenistic church take it over from common usage among the Greek-speaking populace, or even from the use made of it in the worship of Hellenistic rulers and eventually in the cult of the Roman emperor? How, finally, did it become a designation for the first four books in the canonical New Testament? Some of these complex questions lie inevitably in the background of any consideration of the term "gospel." Here, however, we are concerned in the main with the relatively modest matter of the history of the term in the vocabulary of the Galatians.

[128] See G. Friedrich, "*euaggelizomai*"; Stuhlmacher, *Evangelium*, 186–190; and note especially Josephus J.W. 4.618, 4.656. The only secure instance of the noun in the LXX (2 Kgs 4:10) is the plural form. There are a few instances of the singular in non-Christian literature, but the number is small, and there is no reason to think that any of them were known to the Galatians: Josephus J.W. 2.420; Plutarch *Demosthenes* 17.5 (the earliest of Plutarch's writings are from the final years of the first century); an Egyptian papyrus from the third century in which the reference is to the Imperial Cult: Preisigke and Bilabel, *Sammelbuch*, 1.#421.

[129] Dittenberger, *Inscriptiones*, 1.13, 1.20.

[130] G. Friedrich, "*euaggelizomai*."

fected. The term could also refer to personal matters, such as the happy news that an innocent prisoner had been released, that a hated enemy had died, or that a wedding was imminent.

(2) *"Glad tidings" in the emperor cult.* We know of this use from several Greek inscriptions, from the writings of both Philo and Josephus, and from rabbinic tradition.[131] Of the pertinent inscriptions the most famous is a lengthy one found on stones that formed parts of a pillar in the marketplace of Priene, a city in the province of Asia, west of Galatia.[132] Apparently made in 9 B.C., the inscription is concerned with an official decision to reform the calendar, so that the year would begin on the birthday of the emperor Augustus, venerated throughout the text as a god. The pertinent lines say that providence filled the emperor with all virtue and sent him "to us and to the generations after us" as savior. The year should begin on his birthday because, as the divine man, he causes wars to cease and replaces them with peace.[133] Before his birth *glad tidings* (line 37) had been prophetically announced. With his epiphany these *glad tidings* have been more than fulfilled. Thus:

> the birthday of the god [Augustus] was for the world the beginning of the *glad tidings* (line 41) which have gone forth because of him.

If in line 37 glad tidings constituted a *prophecy* of a new and future time of corporate redemption, line 41 announces that the emperor's divine *epiphany* has now been the first of these glad tidings. Other inscriptions, together with the relevant passages in Philo, indicate that chief among the glad tidings subsequent to the emperor's birth were his coming of age and, especially, his accession to the throne.

Since some of the inscriptions come from Asia Minor, it is quite possible that the Galatians were acquainted with the use of the plural noun *euaggelia* in connection with the emperor cult, where claims were made regarding the emperor's power to terminate wars and to restore order, thus benefiting all citizens in the empire. Glad tidings about the emperor declared a salvific event said to change the world.

THE GALATIANS HEAR THE SINGULAR NOUN "GLAD TIDING" FROM PAUL'S MOUTH

An important linguistic event occurred when Paul came to the Galatian cities proclaiming a message he called "the glad tiding," employing the noun without

---

[131] Ibid.

[132] For the text — to some degree restored — see Stuhlmacher, *Evangelium,* 186 n3.

[133] Cf. also Philostratus *Apollonius* 1.28, 8.27, where the verb *euaggelizomai* is used to refer to the arrival of a divine man who brings salvation; G. Friedrich, *"euaggelizomai,"* 712; Strecker, "Evangelium," 189 n.

exception in the singular (*to euaggelion*), and using it both by itself and with such modifiers as "of Christ."[134]

We cannot know with precision the content of Paul's initial message to the Galatians, but we are not wholly in the dark. In 1 Thessalonians we find an encapsulation of Paul's preaching in Thessalonica, and comparison of that encapsulation with passages in Galatians suggests that the glad tiding Paul preached in Galatia was similar.

In 1 Thess 1:5, speaking of the founding of the Thessalonian church, Paul recalls

> that our *glad tiding* did not come to you with words only, but with power and with the Holy Spirit and with much conviction.

A few lines later he presents, as it were, a snapshot from those days:[135]

> . . . you turned from idols, to serve the God who is living and true, and to wait for the coming from heaven of his Son, whom he raised from the dead, Jesus who delivers us from the coming wrath (1 Thess 1:9–10).

And a few lines still further Paul again refers to this message as

> the *glad tiding* of God (1 Thess 2:2).

In Galatians we find Paul using similar motifs to characterize his initial preaching: In bringing to Gentiles the glad tiding of God's Son (Gal 1:16), Paul accented the Son's salvific death (3:1), the call for Gentiles to turn from the worship of lifeless idols to the service of the living God and his Son (4:8), the powerful advent of the Spirit (3:2; 4:6), and the assurance of future deliverance (5:5, 21).

Now, bearing in mind the meanings that the Galatians already attached to the plural noun "glad tidings," we can see that they will have sensed in Paul's use of the singular noun both points of contact and jolting points of disjuncture.

(1) *Points of contact.* The Galatians may not have been astonished to hear Paul attribute worldwide salvation to his glad tiding. Nor will they have been surprised to find him linking it to the word "god," or even to the expression "son of god." All of those things were done in the emperor cult where the Caesar was heralded

---

[134]Paul may also have used the verb *euaggelizomai* in his initial preaching (cf. 1:8, 9, 11, 16, 23; 4:13), but it is doubtless his characteristic use of the singular noun *to euaggelion* that will have seized the Galatians' attention. A similar — but linguistically opposite — event happens in the twentieth century, when one hears references in Shakespeare's Elizabethan English to "these good news."

[135]That 1 Thess 1:9b–10 is in its essence a pre-Pauline tradition has been argued by G. Friedrich, "Tauflied"; cf. Wilckens, *Missionsreden*, 81; Strecker, "Evangelium," 198 n70 (but note the cautious analysis in Holtz, *Thessalonicher*, 54–62). See Malherbe, "Family," 117–118.

as the divine, salvific figure who provided deliverance and thus peace, joy, and wholeness for the entire civilized world. As we have seen, there is a linearity to the sequence of glad tidings in the emperor cult (the emperor's birth, his reaching maturity, his enthronement, his recovery from serious illness, and so on). There is a somewhat similar linearity to Paul's glad tiding, in that the salvific event of the Son's death and resurrection is said to have created a new history that unfolds itself in a series of gospel-events (see Comment #11 and 5:5, 21). In short, even though we cannot say that Paul consciously formulated his glad tiding in relation (either positive or negative) to the glad tidings of the emperor cult, the Galatians are likely to have sensed several points of similarity: news that is good because it announces the arrival of a delivering god, news that is cosmic because it corporately affects the whole world, news that is time-oriented in that it inaugurates a new epoch, thus beginning a new history.

(2) *Points of disjuncture.* Other aspects of Paul's glad tiding will have been strange to the Galatians, and some elements will have been utterly new and foreign to them. That is a matter to which Paul refers in 1:11: "the gospel (glad tiding) preached by me . . . is not what human beings normally have in mind when they speak of 'good news,'" clearly indicating that the Galatians' prior understanding of glad tidings does not serve as the point of departure for Paul's proclamation (Comments #8 and #9).

(a) *Once-for-all.* Paul's glad tiding presents the motif of linearity in a way radically different from that evident both in semipopular usage and in pronouncements connected with the emperor cult. The fact that Paul uses the noun *euaggelion* only in the singular reflects his certainty that his glad tiding is first of all an unrepeatable point, and only after that a line. In the semipopular usage, as noted above, there is no thought of *the* good event that is unrepeatable. On the contrary, glad tidings may be one thing today—a military victory—and another thing tomorrow—an approaching wedding. Similarly, while the emperor may think with one part of his mind that he is immortal, the common citizen knows that the linearity of this emperor's glad tidings (birth, enthronement, etc.) will be replaced upon his death by the story line presented in the glad tidings of the next emperor.

Against that background it is striking that Paul's singular glad tiding is the announcement of the "good new" that will not be repeated. To be sure, like the announcements in the cult of the emperor, Paul's glad tiding creates, as we have seen, a new history that has its own linearity (the parousia is yet to come). The gospel is not, however, one piece of good news alongside others. It begins *the* new history by terminating the old history, together with all its editions of good news. In a word, the Galatians will not have heard Paul preaching *an instance* of good news. They will have heard him proclaiming the thoroughly eschatological, once-for-all good new that breaks the mold of good news.[136] And they will have noted that it does that in several regards:

---

[136]This element of Paul's theology can represent others that arose in part from his drawing on Jewish-Christian traditions that were themselves based on scripture. See below the discussion of Isa 52:7 and other texts. There is no reason, however, to think that the Gala-

(b) *The power to save*. From Philo we know that the glad tidings of an emperor's accession could set off celebrations of a markedly ecstatic sort (*Leg. ad Gai.* 8–13). Nevertheless, the peculiar bond Paul perceives between the *words* of his glad tiding and what he refers to as the demonstrations of *power*, caused by the Spirit, will have set his preaching apart from the imperial announcements (Gal 4:14). Because of the present activity of the Spirit of God's Son, Paul's glad tiding is not a set of words designed to be incised into one of the stone pillars in the marketplace. Like the Spirit that empowers it, the glad tiding of Christ has invaded and continues to invade the Galatians' hearts, happening with power in the common life of their churches again and again (Gal 3:2, 5; 4:6).

(c) *Event*. We can be even more precise. Paul's glad tiding happens because in it God himself steps on the scene, addressing the hearers directly. This glad tiding does become a message (an *akoê*, Gal 3:2), but at no time and under no circumstances can that message be separated either from its real author (God) or from the person about whom it speaks (Christ, the Son of God). On the contrary, this glad tiding is the active power of God, because in it God himself comes on the scene, speaking his own word-event.[137] For this reason Paul draws a contrast between a gospel that would come via a line of tradition and the gospel that came to him by God's own apocalyptic revelation (1:12, 16; Comment #10). Strictly speaking, God's gospel is not an it; the gospel is the good event that God is causing to happen now.

(d) *The cross as glad tiding*. The Galatians may not have been utter strangers to the thought that a god should die and be raised from death.[138] They will have been shocked, however, to find Paul centering his *glad* tiding in the execution of God's Son as a criminal (3:1). And it will have been new to them that this Son of God died "for us," enacting in that hideous death his love for us (2:20), creating true peace in our hearts (1:3).[139] For these motifs there is no preparation in the Hellenistic use made of the plural noun "glad tidings." Indeed, nowhere in any of the many Hellenistic cults do we find a point of contact for the notion that the death of the god is good news.

(e) *Apocalypse*. We have noted the motif of the new epoch in the emperor cult's proclamation of glad tidings. We have also seen, however, that that new epoch was one in a *series* of epochs, not one of only *two* periods of time. Thus, in the emperor cult there is no hint of the apocalyptic dualism that is basic to Paul's glad tiding (Comment #3). The difference is crucial.

---

tians will have sensed this scriptural background, for we have no indication that Paul provided them with an exegetical treatment of scripture passages featuring *euaggelizomai* and *euaggelizomenos* (see again 1 Thessalonians). This is a matter in which the debate between Stuhlmacher and Strecker assumes a certain importance. To some degree, Stuhlmacher's scripture-oriented theses are pertinent to the background of the Jewish-Christian use of the *euaggel* stem in the mission to Jews. But the more Hellenistic analysis proposed by Strecker is fundamental to the question being pursued in the present Comment: How did *the Gentile Galatians* hear Paul's proclamation of the glad tiding?

[137] See Comment #5, and cf. Käsemann, *Romans*, 9.

[138] Affirmed, for example, of Attis, Adonis, and Osiris.

[139] See Cousar, *Cross*.

(f) *Epistemological crisis.* There is no ordinary, visible evidence to support Paul's announcement of the glad tiding. The declaration of peace is not the result of military victories achieved by an army or navy. The joy to which the glad tiding issues an invitation is not connected with a return to economic prosperity, made possible by a safe and efficient road system or by a large merchant fleet. Consequently, Paul's proclamation of glad tiding in a visibly unchanged world creates an epistemological crisis. If the good new is real, yet unattested by visible evidence, where will one look, and how will one look in order to see it? To be sure, in his glad tiding Paul speaks of the advent of the Spirit of God's Son (Gal 3:2–5; 4:6). He speaks also of the Spirit's war against the Impulsive Desire of the Flesh, and of the Spirit's fruit, its power to create even now the loving community of the end-time, the new creation (Comment #49). Thus, God's new deed is to be seen in the miracle of this new community.

Paul is extraordinarily careful, however, to avoid a purely spiritual epistemology, or even one that is fundamentally ecclesiological. Paradoxically, he explicates the new way of knowing, given in the glad tiding, by focusing his major attention on the cross of Christ. The Galatians are sure to have noted that Paul sees the execution of Christ by crucifixion as apocalypse, as the divine, revealing invasion that changes not only the cosmos but also one's way of perceiving it.[140]

None of the strange and difficult elements in these six points of disjuncture, nor all of them taken together, caused the Galatians to turn away from Paul's message. Quite the contrary. In the crucified Christ they saw the one who, loving them, gave his life for their redemption. The glad tiding of this Christ became for them not an object, but rather an occurrence, happening in their midst as though it were a powerful explosion that rearranged the whole of reality (3:1–2). The Spirit of Christ invaded their hearts; they were baptized into this corporate Son of God; and, impelled by the Spirit of Christ, they now cried out to God as their new Father (3:27; 4:6). The glad tiding spoken to them by God himself created them as his new community, and in that New Age community their enthusiasm knew no limit. The love of Christ spawned love of one another, and not least love of Paul, whom they knew to be the messenger God had sent to give them *the* glad tiding (4:14–15).

THE GALATIANS HEAR A GLAD TIDING FROM THE TEACHERS

After Paul's departure the members of the Galatian churches entrusted with catechetical responsibility (6:6) doubtless continued to speak of the glad tiding of Jesus Christ as Paul had done. With the arrival of the Teachers, however, there were significant linguistic and theological changes. In Comment #6 we have already seen that the Teachers did in fact employ the expression "glad tiding," and doubtless in the singular as Paul had done. In their message, however, the churches began to hear the term used in a quite different way. In Comment #33 we will consider the major motifs in the Teachers' message. Here, then, we ask only whether the Teachers' use of the term "glad tiding" may itself give us additional guidance.

---

[140] See J. L. Martyn, *Issues,* 89–110.

(1) *The glad tiding is in accordance with the scripture.* In Comments #33 and #46 we will see good reasons for thinking that the Teachers claimed to be preaching the glad tiding formulated by the apostles in the Jerusalem church. From numerous data—notably from 1 Cor 15:3–4 and Rom 1:2—we know that this Jewish-Christian tradition emphasized the continuity between the glad tiding of Jesus Christ and the scriptures. And from the two exegetical sections of Galatians (3:6–4:7 and 4:21–5:1), we know that exegesis played an essential role in the Teachers' proclamation of the glad tiding. Will their use of the term "glad tiding" itself have been basically affected by the link they draw between scripture and their glad tiding?

(2) *The glad tiding is preached by numerous apostolic evangelists.* As regards the Greek noun *euaggelion*, the question is easily answered. As we have seen above, the LXX contains not a single instance of the noun in the singular with the meaning of "good news." The picture is changed, however, when we take into account the verb *euaggelizomai*, "to bring glad tidings" (Hebrew *biśśar*), and especially when we consider the substantive participle *euaggelizomenos*, "the one who brings glad tidings" (Hebrew *měbaśśēr*). Notably in some passages of 2 Isaiah, and in streams of tradition emanating from—and parallel to—those passages, we find these terms employed to refer to the eschatological proclamation of salvation. Two examples will suffice:

> How beautiful upon the mountains are the feet of *the one who brings glad tidings*, publishing peace, *bringing good news,* publishing salvation, saying to Zion: Your King reigns (Isa 52:7; cf. 1QH 18:14; 11QMelch).

> And it shall be that everyone who calls on the name of the Lord will be saved; for in Mount Zion and in Jerusalem there shall be those who are delivered, just as the Lord said, and there shall be *those who bring glad tidings,* whom the Lord had called to do that (Joel 3:5; LXX).

Whereas the reference in Isaiah 52:7 is to a single figure (the prophet), the LXX of Joel foresees the arrival of a host of messengers called by God to bring redemptive glad tidings (*euaggelizomenoi*).[141]

The pertinence of these observations for our reconstruction of the Teachers' message lies in the probability that the picture of a company of "those who bring glad tidings" made its way into early Jewish-Christian circles, where, by reading the plural *into* Isa 52:7 itself, Jewish Christians found there a reference not to the Messiah, but rather to the apostolic evangelists called by God to bring the glad tiding of the Messiah:

> How beautiful upon the mountains are the feet of *those* who bring glad tidings
> . . . (a Jewish-Christian reading of Isa 52:7 quoted by Paul in Rom 10:15).[142]

---

[141] The reference to a host of messengers seems to have become a tradition, found also in Ps 67:12 (LXX; see below), in the Targum of Isa 40:9, and in some rabbinic texts: G. Friedrich, "*euaggelizomai*," 715–716.

[142] That the plural reading of Isa 52:7 is a Jewish-Christian interpretation antedating Paul is well argued by Stuhlmacher, "Gospel," 162–165.

We cannot say that the Teachers conveyed this reading of Isaiah to the Galatians, but we can surmise that as Jewish-Christian evangelists they knew of it or its equivalent. Like other Jewish Christians, they may have used the verb *euaggelizomai*, "to bring glad tidings," and the substantive participle *hoi euaggelizomenoi*, "those who bring glad tidings," to refer to the eschatological task laid on the apostles in Jerusalem, and on themselves as well.

(3) *The glad tiding is the covenantal Law of God presented to the Gentiles.* For the Teachers, Christian-Jewish evangelists to the Gentiles, what was the content of the glad tiding? In Comments #6 and #33 we see that, even though the Teachers understand themselves to be evangelists of the Messiah, Jesus, the essence of their mission is the task of bringing the good news of the Law to Gentiles. In a word, as they preach to Gentiles, they say not only that their glad tiding is in accordance with the nomistic scriptures. They also say that the glad tiding *is* "the covenantal Law of Sinai," as the Law has been confirmed by the Messiah, Jesus.[143] The equation of the glad tiding with the Law emerges in later Jewish tradition, and precisely in connection with the expectation that a company of evangelists will appear at the end-time, a motif we have found in the Jewish-Christian reading of Isa 52:7. Ps 68:12 (LXX 67:12) links the giving of *the Law* to the presence of numerous bearers of *glad tidings*:

> The Lord gives the word [i.e., the Law]; great is the company of those who bore the tidings (*haměbaśśěrôt; hoi euaggelizomenoi*).

In the *Midrash on Psalms* — a late rabbinic work — this text is then interpreted in such a way as to combine all three of the motifs mentioned thus far: The Law itself constitutes the glad tidings; the evangelists who conveyed the tidings of the Law are numerous; and they brought the nomistic tidings to the Gentiles:

> "The Lord gave the word [i.e., the Law]; great was the company of those who bore the tidings." When the Holy One, blessed be He, . . . gave forth the divine word, the voice divided itself into seven voices, and from the seven voices passed into seventy languages of the seventy nations, so that everyone understood it. Hence it is said, "Great was the company of those who bore the tidings."[144]

In a similar way the Teachers may have told the Galatians that their bringing the covenantal Law to Gentiles is the act of speaking the glad tiding to the seventy peoples of the earth (cf. Acts 2:1–11).

(4) *Indeed, the glad tiding of the covenantal Law is actually being proclaimed to the Gentiles by an angel.* From Gal 1:8–9 we have seen that the Teachers are

---

[143] As Paul uses the word "Sinai" only in Galatians (4:24–25), it may be that he employs it because the Galatians are hearing about "the covenant of Sinai" from the Teachers.

[144] The translation, slightly changed, is that of Braude, *Midrash*, 541. The basic tradition is also preserved elsewhere, for example *t. Sota* 8:6; *b. Shabb.* 88b. Cf. Stuhlmacher, *Evangelium*, 150; Callan, "Midrash," 551–552; Gaston, *Torah*, 40.

probably making a serious claim about a connection between their glad tiding and an angel: it is actually an angel who speaks their gospel to the Gentiles. In light of the Teachers' equating their glad tiding at its core with the Law, interpreters commonly and reasonably see behind 1:8–9 (and 3:19 as well) the traditions in which angels are said to have played a significant role at Sinai in the giving of the Law.[145]

But 1:8–9 may reflect the Teachers' claim that their *present* proclamation of the nomistic glad tiding is in actuality the work of an angel (or angels). Do we have grounds for thinking that claim to be characteristic of some strands of Jewish-Christian tradition?

An affirmative answer is suggested by Rev 14:6, for that text (quoted in the Note on 1:8) reflects the Jewish-Christian picture in which an angel preaches the gospel to all of the nations at the end of time.[146]

Conclusion. Under the tutelage of the Teachers, then, a number of the Galatians are acquiring a new view of the gospel. They are learning that *the glad tiding of God* to all of humanity is *the wonderfully venerable and angelically glorious Law of Sinai,* embodying God's covenantal blessing of Abraham and now confirmed by Christ. They may even be hearing from the Teachers that God's ancient promissory blessing of Abraham was the nomistic glad tiding preached to the patriarch ahead of time by an angel.[147]

THE GALATIANS HEAR PAUL'S GLAD TIDING AGAIN AS HIS MESSENGER READS THE LETTER TO THEM

Given these developments, Paul opens the body of his letter by differentiating the Teachers' counterfeit gospel from the true gospel of Christ (1:6–9). Thereaf-

---

[145]Gaston, *Torah,* has argued that there are no Jewish traditions showing the angels actually participating in the giving of the Law, that event being God's deed. He also argues that the angels said to have been present at the giving of the Law were those allotted by God to the nations. See, however, Deut 33:2 (LXX); Josephus *Ant.* 15.136; Philo *de Somn.* 1.141–143. These and other texts preserve various forms of a tradition in which the glorious nature of the Law is signaled by the affirmation that, in giving it, God was accompanied — and in some cases assisted — by angels. See the Note on Gal 3:19.

[146]Cf. Stuhlmacher, *Evangelium,* 130, 138; J. Jeremias, *Promise,* 22: "We are to understand that 'the proclamation to all the world' will not be by men . . . but by God's angel at the last day"; Lohmeyer, *Offenbarung,* 124.

[147]We know that the Teachers gave a central place in their preaching to traditions about Abraham (Comment #33). Did they include traditions connecting Abraham to the term "glad tiding," perhaps speaking explicitly of God's promise of a son to Abraham as God's glad tiding? We cannot be certain, but it is worth pointing out that that connection is found in later Jewish tradition: God's promise of a son to Sarah and to Abraham is *the angelic declaration of glad tidings* (Gen 18:1–15; *b. B. Mes.* 86b; *Mek.,* Pischa 14; cf. Fragment Targum to Gen 21:7 and *Gen. Rab.* 50:2; Stuhlmacher, *Evangelium,* 138, 130). Given the elements in the Teachers' message sketched above, it would have been a short step for them to affirm that the covenant God made with Abraham was the first form in which the nomistic gospel was declared through an angel. It is even possible, then, that it was the Teachers, rather than Paul, who first connected Gen 12:3 to the expression "to preach the gospel ahead of time" (*proeuaggelizomai*), for they may have said in essence: "An angel of God preached the glad tiding to Abraham ahead of time, promising him a son, thus giving him assurance even before Sinai that via the holy rite of circumcision

ter, he displays the contrast between the two messages through the entire letter, consistently denying that the Teachers' message is in any sense the glad tiding of Christ. There is only one gospel, and it is the one Paul brought to the Galatians at the beginning.

In the course of the letter Paul returns the gospel to the motifs characteristic of his original proclamation. In the form of an argument he preaches again the glad tiding, insisting that in the cross of Christ — not in the Law — God has invaded the human orb, victoriously liberating enslaved humanity, and thus setting right what has gone wrong (2:16). In two exegetical sections he shows the true sense in which the gospel is in accordance with the scripture (3:6–4:7; 4:21–5:1). He provides faithful guidance for behavior in the community made up of persons whose hearts have been invaded by the Spirit of Christ (5:13–6:10). And, striking a parting blow against the counterfeit gospel of the Teachers, he speaks of the death of the old cosmos and of God's new creation that has taken the place of that old cosmos (6:11–18).

Regarding the history of the Galatians' linguistic experience with the term "glad tiding," then, the final step is the one to which we have secure access: their exposure to it as Paul's messenger read the letter aloud to them.

1:10–12 THE GOSPEL AND RHETORIC: FIRST THESIS

TRANSLATION

1:10. Am I now engaged in rhetorical arguments designed to sway the crowds; or am I intent on pleasing God? Do I seek merely to please human beings? If I were still doing that, I would not be a slave of Christ.

11. For, concerning the gospel preached by me, I want you to know, my brothers and sisters, that it is not what human beings normally have in mind when they speak of "good news." 12. For I did not receive it from another human being, nor was I taught it; it came to me by God's apocalyptic revelation of Jesus Christ.

LITERARY STRUCTURE AND SYNOPSIS

Paul knows as well as the Teachers that the message cannot be separated from the messenger. Thus, before stating his initial thesis in 1:11–12, he composes in

---

God's pronouncement of a blessing would one day be extended to all the nations: 'In you all the Gentiles will be blessed.'" Assuming the Teachers to have spoken of a *nomistic* preevangel to Abraham, one would find Paul typically standing their interpretation on its head in Gal 3:8.

v 10 a brief transition in which he speaks of his own identity by restating in rhetorical terms the basic antinomy of the letter's first sentence. His identity as apostle and slave of Christ is given him by God, not by a crowd that is pleased with his preaching. In vv 11–12, then, Paul uses an epistolary disclosure formula — "I want you to know" — to introduce the letter's initial thesis, thus commencing his formal explication of the gospel theme stated in vv 6–9. His message is the gospel of Christ apocalyptically revealed to him directly by God, not taught him by another human being.

NOTES

1:10. *Am I now engaged . . . a slave of Christ.* Paul begins each of several sentences (vv 10, 11, 12, and 13) with the little word *gar*, generally used to introduce a sentence or clause in which grounds are given for a preceding affirmation, and thus often rendered "for." That is clearly its force in vv 11, 12, and 13. Some interpreters have read it that way also at the outset of v 10, usually finding thereby a logical connection between vv 8–9 and v 10. The result is to hear in the first two rhetorical questions of v 10 something like this:

> For consider the following. In pronouncing the curse (vv 8–9) am I seeking to persuade human beings, or even, inconceivable as it may seen, am I seeking to persuade God, calling on him to effect the curse? Of course not! For there is no connection between cursing and persuading.[148]

But this reading produces what one must call a truly tortured line of thought. A better route is to take v 10 as an instance in which *gar* is little more than an emphatic particle or a loose connective (not unusual in questions). Hence, it plays no role in the translation.

More vexing is the problem of understanding the line of thought internal to v 10. Rendered literally, the verse consists of three rhetorical questions:

(1) Am I now persuading human beings?
(2) Or (am I persuading) God?
(3) Or am I seeking to please human beings?

Paul then follows these questions with a conditional sentence which is obviously closely related to the third of them:

> If I were still doing that (seeking to please human beings), I would not be a slave of Christ.

To say that the questions are rhetorical is to say that Paul has certain answers in mind, and that he expects the Galatians themselves to provide precisely those answers. Has he given hints sufficiently clear to facilitate this process?

---

[148] See, for example, Becker. Without being altogether convincing, Vos has recently penned an argument for the causal reading of *gar* in v 10 that is stronger than those previously given ("Argumentation," 9).

We begin with the third question, for it is simply repeated in the protasis of the conditional sentence, and that protasis is contrary to fact, thus implying: "I am *not* still seeking to please human beings!" Hence, Paul expects the Galatians to answer the third question in the negative, saying in effect, "We agree, of course, that you are not seeking to please human beings!"

What response, then, does Paul expect to the first question, "Am I persuading human beings?" There are three major clues, all pointing to a negative answer for this question as well:

First, the initial question differs from the third only in that its verb is "persuade" (*peithô*) rather than "please" (*areskô*), and these verbs can have virtually the same force, since the orator often seeks to persuade his audience by pleasing them.[149] If Paul is not pleasing human beings, neither is he persuading them.

Second, the expression "to persuade the crowd" (e.g., *peithô ta plêthê* in Plato *Gorgias* 452E) was functioning in Paul's time as a definition of the art of rhetoric. As such, the formulation had come to have a decidedly negative connotation in the mouths of some serious thinkers, serving to characterize numerous traveling street preachers who merely flattered and entertained the crowds, hoping solely for popularity and financial gain (see, e.g., 1 Thess 2:4–6; 1 Cor 1:17; 2:1–2; 2 Cor 4:2). Although the Teachers are probably portraying Paul as just that sort of sophist, Paul expects the Galatians to know very well that the portrait does not fit him.

Third, at one other point in his letters Paul speaks of persuading human beings, 2 Cor 5:11. There, conceding that the expression can be used of him, he insists that it represents a merely human perception of his activity. What he really does as a preacher of the gospel is perceived only by God.

Given these three clues — the first two were available to the Galatians — we can be confident that Paul expects the Galatians to answer both the third and the first of his questions in the negative:

> No, of course you are seeking neither to please nor to persuade the crowds by the mere art of rhetoric![150]

What answer, however, does Paul want for the second question, "Am I persuading God?"[151]

Citing passages from Euripides, Plato, and others, H. D. Betz has argued that Paul expects a negative answer to this question no less than to the other two. Who is it, Betz asks, who seeks "to persuade the gods"? It is untrustworthy soothsayers and magicians. According to Betz, read in light of this tradition — one with which the Galatians may indeed have been familiar — the three questions prove to be Paul's way of saying that he is neither a crass rhetorician seeking to please the

---

[149]H. D. Betz 54 n103, 55 n111; B. J. Dodd, "Christ's Slave," 90.

[150]That Paul gives careful attention to the rhetorical structure of this letter itself is not at issue here. See Comment #8.

[151]Grammatically, this second question shares the verb given in the first; but in Greek, as in English, that fact does not necessitate that both questions receive the same answer.

crowds (questions 1 and 3) nor an irrational soothsayer blabbering in the direction of heaven (question 2).

For three reasons, however, one may be led to read the text differently:

(a) In the course of the present volume we will see that Paul has expressed in the letter's opening sentence an antinomy that proves central to the whole of the document. He says he did not receive his call to be an apostle

from human beings, but rather from Jesus Christ and God the Father.

In vv 11 and 12 he repeats this antinomy, insisting that he did not receive his gospel

from another human being, nor was I taught it; it came to me by God's apocalyptic revelation of Jesus Christ.

We have, then, to ask whether the context of v 10 will not have caused the Galatians to sense the first two rhetorical questions as antithetical:

Is it human beings I am persuading, or is it God?

(b) In the same vein one notes that, in the second half of v 10 itself, Paul speaks yet again of the antinomy with which he began the letter:

Do I seek merely to please human beings? If I were still doing that, I would not be a slave of Christ.

Will not the structure of v 10b have inclined the listeners to interpret the questions of v 10a as alternatives?

(c) There is a passage in 1 Thessalonians that offers close linguistic and conceptual parallels to Gal 1:10, and in it Paul clearly says that pleasing human beings and pleasing God constitute an antithesis:

. . . but just as we have been approved by God to be entrusted with the message of the gospel, even so we speak, not to please (*areskein*) human beings, but to please God who tests our hearts. As you know and as God is our witness, we never came with words of flattery or with a pretext for greed, nor did we seek praise from human beings, whether from you or from others (1 Thess 2:4–6).

Here we see that for Paul the antithesis to cheap rhetoric designed to please and flatter human beings is his apostolic labor which is directed toward pleasing God.[152]

---

[152] It is true, as we have seen, that the verb in Gal 1:10a is *peithô* (persuade). We have also noted, however, that this verb can have virtually the same force as *areskô* (please) in contexts drawing on the metaphors of rhetoric.

The three observations outweigh the suggestion that with the second of his rhetorical questions Paul intends to refer to an unworthy activity, that of seeking to persuade God by means of magic.[153] On the contrary, using in a positive sense the expression "to persuade [or please] God," Paul intends to elicit an affirmative answer to his second question, thus calling on the Galatians to say in effect,

> Free of the practice of trying to sway the crowds by pleasing them [negative answers to questions 1 and 3], you are, as we well know, intent on pleasing God [positive answer to question 2].

In a word, just as Paul has said in v 1 that the source of his apostolate is not any other human being, but rather God; and just as he will shortly say the same of his gospel (v 12), so in v 10 he says that the purpose of his preaching that gospel — and of his opposing its adulteration (vv 8–9) — is not to please any of his fellow human beings, but rather to please God.[154]

If I were still doing that. Lit. "If I were still pleasing human beings." As we have seen, the condition is contrary to fact. Paul categorically denies that he is a "human-pleaser" (*ho areskos*), for it is impossible simultaneously to be a human-pleaser and the obedient slave of Christ.

More is involved, however, than a timeless aphorism. With the expressions "Am I *now* engaged in . . ." and "If I were *still* doing that . . ." Paul draws a contrast between two parts of his own life. Referring to his earlier consumptive zeal to please his nomistic teachers (1:14), he implies that in that life he was, as Epictetus would have said, the slave of those he was trying to please (*Diss.* 4.1). Now, with the termination of that period, he has oriented himself solely to Christ, being in fact Christ's slave and therefore liberated from the impulse to please other human beings.

From Rom 1:1 we know that when Paul refers to himself with the expression "slave of Christ," he has in mind his own apostolate. In preaching the gospel to Gentiles Paul is precisely free of the attempt to please them. He now looks solely to Christ as his master; having what one might call a new "towardness," he lives "to the Lord."[155]

slave of Christ. Galatians is characterized by a number of emphatic references to slavery and freedom. Slavery was a central mark of the past, the period before the advent of Christ, the period that still exists anomalously as "the present evil age" (1:4). Freedom, by contrast, characterizes existence in Christ (4:3–7; 5:1). It presents a striking paradox, then, that Paul should here characterize himself, the messenger of the new liberation, as a slave. Equally striking is the paradox

---

[153] In his review of the commentary by H. D. Betz, Aune correctly points to instances of antithetical style in Galatians, 1:11–12; 2:6–7; 3:20 being among them (Review of H. D. Betz, 325).

[154] This verse played its role, along with others (notably in the Corinthian letters), in founding the patristic theory that the power of the Christian message lay in God, not in human eloquence. See Malherbe, "Seneca."

[155] Cf. Rom 14:4 and the dative "to the Lord" in Rom 14:6–8; also Gal 2:6; Phil 3:12–14.

created by 5:1 and 5:13. In the first Paul tells the Galatians never again to submit to the burden of slavery, whereas in the second he commands them to relate to one another in love by serving one another as slaves (5:13). The paradox involves three motifs: (a) Redemption from enslavement to the power of the present evil age — and from its representatives (2:5) — is not a matter of being liberated so as to strike out on one's own. Redemption happens when one is freed into a new slavery, slavery to Christ and to one's neighbor. (b) A slave derives power from association with his owner.[156] (c) Slavery to Christ involves freedom from all other "lords," including self-glorification (5:26).[157]

As the context shows, Paul sees his enslavement to Christ as his call to preach the gospel (1:11, 16). And it is solely as the slave of Christ that Paul is given the power to resist the temptation to preach a gospel pleasing to the crowd. See further Comments #22, #8, and #9.

11. *For.* Here, and in v 12, this word has its usual force as an inferential conjunction. Paul's freedom from the need to please his audience, his new identity as the slave of Christ, has its ground in the gospel itself.[158]

the gospel preached by me. When he is referring to the *true* gospel (cf. 2:5, 14), Paul uses in the main three expressions: "the gospel" (e.g., 1 Thess 2:4; Rom 1:16), "the gospel of God" (e.g., 1 Thess 2:2; Rom 1:1), and "the gospel of Christ" (e.g., 1 Thess 3:2; Rom 15:19). He can also speak of "my gospel" (Rom 2:16; 16:25), an expression similar to the one emphasized in the present verse. The personal dimension ("my") does not reflect possessiveness; it is here a locution necessitated by the fact that the Teachers have attacked Paul's preaching, characterizing it as a fundamental error. Given that attack, Paul takes two steps. First, he makes a few statements about his gospel (1:11–12); second, he traces the history that has been and is being caused to happen by the gospel's march into the world (1:13–3:5).

Following the Hebraic expression *biśśar bĕśōrâ*, Paul speaks literally of "the gospel gospeled by me" (cf. 1 Cor 15:1; 2 Cor 11:7; Rev 14:6).[159] It is an indication of the verbal character of the noun "gospel." The gospel *happens* as it is gospeled. See Comment #7.

I want you to know. Using the verb *gnôrizô*, "to make known" or "to reveal," Paul addresses the Galatians quite personally, as he did earlier in v 6: "I disclose to you." The expression is an epistolary cliché, but Paul's use of it may also reflect its employment in the LXX where it can even take God as its subject.[160] One thinks, for example, of Ps 15:11, "You have made known to me the path of life" (cf. Rom 9:22, 23).[161] The Galatians are already familiar with the content of

---

[156] See notably D. B. Martin, *Slavery*.
[157] Käsemann: "This is our redemption, that we belong to one God, and to no one else" (*Jesus*, 76). B. J. Dodd suggestively relates this motif to Paul's confrontation of Peter in the Antioch episode, 2:11–14 ("Christ's Slave," 100–103).
[158] Cf. Hester, "Structure," 225.
[159] Cf. Stuhlmacher, *Evangelium*, 265; idem, "Gospel."
[160] On the epistolary disclosure formula, see Introduction §10.
[161] Bultmann, "*ginôskô*," 718; Malherbe, "Seneca," 418.

Paul's gospel. Thus, in the sentences he is now introducing, Paul speaks discursively, responding to charges lodged against him by the Teachers.[162]

my brothers and sisters. In accordance with ancient usage Paul dictates here as elsewhere the single word *adelphoi*, lit. "brothers." But we can be confident that in the Galatian churches the women understood themselves to be fully addressed by this term. And that was what Paul intended. Indeed, as we shall see from 3:28, Paul is sure that in some real (but as yet dialectical) sense those who have been brought into the body of Christ have left behind the distinction between the sexes.[163] At the least, the disappearance of that distinction means that Paul can address the church as the eschatological family of God (cf. 4:6–7).

it is not what human beings normally have in mind when they speak of "good news." Lit. "it is not according to man" (*ouk estin kata anthrôpon*). Although mirror reading can be overdone, some of Paul's emphatic negatives constitute direct polemics with the Teachers, and the present clause is a case in point.[164] As we have already noted in considering v 10, the Teachers have probably charged Paul with trimming his message to the pleasures of the crowd for the sake of quick and easy success among the Gentiles. To some extent, the Teachers may very well take their bearings from a striking and impressive antinomy:

according to human beings / according to God's Law (cf. 1 Cor 9:8).

Whoever severs himself from God's revealed will, as God elected to make that will known at Sinai, falls clean out of touch with the divine orb and is therefore tossed to and fro by the impulses of human beings (contrast Gal 5:4). It follows, in the Teachers' view, that Paul's so-called gospel, having no anchor in God's Law, must be a message "according to human beings."[165]

It is a charge Paul denies categorically, stating the ground of his denial in v 12. Before we attend to that ground, however, we pause for a moment over the matter of epistemology. When Paul says that his gospel is not what human beings normally have in mind when they speak of "good news," he also says clearly enough that his gospel effects an epistemological crisis. What human beings call good news cannot serve as the norm for assessing the glad tiding of Christ, even — or should one say especially — if they discern their good news on the basis of the Law![166] See Comments #3 and #9.

12. *For I did not receive it from another human being, nor was I taught it.* Here, as in v 11, the word *gar*, "for," has its full force as an inferential conjunction. Paul

---

[162] In all four instances of Paul's saying "I disclose to you (plural)" the apostle addresses a situation in which the gospel itself is at stake (Gal 1:11; 1 Cor 12:3; 15:1; 2 Cor 8:1). Cf. Stuhlmacher, *Evangelium*, 69–70.

[163] See Comments #40 and #41; Meeks, "Androgyne."

[164] See Barclay, "Mirror-Reading"; Sumney, *Opponents*. See also reviews of Sumney: *CBQ* 54 (1992) 175–177 (Tyler); *JBL* 111 (1992) 347–350 (Hafemann).

[165] See Marcus, "Scripture and Tradition in Mark 7," especially the interpretation of *T. Asher* 7:5 and *T. Levi* 14:4–8.

[166] See J. L. Martyn, *Issues*, 89–110, 209–229.

now states the ground on which he knows, and wishes the Galatians to know, that his gospel is not to be measured by human norms of what might constitute good news. This ground involves an antinomy familiar to us from 1:1, "I did not receive the gospel from another human being, nor was I taught it." On the contrary, "it came to me by God's apocalyptic revelation of Jesus Christ."[167]

In stating the negative part of this argument, Paul employs a technical expression. The words

> to receive (tradition) from someone
> *paralambanô (paradosin) para tinos,*

while attested in Greek writings (e.g., Plato *Philebus* 16c), constitute a literal rendering of the first half of a firmly set Hebrew formula:

> to receive (tradition) from someone and
> to hand (it) on to someone else
> *qibbēl min . . . ûmāsar lĕ . . .*

One notes, for example, the role of this formula in *m. 'Abot* 1:1:

> Moses received the law from Sinai, and he handed it down to Joshua, and Joshua to the elders [the Judges], and the elders to the prophets [Samuel to Malachi], and the prophets handed it down to the men of the Great Assembly [the sages of Ezra's time].

Of course the Galatians will not have known that Mishnaic tractate; but, especially given Paul's supplementary clause, "nor was I taught it," they will have sensed that he has selected the key expression of the traditioning process in order to say with maximum emphasis:

> I did not receive the gospel in a line of tradition![168]

In the first instance, as we have seen, this emphatic clause clearly provides the basis for the preceding sentence. Paul's gospel is not subject to measurement by human norms (v 11) because he did not receive it from a human being in a line of tradition (v 12). Several problems arise, however, not least when one compares this assertion with the one Paul has just made in v 9, for there he indicates that the Galatians are to remain with the gospel tradition he delivered to them. See Comment #10.

it came to me. Paul ends the sentence with a prepositional phrase, "by God's

---

[167] Baarda, "Openbaring," reads v 12a–b as a parenthesis, thus finding the antithetical contrast (*alla*) in vv 11d and 12d. The suggestion would be stronger were the preposition in v 11d *apo, ek,* or *dia.* See also Lyons, *Autobiography,* 155.

[168] Cf. Keck, "Thinker," 28.

apocalyptic revelation of Jesus Christ," not with a clause having its own verb. He means to carry over one of the previous verbs, "receive" or "taught"; or he assumes the simple "came."

by God's apocalyptic revelation of Jesus Christ. This prepositional phrase — lit. "by apocalypse of Jesus Christ" — poses two interrelated translation problems, both having to do with the verbal noun *apokalypsis:* (a) How are we to render the word itself, and (b) how are we to understand the following genitive construction *Iêsou Christou,* "of Jesus Christ"?

(a) There is a long tradition for translating the word *apokalypsis* as "revelation," the verbal thought being that, at a certain juncture, something (or someone) previously hidden is unveiled (Latin, *revelo*). The notion of unveiling is certainly possible in the present instance, especially if one assumes that Jesus Christ is the subject of the revealing action and the gospel is the object:

> I did not receive the gospel from another human being, nor was I taught it; on the contrary, it came to me when Jesus Christ unveiled it to me (cf. 1 Cor 2:7–10; Rom 16:25–26; Col 1:26; Rev 1:1).

In considering apocalyptic theology in Galatians (Comment #3), however, we have seen that the letter contains several passages in which the thought of an unveiling is basically qualified by the assertion that apocalypse is the *invasive* act that was carried out by God when he sent Christ and Christ's Spirit into the world and into human hearts (3:23; 4:4, 6).[169] Could the thought of an invasive act on God's part be the basic motif in the present verse? That question brings us to the second translation issue.

(b) With the genitive construction "of Jesus Christ," does Paul intend to refer to an apocalyptic act carried out by Christ or to an act done to Christ? The major clue emerges a few sentences later in v 16, for there Paul links his gospel to the event of apocalypse just as he does in v 12:

> So when it pleased him [God] apocalyptically to reveal his Son to me, in order that I might preach him among the Gentiles, I immediately kept to myself . . .

In this sentence there is no syntactical ambiguity. God is the subject of the verb *apokalyptô,* being the actor who carried out the invasive revealing. Christ is the object of God's revelatory act. And Paul's receipt of the gospel is the result. If v 12 is explicated in v 16, as seems likely, then in both of these verses Paul refers to God's act of invasively revealing Christ to him. It was in that event that Paul received the gospel he preaches to the Gentiles. In a word, the gospel *happened* to Paul when God stepped on the scene, invading his life in Christ (Comments #7 and #10).

---

[169]The family of words built on the stem *phaner,* "make visible," is absent from Galatians.

COMMENT #8
RHETORIC AND THE SERVICE OF GOD

In Gal 1:10, using an expression that is virtually a definition of rhetoric, Paul denies with great emphasis that, in preaching the gospel, he is seeking to persuade human beings (*anthrôpous peithô*).[170] At numerous junctures, however, the letter shows us an author who is a rather sophisticated rhetorician (Introduction §10). Is the emphatic denial in 1:10, then, nothing more than an example of the widespread ploy in which the rhetorician denies that he is practicing the art of rhetoric? A number of interpreters have thought so.

Before reaching that conclusion, however, one does well to consider another question: Does Paul deny involvement in the art of persuasion in order to affirm his involvement in something else, perhaps in something he considers quite distinct from persuasion? That proves to be a significant question. For, returning to the text, one sees Paul's insistence that the reason for his not being a rhetorician, focused on the task of persuading others, lies in his being instead a slave of Christ.

We have here, in fact, a traditional pattern. Before and during Paul's time, the rejection of rhetoric is often accompanied by a contrasting affirmation of something else. In the *Gorgias*, for example, Plato has Socrates place rhetoric on a very low plane. It is nothing other than the art by which the rhetorically talented and often ignorant speaker quickly persuades the rhetorically seduceable and largely ignorant crowd. In place of rhetoric, then, Plato's Socrates exalts teaching, for, unlike rhetoric, teaching is designed patiently to nurture the hearers' ability to discern the truth itself in matters of right and wrong.[171] Similarly, Paul's contemporary Philo, sharing Plato's portrait of rhetoric in the *Gorgias*, affirms in its place what he considers to be the persuasion that comes from the spirit of God. When Abraham, for example, was possessed by God's spirit, his voice was invested with true persuasiveness and his hearers were given understanding (*de Virt.* 217).[172]

The pattern of rejecting rhetoric in favor of something else is, then, a tradition used by Paul, as by Philo, in a distinctly theological way. In the rhetorical questions of 1:10 Paul makes affirmative statements about God, about Christ, and about the gospel of Christ. He means to say, that is, that, in making him Christ's slave, God called him to preach the gospel of Christ to Gentiles (1:16), while

---

[170]The classic definition of rhetoric appears in Plato's *Gorgias*; see also H. D. Betz 54 n103. In writing to his Corinthian church Paul later repeats his denial that he is a rhetorician and that his gospel is an instance of rhetoric (1 Cor 2:4; cf. Col 2:4). See also, however, 2 Cor 5:11.

[171]In the *Gorgias*, rhetoric proves to be an unworthy branch of flattery, producing unreflective belief (*peithous . . . pisteutikês*). It is not directed toward the time-consuming goal of instruction in the matter of right and wrong (*ou didaskalikês peri to dikaion te kai adikon*), but simply toward persuasion of the crowd on whatever subject is at hand (454E–455A). Cf. Plato *Apology* 17A–18A.

[172]In light of the portrait of rhetoric in the *Gorgias*, it is important to add that Plato could speak of rhetoric being used "in a manner which will be acceptable to God" (*Phaedrus*). In reading Augustine one can pursue a distinction between mere instruction and the affecting power of the Spirit. See Meyer, "Letter."

denying him the task of persuading the very Gentiles to whom he preaches the gospel! Clearly more is involved than a negative portrait of a rhetorician. Paul combines the assertion of gospel-mission with the denial of gospel-persuasion, and that combination causes one to ask what Paul is saying about *the gospel* God has called him to preach.

The problem, moreover, is compounded when one recalls, as noted earlier, that having issued his assertion and his denial, Paul proceeds in this letter itself to employ various rhetorical forms, designed, one would suppose, to persuade the Galatians. With theological rigor, then, we have to ask — in the next Comment — what Paul can actually mean when he says that his gospel is preached apart from attempts to persuade.

COMMENT #9
THE GOSPEL, HUMAN NORMS OF JUDGMENT, AND THE NATURE OF EVANGELICAL ARGUMENT

How can Paul affirm as his God-given vocation the preaching of the gospel to the Gentiles, yet say that that very vocation precludes all attempts to persuade? In fact, this paradox stands on two grounds, both having to do with the character of Paul's message.

First, in 1:11 Paul says that the gospel he preaches is not "what human beings normally have in mind when they speak of 'good news.'" That statement erects a clear roadblock to the normal use of rhetoric. For the rhetorician, knowing that both he and his hearers are human beings, builds his argument — to a large extent — on the basis of various cognitive and emotional elements that are already present in the minds and hearts of his hearers. All people, for example, have notions of justice, of guilt and innocence, of unrighteousness and righteousness, and so on. Paul himself knows that his hearers already have such ideas (see Comment #28). Were he to take these notions and ideas as his point of departure, he could indeed speak in a persuasive way, causing his auditors to say, "Yes, that makes sense."

This, however, Paul cannot do, for the foundation of his message is something that is not already present in the minds and hearts of his hearers. He does not and cannot build his sermon on the basis of his hearers' notions and ideas, for, to repeat his own words, what human beings have in mind when they speak of "good news" is not the gospel. In short, what human beings already have in their minds cannot serve as the point of departure from which one can book a through train to the gospel. And that fact necessarily precludes one of the basic stratagems normally used in the art of persuasion.

Second, there is the matter of the genesis of faith. Although Paul is consistent in saying that God called him to preach the gospel to Gentiles (1:16), he is equally consistent in his certainty that it is not his powers of persuasion that elicit faith (1 Cor 2:4). The power to kindle faith resides solely with God's gospel (Gal 3:2; Rom 1:16–17), and that gospel does not make sense. It is, in fact, "a stumbling block to Jews and foolishness to Gentiles" (1 Cor 1:23). But that means that the gospel Paul preaches — bringing its own criteria of perception and plausibility[173] — is not and cannot be a message by which he seeks in the rhetorical sense to persuade.[174]

With these two observations we begin to understand Paul's insistence that, in preaching the gospel, he is not a rhetorician. We still have to face the fact, however, that in composing his letter to the Galatians (the same can be said of his other letters) Paul employs various rhetorical stratagems. He formulates arguments.[175] We return, then, to our earlier question. How are we to explain the presence in the letter of rhetorical forms?

One might suggest that Paul distinguishes an initial and nonrhetorical proclamation of the gospel from a later and rhetorically sophisticated formulation of a written argument addressed to persons who are already Christians. In short, does Paul consider rhetoric to be both useful and appropriate when the communication is being carried out within the bosom of the church? And can we say, then, that Paul considers the notions put into the Galatians' heads by the Teachers to be a useful argumentative point of departure, being essentially different from the notions the Galatians held when he first came to them? Does he therefore accept the Teachers' questions and their basic frame of reference, in order to formulate a rhetorically effective counterargument, correcting them on their own ground? For example, does he take the Teachers' presentation of "covenantal nomism" as his own fundamental category, in order to correct the Teachers' too-narrow view of it?[176]

In fact, every one of these questions must be answered in the negative. There is ample evidence that Paul does not allow the Teachers' theology to provide the point of departure and thus the basis for his argument. For he does not consider their notions to be in any significant degree different from the notions the Galatians had when he first came to them (see Gal 4:8–9 and Comment #41).[177] The presence of rhetorical forms in Galatians — in spite of the denial of 1:10 — cannot be explained merely as the result of the letter's being an argument.

---

[173] Paul would have agreed with Philo that divine-human communication involves a change both in the mediator of God's message (whether patriarch or apostle) and in the hearers of it (Philo *de Vita Mos.* 2.70; *de Virt.* 217). For, as noted above, neither to the apostle nor to his audience is the gospel explicable by means of norms and criteria already in their minds.

[174] As we have noted in the Introduction (§10), for Paul the gospel is not and can never be subject to ratiocinative criteria that have been developed apart from it. It is for this reason that, in his initial proclamation, Paul cannot take as the foundation of his rhetoric substantive presuppositions he knows to be already present in the minds of his hearers. He does not speak, however, "in tongues" (1 Cor 14:2). In his communication he employs the everyday Greek of the city streets, observing, for the most part, the normal rules of grammar, and using some of the argumentative forms we know to have been taught by the rhetoricians of his day.

[175] See Siegert, *Argumentation*.

[176] The expression "covenantal nomism" is drawn from E. P. Sanders, *Palestinian Judaism.* Cf. Dunn, "Theology"; Comment #37.

[177] As we will see in a careful reading of Galatians 4, 5, and 6, Paul considers the Law itself to be qualitatively different from, say, the religion of the Great Mother (Comments #45 and #48). It cannot serve, however, as the point of departure for the proclamation of the gospel. See J. L. Martyn, *Issues,* 209–229.

We are left, then, with the simple and profound fact that, in writing this letter, Paul begins his evangelical argument precisely where he began his initial proclamation among the Galatians, namely at the center of his gospel, Christ's faithful death and resurrection in our behalf (1:1, 4; 2:26; 3:1; etc.). From that center — which he knows to be the divine and therefore nonrhetorical point of departure — Paul unfolds his argument in ways that make effective rhetorical contact, linguistic and conceptual, with the Teachers' message, thus modulating the terms of argument onto a radically new level of discourse consonant with his different point of departure. And he does all of this, in order to arrive at a conclusion that ultimately replaces the Teachers' themes with those of the true gospel, not simply by contradicting the Teachers, properly speaking, but rather by constructing an argument that is composed, as it were, on a radically different musical scale (see again Comment #41).

Paul is entirely in earnest, then, with what he says in 1:10. Both in his original oral proclamation and in his letter, he understands himself to be a slave of Christ rather than a rhetorician who is seeking to persuade those to whom he speaks. For, as we have seen, the power to persuade — specifically the power to elicit faith — resides in the glad tiding of Christ's death in our behalf, and only in that glad tiding (3:2; Comment #31). When this gospel is proclaimed, it is not Paul, but rather God, who calls and re-calls churches into existence as his new creation (1:6; 6:15).[178]

In writing this letter, therefore, Paul is free to use all the rhetorical skill he can muster, taking every rhetorical stratagem captive to Christ, so as to repreach the gospel itself in the form of an evangelical argument (cf. 2 Cor 10:5). But he has this freedom for two reasons. First, he can use his rhetorical skill as though not using it (1 Cor 7:29–31), because, precisely in the polemical situation into which the Teachers' work has thrown him, he finds that the gospel liberates him from the game one might call "my rhetoric versus your rhetoric." And, second, Paul's rhetorical freedom comes quite specifically from the cross of Christ. That is to say, consistently holding the cross as his point of departure, Paul does not suffer under the illusion that it is his rhetorical skill that elicits faith. He knows, on the contrary, that, when he first came to the Galatians, it was God who kindled their faith via the event of the oral gospel, and — with most of his mind — he is confident that God will rekindle the Galatians' faith via the evangelical argument of the letter (note the term *theodidaktoi*, "ones taught by God," in 1 Thess 4:9).

COMMENT #10
THE GOSPEL, TRADITION, AND APOCALYPSE

In the short span of 1:8–12 Paul speaks about the gospel in two different ways. First, calling on God to place the Teachers under a curse, he refers in vv 8–9 to

---

[178]Crucial, therefore, is Paul's understanding of the difference between the antinomies God causes to be fundamental to his new creation — for example, the Spirit versus the Flesh; 5:17 (Comment #49) — and simple rhetorical antitheses. Rhetorical analysis may identify as an antithesis Paul's reference in 3:2 to the message that elicits faith versus observance of the Law. Paul understands that opposition to be the work of God in Christ, and

the true gospel as *tradition,* connecting the gospel with the verb *paralambanô,* "to receive":

> . . . if someone is preaching to you a gospel contrary to the one you originally *received* (from me), let him stand under God's curse (v 9b).

In v 12, however, he speaks of the gospel as *apocalyptic event,* saying indeed that its apocalyptic identity is antithetical to its being a tradition:

> . . . I did not *receive* it from another human being, nor was I taught it; it came to me by God's apocalyptic revelation of Jesus Christ.

True, in v 9 Paul refers to the gospel the Galatians received *from* him, while in v 12 he speaks of the gospel's coming *to* him. Interpreters have nevertheless been correct in sensing a significant tension between these two ways of referring to the gospel, especially in light of the fact that in 1 Cor 15:1–3 Paul uses the full form of the traditioning language of Gal 1:9, declaring *himself* to have been a link in a *line* of gospel tradition that reached from traditioners *before* him to the Corinthians *after* him. The three passages call for comparison:

The Gospel as Tradition

Gal 1:8–9	1 Cor 15:1–3
. . . if someone should preach to you a gospel contrary to the gospel *I preached to you,* let him stand under God's curse. As I have said before, I say now once again, if someone is preaching to you a gospel contrary to the one *you originally received,* let him stand under God's curse.	For I make known to you, brothers and sisters, the gospel *I preached to you* . . . I handed over to you . . . that which *I also received* . . .

The Gospel as the Apocalyptic Event, Not as a Tradition

Gal 1:11–12

For I make known to you, brothers and sisters, the gospel preached by me . . .

I *did not receive* it from another human being, nor was I taught it; it came to me by God's apocalyptic revelation of Jesus Christ.

---

thus an apocalyptic antinomy. See Comments #31 and #51; Glossary; Morgan, *Nature,* 34–35.

The tensions between Gal 1:12 and 1 Cor 15:1–3 have occasioned a large litera-ture.[179] One does well, however, to take one's initial bearings in the matter from the problem posed by the two passages in Galatians itself. How can Paul say in one breath that the Galatians received the gospel from him in a form of tradition (v 9), whereas he himself did not receive it in that way (v 12)? Several points stand out:

(1) Did Paul know nothing of the gospel until it happened to him in God's revelation of Christ to him? We can be sure that he knew a considerable amount about it, for the gospel was the cause of his persecuting the church. Here we see exposed the difference between the gospel as tradition and the gospel as event. In or near Damascus God caused the traditioned gospel (the gospel Paul found odious) to happen to Paul as (liberating) apocalypse (1:15–17).

(2) When the gospel *happened* to him as event, Paul saw a reversal of the order of tradition and apocalypse. Specifically, he sensed some degree of analogy between himself and the inaugural step in a traditioning line, because the gospel happened to him from its author, God, not from another human being. One thinks of the picture of Moses in the opening sentence of *m. 'Abot*, cited above in the Note on 1:12.[180] Like Moses, Paul received the message directly *from God*; then, passed along *by him* to others, it became after him a tradition. In a word, the gospel is both divine apocalypse (v 12) and after that tradition (v 9).

(3) That is far from being the whole of the matter, however, as one might sense from the fact that, although Paul can compare himself to the prophets Jeremiah and Isaiah (1:15), he never connects himself in any way with Moses. When we look ahead to the revelatory history Paul narrates in 1:13–2:21, we see that the preceding point must be immediately qualified. The gospel does not begin as divine apocalypse, thereafter becoming tradition *instead*.[181] Indeed, Paul's ac-count of the history created by the gospel does not even support the thesis that the gospel involves in the strict sense a dialectic between apocalypse and tradition, as though these formed — in relationship to one another — the foundation of the church. On the contrary, in his historical narrative Paul shows that the gospel marches through the world under the banner of apocalypse and not under the constraints of tradition (1:12; 1:16–17; 2:2; 2:5–6; 2:14). As the gospel moves into the whole of the world, it subjects tradition to itself; it does not subject itself to tradition.

(4) True enough, as we have seen, for the Galatians there is a gospel tradition that began with Paul's proclamation to them (1:8–9). It had a definite linguistic form; Paul knows what that form was, as do the Galatians; he can therefore refer back to it (3:1; cf. 1 Cor 15:1–3). Yet, as we have also seen, the gospel did not come to Paul himself as tradition (1:12); and that fact *permanently* affects his understanding of it. When — at the Jerusalem conference — he finds the gospel

---

[179]In addition to commentaries on Galatians and 1 Corinthians, see the excursus in H. D. Betz (64–66); Cerfaux, "tradition"; Wegenast, *Tradition*; Lührmann, *Offenbarungsver-ständnis*; Stuhlmacher, *Evangelium*; Winger, "Tradition."

[180]Cf. A. I. Baumgarten, "*Paradosis*."

[181]One thinks of the explicit denial in the Passover Haggadah that the exodus is a merely past event. See Davies, *Paul*, 102–104.

under attack, he marshals his own witness under the banner of apocalypse, not under the banner of tradition (2:2), for his apocalyptic gospel cannot be measured by tradition.

(5) It cannot be measured by any tradition, for at every juncture without exception apocalypse takes primacy over tradition. In his account of the Jerusalem conference (2:1–10) Paul says both that his participation was an apocalyptic matter (2:2) and that he categorically rejected the attempt of the False Brothers to subject "the truth of the gospel" to their tradition. But he says that he maintained an equally apocalyptic stance vis-à-vis the Jerusalem leaders. When they shook hands with him, he did not understand them to have approved his gospel, as though these leaders were the guardians of a primal and normative gospel tradition that enjoyed primacy over apocalypse. Rather, having placed the whole of his account under the banner of God's apocalypse (2:2), Paul uses verbs of perception to say with emphasis that *the* issue was whether the leaders would *see* God's work among the Gentiles or not. He is happy to report that the task God gave him in God's apocalypse to him of Jesus Christ — the task of preaching the gospel to Gentiles without circumcision — was something the leaders "saw clearly" (v 7), thus "coming to perceive the grace" of God in his work (v 9). In this narrative Paul shows tradition coming into line with apocalypse, not apocalypse coming into line with tradition.

(6) The thrust of Paul's account of the Jerusalem meeting is characteristic of the whole of Galatians. As we have noted in Comment #7, Paul insists throughout that the gospel was and is God's immediate word — the word God himself speaks in the present moment — and this fact guards the gospel from ever becoming in its heart a tradition. At stake, one might say, is the matter of the gospel's *permanent* origin. That origin is *and remains* God himself, not any ecclesiastical group wherever located. The gospel can never be turned, therefore, into a tradition as distinct from an immediate apocalypse.[182]

1:13–16 PAUL'S APOSTOLIC CALL

TRANSLATION

1:13. I can give the grounds for that assertion by tracing God's way with me. You have already heard some things about my past, the course and nature of my life when I lived in the religion of Judaism. You know that for some time

---

[182]Nor can the gospel be identified as *an* apocalyptic revelation, one instance of a genus of which there are other examples. The result is an antinomy between *the* apocalypse *of Christ* and religion. God has stepped on the scene — and continues to step on the scene — not in religious tradition, but rather in *the event,* the cross/resurrection of his Son. See Introduction §17.

I persecuted the church of God to an extreme degree; I even had it as my goal to destroy it entirely. 14. And my doing that sprang from the fact that in regard to matters of the Jewish religion I outstripped many of my fellows, being far more zealous than they for the traditions handed down from my forefathers. 15. But all of that came to an end. God had in fact singled me out even before I was born, and had called me in his grace. So when it pleased him 16. apocalyptically to reveal his Son to me, in order that I might preach him among the Gentiles, I immediately kept to myself, not asking advice from anyone.

LITERARY STRUCTURE AND SYNOPSIS

Having stated in 1:11–12 the initial thesis of his letter, Paul begins his demonstration of that thesis with a narrative (1:13–2:14), completing the demonstration with the ratiocinative argument of 2:15–21. Both in the thesis and in the demonstration, Paul allows a certain alternation between negative and positive, thus both refuting charges laid against him by the Teachers and repreaching the gospel:

Thesis (1:11–12)

Negative: the gospel I preach is not what human beings normally have in mind when they speak of "good news";
Negative: for I did not receive it from another human being;
Negative: nor was I taught it;
Positive: it came to me by God's apocalyptic revelation of Jesus Christ.

Demonstration (1:13–2:21)

Positive (1:13–16): Using a reference to his life in the religion of Judaism as a foil focused on the process of tradition taught by one human being to another (1:13–14), Paul speaks directly of the time at which it pleased God apocalyptically to reveal his Son to him, so that he might preach this Son among the Gentiles (1:15–16).
Negative (1:17–24): Before continuing to explicate that positive reference to his vocation, Paul develops the negative clauses of his thesis in such a way as to refute the Teachers' charge that he is an unfaithful student of the Jerusalem apostles: "Contrary to what the Teachers say, I was not taught the gospel, for I was constantly at a great distance from Jerusalem, going there in fact only once for a brief and personal visit with Peter."
Positive (2:1–10): Paul then returns to the positive part of the thesis, while retaining a warning note drawn from his refutation of the Teachers. Stating that he is referring to an apocalyptic development (2:2), Paul gives an account of a conference in which the truth of the gospel was victorious over its enemies: In spite of the efforts of the False Brothers to terminate his circumcision-free mission, the gospel he preached to the Gentiles was perceived by the Jerusalem leaders to be one of the two lines of God's salvific activity in the world.

Positive (2:11–14): He then recounts an event in the life of the Antioch church, in which the truth of the gospel was again at stake, making it necessary for him to speak sharply to Peter in the presence of the whole of that church. *Positive* (2:15–21): Finally, silent about his political defeat in Antioch, Paul develops the speech he made on that earlier occasion into a complex ratiocinative argument that he now directs offensively to the Teachers in Galatia.

In 1:13–2:14 Paul uses narrative form to tell four stories (see also Literary Structure and Synopsis for 1:17–24). The initial story, 1:13–16, is certainly not the only part of the connected narrative that the Galatians have already heard in some form, but it is the place at which Paul chooses to begin. For it displays one of Paul's major points: the contrast between the traditional/human religion of the Teachers and apocalyptic vocation at the hands of God.

NOTES

1:13. *I can give the grounds for that assertion by tracing God's way with me.* These words are intended to convey the full force in the present instance of the causal conjunction *gar,* "for," coupled with the epistolary disclosure formula, "you have heard." The word "for" is a term Paul has now used four times in as many verses (if we accept it as original in v 11). Here it introduces not only a sentence, as in vv 10, 11, 12, but also a series of paragraphs stretching all the way to 2:21. That is to say, Paul now gives the grounds for the thesis statements of 1:11–12 by providing an historical narrative of some length, climaxed by the argument of 2:15–21. Hence the need for the paraphrastic translation of the single word *gar.*

You have already heard. This is Paul's second use of a disclosure formula (cf. v 11). Here it is surely to be taken literally. We do not know when or even from whom the Galatians have heard of Paul's life prior to his call. From Galatians itself (1:22–23) we can see that already in Paul's own time stories about him began to enjoy circulation among members of the Jewish-Christian churches of Judea; and we know from second-century sources that such accounts were embroidered by anti-Paulinists of later times.[183] Thus, it is quite possible that the Teachers made remarks to the Galatians about Paul's pre-Christian activity, accenting perhaps his persecution of the church. In his initial preaching to Gentiles — that is to say, in all of his initial preaching (2:7, 9) — Paul is unlikely to have spoken in any detail of his life as a Jew or even of Judaism itself.

my past. Paul uses the first of two temporal particles by which he distinguishes from one another his former life and the life to which God has called him in Christ. In the present verse the temporal particle is *pote,* "formerly," whereas in v 15, beginning to speak of his life after his call, he will use the expression *hote de* (rendered below "But all of that came to an end"). By this temporal distinction does Paul mean to suggest that the eschatological dualism between "the present evil age" (1:4) and "the new creation" (6:15) has a correspondence to two periods

---

[183] Note Peter's reference to "the man who is my enemy" in *Ep. Pet. Jas.* 2:3 (HS 2.112).

in his own life? And if he does think of such a correspondence, what understanding does he now have of Judaism? See Comment #13 and Introduction §17.

in the religion of Judaism. The term *Ioudaïsmos,* "Judaism," was coined in the Hellenistic period to refer to the religion of the Jews as distinct from the religions of other peoples (e.g., 2 Macc 2:21; 8:1). In the NT it occurs only in Gal 1:13 and 14. The cognate expressions *Ioudaïzein* and *Ioudaïkôs zên,* both of which mean to live in a Jewish manner, are also found — in the NT — only in Galatians (2:14). Galatians is thus the letter in which Paul speaks directly and explicitly and repeatedly about Judaism as a *religion.* With these references, then, Paul clearly indicates that he cannot give an account of the path along which God has now led him without addressing the issue of religion.[184] See again Comment #13 and Introduction §17.

for some time I persecuted the church of God to an extreme degree; I even had it as my goal to destroy it entirely. The verbs *ediôkon,* "I persecuted," and *eporthoun,* "I tried to destroy," are both in the imperfect tense, the first pointing to continuance of action in the past, the second denoting volitional intention.[185] Paul's activity as a persecutor extended over some period of time, and by that activity he intended to exterminate the church.[186] Both here and in 1:23 an early scribe altered "tried to destroy" into "fought against," doubtless feeling the stronger expression to be an inappropriately harsh portrayal of the intentions of "the holy apostle." In fact, in Galatians Paul's extremely zealous persecution of the church is the initial item that comes to his mind when he thinks of his former life as an intensely observant Jew (cf. 1 Cor 15:9; Phil 3:6).

the church of God. The word *ekklêsia,* "congregation," "assembly," "church," is the term the early Christian community used to designate itself in the Greek language. For three reasons — explicated in Comments #12, #37, and #52 — Paul uses here the full expression "the church *of God.*" (a) That was a locution used by members of the church who spoke Aramaic and/or Hebrew, the church Paul persecuted. They understood themselves to be the new "congregation of Yahweh" (*qĕhal yahweh*; Deut 23:2 etc.).[187] (b) Paul himself took over the expression to refer to the church as a fundamentally political entity, God's expanding beachhead in the world, and that is a matter he wishes to emphasize in writing to the Galatians. (c) In the present instance he also wants to accent the fact that his persecuting activity was an act taken in conflict against God himself.

14. *And my doing that sprang from the fact.* Paul says simply, "and in regard to matters of the Jewish religion I outstripped many of my fellows," thus giving no

---

[184]Cf. Hengel, *The Pre-Christian Paul.*
[185]Conative imperfect, BDF §326; MT 65. As is indicated in Gal 1:13c, in Gal 1:23, and in Acts 9:21, the verb *porthein* seems to have been used in *reports about* Paul's activity as a persecutor. When not reflecting reports about himself, Paul employs the verb *diôkein* (Phil 3:6; 1 Cor 15:9). In Gal 1:13, then, he combines the two verbs.
[186]Hultgren, "Translating," argues that the expression *kath hyperbolên* "expresses Paul's intensity of zeal [not his intensity of violence] in persecution." But the connection between the Law and violence portrayed in 3:13, for example, suggests otherwise. See now Hamerton-Kelly, *Violence.*
[187]See K. L. Schmidt, "*kaleô,*" 527–529.

syntactical indication of the relationship between this clause and the preceding one. It is almost certainly an instance of subordinating parataxis, typical of Semitic syntax.[188] And while the Galatians probably had no formal knowledge of such Semitic constructions, they will surely have sensed that Paul now speaks of a cause for his intense desire to eradicate the church. That cause was his zeal for the Law. He makes exactly the same causal connection in Phil 3:6: ". . . as regards zeal (for the Law) a persecutor of the church." Precisely how Paul's zeal for the Law led him to persecute the church is a matter discussed in Comment #12.

far more zealous. Does Paul hint that he belonged to the political party of the Zealots? Hardly! He simply means to say that, as a Pharisee of the Diaspora (Phil 3:5), his ardent devotion to the traditions of the Law knew no limit, being the form of his worship of God. In this regard he was almost certainly conscious of standing in the noble tradition of several pious Israelites: Phinehas, whose zeal for God saved Israel from a plague related to idolatry (Num 25:6–13); Elijah (Sir 48:1–2); Mattathias (1 Macc 2:23–26); and so on (cf. 1QH 14:13–15).

The Galatians will not have failed to see that the picture Paul paints of himself prior to his call by God is similar to the picture the Teachers are now presenting of themselves. Paul is saying that, from the course of his own life, he himself is well acquainted with the most intense devotion to the Law. And he is adding that, in his case, that nomistic devotion led him to persecute *God's* church, something the Teachers are doing in their own way at the present time (4:29).

the traditions handed down from my forefathers. This is one of the typical expressions by which virtually any Jew of the time referred to the Law, the venerable tradition studied under the guidance of senior scholars. The Law in which Paul was so thoroughly educated was the Law that contained two voices not yet differentiated from one another by Christ (Comment #48). Given Paul's emphasis on apocalypse in v 16 as the termination of the tradition-oriented course of his life (vv 13–14), the undifferentiated Law to which he was so zealously devoted turns out here to be tradition as distinguished from apocalyptic revelation, thus lying on the human side of the divine/human antinomy. For in speaking of these venerable ancestral traditions, Paul gives no indication that they have their origin in a revelatory act of God (contrast *m. 'Abot* 1:1, cited in the Note on 1:12).

15. *But all of that came to an end.* With the expression *hote de* Paul looks back to the word *pote* in v 13. In Comment #13 we will find strong reasons for sensing here an emphatic *contrast* between the past and the present in Paul's own life. The past was characterized by the life of sincere nomistic observance described in the sentence of vv 13 and 14. The present is seen in the life of apostolic preaching to which God has now called Paul, and which he begins to sketch in the sentence of vv 15, 16, and 17. Between the two, there lay, Paul says, a striking caesura.

God had in fact singled me out even before I was born, and had called me in his grace. In what we have as vv 15, 16, and 17 Paul dictates a single sentence, somewhat long and complex, virtually impossible to render into English without making divisions. The basic structure is clear: A subordinate clause — "So when it

---

[188] K. Beyer, *Semitische Syntax*, 271–281.

pleased him to reveal his Son to me" — is followed by the main clause — "I immediately kept to myself, asking advice from no one." It is remarkable that Paul should refer to his revelatory call in a subordinate clause, giving the main clause to the matter of his itinerary. This surprising syntax forecasts the major concern that will emerge in the travelogue of 1:17–24. Beginning with the major clause — "I immediately kept to myself" — Paul is intent on responding to the Teachers' charge that, having gone to Jerusalem to get the true gospel from the Jerusalem apostles, he later adulterated it for the sake of quick and easy success as a pseudo-evangelist among the Gentiles.

The first clause of the sentence plays, however, a weighty role in Paul's tracing of God's way with him, for, in referring to God, Paul uses two substantive participles, each modified by a prepositional phrase: God is

the one who singled me out (participle)
even before I was born;

God is also

the one who called me (participle)
in his grace.

As is usual in such constructions, the two participles illuminate one another, as do the two prepositional phrases. Both the singling out and the calling speak of God's election, and both speak to the question of God's identity. By electing Paul to carry the gospel of his Son to the Gentiles, and by enacting that election in contrast to Paul's nomistic zeal, God has newly identified himself to Paul as the Father of Jesus Christ.[189]

One may still ask whether Paul thinks of God's singling out and God's calling as distinguishable *stages* in his vocation (so H. D. Betz). This question is best attacked by noting the degree to which Paul is consciously drawing on the traditions about the calls of the classical prophets of ancient Israel. He clearly has in mind the call of Jeremiah:

The word of Yahweh came to me, thus:
"Before I had formed you in the womb I chose you;
Before you were born I set you apart,
and appointed you prophet to the nations" (Jer 1:4–5).

When Paul uses the Greek word *aphorizō* to identify God as the one who singled him out, he is probably borrowing from the verb *qādaš* in Jeremiah 1:5.

Equally obvious is the influence on Paul of the "call tradition" as it is employed in the second servant song of Second Isaiah:

Listen to me, you coastlands;
attend to me, distant peoples:

[189] See Walter, "Römer 9–11."

Yahweh has called me from birth;
from the womb of my mother he pronounced my name . . .
"And now," says Yahweh, who formed me from the womb to be his servant . . .
"I will make you a light to the nations, that my salvation may reach the ends
of the earth" (Isa 49:1–6).[190]

Noting Paul's indebtedness to these prophetic "call traditions," we can see that
with his two participles ("the one who singled me out" and "the one who called
me") he is simply reproducing the emphatic parallelism of those traditions. God's
singling him out *is* God's calling him to a mission; and God's acting before Paul's
birth is a sign of God's grace.

Paul does not speak, then, in a biographical fashion, as though it were his
intention to say, "Let me tell you about my life and experiences!"[191] He speaks,
rather, in a prophetic fashion, concentrating attention in the first instance on
God: "Let me tell you about God and about what he has done, singling me out
before my birth and calling me in his grace to proclaim his good news!" Paul is
thus conscious of standing in continuity with the prophetic traditions (cf. Rom
1:1–2; 11:1–6). He knows equally well, however, that those traditions themselves
emphasize the discontinuity of God's elective grace.[192] Thus, in his own case, he
underlines the sharp *discontinuity* between the Old Age of sincere Law observance and the New Age of apostolic vocation (cf. Isa 43:18–19).

had called me in his grace. As is suggested by Paul's use elsewhere of the verb
kaleô, "to call," he thinks here not of God's calling him, as it were, from one
"occupation" to another (he was a tentmaker both before and after God called
him).[193] The God who calls is the God who calls the nonexistent *into existence*
(Rom 4:17). The same point is underlined by Paul's placing in parallel with one
another the two prepositional phrases "before I was born" and "in his grace."
With Jeremiah and Second Isaiah, Paul is saying that God's elective grace is
God's act of new creation. It has no basis in the human side of the picture. Having not yet been born, Paul could have done nothing to merit or warrant God's
calling of him (cf. Rom 9:11). Was there nothing, then, in his learned mastery
of the nomistic traditions that served to prepare him for God's call? See Comments #13 and #48.

So when it pleased him. The juncture at which the old gave way to the new
was fixed by God's pleasure, neither by a decision on Paul's part to convert to a
new religion nor by the maturing of the cosmos (cf. 4:4).

16. *apocalyptically to reveal.* Having said that God elected him before he was
born, Paul now speaks of the concrete act in which God carried out that gracious
election in time and space. At a specific time ("when it pleased him") and in a

---

[190] Cf. the use of the prophetic "call tradition" in Qumran by the Teacher of Righteousness
or by his disciples (1QH 9:29–32).
[191] The study of Lyons, *Autobiography*, is of considerable value, as is the essay of Gaventa,
"Autobiography." One may emphasize, however, that in 1:13–2:21 Paul transforms the
category of biography into a theological witness focused on *God's* activity in the gospel.
[192] Cf. J. L. Martyn, *Issues*, 209–229.
[193] Hock, *Tentmaking*.

specific place ("Damascus"; v 17) God invaded Paul's life, calling him into existence as an evangelist to the Gentiles and thus as a slave of Christ (v 10). To speak of this invasive action, Paul uses the verb *apokalyptô*, consciously looking back to his use of the noun *apokalypsis* in v 12. One is thus reminded of the linguistic problem noted in that earlier instance. We cannot well translate either the noun or the verb by means of a single English word. Hence "apocalyptically to reveal," for Paul emphasizes once again that God's good news is fundamentally apocalyptic in the sense of being the event of God's stepping powerfully on the scene from beyond.

One notes also, however, that the precise contours of the apocalypse of Christ, the crucified Messiah, cause Paul to employ certain aspects of Jewish apocalyptic while suppressing others. Thinking of the event in which God first made Christ present to him, Paul says not a word about his receiving a vision of heaven, or of angels, or of a future judgment and so on (cf. 2 Cor 11:21b–12:10; contrast 1 Thess 1:10). In Galatians the content of God's revelation proves to be in the first instance the Son whom God has sent invasively into the world (4:4).

his Son. This is a title of considerable richness in Galatians. In developing his picture of God's Son, Paul draws on formulations already current in Jewish Christianity, themselves developments of ancient Israelite motifs (4:4). He also formulates new accents that he uses to make connections with the Galatians' interest in the motif of descent. See Comments #14 and #42.

to me. On the one hand, a strong argument has been made for the rendering "in me," seeing in the phrase an indication of Paul's certainty that God was revealing Christ to the Gentiles not only in Paul's proclamation but also *in* his person (cf. 4:14).[194] On the other hand, the phrase *en emoi* can be taken here as nothing more than an emphasized equivalent to the simple dative *moi*, "to me." For (a) that rendering is harmonious with v 12 above; (b) in the common Greek of Paul's day there are numerous instances in which *en* is added to the dative without altering its meaning;[195] and (c) Paul uses exactly the same phrase eight verses later, saying that the churches of Judea ascribed glory to God *en emoi*, "because of (or for) me." Certainty in this matter eludes us, but the translation given is the more probable.

in order that I might preach him. The direct object of the verb "preach" is a surprise. The thesis Paul has stated in 1:11–12 has prepared the reader to hear more about the revelation and preaching of his *gospel*. The last clause of v 14 has then heightened the expectation that Paul will now speak of the revealed gospel as the entity that stands in contrast to the traditions he received from his forefathers. Instead, surprisingly, he says that God's pleasure was to reveal to him his Son, in order that he might preach *that Son*. What stands opposite tradition is God's Son.

The jolt is doubtless intended. Paul wishes to say that at its foundation God's

[194]See Gaventa, "Autobiography"; Hays, "The Law of Christ," 281.
[195]See BAGD, "*en*," iv.4.a.; and note the reference there to a passage in Aristides (second century A.D.) in which the god is said to have shown wonderful things *en Neritô*, "to Neritos."

good news *is* the revealed and proclaimed Christ, the apocalypse and proclamation of whom precedes and permeates all forms of Christian tradition. It is, indeed, for this reason that the gospel can and must be differentiated from tradition (1:12; Comment #10). What is at stake in the Galatian crisis is the Galatians' bond to Christ himself (5:4). Thus, Paul does not say that his mission began with the preaching of a wiser path of life, a better route to happiness, and so on. He does not even say that his task was to preach a non-Law gospel in contrast to the Law. God called him to preach Christ, the good news being Christ's advent into the world (3:22–4:7).

among the Gentiles. Paul did not initially understand God to be calling him to preach Christ to his fellow Jews, only later being convinced that the gospel was also for Gentiles (contrast Luke's portrait of clearly distinguishable stages in Peter's vocation, Acts 2:22–40; 10:34–35). On the contrary, from the very beginning of his life as a "slave of Christ" (1:10), Paul knew that God was calling him to preach Jesus Christ to Gentiles (see further 2:7, 9; Rom 15:16).

I immediately kept to myself. The dynamism of the preceding clauses has prepared the reader for a final clause equally dynamic and emphatically positive, such as,

> . . . immediately I got on with the business of preaching Christ!

Instead, Paul speaks of a period of retreat from human company, emphasizing the motif of the loner already struck in 1:12.

not asking advice from anyone. The verb *prosanatithêmi* can mean "to ask advice from someone," as it does here, or "to add something to someone by giving him instructions or information," as it does in 2:6. Paul employs it these two times (its only occurrences in the NT) in a decidedly polemical fashion in order to specify further the fundamental antimony of 1:1:

> not from human beings / but rather from God.

The absolute nature of God's revelation to Paul precludes the possibility of his supplementing that event by seeking advice or instruction from other human beings (lit. "flesh and blood," a Hebrew idiom). Precisely who the people were to whom Paul might have turned immediately after experiencing the invasive event of God's revelation he does not say. But since it is only in the next clause that he mentions the possibility of a trip to Jerusalem, he may here be thinking in the first instance of Christians in Damascus. Does he know that stories are being passed about in which he is said to have received supplementary instruction from "the disciples in Damascus" (cf. Acts 9:19b)?

COMMENT #11
THE HISTORY CREATED BY THE GOSPEL

We have seen that the letter's first major section (1:11–2:21) consists of the initial thesis (1:11–12) followed by a narrative in which Paul demonstrates that thesis.

The initial step in the narrative is Paul's account of his being called to his life task by God, the foil for that event being his earlier life as a religious zealot. The later parts of the narrative will be analyzed as we come to them. Here we note four stylistic factors that, threading their way through the entire section, can serve to emphasize its basic character:

(1) Paul uses numerous verbs in the simple past tense (aorist), often in reference to himself: "I went away (1:17) into Arabia," "I went up again (2:1) to Jerusalem," "they shook hands (2:9) with me and with Barnabas," "I said (2:14) to Cephas in front of everyone."

(2) He several times employs the adverb "then"/"thereupon" (*epeita*) (1:18; 1:21; 2:1).

(3) Similarly, he uses the temporal particle "when" (*hote*) in 1:15; 2:11; 2:12; 2:14, thus developing his narratives in chronological order. The result of these three stylistic markers is a first-person narrative of past events that feature Paul as a major actor, that he has arranged in chronological order, and that occurred prior to his ever seeing the Galatians.[196]

(4) In his first-person narrative Paul exhibits a fourth stylistic feature: he speaks three times, and with great emphasis, of revelation enacted by God (1:12; 1:16; 2:2). The third of these is particularly noteworthy. Using the verb "to go up" in the past tense, Paul says simply, "I went up to Jerusalem (the Jerusalem church)." He then repeats the verb "I went up" in order to add with emphasis that he went up as a result of an apocalypse that came from God. Thus, Paul's narrative of *his own activities* is punctuated by references to *God's activity*. Do these two observations tell us something important about the literary nature of 1:13–2:21?

Comparison with ancient Hebrew writings suggests an affirmative answer. In the Persian period a literary genre emerged that was new to Israel, *revelatory history* in the form of a *personal memoir*. It is instructive to read Galatians 1:13–2:21 alongside the Memoirs of Ezra (Ezra 7:1–9:5) and the Memoirs of Nehemiah (much of Neh 1:1–7:5; 11:1–2; 12:27–13:31), not least because a considerable amount of the material in these memoirs consists of historical travelogues in the first person, written so as to attest to the leading of "the good hand of our God."[197] What causes these accounts to be more than autobiographies or personal memoirs is the consistent emphasis on the activity of God.[198]

Turning back to Galatians 1 and 2, we see that Paul employs the first-person narrative in a somewhat similar fashion, producing an apocalyptic/revelatory history narrated in the first person. To be sure, there is no reason to think that Paul consciously drew on the Memoirs; but in his own way he composes in 1:13–2:21

[196]Pertinent comparative material can be found in Greco-Roman autobiographies (Isocrates, Demosthenes, et al.) and especially in autobiographical remarks in letters (Seneca, Pliny, et al.). On the former, see Lyons, *Autobiography*; regarding the latter, see Gaventa, "Autobiography."

[197]See Eissfeldt, *Old Testament*, 542–551.

[198]In their own ways both Lyons, *Autobiography*, and Gaventa, "Autobiography," recognize this; and the conclusions of their studies are similar: In his Galatians narrative Paul "not only defends himself and his gospel, but also offers himself as a paradigm of *the work of the gospel*" (Gaventa, "Autobiography," 326; emphasis added).

a witness to God's activity, much in the Hebraic sense, with his eyes tightly focused on God's invasive transformation of the cosmos in the gospel of Jesus Christ.[199] In order to repreach the truth of the gospel to the Galatians in their current setting, he traces the path along which that invasive God has led him. Far from being basically concerned to formulate a judicial defense before a panel of judges competent to decide the issue, Paul is intent on supplying the Galatians' fundamental need, that of being once again swept off their feet by the gospel, the word that lies beyond the criteria of human judgment (Comment #9). The result is an historical witness without true parallel in Paul's other letters.

COMMENT #12
PAUL'S PERSECUTION OF THE CHURCH

In Gal 1:13 Paul mentions as the first characteristic of his earlier life "in the religion of Judaism" his persecution of the church to an extreme degree, indeed his attempt to destroy it. From this statement four closely interrelated questions arise: (1) Why did the Pharisee Paul persecute the church? (2) Which church, or part of the church, did he persecute? (3) What was this church doing that was so unacceptable as to call for its annihilation? (4) Assuming that Paul mentions his earlier persecution of the church because he feels it to be pertinent to developments in Galatia, of what exactly does that pertinence consist?[200]

(1) The first question is fundamentally answered by Gal 1:14, and that answer is fully confirmed by Phil 3:6 (cf. 1 Cor 15:9). On the basis of his zeal for the Law, Paul identified the nascent church as a group of Jews that was in some way radically unfaithful to God, and he saw in that unfaithfulness a threat to corpus Israel so serious as to demand the group's annihilation. The zealous deed of Phinehas, cleansing Israel from idolatry (by executing a fellow Israelite and his Midianite consort) and thus saving Israel from God's wrath (Num 25:6–13), was one of the best-remembered examples of a zeal for God's commandments enacted for the sake of Israel's well-being (Sir 48:1–2; 1 Macc 2:23–26; etc.). Whether Paul consciously thought of that example or not, when he was faced with the emergence of the church, he listened to the voice of the Law, and in that voice he heard God calling for the end of a group that was in some sense a basically aberrant sect of Jews.

(2) With that observation we have essentially identified the church Paul persecuted. It is very unlikely to have had any Gentile members. In any case, to him it was a peculiar group of Jews, a *Jewish* sect so fundamentally in violation of

---

[199]Note that Paul is tracing the history created by the advance of the *gospel* into the world, and, in Galatians, the gospel has only one form prior to the advent of Christ, God's punctiliar promise to Abraham (3:8). See Comment #37 and the Note on 3:3.

[200]One can also ask about the measures Paul took against the church, even though that is a matter he addresses neither in Galatians nor in others of his letters. One may suppose that he employed the kinds of synagogue discipline to which he was himself later subjected (2 Cor 11:24; 6:8–9). But the verb *eporthoun*, "tried to destroy," could also include some degree of participation in the killing of Christian Jews (Acts 9:1). With regard to the factor of violence, see both Hultgren, "Persecutions," and Hamerton-Kelly, *Violence*.

God's Law as to pose a dangerous threat to Israel from within. Geographically, we can be confident that Paul was not active in Judea (Gal 1:22), but Gal 1:23 shows that the Judean churches stood in such solidarity with the Jewish-Christian churches he did persecute as to refer to him as "the man who formerly persecuted *us*." Perhaps Paul's main activity was in the north, in and near Damascus.

(3) How did the Jewish-Christian churches seem to Paul to be in violation of God's Law? This question has received a number of answers. If we were able to trust Luke's picture in Acts 7 and 8, where Paul is shown to focus his hostile efforts on "the Hellenists," we could conclude that it was the explicit critique of the Law formulated by this wing of the Jerusalem church that struck him as intolerable.[201] As we have just seen, however, Paul says in Gal 1:22 that he was unknown by sight to the churches of Judea, surely including the one in Jerusalem. We can also doubt that Paul would employ the expression "God's church" to refer to only one part of one local church. The picture Luke paints of Paul's activity in Acts 7 and 8 cannot be credited. Presumably, the Jewish-Christian churches persecuted by Paul were fully observant of the Law in their daily life.

Why, then, should a Jew, zealous for the Law, persecute other Law-observant Jews? Even here a number of answers can be given, but there is a strong hint in Gal 3:13 that Paul viewed the church as a Jewish sect that was intent on venerating as though he were God's Messiah a man who had been crucified as a criminal, and who therefore stood under the curse of God's Law.[202] In a word, Paul probably saw in the church's *christology* a truly significant threat to the Law. Thus, however observant the members of this sect might have been in their day-to-day lives, they seem to have represented, in Paul's view, an intolerable cancer in the body of God's elect people (see further the Notes on 1:23 and 3:13).

(4) Finally, we have to ask why, in writing to his Galatian churches, Paul should commence his portrait of his former life by mentioning his activity as a persecutor of the church. In his identification of himself one might expect him to begin at the beginning, so to speak, mentioning his belonging to the tribe of Benjamin (Phil. 3:5). In writing to the Galatians, however, Paul has a peculiar reason for accenting a link between Law observance and persecution of the church: That link not only characterized a period in his own life; it is also characteristic at the present time of the life and work of the Teachers. In a significant sense these zealous observers of the Law "persecute" the churches in Galatia, undermining the work of God's gospel by requiring Gentiles to observe the Law.

With that observation we have answers to all four questions, but there is reason to return briefly to the second of them. If, at a theological level, we ask about the identity of the church Paul persecuted, we recall that he identifies that group as "the church *of God*." With that expression he doubtless recalls the major issue that faced him in that earlier period of his life: Where is God? An odious Jewish sect was confessing the crucified Jesus to be the Messiah *of God*, and it identified itself as the church *of God* (the *qĕhal yahweh*). Paul knew, however, that the Law

---

[201] So Hengel, *Acts*, 74; Hill, *Hellenists*.
[202] See Hultgren, "Persecutions," 103.

was the Law *of God*, and he was sure that God's Law condemned a man crucified as a criminal (Deut 21:23; Gal 3:13). In the collision between the crucified Jesus and the Law, then, there was in the mind of this zealous Pharisee no doubt at all as to where God stood. God stood on the side of the Law. Hence, Jesus, the Law-cursed criminal, could not be God's Messiah, and the church that venerated him as such could not be the church of God.

In speaking of his call to be an apostle (1:15–16) Paul confesses that God turned this nomistic picture exactly on its head. Having an apocalyptic encounter with the resurrected Jesus (1:12), Paul was compelled to see there the clear sign that God stood and stands on the side of the crucified Messiah, that this Messiah is in fact the Messiah *of God*, and that the church is in fact the church *of God*. Paul had, then, to rethink the whole of the conceptual world in which he had been living, not least the assumption that the Law was monolithically the Law *of God*. When Paul says that in the earlier period he persecuted the church *of God*, he confesses that in his nomistically oriented activity he was acting in opposition to God himself.

Does Paul now think, then, that God stands with the crucified Messiah and not with the Law? Yes! (3:13) and No! (4:21b; 5:14; 6:2). See Comments #41, #48, and #50.

COMMENT #13
HUMAN, TRADITIONAL RELIGION AND APOCALYPTIC VOCATION

In Comment #3, considering at length the apocalyptic theology that threads its way through the whole of Galatians, we noted as one of its chief elements the dualistic thought of two ages, a dualism that Paul expresses by referring to "the present evil age" and "the new creation." An issue of importance is raised, then, by Paul's use in 1:13–15 of two temporal expressions by which he distinguishes from one another two periods in his own life. In v 13 he uses the particle *pote*, "formerly," to speak of the period prior to his being called by God. In v 15, employing the expression *hote de*, he begins to speak about the period that followed that call. For the locution *hote de* there are two possible translations: "but when," indicating a sharp contrast between the two periods in Paul's life; and "and when," pointing to a continuity in which the second period is a supplement to the first.

There are two strong reasons for electing the first of these translations, seeing here a sharp contrast. (1) In v 12 Paul emphasizes a contrast between tradition and apocalypse. He then continues that contrast in the next two sentences. In the one comprising vv 13–14 — Paul's description of the period in which, being zealous for the Law, he persecuted the church — he speaks exclusively of his fidelity to religious *tradition*, doubtless thinking of the Law in its paired existence with the Not-Law, the Law whose two voices had not yet been distinguished from one another by Christ (see again Comments #41 and #48). And in referring to his call by God (vv 15–16) he speaks emphatically and exclusively of *apocalypse* directly at the hands of God. (2) As we have noted earlier, it is only by looking back that Paul can say he was earlier persecuting the church *of God* (v 13). At the time, sure that God was active in the nomistic traditions he had received in the religion of Judaism, he was altogether certain that God could not possibly be active in the messianic sect whose members confessed as God's Messiah a criminal put to death by crucifixion (cf. 3:13). With God's apocalyptic call, however, he saw that in his earlier life he had been tragically mistaken as to the locus of God's activity. It did not lie in the traditional, nomistic zeal that led him to persecute the church; it lay in the church! By the expression *hote de*, Paul means to refer to a contrast, "but when"; thus the translation with which v 15 begins: "But all of that came to an end."

Speaking, then, of a sharp contrast between these two periods in his life, does Paul think that they form an analogy to the contrast between the present evil age and the new creation? Some degree of analogy is unmistakable. We can be confident that when Paul was a zealous Pharisee, he viewed "the religion of Judaism" as the one true way of worshiping and pleasing God. After his apocalyptic call at God's own hands, however, he saw that Judaism was now revealed to be a *religion*, as distinguished from God's apocalyptic and new-creative act in Christ (Introduction §17). The watershed of this radically changed perception is easily located, as we have seen in Comment #12: When God himself stepped on the scene of Paul's life, Paul saw that in the head-on collision between the Law and Jesus, God had stood on Jesus' side, not on the side of the condemning Law. Paul's call to be an apostle did not come, then, in what he perceived to be a human religion, but rather in God's immediate apocalypse of his own Son.

Was there nothing, then, in Paul's learned mastery of the nomistic traditions that served to prepare him for God's call? The question is to be answered both in the negative and in the affirmative. On the negative side, we have already noted several strong indications of discontinuity. Paul does not draw for the Galatians the picture of a path leading *from* his traditional education *to* his call to be God's apostle to the Gentiles. Precisely the opposite. On the affirmative side, however, one sees from 1:15 that Paul heard God's call in the language of the prophets of Israel (cf. Isa 54:1 in Gal 4:27 and Comment #48). The God who called him *is* the God of the prophets (and of Abraham; 3:6–29). Thus, grasped by God's apocalypse of Jesus Christ, Paul found a witness to God's presuppositionless grace in scripture (cf. also 3:8), specifically by noting an analogy between his own call at the hands of God himself and the calls of Jeremiah and Second Isaiah.

It follows that Paul does not speak in 1:15–16 of being converted from one religion, Judaism, to another, Christianity. Nor, in speaking to the Gentile Galatians, does Paul denigrate Judaism. As the whole of the letter shows, he is consistently concerned to say that the advent of Christ is the end of religion. With his call, then, he neither remained in the religion of Judaism nor transferred to a new religion, from which vantage point he could comparatively denigrate his earlier religion. Referring to God as *ho kalesas* ("the One who calls"; 1:15), Paul speaks of God's *calling him into existence* as an apostle of Jesus Christ. That call is not for Paul a religious event; it is the form taken in his own case by God's calling into existence the new creation.

COMMENT #14
GOD'S APOCALYPSE OF HIS SON TO PAUL

We have noted that Paul identifies as the content of God's vocational revelation to him nothing other than "his Son" (1:16). In a functional way this title — together with related motifs — has considerable importance in Galatians.[203] There are three major elements in the background, and all three play a role in Paul's references.

(1) In ancient Israel the king was said to become God's son at his *enthronement* (Ps 2:7). From the formula quoted by Paul in Rom 1:3–4, we can see that Jewish Christians prior to him celebrated Jesus' resurrection as, in effect, his enthronement. For these Jewish Christians, Jesus was already descended from King David according to the flesh. When, then, God raised him from the dead, God declared him to be "Son of God" with power.[204] Applied to the resurrected Christ, the title "Son of God" emphasized both the close relation the Son has to God and the resulting power he has as the exalted ruler of the cosmos.

(2) In addition, by the eighth century B.C., ancient Israel sometimes understood herself to be *descended* from God, being corporately identified as God's firstborn son delivered from bondage in Egypt (Hos 11:1; Exod 4:22–23).

(3) There were also traditions about God's *sending* Moses and the prophets to Israel (Exod 3:10; Isa 6:8; Wis 9:10, 17).[205] Similarly, we find references to God's sending from heaven into the world his angel, his wisdom, his spirit (e.g., Gen 24:40; Wis 9:10, 17). Among Jewish Christians these traditions were applied to Jesus, thus serving to spawn a sort of sending formula, evident both in Paul's letters and in the Johannine literature (Gal 4:4–5; Rom 8:3; John 3:16–17; 1 John 4:9; see also Mark 9:37; Luke 10:16; Mark 12:1–12): In the first clause God is the subject of a verb in the past tense, usually "sent"; the object of the verb is "his Son"; and there is a final clause stating the purpose of God's sending act, explicitly or implicitly relating that act of God to Jesus' death.[206]

All three elements in the background of the title "Son of God" are reflected in Paul's references to the Son in Galatians. Indeed, there is also a fourth, the Son's love unto death, that is to say the Son's faith.

Enthronement. The presence of the resurrected and powerful Son of God must have been keenly felt by members of the Damascus church in their services of worship. His presence was also sensed, then, by Paul when God apocalyptically revealed the Son to him, sending the Son into his life (Gal 1:16, where *apokalypsai* is similar to *apostellein*). This Son of God, that is to say, was not the earthly

---

[203]I have said "in a functional way" in order to take into account some of the dimensions of Keck, "Renewal."

[204]The tradition preserved in Ps 2:7 may have served as the root — or one of the roots — from which "Son of God" became a messianic title, even though it can be debated whether that happened in pre-Christian lines of tradition (such as Qumran: 4QpsDan Aa (4Q246); 4QFlor 10–14) or only in the early Jewish-Christian church. See Fitzmyer, "Qumran Aramaic," 391–394; Hengel, *Son of God*; Lührmann, "Christologie," 357.

[205]Cf. Philo's equating of the *logos* with God's son (*de Conf. Ling.* 145–147).

[206]See especially Schweizer, "God Sent His Son"; Comment #42.

Jesus, but rather the one who was now the Lord, alive, present, and enthroned by God's having raised him from the realm of those who have died (1:1, 3). Henceforth, the presence of the crucified, resurrected, and powerful Son of God determined, for Paul, the nature of Christian worship, the life of the church, and specifically Paul's daily work as an evangelist.

Descent. Elsewhere in Galatians Paul connects the title "Son of God" to the motif of descent, a matter to which the Teachers have already given their own attention. We do not know that the Teachers made much of the title "Son of God," but we can be sure that they told the Galatians they could become "sons [descendants] of Abraham" (*sperma Abraam*) by observing the Law. Against the Teachers Paul makes two decisive changes. First, although willing to speak of the Christians' descent from Abraham, he places his accent on their descent from God (Comment #33). He thus draws on Jewish traditions in which the merciful and righteous person is called God's son (Sir 4:10; Wis 2:18), but probably even more on the ancient Israelite portrait of corporate Israel as God's son. Second, Paul insists with great emphasis that the church has become the community of God's sons by its incorporation into God's Son.[207] The sons of God have come into being through the Son of God.

Sending. In speaking of the Son's being sent into the world, Paul draws on the Jewish-Christian sending tradition mentioned above. He also shapes this tradition to the issues at stake in Galatia, accenting the motif of God's redemptive invasion of the cosmos in the sending of his Son (Comment #42).[208]

Faithful love unto death. This motif plays a central role in Paul's reference to the Son in 2:20, for there he speaks of the Son's love and of the Son's faith, both being enacted in his giving up his life for us (Comment #28). In a word, the Son whom God sent into the world (4:4–5), and whom God raised from the dead (1:1), this Son mysteriously remains the crucified Christ who enacted his faithful love of us by dying for us in collision with the Law's curse (2:20; 3:13). The resurrection of the Son does not eclipse the Son's cross.[209]

COMMENT #15
PAUL'S VIEW OF THE LAW IMMEDIATELY AFTER HIS APOSTOLIC CALL

The data do not allow us to draw in detail and with great confidence a picture of Paul *immediately* after his call, prior, that is, to his affiliation with the church in Antioch. He implies that he was grasped by God while he was in contact with Christians in Damascus, that he immediately went to Nabatea, and that he subsequently returned to the Damascus church (1:17). He says that, from the begin-

---

[207] For this reason the translation of Gal 3:26 and 4:6–7 cannot dispense with the word "sons" in favor of, let us say, "children" (NRSV).

[208] In a similar way Paul shapes the formula of Rom 1:3–4 by placing before it the phrase "concerning his Son," thus affirming Jesus' sonship prior to his being raised from the dead (Schweizer, "God Sent His Son," 306 n28).

[209] Cousar, *Cross.* One might add that Paul uses the title "Son of God" mostly in Galatians and Romans, the letters in which he gives great attention to the matter of rectification; see Lührmann, "Christologie," 356.

ning, his work was among Gentiles. What view did he have of the Law in this earliest period? We cannot be sure, but several suggestions can be offered:

(1) First, a question arises in connection with Gal 1:15–16: Why, in speaking of his call, is Paul silent about the Law? In place of the sentence we now have as 1:15–16 he could have said, for example,

> But all of that came to an end. God had in fact singled me out even before I was born, and had called me in his grace. So when it pleased him apocalyptically to reveal his Son to me, in order that I might preach him among the Gentiles, I did so *quite apart from the Law that had played its own role in my earlier misguided persecution of God's church.*

Such a sentence (cf. "apart from the Law" in Rom 3:21) would have fit very well into the Galatian letter, for it would have accented the antinomy between nomistic tradition and gospel-apocalypse already expressed in the transition from Gal 1:14 to 1:15.

(2) We know that, in time, Paul's passage from persecutor of the church to evangelistic apostle involved a reassessment of the Law. Grasped by God, he came to see that in the event of Jesus' crucifixion God had stood on the side of the condemned victim rather than on the side of the condemning Law (Comment #13). Again, then, why does he not mention this reassessment of the Law in 1:15–16?

(3) We have also noted that — aside from its christology — the church persecuted by Paul was Law-observant in its daily life. One ponders the fact, then, that after Paul's call members of this Law-observant church did not say that their former persecutor was preaching a Law-less gospel. On the contrary, these Law-observant Christians reported among themselves that he was now preaching precisely the faith which he had earlier tried to destroy (1:23–24), scarcely indicating that he held a view of the Law which they perceived to be materially divergent from their own.[210] Was Paul's activity perceived to be no threat to Law-observant churches in Judea because in his preaching he did not even mention the Law?

(4) At a later point in the letter, and as a rather sudden outburst, Paul says,

> As for me, brothers and sisters, if, on occasion, I am preaching, as part of the gospel message, that one should be circumcised — as some wrongly report to you — why am I being persecuted to this day? My preaching circumcision would amount to wiping out the scandalous character of the cross (5:11).

In the Note on this verse we will see that the second clause can be translated "if I am *still* preaching that one should be circumcised," indicating the existence of

---

[210]It is often assumed that Paul immediately adopted as his own the loose stance toward the Law characteristic of the pre-Pauline Hellenistic church. We can be indeed confident that Paul was not the first to preach Christ to Gentiles. There was, however, no monolithic "Hellenistic church," and thus no taken-for-granted Hellenistic attitude toward the Law, ready-made and available for Paul to adopt. See Räisänen, *Law,* 254–256; cf. Jervell, *Unknown Paul,* 52–67; Hill, *Hellenists.*

a report that at some time in the past Paul advocated circumcision of Gentile converts to the church. We will also see reasons for preferring the inset translation above. Even so, Gal 5:11 seems to reflect a simple fact: In Paul's own lifetime, someone said that, at some time, the apostle preached in such a way as to leave one uncertain about his understanding of the Law.[211] Could that report have reflected nothing more than Paul's failure to mention the Law with palpable emphasis in his earliest preaching to Gentiles (cf. 1 Thessalonians)?

1:17–24 Paul and the Jerusalem Apostles

Translation

1:17. Nor did I make a trip up to Jerusalem to see those who were already apostles before I became one. On the contrary, I went away to Arabia, and later I returned to Damascus.
18. Then, after three years had passed, I did go up to Jerusalem in order to visit Cephas, and I stayed with him two weeks. 19. I saw none of the other apostles, except James, the brother of the Lord. 20. What I am writing to you now is no lie, God being my witness! 21. Then, I went to the regions of Syria and Cilicia. 22. And through the whole of this time, I was still unknown by sight to the churches of Judea which are in Christ. 23. They only heard it said about me that "the man who formerly persecuted us is now preaching the faith that he had earlier tried to destroy"; 24. time and again they ascribed glory to God because of me.

Literary Structure and Synopsis

We have seen that Paul builds the first major section of the letter (1:11–2:21) by stating his initial thesis and by taking five steps in which he explicates it, almost totally in narrative form. The positive element of the thesis,

> On the contrary, the gospel I preach came to me by God's apocalyptic revelation of Jesus Christ,

is developed in part by a sharp narrative contrast between Paul's life in the religion of Judaism and his life as an apostle called to preach Christ to the Gentiles (1:13–16). Following that, Paul now takes the second step in 1:17–24, continuing his narrative in a way that explicates the negative elements in his thesis:

[211]Cf. Linton, "Aspect"; see now Hengel, "Stellung."

The gospel I preach is not what human beings normally have in mind when they speak of "good news"; for I did not receive it from another human being; nor was I taught it.

It is in this second section of the narrative that one learns why the negative parts of the thesis are necessary: The Teachers have charged that Paul is unfaithful to the gospel that he received from the leaders of the Antioch church, the gospel he also studied by traveling to Jerusalem, where he sat at the feet of the Jerusalem apostles. Paul's response thus takes the form of a negative travelogue designed to prove his distance from Jerusalem. See Comment #16.

NOTES

1:17. *Nor did I make a trip up to Jerusalem.* Paul is now doing more than continuing the motif of the apostolic loner. This negative is both specific and climactic: he tells the Galatians specifically where he did not go. Moreover, before he completes the paragraph at 1:24, he will employ the negative three more times ("I saw none," v 19; "no lie," v 20; and "unknown," v 22; see again Comment #16).

Jerusalem. There were two widely used Greek transliterations of this place-name. Paul regularly employs the less Hellenized of the two (e.g., Gal 4:25, 26); but here, in the next verse, and at 2:1 he employs the form that has as its initial component the Greek word "holy" (*hieros*, as early as Polybius; BDF §56). Whether he does so intentionally is impossible to say. What we can affirm is that Jerusalem is important to Paul *the apostle* neither as the center of Judaism, with its Temple and priestly cultus, nor as the locus of his early education to be a scribe of the Pharisees (so Acts 22:3). For Paul Jerusalem is now the place of the Jerusalem church, its poor (2:10), its leaders (2:9), and, unfortunately, its "False Brothers" (2:4). In short, for Paul the word "Jerusalem" is dominantly a metonym for the Jerusalem *church*, functioning in a way not altogether different from the way "Rome" functions nowadays in the vocabulary of Roman Catholic clerics (see Comment #46).

those who were already apostles before I became one. Having accented the lone-wolf nature of his apocalyptic, apostolic calling at the hands of God himself, Paul now acknowledges the existence of a circle of Christian apostles that had its origin before he was called (Comment #1). One does well to speak here of *Jerusalem apostles,* for the way in which Paul refers to this group, both here and in 1 Cor 15:7, indicates a circle located in Jerusalem and occupied with the leadership of the Jerusalem church and thus with the mission to the Jews (Gal 1:19; 2:7, 9). Paul can and does acknowledge members of this apostolic circle. The link between vv 16 and 17 shows, however, that he places them under the rubric of "flesh and blood," emphasizing that they are human beings, not beings of some supra-human order (cf. 2:6).[212] Putting 1:1 together with 1:17, we can see

[212] Regarding Paul's distance from the Jerusalem church, one may add with confidence that at the time of his call that church did not have a mission to Gentiles of any sort, whereas he knew his call to be focused exclusively on taking the gospel to Gentiles (2:7, 9).

that Paul wishes to say three things: (a) I am the lone-wolf apostle to the Gentiles, called to that task directly by God when he revealed his Son to me. (b) God thereby placed me in the company of his church (1:13) in which apostles already existed. (c) As God's apostle, however, I have never been and am not now subject to instruction from the other apostles.[213]

I went away to Arabia. If the Galatians asked Paul's messenger about the location of Arabia, he probably referred to the kingdom of the Nabateans, stretching "from the Hauran down through Moab and Edom and expanded on both sides of the Gulf of Aqaba."[214] We should like to know to what part or parts of the Nabatean kingdom Paul went, what his positive motive was for going there, and precisely what he did there. We might ask, for example, whether he tried unsuccessfully to establish churches (the earliest Christian remains discovered in Nabatea by archaeologists are dated in the fourth century).[215] Did some aspect of his work eventually anger Nabatean authorities (2 Cor 11:32-33)?[216] Probably, but we cannot be certain. For in wording the present verse Paul intends only to say what he did not do: go to Jerusalem for "Christian education" (contrast Acts 26:20).

and later I returned to Damascus. Again it is particularly modern readers who note that there is much Paul does not say. How long did he remain in Nabatea? Why did he return to Damascus? If his activities in Nabatea were in some way politically unsettling, so that he was "invited" to leave, did he go back to Damascus while that city was still directly in Roman hands, thus finding there safety from Nabatean forces? How long did he then remain in Damascus? Lastly, was his final departure from Damascus necessitated by the Nabatean acquisition of the city, being thus an event to which we can give a date (cf. 2 Cor 11:32-33)? None of these matters is of interest to Paul as he writes this letter, but see Comment #17.

What Paul does indicate in the present clause is that he was in Damascus before his trip to the south, thus saying indirectly but clearly that God called him when he was in or near that city. This is one of the points at which Luke's account

---

[213]We know that the term "apostle" had several meanings among early Christians, but a detailed arranging of these meanings in the order of their historical origins and developments is a task precluded by the cloudy nature of our sources. The most we can say is that, beyond the use of the term simply to refer to the messengers whom one local church might send to another (2 Cor 8:23; Phil 2:25), there seem to have been two basic meanings. First, the Greek word "apostle" was apparently used very early to refer to Peter and to other members of the Jerusalem church, thus referring to a circle larger than the Twelve (1 Cor 15:5-7). Second, it was employed somewhat later, perhaps in the Antioch church, and especially by Paul, who used it to speak of his own vocation. See Käsemann, "Legitimität"; Barrett, *Signs*; idem, *Second Corinthians*, 28-32; H. D. Betz, "Apostle"; Note on 1:1 and Comment #1 above.

[214]Murphy-O'Connor, "Arabia," 733.

[215]Regarding Nabatean archaeology, see Schwank, "Funde"; Graf, "Nabateans."

[216]The fact that Aretas, king of Nabatea, became at one point very angry with Paul (2 Cor 11:32-33; cf. Acts 9:23-25) may be hint enough that Paul preached a message that was in some way unsettling to civic order. See again Murphy-O'Connor, "Arabia."

in Acts coincides with Paul's own testimony: Luke places the event near Damascus (Acts 9:3; 22:6; 26:12, 20). Paul gives no hint, however, that his apocalyptic call happened as he was journeying *from* somewhere else (say Jerusalem) *to* Damascus. The lone-wolf character of Paul's call is further accented by his saying nothing at all about the makeup and beliefs of the church in Damascus or about roles played by any of its members, such as Ananias (Acts 9:10). Paul heard God's call in the context of Syrian Christianity, but his own self-portrait does not at all accent that fact.[217] It is as though Paul had neither teachers (1:12) nor companions (1:17) on the early part of the way along which God chose to lead him.

18. *Then, after three years had passed.* This is the first of three sentences in which Paul uses the adverb *epeita,* "then" or "thereupon," to present a series of events in narrative form (1:18; 1:21; 2:1). In the second instance he allows the adverb to stand alone, so that it simply connects the event just narrated with the next one:

> I went to Jerusalem to visit Cephas for a couple of weeks. 21. After that (*epeita*) I went to the regions of Syria and Cilicia.

In the other two instances, however, Paul combines the adverb with a notice of a specified number of years (1:18: "after three years"; 2:1: "after fourteen years"). From what point or points are these two measurements to be taken?

In Comment #17 we will see grounds for thinking that in both of those cases Paul measures from the date of his call. In the present verse, then, Paul indicates that about three years passed between his call and his trip to visit Peter in Jerusalem.

I did go. The verb is the simple past tense, "I went," but the nuanced translation is called for by the context, which shows Paul somewhat grudgingly admitting that during this period he did make one trip to Jerusalem.

in order to visit Cephas. A great deal has been written about the verb *historeô,* centering on the question whether it means in the present instance "to get information (about Jesus?)" or simply "to visit, thereby becoming acquainted with." Both meanings are philologically possible, but if we wish to grasp Paul's intention, and if for that purpose we take our bearings from the context, the former meaning is almost certainly to be excluded. Paul has taken great care to say that his gospel and his call came by revelation directly from God, and that neither was, therefore, in need of supplementation by the sort of instruction he could have received from another human being, even one of the Jerusalem apostles (vv 13 and 17). In 1:16 Paul says that following his call, he kept to himself, "not asking advice from anyone," and in 2:6 he insists that the leaders of the Jerusalem church did not in any way supplement the truth of the gospel revealed to him by God. Hence, it must be Paul's intention now to admit only that he visited Cephas.

It is, of course, inconceivable that during the visit Cephas was silent about

---

[217]Cf. Bousset, *Kyrios Christos.*

Jesus the Christ, about God's having raised him from the dead (cf. 1 Cor 15:5), and about the work among his fellow Jews to which God had called him. Moreover, we can easily imagine that when the Teachers gave the Galatians their own comments on Paul's letter, they cited this visit as one of the occasions on which Paul was sure to have received instruction from Peter. If, however, he received from Cephas information about Jesus, he clearly did not consider that to be instruction in "the gospel."

But what about communication on this occasion from Paul to Peter, the man who was at this time a major leader of the Jerusalem church, and the key actor in the mission to the Jews?[218] We can be sure that Paul made clear his call by God to preach Christ to the Gentiles; and, following that communication, there will certainly have been some discussion between the two men of the two missions, the older mission to the Jews and the younger one to the Gentiles. Paul and Peter may even have reached — between the *two* of them — at least an embryonic understanding of God's plan to advance his gospel into the world along two parallel paths. If so, it is possible that, in the later conference involving the churches of Antioch and Jerusalem (2:1–10), Peter and Paul worked with members of their respective delegations to secure universal assent to the embryonic agreement they had themselves reached during this earlier visit.[219] In any case, an early perception of God's worldwide plan was shared by Peter and Paul as persons each of whom knew himself to have been commissioned directly by God through the risen Christ.[220]

Cephas. "Cephas" and "Peter" (the latter being an inferior manuscript reading here) are Aramaic and Greek words respectively for "rock," the sobriquet of one of Jesus' disciples (1 Cor 15:5; Mark 3:16). To refer to this man, Paul uses the Aramaic name, "Cephas," four times in our letter and an equal number of times in 1 Corinthians (eight of the nine times in the NT). The Greek form of the man's name, "Peter," occurs in the gospels and Acts more than 150 times, whereas the Aramaic form, clearly favored by Paul, emerges there only once (John 1:43). The practice established in the gospels makes it best for us to follow convention in using the name "Peter," reminding ourselves only that Paul's custom is to use the Aramaic name "Cephas," the sole exception in his letters being the references to "Peter" in Gal 2:7–8.[221]

To Paul, Peter was a person of great importance in God's plan. In 1 Cor 15:5

---

[218]Klein suggests that the major leadership of the Jerusalem church passed to James before the conference between that church and the one in Antioch ("Galater 2, 6–9"). Cf. Hahn, *Mission*, 80 n1.

[219]Luedemann, *Chronology*, 64–71. Building on Luedemann's reading, A. Schmidt even thinks it possible that 2:7 contains *words* of an agreement reached by Paul and Peter on the occasion of Paul's early visit: "Paul is entrusted with the gospel as it is directed to those who are not circumcised, just as Peter [as the leader of the Jerusalem church] is entrusted with the gospel to those who are circumcised" ("Missionsdekret").

[220]Cf. Satake, "1Kr 15,3."

[221]In a fascinating and unconvincing argument Ehrman has vigorously questioned the assumption that Cephas and Peter were the same man: "Cephas." See now Allison, "Peter."

Paul names him as the first witness to the resurrected Christ. In the formula of Gal 2:7–8 Peter is Paul's exact counterpart, the two being identified as the heads of the two gospel missions, one to the Jews, one to the Gentiles. We have to ask, however, why in the present verse Paul specifies that his visit was with Peter, rather than with the Jerusalem church as such. The first reason, one supposes, is that that limitation is simply true. In 1:22 Paul says that prior to the Jerusalem conference he was personally unknown to the *churches* in Judea, presumably including the one in Jerusalem. A second reason appears when one notices that Paul does not have to tell the Galatians who Peter is. Perhaps the Teachers have already spoken to them about Peter, saying not only that Peter played a major role in the Jerusalem church, being a dependable tradent of the true gospel, but also that he functioned as one of Paul's teachers in the gospel tradition, before Paul began to deviate from it.

stayed with him. By saying that he was Peter's houseguest (*menein pros tina*, Acts 18:3 [D]; *Did.* 12:2), Paul may intend to emphasize that his visit was essentially personal rather than official. If so, one should pause before attempting to relate this trip to the famine visit portrayed in Acts 11:27–30 (and note again Gal 1:22, with its insistence that Paul was throughout the whole of this time unknown to the churches of Judea, surely including the church of Jerusalem). The unofficial nature of the visit should also warn one not to use the categories of superior/inferior in depicting the relationship between Peter and Paul.[222] Paul intends to mention precisely a personal visit with Peter, not an official conference with powerful authorities of the Jerusalem church.

two weeks. Lit. "fifteen days." Again the context shows that Paul is emphasizing the brevity of the visit.

19. *I saw none of the other apostles.* Paul returns to the negative tone characteristic of the formal denial. As we have observed, he does not deny the existence of a circle of apostles in the Jerusalem church (v 17). He says only that he did not go to that church in order to receive gospel instruction from them. Being Peter's houseguest for two weeks, he did not even meet the persons the Teachers consider to be the leading repositories of the gospel tradition, the apostles in what the Teachers themselves refer to as the "mother church" (Comment #46). Paul seems to have been consciously concerned to limit his stay to a personal visit with Peter, and, for reasons about which we can only speculate, Peter agreed to that limitation.

except James, the brother of the Lord. This final clause of v 19, introduced by the words *ei mê* and apparently simple and straightforward, is in fact difficult to interpret and thus to translate. To no small extent the way in which the Galatians will have understood the clause is certain to have depended on the tone of voice employed by Paul's messenger in reading it aloud, a factor inaccessible to us. There are two major alternatives:

(a) Taking the words *ei mê* to mean "except," one would have an instance in which Paul is admitting to an exception:

[222]*Pace* R. E. Brown et al., *Peter*, 29–30.

I saw none of the other apostles; well, true enough, I did see one of them, namely James.

We might compare 1 Cor 1:14, where Paul again follows a denial with a clause introduced by *ei mê:* "I am thankful that I did not baptize a single one of you! Oh yes, true enough, I did baptize Crispus and Gaius." In both of these instances Paul may intend grudgingly to admit that he has to reckon with one or more exceptions to the claim he makes in the major clause (in 1 Cor 1:14 Crispus and Gaius; in Gal 1:19 James). On this reading Paul considers James to be an apostle, and he admits that, in regard to James, his claim in the preceding clause has to be qualified.

(b) But the Greek expression *ei mê* can also denote contrast; taking it in that meaning, one arrives at a different paraphrase:

I saw none of the other apostles, and thus I cannot be said to have received instruction from them; but, by contrast, leaving aside the category of the apostles, I did see James.

It is difficult to be altogether confident of either reading. Forced to choose, however, one would prefer the first. We have already noticed that the major thrust of 1:17–24 is that of a formal denial. It seems likely, then, that in the last clause of v 19 Paul is punctuating the denial with a sort of parenthetical admission to an exception; he did see a second apostle, James the brother of Jesus.[223] In short, it seems probable that Paul's intention throughout is simply that of distancing himself from the Jerusalem church as regards instruction in the gospel. It is even worth noting that Paul uses different verbs to speak of his contacts with Peter and James. He visited Peter, staying in his house for two weeks; he merely saw James, adding no information as to the length of that contact.

20. *What I am writing to you now is no lie, God being my witness!* Paul pauses to take an oath, saying that he is composing the entire passage in the presence of God, who knows all things, and that he is willing to call upon God to certify the truth of his lengthy denial. It thus becomes doubly clear that the Teachers have given the Galatians their own account of Paul's early years as a preacher of the gospel, speaking particularly of the relationship they say he had with the Jerusalem apostles during those years. By calling God as his witness, Paul wishes to tell the Galatians once again (cf. 1:6) that adherence to the Teachers' message involves them in defection from God. One may note similar oaths of certitude in 1 Thess 2:5, 10; 2 Cor 1:23; 11:31; 12:19; Rom 1:9; 9:1; Phil 1:8.

---

[223]The fact that Paul supplies James with an appellative, "the brother of the Lord," is sometimes mentioned — along with other data — in support of the thesis that he intends to deny James's status as an apostle. But Paul's reference to James in 1 Cor 15:7 can be taken to indicate that Paul did consider him an apostle: ". . . he [the risen Christ] was seen by *Cephas,* then by *the twelve* [of whom Cephas was certainly one] . . . then he was seen by *James,* then by all the apostles [of whom James was presumably one]." However others may have seen James (Clementine *Hom.* 11.35.4), Paul probably considered him to be not only the Lord's brother but also one of the apostles.

21. *Then.* See the Note on 1:18 and Comment #17.

the regions of Syria and Cilicia. From Paul's accounts of the later meeting in Jerusalem and of the still later incident in the Antioch church (2:1–10 and 2:11–14), we can see that after his visit with Peter he went to Antioch, where he was able to attach himself to a church that had already embraced — in some form — a mission to Gentiles. Functioning then as an evangelist of this church, he labored in its vicinity (Syria) and immediately to the west in Cilicia.[224] In this period he did not journey to Galatia; see Comment #17.

Was Paul still pursuing his work alone? Again it is the narratives in Galatians 2 that supply an answer. In the pre-conference period, Paul worked shoulder-to-shoulder with Barnabas, both men being sponsored in a significant sense by the Antioch church.

22. *And through the whole of this time.* In the travelogue proper, Paul has regularly employed aorist verbs (simple past tense). In dictating vv 22–24 he puts two of the main verbs in the imperfect periphrastic and a third in the simple imperfect, thus emphasizing that he is describing a state of affairs that obtained over a period of time prior to the event he will narrate in 2:1–10. By describing this state of affairs Paul draws a conclusion to vv 16–21, and in so doing makes three points:

(a) During this period (a decade and a half of my missionary activity) *I remained unknown* by sight to the Judean churches, and thus it cannot be said that I received instruction from the Jerusalem apostles (contrast Acts 9:28).

(b) *They only heard it said about me* that "the man who formerly persecuted us is now preaching the faith that he had earlier tried to destroy," thus indicating their agreement with my gospel.

(c) Indeed, *they gave glory* to God for me, thus showing that they viewed my activity as work inspired by God.

I was still unknown by sight to the churches of Judea. From Acts we have confirming evidence of thoroughly Jewish-Christian churches in Judea, the members of the one in Joppa being explicitly identified, for example, as "the believers drawn into the church from the Jewish nation" (Acts 10:45; cf. Comment #25). There is, moreover, no good reason to exclude the church of Jerusalem from Paul's comprehensive expression "the churches of Judea." It follows that this verse is incompatible with Luke's account of Paul's passive participation in the stoning of Stephen (Acts 7:58–81) and especially with Luke's statement that shortly afterward, in Jerusalem itself, Paul "was ravaging the church" (Acts 8:3). It is true that in Luke's account the outbreak of persecution that began with the

---

[224]The place-names "Syria" and "Cilicia" are twice linked in the book of Acts, namely at 15:23 (the churches addressed in the "apostolic decree") and at 15:41 (Paul's itinerary immediately after the Jerusalem conference portrayed in Acts 15). Neither reference is of much significance for understanding Gal 1:21. If some of the Galatians may have needed a verbal gloss from Paul's messenger in order to be sure about the location of Arabia (1:17) and even of Syria, they will have had no similar trouble knowing the whereabouts of Cilicia, an area immediately to the south of them.

killing of Stephen was directed mainly toward one part of the Jerusalem church, the Greek-speaking "Hellenists"; and this Lucan distinction has recently been used to bring Gal 1:22 and Acts 8:3 into harmony with one another: Paul was personally unknown to the wing of the Jerusalem church that was able to remain in the city, immune to persecution, namely those who were Aramaic-speaking.[225] But this interpretation may be more clever than convincing. In any case, the Galatians will have understood Paul to say that until the trip pictured in 2:1–10 he had no contact with any of the churches of Judea as communities, including the one in Jerusalem.[226]

the churches of Judea which are in Christ. The formulation is somewhat elaborate, as H. D. Betz notes. An even more elaborate one emerges in the midst of a paragraph of 1 Thessalonians that has been suspected by some, probably wrongly, of being a post-Pauline interpolation, "the churches of God which are in Judea in Christ Jesus" (1 Thess 2:14).[227] Taken together, the Galatians passage and the one in 1 Thessalonians leave us with the impression that Paul was consistently careful to refer with great respect to those thoroughly Jewish-Christian churches whom he did not know personally and to whom he was personally unknown. At the time of Galatians those congregations made up the vast majority of the local churches in the "church of God," Gentile Christianity (and mixed churches such as the one in Antioch) being a distinct minority.

By placing the prepositional phrase "in Christ" at the end of the sentence (both in the present verse and in 1 Thess 2:14), Paul emphasizes it, showing that literal location — and doubtless ethnic derivation as well — are of far less consequence than the theological location of these churches in Christ. That is to say, we meet here an instance of Paul's theological use of spatial language (cf. Rom 5:2). He thinks of Christ as the new realm God is now establishing in the world. Thus, while the churches are geographically located in Judea, they are more importantly located in Christ.

23. *They only heard it said about me.* Stories both about Paul's past life and about his present activities circulated in the Judean churches, a fact Paul can now use as the forceful finale to his formal denial.[228] For by adding the little adverb "only" (cf. 2:10), he says once again that he cannot have been a student in one of these churches, learning the gospel tradition there.[229]

"*the man who formerly persecuted us.* The last clause of v 23 is introduced by the Greek word *hoti*, very probably indicating in this instance a direct quotation, or something close to it. Paul encapsulates the stories by employing the same verbs used in v 13, "persecute" and "try to destroy." To some degree the vocabulary of the quotation may be his own. The participial expression, however, "he

---

[225] So Hengel, "Ursprünge," 24 n35.
[226] Hultgren has argued, unconvincingly I think, that Paul was not known *as an apostle* to the churches in Judea, but was known to them as their persecutor ("Persecutions").
[227] See the recent argument for authenticity in Schlueter, *Measure.*
[228] Cf. Lindemann, *Paulus*; Babcock, *Legacies.*
[229] Cf. Gnilka, *Philipperbrief,* 97.

who persecuted us" is probably a faithful representation of an appellation the Judean Christians used to refer to Paul.[230]

But why, if they have never seen him, should they identify him as the one who persecuted "us"? We can imagine two stages of development: Christians from the north (Damascus and environs), traveling among and speaking to the Judean churches, tell stories about Paul's transformation, identifying him literally as "the one who formerly persecuted us." Subsequently, the Judean Christians, passing the stories about, include themselves with their fellows from the north. Paul's activity as a persecutor was certainly directed against Jews who confessed Jesus as God's Messiah (1:13). In such a matter geography might be considered a factor of no great significance. To all Jewish Christians, then, Paul became "the one who formerly persecuted us."[231]

is now preaching the faith that he had earlier tried to destroy." Here there are two further grounds for thinking that Paul is using some of the expressions actually employed in the stories about him. (a) The verb *euaggelizomai*, "to preach," seems to have been somewhat more frequently used by the Jewish-Christian churches of Paul's time than by Paul, who preferred the noun (see Comment #7). (b) Jewish Christians are also more likely to have been the ones who used the noun "faith" with the definite article to refer to the gospel message. Composing on his own, Paul speaks not of preaching "the faith," but of preaching "the gospel" (Comment #7).

In the present context what is important to Paul is the opportunity to say that these Jewish Christians identified their good news with the good news he was preaching in his own work, even though that work was geographically and ethnically far removed from their own. In short, knowing that he will momentarily have to refer to the False Brothers in the Jerusalem church, Paul is more than glad to affirm that throughout the period prior to the Jerusalem meeting he was generally seen by Christians in Judea as anything but a threat.

24. ascribed glory to God because of me. On the contrary, when Christians in Judea circulated stories about him, they thanked God for him!

---

[230]The substantive *ho diôkôn* is an instance of the present participle being used to refer to an action prior to that of the main verb. See Meecham, "Present Participle" (cf. Gal 6:13, although in that case the participle is passive). See also Bammel, "Galater." On stories about Paul that were circulated among Judean Christians, see Acts 21:21; and cf. "the enemy man" as a reference to Paul in the *Ascents of James* 1.70.1 (Van Voorst, *Ascents*, 73; F. S. Jones, *Source*, 106); *Ep. Pet. Jas.* 2:3 (HS 2.112).

[231]Again one might note that, in writing the Acts of the Apostles, Luke reverses the picture. There Paul first persecutes Christians in Jerusalem, and stories of his activity subsequently make their way north to Damascus (Acts 9:13). The reversal is surely the work of Luke, in whose view all important Christian tradition flowed from the Jerusalem church rather than to it.

COMMENT #16
THE NEGATIVE TRAVELOGUE; PAUL THE APOSTLE AND THE APOSTLES IN THE JERUSALEM CHURCH; THE MISSIONS TO THE JEWS AND TO THE GENTILES

THE NEGATIVE TRAVELOGUE

Having begun in 1:13–16 to demonstrate the positive statement in the thesis (1:12c), Paul turns in 1:17–24 to an explication of the negative elements of the thesis, showing by means of a travelogue with a consistently negative tone that he was not taught the gospel by another human being. Immediately after mentioning his apocalyptic call in v 16 he says that he asked advice from no one. In the next verse he gives specificity to that denial:

> Nor did I make a trip up to Jerusalem to see those who were already apostles before I became one (v 17a).

In this manner, before he completes the paragraph at 1:24, Paul employs the negative three more times. Fully displayed, the line of negation runs as follows:

v 11	The gospel I preach is *not* what human beings normally have in mind when they speak of "good news."
v 12	I did *not* receive it from another human being.
v 12	I was *not* taught it.
v 16	I did *not* ask advice from anyone.
v 17	I did *not* make a trip to Jerusalem.
v 17	*On the contrary*, I went away to Arabia.
v 17	I returned to Damascus (traveling there directly, that is to say, *not* passing through Jerusalem).
vv 18–19	After three years had passed I did go up to Jerusalem . . . but, aside from Cephas, I did *not* see any of the other apostles, except James.
v 20	What I am writing to you is *not* a lie.
v 21	Then I went to the region of Syria and Cilicia (*far* from Jerusalem).
vv 22–23	Thus, through the whole of this period the Christians in the churches of Judea (including the one in Jerusalem) did *not* even know me by sight; they only heard stories about me.

The length and concerted nature of this narrative compel one to speak of a formal denial, made necessary because — giving, one supposes, their own account of Paul's first Jerusalem visit (vv 18–19) — the Teachers are telling the Galatians something like this:

> The man called Paul spent a significant amount of time in Jerusalem receiving accurate instruction in the gospel-tradition from the apostles in the mother church. Later, pursuing a pseudo-mission among Gentiles — including you yourselves — he deviated seriously from that true line of tradition, and he continues to do that to this day.

Faced with such an accusation, Paul composes what we might call a *negative travelogue,* for in it he is intent primarily on saying where he was *not* (Jerusalem), where he was only *very briefly* (Jerusalem), whom he did *not confer with* (the circle of apostles in the Jerusalem church), and whom he did *not* see (members of the churches in Judea, including the one in Jerusalem). The result is a formal defense.

But while the term "defense" is appropriate as a description of the negative travelogue (1:17–24), one significant qualification is necessary. The motif of independence is more than Paul's defense against charges brought by the Teachers. Fundamentally, it reflects Paul's understanding of the relationship between his own apostolate and that of the apostles in the Jerusalem church, and thus the relationship between the mission to the Gentiles and the mission to the Jews.

THE APOSTLE PAUL AND THE APOSTLES IN THE JERUSALEM CHURCH

The fact that the Teachers falsely portray the Jerusalem apostles as Paul's teachers does not cause Paul either to deny the existence of those apostles or to negate their place in God's salvific plan. Both here and elsewhere in his letters Paul freely speaks of the Jerusalem apostles, including Peter, probably also James, Andronicus and Junia (Rom 16:7), and doubtless others as well.[232] A closed circle, this group did not encompass all witnesses to the resurrection (1 Cor 15:6). It was made up of members of the Jerusalem church who had been called by the resurrected Lord to the apostolate that would evangelize the Jews (1 Cor 9:1). Paul acknowledges the apostolic calling of these persons.

One notes, however, that Paul follows a practice apparently characteristic of the churches in Syria by allowing the word "apostle" to have a reference reaching beyond the circle of the apostles in the Jerusalem church. At least some of the pneumatic evangelists sent out by the church in Antioch were designated by that same term. Paul and Barnabas were examples, both being Antioch apostles, equipped for a Spirit-oriented mission and sent out from the Antioch church specifically as evangelists to the Gentiles (Gal 2:1–13; Acts 13:1–3). In the case of Paul one sees, then, an apostolate that had in the early period of his work two foci. He was sure of his having been called to his Gentile mission by the resurrected Lord himself; and in that early period he was also conscious of being sent out on that mission by the Antioch church, just as was Barnabas. Hence, had someone asked Paul at the time of the Jerusalem meeting whether he was an apostle sponsored by the Antioch church, he would surely have answered in the affirmative, seeing no conflict between that identity and the one given him directly by the risen Lord.

Later, after the painful breach with the church in Antioch, a development in which messengers from the Jerusalem church played a role (2:11–14), Paul reverted solely to his call by the risen Lord, conscious of being an apostolic evangelist sent by Christ into the whole of the Gentile world, and receiving regular support neither from a "home church" nor from those to whom he preached

---

[232]On "apostle," see Comment #1 and Notes on 1:1 and 1:17; on the reading of the names in Rom 16:7, see Fitzmyer, *Romans.*

(1 Cor 9:6). In writing to the Galatians Paul speaks of his call in terms that accent the motifs of the loner and of world-foreignness, doing that for two reasons: First, the Teachers have charged him with being an unfaithful student of the Jerusalem apostles. Second, he has now had a painful history with the churches in Antioch and Jerusalem (see Comment #46).

THE MISSION TO THE JEWS AND THE MISSION TO THE GENTILES

By the time he writes to his Galatian churches—and even as early as the Jerusalem conference—all of these factors converge in the clarity with which Paul sees the relationship between the mission to the Jews and the one to the Gentiles, a matter to which we will return in Comment #19. Here it will suffice to say that already in the negative travelogue of 1:17–24 Paul shows a dual conviction: (1) Both of these missions are being carried out by apostles sent to their work by God himself, and (2) it is God's will that these missions proceed along two lines completely parallel to one another. The priority of the mission to the Jews, that is to say, is chronological, not essential. God did not choose to found the Jewish mission in order, then, to build the Gentile mission on that earlier foundation. Nor did he choose to cause the gospel to radiate out into the whole of the world from Jerusalem (*contra* Luke's picture in Acts). Along parallel lines God is at work in both missions, creating his church by *simultaneously* drawing into it former Jews and former Gentiles, thus making it his new creation.[233]

COMMENT #17
CHRONOLOGY AND GEOGRAPHY: PAUL'S LABORS PRIOR TO THE MEETING IN THE JERUSALEM CHURCH

Recent decades have seen several serious attempts to write comprehensive accounts of Pauline chronology, that matter becoming among NT scholars virtually a field of subspecialization (Introduction §4). The present Comment is designed to make only two observations about Paul's pre-conference labors as they are presented in Gal 1:17–2:1.[234]

CHRONOLOGY: THE ADVERB "THEN"

In the Note on 1:18 we have mentioned Paul's use of the adverb "then" in that verse, and in 1:21 and 2:1 as well. These three references show that Paul intends to give a chronologically linear account of his travels and activity over a period of some length:

Galatians 1

16. [After God's call sent me to preach his Son among the Gentiles] I immediately kept to myself, not asking advice from anyone. 17. Nor did I make a trip

---

[233]The refrains "the Jew first, and also the Gentile" (Rom 1:16) and "there is no distinction" (Rom 3:22) have been well analyzed by Bassler, *Impartiality*; idem, "Impartiality."
[234]The place of Galatians within the chronological order of Paul's letters will be discussed in Comment #24.

up to Jerusalem to see those who were already apostles before I became one. On the contrary, I went away to Arabia, and later I returned to Damascus. 18. *Then*, after three years had passed, I did go up to Jerusalem in order to visit Cephas, and I stayed with him two weeks. 19. I saw none of the other apostles, except James, the brother of the Lord. 20. What I am writing to you is no lie, God being my witness! 21. *Then*, I went to the regions of Syria and Cilicia. 22. And through the whole of this time, I was still unknown by sight to the churches of Judea which are in Christ. 23. They only heard it said about me that "the man who formerly persecuted us is now preaching the faith which he had earlier tried to destroy"; 24. time and again they ascribed glory to God because of me.

Galatians 2

1. *Then*, after fourteen years, I went up to Jerusalem again, accompanied by Barnabas . . .

Given the structure of the narrative, one's first impression may be that Paul depicts that sequence in a simple way, relating each event to its predecessor: First "A" happened; then "B"; then "C"; then "D." But what is one to make of the fact that in two instances Paul combines the adverb "then" with a specific number of years?

1:18. Then, after three years . . .
2:1. Then, after fourteen years . . .

Does Paul intend in these two instances a simple narrative sequence, measuring an interval between consecutive events? Or does he, in one or both cases, measure a specific number of years from the first event in the sequence? This question has been extensively and sharply debated.[235]

We do well to approach the question by taking into account not only Paul's use of the adverb *epeita* but also the instance in v 16 of the adverb *eutheôs*: "*immediately* after that [my call], I kept to myself . . . ; nor did I make a trip to Jerusalem . . ." In this sentence Paul is clearly taking his call as the point from which chronological measurement is to be made, and he is using the adverb *eutheôs* to indicate the temporal measurement between his call and a trip to Jerusalem. He says, that is, that *immediately* after his call he kept to himself, not going to the Jerusalem church. It is highly probable, then, that he uses the adverbial expression in v 18 — "then, after three years" — in the same way, indicating the length of time between his call and his actually making a trip to Jerusalem. One may paraphrase the two references to a Jerusalem trip as follows:

[235]Beyond the commentaries, see the specialized studies mentioned in Introduction §4. In favor of the simple reading, one could point out that in 1 Corinthians 15 Paul five times uses the adverb *epeita* in the simple way to indicate a sequence of events (vv 5, 6, 7, 23, 46). The comparison is of no real help, however, for in these instances Paul does not combine the adverb with a time measurement.

16. *Immediately after* my call, I kept to myself. 17. I did not make a trip up to Jerusalem to see those who were already apostles before I became one. 18. Then, not having gone up to Jerusalem immediately after my call, *when about three years had passed since that event,* I did go up to Jerusalem in order to visit Cephas.[236]

And the same intention seems to be expressed in 2:1:

Then, *about fourteen years after my call,* I went up to Jerusalem again, accompanied by Barnabas . . .

The results can be easily sketched:

(1) Paul was called by God when he was persecuting the church in Damascus (1:13, 17).
(2) For about three years after his call, he was distant from Jerusalem, working in Arabia and Damascus (1:18).
(3) Leaving Damascus, he took a two-week trip to visit Peter in Jerusalem (1:18).
(4) After that trip, attaching himself to the church in Antioch, he worked out of that church, preaching the gospel to Gentiles both nearby, in Syria, and as far west as Cilicia (1:21).
(5) About fourteen years after his call, the Antioch church sent him as one of its representatives to a conference held in the church of Jerusalem (2:1).
(6) Shortly after that, there was a painful incident in the Antioch church, leading Paul to inaugurate his own work (in his own circle) as an independent apostle to the Gentiles (2:11–14).[237]

---

[236]The translation *"about* three years" is necessary because in Paul's day there were several ways of counting years, one being to count as the first of several years the calendar year *in* which the first event occurred (see, e.g., *m. Rosh Hash.* 1:1). In terms of the modern calendar it is as though an event occurring shortly after Christmas were to be considered to begin its second year on January 1. Thus, it is possible that when Paul says "three years," he means two years plus several days, weeks, or months. Nothing in the text of Galatians provides greater precision.

[237]If one is concerned to fix absolute dates, the safest point from which to take one's bearings may be Gal 1:18. Assuming that the trip to Jerusalem mentioned there was taken from Damascus, as seems almost certain, we can reasonably equate it with the reference to a departure from Damascus mentioned in 2 Cor 11:32–33. And since the latter reference includes the notice that this departure happened when Aretas was king in Damascus, we can place Paul's first trip to Jerusalem between A.D. 37 and 39 (Jewett, *Chronology,* 32, followed by Murphy-O'Connor, "Missions," 74). Given the scheme laid out above — and anticipating the remainder of the present Comment — dates could then be assigned as follows: (a) About A.D. 35, persecuting the church in Damascus, Paul is called by God to be an evangelist to Gentiles. (b) From about A.D. 35 to 38 he works in Damascus and Arabia. (c) About A.D. 38 he leaves Damascus, visiting Peter for two weeks in Jerusalem, and going from Jerusalem to Antioch, instead of returning to Damascus. (d) For the decade from ca. A.D. 38 to A.D. 48, having the empathetic Antioch church as his base and Barnabas as his trusted coworker, Paul preaches the gospel to Gentiles in Syria and as far west as his native Cilicia. (e) In ca. A.D. 48, as a trusted delegate of the Antioch church, he travels a second time to Jerusalem, with his colleague Barnabas, in order to participate

GEOGRAPHY

We have noted that the nature of 1:17–24 as a negative travelogue shatters all hope of drawing from it a highly detailed and precise account of the places and temporal junctures of Paul's activities in the period prior to the Jerusalem conference. About matters that would be of no help in demonstrating his distance from Jerusalem Paul says nothing. Two instances of his silence nevertheless demand our attention: In composing the travelogue Paul nowhere mentions the church of Antioch; he also fails to speak of the founding of the Galatian churches.

(1) *Paul and the church in Antioch.* Everything in 2:1–14 indicates that prior to the painful incident in the Antioch church, Paul was functioning, alongside Barnabas, as one of Antioch's evangelists to the Gentiles. An event of considerable importance must therefore be supplied between Paul's visit with Peter (1:18–20) and his commencing his work in Syria and Cilicia (1:21). After conferring with Peter, that is, Paul must have journeyed to Antioch, rather than returning to Damascus. And in Antioch he must have attached himself quite closely to a church that may have had, already at that time, a Gentile mission, being thus drawn — along with its daughter churches — both from Jews and from Gentiles (2:13). Already an apostle sent into his work by Christ, Paul now became an apostle sent by Christ through the Antioch church. We can be confident that in 1:21 Paul refers to labors he carried out shoulder-to-shoulder with Barnabas, both in the area surrounding Antioch (Syria) and somewhat further to the west (Cilicia). It is, then, the later and deeply painful break with the church in Antioch (2:11–14) that explains Paul's silence about that church in his travelogue, and specifically his failing to mention his Antioch attachment at the outset of 1:21.

(2) *Paul's founding of the Galatian churches.* Having concluded in the Introduction (§3) that the Galatian churches were very probably located in the cities of Ankyra and Pessinus (perhaps also in the trading center of Tavium), we must now ask about the date of their birth. Here three matters demand our attention: First, we look yet again at 1:21, Paul's reference to his work in the period preceding the Jerusalem conference. Then we consider his statement about preserving the truth of the gospel by withstanding the False Brothers at the Jerusalem conference (2:5). Finally, we take into consideration Paul's references to Barnabas in 2:1, 9, 13.

(a) *Galatians 1:21 (Paul's work in Syria and Cilicia).* Reading this verse in the context of the travelogue, exegetes commonly take three steps: First, they relate the verse to Paul's intention mentioned above. Since he wishes to emphasize his

---

in the conference between the churches of Antioch and Jerusalem. (f) From ca. A.D. 48 onward, following a bitter estrangement from the Antioch church and from Barnabas, Paul turns to the west, founding churches in Galatia and in several of the cities surrounding the Aegean Sea (Philippi, Thessalonica, Corinth, Ephesus). We have only to note serious disagreements among the experts in Pauline chronology, however, to conclude that our confidence in absolute dating cannot be great. And noting that in Acts Luke mentions neither the founding of the Galatian churches nor their invasion by the Teachers, the student of Galatians can expect little help from that source. See the caveat of Slingerland, "Acts 18:1–18."

distance from Jerusalem, Paul says simply that after his brief visit with Peter, he "went to the regions of Syria and Cilicia." Second, having noted that intention, most interpreters add, quite reasonably, that it precludes Paul's giving a complete itinerary for this pre-conference period. Thus, his silence regarding Galatia in Gal 1:21 is considered to have no significance. Third, given what we know from the other letters — not to mention Acts — many interpreters say next that Paul must have been active in this period far beyond Syria and Cilicia. Following a now-famous comment of J. Weiss, the majority of interpreters supply what Paul fails to say in Gal 1:21, thus concluding that — in spite of this instance of silence — Paul's work *prior* to the conference must have included the founding of the churches in Galatia, Macedonia, and Achaia.[238]

But this line of argument has only the appearance of reading Gal 1:21 in its context. In fact, it bends that verse to fit chronological/geographical conclusions reached on the basis of data found elsewhere (in Acts, in others of Paul's letters, or in both), thus violating the simple rule of Pauline chronology mentioned in the Introduction (§4). To read Gal 1:21 as an element in Paul's Galatian letter — to read it, that is, in the context of the negative travelogue — is to see that the absence of a reference to Galatia is highly significant.

Everyone agrees that one of Paul's major intentions in composing the travelogue is to demonstrate his distance from Jerusalem. What is commonly overlooked is that nothing would have offered the Galatians stronger proof of that distance than for Paul to have said:

Then, I went to the regions of Syria and Cilicia, far removed from Jerusalem, coming even to the cities of Galatia, as you yourselves well remember.

Had Paul been able to say that, he would certainly have done so.[239] His silence in 1:21 regarding the founding of the Galatian churches is, then, far from insignificant. It is the strongest indication that, when he went to the Jerusalem conference — in the company of his coworker Barnabas — he had not yet traveled to Galatia.[240]

---

[238]Weiss, "The statement of the Apostle . . . (Gal 1:21) . . . has merely the *negative* purpose of showing that he had removed himself far from the 'sphere of influence' of the original Apostles" (*Christianity*, 1.203; emphasis added).

[239]See FBK 193. Had Paul been in Galatia prior to the conference, he would have been able to prove his distance from Jerusalem by calling on the proverbial *two* witnesses: the churches in Galatia and the churches in Judea (1:22–24).

[240]Luedemann has been willing to identify the pre-conference dating of Paul's westward mission as the major thesis of his remarkably detailed and sometimes insightful book on Pauline chronology (*Chronology*, 291). His interpretation of Gal 1:21, however, is no more convincing than previous arguments have been, for it does not truly take into account Paul's intention to compose a travelogue that will *prove* his distance from Jerusalem (59–61). One is disappointed, then, to see that Luedemann's treatment of Gal 1:21 is followed by Murphy-O'Connor in an otherwise helpful study ("Missions," 79). According to Jewett (*Chronology*, 2), Suggs showed years ago that "the second missionary journey came before instead of after the Apostolic Conference" (the reference is to Suggs, "Date"). See further the postscript Luedemann wrote for the English translation of his work on

(b) *Galatians 2:5 (the preservation of the truth of the gospel)*. In the Note on this verse we will see that the Greek construction easily allows the translation

[In resisting the enslaving attempt of the False Brothers, Barnabas and I acted] so that the truth of the gospel might remain, coming eventually to you [Galatians].

This rendering does not have great probative value in itself, but in light of the conclusion we have reached on the basis of 1:21, it is to be preferred.

(c) *Galatians 2:1, 9, 13 (Barnabas)*. The dating of the birth of the Galatian churches after the conference — and, as we will see below, after the painful incident in Antioch — would become very questionable, however, if we could show that the churches were founded while Paul and Barnabas were working as a team. For from Paul's references to Barnabas (2:1, 9, 13) it is clear that that teamwork was limited to the period before Paul's break with the church in Antioch.[241] But in the passages in which Paul speaks of the birth of the Galatian churches, he gives no hint at all that on his trip into Galatia he was accompanied by Barnabas. On the contrary, he speaks consistently as though he had been at that time alone (1:8–9; 4:13–15).[242]

Could one perhaps argue that he speaks in that way merely because he is estranged from Barnabas as he writes the letter? Hardly. That estrangement is reflected in Paul's report of the Jerusalem conference (see Comments #18 and #20); but it does not bring Paul to eclipse Barnabas entirely from his account of that event, for Barnabas was in fact there playing his part. Similarly, on the hypothesis that Barnabas was involved in preaching the gospel in Galatia, one can imagine Paul's reducing his colleague's role; but it is scarcely credible that, in writing 4:13–15, he would erase Barnabas's role entirely, virtually inviting the Galatians to correct his account. We have here another indication that Paul's work in Galatia came after his estrangement from Barnabas, therefore after the incident in the Antioch church, and thus after the Jerusalem conference.[243]

Conclusion. Observations primarily focused on data in Galatians itself leave us, then, with one conclusion: Paul founded the Galatian churches (and thus

---

chronology; recent studies of Suhl, "Beginn"; idem, "Chronologie"; Georgi, *Remembering*, 128–137. The argument of Mitchell, by which, following Bruce, he harmonizes Galatians and Acts, runs aground on Paul's silence in Gal 1:21 (*Anatolia*, 5).

[241] One might pause momentarily over the possibility that Paul and Barnabas traveled to Galatia between the conference and the Antioch incident. Again, however, one would have to explain Paul's failure to mention such a development in Galatians 2.

[242] Was Paul accompanied in Galatia by a distinctly junior partner, Silvanus (cf. Acts 15:36–16:3a)? We cannot know, but Gal 4:13–15 scarcely suggests such a picture.

[243] The change in Paul's working companions after the Antioch incident is reflected with partial accuracy in Acts 15:36–16:3a. Luedemann's attempt to revive the view that the Antioch incident preceded the Jerusalem conference (*Chronology*, 75–77) has found little support. See Georgi, *Remembering*, 128–137.

those in Macedonia and Achaia as well) after the Antioch incident had led to his break with Barnabas, and indeed with the Antioch church itself.[244] The Galatian congregations were not founded, then, as daughter churches of the church in Antioch. From their birth they bore the peculiar marks of the theology Paul developed after his painful break from that great church in the east.[245]

[244]The chronological difficulties that arise from this conclusion are real: By beginning not only with Paul's letters but also and emphatically with Galatians itself, we have arrived at a picture in which the extensive and complex labors of Paul in the cities of Galatia, in Philippi, Thessalonica, Corinth, and Ephesus fall in the period after the Jerusalem conference. But that period may have been eight years or more in length. Thus the problems are not insoluble, as one can see from FBK 180; Lührmann 10 (German edition); Georgi, *Remembering*; and Suhl, "Beginn," to cite a few scholars who agree in placing the founding of the Galatian churches after the conference.

[245]There is no good reason to think that, in preaching the gospel to the Galatians, Paul mentioned the Antioch incident. On the contrary, it was very probably from the Teachers that the Galatians first heard of both the Jerusalem conference and the Antioch incident. We can be confident, however, that Paul's preaching in Galatia was theologically informed by these events. Having seen the virus of nomistic rectification spread from the False Brothers in the Jerusalem church to his home church in Antioch, Paul was doubly careful, we can be sure, to found the Galatian churches on the basis of the gospel of grace, centered in the cross of Christ (3:1). One can understand, then, the depth of his dismay and anger on learning that that same virus had been carried to those churches by the Teachers, persons presenting themselves as representatives of the Jerusalem gospel.

2:1–10 A CONFERENCE INVOLVING
TWO CHURCHES

TRANSLATION

2:1. Then, after fourteen years, I went up to Jerusalem again, accompanied by Barnabas; and I also took along Titus. 2. I went up as a result of revelation. And I communicated to them the gospel that I preach among the Gentiles; then I did the same thing in a private setting with those who were the acknowledged leaders, lest it should somehow turn out that in my work I was running or had run in vain. 3. But my anxiety proved baseless, for Titus, who was with me, was not compelled to be circumcised, even though he was a Greek. 4. Yet, because of the False Brothers, secretly smuggled in, who indeed came in stealthily in order to spy out our freedom that we have in Christ Jesus, their purpose being to enslave us, 5. to whom we did not give in even momentarily, so that the truth of the gospel might remain, coming eventually to you. 6. Moreover, from the acknowledged leaders of the Jerusalem church — what sort of persons they were is to me a matter of no consequence; God does not play favorites — those leaders did not add anything to my gospel. 7. On the contrary, they saw clearly that I had been entrusted by God with the gospel as it is directed to those who are not circumcised, just as Peter had been entrusted with the gospel to those who are circumcised. 8. For he who was at work in Peter, creating an apostolate to those who are circumcised, was also at work in me, sending me to the Gentiles. 9. Coming to see that fact, and thus coming to perceive the grace given to me by God, James and Cephas and John — those held by the Jerusalem church to be "the pillars" — shook hands with me and Barnabas, signifying that, in fellowship with one another, we were to go to the Gentiles and they to those who are circumcised. 10. The only other move on their part was a request that we remember "the poor," and this was a request which I was eager to carry out.

LITERARY STRUCTURE AND SYNOPSIS

Explicitly commencing his account of the Jerusalem conference with the statement that his attendance at the meeting was itself an apocalyptic development (2:2), Paul narrates an event in which the leaders of the Jerusalem church came to perceive the divine origin of the gospel he preaches to the Gentiles. With this account, then, Paul demonstrates the final statement in the thesis of 1:11–12:

[The gospel I preach] came to me by God's apocalyptic revelation of Jesus Christ.

But since the Jerusalem leaders came to share that perception in spite of a contrary opinion on the part of others in that community (2:4), it is not surprising that in a polemical tone Paul continues the use of negatives we saw to be characteristic of the travelogue (Comment #16). To that earlier line of negation Paul now adds:

2:3. Titus was *not* compelled to be circumcised.
2:5. To the False Brothers we did *not* give in even momentarily.
2:6. The leaders of the Jerusalem church did *not* add anything to my gospel.

The dramatic tension created by these emphatic negations is reinforced by Paul's presenting a series of scenes marked off by changes in the dramatis personae:

Scene 1 (v 1). Actors: Paul, Barnabas, and Titus. They journey from the Antioch church to the church in Jerusalem.

Scene 2 (v 2a). Actors: Paul and the members of the Jerusalem congregation. Paul communicates his gospel to the Jerusalem church as a whole.

Scene 3 (v 2b). Actors: Paul and the Jerusalem leaders. Paul communicates his gospel in a private setting.

Scene 4 (vv 3–5). Actors: The "False Brothers," Titus, Paul, and Barnabas (note the "we" of v 5). In this scene Paul first gives the outcome of a process (v 3); then he portrays the process itself (vv 4–5).

Scene 5 (vv 6–10). Actors: The leaders of the Jerusalem church (Peter, James, and John) and Paul and Barnabas. The Jerusalem leaders come to perceive that God is no less active in Paul's Gentile mission than he is in Peter's work among the Jews. An official agreement is worded; all acknowledge it; the Jerusalem leaders add only one thing, a request that Paul and Barnabas remember "the poor."

NOTES

2:1. *Then.* For the third time Paul employs the adverb *epeita* (1:18, 21), thus introducing yet another episode in the revelatory history that he writes in the form of a personal memoir.

after fourteen years. This phrase is of some importance for one's attempt to piece together a chronology of Paul's life and work. Scholars expert in that matter have read the reference in various ways. In Comment #17 we have seen reason to think that Paul refers to an event fourteen years after his call (1:15–16).

I went up to Jerusalem. Modes of land transportation in ancient times — mostly one's legs — caused people to refer to a trip as "up" or "down" according to physical elevation. Paul uses the common expression for a journey to Jerusalem, a city on the elevated Judean ridge. When we note, however, that the antecedent of the pronoun "them" in v 2 must be the members of the Jerusalem church (certainly not the residents of the city of Jerusalem), we see that when Paul uses the word "Jerusalem," he thinks both of the city and — emphatically — of the Jerusalem church. See Comment #46.

From what region or city did he begin this second trip to Jerusalem? A single factor indicates that this journey was begun in Antioch. Paul indicates that he was accompanied by Barnabas, and, as we shall see later (notably in 2:13), at the time of the Jerusalem meeting Barnabas was a weighty leader of the church in Syrian Antioch. Moreover, there are several indications in 2:1–10 that the meeting Paul now recounts was understood by all of the participants — at least at the time it was held — to be a conference in which *two churches* were dealing with one another via their representatives. Barnabas and Paul represented the church of Antioch; James, Peter, and John represented the church of Jerusalem. It follows that when Paul actually commenced this second trip to Jerusalem, he was back in the east, specifically in Syrian Antioch, being as yet on good terms with the Antioch church, still functioning as a missionary sponsored by that church.

It is therefore striking that Paul speaks of this trip and of the meeting in Jerusalem without mentioning either Antioch or its church. This instance of silence is at least as significant as Paul's failure to mention the Antioch church at any point in the travelogue of 1:17–24. In order to sense its significance, we will be helped by bearing in mind several questions: (a) What was the precise nature of the meeting? (b) In his account does Paul suppress dimensions of the meeting other participants would have mentioned? (c) If he does engage in such suppression, what are his motives? See Comment #18.

accompanied by Barnabas. Where Paul could have written "Barnabas and I went up to Jerusalem," he says instead, "I went up to Jerusalem, with Barnabas." That is to be explained in part by noting that Paul adheres to the form of the personal memoir, employing verbs in the first person. But we see also that after this initial and rather casual reference to Barnabas, Paul causes his colleague to drop from sight until v 9, where he portrays the final stance taken by the Jerusalem leaders (on the plural verb in v 5, see below). Moreover, he says in the final clause of v 1 that it was he, not he and Barnabas, who "took Titus along," and he refers to Titus as having been "with me," rather than "with us" (v 3). More is involved than the style of the personal memoir. Again see Comment #18.

and I also took along Titus. As we have hinted above, Paul portrays Titus as a convert not of himself and Barnabas, partners active in the mission of the Antioch church, but rather as a convert of himself alone. Crucial to Paul as he writes to the Galatians is not that the Antioch church and its mission were made present at the conference by that church's representatives (himself and Barnabas), but rather that *his gospel* was made present by a piece of its fruit, Titus.[1]

2. *I went up as a result of revelation.* Were Paul writing an account similar in style to that of Acts 15, he might have said,

> and Barnabas and I went up as a result of the Antioch church's concern that certain people in the Jerusalem church were spying on the Antioch church's Gentile mission. That church therefore deputized us to be its representatives in a conference it was to have with the church of Jerusalem.

By contrast, Paul makes his memoir emphatically lean. He says that God was the cause of his making the journey: "I went up because God revealed to me that I should go."[2]

This is the third point in the memoir at which Paul speaks of God's activity in revelation (1:12, 16). What is at stake in the whole of the memoir is Paul's gospel, and that gospel is God's activity, not a collection of human traditions that could be rationally discussed and debated by a group of human beings, acting as a kind of judicatory. On the contrary, the gospel is the event by which God is now creating history! Just as it is the event that *begins* with God's revelation of his Son (1:12, 16), the point at which God powerfully steps on the scene, so the event of the gospel *continues*. One can even say that the gospel has a future, because God repeats his apocalyptic presence.

I communicated to them. In the middle voice, as here, the verb *anatithêmi* can mean "to refer a matter to a deliberative body for its consideration" (Polybius Frag. 21.46.11). Hence the common paraphrase of the present clause as "I submitted my gospel for their consideration." But the verb can also have the simple force of communicating something that is one's own, with a view to consultation (e.g., Plutarch *Mor.* 2.772d), and that is the meaning intended here. Dunn is right: Paul is careful to indicate that he did not go to the Jerusalem church cap in hand.[3] He is consulting with the Jerusalem church ("them") in the proper sense of taking counsel together, but there is no indication that he thinks of submitting his gospel to the judgment of higher authorities. We will note below his emphatic use of verbs of perception in connection with the leaders of the Jerusalem church. It follows that upon his arrival he must first have pondered the question

---

[1]Titus was very probably a member of one of the Gentile daughter churches of the church in Antioch. He might even have belonged to a congregation as far afield as one of the cities in Cilicia (cf. 1:21). Although Acts has no reference to Titus — none even in the account of the Jerusalem meeting — we know that, in a later period, Titus was a close companion of Paul in the work in Corinth (2 Cor 2:13; 7:6, 13, 14; 8:6, 16, 23; 12:16). Luedemann's argument (*Chronology,* 106) that Titus was from Greece itself, and that that indicates a Pauline mission on the Greek mainland prior to the Jerusalem conference, has been correctly questioned by several reviewers, including Fitzmyer (Review of Luedemann).

[2]On *kata* plus accusative as "because of, as a result of, on the basis of," see BAGD II.5.δ.

[3]Dunn, "Relationship," 467; cf. Satake, "1Kr 15,3."

Will they perceive the truth of the gospel revealed to me by God himself, or will they fail to perceive it?

Paul put his gospel before them, doubtless to some extent in sermonic form, for the gospel is preached event. And he did so in the hope of their perceiving the truth: God was at work in it.

them. Strictly speaking, this pronoun has no antecedent, but the intended reference is clear. The "them" to whom Paul presented his gospel is the Jerusalem church. Thus, in 2:1 Paul has used the word "Jerusalem" as a metonym for the church there, a locution that will prove important to the interpretation of 4:25 (see Comment #46).

the gospel that I preach. Here again, rather than including Barnabas, Paul uses the first person singular. The formula in 2:9 shows clearly that at the time of the conference Barnabas was Paul's evangelical partner, preaching the same gospel to the same people, Gentiles. In Galatia, however, Barnabas's preaching and his vocation are not at issue; and, in addition, Paul has meanwhile suffered a divorce from Barnabas. If an account of the conference can now serve for the advancement of the gospel in Galatia, Paul will have to focus matters on *his* gospel, referring to it in the present tense: the gospel that I preach.

among the Gentiles. See the discussion of the expression "to those who are not circumcised" in the Note on v 7 below.

in a private setting. The context implies that the initiative for this additional arrangement lay with Paul. Even before the meeting, he was aware of the presence within the Jerusalem church of several identifiable groups with different tendencies, notably the leaders (vv 6 and 9) and the False Brothers (v 4), the latter having already journeyed north to see what was happening in the daughter churches of the Antioch congregation (Comments #21 and #25). He thus wished the acknowledged leaders of the Jerusalem church to hear his gospel apart from the possibly influential presence of others. Fully convinced, as we have seen, that his gospel had come — and continued to come — by God's revelation, Paul was willing to engage in the politics of God, concerned that the leaders of the church in Jerusalem have every chance to perceive God's work in his mission.[4]

those who were the acknowledged leaders. The substantive participle *hoi dokountes* is an abbreviation for the expression used in v 6a, *hoi dokountes einai ti,* "those who seem to be something," that is to say persons held in high esteem (repeated in v 6b). In v 9 Paul refers a fourth time to the same circle, finally employing the full expression, *hoi dokountes styloi einai,* "those who seem to be pillars," and giving the persons' names, "James, Cephas, and John." All three expressions reflect a language pattern employed in the Jerusalem church to refer to its leaders. Leaving aside for the moment the import of the term "pillars," one might compare the Hebrew expression "Men of Name" (*'anšê haššēm*) used for essentially the same purpose in the Qumran community (e.g., 1QM 2:6; 1QSa 2:11).

What is Paul's stance toward these men? Noting that he uses the expression

---

[4]Regarding the politics of God, cf. Lehmann, *Transfiguration.*

four times in the present paragraph (in the NT it emerges only here), not always in what one would call the same tone of voice, we are prepared for some ambivalence.[5]

On the one hand, it is clear that Paul does see these persons in a special light. Had he not acknowledged their difference from the rank-and-file members of the church in Jerusalem, he would not have taken the initiative to arrange a private conversation with them. Moreover, although Paul does not use the term "apostle" at any point in his account of the Jerusalem conference, we know that there were apostles among these leaders, and we have already noted Paul's readiness to acknowledge both the special character of apostles and the fact that others were called by God to be apostles before he was (Comment #16).

On the other hand, Paul is equally firm that God's *eschatological* vocation is the only authorization to be acknowledged among human beings. If some church members slide into the habit of referring to God's apostles as "men of impressive reputation" — was this done not only by members of the Jerusalem church but also by the Teachers? — Paul will express only his own stinging disdain, saying that God pays no attention at all to human reputation (2:6). We are again reminded of the degree to which Paul allows Galatians to be permeated by the antinomy struck in its first verse:

from human beings / from God.

Insofar as the Jerusalem leaders play their role as a result of God's vocation, Paul will gladly acknowledge their special responsibility. And in his account of the meeting he will emphasize that in that setting it is their responsibility to recognize God's gospel when it is laid before them.

lest it should somehow turn out that in my work I was running or had run in vain. In light of the Note above on the expression "I communicated to them," we might now expect Paul to contemplate the possibility that the meeting would end in a failure of perception on the part of the Jerusalem church. He could say, for example, that he arranged a private meeting with the leaders "lest it should turn out that the obstinacy of certain persons in the Jerusalem congregation should blind the entire company to the power of God at work in my gospel." Instead, at least on the face of it, he speaks not about the possibility of a failure of perception on the part of the Jerusalem church, but rather about the possibility of his having to conclude that his own work had been carried out in vain, bearing no true fruit ("running" is a widespread metaphor for exerting oneself strenuously). On any reading, Paul speaks here of a danger he saw on the horizon. What was its precise nature?

The danger is not difficult to define if we bear in mind that the conference was in point of fact a meeting in which two churches were negotiating with one another. At stake in the meeting was the gospel being preached to Gentiles by a number of missionaries sponsored by the Antioch church. It follows that the anxi-

---

[5]In classical usage a note of irony is sometimes present: those who *seem* to be something but in fact are not; for example, Plato *Gorgias* 472A.

ety which Paul emphatically personalizes — "lest it should somehow turn out that in *my* work *I* was running or had run in vain" — was first of all an anxiety experienced by the Antioch church as a congregation. For a negative stance on the part of Jerusalem would leave Antioch with only two paths: to abandon its circumcision-free mission to Gentiles, or to maintain that mission at the price of a rift with Jerusalem that would have produced two churches, one drawn from Jews and a second drawn to an increasing extent from Gentiles. In reporting to the Galatians Paul personalizes what was at that earlier time a corporate anxiety on the part of the Antioch church.

Had the Jerusalem leaders actually spoken the fateful words — "We conclude that the circumcision-free message preached to Gentiles by the church of Antioch is no gospel!" — would the Antioch church have abandoned that work? The question cannot be answered, though on the basis of 2:11–14 one would not be able to exclude the possibility that the Antioch church would have essentially acquiesced, altering its Gentile mission fundamentally. If, however, following Paul's lead, we personalize the matter to the apostle himself, the answer is both clear and emphatically negative: Everything he has said about God's way with him in 1:15–24 indicates that he could not have abandoned his call; and everything he will now say about the conference only places his vocational certainty in italics. The danger of which he speaks cannot have been that of his having to conclude that God had not called him to his work. The danger lay in the possibility that the Jerusalem leaders would *fail to perceive* something that was to Paul an absolute certainty: God's powerful work in his own preaching to Gentiles.

Why does he speak, then, of the prospect that developments might lead him to think he had worked in vain? The answer lies in his view of the church of God. The danger of a rift in the one church is fully as horrifying to him as he writes to the Galatians as it can possibly have been both to the Antioch church and to himself at the time of the meeting.[6] If the Jerusalem leaders had uttered those terrible words, Paul would surely have stood firmly by "the truth of the gospel," as he will show in the next episode (2:11–14). But he would have been shaken to his roots, for that development would have destroyed his assumption that the one "truth of the gospel" is in fact bringing into being one church of God made up of former Jews and former Gentiles (3:28; 6:15). If the Jerusalem church had failed to perceive that grand picture, the result would have been that his work was not bearing fruit *as a branch of the one vine.* That is the danger he considers in the words "lest . . . I was running or had run in vain."

3. *But.* By this strong adversative (*alla*) Paul indicates immediately that the anxieties he had at the outset of the meeting — and probably at several junctures in its course — proved groundless. And with the sentence thus introduced he begins to speak of the activity of a discrete group within the Jerusalem church, the persons he will shortly call the False Brothers. Verse 3 thus commences a scene (vv 3–5) marked off by its dramatis personae: the False Brothers, Titus, and Paul (with Barnabas included in the plural verb of v 5a).

Titus. Paul is sure that the fruit of his gospel is altogether acceptable to God,

[6]Cf. Achtemeier, *Quest*; Dunn, *Unity.*

because he knows that the Gentile Christians represented in Titus constitute one arm of God's unified outreach into the whole of the cosmos. When, then, he takes Titus into the Jewish church of Jerusalem, Paul causes the whole of the *one church* to be present in one locale, thus facing the leaders in Jerusalem with the question "Will you perceive the presence here of the wholeness of God's one church, drawn as it is both from Jews and from Gentiles?"

who was with me. Eclipsing Barnabas by not saying "who was with us," Paul again focuses his account on his own gospel.

was not compelled to be circumcised. In writing to the Galatians Paul gives a significant role to the verb "compel," twice in the construction "compel [a Gentile or Gentiles] to be circumcised" (here and at 6:12) and once in the expression "compel Gentiles to live in a Jewish manner" (2:14). In the present instance the next sentence gives the identity of the persons who attempted to compel the circumcision of Titus: the False Brothers. When, then, we note that at 6:12 Paul uses the same expression to refer to the present activity of the Teachers in Galatia, we see the character of his account of the Jerusalem meeting as a two-level drama marked by words and constructions that spring to his mind because of current developments in Galatia (Comment #18). The False Brothers act both their own once-upon-a-time role and the contemporary role of the Teachers. And the emphatic negative gives the message for the contemporary setting in Galatia: "As I withstood the False Brothers' attempt to compel the circumcision of Titus — doing that to preserve the truth of the gospel for you — so you are to do the same vis-à-vis the corresponding attempt of the Teachers at the present time."[7]

to be circumcised. For reasons just stated, Paul uses the once-upon-a-time attempt to compel the circumcision of Titus to introduce one of the letter's major motifs, circumcision (see 2:7, 8, 9, 12; 5:2, 3, 6, 11; 6:12, 13, 15; cf. 3:28). In Galatians all of Paul's references to circumcision are literal (contrast Phil 3:3; Rom 2:25–29; Col 2:11; cf. Philo *de Spec. Leg.* 1.8).[8] Indeed, in Galatians 3 Paul will subtly link the matter of circumcision to the term "flesh," taking advantage of the obvious connection. In these literal references Paul consistently sees circumcision as *the sign par excellence* of adherence to the Law.[9] One of the letter's chief issues is whether the church of God is the prolongation of ethnic Israel (see Comments #37 and #52).

4. *because of the False Brothers.* Paul begins the sentence of vv 4–5 with this prepositional phrase, but he does not complete the sentence in the manner required by the rules of grammar. He should say something like,

---

[7]A few exegetes have suggested that, after halting the False Brothers' *demand*, Paul may have acquiesced voluntarily, circumcising Titus for the sake of peace in the Jerusalem church, or for some similar reason (e.g., Duncan). That reading has the advantage of appearing, at least, to ease the problem of 5:11. For reasons given in the Note on 2:5 below, however, it is almost certain that Paul made no compromise at all with the False Brothers.

[8]On Borgen's interpretation of Gal 5:11, see the Note there.

[9]See, however, the different reading proposed by Klumbies, "Zwischen": the Teachers demanded circumcision, without intending to impose the whole of the Law.

But, because of the False Brothers . . . we found it necessary to fight for the truth of the gospel.

Instead, he allows his sentence to become a grammatical shipwreck, an anacoluthon lacking grammatical continuity. Doubtless every one of the following clauses is intended, but the relationships among them are in some instances difficult to discern, because Paul piles them onto one another without consistent attention to sentence structure.

Three points are worth noting: (a) This is the first of two glaring syntactical slips in Paul's account of the Jerusalem meeting, the other emerging in vv 6–9, a scene in which a major role is played by the leaders of the Jerusalem church. (b) Each of these grammatical non sequiturs emphasizes a negative clause:

Yet, because of the False Brothers . . . to whom we did *not* give in even momentarily . . .

Moreover, from the acknowledged leaders of the Jerusalem church . . . those leaders did *not* add anything to my gospel.

(c) Each anacoluthon occurs at a juncture at which Paul turns his attention to a group of actors who caused — and cause — an increase in his pulse rate. Had the False Brothers been able to convince the Jerusalem leaders that the circumcision of Titus was a necessary condition for the continuation of the meeting, the result would have been a tragic split in the church. Had the Jerusalem leaders insisted on adding a qualification to Paul's gospel, he would have had to reject it, and that, too, would have opened a wound in the church from which it might not have recovered. When Paul pictures these groups in his mind, he experiences a degree of mental suffering, and his syntax suffers as well.

the False Brothers. In the NT the expression occurs only in Paul's letters (here and in 2 Cor 11:26). It may be his own coinage, indicating one who, without being a real brother, "bears the name of brother" (1 Cor 5:11). We have noted above that Paul gives his attention to these men in a parenthetical scene (vv 3–5), before he returns to consider at greater length his exchange with the acknowledged leaders (vv 2, 6–10). He may very well refer to these same persons in 2 Cor 11:26, listing them among people who have persecuted him (see also Notes on Gal 4:29 and 5:11). In Comments #25, #45, and #46 we will see reasons for thinking that Paul includes the False Brothers in his reference to "the circumcision party" within the Jerusalem church (2:12). We will also conclude that — at the time of the writing of Galatians — he dares to link the Jerusalem church with slavery (4:25) because of the influence wielded in that congregation by the False Brothers.

secretly smuggled in. Polybius uses the verb, from which this passive adjective is derived, to refer to the action of admitting some Galatians secretly into a city (Frag. 2.7.8; cf. 1.18.3). Paul can count on his readers to grasp the sinister sense he intends. Perhaps certain members of the Antioch church, not truly supportive of its circumcision-free Gentile mission, facilitated the spying activity of the False Brothers.

came in stealthily. Paul pictures the False Brothers sneaking into some setting in which they had no proper business.[10] Into what setting did they enter? The fact that the meeting brought together the church of Antioch and the church of Jerusalem suggests that the False Brothers had on occasion journeyed to Antioch, where, slipping into meetings of Antioch's daughter churches, they had taken note of the pattern of life in those churches.[11]

in order to spy out. The False Brothers doubtless understood their monitoring activity to be a necessary consequence of their conviction that, at the day of judgment, God will judge all human beings on the basis of the Law.[12] They found it necessary, therefore, to see whether the Antioch church's circumcision-free mission might be compromising the legal purity of the church. If nonobservant Gentiles are brought in, the community is itself polluted and subject to judgment.[13]

Paul does not pause in order to assess the False Brothers' motives in a charitable way. He sees only something sinister, using a verb sometimes employed to refer to espionage (BAGD).

our freedom that we have in Christ Jesus, their purpose being to enslave us. When Paul's messenger had completed the reading of the letter, the Galatians will have sensed that, in writing to them, Paul had chosen to place great weight on the noun "freedom" (here, once in 5:1, and twice in 5:13), on the corresponding verb, "to set free" (5:1), on the adjective, "free," mostly used as a noun (3:28 and five times in 4:22–31), and on other terms with closely related meanings (e.g., "snatch out of the grasp of," 1:4; "redeem [out of slavery]," 3:13; 4:5). Freedom, in short, is a very large part of the message of the letter taken as a whole.

But the Galatians' experience with this motif will scarcely have begun with the hearing of Paul's letter; and we will be better able to sense the impact of Paul's references to it when we have at least a partial grasp of the pertinent elements of the Galatians' linguistic history. See Comment #22.

5. *to whom we did not give in even momentarily.* Having identified the False Brothers on the basis of their activity prior to the meeting (v 4), Paul returns to their corresponding attempt to compel the circumcision of Titus at the meeting itself (v 3). Presumably, there was a struggle witnessed by at least part of the Jerusalem church. Perhaps it was this struggle that caused Paul to take the initiative to meet privately with the recognized leaders (v 2). In any case, Paul's manner of expression shows that he had a genuine battle with adversaries who were able to bring to bear considerable pressure. Surprisingly enough, the textual history of v 5 raises the question whether in the face of such pressure, Paul gave way, at least to some degree. Four readings are attested:

---

[10]It is worth noting that Paul uses this same verb (*pareiserchomai*) when, in Rom 5:20, he speaks of the advent of the Law: "The Law came in by a side door . . ." See Comment #38.

[11]Cf. Georgi, *Remembering*, 23.

[12]Stuhlmacher, *Evangelium*, 89.

[13]The False Brothers may also have thought that the circumcision-free mission of the Antioch church was endangering the Jerusalem church in its thoroughly Jewish setting. See Jewett, "Agitators."

(1) to whom we did not give in even momentarily
(2) we did not give in even momentarily
(3) to whom we did give in momentarily.
(4) we did give in momentarily.[14]

Readings 2 and 4 can be quickly put aside. Lacking the expression "to whom," they constitute a scribal attempt to erase the roughness of the anacoluthon mentioned above in connection with the words "because of the False Brothers." We are left, then, with readings 1 and 3, and here a decision is once again easy. The third reading is almost certainly the work of a copyist intent on portraying Paul as a reasonable man, capable of compromise.[15] Moreover, since it is clear that Paul views the circumcision movement in Galatia as a development that is threatening to the gospel, it is inconceivable that he would report having defended the gospel at an earlier juncture by yielding momentarily to the demand for the circumcision of Titus! Reading 1, then, best preserves the words of Paul. Vis-à-vis the False Brothers, Paul was an uncompromising warrior.

Even in the Jerusalem meeting the gospel thrusts its preachers not into a state of otherworldly peace, but rather into battle. In this battle Paul was triumphant. The False Brothers did not succeed in persuading the leaders of the Jerusalem church to take their position.

we. However shaken Paul was by Barnabas's later behavior during the incident in Antioch (2:11–14), he is willing — perhaps happy — to portray Barnabas as his steady comrade in struggling against the False Brothers.

the truth of the gospel. This is an expression that Paul constructs with care, so as to lay more or less equal weight on the two nouns "truth" and "gospel." One is reminded of the fact that only in Galatians does Paul refer to himself as one

---

[14]Reading 1 is the statement of a radical and wholly uncompromising theologian, while reading 3, supported by the western text and a number of the Church Fathers, is that of a man given, at least on occasion, to flexibility, presumably for the sake of peace within the church. The weight of manuscript evidence favors reading 1, for it is very widely attested, except for D*. Transcriptional probability also supports that reading, as we will see.

[15](a) In the early history of the Church, we can easily find theologians who would gladly have changed the first reading into the third, for one of the major developments in the early interpretation of Paul is the tendency to domesticate his radicality (Lindemann, *Paulus*; de Boer, "Images"). Moreover, that tendency is apparent in the Acts of the Apostles, and it is worth noting that the third reading makes the author of Galatians look somewhat like the Paul of Acts. For, even if Timothy was considered a Jew by birth, having a Jewish mother, he had not been circumcised. According to Acts, then, finding Timothy to be a faithful Christian, Paul wanted Timothy to accompany him, *and* "because of the Jews in those places (Cilicia)," Paul circumcised him (Acts 16:3). (b) The third reading does not fit well into the form of the denial that stretches all the way from 1:12 to 2:6, whereas the first reading continues the motif of the denial. Just as Paul will deny in v 6 that the leaders of the Jerusalem church provided an addendum to his gospel, so he now denies that he and Barnabas gave in to the False Brothers even momentarily. (c) There is finally the matter of the relationship between the two clauses of v 5. Paul does not say that he walked a path designed to keep peace in the church (he does not consider the False Brothers really to be in the church). He says that the action of himself and Barnabas was taken "so that the truth of the gospel might remain."

who "speaks the truth," doing so in order to contrast himself with the Teachers (4:16–17; cf. 1:20), saying also that the Teachers are causing the Galatians to waiver in their obedience to "the truth" (5:7). What is at stake in Galatia is the truth.

Paul is far from concerned, however, to offer a philosophical discourse on truth. Here, in his initial use of the noun (as also later in 2:14), he allows the term "truth" to be defined by the term "gospel." When he links the nouns "truth" and "gospel," he does two things to the former: First, he gives to it a specificity it does not have in common parlance, by saying that the truth *is* the gospel of Jesus Christ. Second, he reflects his perception of a crucial antinomy not really grasped by placing opposite one another truth and falsehood. Were the truth of the gospel not to remain, the result would not be falsehood, but rather disaster in the form of apocalyptic judgment (cf. 2 Cor 2:14–16 and Gal 5:21).

We have, then, an instance in which Paul brings to bear the eschatological force of the major Hebrew term for truth (*'ĕmet*). The truth of the gospel is not a thing. Truth is, rather, the end-time *event* of God's redemption in Jesus Christ. For that reason its genuine opposite is not human falsehood, but rather judgment at the hands of the God who judges in his truth-event (cf. 1:8–9; 5:10b).[16]

might remain, coming eventually to you. In speaking of the truth of the gospel, Paul allows an explicit coalescence between the two levels of the drama. Having said that he and Barnabas waged a battle in *Jerusalem* against the False Brothers, he tells *the Galatians* that the battle was waged in their behalf. That much is obvious. Not immediately clear is the force of the prepositional phrase *pros hymas* in the expression *diamenō pros hymas*. Does the expression mean "remain with you," or does it mean "remain for you"? That is to say, thinking his way back into the various scenes of the Jerusalem conference, does Paul intend to say that he and Barnabas did battle so that the truth of the gospel might remain *with* the Galatians, their having already received it? Or does he mean that the battle was waged so that the truth of the gospel might remain *for* the Galatians, in the sense that, being thus preserved, it would make its way *to* them in due time?

Because linguistic considerations do not settle the matter, the observations we have made about the force of 1:21 are our best guide (see Comment #17).[17] They have led us to conclude that Paul did not found the Galatian churches prior to

---

[16]Stuhlmacher (*Evangelium*, 90 n2) has quoted a memorable comment of H. von Soden: "Truth is not something that lies somehow beneath or behind things, as though one could find it by penetrating matters to their innermost parts. Truth is that which will be revealed in the future (*sich herausstellen*). In essence the opposite of truth is not deception (*Täuschung*), but rather disappointment (*Enttäuschung*)."

[17]Taking the prepositional phrase by itself, Murphy-O'Connor notes that the word *pros* (with accusative) means "with" in Gal 1:18; 4:18, 20 ("Missions," 78–79). Indeed, one might add that Paul sometimes employs *pros tina* with other compounds of *menō* (namely, *katamenō* and *epimenō*) to mean "with" (in addition to Gal 1:18, see 1 Cor 16:6, 7), a fact that is presumably responsible for BAGD's finding "with you" in Gal 2:5. One may still pause, however, for *diamenō pros tina* occurs nowhere else in the NT; nor does LSJ provide an example. Moreover, the most common use of *pros* with accusative, "toward," gives a perfectly understandable meaning in Gal 2:5. Those who read "with you" (or something similar) seem already to have committed themselves on other grounds to a Galatian mis-

the Jerusalem conference; and that conclusion can be sustained here without resorting to procrustean linguistics. The most common meaning of *pros* with accusative is "toward," and that meaning gives a perfectly understandable sentence in this case. In resisting the False Brothers, Paul and Barnabas preserved the truth of the gospel, and looking back at that deed, Paul can say that it was an act taken so that the gospel might eventually make its way to Galatia in the course of his own labors.

6. *Moreover, from.* In the Note on v 4 we observed that, when Paul thinks of the False Brothers, his command of grammatical niceties partly disappears in a cloud of emotional heat. Something similar happens when he turns his attention to the acknowledged leaders of the Jerusalem church. His ambivalent feelings about these persons produce a long sentence (vv 6–10) that is syntactically somewhat disjointed. The relationships among its major parts are, however, essentially clear. The initial prepositional phrase "from the acknowledged leaders" is picked up later in the sentence by the clause "those leaders did not add anything to my gospel."

the acknowledged leaders. See the Note on v 2 above.

what sort of persons they were. We note three linguistic factors: (a) the tense of the verb, "they *were*," (b) the presence of an enclitic particle (*pote*) that can mean "formerly," and (c) the change of tense in the next clause, "*is* a matter of no consequence to me." From these factors some interpreters have thought that with the expression "the acknowledged leaders" (*hoi dokountes*) Paul intends to speak of a status he himself "formerly" accorded to these men at the time of the meeting (doing so no longer).[18] It is more likely that he uses the past tense and the word *pote* for the simple reason that he is telling a story of past events. The change to present tense in the next clause would then have some such force as the following: "remains a matter of indifference to me today, a fact I cite in the face of the Teachers, whom you constantly hear extolling the Jerusalem leaders."

God does not play favorites. The Greek renders a Hebrew idiom *nāśā' pānîm,* meaning "to lift the face of someone." The image is that of a powerful person who, being surrounded by a group of competitive supplicants, steps forward to lift the face of one, thus showing favor to that one. In the present instance, as in numerous others (cf. 2 Chr 19:7; Deut 10:17; Job 24:19; Acts 10:34; Jas 2:1; Rom 2:11), the picture is invoked precisely in order to deny its pertinence to God. Even with regard to the leaders of the church in Jerusalem, God is free of partiality.[19]

those leaders did not add anything to my gospel. For a second time in his string of denials Paul employs the verb *prosanatithêmi* with the negative. In 1:16–17 he said that immediately after he received God's revelatory call, he did not *consult*

---

sion prior to the conference (e.g., Luedemann, *Chronology,* 71). It is unlikely that the expression is timeless (Mussner)!

[18]For example, Dunn.

[19]Later, in writing to the Roman church, Paul will make God's impartiality a central axiom with broad results: As God is free of partiality, it follows that Jews and Gentiles are treated as equals. Pertinent materials from rabbinic literature and from Philo are collected in Bassler, *Impartiality*; see also her "Impartiality."

with the Jerusalem leaders, as though words spoken by a human being could supplement God's apocalypse. So also here, conscious of having gone to the Jerusalem meeting as a result of God's apocalyptic revelation that he should go (v 2), and having communicated to the Jerusalem leaders his gospel, Paul denies that the leaders of the Jerusalem church gave him instruction of any kind. God's revelation of his Son cannot be supplemented by human teaching (cf. 1:11–12).

Does Paul intend specifically to deny something the Teachers are presently claiming to have happened at the meeting? That question leads us to the picture Luke paints in Acts 15, where we note two pertinent elements: (a) Although the Christian Pharisees (Acts 15:5) — like the False Brothers in Paul's account — do not get their way in demanding circumcision of Gentile Christians, the leaders of the Jerusalem church are portrayed by Luke as issuing a decree that constitutes a supplement to the circumcision-free gospel of the Antioch church: Gentile Christians are not required to be circumcised, but they are henceforth to observe certain food laws and to abstain from sexual immorality (Acts 15:23–29). (b) In the decree itself the Jerusalem leaders mention Paul by name (Acts 15:25), showing that — in Luke's view — he was included in those on whom the supplement was imposed. Thus, as Luke tells the story, immediately after the meeting, Paul visits his churches, causing them now to observe "the decisions (dogmas) which had been reached by the apostles and elders who were at Jerusalem" (Acts 16:4). In a word, Luke portrays the Jerusalem leaders as imposing a supplemental requirement focused in part on food laws, and he says that Paul accepted this supplement.

Returning to Paul's account in Galatians, we can see that the apostle is denying a turn of events very like that portrayed in Luke's picture.[20] He says that the leaders of the Jerusalem church did not add anything to his gospel (lit. "to me," the pronoun being emphatic in form and placement in the Greek sentence). Whether Paul ever knew of the "decree" mentioned in Acts 15 cannot be discussed here.[21] But the specificity of Paul's denial in Gal 2:6 seems to indicate that the Teachers are conveying to the Galatians a picture of the meeting not altogether unlike that of Acts 15.[22]

7. *On the contrary.* Paul says that what happened was the opposite (*enanti*) of the picture given in v 6.

they saw clearly. However syntactically disjointed it may be, the long and complex sentence of vv 6–10 is consistently focused on the leaders of the Jerusalem church. At the end of v 6 Paul first makes them the subject of a finite verb:

those leaders did not add anything to my gospel.

In vv 7–9 he then continues the focus on these leaders with two participial clauses (literally rendered):

[20]Cf. Linton, "Aspect."
[21]See Hurd, *Origin*; Luedemann, *Chronology*; Jewett, *Chronology*.
[22]Cf. Georgi, *Remembering*, 30.

On the contrary, *coming to see* that I had been entrusted by God with the gospel . . .

and

coming to perceive the grace given to me by God . . .

Finally, in v 9 he closes the sentence by allowing the Jerusalem leaders to be again the subject of a finite verb:

James and Cephas and John . . . shook hands with me and Barnabas . . .

Why does Paul focus the Galatians' attention on the leaders of the Jerusalem church?

To a great extent our interpretation of 2:1–10 turns on our answer to this question. There are three major interpretive alternatives: (a) Some exegetes see a reflection of the Jerusalem leaders' authority. Paul has to put them in the center of the picture because, however reluctant he may be to do so, he has to reflect in his account the fact of their power over him.[23] (b) Alternatively, one may suggest that Paul focuses attention on these leaders not because he considered them to have institutional authority, but because he considered them to be, in a sense, on trial by God. For in his view the major issue of the meeting was whether they would perceive the action of God that lay before their eyes, or would fail to perceive it. (c) Similarly, one may propose that Paul places the Jerusalem leaders in the spotlight because the issue of the meeting was quite specifically whether they would come to share a perception already reached by himself and Peter when he visited the latter in Jerusalem a number of years earlier (1:18).[24]

The two parallel participles, "seeing" and "perceiving" (see literal rendering above), speak strongly for the second and/or third interpretations. Both participles show the inceptive use of the aorist tense: "they came to see clearly" and "they came to perceive" (BDF §318 (1), §331). The resulting picture is entirely harmonious with Paul's emphatic insistence in v 2 that he went to the meeting because God revealed to him that he should go. Paul knows the meeting to have been one juncture, among others, along the line of the apocalyptic march of God's gospel into the world. And the twin of God's apocalyptic march is the event in which human eyes are opened to see what God is doing (Comment #3).

Thus, Paul's account of the meeting is fundamentally informed by the relationship between apocalyptic and new epistemology. Happily, he can say that all of the Jerusalem leaders came to perceive God's hand in the work he and Barnabas were pursuing among the Gentiles.

I had been entrusted by God. For the first time in Galatians, Paul here employs the verb *pisteuô*. This passive use of the transitive construction means "to be

[23] Cf. Holmberg, *Power*; Klein, "Galater 2, 6–9."
[24] As noted earlier, building on a pregnant suggestion made by Luedemann, A. Schmidt has advanced this thesis ("Missionsdekret").

entrusted" by someone with something (divine passive; cf. v 8). Paul was entrusted with the gospel by God's apocalyptic act, not by an ecclesiastical decision (1:1, 11–12). Hence, that entrustment is not subject to the deciding powers of any group of human beings (cf. 1 Cor 9:17).[25]

the gospel as it is directed to those who are not circumcised. In the Greek expression *to euaggelion tês akrobystias* the noun *akrobystia* ("foreskin," thus "men having the foreskin, Gentiles") is an objective genitive; it identifies the persons who are being evangelized in Paul's work, the Gentiles (BDF §163). The same thing is true for the genitive noun *tês peritomês* at the end of the verse: Peter has been entrusted with the gospel as it is directed to those who are circumcised, the Jews. In these parallel clauses, then, Paul in no way suggests that there are two gospels. There are, rather, two missions in which the one gospel is making its way into the whole of the cosmos.

But how, exactly, was the distinction between these two missions understood? Was that distinction a matter of geography, Peter preaching in the land of Israel, where Jews were in the majority, while Paul went outside that land, where the vast majority was Gentile? Or did the participants in the meeting think of an ethnic distinction, Peter preaching to Jews, Paul to Gentiles? In Comment #19 we will see that the text resembles a verbal formula that came to represent an ethnic division of labor.

8. *he who was at work.* Although vv 7 and 8 say nearly the same thing, there are here three new accents:

(a) Rather than referring to God, and specifically to God's action, merely by means of a passive verb, "I had been entrusted," Paul now identifies God by a substantive participle. It is a pattern he frequently employs in Galatians:

The one who called you	1:6
The one who singled me out	1:15
The one who called me	1:15
The one who was at work	2:8
The one who supplies the Spirit	3:5
The one who works miracles	3:5
The one who called you	5:8.

By this means, Paul emphasizes the crux of the meeting: the issue was not that of devising a set of humanly conceived plans, but rather a matter of perceiving God's identity, by learning what God is actually doing. God is *the* actor; the church's task is to see what God is doing and to follow in his way.

(b) Whereas in v 7 the expressions employed to speak of the two missions are identical, there is now a linguistic imbalance. The goal of God's activity in Peter

---

[25]The institution of the *šālîaḥ/apostolos* lies in the background, for that person is obliged to subordinate his own will to that of the one who has sent him (see Note on 1:1). The Teachers understand Paul to be an apostle who, following his own will, is unfaithful to the commission he received from the Antioch church. Paul understands himself to be true to the commission he received from God. See Comment #1.

is now said to be "an *apostolate* to those who are circumcised," whereas about God's activity in himself Paul says only that it was directed to the Gentiles. Whether it was Peter at the time of Paul's personal visit with him, or the Jerusalem leaders at the time of the meeting, someone seems to have seen to it that the formula acknowledged *the activity of the same God* in Peter's *apostolate* and in Paul's *work*, thus subtly but unmistakably failing to grant formal apostolicity to Paul's labors. If that be so, Paul does not bridle at the imbalance. He simply accents the parallelism of God's activity, and in doing so he doubtless reflects the note that was of major significance to all participants.

(c) Instead of employing for a second time the expression "those who are not circumcised," Paul speaks of "the Gentiles," as he frequently does when he refers to the task given to him by God (*eis ta ethnê*; cf. 1:16; 2:2; 1 Thess 2:16; Rom 1:5; etc.). The Galatians will have readily sensed that Paul includes them in this expression, thus saying, first, that *he* — not the False Brothers — is the one in whom God causes the gospel to march to the Gentiles; and, second, that the Jerusalem leaders perceived that arrangement as divinely ordained.

9. *Coming to see that fact, and thus coming to perceive.* Two words often used by interpreters to encapsulate the result of the meeting prove, in fact, to be inadequate taken by themselves. (a) The meeting did not end simply with an "agreement," in the usual meaning of that term. As we have noted above, Paul places great emphasis on the Jerusalem leaders' being granted a new perception of God's work in the world. There was, then, an agreement, but not in the sense of a prudent and efficient arrangement. That agreement was rather a *confession* oriented to God's activity. (b) The result of the meeting is also misstated when one says that the formula of v 9 reflects Paul's achievement of "independence."[26] Again, that formula records, rather, a *perception* that came to be held in common among the members of two churches, the one in Jerusalem and the one in Antioch. And given the banner under which Paul understood the meeting to take place (God's apocalypse; v 2), that perception was not Paul's achievement of independence, but rather an *acknowledgment* of God's evangelical action in the world, an acknowledgment doubtless gained in God's enabling presence.

the grace given to me by God. Where Paul could have said that the Jerusalem leaders arrived at a true understanding of *the task* given him by God, he speaks rather of God's grace. The term summarizes what Paul knew to be at stake in the meeting (and what he sees to be now at stake in Galatia; cf. "grace" in 1:6, 15; 2:21; 5:4). The issue between himself and the False Brothers was not whether there would be a mission to the Gentiles (and that is far from being the issue between himself and the Teachers). The issue, as he says with emphasis, was the fundamental character of that mission, and thus the truth of the gospel: whether God's deed in Jesus Christ is entirely devoid of prior requirements, such as circumcision.

And the answer to that question is "grace." Neither the missionary himself (see the Note on the term "grace" in 1:15) nor those who hear his preaching are addressed by God because of any worthiness they possess or because of any pre-

---

[26]Cf. Georgi, *Remembering*, 31; Holmberg, *Power*, 29.

condition they have fulfilled. Paul wants the Galatians to see, therefore, that the *presuppositionless character* of God's gracious good news in Christ was *the* issue at the conference. This fundamental character of the gospel was seen by the Jerusalem leaders to be the way God is at work in his circumcision-free mission to Gentiles.

James and Cephas and John. After his reference to the False Brothers in vv 4–5, Paul allows those men entirely to disappear. He can claim neither that they came to the true perception of the gospel nor that they were put out of the church by the three Jerusalem leaders. In vv 6–10 his attention returns to those leaders. Having previously referred to these men only as "those acknowledged to be leaders" (vv 2 and 6), Paul now adds three further notes: He gives them their names. He lists the names in a certain order.[27] And he identifies the three men as "the pillars." If, on the occasion of Paul's two-week visit with Peter (1:18), these two evangelists had reached a common understanding of God's two-pronged work in the world, then Paul now names the Jerusalem leaders who came to share that understanding at the time of the conference.[28]

James. Paul has already once referred by name to James (1:19), and, in recounting the incident at Antioch, he will mention him a third time (2:12). Is it significant that in v 9 his name is placed at the head of the list?[29] In 1:19 Paul mentions James after Peter, and more or less in passing, having said that the purpose of his first trip to Jerusalem was to visit Peter. Presumably, the major subject discussed by these two men was world evangelism, not organizational arrangements in the Jerusalem church. As we have seen, however, in 2:1–10 Paul is recounting a meeting that was in a significant sense an ecclesiastical conference: two churches were conferring with one another. Hence, here the order of the names — James, Peter, John — probably does reflect the organization of affairs in the Jerusalem church. James was the chief leader, or was in the process of becoming that (cf. 2:12).[30] It may also be, however, that Paul has placed James's name in the position of emphasis in order to say that even the leader known to be a strict adherent of the Law came to see that God was at work in Paul's circumcision-free mission to Gentiles.[31]

Cephas. Regarding Peter's Aramaic name, Cephas, see the Note on 1:18.

John. This man is named nowhere else in Paul's letters. One assumes that the reference is to John the son of Zebedee, who was one of the Twelve, who plays a minor role in Acts (standing mostly in Peter's shadow), and whom Luke does not even mention in connection with the meeting of Acts 15.

those held by the Jerusalem church to be "the pillars." Paul apparently borrows an expression used in the Jerusalem church; it is there that James, Cephas, and John are referred to as "the pillars." But by also repeating the expression *hoi dokountes einai ti,* lit. "those who seem to be something" (2:2, 6 [twice]), Paul

---

[27]The western reading, giving precedence of place to Peter, is secondary. See Lightfoot 109.

[28]See again A. Schmidt, "Missionsdekret."

[29]On the variant readings, see R. E. Brown et al., *Peter,* 31 n69.

[30]Ibid., n71.

[31]Conzelmann, *History,* 55.

avoids explicitly participating in the linguistic pattern himself (cf. the middle clause of v 6). Between the meeting and Paul's writing Galatians, further developments have troubled his relationship with the Jerusalem leaders — especially with James — perhaps confirming some marginal reservations he had about the way in which members of their church extolled them (see the Note on 2:12 and Comment #46). At the time of the conference, however, Paul was in untroubled fellowship with these leaders themselves.

"the pillars." The image (occurring nowhere else in Paul's letters) is that of a building, having as a major feature several pillars supporting the roof. The metaphorical use can be seen as early as Euripides (*I.T.* 57), and it emerges in rabbinic traditions to refer to the three patriarchs, Abraham, Isaac, and Jacob, pillars of Israel and indeed of the world.[32] Members of the Jerusalem church may have viewed James, Cephas, and John as the new patriarchs, and thus as the pillars, because they formed the indispensable connecting link between Jesus of Nazareth and his church.[33] In any case, it was doubtless easy to think of these three men as the pillars of the eschatological temple that would shortly house the congregation made up of God's new people at the end of time.[34] Regarding Paul's own stance toward this metaphor, see the preceding Note and the one on 2:2.

shook hands . . . signifying that, in fellowship with one another. Lit. "gave the right hand of fellowship" (*dexias edōkan koinōnias*). The Jerusalem leaders now step forward, offering their hands in acknowledgment that all delegates at the meeting — and thus the churches they represent — are bound to one another by their common participation (*koinōnia*) in God's work. That is to say, God's eschatological people is bound together by the integrity of God's eschatological activity through them. In this matter the Jerusalem leaders take the initiative — as Paul portrays them — not because they have authority over Barnabas and him, but rather because it is they who have been given new insight into God's activity.[35]

with me and Barnabas. As we have noted above, Paul portrays the meeting as though it were focused almost exclusively on his own mission. Here, however, as he speaks first of the formula that expressed a common perception of God's work, and second of the climactic gesture of the handshake that signaled that common perception, he reflects the fact that the leaders of the Jerusalem church were dealing not simply with him but with him and Barnabas. See Comments #18 and #20.

we were to go to the Gentiles and they to those who are circumcised. The significance of the shaking of hands is something Paul indicates in three ways: (a) by the noun "fellowship" noted above, (b) by the final clause of v 9, lit. "in order that we to the Gentiles, they to the circumcised," and (c) by the first clause of v 10, "The only other move on their part was a request . . ." The second of these,

---

[32] See Aus, "Pillars."
[33] Cf. Barrett, "Pillar," 18.
[34] In *1 Clem.* 5:2–4 Paul and Peter are identified as "the most righteous pillars of the church."
[35] Sampley suggests that the Jerusalem leaders understood their initiative in the handshake to signify superiority, whereas Paul and Barnabas saw a sign of equal partnership (*Partnership*, 50).

the final clause of v 9, is introduced by the conjunction *hina*, "in order that," used elliptically without an expressed verb. The context supplies the verb: Representing the church in Antioch, Paul and Barnabas are to (continue to) *preach the gospel* to the Gentiles, free of the requirement of circumcision, while the leaders of the Jerusalem church (continue to) *preach the gospel* to the Jews. Thus, the conjunction "in order that" is purposive with regard to God's intention. For that reason one does well to avoid the translation "with the agreement that." The shaking of hands does not indicate merely that a sensible, political division of labor had been reached. It signifies, as we have seen, a common perception of God's activity.

we . . . they. This is again one of the points in Paul's account at which the fact peeps through, so to speak, that the meeting was held in order to bring two churches into conversation with one another. The "we" are Paul and Barnabas, as representatives of the church in Antioch; the "they" are James, Peter, and John, as representatives of the church in Jerusalem.

to the Gentiles . . . to those who are circumcised. With this formula, the participants recognize as God's work only one mission to the Gentiles, the circumcision-free mission of the Antioch church. Paul thus sees God's hand in the formula, for in it all participants faithfully confess the truth of the gospel (v 5). In fact, however, the formula will quickly prove to be very problematic by being subject to various interpretations. See Comment #23.

10. *The only other move on their part.* The Jerusalem leaders did make a request, but, in doing that, they did not in any way try to provide a supplement to Paul's message (v 6). On the contrary, they emphasized the fellowship signaled in the handshake by asking that the bond between the Jerusalem church and the church in Antioch find concrete expression in a form of remembrance.

that we remember "the poor." The verb *mnêmoneuô* is fairly widely attested with the simple meaning "to remember," "to keep in mind," "to think of." Reporting words spoken by the Jerusalem leaders, Paul puts the verb in the present subjunctive following the conjunction *hina*, that construction being used here to express an imperatival/urgent request (BDF §387.3). Further, the continuous force of the present tense indicates a request to "remember the poor" regularly.[36] In short, one can imagine that, while shaking hands, the Jerusalem leaders said two things: "We see that God is himself active in both lines of mission, yours to the Gentiles and ours to the Jews. We ask only that you regularly remember the poor!"

What is specifically involved in this remembering is indicated by the plural pronoun "we" and by the expression "the poor," both of which continue the pic-

---

[36]Two misreadings are to be avoided. (a) Luedemann has seen in the present subjunctive verb *mnêmoneuômen* — and even in the aorist verb *espoudasa poiêsai*! — evidence that "the collection is still fully in progress" as Paul writes to the Galatians (*Chronology*, 80). In fact, the tense of the verb *mnêmoneuômen* gives no indication as to the state of affairs with the collection at the time at which Paul is writing the letter. See Georgi, *Remembering*, 45. (b) The motif of regularity has been taken to point to an annual subvention analogous to the Jewish temple tax. On these matters, see Keck, "Saints"; idem, "The Poor"; idem, "Poor"; Hanks, "Poor, Poverty (NT)."

ture of two churches in conversation with one another. Speaking for the church in Jerusalem, James, Peter, and John address their request to Paul and Barnabas as representatives of the church in Antioch. And by mentioning "the poor," the Jerusalem leaders refer to their own church, or to a circle of persons within that church. The Antioch church is to remember the Jerusalem church in the sense of regularly collecting and forwarding funds. That is the conclusion we can draw from a passage in Romans in which Paul uses the term "the poor" while thinking of the Jewish Christians in Jerusalem. Discussing his travel plans toward the end of his letter to Rome, he says:

> At present . . . I am going to Jerusalem with support for the saints. For [the churches in] Macedonia and Achaia have been pleased to make a contribution for *the poor* among the saints in Jerusalem; they [the Gentile churches I founded in Macedonia and Achaia] were pleased to do it, and indeed they are in debt to them, for if the Gentiles have come to share in their spiritual blessings, they ought also to be of service to them in material blessings (Rom 15:25–27).

There Paul clearly uses the term "the poor" to speak of members of the church in Jerusalem, and he refers to a collection of money being assembled among (some of) his churches for delivery to these poor ones.[37] In Comment #24 we will see grounds for thinking that, between the Jerusalem leaders' request — directed to the church in Antioch — and the collection Paul later assembled among his own churches, there is a long and somewhat complicated history. For the moment the point is that with the expression "the poor," James, Peter, and John refer to the church in Jerusalem, and their request is for regular financial assistance from the church of Antioch, probably including its daughter churches.

a request which I was eager to carry out. Two factors call for attention in connection with Paul's verb, *espoudasa poiêsai*, "I was eager to carry [it] out" or "I hastened to carry [it] out." (a) The verb is singular, with Paul alone as the subject, whereas Paul has just said that the request for aid was directed to Barnabas and himself, and thus in actuality to the church of Antioch. Why does he suddenly focus attention on himself, neither speaking of Barnabas's response nor describing the process of the collection in the Antioch church? And (b) the verb is in the simple past tense, with no indication of continuance, whereas the verb with which the Jerusalem leaders express their request — *mnêmoneuômen*, "that we remember" — has the continuous force of the present tense, as noted earlier. Why, having mentioned the request for continuous support, does Paul refer to his own role with the simple past tense? In Comment #24 we will see grounds

[37] In Gal 2:10 ("the poor") *and* in Rom 15:26 ("the poor among the saints in Jerusalem") Paul probably thinks both of literal poverty and of the Jerusalem church's eschatological role. Cf. Georgi, *Remembering*, 114; Fitzmyer, "Jewish Christianity"; Theissen, *Social Setting*; Holmberg, *Power*, 35–36.

for thinking that, as Paul writes to the Galatians, he is no longer involved in the Antioch church's regular support for the church in Jerusalem.

COMMENT #18
THE CONFERENCE HELD BY THE CHURCHES OF JERUSALEM AND ANTIOCH NARRATED AS A TWO-LEVEL DRAMA

Was the meeting actually convened under the auspices of two churches, for the sake of discussions between those corporate bodies? Paul's repeated use of verbs in the first person singular suggests no such thing. But his portraits of the actors in the drama show that the meeting was in fact a formal conference involving the churches of Jerusalem and Antioch as negotiating parties:

In 2:5 Paul says that the False Brothers tried to enslave "us," and he emphasizes that "we" did not give them so much as an inch. Who are the "we"? In spite of the fact that he has not mentioned Barnabas since v 1, Paul surely intends to refer to himself and Barnabas. But the possibility must be at least entertained that the plural reaches also to a wider circle, the Antioch church made present at the meeting by its representatives, Paul and Barnabas.

That possibility becomes almost a certainty when we read carefully v 9, where Paul says three things about the Jerusalem leaders: James and Cephas and John, those who were held in respect by the Jerusalem church as though they were the pillars on which it stood, perceived the grace that had been given *to me*. They therefore extended the right hand of fellowship *to me and to Barnabas*. They did this as a sign that *we* should go to the Gentiles and they to the circumcised.

Although the syntax is clear, the change in the pronouns is strange, until one sees that Paul is suppressing certain dimensions of the proceedings. James and Cephas and John are the acknowledged leaders of the Jerusalem church, empowered at least to some degree to speak for that church. With whom are these representatives of the Jerusalem church dealing? In the first of the three clauses of v 9 Paul implies that they are dealing with him, the result being their perception of the grace that God has given to him (cf. vv 7 and 8). But in the next clause he portrays the representatives of the Jerusalem church standing face-to-face with himself *and Barnabas*; and in the final clause he cites words that obviously constitute a formal agreement between two corporate groups, "we" and "they": "we to the Gentiles; they to the circumcised." Grammatically, the antecedents of the pronouns are clear: "we" are Paul and Barnabas, and "they" are James, Cephas, and John. Clearly, "they" represent the *Jerusalem* church, *as it sponsors the gospel mission to Israel*. It follows that these representatives of the Jerusalem church very probably saw Paul and Barnabas as men who represented another church, *as it sponsored the burgeoning gospel mission to Gentiles*.

We should therefore paraphrase 2:9 by rendering "they" as the church in Jerusalem and "we" as the Antioch church.[38] At the time of the meeting Paul was functioning, with Barnabas, as a representative of the church in Antioch, and these two men took the trip to Jerusalem in order to attend a formal conference

[38] See Georgi, *Remembering*, 21–25; Schütz, *Anatomy*, 147.

designed to bring into conversation with one another two churches that were actively pursuing two distinct missions.

Further pondering Paul's account, one sees that he is suppressing more than the fact that he and Barnabas went to Jerusalem as representatives of the Antioch church. Indeed, taking some clues from the next paragraph (2:11–14), we can show that Paul shapes his account quite extensively. Only a pinch of imagination is needed, in fact, to compare his rendering with a picture of the Jerusalem meeting as it might have been drawn by Barnabas or Peter:

The Once-upon-a-Time Meeting	Paul's Dramatic Rendering
The attempt of the False Brothers to compel the circumcision of Titus is unlikely to have been the first such move on their part.[39] The meeting was arranged to take up tensions that had arisen over time concerning the Antioch church's circumcision-free mission to the Gentiles. It seems probable that the False Brothers had been spying on Antioch's daughter churches, and that that was a major reason for convening the conference.	Paul says nothing about developments that led up to the meeting.
The major actors were the church in Antioch — the community that gave birth to the first organized mission to the Gentiles — and the church in Jerusalem, these two churches having thought it wise to confer.[40]	In Paul's drama the major actors are himself, the False Brothers, and the leaders of the Jerusalem church.
Barnabas was seen by the Jerusalem leaders — and by the Antioch church as well — as Paul's partner. Indeed, he may have been considered the leader of the Antioch church and thus the senior partner in the Antioch delegation. For this reason he is named alongside Paul in the official agreement (v 9).	As far as is possible, Paul gives Barnabas a relatively insignificant role as a sort of "tagalong."

[39]Cf. Georgi, *Remembering*, 23.
[40]If the kernel of the formula used in v 9 had already been a matter agreed to by Paul and Peter on the occasion of Paul's two-week visit to Jerusalem (1:18), then the wisdom of convening a conference may have lain mainly with these two men.

The conference was focused on the gospel preached among Gentiles by missionaries of the church of Antioch, two of whom, at least, had been working side by side, Barnabas and Paul.	The focus in Paul's account is the gospel he preaches among Gentiles.
The major outcome was an agreement that the Antioch church should pursue its circumcision-free mission to Gentiles, while the Jerusalem church should preach to Jews.	The major outcome, as Paul presents it, is that the Jerusalem leaders come to see the divine origin of his gospel. Given that perception, all participants saw both the unity of the church in one *koinônia* and the intention of God to extend the church-creating gospel into the world along two parallel lines.[41]

Should we then give Paul a failing grade in the subject of history? To do that would be to miss the challenge of his remarkable account. For the points of divergence between the two columns are useful, in that they pose the much-discussed question "What is history?" And while the present volume is not the place to attempt even a sketchy discussion of that question, we can say at least one thing: For Paul the history of the gospel is the story of the repeated presence of God, as he causes the gospel to progress victoriously into the world of enslavement (note Phil 1:12). The apostle is thus sure that past episodes in this victorious history can never be talked about as though the forward march of the gospel were merely a matter of the past. On the contrary, what God is now doing in the victorious progress of the gospel in Galatia constitutes the reason for giving a narrative of events that took place in Jerusalem.

And in Galatia what is at stake is not the mission to the Gentiles carried out by the Antioch church, but rather Paul's own mission. Barnabas is not — and has not been — an actor in the Galatian setting.[42] The Paul known to the Galatians is not an evangelist working shoulder-to-shoulder with Barnabas; nor is he a missionary acting under authorization from any church (1:1). It is *his gospel* that he must now repreach to the Galatians, and in his account of the meeting in Jerusalem he does that by telling a story about the conference in a *form suited to the Galatian setting*. He presents, in a word, a two-level drama in which there is one major point of correspondence between the once-upon-a-time and the present: In Jerusalem *the truth of the gospel* demanded of him that he wage a war against the False Brothers who were intent on *compelling* the circumcision of Titus (2:3). In Galatia that same *truth of the gospel* now makes necessary his waging war

---

[41] See Schütz, *Anatomy*, 147.
[42] In giving the Galatians their own account of the Jerusalem meeting and the Antioch episode, the Teachers almost certainly *mentioned* Barnabas, but Paul does not see him as an actor in the matters at stake in Galatia.

against the Teachers who are intent on *compelling* the circumcision of the Galatians (6:12).

His dramatic account of the meeting is thus a witness to the history of the gospel, not a matter of being evenhanded with all of the participants. The event itself was an episode in which the truth of the advancing gospel was preserved for the Galatians (v 5). Paul's account of the event is therefore an historical witness in which the truth of the gospel is once again unleashed, this time against its foes in Galatia. And since the truth of the gospel is a matter of God's ever-new activity, it would be betrayed were one to speak of it solely in terms of the once-upon-a-time. We see, then, that Paul has only one question in mind as he shapes his account: "What was God doing in Jerusalem that is revealing as to what God is doing now in Galatia?"[43]

COMMENT #19
THE CONFERENCE AND EARLY CHRISTIAN MISSIONS

A FORMULA REFLECTING A COMMON PERCEPTION OF GOD'S ACTIVITY IN TWO PARALLEL LINES OF GOSPEL MISSION

At a conference dealing with such important matters, certain words must have passed back and forth among the participants, including some sort of formulation that came to represent a common perception. Does the text contain clues pointing to the actual words of that formulation? In fact, there are five:[44]

(1) *Peter.* In eight of his ten references to Peter, Paul uses the Aramaic form of his name, "Cephas." Only in Gal 2:7–8 does he employ the Greek form, a departure from his practice that is explicable by the hypothesis that in this instance he is quoting from a formulation not entirely of his own making.

(2) While the formula of v 9 is quite similar to that of vv 7–8, there are significant differences.

Verses 7–8	Verse 9
7. On the contrary, they saw clearly that I had been entrusted by God with the gospel as it is directed to those who are not circumcised, just as Peter had been entrusted with the gospel to those who are circumcised. 8. For he who was at work in Peter,	9. Coming to see that fact, and thus coming to perceive the grace given to me by God, James and Cephas and John—those held by the Jerusalem church to be "the pillars"—shook hands with me and Barnabas, signifying that, in

[43]Thus, the futility of asking Paul for an "objective historical report" is at least matched by the reductionistic rigidity of assuming that he is concerned to bring out the "relevance" or "significance" of a past event. He does not ask, for example, about the relevance of the agreement (v 9) for the situation in Galatia, but rather about the activity of *God* then and now. In a word, for Paul the history of the gospel is what it is because the God who acted in it is the God who is now acting in it. The theological issue, as it arises in the Gospel of John, is discussed in J. L. Martyn, *History*; Ashton, *Understanding*; Smith, *Theology.*
[44]Dinkler, "Schlier."

creating an apostolate to those who are circumcised, was also at work in me, sending me to the Gentiles.

fellowship with one another, we were to go to the Gentiles and they to those who are circumcised.

In vv 7–8 there are two actors in God's evangelistic plan: Paul to the Gentiles, Peter to the Jews. In v 9, however, "we [Paul and Barnabas] were to go to the Gentiles and they [James and Peter and John] to those who are circumcised." We have already encountered the suggestion that vv 7–8 contain the kernel of an earlier agreement reached by Peter and Paul on the occasion of Paul's first trip to Jerusalem (1:18), while v 9 reports that at the time of the meeting that earlier agreement was also adopted (and adapted) by James and John, representing the Jerusalem church with Peter, and by Barnabas as one of the Antioch representatives.[45]

(3) Both v 7 and v 9 are introduced by participles of perception (inceptive aorist), "[the leaders] *coming to see* . . . [the leaders] *coming to perceive* . . ." The second of these participles is followed by a summary that rewords the formula of vv 7 and 8, as we have just seen. In a word, then, these participles introduce what the Jerusalem leaders *came to perceive* in the course of the meeting. Did they come to see something already seen by Peter and Paul and already expressed in a formula worded jointly by these two men?

(4) In fact, three of the key expressions in the formula of vv 7–8 have been correctly identified as un-Pauline: "gospel of the circumcision," "gospel of the uncircumcision," and "apostolate of the circumcision" (the third, emerging in v 8, is rendered in our translation as "creating an apostolate to those who are circumcised").[46] This third expression is particularly striking, for, as we have seen in the Note, its use in v 8 results in a linguistic imbalance, linking the term "apostolate" to Peter but not to Paul. Is Paul — the author of Gal 1:1 — likely to have created that imbalance?

(5) One notes furthermore the order of the names in v 9, that of James preceding that of Peter. If vv 7–8 contain the germ of an earlier agreement, that agreement may reflect a time when Peter was the major leader of the Jerusalem church, v 9 showing that, by the time of the meeting, James was ascending to the helm.

All in all, it seems best to find at the core of vv 7–8 the central motifs, and even some of the actual terms, of a formulation arrived at by Peter and Paul prior to the conference. Verse 9, then, reflects the adoption of that earlier formula by all participants in the conference itself. We cannot reconstruct in detail a verbal quotation, but we can sense that Paul is functioning here as a reporter. All participants saw that God was causing the gospel to advance into the world along two parallel lines, the older and unquestioned one being the Jerusalem church's evangelistic labors among Jews, the newer but no less God-empowered one being the work among Gentiles radiating from the church in Antioch.

---

[45] See again A. Schmidt, "Missionsdekret."
[46] See H. D. Betz 97–98.

Two Simultaneous Lines of Mission Distinguished from One Another Ethnically

Nothing in the texts of vv 7–9 would have suggested to the Galatians that the two lines of mission were different from one another by virtue of geography, the Jerusalem church having responsibility for Palestine, the Antioch church being responsible for the rest of the Mediterranean basin. On the contrary, the distinguishing mark is consistently ethnic: one line of mission to the Jews, a second and simultaneous line to the Gentiles.

It is true that, in writing the book of Acts, Luke paints a different picture, even of Paul's own work. Understanding the two lines of mission to be essentially sequential rather than simultaneous, Luke has Paul regularly begin his mission in the local synagogue, turning to Gentiles only after severe difficulties have developed in the synagogue. And even then the Lucan Paul stays close to the local Jewish community, commencing his further work with the Gentile "God-fearers" who had attached themselves to the synagogue (see, e.g., Acts 17:1–15).[47]

A number of interpreters point out that this picture in the Acts of the Apostles seems to be supported by two passages in Paul's Corinthian letters:

In 1 Cor 9:19–23 Paul speaks both of his *unvarying* task of proclaiming the gospel and of his *flexibility* regarding personal Law observance:

> For though I am free with respect to all, I have made myself a slave to all, that I might win more of them. To the Jews I became as a Jew, in order to win Jews. To those under the law I became as one under the law (though I myself am not under the law) so that I might win those under the law. To those outside the law I became as one outside the law (though I am not free from God's law but am under Christ's law) so that I might win those outside the law. To the weak I became weak, so that I might win the weak. I have become all things to all people, that I might by all means save some. I do it all for the sake of the gospel, so that I might share in its blessings (NRSV).

According to one reading of this text, Paul means that he preaches both to Jews and to Gentiles.

In 2 Cor 11:22–28, in the course of listing his sufferings, Paul mentions that he five times received "at the hands of the Jews the thirty-nine lashes" (11:24).[48] Since the other sufferings are clearly cited by Paul as evidence of his work in preaching the gospel, some interpreters have assumed the same for this one: in the course of evangelizing in synagogues, Paul aroused violent opposition and had to suffer the consequences.

There are strong reasons, however, to reject the line of interpretation drawn from Acts and apparently supported by these two Pauline passages, not the least being that it involves accepting Luke's portrait as the primary evidence, while ignoring almost all of the pertinent data in Paul's letters, save the two texts from the Corinthian letters. An assessment of the evidence by E. P. Sanders is worth quoting:

[47] Nearly every time the term "synagogue" appears in Acts, Paul is involved.
[48] Cf. Gallas, "Synagogalstrafen."

. . . we should apply to the question of Paul's missionary practice the principle established by John Knox for defining his chronology and travels: the primary evidence is Paul's letters. Acts should be disregarded if it is in conflict. If we look simply at Paul's letters quite a different picture emerges.

Paul, in discussing his ministry, speaks exclusively of Gentiles (with the exception of 1 Cor. 9:20). He is apostle to the Gentiles (Rom. 11:13), and he was called in order that he might preach Christ among the Gentiles (Gal. 1:16; cf. 2:2: "the gospel which I preach among the Gentiles"). The agreement between himself, Peter and James was that he, Paul, would go to the "uncircumcised" or "Gentiles" (Gal. 2:7, 9), not simply to areas outside of Palestine. His task was to win obedience among all the Gentiles (Rom. 1:5), and he could report success: Christ had worked through him to win obedience from the Gentiles (Rom. 15:18). He wished to go to Rome in order that he might "reap some harvest among [the Romans] as well as among the rest of the Gentiles," since he was under obligation to all Gentiles, both Greeks and barbarians (Rom. 1:13–14). He does not say that Jews disrupted his preaching to Jews (as Acts has it), but rather that they hindered him in his efforts to preach to Gentiles (1 Thess. 2:16). Whatever Peter thought of the agreement with Paul, Paul himself appears to have taken it in the ethnic sense. His mission was "to be a minister of Christ Jesus to the Gentiles . . . so that the offering of the Gentiles would be acceptable" (Rom. 15:16).[49]

The picture does not vary significantly when we consider Paul's characterizations of his converts. With very few exceptions, none can be identified from the Pauline letters as being Jewish. Timothy may have been considered a Jew, as, according to Acts 16:1–3, his mother was Jewish, but there is no hint of this in Paul's letters, nor an unambiguous indication that Timothy was a convert of Paul.[50] The case of Crispus could support the thesis that Paul preached to Jews. Acts identifies Crispus as Jewish (18:8), and Paul says that he himself baptized this man (1 Cor 1:14). As noted above, however, on at least five occasions Paul had to defend himself (unsuccessfully) in a synagogue examination, the charge evidently being that he preached the gospel to Gentiles (2 Cor 11:24; 1 Thess 2:16). Was it in one of these defenses that his words resulted in the conversion of Crispus? In any case, while we must reckon with Paul's having in a few contexts shared the gospel with at least a few Jews, these are exceptions that prove the rule. If one credits Acts' portrait of Prisca and Aquila as Jewish, one should also note that even Acts does not explicitly identify them as Paul's converts, and the same is true of Sosthenes (Acts 18:2, 17; 1 Cor 1:1; cf. Rom 16:3; 1 Cor 16:19).

[49]E. P. Sanders, *Law*, 181; cf. Meeks, *Urban*, 25–32. Note the comment of Barclay, ". . . at least at his defense [prior to receiving the thirty-nine lashes in five synagogues; 2 Cor 11:24], *if at no other time*, he [Paul] must have given some account of his convictions to an audience of Jews" ("Diaspora Jews," 116 n53; emphasis added). As the qualifying clause shows, this cogent observation is far from supporting the thesis that Paul regularly preached to Jews.

[50]Cf. Cohen, "Timothy."

Another missionary couple, Andronicus and Junia, is said by Paul to be Jewish, but he adds that they were "in Christ before me" (Rom 16:7; cf. 16:11).

Further, Paul's descriptions of the former lives of his converts is consistent with the view that they were Gentiles.[51] The argument that exegetical passages in Paul's letters presuppose readers familiar with elements of "synagogal study" neglects the degree to which Paul's opponents initiated his Gentile converts in the rudiments of exegetical practice, not to mention instances in which he may have been the teacher himself. In a word, concentration on 1 Cor 9:19–23 and 2 Cor 11:22–28 can be misleading. The vast preponderance of the evidence in Paul's own letters shows him preaching to Gentiles, not to Jews and Gentiles.

What are we to say, then, of the Corinthian passages? Closely examining 1 Corinthians 9, one notes that, to a remarkable degree, the persons Paul mentions there correspond to the persons he mentions at the Jerusalem meeting:

1 Cor 9:5–6	Gal 2:1–10
Paul, Barnabas	Paul, Barnabas
the other apostles	John (an apostle)
the brothers of Jesus	James (Jesus' brother)
Cephas	Cephas

Luedemann is probably right to suggest that, when he penned 1 Corinthians 9, Paul had part of his mind on the Jerusalem meeting.[52] Indeed, one may be yet more specific, paraphrasing 1 Cor 9:20–21 in relation to that meeting (during which Paul was certainly observant) as follows:

At the time of the conference in the Jerusalem church, I became as one under the Law, in order that I might win those under the Law (the "pillars") to the holistic vision of the worldwide march of God's gospel. To those in the Antioch church's daughter communities—Gentiles outside the Law—I became as one outside the Law, in order that I might also win them to that holistic vision of the gospel.[53]

And what of 2 Cor 11:24? If one reads that text against the background of the Lucan portrait of Paul, one thinks of the apostle, as I have said above, suffering severe consequences for preaching to Jews in their synagogues. To stay with Paul's letters, however, is to read the text differently, by comparing it with 1 Thess

[51] Regarding Galatia, see Introduction §3. From 1 Cor 7:18 one can suggest that Paul occasionally evangelized Jews, but, as a specification of 7:17, that text seems to pertain in the first instance to the Corinthian church, an almost totally Gentile congregation (1 Cor 12:12) with, at most, a sprinkling of Jews (1 Cor 1:14).
[52] Luedemann, *Paulus*, 2.113.
[53] To this argument one may add yet another. To read 1 Cor 9:19–23 as a literal description of Paul's regular practice *in his mission field*, we would have to suppose that in a given city he switched back and forth to and from the laws of kashrut, as though vacillation were his major business (so E. P. Sanders, *Law*, 186).

2:16.[54] There Paul says that his persecution at the hands of Jews resulted not from evangelistic activity carried out among them, but rather from his preaching to Gentiles. If we interpret 2 Cor 11:24 in light of that statement, we will conclude that, on more than one occasion, it was precisely Paul's *Gentile* mission that evoked the wrath of his fellow Jews.[55]

To listen to Paul's own testimony, then, is to see in Gal 2:7–9 a clear and unequivocal reference to two missions that are in the precise sense of the term ethnically parallel to one another: that of the Jerusalem leaders to the Jews and that of Paul and Barnabas to the Gentiles.[56]

COMMENT #20
BARNABAS AND PAUL

We have noted the shrinkage of Barnabas's role in Paul's account of the Jerusalem conference (Comment #18). That part of the picture is brought into even greater relief when we recall that, in addition to references to Barnabas in Paul's letters (Gal 2:1, 9, 13; 1 Cor 9:6; cf. Col 4:10), we have some fairly reliable data in the Acts of the Apostles.

Luke portrays Barnabas as one of the giants in the earliest church. According to Luke, his name from birth was Joseph, but his fellow Christians called him by the Aramaic surname "Barnabas," given him by the apostles in Jerusalem, and translated by Luke for his Greek readers: "son of encouragement" (Acts 4:36). Thus, Luke portrays a man of thoroughly Jewish lineage, a prosperous Levite, who functions as a well-known leader among the Jews making up the Jerusalem church. Indeed, Luke shows him to be deeply trusted by his fellow members in that church (Acts 9:27).

When news reaches Jerusalem that the Hellenists have broken the boundary of Judaism by preaching the gospel to Gentiles in Antioch, the Jerusalem church dispatches its trustworthy Barnabas to look into the matter (Acts 11:22). Investigating the makeup and activity of the Antioch church, Barnabas perceives there "the grace of God," moves to Antioch, and enters himself into the Gentile mission as it is pursued by that church, becoming one of its leading members, perhaps referred to in Antioch as an apostle (Acts 12:25–13:3; 14:4, 14). Now held in high respect by the Antioch church, Barnabas is dispatched on more than one occasion back to Jerusalem (11:30; 15:2).

---

[54] See now the argument for the authenticity of 1 Thess 2:14–16 in Schlueter, *Measure.*

[55] In the whole of Romans 9–11, with its note of deep anguish over Israel's unbelief, there is not a single hint that Paul portrays a development that has occurred in spite of his efforts to "win" Jews.

[56] Especially in light of Peter's activity in Syrian Antioch (Gal 2:11–14) and perhaps later in Corinth (1 Cor 1:12; 3:22; 9:5), we may still ask, to be sure, whether all participants at the conference understood the formula in the same way. There may be something to the thesis of Barrett that Peter is the opponent Paul mentions in 2 Cor 10:7; 11:4–5 ("Cephas," 11–12 [critique in R. E. Brown et al., *Peter,* 37]). Did Peter become more and more active among Gentiles as time passed, perhaps preaching *a partially* Law-observant gospel to them? Cf. Hengel, "Ursprünge," 21n; R. E. Brown, "Types," 77 n10.

In a word, Luke's portrait is that of a highly regarded leader, first by the Jerusalem church and later by the church in Antioch. Given our conclusion that the meeting described by Paul in Galatians 2 brought together the church of Jerusalem and the church of Antioch, Luke's portrait of Barnabas acquires added interest. For, according to Luke, Barnabas had proved himself trustworthy in both of these churches. Would not such a person play in the meeting a much more important role than is given to him in Paul's account?

We may note also that, when Luke portrays the extensive evangelical teamwork carried out by Barnabas and Paul, he presents the former, at least initially, as the senior partner, giving the honor of place to Barnabas ("Barnabas and Paul"). Here we may be in touch with Luke's tendency to domesticate Paul into the one true line of expansion radiating from the Jewish-Christian church in Jerusalem. It is also possible, however, that Barnabas's initial place of seniority reflects an aspect of the relationship between the two men that Paul thoroughly suppresses in writing to the Galatians.[57]

Finally, there is Paul's own reference to Barnabas in 1 Cor 9:6, suggesting, first, that by the time Paul wrote 1 Corinthians he and Barnabas were back on reasonably good terms and, second, that their comradeship prior to the Antioch breach was based in part on their mutual decision that, unlike other Christian missionaries, they would consistently earn their own living, rather than receive material support from the people to whom their evangelistic mission was directed.[58] The fact remains that as Paul writes Galatians, he is essentially estranged from Barnabas.

COMMENT #21
THE FALSE BROTHERS IN THE JERUSALEM CHURCH

In his account of the Jerusalem conference Paul gives a fairly clear picture of the False Brothers:

(a) They claim to be brothers in the church of God, and some members of the church grant them this identity.

(b) In Paul's view, that claimed identity is altogether false, and false in a quite specific way; see (f) below.

(c) At the Jerusalem meeting, these persons attempted to compel the circumcision of Titus (2:3).

(d) Someone smuggled them into a setting in which, in Paul's opinion, they should not have been present (2:4).

(e) They entered that setting stealthily in order to spy on the kind of freedom characteristic of the mission of Paul and Barnabas, intending to terminate that mission in the form in which it was being pursued.

(f) That spying activity proved them to be enemies of the truth of the gospel, hence false brothers; but their attempt to enslave the circumcision-free mission to the Gentiles was successfully withstood by Paul and Barnabas.

[57] See Daniels, "Barnabas."
[58] Cf. Theissen, *Social Setting*, 27–59; Hock, *Tentmaking*.

This list leaves unanswered three questions of importance:

(1) Were the False Brothers non-Christian Jews? Against this suggestion, advanced by Schmithals, it must be said that non-Christian Jews are referred to by Paul as "my brothers . . . according to the flesh" (Rom 9:3), an appellation free of the charge of deception.[59] In Gal 2:4, however, Paul speaks of a group who claim to be brothers in Jesus Christ (cf. 1:22), but who, in his judgment, are not. In the perspective of the history of religions we can designate them as Christian Jews rather than as Jewish Christians (thus emphasizing their theological kinship to the Teachers in Galatia), and specifically as members of the church in Jerusalem (cf. Comment #6; Glossary).

(2) Did these persons function for the first time as spies in the meeting in Jerusalem, or did they carry out that activity at an earlier point and in another setting? We cannot be completely certain, but several literary characteristics of 2:4 provide a hint. First, vv 3–5 constitute a parenthesis focused primarily on the attempt of the False Brothers to compel the circumcision of Titus during the meeting. Verse 4 is then a sort of parenthesis within that parenthesis, identifying the False Brothers not as actors bent on compelling circumcision, but as persons who at some time and in some setting functioned as spies. It is certainly possible, then, that they engaged in that activity prior to the meeting. And if so, the reference is probably to reconnaissance they carried out by slipping into meetings of daughter churches of the church in Antioch, thus playing a significant role in precipitating the Jerusalem meeting itself.

(3) After the failure of the False Brothers' attempt to compel the circumcision of Titus — it was decisively negated in the formula of agreement (2:9) — did these persons disappear, thus causing Paul no further difficulty? We can be quite confident of the opposite assumption. At the time of the meeting, they already had in the Jerusalem church a following large enough to attempt to compel even *the pillars* to require the circumcision of Titus. And considerable probability attaches to the thesis that they continued to function in the Jerusalem church as leaders of the "circumcision party" (2:12), a powerful group that acquired over time yet greater influence with James (Comment #25). That thesis would go a long way toward explaining Paul's reference in 4:25 to a Jerusalem that is in a state of slavery together with its children (see Comments #45 and #46).

We cannot be sure that the False Brothers functioned as sponsors of the Teachers, but some relationship between the two groups seems highly probable. The Teachers' claim to represent the Jerusalem gospel implies a significant connection with a powerful part of the Jerusalem church.[60] Thus, in his account of the Jerusalem meeting, Paul says to the Galatians in effect, "The Teachers correspond to one element in the Jerusalem church, a group of men who claim to be brothers, but in fact are not."

---

[59]Schmithals, *Gnostics*, 14; cf. Wegenast, *Tradition*, 47 n1; Stuhlmacher, *Evangelium*, 90.
[60]As Käsemann has aptly remarked, "Only the authority of the church in Jerusalem could shake the authority Paul had in his own churches" ("Legitimität," 490). Barrett is right to say that many of the points made by Käsemann in his study of 2 Corinthians apply equally to Galatians (Barrett, *Freedom*, 60).

Finally, looking at the development of anti-Paulinism in the second century, one can consider the possibility that the False Brothers formed the initial group from which at least some of the later strands of anti-Paulinism arose.[61]

COMMENT #22
SLAVERY AND FREEDOM

As the whole of the letter is a comment on this topic, we will limit the present discussion to four points pertinent to the interpretation of 2:4: ". . . the False Brothers . . . came in stealthily in order to spy out our freedom that we have in Christ Jesus, their purpose being to enslave us."

(1) It is likely that the Teachers offered the Galatians impressive discourses on the matter of slavery and freedom. In 5:16 we find a strong indication that they informed the Galatians both of the Impulsive Desire of the Flesh and of the Law as its antidote. Thus emphasizing that Gentile life is the perfect showplace of the effects of enslavement to the Impulsive Desire of the Flesh, the Teachers also proclaimed a message of freedom: In his Law God has provided liberation from that enslaving monster (see Comments #32 and #49). They must have shared with the Galatians traditions similar to the following:

. . . and it is written (Exod 32:16) "And the tables were the work of God, and the writing was the writing of God, graven upon the tables." Read not "graven" (*ḥārût*) but "freedom" (*ḥērût*), for no man is free but he who occupies himself with the study of the Law (*m. 'Abot* 6:2; cf. Sir 6:23–29 and Philo *Quod Omn*. 45).

Precisely the same motif is evident in the type of Jewish-Christian theology enshrined in the epistle of James, where one hears that the Law is not only royal (Jas 2:8) but also perfect, in that it bestows freedom (Jas 1:25; cf. L. T. Johnson, *James*).

(2) Given this kind of instruction, the Galatians are sure to have been greatly shocked when they noted that Paul was intent on standing the Teachers' picture exactly on its head. This radical reversal is begun in 2:4, where Paul says that to impose the Law on Gentiles is not to free them. It is to enslave them. In the mission to Gentiles, that is, Law observance falls on the side of slavery, not on the side of freedom, a matter to which Paul returns at numerous points in the course of the letter.

(3) Especially important is the fact that Paul does not speak of freedom as an abstraction, as an ideal, or as a state of mind that can be achieved, let us say, by learning to view all things external to the real self as matters of no consequence (the Stoic *ta adiaphora*).[62] On the contrary, he speaks of the freedom that God has enacted in Christ Jesus, and he is willing to define in some detail the forces of slavery from which Christ has set us free. See Comments #39 and #41.

[61] Cf. Luedemann, "Antipaulinismus," especially 443; idem, *Paulus*, 2.60–61.
[62] Fundamentally, the adiaphorous formulations of 5:6 and 6:15 are derived from Jewish apocalyptic, not from Stoic tradition. See Comment #51.

(4) Finally, just as freedom in Christ is not an abstract ideal, so it is not autonomous. On the contrary, freedom is known by the one who is Christ's slave (1:10), and it is lived out in the community in which each is the slave of the neighbor, serving the neighbor's need (5:13).

COMMENT #23
ISSUES LEFT UNATTENDED AT THE CONFERENCE

The grandeur of Paul's portrait of the conference is accompanied by a remarkable silence regarding difficult developments that were waiting just over the horizon. At the conclusion Paul and Barnabas, the Antioch delegates, acknowledge as one line of God's work a mission to Jews presupposing continued Law observance. The Jerusalem leaders come to perceive as another line of God's work a circumcision-free mission to Gentiles. No participant thought God was about the business of creating two churches. Yet, there is no hint that either party thought through in a rigorous way the problems that would inevitably arise at an intersection of these two lines of mission. Indeed, already at the time of the meeting, the Antioch church was drawn in part from Jews and in part from Gentiles (2:12–13). How should one explain the naïveté reflected in the fact that the delegates left unattended issues posed by the existence of such a mixed church?

In the case of the Jerusalem leaders it may be pertinent to recall the Jewish conviction that God's causing the Gentiles to stream into the company of his people would be an event of the end-time.[63] If Peter, James, and John were energetic participants in the formula of 2:9, then with an enthusiasm that is a stranger to meticulous foresight, they may have thought in essence,

> Now is the end-time; it can be no surprise, then, that the inflow of the Gentiles has already begun.[64] Let the gospel therefore advance into the whole of the world, to the Jews and to the Gentiles.

This is, at any rate, the sort of enthusiasm that would have left several further questions unanswered.

(1) If, as just suggested, the Jerusalem leaders thought that God would soon — somehow — bring the Gentile Christians into his already-existent people Israel, we can be sure that they did not say this to Paul (see Comment #37). Strange as it may seem, the manner in which God would ultimately accomplish the palpable unity of his church, and the ultimate relationship between that end-time church and Israel, were matters left unresolved at the conference (cf. Rom 11:25–36).[65]

[63] See, for example, J. Jeremias, *Promise*, 22.
[64] When Paul wrote Galatians, he categorically rejected the thought that the gospel was bringing the Gentiles into an already-existent people of God. See Comment #37. At the conference this matter did not arise as an issue.
[65] Achtemeier, *Quest*; Dunn, *Unity*.

(2) What view of the Law is implied by the two parallel lines of mission? Pondering that question, one sees that the Antioch and Jerusalem delegates almost certainly interpreted in different ways the common formula itself.

Paul, we can be sure, understood the formula to imply that observance and nonobservance of the Law are matters of insignificance, being nothing other than indications of the state in which one existed when one was called by God in Christ (1 Cor 7:20–24). Was one a Jew when called, one remained observant. Was one a Gentile when called, one remained nonobservant, knowing that observance and nonobservance were matters of no true significance.

At least some of the Jerusalem leaders will have had a different reading of the formula. We cannot define it with precision, but we can reemphasize the point mentioned above. Holding the Law to be God's gift, and thinking in corporate terms of Jews and Gentiles, they will probably have been able to accept as God's work a mission parallel to their own, and directed to Gentiles, because they believed that, in some way, God would shortly bring the nonobservant Gentile congregations into Law-observant Israel.[66]

(3) Given these different points of view, one begins to see that the formula was both a momentous recognition of the character of God's outreach into the whole of the world and a bomb waiting for a spark to ignite its fuse. For in fact the formula itself had the effect of silently posing a crucial question: What is the point of departure for the doing of theology in God's church, the Sinaitic Law or Christ? Taken by itself, the formula provided no answer. Indeed, as subsequent events were to show, the formula could serve as an expression of common conviction because, leaving that question unaddressed, it allowed each of the major parties to interpret the two parallel lines in a way that reflected that party's *unspoken assumption* about the point of departure for Christian theology.

Paul saw the formulation of two lines to be a victory for the circumcision-free gospel to the Gentiles, because he took it to imply that the foundation of the whole of the church, as God's new creation, was rectification by the faith of Christ, apart from the Law. For him the announcement of God's good news in Christ, without any presupposition whatsoever, was the point from which one began all thinking and practice in the church (see Comments #28 and #48).

At least some of the Jerusalem leaders, on the other hand, saw the formulation of two lines to be an acceptable pattern, as we have noted above, because they assumed a final harmony — in some form — between observance of the Law and faith in Christ for the whole of the church. That this assumption actually came to be entertained by some persons in the churches of Jerusalem and Antioch is clear from the so-called Apostolic Decree of Acts 15, not to mention the outcome of the Antioch episode (Gal 2:11–14).[67] But when the formula of Gal 2:9 is read in this way, the door is at least opened for taking the Law to be the immutable point of departure for the working out of theology in God's church. Here it is important to notice that something Paul came in time to regard as an antinomy

---

[66]Davies, "People"; cf. E. P. Sanders, *Law*, 177.
[67]Regarding the Apostolic Decree, see Callan, "Decree."

characteristic of the Old Age was written right into the formula: the distinction between Jew and Gentile (see 3:28). Thus, the seeds of further battles were sown in the concordant language of the common formulation itself!

(4) Where will those further battles emerge? When one poses that question, one returns to the astonishing observation that no one in the Jerusalem meeting seems to have thought to word the formula in a way that took into account problems that might arise in mixed churches. And, as we have noted earlier, it will not suffice to say that such questions lay as yet far in the future. One of the two churches represented at the meeting, that of Antioch, was a mixed church already! Moreover, from Gal 2:11–14 we know that at the time of the Jerusalem meeting the church of Antioch was ordering its common life on the assumption that Law observance was a matter of indifference. Hence, while the formula itself contained as one of its foundation stones, a point which the Jerusalem leaders presumably saw as nonnegotiable, the distinction of Jew from Gentile, the other ecclesiastical party to the formula, the church of Antioch, was already living in a way that to a large extent identified that distinction as a matter of no consequence. Again, therefore, we see that the formula set the stage for further struggles, and precisely in locales in which the two lines of mission could not be kept separate.

COMMENT #24
THE COLLECTIONS FOR THE JERUSALEM CHURCH AND THE CHRONOLOGICAL PLACE OF GALATIANS IN THE PAULINE LETTER CORPUS

In Comment #17 we noted strong reasons in the Galatian letter itself for thinking that Paul founded the Galatian churches after the painful confrontation with Peter had led to his separation from the Antioch church and from Barnabas as well. Are there similar data in the letter that enable us to reach a trustworthy conclusion about its place in the chronological order of Paul's letters? The most secure basis for an attempt to answer this question lies in Paul's statement about the collection for Jerusalem in 2:10. For that statement is clearly related to certain passages in others of Paul's letters; and careful comparison enables us to fix the relative date of Galatians.

Closing his account of the Jerusalem conference with the report that the leaders of the churches of Jerusalem and Antioch shook hands, thus signaling a shared perception of God's two-pronged activity in the world, Paul adds in 2:10:

> The only other move on their part was a request that we remember "the poor," and this was a request which I was eager to carry out.

In the Note on this verse we have identified two questions that call for discussion. Having said in the first half of the verse that the Jerusalem leaders' request for aid was directed both to Barnabas and to himself, as representatives of the Antioch church, why does Paul use a singular verb in the second half, speaking only of his own active passion to fulfill the request? And why, in referring to this instance of his zeal, does he put the verb in the simple past tense — "a request which I *was* eager to carry out"?[68]

Pondering 2:10 with its attendant questions, one recalls, as noted above, that Paul's letters contain several references to a collection for the Jerusalem church. Three of these prove to be of immediate pertinence to an attempt to find the place of Galatians in the chronological order of Paul's letters:

Gal 2:9–10. Coming to see that fact, and thus coming to perceive the grace given to me by God, James and Cephas and John — those held by the Jerusalem church to be "the pillars" — shook hands with me and Barnabas, signifying that, in fellowship with one another (*edôkan dexias koinônias*), we were to go to the Gentiles and they to those who are circumcised. The only other move on their part was a request that we remember "the poor," and this was a request which I was eager to carry out.

1 Cor 16:1–4. Now concerning the collection (*logeia*) for the saints: you should follow the directions I gave to the churches of Galatia. On the first day of every week, each of you is to put aside and save whatever extra you earn, so that collections (*logeiai*) need not be taken when I come. And when I arrive, I will send any whom you approve with letters to take your gift to Jerusalem. If it seems advisable that I should go also, they will accompany me (NRSV).

Rom 15:25–27. At present . . . I am going to Jerusalem with support for the saints (*diakoneô*). For [the churches in] Macedonia and Achaia have been pleased to make a fellowship-establishing contribution (*koinônia*)[69] for the poor among the saints in Jerusalem; they [the Gentile churches I founded in Macedonia and Achaia] were pleased to do it, and indeed they are in debt to them, for if the Gentiles have come to share (*koinôneô*) in their spiritual blessings, they ought also to be of service to them in material blessings.

These references virtually demand that we attempt to reconstruct the history of the collection, or, as we shall see, the history of the collections. Guided to a considerable extent by the perceptive work of Georgi, we can arrive at a sketch:[70]

[68]This second question is as important as the first. One recalls that in 1:22–23 Paul used the imperfect tense to speak of something that happened — and continued to happen — over a period of some duration. The same temporal linearity is conveyed by the present-tense verb in 2:10: the Jerusalem leaders' request was that funds be assembled for their church regularly (*mnêmoneuômen*). By contrast, Paul refers in a punctiliar fashion to his own role in this collection. Characterizing his past, he says simply, "I was eager to carry out their request." A detailed and convincing consideration of this aorist verb (*espoudasa poiêsai*) is one of the major desiderata lacking in the analysis of Luedemann, *Chronology*, 77–87.
[69]See Peterman, "Romans 15.26"; Hainz, "Koinônia bei Paulus."
[70]Georgi, *Remembering*. At some points I have not been able to follow Georgi's reconstruction (by the same token, he will surely disagree with some aspects of the picture I present below). In the following sketch, however, I am extensively indebted to Georgi's proposal. Critiques of his work made by Jewett (*Chronology*, 67–68) and by Luedemann (*Chronol-*

(1) The history of the collection began with the request directed by the Jerusalem church to the church in Antioch, probably including its Gentile daughter churches. As representatives of the Antioch church, Barnabas and Paul gladly committed that congregation to the task, understanding it to be an endeavor that would extend over a period of some time. All who were involved surely saw also that the collection had two essential elements. It would supply a genuine need on the part of the Jerusalem church; and its delivery would concretely reflect the unity of God's church, drawn both from Jews and from Gentiles.[71]

(2) There is no reason at all to think that the Antioch church refused to honor the agreement to which it was committed by its representatives. Presumably, the collection went forward in that church with some regularity, energized by the efforts of Barnabas and Paul.[72]

(3) Then came, however, the Antioch visit of the delegation from James as head of the Jerusalem church, and the painful developments that ended with Paul's withdrawal from the church of Antioch (and some degree of mutual mistrust between Paul and the Jerusalem church). Clearly, that was an event of momentous proportions for Paul, impelling him into his own mission far to the west (Comment #17). It is sure also to have terminated his active participation in the life of the Antioch church, including its collection for the church in Jerusalem. One can imagine that Paul now felt no very warm bond with either of those churches.

(4) It also takes no great powers of fantasy to enter imaginatively into the minds of the leaders of the Antioch church, not to mention James's delegation that returned to the church in Jerusalem. Paul now had enemies in both churches; and, if he had angry words about them (2:14), they must have had words no less angry about him:

Look! Paul participated in the collection for a time, but now he has ceased to do so, reneging, in fact, on the agreement reached at the Jerusalem conference! In this way he has shown not only his deviation from the true gospel but also his callousness with regard to the financial suffering of the saints in Jerusalem and his lack of a steady commitment to the unity of the worldwide church under the leadership of the mother church in Jerusalem.

---

ogy, 77–99), while worthy of attention, are fundamentally unconvincing. For example, Luedemann's contention that the Galatians are sure to have been informed of Paul's consistent zeal in carrying out the Jerusalem leaders' request is probably the opposite of what happened, as we will see in point 5 below. See further Lightfoot 55; Borse, *Standort*, 37–38, 145; Hurtado, "Collection." Hainz represents several other interpreters when he says that Georgi's proposal is burdened by a series of hypotheses. In effect, he also speaks for others when, having appreciatively identified that proposal as fundamentally informative, he largely leaves it aside, focusing his attention on his own subject, the term *koinōnia* (*Koinōnia*, 151; cf. his "Koinōnia bei Paulus," 375 n4). But it is only by hypotheses and their testing that progress is made.

[71]The unity of God's church drawn both from Jews and from Gentiles is also presupposed — in a certain form — in James's decision somewhat later to send a delegation to Antioch (Gal 2:12).

[72]Cf. Acts 11:27–30, and the commentaries on Acts by Haenchen and Conzelmann.

(5) With equal probability we can imagine that, when the Teachers came into Paul's Galatian churches sometime later, they said essentially the same thing: "Paul's withdrawal from Antioch's collection for the Jerusalem church reflects his theological bankruptcy, his disrespect for the pillars on whom God has elected to build his church, and his hard-hearted disregard for the mother church in her suffering."[73]

(6) At this point we return to Gal 2:9–10, where, having said that the Jerusalem leaders' request was directed both to Barnabas and to himself, Paul immediately ignores Barnabas, referring only to his own reaction. To read Paul's statement in Gal 2:10 against the background sketched above is to see that the shift to the first person singular gives it the ring of a protest: "What the Teachers are telling you is false. The request conveyed to Barnabas and me by the leaders of the Jerusalem church is a matter to which I, no less than Barnabas, immediately turned my active and enthusiastic attention." Indeed, taking 2:10 and 2:11 together, one hears Paul saying:

> The only other move on the part of the leaders of the Jerusalem church was to ask Barnabas and me to convey to the church in Antioch a request that we all continually remember "the poor." And, contrary to what you have heard about my stance toward this collection, I, no less than Barnabas, immediately gave my active and enthusiastic attention to this matter. *But*, when Peter came to Antioch . . .

(7) Given this reading, one can also understand why Paul puts the verb of "I was eager to carry it out" not only in the first person singular but also in the simple past tense. As he writes to the Galatians, Paul cannot say that he is still participating in the Antioch collection, and nowhere else in the letter does he mention that matter.[74] For, enthusiastic as his participation in the Antioch relief effort was, that participation now lies in the past. Nor is there the slightest hint in Galatians that Paul has commenced his own collection to take the place of his earlier participation in that of the Antioch church.[75]

(8) Sometime after dispatching his volatile letter to the Galatians, Paul conceived the idea of assembling a collection for Jerusalem from his own essentially Gentile churches. What brought him to this thought we cannot say with certainty, nor can we be entirely sure about all of the steps he took to implement

---

[73] Regarding the thesis that the Teachers referred to Jerusalem as "our mother," a suggestion made a century ago by Holtzmann (*Einleitung*, 243), see the Note on 4:26 and Comment #46.

[74] Mussner glosses Gal 2:10 to read, "as you yourselves know" (125 n125), thus supplying exactly what Paul does not say. The thesis of Trobisch that Paul himself combined Galatians, 1 and 2 Corinthians, and Romans into a literary whole (*Letter Collection*) provides data pertinent to ancient letter combinations, without proving convincing with regard to Paul's letters. For, while contending that Paul could stitch these letters together on the basis of their references to "the" collection (70 and passim), neither in *Letter Collection* nor in *Paulusbriefsammlung* does Trobisch provide an assessment of the work of Georgi.

[75] Read on its own, Gal 6:6 is a reference neither to the Antioch collection nor to one conceived by Paul himself. See the Note there.

this new collection.[76] We can be confident, however, of the fundamental conviction that informed this move. In spite of all the difficulties caused by the False Brothers and their allies, Paul knew that his Gentile churches were bonded to the Jewish church in Jerusalem by the fact that all were local outposts of God's redemptive invasion of the world in Jesus Christ.[77]

Paul quickly launched his collection with at least three moves. (a) Concerned at this time with the church in Corinth, he directed his first collection communication to that congregation (via either the letter mentioned in 1 Cor 5:9 or an oral communication). (b) His next word about the collection was directed to his churches in Galatia, presumably by means of a letter now lost (let us call it Galatians B). In communicating with the Galatians it occurred to Paul to speak not only of the collection but also of a procedure by which the Galatians were to assemble their share of the funds: "On the first day of every week, each of you is to put aside . . ."[78] (c) At this same time the Corinthians raised a few questions about the collection, and Paul responded to them, repeating the procedural instructions he had just given to the Galatians (1 Cor 16:1-2).[79]

[76] It is easy to imagine that the idea of a collection from his own churches materialized in Paul's mind as he thought over the various effects of the intemperate letter he had sent to the Galatians. He was almost certainly aware of a link between the Teachers and a powerful wing of the Jerusalem church, and thus of the probability that a report would soon make its way to Jerusalem regarding the letter in which he had portrayed the church there as the locus of slavery (Gal 4:25; Comment #46; J. L. Martyn, "Jewish-Christian Interpreters"). In any case, some development of this sort revived in Paul the passionate ecumenical feelings he had had when he and Barnabas attended the conference. Georgi suggests that causative factors emerged in Paul's difficulties with his church in Corinth, including Paul's conviction that some of the troubling developments in Corinth stemmed from a lack of close connection with the Jerusalem community's witness to Jesus' resurrection (*Remembering*, 49–52).

[77] In writing to the Romans Paul went a step further, saying that his Gentile congregations were in debt to the Jewish church in Jerusalem (Rom 15:37).

[78] Given Paul's relationship with Galatia, we can assume that he took this step with considerable anxiety. But the participation of the Galatian churches must have seemed to him of special importance, in light of the Teachers' relations with a wing of the Jerusalem church and his having told the Galatians that the Jerusalem church was linked with slavery (Gal 4:25).

[79] Did Paul approach the Galatians about his collection after hearing that his angry letter had been at least partially successful (Georgi, *Remembering*, 49)? Or, as suggested above, did he do that soon after sending the angry letter, perhaps thinking that the idea of a collection for Jerusalem could itself increase the likelihood of his letter's being heard as he wished it to be heard? The latter is an attractive interpretation, although certainty in the matter escapes us. More important, however, is the recognition of another limit to our knowledge. From 1 Cor 16:1-2 we can say nothing at all regarding the Galatians' reaction to Paul's communication about his collection. Contrary to an often repeated reading of 1 Cor 16:1-2, Paul does not speak there about an "exemplary participation" on the part of the Galatians. He says only that he has given them instructions in the matter of procedure. That passage, therefore — and thus the whole of 1 Corinthians — could have been written within a day or two of Paul's having broached with the Galatians the matter of his collection, and thus before he knew anything about the Galatians' inclinations. The *series* of collection communications in the case of the Corinthian church — (a) Paul's announcement, (b) the Corinthians' questions about the collection (1 Cor 16:1), (c) Paul's instruc-

With this sketch, then, we have reached the first conclusion about the place of Galatians in the Pauline letter corpus. It precedes 1 Corinthians, and thus all of the Corinthian letters that have been preserved.[80]

(9) Finally, what is one to say of Paul's reference to his collection in Rom 15:25–27? For our present purpose the most striking element in this passage is Paul's silence about the Galatian churches, for that silence supports what has been said above on the basis of 1 Cor 16:1–2.[81] When Paul mentioned the Galatians to the Corinthians, he may have been to some degree whistling in the dark, hoping against hope that the Galatians would participate in his newly formed plan, and viewing that plan as a move that helpfully modified his angry letter. By the time he wrote to the church in Rome, it was clear to him that the Galatians would do no such thing. From a study of the history of the two collections for Jerusalem, then, we can recover the chronological order of Galatians, the Corinthian letters, and Romans.

Conclusion: At some point prior to the writing of 1 Corinthians — prior even to his earlier Corinthian letter (1 Cor 5:9) — Paul received news of horribly distressing developments in his Galatian churches. Presumably in Macedonia or Achaia at the time — and not long away from Galatia itself (Gal 1:6) — he composed an extraordinarily vituperative letter in which he referred in a decidedly negative way to the Jerusalem church (Gal 4:25). Thereafter, perhaps especially in view of that potentially explosive reference, it occurred to him to organize a collection among his Gentile churches for delivery to the church in Jerusalem,

---

tion about the method for assembling the funds (1 Cor 16:2; still later 2 Corinthians 8 and 9) — has led to the unwarranted assumption of a similar series of communications in the case of the Galatian churches. It seems likely, as suggested above, that, in his collection communication to the Galatians (the now lost Galatians B), Paul informed the Galatians both of the collection and of a method of assembling the funds (1 Cor 16:2).

[80]Regarding the widely accepted theory that 2 Corinthians consists of several letters, see, for example, Furnish, *II Corinthians*; H. D. Betz, *2 Corinthians 8 and 9*. We can pass over the numerous and complex stages through which Paul's collection plans went as a result of manic-depressive developments in the Corinthian church. On that matter, see Georgi, *Remembering*, 59–109.

[81]There is also no reference in Romans to the church in Ephesus. On the basis of Acts 20:4 (cf. also Acts 21:29), Georgi thinks it probable that the church of Ephesus did participate; and he speculates that Paul's silence about Galatia may indicate that the Galatians' representatives had not yet arrived in Corinth, as Paul was writing to the Romans, or that at that time the Galatians "had not made a final commitment" (123). To me it seems far more likely that they had already told Paul of their refusal to participate. Perhaps by this time the Teachers had succeeded in replacing all of the Pauline catechetical instructors (Gal 6:6), thus persuading the Galatian churches to destroy Paul's collection communication (Galatians B) and, in any case, to avoid being perceived in Jerusalem as congregations belonging to the Pauline orb. That would help to explain both the loss of Galatians B and the depth of the anxiety Paul expresses in Rom 15:25–27. His anxiety over the possibility of his collection's being rejected is also a strong indication that the funds of which he speaks in Romans 15 are not being assembled in response to an urgent request made by the Jerusalem leaders. Contrary to Luedemann's concerted attempt to refute Georgi (especially *Chronology*, 80–87), there seem to have been in essence two collections, however much — as Georgi himself stresses — Paul may have thought of his own effort as a continuation of the work undertaken earlier in the Antioch church.

thus signaling the unity of God's church and responding to genuine poverty in the Jerusalem congregation.[82] He communicated this plan both to Corinth and to Galatia. Sometime later, after the Galatians' refusal had become clear, he mentioned the matter to the Romans, emphasizing his anxiety about the reception his collection would get in the Jerusalem church, an anxiety that may have been partly caused by the Galatians' refusal to participate. Romans, then, is later than both Galatians and the Corinthian letters. And since there is no clear reference to a collection in 1 Thessalonians, Philippians, and Philemon, we arrive at the following order:[83]

Letters written prior to Paul's beginning his own collection for Jerusalem are 1 Thessalonians, Galatians, and Philippians.[84] Communications after Paul had conceived that plan are the letter mentioned in 1 Cor 5:9 (assuming it to have included the news of his collection plans), Paul's collection communication to Galatia (Galatians B), the letters now contained in 1 and 2 Corinthians, and finally Romans.[85] At a number of points in the present commentary, we will see that the order of Galatians, the Corinthian correspondence, and Romans is important for the reading of Galatians itself. One hardly needs to add that it is a matter of considerable consequence for our efforts to understand the unfolding of Paul's theology in the midst of the strains and stresses in his various churches. It is especially important for our attempts to understand Paul's view of Israel (Comments #37 and #52).

2:11–14 AN INCIDENT IN THE ANTIOCH CHURCH

TRANSLATION

2:11. But when Cephas came to Antioch, I opposed him to his face, because in fact he stood condemned. 12. It happened in this way: Before the arrival

[82] Since Paul did not consider the False Brothers to be genuine members of God's church, he may have hoped that, in delivering his collection, he could drive a wedge between them (the enslaving Jerusalem church of Gal 4:25) and the remainder of the Jerusalem congregation ("the poor among the saints in Jerusalem").

[83] Once Paul had conceived the plan for his collection, it occupied a place in his thinking so large as to make it unlikely that he would subsequently write a letter to any of his churches without mentioning it.

[84] The character of Paul's letter to Philemon precludes our dating it by reference to Paul's collection. Moreover, the order of 1 Thessalonians, Galatians, and Philippians with respect to one another has to be discerned on grounds other than the collection, for the attempts to find indirect collection references in them are more ingenious than convincing.

[85] In light of the line of analysis presented above, the arguments of Borse for placing Galatians between the two letters now contained in 2 Corinthians must be said to be interest-

of some messengers from James, Cephas ate regularly with the Gentile members of the Antioch church. But when those men came, he drew back and separated himself from the Gentile members, because he was afraid of the circumcision party. 13. The other Jewish members of the Antioch church joined him in playing the hypocrite, so that even Barnabas was carried away by their hypocrisy. 14. But when I saw that they were not living out the truth of the gospel in a single-minded fashion, I said to Cephas, in front of the whole church, "You, a Jew by birth, are living like a Gentile, not like a Jew. How can you then compel the Gentile members of the church to live in the Jewish manner? . . ."

LITERARY STRUCTURE AND SYNOPSIS

At 2:11 Paul commences yet another episode in the revelatory history that he casts in the form of a personal memoir. As at earlier transitions there is a change of locale (cf. 1:17, 18, 21; 2:1), in this instance from Jerusalem to Antioch. With this story Paul takes his hearers to the church that was living at the time on the frontier of the circumcision-free mission to the Gentiles.

To a considerable extent there is a new set of characters, as was the case at 2:1, and among them sharp tensions arise, making one aware that this episode is an important juncture in the history of the church. Corresponding to these tensions, there are two further notes of discontinuity with the earlier parts of Paul's revelatory history: (1) The trip that transports the reader of Galatians to the new locale is taken, for the first time, by someone other than Paul, so that the new episode does not continue the Pauline travelogue. (2) The episode is introduced by the expression "but when," rather than by the connecting adverb "then" (contrast 1:18, 21; 2:1), raising the question at the outset whether — or in what way — this new turn of events will actually prove to be another step in the victorious march of God's gospel into the whole of the world.

Attempts to locate the end of the episode present a famous puzzle, sensed even by the earliest interpreters of the letter. In v 14 Paul reports an incisive comment he made to Peter in front of the Antioch church, doing so with a clarity that enables one confidently to place the first of the quotation marks — "You, a Jew by birth, are living . . ." But he gives no clear indication as to where his remark to Peter ends, although by the time the reader comes to the final verses of chapter 2, he knows that he is no longer hearing the speech that Paul made to Peter in Antioch. Indeed, as regards literary form, the concluding verses of the chapter are unlike anything the reader of Galatians has encountered earlier. They present a carefully reasoned discourse, and the discourse is without formal indication of the addressee(s) Paul has in mind (contrast 2:14 and 3:1).

In fact, Paul's failure formally to close the quotation begun in v 14 is no accident. It reflects his determination to connect his account of the Antioch incident

---

ing but not convincing (*Standort*; cf. his commentary). Thematic and linguistic congeniality proves nothing when it is not accompanied by a sophisticated consideration of the various opponents Paul had to face.

to the situation in Galatia. Every episode in the revelatory history is narrated for the sake of its pertinence to developments in Galatia. As we have seen, in recounting the meeting in Jerusalem Paul could display the victorious march of God's gospel toward Galatia (2:5) by making his narrative a two-level drama, some of the characters playing parts both on the stage in Jerusalem and on the stage in Galatia. Moreover, the power of that drama vis-à-vis the Galatian crisis lay in the fact that Paul was able to end it by presenting a scene in which the leaders of the Jerusalem church shake hands with him and voice a perception of God's activity that points clearly to the victorious advance of the circumcision-free gospel into the Gentile world, not least into Galatia.

To develop the Antioch narrative into a full-fledged two-level drama—with numerous actors playing roles simultaneously both on the Antioch stage and on the one in Galatia—was not an option for Paul. There is no doubt, as we have noted, that in this case also he recounts the incident for the sake of its impact on the crisis in Galatia. And there is some degree of correspondence between the messengers from James (v 12) and the Teachers. Both come into churches that are faithful to the truth of the gospel, and in each case this arrival disrupts that faithful pattern of life. In the Antioch drama itself, however, no actor other than Paul himself stood steadfastly by the gospel. Paul cannot present a final scene marked by yet another victory for the gospel. Indeed, in political terms the Antioch incident ended in tragedy. Hence, in presenting his account to the Galatians Paul must achieve the contemporary impact of the narrative—for the most part—in some way other than that of the two-level drama.

He accomplishes this impact by allowing his speech to Peter to become without notice a speech addressed to the Teachers in Galatia. Built on tradition accepted by all Jewish members of the church, the speech is addressed to Jewish Christians (initially Peter, then the Teachers), not to the Gentile Christians in Galatia (see Literary Structure and Synopsis for 2:15–21). Moreover, just as the speech to Peter was made lit. "in front of them all" (the Antioch church, v 14), so Paul's extension of the speech is made to the Teachers in front of the contemporary "all," that is to say in front of the Galatian churches. And in that way, Paul causes the subtle transition to do its work. Close reading of the text shows where this almost imperceptible transition lies. Verses 15 and 16 constitute an overlap between the once-upon-a-time remark to Peter and the contemporary speech to the Teachers. Even in vv 17 and 18 there is a hint of a two-level drama; for, in charges now being laid against him by the Teachers, Paul hears echoes of criticisms that were directed to himself and Peter by James's messengers in Antioch. But, as stated above, in composing vv 15–21 Paul accomplishes most of the contemporary impact by modulating his once-upon-a-time speech to Peter into a speech addressed to the Teachers in the presence of the Galatian churches.

If the inner structure of Paul's Antioch narrative and extended speech is a bit difficult to grasp, its end is, by contrast, easily discerned. In 3:1 Paul returns to a style he has employed earlier (1:6–9), addressing not the Teachers, but rather the Galatians, this time explicitly naming them. Thus, the literary unit begins at 2:11 and ends at 2:21; in it Paul presents the final episode in the revelatory history.[86]

This analysis is confirmed when we return briefly to the matter of the dramatis personae. In addition to Cephas, James, and Barnabas — mentioned already in the account of the Jerusalem conference — there is now the whole of the Antioch church, a community that is mixed as regards the ethnic origin of its members, a minority being Gentiles by birth (vv 12 and 14), most being by birth Jews (v 13). There is also a group of messengers who come to Antioch from Jerusalem, specifically from James (v 12), and there is a group whom Paul calls "those of the circumcision" (v 12). The members of this latter group remain offstage, but they are sufficiently powerful to cause an actor on the stage, Cephas, to act his part out of fear.

It is striking that Paul mentions none of these persons in the ratiocinative argument of vv 15–21. That instance of silence is yet another indication that at v 15 Paul allows the dramatic narrative imperceptibly to pass into a discourse loosed from the setting in Antioch.

NOTES

2:11. *But when.* Up to this point Paul has introduced every major episode in his historical sketch by the adverb "then" (*epeita*; 1:18, 21; 2:1), thus pointing to linear continuity. Here, however, with the expression *hote de* he strikes a note of discontinuity that is reinforced by the same expression in v 12 (cf. 2:14; 1:15; 4:4). The formula of concord sounded at the close of the Jerusalem meeting was the result of God's work, but it did not preclude setbacks.[87]

Cephas. Regarding the variant "Peter," see the Note on 1:18. A number of the manuscripts that here read "Peter" do the same at 2:14. They are almost certainly secondary.

came. Paul shows no interest in the reason for Peter's trip to Antioch. Did Peter come in order to carry back the first of the funds collected for the church in Jerusalem? And did the assembling of funds take some time, during which he turned his energies to the evangelization of Jews in the great city?

Antioch. The first church to arise in one of the truly great metropolitan centers of the Roman Empire, the Antioch congregation was a community of some

---

[86] H. D. Betz calls 2:15–21 the *propositio*, a section following the *narratio* (1:12–2:14) and preparing for the *probatio* (3:1–4:31). It is an instance of bringing a rhetorical category to the structural analysis of Galatians without having a rhetorical marker in the text of the letter. See Introduction §10.

[87] Luedemann is the latest to suggest that the Antioch episode occurred prior to the Jerusalem conference (*Chronology*, 75–77). Against this highly improbable reading, see, for example, Jewett, *Chronology*, 83–84; Murphy-O'Connor, "Missions," 81 n14. Paul's confidence in Barnabas and, even more important, the confidence of the Antioch church in Paul — necessary presuppositions of the conference — were hardly still intact after the Antioch episode. The coup de grâce to Luedemann's reading is the absence of all reference to food laws in 2:1–10.

means, able to assemble funds for the church in Jerusalem.[88] It also became the initial testing ground for the formula that speaks of two parallel lines of mission, one to the Jews and one to the Gentiles (vv 7, 9). Its major leaders, Barnabas and Paul, were Jews by birth (in Acts all of the named leaders in Antioch are Jews; cf. Gal 2:12–14). Yet, it had an active mission to Gentiles, pursued mainly by Barnabas and Paul, and resulting in a mixed congregation clearly distinct from the local synagogues.[89] Mixed as it was, it was different, in fact, not only from its neighboring synagogues and from the Jewish church in Jerusalem. It was also different from those of its daughter churches that were drawn solely from Gentiles. In short, this congregation of born Jews and born Gentiles was more than interesting. It was a sort of time bomb, being the locus in which the two parallel lines of mission threatened to cross in such a way as to pose unexpected problems.

I opposed him to his face, because in fact he stood condemned. Paul summarizes the incident before providing details, and in doing so he indicates that his own opposition to Peter was subsequent and secondary to a prior act of God. He speaks, to be sure, of hypocrisy (v 13), but he also indicates that the fundamental cause of God's condemnation was Peter's failure to order his daily life by "the truth of the gospel" (v 14).

12. *It happened in this way.* These words are added in order to reflect the fact that Paul now turns to his narrative only after he has summarized the whole of it in one sentence.

Before the arrival . . . Cephas ate regularly with the Gentile members of the Antioch church. The Jerusalem church, truly observant of the Law, held its common meals — including the eucharist — in accordance with the Jewish food laws, doubtless keeping to that practice during the conference. In the Antioch church, however, the meals — again including the eucharist — were arranged by an adjustment on the part of the members who were Jews by birth. At least by implication, the food laws were declared to be essentially a matter of no consequence in the church. By putting the verb "ate" in the imperfect tense, Paul indicates that over a period of some length Peter was fully at home in the Antioch church, adopting its meal practice.

the Gentile members of the Antioch church. From 3:28 we can see that, when he wrote Galatians, Paul held the church of God to be made up of former Jews and former Gentiles. And that was doubtless a conviction he cherished at the

---

[88]On the Antioch church, see Meeks and Wilken, *Antioch*; R. E. Brown and Meier, *Antioch and Rome*; Norris, "Antioch."

[89]The term "Christians" was a Latin title coined by Gentiles who took "Christus" to be a proper name (R. E. Brown and Meier, *Antioch and Rome*, 35). In Luke's time it served to distinguish members of the church from both Jews and Gentiles. Luke's projection of this usage back to the early days of the Antioch church (Acts 11:26) may not be historically accurate, but it is a true index of the nature of that congregation, which, because of its mixed membership, was neither a synagogue nor a Gentile association of some sort. After Paul's founding of it, the church in Corinth came to include former Jews as well as former Gentiles, but Paul's other churches seem to have remained almost totally Gentile in ethnic origin.

time of the incident he is now narrating. To be sure, "the uncircumcision" and "the Gentiles" are expressions Paul uses to refer to the people God called him to evangelize, just as "the circumcision" serves to denote the mission field of the leaders of the Jerusalem church, and especially of Peter (1:16; 2:2, 7, 8, 9; cf. 3:8, 14). But once a person enters the church, ethnic origin becomes for Paul and his fellow workers a matter of no importance.

In the present verse, however, and again in v 13 (the "Jewish members of the Antioch church"; cf. vv 14 and 15), Paul uses a locution that reflects a fact about the life of the Antioch church. Although its members were committed to a circumcision-free mission to Gentiles, and although they ignored the Jewish food laws in their common meals, they remained to some degree conscious of their ethnic derivation.

But when those men [some messengers from James] came. For the second time in two verses (cf. "But when" in v 11) Paul sounds in an ominous way the note of discontinuity. With the arrival of the messengers from James, a series of events begins to unfold that does not belong transparently to the victorious forward march of the gospel.

some messengers from James. Although Paul uses a colorless expression, "some persons from James," the ensuing course of events shows that they constituted an official delegation, empowered by James to journey to Antioch and to deliver a message to Peter.[90] We can be sure that the message did not directly and explicitly rescind the formula of the Jerusalem conference with its acknowledgment of the Antioch church's circumcision-free mission. Had it done so, Paul would certainly have pointed that out, and he would have launched a direct attack on James rather than on Peter. The issue of circumcision was not reopened. The issue was changed to the matter of Jewish-Gentile association at meals.[91]

he drew back and separated himself from the Gentile members. The first verb, "drew back," sometimes describes a military or political maneuver designed to bring one into a sheltered position of safety. The second refers here to cultic separation.[92] Since the eucharist was part of the common meal, Peter's withdrawal from the latter brought with it his withdrawal from the former. He has now separated himself from the Gentile members, as they eat the Lord's Supper.

because he was afraid of the circumcision party. Peter surely saw his separation from the common table as a reasonable adjustment necessitated by an argument delivered to him by James's messengers (see Comment #26). He may have wished to avoid what he considered an unnecessary offense to a highly significant part of the Jerusalem church, including James himself (cf. Paul's own stance in Rom 14:21–22; 15:1). Paul, however, does not hesitate to attribute Peter's move

---

[90] F. Watson, *Paul*, 58, holds that the messengers from James are the same as the Teachers who invaded Paul's Galatian churches. Why does Paul not say so?

[91] A similar modulation of issues is portrayed in Acts 15. See Mussner. A provocative reading is now offered in Esler, "Breaking."

[92] Paul's use of the imperfect tense for these two verbs may indicate that he waited for some time to see whether Peter's withdrawal from the common meals would prove to be Peter's steady position. If so, his own act in confronting Peter was not taken impulsively, but simmered to a boil.

to fear, probably seeing a partial parallel between Peter's acting out of fear and the Galatians' present tendency to act on the basis of their fear of the Teachers (cf. 1:7; 4:17; 5:10).

the circumcision party. In the context one might have expected to hear that Peter was afraid of "the food-laws party." Instead, Paul identifies the persons involved as *hoi ek peritomês,* literally "those from the circumcision." On this expression, see Comment #25. Paul draws on the vocabulary of the Jerusalem church in order to refer to a party within that congregation whose members derive their basic identity from their ethnic (Jewish) heritage and who are sure that all members of the church have to be taken into this ethnic heritage, at least to some degree.[93]

13. *The other Jewish members of the Antioch church joined him.* Peter's act did not remain the deed of an individual. Others followed him. And the context, and especially Paul's reference in v 12 to "the Gentiles," makes clear that in speaking literally of "the other Jews," Paul thinks of the members of the Antioch church who share with Peter the characteristic of being Jews by birth. In the Note on v 11 we have seen that most of the leaders of the church in Antioch were drawn from this ethnically distinguishable group. It is, then, the powerful kernel of the church that has left the table.

in playing the hypocrite. Paul further darkens the picture, speaking indeed of the absence of integrity. He says that, as he looks at Peter and the others, he sees actors reciting lines written by someone other than themselves.[94]

so that even Barnabas was carried away. The crowning blow to Paul is the defection of Barnabas, his otherwise faithful coworker who had stood solidly beside him in the earlier battle with the False Brothers (2:5). At a later time Paul will speak both of Barnabas and of Peter in an even tone of voice and without rancor (1 Cor 9:5–6). For the moment, thinking only about their actions in the Antioch church, he is filled with anger and disappointment.

14. *not living out . . . in a single-minded fashion.* The verb *orthopodeô* is rare in the literature that has come down to us, but the Galatians will have grasped the major force of it, even if, never having heard it before, they had to proceed on the basis of etymology. They will have seen, namely, that Paul changes the damning metaphor from that of actors hypocritically playing false parts on a stage (v 13) to that of pedestrians who fail to walk — or runners who fail to run — in a straight line, thus showing the lack of consistent fidelity.

the truth of the gospel. The fidelity that is lacking is quite specific, being focused on the gospel.[95] Thus, Paul finally comes to the crux of the matter, by

---

[93]Regarding the use of the term "identity" here and in 3:7, 9, 10, see the close of the Note on 6:14. Vouga locates the circumcision party within the Antioch church ("Der Galaterbrief," 249).

[94]Paul finds in Peter's withdrawal an act in which Peter himself does not fully believe. Peter and the others are rebuilding something they had earlier torn down: the legal wall separating Jew from Gentile. Cf. 2:18 below; Wilckens, "*hypokrinomai*"; and note the use of the verb in Epictetus *Diss.* 2.9.19.

[95]Preceding "the truth of the gospel," the preposition *pros* means here "in accordance with" (BAGD, "*pros*," III.5.d.).

speaking no longer of hypocrisy, but rather of unfaithfulness to "the truth of the gospel," an expression to which he had given a weighty role in his earlier account of the conference in Jerusalem (2:5). But his use of that expression here poses one of the vexing puzzles of his account of the incident in Antioch: How can he possibly hold that the actions of Peter and Barnabas in leaving the common table are as much in violation of God's good news as was the attempt of the False Brothers to compel the circumcision of Titus? See Comment #26.

I said to Cephas, in front of the whole church. Whether Paul first remonstrated with Peter in private we do not know (cf. Matt 18:15). Commentators rightly compare Paul's public confrontation of Peter with the instructions he gives at a later point to the Galatian congregations themselves:

> Brothers and sisters, if someone should be caught committing a transgression of some sort, you who are spiritual are to restore that person to his former condition in the community, doing so in a spirit of gentleness, taking care, lest you yourself be tempted (6:1).

Vis-à-vis Peter, Paul displays anything but gentleness![96] It is clear, however, that he does not see Peter's withdrawal as an instance of mere "transgression." Peter's act is the effective preaching of an anti-gospel in the midst of the Antioch church. For that reason Paul has no alternative but to address the issue in a plenary meeting of the church with the messengers of James also being present.

"You. With the singular pronoun and a verb in the second person singular, Paul now begins to quote the remark he made to Peter. Many modern translations, and the majority of the commentators who employ quotation marks, place the second set of marks at the end of v 14. That practice is probably inevitable, but one does well to note that, although Paul begins with remarks he made to Peter in Antioch, he then moves imperceptibly to an argument addressed to the Teachers and thus formulated as part of the letter (see Literary Structure and Synopsis above).

are living like a Gentile, not like a Jew. With these words Paul introduces the matter of Law observance, for that is what distinguishes Jewish life from Gentile life. Why, however, does he use the present tense? Perhaps because he wishes to emphasize again (v 12) that Peter's earlier departure from the requirement of the food laws had become a pattern stretching over a period of some length. And being a pattern, it could not be terminated with the blink of an eye.

compel the Gentile members of the church to live in the Jewish manner. The verb "to compel" is a term of great significance in the Galatian setting, as we have discovered in the Note on 2:3. When Paul sees that the Galatians are being compelled by the Teachers to take up Law observance (6:12), he recalls two earlier instances of compulsion: (a) At the meeting in Jerusalem the False Brothers attempted in vain to compel the circumcision of Titus (2:3); and (b) at one point in the history of the Antioch church Peter acted in a way that involved a similar

---

[96]To ask whether Paul now feels himself superior to Peter, whereas he was earlier inferior to him, is to introduce a frame of reference foreign to the text (R. E. Brown et al., *Peter,* 29–30). For Paul the norm is not personal authority, but rather the truth of the gospel.

compulsion, this time successful (2:14). Under the pressure of the leading members of the Antioch church — Jews by birth — the Gentile members agreed (reluctantly?) to a common meal prepared essentially in accordance with the Jewish food laws.[97]

To describe that development, Paul employs the verb "to live in the Jewish manner" (*ioudaïzein*).[98] As it is found nowhere else in the NT, we do not know how it may have been employed, if it was used at all, by other Christians of Paul's time.[99] In the book of Esther (8:17) and in the writings of Josephus (*J.W.* 2.454, 463) it seems to have about it a ring that is artificial — perhaps even somewhat false — referring to Gentiles who take up wholly or in part the Jewish way of life, without thoroughgoing conviction from the heart.[100] While Peter's eyes are fixed on the messengers from James (and, behind them, on the circumcision party in the Jerusalem church), Paul sees what is happening to the Gentile members of the Antioch church.[101] It clearly did not occur to Paul to call these members to his side, leading them out and thus founding a separate and exclusively Gentile church. The apostle never wavered in his conviction that God was making a new creation by drawing into one church both Jews and Gentiles (see not only Gal 2:7–10 but also Rom 15:25–31).

No less than later interpreters of our letter, the Galatians will have noticed that, whereas Paul quotes his own caustic remark to Peter, he does not cite Peter's response. Nor does he say what ensued in the Antioch church as a whole. Recalling the uninhibited way in which he reports his victory vis-à-vis the False Brothers (vv 3–4), one is bound to conclude that the Antioch incident ended in political defeat for Paul. Given that development, the route open to him as he writes to the Galatians is simply to bear witness to the truth of the gospel yet again, and that is what he does in the argument of vv 15–21.

COMMENT #25
THE CIRCUMCISION PARTY AS A GROUP OF CHRISTIAN JEWS IN THE JERUSALEM CHURCH

Having said that Peter withdrew from the common meals in the Antioch church only after messengers brought word from James, Paul adds that Peter's act of cultic separation was the result of his fearing *hoi ek peritomēs*, "persons from among

---

[97]"To compel to live in the Jewish manner" is not an anti-Judaic expression. See Introduction §17.
[98]In the history of the interpretation of Galatians the Teachers have most often been referred to as "Judaizers," that is to say people who compel others to live in the Jewish manner. In the Introduction (§6) and in Comment #6 I have given reasons for abandoning this practice, using instead the expression "the Teachers." One may add that the verb *ioudaïzein* means to live in the Jewish manner, not to cause someone else to do that.
[99]In the early second century see the use Ignatius makes of the expressions *ioudaïzein* and *zaô kata Ioudaïsmon* (*Magn.* 10:3; 8:1).
[100]Cf. MH 409: "*Ioudaïzô* follows the well-known type of 'imitatives,' *mêdizô*, *lakônizô*, and even *philippizô*, 'to ape the Mede,' 'to imitate the Spartan manners,' 'to side with Philip.'"
[101]See E. P. Sanders, *Law*, 176–178.

those who are circumcised" (Gal 2:12). Does this expression refer to non-Christian Jews (so numerous interpreters) or to Jews who have come into the church? A brief consideration of the use of the expression in Paul's letter to the Romans, in Eusebius's *Ecclesiastical History*, and in the Acts of the Apostles will provide guidance.

ROM 4:11b–12

In the course of a complex argument about Abraham's rectification, Paul constructs a sentence that reflects in part the view of God's activity that prevailed at the Jerusalem conference. God has empowered two parallel lines of mission, one to the Gentiles and one to the Jews:

> [God's ancient purpose, now brought to completion, was] that Abraham should become the father of all who believe while they are in the state of uncircumcision . . . and also the father of the circumcised ones, who are characterized not only by the fact that they are those drawn from the circumcised (*hoi ek peritomês*) but also by their walking in the steps of the faith held by Abraham before he was circumcised (Rom 4:11b–12).

Here Paul employs the same expression we find in Gal 2:12, using it in a way that presupposes a mission to Gentiles. With the presence of Gentiles in the church, one can refer in a differentiating way (1) to persons who have come into the church from the Gentile world and (2) to persons who have come into the church from the Jewish world, "those drawn from the circumcised." In the second expression the absence of the noun "believers" is of no consequence. By that expression Paul refers in Rom 4:12 to those who have come into the church from the Jewish people.[102]

EUSEBIUS ECCLESIASTICAL HISTORY 4.5.3

Eusebius (fourth century) employs the expression *ek tês peritomês* several times, always enclosing it between an article and a noun, and consistently using it to refer to Jews who have been drawn into the church. Stating, for example, that prior to the Jewish revolt of A.D. 132, all of the Jerusalem bishops, beginning with James, were Jews by birth, Eusebius then refers to them as *hoi ek peritomês episkopoi*, "the bishops from the circumcision" (*EH* 4.5.3; cf. 4.5.4), thus using the prepositional phrase *ek peritomês* as a partitive expression equivalent to "drawn from the Jewish nation into the church."

ACTS 10:45

In the first of two instances in Acts, Luke employs the expression in exactly the same way, and in a context in which the issue is strict adherence to the Jewish

---

[102]Paul does not recognize these people to be children of Abraham solely by virtue of their ethnic origin (cf. Matt 3:9). For Paul "those drawn into the church from the circumcised" are children of Abraham because they are also those who find their true origin in Abraham's faith (*to sperma ek pisteôs Abraam*, Rom 4:16).

food laws. At its heart Acts 10 is the story of Peter's conversion as regards mealtime association with Gentiles (cf. Gal 2:12). Prepared by a vision from God, Peter enters the ritually "unclean" home of the Roman centurion Cornelius, eats with the Gentiles there (Acts 11:3), preaches the gospel, and finds that God pours out the Spirit even on the Gentiles. This development is a source of amazement to Peter and to his traveling companions, members of the church in Joppa identified by the expression *hoi ek peritomês pistoi*, "believers drawn into the church from those who are circumcised" (10:45). The locution is used as it is in Rom 4:12 and in Eusebius: It does not refer to Jews, but rather to Jews who have made their way into the church. And in the sense in which it is used in Acts 10 it would not have been employed at all until the church also contained Gentiles.[103]

Acts 11:2

The second reference in Acts follows immediately after the first. News of Peter's mealtime association with the Gentile Cornelius reaches the Jerusalem church, exactly the thing that seems to have been feared by James in the story of Gal 2:10–14. And upon Peter's return to Jerusalem, he is criticized by a group in that church identified by the precise expression used in Gal 2:12, *hoi ek peritomês*, "the persons drawn from those who are circumcised" (Acts 11:2). Moreover, the form of this group's criticism is noteworthy: "You, Peter, have visited uncircumcised people and have eaten with them!" Again, then, the expression *hoi ek peritomês* refers not to Jews, but rather to Jews who have been drawn into the church, and whose concern is focused on association with uncircumcised Gentiles in the form of a common meal.

Here, however, a problem arises. All members of the Jerusalem church have come into it from the Jewish nation. Like the members of the church in Joppa, they could all be called "believers drawn into the church from those who are circumcised" (Acts 10:45). Yet in Acts 11:2 Luke clearly refers to a distinct group within the Jewish-Christian congregation in Jerusalem. Peter, a Jew by birth, does not belong to this group. He is in fact subject to its criticism. How could this situation and this locution have arisen?

Apparently in addition to the usage in which "the persons drawn from those who are circumcised" refers to Jewish Christians in general (so Rom 4:12, Eusebius, and Acts 10:45), the expression had acquired the status of a technical term in the vocabulary of the Jerusalem church, referring in fact to a *party* within that community. Unlike the other members of the church, the circumcision party retained its Jewish derivation as an essential mark of its identity. And it attempted to preserve that derived identity for the whole of the church by demanding consistent and — within the church — universal separation from Gentiles at meals.[104]

---

[103]There is, moreover, an added note: These believers who have been drawn into the church from the Jewish nation come to a new understanding as regards "unclean foods" and "unclean persons" (Acts 10:14–15, 28). They learn, in a word, that "God shows no partiality" (10:34).

[104]In Luke's story Peter wins the day, bringing even the circumcision party to see God's hand in the conversion of Cornelius. That outcome — certainly pleasing to Luke, if not created by him — does not lessen the portrait of genuine tensions internal to the Jerusalem

GAL 2:12

It is a short step from that conclusion to Gal 2:12, where we find, in fact, the earliest reference to this group. To be sure, when we compare Gal 2:11–14 with Acts 10–11, we see that the winners and the losers are reversed in the two stories. In Acts Peter is converted to the view that "what God has cleansed [must not be called] common" (Acts 10:15; 11:9). And, upon his return, far from fearing the circumcision party in the Jerusalem church, Peter silences this group with his powerful testimony (Acts 11:18). The issues in the two stories are essentially the same, however, involving tension in the matter of meal practice between Peter and "those drawn from the circumcision."

We can surmise, then, that after the inception of a mission to Gentiles, the expression *hoi ek peritomês* was used in two ways: (1) Largely devoid of affect, it functioned as a general term for identifying the congregations — or groups within congregations — made up of born Jews (Rom 4:12 and Acts 10:45; cf. Col 4:11). (2) In the Jerusalem church it was also employed, however, as a technical term to refer to a party within that congregation intent on a mission to Gentiles that was at least partly Law-observant (Gal 2:12 and Acts 11:2).

It follows that, in recounting the Antioch incident, Paul borrows from the Jerusalem church the expression by which it refers — in a differentiating way — to this zealous party in its midst, a party to which the False Brothers must have belonged. And in writing to the Galatians Paul is concerned to emphasize that the members of this party are persons who receive their distinctiveness from their ethnic and religious derivation. In short, acting through James to impose the Jewish food laws even on the Antioch church, members of the circumcision party follow a path that reflects their understanding of themselves and of the church of God: Their being drawn from the Jewish nation — *hoi ek peritomês* — is the fact most consequential for their identity. And in their view the same is true for the identity of the whole of the church. It is a mistake to say that they are Jews. They do hold, however, to a form of theology that warrants calling them Christian Jews rather than Jewish Christians.[105]

The story Paul tells in Gal 2:11–14 is focused on events in the church of Antioch, and especially on the actions of Peter and Barnabas. This incident is also, however, an event in the history of the Jerusalem church, and specifically in the history of the relationship of that church to missionary work among Gentiles, not least the work of Paul (cf. Comment #46). With Peter's fear of the circumcision party in the Jerusalem church, an ominous shadow fell across the stage of early Christianity, and that shadow surely deepened Paul's concern about developments internal to the Jerusalem church itself. He could still look back to the happy conclusion of the conference, but he had now to reckon with the fact that, subsequent to the conference, the circumcision party had increased its power

---

church. Are the traditions behind Acts 10–11 in some way related to the incident in Antioch narrated by Paul in Gal 2:11–14?

[105] On the nomenclature, see Comment #6 and the Glossary. It is when we ask about the motivation of the circumcision party that we come into the area suggestively explored by Jewett in "Agitators."

in the Jerusalem congregation, even bringing James around to its position in some degree.

Indeed, it would seem quite probable that, when James's messengers returned to the Jerusalem church with their report, James himself was pleased, insofar as the report included an assurance of Peter's compliance with the request that he not enter into close association with persons failing to keep the food laws. James may have regretted the breach with Paul, but, like Peter and the Jewish members of the Antioch church, he surely held Paul responsible for it. There is, moreover, no indication that he did anything to curb the False Brothers. On the contrary, having complied with their request that he send messengers to the Antioch church, he may have been open to further suggestions from them.

The importance of these developments for Galatia is heightened when we ask again why Paul included an account of the Antioch incident in his letter. Given three facts—Paul's political defeat in Antioch, his breach with the Antioch church, and not least the increased influence of the circumcision party in the Jerusalem church—we can be confident that Paul would have preferred to include no reference to the incident at all. We must surmise that the Teachers had already given the Galatians their own account, and that Paul knew they had done so. Paul speaks of the incident, then, in order to say that the Teachers' account fails to address, in the light of the truth of the gospel, the theological issue that was—and is—at stake. He therefore sharpens that issue in a speech directed to the Teachers themselves, doing so in such a way as to begin his consideration of the matter of God's making things right in the world (2:15–21; Comment #28).

Powerful as the theological essay of 2:15–21 proves to be, however, one senses behind Paul's account of the Antioch incident the dark developments internal to the Jerusalem church that led to it. Specifically, the reader of Galatians suspects that he has not heard the last of the ways in which the False Brothers and the circumcision party will affect the history of their church, and even of churches beyond their own. One is prepared, then, to find Paul later referring to the Jerusalem congregation in a manner that reflects its history subsequent to its role in the Antioch incident (4:25 and Comment #46).

COMMENT #26
PETER IN ANTIOCH AND INFIDELITY TO THE TRUTH OF THE GOSPEL

Paul's narration of the incident in Antioch shows that in his view that event differed from the Jerusalem conference in three major ways. There was a radically unsettling change in Peter. There was a change in the bone of contention from circumcision to food laws. The final scene, instead of being marked by the shaking of hands and a formula of concord, brought a painful confrontation, a stinging political defeat for Paul, and a traumatic parting of ways. Paul severed his relationship with the Antioch church. It is that concluding scene that Paul turns to his own use, developing his once-upon-a-time remark to Peter (v 14) into a speech he now addresses to the Teachers who have invaded his Galatian churches (vv 15–21). Finally, important as these three differences may be, Paul insists that both pictures have a common center. The fundamental issue that was at stake in Antioch is the issue that had earlier been at stake in Jerusalem: fidelity or infidelity to the truth of the gospel. And in developing his speech to the Teachers, Paul insists that that issue is also the crucial matter currently at stake in Galatia.

THE UNSETTLING CHANGE IN PETER

Paul's dynamic portrait of Peter in Antioch is easily described, having four major features: (1) In that picture Peter remains one of God's apostles. We can assume that Paul initially welcomed Peter to the Antioch church, continuing the cordial relationship the two men had had for more than a decade. There is no indication that Paul was suspicious of Peter or in any way critical of him for coming, whereas he certainly would have opposed a visit from the False Brothers.[106] (2) Paul draws no connection, however, between Peter's trip and God's revelatory leading (contrast 2:2). (3) The absence of that connection becomes more impressive when Paul portrays Peter as a man who was afraid, not of God, but rather of a group within the Jerusalem church (contrast 1:10). And (4) Paul indicates that this fear led Peter to separate himself from the Gentile members of the Antioch church, even though the final outcome of that separation caused him — in Paul's view — to be unfaithful to the truth of the gospel (vv 12–14). In the final analysis Paul's portrait is that of a "pillar" that could be and was severely shaken.[107]

THE BONE OF CONTENTION

Another difference between Paul's account of the Jerusalem conference and his picture of the incident in Antioch is the change of the bone of contention. In the conference the open battle was focused on the False Brothers' attempt to compel the circumcision of Titus. Now, in the Antioch incident, the fight develops in such a way as to be focused on the arrangements for the church's common meals.[108] We can be sure that this shift had its own history, involving at least three factors.

(1) In the first place, it was probably related to some degree of change in the leadership of the Jerusalem church. Peter has left Jerusalem, at least temporarily, and John is no longer mentioned. Political unrest in Judea that would eventually lead to a zealotic uprising may have caused the Jerusalem church to put at its head the man most strict in his zeal for the Law, James.[109] And these develop-

---

[106] Peter lived for some time in the Antioch church, perhaps evangelizing Jews in Antioch, as Paul and Barnabas evangelized Gentiles. Did he later travel still further afield, even to Corinth (1 Cor 1:12; 3:22; 9:5; Barrett, "Cephas"; R. E. Brown et al., *Peter*, 37; Perkins, *Peter*)?

[107] R. E. Brown et al., *Peter*, 29–30.

[108] Esler has recently argued that, in direct breach of the Jerusalem agreement, Peter eventually advocated the circumcision of the Gentiles in the Antioch church, the verb *ioudaïzō* in 2:14 meaning "to become Jews (through circumcision)." I am not convinced of this portrait of Peter, but one element of Esler's argument is suggestive: In terms of some strains of Mediterranean culture, the False Brothers, having experienced "shame" and loss of "honor" at the conference, doubled their efforts thereafter ("Breaking," 305–306). See Comment #46.

[109] See Jewett, "Agitators," especially 206; Eusebius *EH* 2.23; Josephus *Ant.* 20.199–203; Reicke, "Hintergrund," 185–186.

ments may have encouraged the False Brothers and other members of the circumcision party to make another attempt to bring the Gentile mission of Antioch under the Law, at least to some degree.

(2) The shift was directly related to actions on the part of Peter. The Jerusalem conference had ended with a formula of concord in which Peter was credited with the central role in the mission to the Jews (2:7, 8). At the present time, however, this chief figure of the Jewish mission was not working on the *purely* Jewish frontier. Even if Peter was keeping to the Jerusalem agreement, preaching only to Jews in the city of Antioch, he had as his local base the mixed church in that city, and he was regularly entering fully into the nonkosher pattern of its life. That was exactly the sort of development that would trouble both James and the circumcision party in the Jerusalem church (though perhaps for somewhat different reasons; see Comment #46). Almost surely influenced by that party, then, James decided to remind Peter, in a warning tone of voice, that the Jerusalem formula recognized two completely *parallel* mission paths, and that the first of these, his mission among the Jews, would be placed in jeopardy if he continued to have decidedly close relations with Gentiles on Gentile terms.[110] James's argument may have been quite simple and, on its face, quite innocent:

> Peter, your God-given work among our people is threatened by your associating closely with Gentiles, especially your regularly eating some of their foods. It is a serious problem. But it is also one that can be solved. If, for a time, you are going to pursue the Jewish mission from the Antioch church, you are to withdraw from the common table in order not to jeopardize that mission.[111]

In a later period Paul indicates that some circles of Jewish Christians came in time to hold him responsible for the slim results of the Jewish mission.[112] It is easy to imagine that at an earlier date a similar concern for the future of the Jewish mission was aroused by Peter's behavior at Antioch. That would explain the shift from the demand for circumcision to a concern with Peter's manner of association with Gentiles.

(3) The Jerusalem conference had also closed with a request by the church in Jerusalem that funds be regularly forwarded from the church in Antioch. Only a short time may have passed before James realized that the position of the Jerusalem church among zealous observers of the Law could be made fundamentally untenable if that congregation gladly and regularly received money from unrighteous Gentiles. It is possible, therefore, that James also thought along these lines:

> The receiving of contributions from unrighteous Gentiles is a serious problem, but perhaps my message to Peter will lead eventually to a solution for it as well.

---

[110]See the cogent argument of E. P. Sanders, "Gal 2:11–14."

[111]This message sent by James is not likely to have been in any way related to the so-called Apostolic Decree of Acts 15:29 (cf. Catchpole, "Apostolic Decree," 438, the critique by Luedemann, *Chronology*, 123 n100, and the discussion in Achtemeier, "Elusive Unity"). See further R. E. Brown and Meier, *Antioch and Rome*, 3 n3, 42–43.

[112]Rom 9:1–3; cf. Acts 21:20–24; Col 4:11; *Ascents of James* 1.70.4; Van Voorst, *Ascents*, 73; F. S. Jones, *Source*, 170.

Suppose Peter's withdrawal from the common table should become contagious, causing all the Jewish members of the Antioch church to follow his
lead. It is clear that the Gentile members consider the precise arrangements
in the common meal to be a matter of no consequence. Titus showed as much
when he ate our food during the conference. Very well. Let the Gentile Christians be the ones who make the adjustments, holding the common meal according to the more important of the food laws. Members of our church here
in Jerusalem could then say that they require observance of the food laws in
all congregations with whom they have fellowship; and Antioch's funds would
then come from righteous Gentiles.[113]

All three of these suggestions, and especially the third, involve a degree of
speculation. Highly probable, in any case, is the suggestion that James's message
was reasonable, modest, and directed to Peter as an individual. Neither James
nor Peter is likely to have anticipated a major explosion that would engulf the
whole of the Antioch church, and that would eventuate in an extremely hurtful
break with Paul. Both of those developments ensued, however.

Peter's withdrawal from table fellowship proved contagious precisely along ethnic lines; and that was an event which in Paul's view terminated the Antioch
church's witness to the baptismal formula: "In Christ there is neither Jew nor
Gentile" (cf. 3:28). It was thus this corporate move on the part of the Jewish
members of the Antioch church that brought the thunderous explosion from
Paul.

THE TRUTH OF THE GOSPEL

Seeing no grounds for accommodation, Paul spoke to Peter in absolute terms,
identifying him as the actor who was compelling the Gentile members to live in
the Jewish manner. Not satisfied, that is, with the charge of hypocrisy, he ends
up by reaching to the depths of his theological vocabulary, telling the Galatians
that he found in Peter's contagious withdrawal from the common table an act
fully as unfaithful to the truth of the gospel as was the earlier attempt of the
False Brothers to compel the circumcision of Titus! In Paul's view, what had
been faithfully confessed by "the pillars" in Jerusalem had now been unfaithfully
violated in Antioch. Is this not an instance of highly inflated language on the
part of one who rushes to war when a reasonable compromise lies close at hand?

Peter must have thought so, and Barnabas as well, both men being as disappointed in Paul as Paul was in them. Confident that the mixed church in Antioch
could easily observe the Jewish food laws without losing anything essential to its
life and work, they had to endure Paul's accusation that they had become enemies of the gospel! How could Paul be so inflexible and so apparently self-
righteous, sure that, like Elijah, he and he alone saw matters in their true perspective?

Because that question cannot be answered apart from a detailed analysis of the
complex sentence of 2:15–16, together with its explication in vv 17–21, we will

---

[113] See Suhl, "Galaterbrief," 3086.

return to it in due course (Comment #28). Here we can attend to two other matters pertinent to what Paul calls the truth of the gospel. Why does Paul focus his attack on Peter rather than on James? What are the implications of Paul's references to Judaism in the rhetorical question he addresses to Peter in v 14?

PAUL, JAMES, AND PETER

If the truth of the gospel was faithfully presented in the formula of concord to which James was a party (v 9), and if the result of James's message to Peter is an instance of unfaithfulness to the truth of the gospel, why does Paul not attack James? Although we cannot be sure about it, part of the answer probably lies in the nature of James's message. As we have noted above, that message must have been directed to Peter as an *individual,* as the apostle to whom God had entrusted the chief role in the mission to the Jews. Moreover, in wording the message James must have been careful not to dishonor the formula of concord itself. Indeed, he may even have taken that formula as the basis of his message, reminding Peter of his responsibility for one of the lines of mission outlined in it. If so, James's message itself may have elicited a small amount of sympathy in Paul. He surely agreed with James that the mission to the Jews was absolutely crucial to the truth of the gospel (Gal 2:7, 9; Rom 9:1–3). Moreover, James's message itself may have been literally innocent of the corporate dimensions that were given to it when there was a mass exodus from the table by all of the Jewish members of the Antioch church.

We can be sure, however, that the total impact of the Antioch episode left Paul feeling suspicious of James. One notes that Paul did not accompany the messengers back to Jerusalem, hoping in direct conversation to show James that his intrusion into the life of the Antioch church had the effect of nullifying the formula of concord, even though the presenting issue had been shifted from circumcision to food laws. Paul may have thought that he could not bring James around a second time.

However suspicious Paul must have been of James, it is clear that he laid the chief responsibility at Peter's door. Why? Presumably, Paul thought Peter could have complied with James's message while honoring the truth of the gospel, as it was being lived out in the Antioch church's pattern of life. Rather than leading a corporate walkout of the Jewish members of that church, thus altering things in the mission to the Gentiles — the mission to which God had not called him — Peter could simply have returned to Jerusalem. Paul certainly knew that there were different meal patterns in the Jewish and Gentile missions respectively. And for him the maintenance of these different patterns was compatible with the unity of God's church, so long as neither pattern was imposed outside its orb, thus implying that it was itself salvific (cf. 2 Cor 10:12–18). If, instructed by James, Peter came to think that his God-given task would be jeopardized by his associating closely with Gentile Christians, then he was free to leave the common table of the Antioch church by returning to Jerusalem and resuming his task there. What he was not free to do was to lead a corporate walkout. For that corporate move — the little bit of yeast that leavens the whole lump of dough (cf.

Gal 5:9)—had the effect of compelling the Gentile members of the Antioch church to observe the food laws, as though that form of Law observance were God's elected means of making right what had gone wrong in the world.

THE TRUTH OF THE GOSPEL AND COMPELLING GENTILES TO LIVE IN THE JEWISH MANNER

It is precisely the matter of compulsion that emerges in the remark Paul made to Peter in the form of a rhetorical question (v 14):

> You, a Jew by birth, are living like a Gentile, not like a Jew. How can you then compel the Gentile members of the church to live in the Jewish manner?

As we have seen in the Notes, this last expression seems in Paul's time to have had about it a ring that is artificial—perhaps even somewhat false—referring to Gentiles who take up wholly or in part the Jewish way of life without thorough-going conviction from the heart. Paul's remark to Peter is thus not an attack on Judaism. It is a statement about a specific act *in* the Antioch church that compelled the Gentile members to pretend to something that was in a significant sense false.

And that falsity was something Paul underlined by using the verb "to compel" (cf. 2:3; 6:12). One recalls again that at this time the church—taken as a movement in Palestine, Syria, and Cilicia—was predominantly Jewish, Gentile members being a minority. The corporate withdrawal of the Jewish members in Antioch was a move taken by a powerful majority.[114] It had the effect of compelling the Gentile members—a small and weak minority—to observe the Jewish food laws at the common table, as though those laws were essential to the life of God's redeemed community. An untenable conclusion followed: To compel the Gentile members to observe even a part of the Law was to imply that the Law, rather than Christ's atoning death, was God's appointed means of salvation for the whole of humanity (see 2:16, 21).

In all of this Paul saw a singular instance of unfaithfulness to the truth of the gospel. And since the work of the Teachers is now having the same effects in the Galatian churches, compelling them to commence observance of the Law (6:12), he sees the truth of the gospel to be at stake in Galatia, and he attacks the Teachers no less vigorously than he attacked Peter in Antioch. Exactly what the truth of the gospel might be is a subject Paul begins concertedly to address in 2:15–21.

---

[114]Cf. Barrett, "Minorities."

2:15–21 MAKING RIGHT WHAT IS WRONG

TRANSLATION

2:15. We are by nature Jews, not "Gentile sinners." 16. Even we ourselves know, however, that a person is not rectified by observance of the Law, but rather by the faith of Christ Jesus. Thus, even we have placed our trust in Christ Jesus, in order that the source of our rectification might be the faith of Christ and not observance of the Law; for not a single person will be rectified by observance of the Law. 17. If, however, seeking to be rectified in Christ, we ourselves have been perceived to be sinners, then is it true that Christ has become a servant of sin? Absolutely not! 18. For, as the incident in Antioch reveals, the way in which I would show myself to be a transgressor would be to rebuild the walls of the Law that I have torn down. 19. For, I have died to the Law, through the Law, in order that I might live to God. I have been crucified with Christ. 20. It is no longer I who live, but rather Christ lives in me, and the life I now live in the flesh I live in faith, that is to say in the faith of the Son of God, who loved me and gave himself up to death for me. 21. I do not nullify God's grace! For if it were true that rectification comes through the Law, then Christ would have died for no purpose at all.

LITERARY STRUCTURE AND SYNOPSIS

Dealing earlier with the structure of 2:11–21, we noted that the second half of that section (vv 15–21) consists of a concerted argument, the first one of its kind in the letter. In form it is a speech, commenced in the proper sense not with the caustic question addressed to Peter alone (v 14), but rather with a rhetorical convention, the *captatio benevolentiae*, in which the speaker captures his audience by means of a friendly reference to something he shares with them. After verbally striking Peter in the face, that is, Paul makes a new beginning, rhetorically putting his arm around Peter's shoulder: "We, after all, are Jews (Jewish Christians), not Gentile sinners; and as such we are in possession of certain pieces of knowledge" (vv 15–16). As the argument unfolds, one sees, however, that this Jewish "we" comes to envelop not only Paul and Peter in the presence of the Antioch church but also Paul and the Teachers in the presence of the churches in Galatia. Verse 15 is the point at which Paul commences an overlap between these two settings. And the speech thus introduced has two major parts, vv 15–16 and vv 17–21.

PAUL'S CHARGE AGAINST PETER AND THE TEACHERS (VV 15–16)
Both in the speech as it was addressed to Peter and in the speech as it is now addressed to the Teachers, v 15 functions as the friendly introduction, but with v 16 that gracious beginning also becomes a statement of the issue at hand. When one notes in v 16 the content of the knowledge that is shared by Paul, Peter, and

the Teachers (shared indeed by all Jewish Christians), and when one takes account of the way in which Paul makes use of that knowledge in formulating his argument, one sees his strategy. The friendly reference to shared existence as Jewish Christians enables Paul emphatically to level his charge: Jewish Christians such as Peter and the Teachers have simply to listen to their own gospel tradition to know that their acts stand condemned. To Peter and to the Teachers Paul says in effect:

> In view of your actions, I will cite your own gospel tradition, not some form of the gospel said to be peculiar to myself. Listen to it! Our shared Jewish-Christian gospel makes a declaration pertinent to your desire to bring Gentile Christians under the Law. Specifically, one can see from that tradition that God has elected to make things right, not by means of a call to observance of the Law, but rather by means of Christ's own faith.

Formulated as a charge against the actions of both Peter and the Teachers, vv 15–16 constitute the first part of Paul's speech.

THEIR CHARGES AGAINST PAUL (VV 17–21)

The second part of the speech consists largely of Paul's response to charges brought against him. To some extent these charges reach back to the setting in the Antioch church, but in the contemporary scene they reflect things being said in Galatia by the Teachers:

They say that in his mission to Gentiles Paul is taking two steps that bring a horrible result when they are combined with one another. He is claiming rectification solely by Christ without salvific reference to the Law, and he is associating closely with Gentile sinners, failing to require their observance of the Law. Taking these two steps, Paul has himself become a sinner, and — horror of horrors — he has thus made Christ a servant of sin (v 17)!

Since, moreover, the Law *is* for the Teachers the grace of God, they say that these actions on Paul's part show him to be regularly nullifying God's grace (v 21)![115] As always, Paul's argument constitutes more than a response. It is also a repreaching of the gospel. Having emphasized and applied the antinomy between observance of the Law and the faith of Christ (v 16), he explicates that antinomy by means of his own testimony (vv 19–20) and by restating the antinomy itself in such a way as to make clear that the faith of Christ is Christ's faithful death in our behalf (v 21).[116]

---

[115]That the Law — as an essentially undifferentiated monolith — is God's gracious gift to Israel was and is held in all streams of Judaism and in all forms of early Jewish Christianity, save those fundamentally influenced by gnosticism (Strecker, *Judenchristentum*). Cf. Werblowsky, "Torah." Whether, in writing to the Galatians, Paul intends to deny this fundamental affirmation is a very complex question. See Comments #28, #31, #34, #38, #48, and #50.

[116]Regarding the word "antinomy," see the Glossary.

Notes[117]

2:15. We. After the caustic question of v 14, addressed to Peter in the singular, "How can you, a Jew, do such and such?" Paul gives his speech a new beginning, using the plural pronoun "we," placed in the emphatic position, in order to include the Teachers as well as Peter and himself: "We — all of us — belong to the same group, differentiated from those others." Technically, as we have seen above, it is the *captatio benevolentiae*, the introductory means by which a speaker strikes a note that binds him to his addressees in a friendly manner. Here both speaker and addressees are born Jews. Thus, just as the Gentile members of the Antioch church witnessed a remark made by Paul to Peter (vv 14–15), so the members of the Galatian congregations — all of them Gentiles — are now witnesses to remarks that Paul addresses to the Teachers (vv 15–21).

Paul shades this double-level "we" into v 16, speaking of Jewish-Christian tradition shared by himself, Peter, and the Teachers, and referring to the act of putting one's trust in Christ as a step they have all taken. There is a shift, however, at v 17. There Paul momentarily refocuses his "we" on himself and Peter.

are by nature Jews. For a second time in Galatians Paul uses the word "Jews" to refer to members of the church who are ethnic Jews (2:13). New is the subtle but sharp message he communicates with the expression "by nature." For there is no Jewish tradition in which Jews are said to be who they are as the result of a natural process. Indeed, it cannot be an accident that there is no Hebrew equivalent for the word "nature" (*physis*).[118] Speaking in the context of the church (see Introduction §17), Paul introduces a caveat right into the *captatio benevolentiae* itself: Peter has left the common table on the basis of a distinction that has been eclipsed by the truth of the gospel (cf. 4:3, 8; 3:28; Comment #40).

"Gentile sinners." In Jewish tradition Gentiles, not having the Law, are inevitably sinners, who do not hear the call to repentance and thus cannot receive forgiveness.[119] With this standard expression, then, Paul continues to speak of the distinction between Jews and Gentiles, thus using terms with which Peter and the Teachers would agree. It is thus his adopting this frame of reference that poses one of the problems of v 15. In Antioch he has just witnessed the violation of the truth of the gospel precisely by an action predicated on the distinction between Jews and Gentiles *in the church*. And that same distinction underlies the false gospel of the Teachers in Galatia. How can Paul hope to take his stand against this violation of the gospel when in his own speech he adopts its frame of reference? The answer lies in v 16, where, among other things, Paul finds in Jewish-Christian tradition itself a witness to the end of the Jew/Gentile distinc-

---

[117]At several junctures the Notes in this section can be profitably compared with Bultmann, "Auslegung."

[118]The phrase "by nature" can refer to natural endowment inherited from one's ancestors. In Romans Paul speaks of the Gentiles as those who are by natural inheritance uncircumcised (2:27). But it is one thing to say a Gentile is a Gentile "by nature," and quite a different thing to say the same of a Jew! See H. Koester, "*physis.*"

[119]Cf. Pancaro, *Law*, 30–44 and 119.

tion. Verse 15 proves, then, to be the baiting of the trap, so to speak, which will be sprung in v 16.

16. *Even we ourselves know, however.* Paul will not call down on the heads of Peter and the Teachers an esoteric tradition foreign to the Jewish mission God has entrusted to Peter (vv 7 and 8). On the contrary, having noted that he stands with Peter and the Teachers by reason of shared Jewish extraction — they are all Jewish Christians — Paul can expect them to follow him as he cites a Jewish-Christian formula that expresses knowledge held in common by all of them. The subject to which he turns, rectification, is a topic already at home in Jewish-Christian circles. The basic contours of the rectification formula can be studied in part by attending to three other passages in Paul's letters in which the apostle quotes from Jewish-Christian rectification tradition (Rom 3:25–26a; Rom 4:25; 1 Cor 6:11; see Comment #28).

a person. Having joined hands with his Jewish-Christian hearers in vv 15–16a, Paul begins immediately to undercut the distinction between Jew and Gentile. For to his ears the Jewish-Christian formula speaks of the eschatological revelation of *anthrôpos*, the human being, meaning every person.[120] Thus, while Paul speaks formally *to* Peter and *to* the Teachers, he speaks about all human beings, including the Gentile members of the churches in Antioch and Galatia.[121]

is not rectified. What is known about the human being Paul now indicates by using in the present tense the verb *dikaioô*, a word that — with its noun *dikaiosyne* — has occasioned a veritable library of books and articles from the earliest interpreters of Paul to those of the present day. The thrust of the verb and of the noun is exceedingly difficult to grasp, and equally difficult to render in a modern language.

The first problem arises from the fact that, whereas in Greek the verb *dikaioô* and the noun *dikaiosyne* are linguistically cognate, most of the verbs and nouns by which these terms have been translated are not. To render the verb with the English expression "to justify" while translating the noun as "righteousness" — the most common way of proceeding — is to lose the linguistic connection that was both obvious and important to Paul. To be sure, one can compel the verb to draw on the noun, translating *dikaioô* "to make righteous," "to declare righteous," "to rightwise," and even "to righteous." The last two of these, lying outside normal English usage, have the virtue of alerting the hearer to the strangeness of Paul's terms. But that virtue is bought at the price of linguistic clumsiness.

The second problem is substantive. All of the translation options listed above

---

[120]Arguments have been advanced that Paul speaks here exclusively of Gentiles: it is Gentiles and only Gentiles who are not rectified by observance of the Law (e.g., Gager, *Origins*, 233). Had Paul intended this meaning, he would have spoken explicitly of the *hellên*, the Greek, as he does in 3:28, saying something like "We who are born Jews know that a Gentile (*hellên*) is not rectified by observing the Law . . ." Cf. *b. Sanh.* 59a, where Rabbi Meir is said to have found in the mention of "man" in Lev 18:5 a reference to all human beings.
[121]Cf. Strecker, "Befreiung," 507.

have one weighty liability: they are at home either in the language of the law—where "to justify" implies the existence of a definable legal norm—or in the language of religion and morality—where "righteousness" implies a definable religious or moral norm. As we will see, Paul intends his term to be taken into neither of these linguistic realms. Hence, we will find some advantage in using the verb "to rectify" and the noun "rectification." For these are words that belong to a single linguistic family (*rectus facio*), and they are words that are not commonly employed either in our courtrooms or in our religious and moral institutions.[122] The subject Paul addresses is that of God's *making right what has gone wrong*.

The word family of "rectification" is markedly uneven in the Pauline corpus. In 1 Thessalonians Paul does not employ it at all, and he gives it no great role in either 1 or 2 Corinthians.[123] In Galatians, in Philippians, and in Romans, by contrast, terms in this word family receive great emphasis, doubtless because of the situations in which, and to which, these three letters were written. Of these three, Galatians is almost certainly the earliest (see Introduction §9; Comment #24). It is in Paul's struggle with the Teachers—themselves theologians who spoke at some length about rectification—that we see him formulating his thought on rectification. And that is itself a sharp warning against the practice of analyzing Paul's thought on rectification as a teaching which in its essence is a polemic against Pharisaic Judaism.[124] The issues raised by Paul's use of the language of rectification in Galatians are of such importance and of such complexity as to require extended treatment in Comment #28.

by observance of the Law. The Jewish Christians whose tradition forms the basis of v 16 did not pose as an issue the means God chose to employ in his act of rectification. Hearing that tradition in light of the odious labors of the Teachers, however, Paul discerns an antinomy directed to that question: In what way has God chosen to make things right? And Paul expresses this antinomy by prepositional phrases, presenting the antinomy three times in this one sentence:

The human being is not rectified
(a) by observance of the Law, but rather
(b) by the faith of Christ Jesus.
Thus, even we Jewish Christians have placed our trust in Christ Jesus, in order that we might be rectified
(b') by the faith of Christ and not
(a') by observance of the Law;
for not a single person will be rectified
(a") by observance of the Law.

---

[122]Cf. Keck, *Paul and His Letters*, 111–112.
[123]See the table in Reumann, *Righteousness*, 42. The adverb *dikaiôs* in 1 Thess 2:10 is of no direct pertinence. On 2 Cor 5:21, see particularly Wilckens, *Römer*, 1.207.
[124]The practice is time-honored and widespread, being followed even by very capable scholars, for example Becker, *Heil*, 252–256.

Paul uses the preposition *ek* in all of these cases except (b), where he writes *dia*. The result is a compact expression focused on the means of rectification, including perhaps some concern with the source as well.[125] See Comment #27.

but rather. Paul dictates *ean mê*, an expression that in the present context signifies absolute opposition to that which precedes.[126] As regards rectification, the faith of Christ Jesus does not serve as a supplement to observance of the Law, either for Christians of Jewish lineage or for those from among the Gentiles. On the contrary, as regards salvation, observance of the Law and the faith of Christ constitute a genuine antinomy. A major question is whether Paul thinks of this antinomy as so thoroughly harmonious with those of 1:1 and 1:11–12 as to imply that Law observance is a merely human act, whereas the faith of Christ is the deed of God.

the faith of Christ Jesus. Paul writes *pistis Christou Iêsou*, an expression which can mean either the faith that Christ had and enacted or the faith that human beings have in Christ, both readings being grammatically possible.[127] Recent decades have seen extensive discussion of the matter, sometimes even heated debate; and the debate has demonstrated that the two readings do in fact lead to two very different pictures of the theology of the entire letter.[128] Is the faith that God has chosen as the means of setting things right that of Christ himself or that of human beings? Attention to a number of factors, especially to the nature of Paul's antinomies and to the similarities between 2:16 and 2:21, leads to the conclusion that Paul speaks of the faith of Christ, meaning his faithful death in our behalf. See Comment #28 and the Note on 2:20.

---

[125]It appears that Paul was the one who coined the expression *dikaiôthênai ek*, "to be rectified by." The LXX did not provide him with this expression (there one finds *en* and *apo*). But, given Paul's equating "to be rectified" with "to be made alive" (Gal 3:21), and given his fascination with Hab 2:4, it is possible that, in coining the expression *dikaiôthênai ek*, he was influenced by Habakkuk's locution "the one who is rectified by faith will live." More important is the possibility that, often using the preposition *ek* in this construction, Paul sometimes thought of the issue as one of source as well as means. If the latter had been his exclusive concern, he could have consistently employed the prepositions *dia* (the second phrase of Gal 2:16 as noted above) and *en* (Gal 5:4). Or he could have regularly used the dative (Rom 3:28). Perhaps in Paul's view the Teachers' theology poses a question that goes deeper than the means of rectification, posing the issue of source. One sees a reflection of this deeper dimension in Paul's rectification polemic in Philippians, where he places opposite one another rectification that has its source in the Law (*dikaiosyne ek nomou*) and rectification that has its source in God (*dikaiosyne ek theou*; Phil 3:9). That is more than a discussion of means. On the hypothesis that a similar concern informs Paul's polemic in Galatians, I have rendered the central clause of Gal 2:16 as ". . . in order that the source of our rectification might be the faith of Christ and not observance of the Law." Cf. further Cosgrove, "Justification."

[126]See BDF, §376, §480.6; and especially K. Beyer, *Semitische Syntax*, 138–139. On Dunn's reading of *ean mê*, see his "New Perspective"; idem, "Works"; the critique by Räisänen, "Galatians 2:16"; and Dunn's commentary, 137–138. See further Comment #28.

[127]The first is probably best classified somewhat loosely as an authorial genitive — Christ is the author of the faith spoken of — whereas the second can be called an objective genitive (BDF §63). See Comment #28.

[128]Note the different encapsulations of the theology of Galatians presented by Dunn, "Theology," and J. L. Martyn, "Events."

Thus, even we. There are not two ways of being rectified. Together with the Gentile, the Jew stands before God with empty hands.

have placed our trust in Christ Jesus. In the first half of the verse Paul has spoken of an antinomy. It is not by means of something the human being does — observe the Law — that God has elected to carry out his rectification, his making that human being right. God's means of rectification is solely the divine act of Christ's faith. Now, however, in a decidedly secondary place, Paul does speak of placing one's trust in this faithful Christ, a matter no less significant for being secondary.[129] Having spoken of God's rectifying deed in Christ, has Paul finally turned to an act done by the human being himself? See Comment #29.

in order that the source of our rectification might be the faith of Christ. Paul adds a clause introduced by the purposive conjunction *hina*, "in order that," speaking then a second time of rectification and of *pistis Christou*. Interpreters who find in the earlier instance of *pistis Christou* a reference to human faith in Christ see the same thing here, thus rendering the first two-thirds of the verse somewhat as follows:

> We Jewish Christians know that the human being is not rectified by works of the Law, but rather by faith in Christ Jesus. Thus, even we have placed our trust/faith in Christ Jesus, in order that we might be rectified by our faith in Christ and not by works of the Law . . .

It is a reasonable reading, for grammatically the purpose clause does modify the verb "we have placed our trust," thus seeming to state the purpose "we" had in mind when we did that: We believe in Christ in order to be rectified, God's act of rectification being, then, God's response to our act of faith.[130] But the argument in Comment #28 leads, as already noted, to the conclusion that, with the phrase *pistis Christou*, Paul refers not to faith in Christ, but rather to Christ's faithful death for us. The "in order that" clause is therefore more reflective of God's purpose than of ours:

> God's act in Christ's faith is our rectification. Thus, we have placed our trust in Christ, in order that the source of our rectification should be what God purposed it to be: Christ's faith.[131]

for not a single person will be rectified by observance of the Law. Paul emphasizes the negative side of his antinomy by stating it a third time, doing so by drawing on Ps 143:2, where the verb is in the future tense (Ps 142:2; LXX). Since

---

[129]The expression *pisteuô eis* with a name in the accusative case (the only time in Galatians) combines the intransitive use of the verb *pisteuô* with a prepositional phrase, thus meaning "believe in someone," in the sense of placing one's trust in that person. See BAGD, "*pisteuô.*"

[130]The dative *pistei* in Rom 3:28 is often read in the same way: God rectifies us in response to our act of faith.

[131]Cf. Käsemann, *Perspectives*, 82.

he later uses the same Psalm verse in Rom 3:20, we may profitably compare the three texts:

Psalm 143:2	Gal 2:16	Rom 3:20
1. for	1. for	1. for
2.	2. by observance of the Law	2. by observance of the Law
3. not	3. not	3. not
4. shall be rectified	4. shall be rectified	4. shall be rectified
5. before you	5.	5. before him
6. everyone (anyone) living	6. all flesh	6. all flesh

Although Paul gives no formal signal that he is quoting scripture, he knows he is doing that, and he can probably assume that the Teachers are also aware of it. What he has to say about God's act of setting things right can be shown not only from rectification tradition at home in Jewish-Christian circles (the first three-quarters of v 16) but also from scripture. To be sure, if Paul's Septuagint read as indicated above, he makes here two significant alterations.

First, in line 6 Paul changes "everyone living" to "all flesh," thus focusing his polemic on the Teachers' claim that one is rectified by commencing observance of the Law with the act of circumcising the flesh of the foreskin.[132] Second, he inserts line 2, thus causing the Psalm verse to fit into his argument about the impotence of Law observance.[133]

17. *If, however, seeking to be rectified in Christ, we ourselves have been perceived to be sinners, then is it true that Christ has become a servant of sin? Absolutely not!* The form of the conditional sentence is clear: Paul takes for granted the facticity of the first two clauses (the protasis), placing in question only the inference drawn in the third (the apodosis):

[132] So correctly Jewett, *Terms*, 98, 112; cf. *1 Enoch* 81:5, ". . . and show all your children that no flesh is righteous before the Lord." From the text in *1 Enoch* and from the term *anthrôpos* in Gal 2:16a, Verhoef follows a different route, arguing that Paul's concern is focused on the human being as a sinful creature (*Geschreven*, 44, 171). But the change may also have linguistic precedents (K. Beyer, *Semitische Syntax*, 189 n4).

[133] The omission of line 5, "before you (God)," shows only that in the highly compact verse of Gal 2:16, Paul focuses his attention on Christ, and not on the subject of God's judgment. The inclusion of these words in Rom 3:20 (altered for the context) reflects Paul's concern to make God's judgment a major motif in the first three chapters of Romans (cf. Gal 3:11). At first glance one may be surprised to see that Paul leaves intact the future tense of the verb in line 4. For in the first clause of v 16 he has spoken of rectification in the present tense, reflecting one of his major convictions about the current scene: in Christ's atoning death God has already commenced making things right. But the role of the promissory Law was precisely that of foreseeing this development: "And the scripture, foreseeing what is now happening — namely, that God is rectifying the Gentiles on the basis of faith — preached the gospel ahead of time to Abraham, saying, 'In you all the Gentiles will be blessed'" (Gal 3:8; see Comment #48). Given this understanding of the promissory voice of scripture, Paul can leave the future tense of line 4 as it is in the LXX. Moreover, although God has commenced setting things right, the fullness of rectification remains a matter of certain hope (cf. 5:5).

We are seeking to be rectified in Christ, and in light of our doing that, we have been perceived by someone to be sinners. From that development can one justly infer that Christ has become a servant of sin? Absolutely not![134]

Vexing problems nevertheless remain, and they have occasioned numerous interpretations.[135] Having referred to rectification as God's gift in Christ, why does Paul speak of it here as something to be sought? Who is the "we"? Who is the they who have done the perceiving? And on what ground did they perceive us to be sinners? Is "servant of sin" an expression Paul quotes rather than coins?

No reading answers all of these questions in a completely satisfactory way, but the best route lies in the assumption that Paul can take for granted comprehension on the part of the Galatians (as they listen to the speech he addresses to the Teachers) because he is borrowing several of his expressions from things the Teachers are saying about him.

seeking to be rectified. With the immediately preceding quotation of Ps 143:2, Paul has prepared his hearers for a reference to the future dimension of the fullness of rectification. And Phil 3:7–9, to take an example, shows that Paul can speak simultaneously both of free grace and of the most strenuous striving toward that future (cf. Gal 5:5). It seems best, then, to hear "seeking to be rectified" as Paul's positive reference to the sure hope of ultimate rectification.[136]

we ourselves. Having given in v 16 no formal indication that he has terminated the remarks he once made to Peter, Paul is now able to speak on two levels, using the plural pronoun in two frames of reference. In regard to the once-upon-a-time event in Antioch, he uses the plural pronoun to refer to Peter and himself in the setting of the Antioch church after the arrival of James's messengers. In regard to contemporary developments, he uses the pronoun to speak of himself in the setting created in his Galatian churches by the arrival of the Teachers (cf. the "I" in v 18).

have been perceived to be sinners. Using the verb *heuriskō* to speak of intellectual discovery based on observation (BAGD), Paul refers on the once-upon-a-time level to the way in which Peter and he himself were perceived by the messengers of James upon the latter's arrival in Antioch. And the basis of this perception is easy to see.

---

[134]See the helpful analysis of Winger, *Law*, 142–144. The conclusion "Absolutely not!" "implies that 2:17 is a question, and that the issue is whether or not the inference it suggests is valid; the premise ['we ourselves have been perceived to be sinners'] is evidently accepted" (144).

[135]See Soards, "Seeking," where, in addition to a helpful survey of various interpretations, a productively provocative reading is proposed. See the next footnote.

[136]Taking *zētountes* ("seeking") with *heurethēmen* ("we have been perceived"), Soards proposes a different reading, by finding the protasis to be "If we have been perceived as those who are seeking to be rectified in Christ" ("Seeking"). That, Soards says, is a reference to a purely human striving after rectification that Paul himself considered sinful and thus antithetical to God's free gift of grace. The major problem with this reading lies in its taking *hamartoloi* ("sinners") in a sense removed from that which the term has in the immediate context (v 15).

If Peter and I were perceived to be sinners by James's messengers on the ground that at table we were indistinguishable from Gentiles . . .

Moreover, the reference on the contemporary level will have been doubly clear to the Galatians because of things they are currently hearing from the Teachers.

If I have been perceived by the Teachers to be a sinner on the ground that I have abandoned the Law, the only God-given antidote to sin . . . (cf. Rom 3:8).[137]

then is it true that Christ has become a servant of sin? Absolutely not! One might have expected a simple denial of the charge he mentions in the preceding clauses: "We, Peter and I — and I myself — have by no means become sinners by affirming rectification in Christ while closely associating with Gentiles apart from observance of the Law!" Instead, Paul speaks of Christ. The inference he denies thus implies that a second charge has been added to the one he has just mentioned. The Teachers are saying that, by linking rectification solely to Christ apart from observance of the Law, Paul has not only become a sinner indistinguishable from a Gentile. He has also in effect turned Christ into one who condones and even facilitates sin, rather than combating it!

servant of sin. Did the Teachers call themselves "servants of righteousness," consequently coining the expression "servant of sin" in order to ridicule Paul's view of Christ (cf. 2 Cor 11:15)? That is a possibility. In any case, Paul seizes the charge laid against him as an opportunity to speak in the next verse about the true definition of sinful transgression.

18. *For.* Shifting to the first person singular, Paul now gives his initial reason for categorically rejecting the charge he has just mentioned. The linguistic shift is occasioned partly by Paul's concern to refute the charge, but in the end (notably in vv 19–20) Paul uses the first person singular pronoun to reveal the identity of the eschatological human being whom God is creating in Christ. See the Note on v 20.

as the incident in Antioch reveals. This is a paraphrastic addition to Paul's sentence, introduced for reasons given below.

the way in which I would show myself to be a transgressor. Thinking again both of the battle in the Antioch church and of its double in his Galatian churches, Paul reflects on the path he would actually have followed had he joined Peter in reintroducing the food laws which both of them had earlier "torn down."[138] In English the concluding clause — lit. "I show myself to be a transgressor" — can be put first (and in the subjunctive mood) in order to emphasize Paul's intention to say that there is now a new route that would have led him into transgression had he followed it. That new route leading to transgression:

[137]Cf. Marcus, "Scripture and Tradition in Mark 7," not least the interpretation of *T. Asher* 7:5 and *T. Levi* 14:4–8.

[138]Literally, Paul writes a second sentence in the form of a real condition, but he treats it as an unreal hypothesis (cf. 1 Cor 8:13): "For if I were to rebuild the things I have torn down," followed by the conclusion, "I would then show myself to be a transgressor."

would be to rebuild the walls of the Law that I have torn down. Paul's language is highly allusive. Literally, he says that the way in which he would show himself to be a transgressor "would be to rebuild the things that I have torn down." His verbs (tear down; build again) paint the picture of an edifice being destroyed and rebuilt, but he does not say explicitly what edifice he has in mind. Apparently, he assumes the Galatians will know from the context — vv 16–17; vv 19–21 — that the edifice is the Law, seen as the wall that separates Jews from Gentiles, providing rectification only to the former (cf. also Eph 2:14).[139] The reference to tearing down the edifice is picked up in the next verse by the expression "die to the Law." One might paraphrase: "The way in which I would show myself to be a transgressor would be to reassert what I have denied: the connection between rectification and observance of the Law."

The result of this sentence is a radical redefinition of transgression, and especially a radically altered view of the relation between transgression and Law observance: The Law *can* play a role leading not to the defining and vanquishing of transgression, but rather to transgression itself![140] Specifically, Peter in Antioch and the Teachers in Galatia uphold the food laws in order, they think, to avoid transgression. In fact, however, they follow a new route toward transgression. Paul himself would have followed that route had he joined Peter in reintroducing the food laws they had earlier "torn down," and he would now follow that route were he to join the Teachers in requiring Law observance of his Gentile converts. For whoever reerects the Law's distinction between Jew and Gentile, as though God were making things right via observance of the Law, rather than in Christ, has thereby shown himself to be a transgressor.

We have here, then, the earliest point in his letters at which Paul begins to analyze in a profound way the strange and insidiously destructive alliance between the Law and Sin (cf. Romans 7).[141]

19. *For.* Paul continues to reject the Teachers' charge that he is a sinner who has made Christ a servant of sin. His own inability to rebuild the legal enclosure that he has torn down is the result of something that has happened *to* him: He has been removed from that enclosure (cf. Rom 7:1–6).

I have died to the Law. Within the NT the expression "to die to something" (*apothnêskô* with the dative) is peculiar to Paul, meaning to be separated from that thing by the event of one's own death (BAGD). What Law was it, specifically, from which Paul was separated by dying? The context provides the answer: It was the Law that distinguishes holy from profane, Jew from Gentile, thus enabling members of the holy people justly to exclude from their company those who are not holy (so the Antioch incident). In a word, it was the Law in its paired existence with the Not-Law (Comment #41). It is crucial to note that Paul speaks

---

[139] Paul may have drawn the verbs "tear down" and "build" from Jewish traditions (so Michel, *"oikos"*). In any case, the view that Paul was one who destroyed the Law was circulated among Jewish Christians already in his lifetime (Rom 3:8, 31; cf. Acts 18:13; 21:21, 28); and it later became a fixed tradition among Jewish Christians (*Ep. Pet. Jas.* 2:4, HS 2.112).

[140] See now Winger, *Law,* 146, 163.

[141] See especially Meyer, "Worm"; Comment #49, Appendix.

about separation from the Law, not about commencing a life that is characterized by violation of the Law (see 5:14, 23; 6:2; Comment #48).

through the Law. This is yet another opaque phrase that has occasioned much comment.[142] Paul had centered his initial preaching to the Galatians in the cross of Christ (3:1), and, in writing his letter, he now does the same (6:14). Thus, the Galatians might have expected him to say, "It was through the cross of Christ that I suffered separation from the Law." Why, instead, does he say that his lethal separation from the Law happened through the Law? Because, as one sees from 3:13, what separated him from the Law in its paired existence was precisely the role that the Law played in the death of Christ. In the event of Christ's crucifixion the Law did not stand idly aside. It pronounced a curse on Christ, effectively taking up its own existence and carrying out its own activity apart from God! Paul's participation in Christ's crucifixion (see the last clause of v 19) was thus a participation in the event in which the Law acted against God's Christ!

in order that I might live to God. The astonishment caused by the first part of the sentence proves to be only a prelude to the shocking amazement occasioned by the last clause. Paul says that the purpose of his being separated by death from the realm of the Law is that he might exist as one who is alive in the realm of God. One can scarcely think of a statement more thoroughly foreign to the theology of the Teachers (and to Jewish and Jewish-Christian theology in general). It is not an exercise in mere fantasy to imagine that, as Paul's messenger finished reading v 18, the Teachers jumped to their feet, loudly charging Paul with blasphemy!

This verse is, however, only the first of several junctures at which Paul portrays a gulf between God and the Law, and in the course of reading later passages we will return to several issues raised by this shocking motif. What was the role of the Law prior to its collision with the Messiah? If the Law had its origin in God, a question not addressed in this verse, then how can it have taken up its own existence apart from God, constituting a sphere of power in some sense antinomously related to that of God? Finally, with the advent of Christ, has the Law been categorically overcome, thus losing its role altogether? On these questions, see the Notes on 3:19–29 and Comments #38, #41, and #48.

At the present juncture it is enough to see that Paul is speaking in a way that is tightly focused on the crucifixion. The antinomy

to live to the Law / to live to God

is a thoroughly apocalyptic antinomy newly created at the cross (Comment #51).
I have been crucified with Christ. See Comment #30.

---

[142]There are three major interpretations: (a) The phrase "through the Law" can be taken as Paul's initial reflection on the theme of the Law's having played an active role in salvation as a sort of pedagogue leading to Christ (3:24). But the required reading of 3:24 is almost certainly wrong. (b) The phrase can be related to the expression "through the commandment" in Rom 7:11, for, in the broad context of that expression, Paul speaks of the Christians' having died to the Law (Rom 7:4). But there Paul explicitly relates mortal separation from the Law to incorporation into the "body of Christ." (c) The phrase can be related to the thought that the Law played an active role in Christ's crucifixion: "Through

20. *It is no longer I who live.* We have already noted one of the reasons for Paul's shift to the first person singular. He is determined directly to refute a charge brought against him by the Teachers. A deeper concern informing the speech of vv 15–21 is indicated, however, by his use of the term *anthrôpos,* "human being," in v 16, a clear signal that he is dealing throughout with the deed of God in which the old human being suffers death and the eschatological human being is made alive. Using the first person, then, Paul presents himself as the paradigm of this human being.[143]

Crucified with Christ and thus experiencing mortal separation from the Law, this *anthrôpos* does not any longer have an identity given by the Law. He is neither Jew nor Gentile. Thus, vis-à-vis the old collectives called Jews and Gentiles, this eschatological human being can no longer say "we," but has rather to say "I," speaking of his own death to these collectives. At this juncture Paul does not yet refer to the new collective, the church (see Comment #40).

but rather Christ lives in me. That old I has not been merely renewed. Having been crucified with Christ, it has been replaced by the risen Christ himself. To say this, Paul employs spatial language of a sort we have encountered earlier (e.g., in 1:22), saying now that Christ lives *in* him.[144] In fact, v 20 is a valuable index to Paul's varied uses of the preposition "in." First he says that Christ now lives *in* him. Then he says that he nevertheless remains a human being who lives *in* the flesh. Finally, he adds that he lives his present life not only in the human orb but also and fundamentally *in* a certain faith, namely the faith of Christ.

In each of these spatial metaphors the accent lies on an orb of power. The risen Lord extends the space of his power by taking up residence in Paul, the paradigmatic eschatological human being. That event does not fully remove Paul from the space of human beings; but it does create a new sphere in which Paul lives, the sphere of Christ's own faith. Having been conformed to Christ's death (cf. Phil 3:10), Paul continues to share Christ's path, finding that the event in which the risen Christ has seized him is in fact his being brought to life (cf. Rom 8:1). The dominant motif, then, is not a mystical union with divine nature, but rather the resurrected Christ's powerful invasion, seen on a personal level. Thus, in 1 Cor 15:45 Paul can say that, at his resurrection, Christ, the eschatological Adam, became an alive-making Spirit (cf. 2 Cor 5:20).

and the life I now live. It is Christ who now lives in Paul, but that does not mean that there is no longer an I. The I has been crucified and re-created by forces other than the self.

in the flesh. Nor is the life of which Paul speaks an other-worldly "solution" to the "problem" of death.[145] It is lived in a place called "flesh," that is to say in the place of everyday human existence. Even in Galatians, Paul's most enthusiastic

---

(i.e., because of) the Law's role in the crucifixion of God's Christ, I was separated from the Law."

[143] Cf. Tannehill, *Dying,* 61.

[144] Cf. Brandenburger, *Fleisch,* 54–57, 197–216.

[145] See Meyer, "This-Worldliness"; de Boer, *Defeat.*

letter, there is the eschatological reservation essential to his apocalyptic perspective (cf. 5:5). But there is also more.

I live in faith, that is to say in the faith of the Son of God. The place in which the I lives this new life is not only that of everyday human existence but also and primarily the place of faith (the stress lies on the end of the sentence). Were it only the former, it would not be life "to God" (v 19). Were it only the latter, it would be a futile attempt to escape the specific place in which one was called (1 Cor 7:20–24).[146]

But what is this newly created faith-place? A linguistic clue is found in the degree of parallelism between Gal 2:20 and Rom 5:15:

Gal 2:20	Rom 5:15
(and the life I now live in the flesh)	(and the free gift abounds)
I live in faith,	in grace,
namely the faith of the	namely the grace of . . .
Son of God . . .	Jesus Christ
(*en pistei . . . tê tou huiou tou theou*)	(*en chariti tê tou . . . Iêsou Christou*)

Just as in Rom 5:15 the life-giving grace is specified as the grace "of Jesus Christ," so here the life-giving faith of which Paul speaks is specified as the faith *of* the Son of God (see Note on 2:16 and Comment #28). Christ's faith constitutes the space in which the one crucified with Christ can live and does live.[147]

who loved me and gave himself up to death for me. Having spoken of the Son's faith as the space of life-giving power, Paul now specifies that power by two participial clauses (aorist tense), speaking of the Son's love and of the enactment of that love in his self-sacrifice. These clauses are drawn from christological formulas (cf. 1:4a; Eph 5:2), but the major point is that Paul uses them here to answer two questions: Who is this Son of God, and what is his faith? He is the one who "loved me and gave up his life for me," and his faith *is* that sacrificial act (see also the latter part of the next Note).

21. *I do not nullify God's grace!* Lacking a connective conjunction, this sentence is an independent statement in which Paul summarizes his refutation of the Teachers' charge against him, thus gathering together the major threads of the entire paragraph begun in v 15. It is not surprising that the Teachers should have charged Paul with nullifying God's grace, for they almost certainly equated that grace with the Law, God's gracious gift *par excellence*.[148]

For Paul, however, the locus of God's grace is defined by the locus of God's

---

[146]See J. L. Martyn, *Issues*, 279–297.
[147]See Hays, *Faith*, 168; idem, "The Law of Christ," 280 n35; idem, "What Is at Stake?"; Dunn, "Once More."
[148]2 *Apoc. Bar.* 44:14 can represent innumerable passages in which one finds celebrations of the Law as God's gracious gift; cf. Werblowsky, "Torah."

rectifying power. Thus, in refuting the Teachers' charge, he returns to the vocabulary of v 16, and specifically to the antinomy showing God's deed of rectification to have been enacted in Christ's faithful death, not in the Law.

For if it were true that rectification comes through the Law. The sentence consists of a conditional clause (*ei* without verb) and a simple conclusion (the inferential particle *ara* with an aorist verb), thus giving no syntactical indication that Paul considers the condition to be contrary to fact. As Winger has argued, however, Paul does not always use the form of a condition contrary to fact when he is refuting an opponent.[149] And in 3:21 Paul uses the conditional clause of the present sentence as a conclusion that is clearly contrary to fact. Rectification does not come from the Law.

then Christ would have died for no purpose at all. Restating the antinomy of v 16, Paul makes clear the identity of the power that stands in stark contrast with the impotence of Law observance. That power is not an act of faith on the part of the human being. The opposites are:

God makes things right through the Law.

God makes things right through Christ's death.

If the first were true, then the second would not be true, and the conclusion would be that Christ's death happened as an inconsequential event, rather than as God's effective enactment of rectification. Here Paul provides the antinomy that will prove to be fundamental to the entire letter: God's making things right by Christ's cross rather than by the Law. And by stating this antinomy as the climax of the speech he makes to the Teachers—in the presence of the Galatians—Paul hurls the Teachers' charge back into their faces:

It is not I who nullify God's grace, but rather you! That is what you do when you preach your so-called gospel of rectification by observance of the Law. For that false gospel amounts to saying that Christ died to no purpose! To demand of Gentiles that they observe the Law is to deny God's grace enacted in Christ's death.

COMMENT #27
OBSERVANCE OF THE LAW

THE EXPRESSION ERGA NOMOU
In order to speak of the means God has *not* used to make things right, Paul employs the Greek expression *erga nomou*, lit. "the works of the Law." It is a locution that has led a great many interpreters to credit Paul with a theology of "faith" versus "works." In fact, a rather different translation is called for, leading to a different picture of Paul's theology.

In this relatively brief letter Paul uses the expression *erga nomou* six times:

---

[149]Winger, "Unreal Conditions."

2:16   In this pithy sentence Paul says three times that *erga nomou* is not the means God has selected for accomplishing rectification.

3:2   He negates the expression a fourth time after posing the question "How and from what source did you Galatians receive the Spirit?"

3:5   A fifth negation of *erga nomou* responds to the question "How is it that God is presently supplying you Galatians with the Spirit and working wonders in your midst?"

3:10   Here Paul gives a negative characterization of persons who derive their identity from *erga nomou* (contrast 3:27).[150]

Although the precise expression *erga nomou* has not been found in any Greek literature prior to Galatians, Jewish Christians of Paul's time — and Gentile Christians instructed by Jewish Christians (the Galatians, for example) — would have had little difficulty grasping its meaning. It refers simply to observance of God's Law. There are numerous parallels in the Septuagint, in Jewish traditions, and in traditions we can trace to Jewish Christians.

Exod 18:20 can serve as an example from the Septuagint. When Moses functions as the mediator between God and Israel in regard to everyday matters, he

> teaches them God's commandments and *his Law*, and makes them know *the way in which they must walk* and the *works they must do* (Exod 18:20; LXX).

The three expressions placed in italics are equivalents of one another: To be taught God's Law is to know the way in which one is to walk, and that, in turn, is to know the works (*erga*) one is to do. Thus, these works are works of the Law, and specifically acts taken along the path of Law observance.

In the Dead Sea Scrolls the expression "works of the Law" emerges in Hebrew with precisely the same meaning. In 1QS 5:21, for example, one who undertakes to enter the covenant community is examined with respect to his understanding and "his deeds in the Law" (*ma'ăśayw battôrâ*; cf. also CD 13:11). The same expression is used to refer to the examination carried out at the end of a year (1QS 6:16), and it plays a significant role in *Miqsat Ma'aseh ha-Torah* (4QMMT), where it refers to the precepts of the Law that are to be done by members of the community.[151] In these cases the locution clearly has nothing to do with "works" in contrast to "faith." Even the word "works" can be misleading here. For the expression simply summarizes the grand and complex activity of the Jew, who faithfully walks with God along the path God has opened up for him in the Law.

---

[150] In his much longer letter to the church in Rome Paul employs the full expression only three times (2:15; 3:20, 28; to which one may add, perhaps, 3:27; 4:2, 6). There, and in the Corinthian letters as well, he also uses the word *erga*, lit. "works," sometimes as a shortened form of the full expression, sometimes — especially in the singular — meaning simply that which human beings do. As we will see in Comment #28, the overlap of these two usages reflects one of Paul's basic convictions: When considered salvific, observance of the Law belongs on the human side of the divine/human antinomy; it is a human deed.

[151] See *Discoveries in the Judean Desert*, vol. 10 (ed. E. Qimron and J. Strugnell; Oxford: Clarendon, 1994); Martinez, *Scrolls*, 77–85 (note 79, line 113); cf. Dunn, "4QMMT."

The expression, or some equivalent, was also used by Jewish Christians. Understanding the Law to be perfect in its strength to liberate one from the power of sin and of the Evil Impulse, the author of James consistently speaks in a positive way of Law observance. He can therefore draw a contrast between the hearer of the Law who forgets and the doer of the Law who acts (*poiêtês ergou*; Jas 1:25). By such expressions he refers to faithful observance of God's Law as the "word of truth," not to human accomplishments by which one earns one's salvation. With a slightly different vocabulary, but in a similar way, Jewish-Christian traditions in Matthew commend observance of the Law (Matt 5:16–20; 23:1–3).

THE GALATIANS' EXPERIENCE WITH THE EXPRESSION ERGA NOMOU PRIOR TO HEARING PAUL'S LETTER

Considering the use of the expression in these and other traditions, we can draw four conclusions pertinent to the Galatians' experience with the expression *erga nomou* prior to hearing Paul's letter:

(1) In all probability the Galatians first heard the expression from the Teachers. (2) In the Teachers' discourses *erga nomou* referred simply to observance of the Law. (3) It follows that, prior to receiving Paul's letter, the Galatians' experience with the expression "observance of the Law" had almost certainly been altogether positive. Presumably, they were instructed by the Teachers to be as thankful to God for the Law as were the Psalmists in ancient Israel, the Covenantors in Qumran, and other Jewish Christians, such as the author of James (cf. Jas 1:22–25). (4) The Teachers may also have taught the Galatians that being observant of the Law is something human beings can do only with the help of God. Here a passage from the Qumran scrolls comes to mind, not least because it connects rectification with that observance of the Law that can be executed by the human being only under God's guidance:

> Rectification, I know, does not belong to man, nor perfection of way to the son of man: to the Most High God belong all rectifying deeds. The way of man is not established except by the Spirit which God created for him to make perfect a way for the children of men . . . (1QH 4:30–31; Vermes, altered).[152]

---

[152] In Qumran two crucial motifs are combined: God's gracious rectification and strict observance of the Law. A superficial reading could lead one to think that this combination involves two separate steps: God acts graciously in the first place, and then God sits back, so to speak, to see what the human being will do on his own. In fact, the God who rectifies by his grace and who demands perfection of way is also the God who accompanies the community along the path of Law observance (cf. 1QS 11:16–17). Required is the strictest observance of the Law that can be imagined. *And* that observant life, that rectifying perfection of way, happens by the active will of God, who alone can do works that are rectifying. In Comment #49 we will see that something similar can be said of the Teachers. They are unlikely to have thought of Law observance as a totally autonomous, human deed. Since, however, they are exhorting Gentiles to *commence* the observant life by the rite of circumcision, they speak of a transfer that must be enacted by the human being (Comment #37).

And the same point is frequently emphasized by Philo. For example,

> . . . so long as the mind supposes itself to be the cause of anything, it is far from making room for God; far also from confessing or making acknowledgment of him. For we must take note that the very confession of praise itself is the work not of the soul but of God who causes thankfulness to appear (*Leg. Alleg.* 1.82; *LCL*, altered).[153]

Prior to hearing Paul's letter, then, the Galatians will not have thought of observance of the Law as a great burden of required "works." Nor are they likely to have thought that by observing the Law they were performing totally autonomous deeds by which they could earn their own salvation, completely without the help of God.[154] Under the tutelage of the Teachers, they will have come to think of Law observance as the way to true life graciously opened up for his people by God, and confirmed to eternity by God's Messiah (Comment #33).

THE GALATIANS ATTEND TO PAUL'S USE OF THE EXPRESSION ERGA NOMOU

Listening then to Paul's letter, the Galatians are sure to have sensed immediately that, in his use of the expression *erga nomou*, Paul is referring to observance of the Law, not to something one might call "works." They will have been shocked, however, to see that the apostle speaks of Law observance in a consistently negative way, and they will have been surprised to note that he identifies observance as a merely human enterprise, emphatically denying, therefore, that it is God's elected means of setting things right, of supplying the Spirit, and of effecting wonders. Why Paul takes these steps is a matter the Galatians will have been able to penetrate only by attending carefully to his statements about rectification. See Comment #28.

COMMENT #28
GOD'S MAKING THINGS RIGHT BY THE FAITH OF CHRIST[155]

PAUL ARGUES ON THE BASIS OF SHARED JEWISH-CHRISTIAN TRADITION

Gal 2:16 is one of the most tightly concentrated theological statements in all of Paul's letters. It is also the earliest of his references to rectification, and thus the text in which we are privileged to see this crucial element of his theology taking shape.[156] Building on some of the results reached in the Notes, we can begin with a somewhat paraphrastic translation:

---

[153]Cf. *Leg. Alleg.* 1.48 and .50. *Human* works are transgressions, as one sees, for example, in 1 Esdr 8:83–84.

[154]The Teachers' adherence to the doctrine of the Two Ways will have had the effect nevertheless of portraying God as the divinity who gives one the *possibility* of nomistic obedience: Comments #37 and #49. Note the expression "forensic apocalyptic eschatology" in the Glossary.

[155]Cf. J. L. Martyn, *Issues*, 141–156.

[156]On the relative date of Galatians, see Introduction §9; Comment #24.

Gal 2:16. As Jewish Christians, we ourselves know that a person[157] is not rectified by observance of the Law, but rather by the faith of Christ Jesus. Thus,
even we have placed our trust in Christ Jesus, in order that the source of our
rectification might be the faith of Christ and not observance of the Law; for
not a single person will be rectified by observance of the Law.

As the initial clause indicates, Paul says that he is citing a tradition about rectification that he shares with all Jewish Christians, including the Teachers. We cannot say precisely where the tradition ends and Paul's situational interpretation
begins. Indeed, one suspects that the sentence is not the sort that recommends
such a literary exercise.[158] Still, the interpreter does well to begin by taking Paul
at his word. It is as though — building on an earlier remark directed to Peter —
Paul had said to the Teachers:

> You and I share a Jewish-Christian tradition about rectification. I cite this
> shared tradition, precisely in order to show that you are currently misleading
> my Galatian churches, by straying from convictions to which you yourselves
> feign allegiance!

A JEWISH-CHRISTIAN TRADITION ABOUT RECTIFICATION
Is Paul referring to a Jewish-Christian rectification tradition to which we have
access, which we know Paul to have known, and which is sufficiently well formed
to enable us to compare it with Paul's reading of it? In fact, his own letters present
us with several snippets of such a tradition, and three of those snippets prove to
be of considerable importance, Rom 3:25; 4:25; 1 Cor 6:11:[159]

---

[157] Lit. "a human being." The identity of this *anthrôpos* is a matter of great import. In the
underlying Jewish-Christian tradition it is the Israelite. In Paul's interpretation the term
refers to all human beings. In neither view, then, is it the Gentile, distinguished from the
Jew, *pace* Gager, *Origins*, 233, who follows the suggestions of Gaston and M. Barth.

[158] In "New Perspective" Dunn argued, to be sure, that such a literary division can be made
(111–113). Taking *ean mê* in 2:16a to mean "except," he suggested that that part of the
verse is Jewish-Christian tradition: ". . . one is not rectified by works of the Law except
[unless] those works be accompanied by faith in Christ Jesus." In 2:16b, Dunn continues,
Paul "pushes what began as a [Jewish-Christian] qualification on covenantal nomism into
an outright [Pauline] antithesis" (113). It is an interesting suggestion, but one that falters,
I think, on three grounds. (a) We can be almost certain that *ean mê* is to be taken here
with its adversative force, "but rather" (see Räisänen, "Galatians 2.16"; Eckstein, *Verheissung*, 21). (b) Exploring the huge realm of possibility, one might indeed entertain the
thought that, on occasion, some Jewish Christians told their Jewish neighbors they would
not be justified by keeping the Law unless they added faith in Christ. In fact, however,
Dunn cites no Jewish-Christian tradition to support such an hypothesis, and support from
data external to Gal 2:16 itself is exactly what is needed. (c) Finally, the Jewish-Christian
rectification tradition known to Paul never refers to a circumstance in which rectification
does *not* occur (Matt 5:20 is another matter). See below the discussion of Rom 3:25; Rom
4:25; 1 Cor 6:11, none of which contains a negative. We conclude that Paul is responsible
for all of the negatives in Gal 2:16 (drawing the third from Ps 142:2).

[159] On pre-Pauline, Christian rectification traditions, see Stuhlmacher, *Gerechtigkeit*, 185–
188; Kertelge, *Rechtfertigung*, 45–62, 242–245; several articles in J. Friedrich et al. (ed.),
Rechtfertigung: Hahn, "Taufe" (104–117); Lührmann, "Christologie" (359); Strecker,
"Befreiung" (501–505). See also Reumann (with responses by Fitzmyer and Quinn),

Rom 3:25 (plus 26a). . . . Christ Jesus, whom God put forward as a sacrifice of atonement by his blood. God did this to demonstrate the power of his rectitude; in his divine forbearance, that is to say, he has forgiven the sins previously committed . . .

Rom 4:25. . . . Jesus our Lord . . . who was handed over to death for our trespasses and was raised for our rectification.

1 Cor 6:11. And this is what some of you used to be [fornicators, idolaters . . . thieves . . . drunkards . . . robbers; v 9]. But you were washed, you were sanctified, you were rectified in the name of the Lord Jesus Christ and in the Spirit of our God.[160]

While these Jewish-Christian formulas show variations, a picture of considerable coherence does emerge from them.

(1) *Rectification is an act of God.* Drawing heavily on traditions in the Old Testament and on strands of Jewish thinking about rectification, the Jewish Christians who worded these formulas speak about an act of God.[161] There are rich traditions, to be sure, having to do with human deeds of rectitude (e.g., Tob 4:5–6; Wis 2:12). The makers of these formulas do not draw on those traditions. They speak about God's action (cf. Judg 5:11; Isa 46:13).

(2) *In that act God sets right things that have gone wrong.* In accordance with the causative force of the *hiphil* of the Hebrew verb ṣādēq (clearly reflected also in Jewish traditions expressed in Greek), the authors of the Jewish-Christian formulas speak of an action by which God changes the human scene, creating integrity where things had gone wrong.

(3) *What has made things wrong is transgressions against God's covenant committed among God's people.* Here we have a point that requires emphasis. The human scene envisaged in these Jewish-Christian formulas is that of the Jewish nation, and in that scene the need of rectification has arisen from the fact that members of God's people have transgressed commandments explicitly issued to them by God, thus proving unfaithful to God's gracious covenant.[162]

Righteousness, 27–40; Schnelle, *Gerechtigkeit;* Hays, "Justification." I leave aside formulas lying outside the letters of Paul. It is impossible to know the relative ages of the three formulas cited below. We can say only that they are of Jewish-Christian origin; the application of the formula in 1 Cor 6:11 to Gentiles (fornicators, idolaters, etc.) is a secondary move on Paul's part.

[160]On the texts in Romans, see particularly the commentaries of Käsemann, Wilckens, Meyer, and Dunn. Dahl has argued that Rom 3:25 and 4:25, along with Rom 8:32 and Gal 3:13–14, reflect the use of Akedah traditions by Jewish Christians ("Atonement"). This hypothesis may have some force in the case of Rom 8:32, but it is of dubious pertinence to the other passages.

[161]Did the formula cited by Paul in Rom 3:25 contain the phrase *dia pisteôs* (NRSV, "effective through faith")? If so, then like the rest of the formula it must have referred to God's rectifying act as *his* active faithfulness to the covenant. See footnote 169 below.

[162]The covenantal theology of the formula cited in Rom 3:25 is noted by numerous interpreters, the pathbreaking work being that of Pluta, *Bundestreue.* See also Käsemann, *Romans,* 100.

(4) *What makes transgressing members of God's people right is God's forgiveness.* Given Israel's sins, the need is for divine acquittal, forgiveness, remission of sins, and cleansing, so that the covenant can be unburdened and a new life begun.[163] Rectification is now accomplished, however, not by a sacrifice executed by a human being (such as the high priest acting on the Day of Atonement), but rather by Christ's death. And in this Jewish-Christian tradition that death is understood to have been God's sacrificial act taken at his initiative. It is the deed in which God has forgiven the sins formerly committed in Israel, wiping the slate clean (Rom 3:25).[164]

(5) *God's rectification is therefore God's mercy.* This definition is one of the points at which the Jewish-Christian formulas are similar to passages in the Qumran scrolls.[165] The formula of 1 Cor 6:11, for example, can be profitably compared with several Qumran texts:

1 Cor 6:11. [There was guilt as the result of many sins] but you have been washed, you have been sanctified, you have been rectified in the name of the Lord Jesus Christ . . .

1QS 11:13–15. He will draw me near by his grace, and by his mercy will he bring my rectification. He will judge me in the rectitude of his truth, and in the greatness of his goodness he will pardon all my sins. Through his rectitude he will cleanse me of the uncleanness of man, and of the sins of the children of men, that I may confess to God his rectitude (Vermes, altered).

1QH 4:34–37. When I thought of my guilty deeds . . . I said "In my sins I am lost . . ." But then, when I remembered the strength of your hand and the fullness of your mercy, I rose again and stood upright . . . for you will pardon iniquity and you will purify man of sin through your rectification (Vermes, altered).[166]

1QS 11:12. As for me, if I stumble, the mercies of God shall be my eternal salvation. If I stagger because of the sin of flesh, my rectification shall be by the rectitude of God which endures forever (Vermes, altered).

---

[163]This is a juncture at which the thesis of Thielman may be taken into account (*From Plight to Solution*), for that thesis may have some pertinence to the Jewish-Christian authors of the rectification formulas. *They* may have worked to some degree from plight to solution, though the terms would be better put by speaking of sin and salvation. In any case, Thielman's thesis is unconvincing as regards *Paul*. It is a matter in connection with which one recalls that K. Barth was an exegete as well as a systematic theologian; for over a considerable period of time he correctly emphasized that Paul saw Adam in the light of Christ, sin in the light of grace, and so on. Note, for example, the comments ". . . it is only by grace that the lack of grace can be recognized as such" (*Church Dogmatics*, 2.2, 92); ". . . the doctrine of election . . . defines grace as the starting-point for all reflection and utterance . . ." (93). In recent decades Barth's point has been emphasized in a certain way by E. P. Sanders, *Palestinian Judaism*, 442–447.

[164]Cf. Breytenbach, "Versöhnung," 78; Hamerton-Kelly, *Violence*, 142.

[165]See O. Betz, "Qumran"; E. P. Sanders, *Palestinian Judaism*, 305–312.

[166]On the understanding of sin in Qumran, see Becker, *Heil*, 144–148, and the critique of Becker's work in E. P. Sanders, *Palestinian Judaism*, 272–284.

The last passage is of particular importance because it places in parallel God's mercy and God's rectification. The Jewish-Christian formulas do something similar, equating rectification with God's forgiving initiative in cleansing one from sins. They thus stand in a long and impressive line of tradition: God's deed of rectification is God's merciful forgiveness of transgressions for which atonement has been made (cf., e.g., *Pss. Sol.* 3:3–12).

(6) *The Law is not mentioned because its continuing validity is taken for granted.* The ways in which the Jewish-Christian formulas draw on OT traditions, and the fact that they were made by Christians who were distinctly Jewish, tell us that the transgressions referred to were identified as transgressions on the basis of the Law.[167] Moreover, while it may seem obvious, we must reiterate that, for the Jewish-Christian authors, the God who has now enacted his rectifying forgiveness is the God of Israel, the God of the covenant, the author of the Law. By enacting his rectifying forgiveness in the death and resurrection of Christ, God has established his right over his creation Israel, thus restoring the integrity of the nomistic covenant.

There is, therefore, no thought that God's rectification removes one from the realm of God's Law.[168] The three rectification formulas do not mention the Law

---

[167]In "Types" R. E. Brown has made some suggestions that are helpful for the identification of churches outside of Palestine. The church of Jerusalem was, however, another matter; and the same is true of the churches in Judea that were children of "the gospel to those who are circumcised" (Gal 1:22; 2:7, 9). In their own eyes all of these churches were thoroughly observant, Jewish-Christian communities, and the formulas we are discussing seem clearly to have been authored in them.

[168]The thought of being removed from the realm of the Law would have horrified both the Qumran Covenantors and the Jewish-Christian authors of the three rectification formulas. The God whom the Qumran psalmist praises because he will "pardon iniquity and purify from sin by . . . [his] . . . rectification" (1QH 4:37) is the God who has engraved his Law on the psalmist's heart (1QH 4:10). Similarly, for Jewish Christians the God who has graciously rectified Israelite sinners in the sacrificial death of his Son is the one who graciously gave the Law, engraving it forever on the hearts of his people. At this point one may pause in order to ask an important question about the assumption that God's rectification is an act taken by him in the context of the Law. Does this assumption mean that the authors of the Jewish-Christian formulas fail to present God's rectifying deed in Christ as an act of grace? By no means! Like the Qumran Covenantors (and other Jewish sages who deal with the subject of rectification), these Jewish Christians celebrate a new instance of God's grace in the undisturbed context of God's gracious Law. Just as the Covenantors could throw themselves on the merciful rectification of God, without dreaming of abandoning God's Law, so the authors of the traditions preserved in 1 Cor 6:11, Rom 3:25, and Rom 4:25 celebrate rectification in Christ without contemplating the possibility that that deed of God might stand in tension with God's giving of the Law, or with their observance of it. Modern Christian interpreters sometimes say of Qumran that strict adherence to the Law spoils the confession of hope solely directed to God's rectification, turning it into something other than true *sola gratia*. But that is a reading forgetful of the fact that Qumran exemplifies the way in which Israel traditionally put together the deepest belief in God's mercy and the strictest observance of God's Law (cf. E. P. Sanders, *Palestinian Judaism*, 292). In a word, the Covenantors do not move *away from* the confession of God's gracious rectification *to* the demand for punctilious observance of the Law, thus allowing the latter to "spoil" the former. On the contrary, they are representative Jews in holding the two together: observance of the Law and confession of God's mercy. *Mutatis*

either positively or negatively, because taking the Law for granted, they express the *novum:* God's gracious and rectifying forgiveness of sins in Christ.

(7) *God has accomplished his rectifying forgiveness in Christ, specifically in Christ's death and resurrection.* Just as the formulas' silence about the Law shows that the Law's continuance is taken for granted, so that silence also indicates that rectification is not attributed to the Law (a point that will prove crucial to Paul). God has provided his rectifying forgiveness by acting in the atoning blood sacrifice that is Christ's death (Rom 3:25), or in the event of Christ's resurrection (Rom 4:25). And that accomplishment of God is made real for those who are being baptized when the name of the Lord Jesus is pronounced over them and the Spirit of Christ descends on them (1 Cor 6:11). Thus, the Jewish Christians responsible for these formulas see an indelible connection — even an identity — between God's deed of rectification and God's deed in Christ.

(8) In these formulas one finds, then, *God's messianic grace in the context of God's Law.* For that reason the authors of these formulas would have found a polemic against rectification by Law observance entirely beside the point. They were making no such claim. Indeed, the Jewish-Christian tradition about rectification is a stranger to polemics. It seems to have been formulated in Jewish-Christian churches largely free of internal strife.

(9) *God's rectifying forgiveness in Christ is confessed without explicit reference to faith.* Just as the formulas make no reference to the Law, so they do not mention faith, either on the part of members of the Jewish-Christian communities or on the part of Jesus Christ.[169] There is, therefore, no hint of a polemical antinomy that would place opposite one another Christ's faithful deed in our behalf and our observance of the Law.

In these nine points we have, with a reasonable degree of probability, the major outlines of a Jewish-Christian rectification tradition that antedated both Paul and the Teachers, a tradition that was shared by both of them, indeed a tradition that both claimed to revere. Can we speak with some confidence about the ways in which the Teachers and Paul interpreted this shared tradition?

THE TEACHERS' INTERPRETATION OF THIS JEWISH-CHRISTIAN TRADITION

Here two points are of major importance. First, we can be confident that the Teachers find in the tradition what we have seen actually to be there: the affirmation of God's forgiveness of Israel's sins in the sacrificial death of his Messiah. For the Teachers, as for the Jewish-Christian authors of the tradition, Jesus' death is

---

mutandis the Jewish Christians from whom Paul inherited 1 Cor 6:11, Rom 3:25, and Rom 4:25 did essentially the same.

[169] The question whether the phrase *dia pisteôs* (NRSV, "effective through faith") was included in the pre-Pauline formula of Rom 3:25 is an issue much discussed and unlikely ever to be settled to the satisfaction of all interpreters. In any case, if *dia pisteôs* is to be taken as part of the Jewish-Christian tradition, Pluta's argument in *Bundestreue* stands: That phrase referred, *as did the formula as a whole,* to God's trustworthy deed in Christ, his rectifying act of faithfulness to his covenantal people. In that tradition it meant neither Jesus' faith nor faith on the part of the human being.

the totally adequate sacrifice made by God himself, the sacrifice in which God accomplished the forgiveness of sins for Israel, the people among whom observance of the Law was and is taken for granted.

Second, however, as missionaries to Gentiles, the Teachers hear the Jewish-Christian tradition in a new context in which observance of the Law is not — and cannot be — taken for granted. And because they carry out their mission by inviting Gentiles to *enter* the people of Israel, they necessarily posit an explicit relation between rectification and observance of the Law. Where the Jewish-Christian tradition affirmed God's deed in Christ for an Israel in which Law observance was taken for granted, the Teachers understand God's act of forgiveness in Christ to be God's gracious deed for Israel, *including* all Gentiles who *transfer* from their pagan existence into God's Law-observant people. That rectifying transfer, then, clearly requires that Gentiles take up observance of the Law.

PAUL'S READING OF THE TRADITION IN LIGHT OF DEVELOPMENTS IN GALATIA

Paul's interpretation of this Jewish-Christian rectification tradition is more complex, involving seven crucial points.[170]

(1) The Teachers' use of the Jewish-Christian tradition does not cause Paul to give it up. Nor does he provide the slightest hint that he disagrees with the tradition itself. Precisely the contrary; he calls the Jewish-Christian rectification tradition down on the heads of the Teachers. The way in which he does that proves to be of considerable interest.

(2) As he writes to his Galatian churches, the setting in which Paul hears this Jewish-Christian tradition is both similar to and fundamentally different from the setting in which the Teachers hear it. On the one hand, since both Paul and the Teachers are active in missions to Gentiles, like the Teachers Paul necessarily hears the tradition in that new context.

On the other hand, however, even that context is quite different for Paul. In stark contrast to the Teachers, Paul perceives every day that in his Gentile mission field God is creating churches — actively beginning to make things right in the whole of the world — *apart from* observance of the Law. It is easy to see, then, that Paul does not hear a rectification tradition that speaks about the Israelite, the Jew, the transgressor of God's covenantal Law who, because of his transgression, stands in need of forgiveness. As we have noted, Paul hears a tradition that speaks to and about *anthrôpos*, the human being, both Jew and Gentile, without any distinction between the two (cf. 2:16a and 3:28). Exactly how can he hear the tradition in this way?

(3) He notes in the Jewish-Christian rectification tradition a striking instance of *silence*. As we have seen, the tradition, referring emphatically to God's deed of rectification, does not even mention the Law. Specifically, it does not attribute rectification to observance of the Law. In the light of God's work as Paul observes it in his own mission, he sees, then, that the tradition's silence about the Law is

---

[170]See again the works on justification/rectification by Stuhlmacher, Kertelge, Reumann, and Hays cited in footnote 159 above.

no mystery. Indeed, in this silence he senses not only that the tradition itself is speaking generically about the human being; he senses also that it is saying, "the human being is not rectified by observance of the Law."

(4) Silent with regard to the Law, this Jewish-Christian tradition is eloquent with regard to Christ; and Paul is as sensitive to the eloquence as he is to the silence. For, given his theological anger at the Teachers' work in his Galatian churches, Paul hears the tradition's nomistic silence and its christological eloquence in a new way. He now hears God's voice formulating a new antinomy that links the verb "to be rectified" both to a negative statement and to a positive one: The human being

is not rectified by observance of   but rather by *pistis Christou Iêsou.*
the Law

And, to formulate the positive member of this gospel antinomy, Paul coins an eloquent expression of his own, *pistis Christou.*

(5) Recent decades have seen an extended and vigorous debate as to the force of this expression, some interpreters taking it to mean human faith in Christ (a construction they usually call an objective genitive), some finding a reference to the faith of Christ (usually termed subjective, but best identified, somewhat loosely, as an authorial genitive).[171] Supplementing arguments of Hays and others, one can mention two observations that tilt the balance decisively in favor of rendering *pistis Christou* as "the faith of Christ."

(a) The Jewish-Christian rectification tradition on which Paul is drawing had spoken about an act that God carried out in Christ. If Paul is hearing that tradition anew, without violating it fundamentally, a simple conclusion is to be drawn: When he says that God has made things right by *pistis Christou Iêsou,* he is referring to God's rectifying act *in Christ* (centrally in his death, which Paul always understands to be part of a holistic event including his resurrection). *Pistis*

---

[171] To trace this debate, one will do well to begin with Kertelge, *Rechtfertigung,* 162–219, noting Haussleiter's move from subjective genitive to genitive of authorship (*Glaube*). From Kertelge one can then make one's way to Howard's articles in *HTR* and *ExpTim;* to the items mentioned in the papers of Hays, "What Is at Stake?" and of Dunn, "Once More"; to those papers themselves; to Longenecker, "*Pistis*"; and to D. A. Campbell, "Romans 1:17." As P. W. Meyer pointed out in remarks made at the meeting of the Society of Biblical Literature in 1991, the objective genitive, strictly defined, demands not only a verbal ruling noun but also one whose cognate verb is transitive. The verb *pisteuô* is itself transitive only with the meaning "to entrust" followed by two accusatives. In the case of *pistis Christou* one may be well advised, then, to speak of a genitive of authorship or of origin. Everyone must agree that Paul sometimes speaks of the faith had by human beings; and in Gal 3:2 and 3:5 he identifies the generative source of that faith: the proclamation of Christ's death. From those references, then, and also from Gal 3:22–25, one could draw a conclusion not far from that of Haussleiter: "Christ accomplishes faith, in that he communicates himself . . . And then he remains active behind our faith, so that the redeeming power of faith lies in the fact that the living Christ is both the one who originates it and the one who consistently carries it along" (cited from Kertelge, *Rechtfertigung,* 164 n18).

Christou, in short, arises in Paul's vocabulary as his way of reflecting the tradition's reference to *Christ's* role in God's deed of rectification.[172]

(b) That interpretation is firmly supported by a comparison of Gal 2:16 with Gal 2:21. Gal 2:16 is the opening sentence in the first rectification passage in the letter, the final sentence of that passage being 2:21. Both are pithy references to God's deed of making things right, and both are antinomous in form:

2:16. . . . the human being is not rectified by observance of *the Law,* but rather by *pistis Christou Iēsou.*	2:21. . . . if rectification were through *the Law,* then *Christ died* for no purpose at all.

If beginning corresponds to end, then in 2:16, as in 2:21, Paul is referring to an opposition between rectification by Law observance and rectification by the deed of God in Christ. It follows that *pistis Christou* is an expression by which Paul speaks of Christ's atoning faithfulness, as, on the cross, he died faithfully for human beings while looking faithfully to God.

(6) The result of this interpretation of *pistis Christou* is crucial to an understanding not only of Galatians but also of the whole of Paul's theology. God has set things right without laying down a prior condition of any sort. God's rectifying act, that is to say, is no more God's response to human faith in Christ than it is God's response to human observance of the Law. God's rectification is not God's response at all. It is the *first* move; it is God's initiative, carried out by him in Christ's faithful death.

The antinomy of Gal 2:16, then — *erga nomou* versus *pistis Christou* — is like all of the antinomies of the new creation: It does not set over against one another two human alternatives, to observe the Law or to have faith in Christ. The opposites, as one sees from Gal 1:1 onward, are an act of God, Christ's faithful death, and an act of the human being, observance of the Law. The one has the power to rectify, to make things right; the other does not.

To be sure, as Paul will say in 3:2, Christ's faithful death for us has the power to elicit faithful trust on our part (see Comment #29). Thus in 2:16 itself he speaks *in the second instance* of our placing our trust in Christ:

Thus, even we have placed our trust in Christ Jesus, in order that the source of our rectification might be the faith of Christ and not observance of the Law.

The point is that the Christ in whom we faithfully place our trust is the Christ who has already faithfully died in our behalf (cf. Rom 5:8) and whose prevenient death for us is the powerful rectifying event that has elicited our faith.[173]

---

[172] In theory one could consider the possibility that where the tradition spoke of an act of *God,* making things right in Christ's death, Paul heard a reference to an act of *the human being,* having faith in Christ. I see, however, no exegetical ground firm enough to support this hypothesis, and much to oppose it. See also the next footnote.

[173] When we trust God, Paul would say, we signal that we ourselves have been invaded by God's presuppositionless grace, and we confess that the locus of God's invasion is *especially* our will! Far from presupposing freedom of the will (cf. Hos 5:4), Paul speaks of the freeing of the will for the glad service of God and neighbor. And that freeing of the will

(7) Finally, there is the matter of indicating plainly what rectification is. Here one notes that 2:16–21 is only the first of the rectification passages in Galatians. The second is 3:6–4:7. Pondering the differences between the first rectification passage and the second (see further below), we see that, in the first, Paul provides his own arresting instance of silence. He uses the verb "to be rectified" three times in 2:16, a fourth time in 2:17, and, as a fifth reference, he employs the noun "rectification" in 2:21. Yet he speaks in this initial rectification passage only of the means or the source of rectification, giving not a hint as to what rectification itself might be. Why this silence?

It is surely intended for rhetorical effect. In his speech to the Teachers Paul says nothing about the Jewish-Christian definition of rectification as forgiveness, in order to clear the deck for a new definition. And that new definition does in fact emerge in the second rectification passage, 3:6–4:7.

To begin with, one notes the number of actors on the stage on which God's rectifying deed occurs. The Jewish-Christian tradition presents a drama in which there are three actors: sinful human beings, Christ, and the God of the covenant who has accomplished in the blood sacrifice of Christ the true forgiveness of human sins. Without expressing a polemic against this tradition, Paul does go well beyond it in 3:6–4:7, presenting there a new definition of rectification that involves a crucial increase in the number of actors. That is to say, in 3:6–4:7 we find a drama in which there are four actors: human beings, Christ, God, *and anti-God powers*, the last of these actors being variously identified:

the Law that has the power to curse (3:10)
the Law as it pronounces its curse on the crucified Christ (3:13)
Sin functioning as the prison warden over the whole of creation (3:22)
the elements of the cosmos that enslave both Jew and Gentile (4:3).[174]

With the appearance of these anti-God powers, the landscape is fundamentally changed, indicating what has really gone wrong and what is really involved in God's making it right in the whole of the cosmos.[175] The cosmic landscape

---

reflects one of Paul's major convictions: Our trust in God has been awakened, kindled by God's trustworthy deed in Christ. See Schlier, who, in interpreting *akoê pisteôs* in Gal 3:2, speaks perceptively of "revelation that kindles faith" (122).

[174]Note that from Gal 3:10 to 4:5 Paul uses the expression *hypo tina einai*, "to be under the power of someone or something," no fewer than eight times, thus referring seriatim to anti-God powers that enslave all human beings (Comment #39).

[175]In Galatians it is the movement from the first rectification passage to the second that confirms the major thesis of Käsemann: For Paul God's rectification in Christ is "the rightful *power* with which God makes his cause to *triumph* in the world that has fallen away from him . . ." *Questions*, 180; emphasis added; cf. Zahl, *Rechtfertigungslehre*). The fact that the formulaic *dikaiosynê theou* does not appear in Galatians is thus of no consequence. The view of God's rectification as God's deed of *power* is present in a multitude of texts, ranging from pre-apocalyptic traditions in ancient Israel to the Dead Sea Scrolls and beyond. Translators are correct, for example, to render *sidqôt yahweh* in Judg 5:11 (the Song of Deborah) "the triumphs of the Lord" (NRSV). In a word, the institution of the holy war is the deep soil in which cosmological apocalyptic took root in Israel.

now proves to be a *battlefield*, and in that setting the need of human beings is not so much forgiveness of their sins as deliverance from malignant powers that hold them in bondage (cf. Comments #2 and #39).

The change to this battlefield is particularly impressive as regards the way in which Paul perceives the relation of Christ's death to the Law. To be sure, building on Jewish-Christian atonement tradition, Paul still says that Christ died "for us" (3:13). But now Christ's death is seen to have happened in *collision* with the Law, and human beings are not said to need forgiveness, but rather deliverance from a genuine slavery that involves the Law. In this second rectification passage the Law proves to be not so much a norm which we have transgressed — although transgressions are involved (3:19) — as a tyrant, insofar as it has placed us under the power of its curse. And by his death Christ is not said to have accomplished our forgiveness, but rather our redemption from slavery. With the apocalyptic shift to a scene in which there are real powers arrayed against God, rectification acquires, then, a new synonym, *exagorazô*, "to redeem by delivering from slavery" (3:13; 4:5).[176] And, as we have noted, one of the powers from whose tyranny Christ has delivered us is the Law in its role as the pronouncer of a curse on the whole of humanity.

The shifts involved in moving from the first rectification passage to the second provide, then, a major clue not only to Paul's definition of rectification but also to the genesis of his carefully formed thinking on this subject. For in Gal 3:6–4:7, no less than in the earlier passage, Paul is formulating a polemic against the Teachers' discourses on rectification. Specifically, he is circumscribing "the forensic apocalyptic theology of the . . . Teachers with a cosmological apocalyptic theology of his own."[177] Rectification thus remains, for Paul, God's act in the death of Christ. But now, having taken silent leave of the Jewish-Christian concern with the forgiveness of nomistic transgressions, Paul sees in Christ's death God's liberating invasion of the territory of tyranny.

THE PLACE OF RECTIFICATION BY THE FAITH OF CHRIST IN PAUL'S THEOLOGY

Paul's use of rectification language has been thought to constitute a doctrine, and about that doctrine numerous interpreters have made three claims: It was polemical in its very nature. It led to unnecessary divisions in the early history of the church. And, being itself unnecessary, it proves on inspection to have been

---

[176] As we have seen in Comment #2, Paul effects the same kind of shift at Gal 1:4b. Having quoted Jewish-Christian tradition in which Christ is said to have given his life "for our sins" (1:4a), Paul changes the frame of reference to that of apocalyptic deliverance from the powerful grasp of the present evil age (*exelêtai*). While he does not use in this shift the language of rectification, one can say that the theological integrity of the letter warrants taking *exaireomai* ("to snatch from the grasp of") as yet another Pauline synonym for rectification. And when we are speaking of synonyms, we must at least mention two further ones: For Paul God makes things right by bringing life where there was death (Gal 3:21; Rom 4:17) and by creating community where there was division (Gal 3:28; note *heis* ["one"]).

[177] De Boer, "Apocalyptic Eschatology," 185; see Glossary.

marginal to the core of Paul's gospel. Is any light shed on these claims by our consideration of Gal 2:16, and by our comparison of the first two rectification passages in Galatians (the third is 5:4–5)?

The polemical nature of Gal 2:16 is beyond dispute. When Paul says,

> . . . the human being is *not* rectified by observance of the Law, *but rather* by the faith of Christ Jesus,

he is clearly involved in a battle marked by considerable theological fury (cf. Gal 5:12). It is scarcely surprising, then, that the doctrine of rectification did indeed play a role in early Christian tensions (e.g., Jas 2:18–26).[178] Historians have had some reason for suggesting that those tensions — variously qualified and supplemented — had a hand in the ultimate divorce between the largely Gentile church of the Mediterranean basin and the older, distinctly Jewish churches of Jerusalem, Judea, and parts of Syria. None of these developments indicates, however, that Paul was himself an enemy of Jewish Christianity. The truth lies with the precise opposite.

No one in the early church held more tenaciously to the vision of church unity than did Paul, and no one paid a higher price for that vision. At the Jerusalem conference it was Paul, as we have seen earlier, who was consumed by the comprehensive vision of God's great work proceeding along two parallel paths, between which he envisioned only mutual support and respect. In his early work he was at peace with the Jewish-Christian churches of Judea (Gal 1:22–24), and to the end of his life he was certain, first, that the unified church of God was drawn both from Jews and from Gentiles (Rom 9:24) and, second, that that unity demanded concrete expression in the collection he gathered from his own churches for the church in Jerusalem (the delivery of which led eventually to his death; Rom 15:25–32; Comment #24).

Given the history of the interpretation of Paul's letters, then, one can scarcely overemphasize that Gal 2:16 shows Paul formulating a polemic neither against Judaism nor against Jewish Christianity. At the genesis of Paul's doctrine of rectification, the apostle understands himself to be in accord with Jewish-Christian rectification tradition, *as* he hears that tradition anew in light of God's gospel invasion of the whole of the world.

Comparing Gal 2:16–21 with Gal 3:6–4:7, and seeing that the two passages present a theological integrity, we have found in the progression from the first to the second an essential clue to the polemical character of Paul's doctrine of rectification. In the first rectification passage Paul emphasizes the antinomy between Christ's faithful death and observance of the Law. In the second passage he then brings that antinomy into the perspective of cosmic apocalyptic, in which God has set things right by acting in Christ against real enemies (3:13; cf. 4:3–5). But that means that *Paul's* rectification polemic against the Teachers in 2:16 is nothing other than a reflection of *God's* rectifying polemic against his enemies. Among these enemies Paul understandably attends particularly to the

---

[178]See L. T. Johnson, *James.*

curse of the Law. Having earlier said that God does not make things right *by means of* the Law, Paul now says that God has had to make things right by entering into combat *against* the Law, insofar as it enacts its curse (3:10). And Christ's death on the Law-cursed cross is the point at which God has done that (3:13).

It is thus *God's* polemical act in Christ that causes Paul's doctrine of rectification to be polemical, and that means that one cannot minimize the latter without doing the same to the former. We have no evidence, it is true, that before writing to the Galatians Paul ever spoke directly and explicitly on the subject of rectification. Once his combat with the Teachers in Galatia led him, however, to craft that way of preaching the gospel of God's triumph, he never gave it up.

For while Paul may well have been a person to whom compromise was foreign territory, his personal idiosyncrasies do not explain his theological tenacity. At root, he was sure that his call to be an apostolic soldier was a reflection of God's identity as *the* soldier, intent on making things right. It is God's declaration of war in Christ against all of the forces enslaving the human race that formed the foundation of Paul's militant doctrine of rectification. In short, *God's* rectifying declaration of war in Christ is what gave Paul total confidence that in the end Christ will hand over the kingdom to God the Father, *after* he has destroyed every ruler and every authority and power (1 Cor 15:24).

COMMENT #29
PLACING ONE'S TRUST IN CHRIST JESUS

At three junctures in Galatians Paul uses the verb *pisteuô*, once in the construction *pisteuô eis* plus accusative, "to place one's trust in Christ Jesus" (2:16), once as *pisteuô* plus dative, "to have faith in God" (3:6, quoting Gen 15:6), and a final time in the form of a substantive participle, "those who believe" (3:22).[179] In all three instances there is a fluidity of reference, involving trust, faith, and belief. Comparing the three passages with one another, and taking into account pertinent data in Paul's other letters, we can see the major accents Paul has in mind:[180]

(1) The placing of trust is a human deed. Since he allows human beings to be the subject of the verb "to place one's trust," "to have faith," "to believe," Paul must be referring to an act carried out by human beings. One trusts Christ Jesus as the Son whom God sent into the world to give his life in behalf of us, and as the one whom God then raised from the dead, causing him to become the fully trustworthy Lord of the cosmos. This trust, being directed toward the risen Lord who is influentially present in the worshiping community, has about it the character of a confessional prayer, spoken not in the Lord's absence, but rather in his presence. There, in his presence, the worshiper knows this cosmic Lord to be the

---

[179] As far as we know, there is no Jewish background for the expression "to believe in the Messiah" (1QpHab 8:1–3 is another matter). In Judaism one looks for the messianic age and its signs, trusting in God's purposes. As we will see below, with the crucifixion and resurrection of Jesus Christ, this pattern is altered, in that Christ's faithful death elicits faith in him.

[180] Cf. Bultmann, *"pisteuô"*; Lührmann, *Glaube*, 46–59; Keck, *Paul and His Letters*, 80–94; Haacker, "Glaube."

one who fully determines his own life, not least his future, as he lives in the community of faith (1 Thess 4:14; 1 Cor 15:22; Rom 10:9). Belief involves, then, face-to-face obedience, together with the certainty of a hope that is faithfully sustained through thick and thin (cf. Gal 5:5; Rom 8:31–39). If Paul inherited most of these formulations, his own contribution can be summarized in two additional points.

(2) The placing of trust is also more than a human deed. The structure of Gal 2:16 is an important clue to Paul's understanding of faith on the part of human beings. The order of the clauses shows that, for Paul, God's deed of rectifying us by the faith of Christ precedes *our* deed of placing our trust in that Christ. The same order of events is stated in Gal 3:22, where Paul says that God's promise is given via the faith of Jesus Christ to those who believe. Indeed, Christ's faith is not only prior to ours but also causative of it. That point is put beyond doubt when Paul says that the proclamation of Christ's faithful death is what has the power to elicit our trusting faith (3:2). All of these passages, in a word, reflect Paul's keen interest in the issue of the genesis of human faith.

We can reiterate that Paul is serious when he allows human beings to be the subject of the verb "to place one's trust." Those who believe in Christ are not puppets, moved about and made to speak by others (contrast the act of hypocrisy in 2:13, and see Comment #49). But, just as these persons are not puppet believers, so they are not believers as a result of an act of their own autonomous wills, as though the gospel were an event in which two alternatives were placed before an autonomous decider, and faith were one of two decisions the human being could make autonomously.[181] On the contrary, for Paul faith does not lie in the realm of human possibility. Even to speak of faith as a "possibility granted by God" can be misleading. For faith is not an option human beings can choose. Thus, when Paul speaks about placing one's trust in Christ, he is pointing to a deed that reflects not the freedom of the will, but rather God's freeing of the will. In Christ, the Son of God whose faith is engagingly enacted in his death, God invaded the human orb and commenced a battle for the liberation of the human will itself. And in the case of believers, that apocalyptic invasion is the mysterious genesis of faith in Christ (cf. Phil 2:12–13; Gal 4:4, 6).[182]

(3) One trusts the God who is active in the gospel. What Paul says about God's

---

[181]See especially 1 Cor 1:18 and J. L. Martyn, *Issues*, 217–221.

[182]Once Paul's understanding of Christ's faith was lost, it was inevitable that his profound grasp of the relationship between faith in Christ and God's rectification should also disappear, to be rediscovered only from time to time. Certain ones of his own expressions have played their roles in the ensuing confusion. In Gal 2:16, for example, he says that "we have believed in Christ Jesus *in order that* we might be rectified by the faith of Christ and not by observance of the Law." When *pistis Christou* is read as "faith *in* Christ," the conjunction "in order that" falsely assumes a causative role, as though it had been Paul's intention to say, "We have believed in order to be *thereby* rectified, God's act of rectification being God's response to our deed of faith." As we have just noted, Paul's understanding of the primacy of God's rectifying act in Christ's faith and his consequent understanding of the genesis of our faith preclude such a view. By the conjunction "in order that," Paul means to speak of God's *purpose* that we be rectified by Christ's faith, and not by our observance of the Law. Cf. Käsemann, *Perspectives*, 82.

deed in Christ he also says about the proclamation of this deed, reflecting his convictions that God is the immediate and irreplaceable author of the gospel, and that the gospel is itself an invasive event, not merely the offering of a new option. It is in the gospel-event that Christ's faith elicits our faith. Thus, Paul can even include faith in the list of the fruit that is borne by the Spirit of Christ (5:22), suggesting that the act of trust does not have its origin in the human being. On the contrary, as we have noted, that act springs from the proclamation of the risen Lord. It is incited by the preached message (Gal 3:2; Rom 10:17). It is empowered by the Spirit.[183]

COMMENT #30
CRUCIFIXION WITH CHRIST

Paul's statement that he suffered crucifixion along with Christ (Gal 2:19) is strange and difficult to grasp. Three matters call for discussion.[184]

CHRIST'S CRUCIFIXION

This is the first juncture in the letter at which Paul refers to the manner of Christ's death, execution by crucifixion, but it is by no means the first time the Galatians have heard of it. In Paul's preaching to them he painted before their eyes a picture of Jesus Christ as he suffered this vile and obscene death (3:1), an extraordinarily cruel and gruesome form of execution known throughout the Levant, adopted particularly by the Romans, used in Palestine by both the Romans and the Jews, and perhaps employed among the Galatians themselves.[185] In most instances the practice was to nail the condemned person to a wooden pole (often equipped with a crosspiece) while the person was still alive, thus causing him to die a slow and obscene death in a public place, where onlookers could watch him die. While sadistic tendencies doubtless played a role in its invention, the primary motive for crucifixion lay in the assumption that such a gruesome form of execution would instill in the onlookers a respect for law and order, as defined by the crucifiers.

Paul's perception of Christ's crucifixion is thoroughly apocalyptic, in that it is both this-worldly and other-worldly. (1) On the one hand, it is the real death that was carried out with literal nails on a literal piece of wood, a gruesome spectacle that Paul can portray literally in sermonic form (3:1), and about which Paul does

---

[183] Cf. Käsemann, *Romans*, 290: "Faith . . . does not have to discover Christ, because he is always on the scene before us; he is there in the word of preaching" (author's translation). God's liberation of the will involves an invasion of the will, as Hosea knew very well (Hos 5:4; 6:1).

[184] The literature on these subjects is justly immense. See notably Tannehill, *Dying*; Cousar, *Cross*; and the studies mentioned in those works.

[185] The literary evidence is well given by Hengel, *Crucifixion*; the archaeological data and particularly the pertinent texts in the Qumran scrolls are presented and astutely analyzed by Fitzmyer, *Advance*, 125–146. It is Diodorus Siculus (citing Posidonius) 5.32.6 who speaks of the Celts (Galatians?) sacrificing criminals to their gods by crucifying them; Hengel, *Crucifixion*, 23.

not speak with any of the euphemisms that are always ready to hand, such as "go to sleep."[186]

(2) On the other hand, however, the crucifixion of Christ is *entirely* real as the cosmic event that cannot be truly seen by those who look only at human actors who employ literal nails and pieces of wood. One notes, then, that in 1 Cor 2:8 Paul identifies those who crucified Christ as "the rulers of this age," referring to supra-human powers. By the same token it is worth noting that in Galatians Paul does not give a this-worldly identification of the crucifiers. Specifically, he provides not the slightest hint that the Jewish authorities played a role; nor does he speak of the Roman procurator or of the Roman soldiers (contrast 1 Thess 2:14–15). This silence reflects his certainty that the cross is the event that involved the death of the old *cosmos* and the birth of the *new creation* (1:4; 6:14–15).

CHRIST'S CRUCIFIXION AND THE LAW
Although Paul believes that the Law played an active role in the crucifixion of Christ (see "through the Law" in 2:19), he clearly does not view the crucifixion as a Jewish event in the proper sense. True enough, the link Paul draws between Christ's crucifixion and the Law may have a *formal* parallel in 4QpNah, where lines 7 and 8 can be interpreted to speak of the crucifixions of *Israelites* carried out in accordance with the Law (cf. 11QTemple 64:6–13).[187] But in Paul's theology this link between Christ's crucifixion and the Law reflects the conviction that, in its paired existence with the Not-Law, the Law is a cosmic power affecting Gentile no less than Jew. Thus, Paul does not say that the Sanhedrin worked through the Law to bring Christ to his death. He attributes the active role to the Law itself as one of the enslaving elements of the old cosmos (3:13; Comment #41).

PARTICIPATION IN CHRIST'S CRUCIFIXION
The cosmic horizon created by Christ's crucifixion is also the key to Paul's insistence that he himself suffered crucifixion with Christ. The verb "to crucify with" (*systauroô*) is used in the gospels to speak literally of the simultaneous crucifixion of other men along with Jesus. Using the verb in a nonliteral manner, Paul em-

---

[186]The reference in 1 Cor 15:20b to Christ's being the first fruits of "those who sleep" is no real exception, for in his own death Christ did not go to sleep. He joined those who are dead (1 Cor 15:20a).

[187]Yadin suggested that the text in 4QpNah be reconstructed to read: "The Lion of Wrath (Alexander Janneus) . . . has found in the Seekers after Smooth-Things (Pharisees) a crime for which the verdict is death: them he hangs as live men on the tree, *as this is the law* in Israel as of old" (emphasis added). The law in question is, then, Josh 8:23–29 and Deut 21:22 ("Pesher," 10–12). Similarly, 11QTemple 64:6–13 (Martinez, *Scrolls*, 178; J. Maier, *Temple*, 55) speaks of two treasonous crimes against Israel for which the appropriate punishment is almost certainly held to be crucifixion, and the scriptural basis is given by reference to Deut 21:22–23 (see Fitzmyer, who essentially agrees with Yadin, while being somewhat reluctant to say that the author of 4QpNah explicitly justified Janneus's crucifixion of numerous Pharisees as a deed called for by the Jewish Law; *Advance*, 132). At any rate, in Qumran Deut 21:23 was read as a reference to crucifixion as the form of punishment appropriate to an Israelite cursed by God for a heinous crime.

ploys it twice, in Gal 2:19 and in Rom 6:6, referring to one's participation in Christ's own crucifixion by suffering that death with him.

In fact, Gal 2:19 and Rom 6:6 belong to a large complex in Paul's theology marked by his use of the expressions "with Christ" and "in Christ."[188] From the immense modern literature on this language of participation, four further points can be drawn:

(1) It seems probable that the earliest focus in this thought complex lay on the sure hope of participating in Christ's *life* at the parousia, a hope that was probably derived from traditions promising to the righteous an undisturbed eschatological fellowship with the Son of Man.

And the Lord of Spirits will abide with them, and with that Son of Man shall they eat and lie down and rise up for ever and ever (*1 Enoch* 62:14).

The earliest church seems to have seen Christ's resurrection as the beginning of the general resurrection, and thus as an event that would soon affect, in one way or the other, all human beings. Believers alive at the moment of the parousia would experience this general resurrection in the form of the apocalyptic "meeting" (*apantêsis*) with the Lord Jesus in the air, the result being that they would therefore be "with the Lord" in the sense of participating in his life (1 Thess 4:16–17, a pre-Pauline formula).

(2) When was this participatory language expanded to include not only Christ's resurrected life but also his death? It is probable that the *thought* of participating in Christ's death and burial was tied to the act of baptism prior to Paul (Rom 6:3–8). It may have been Paul himself, however, who forged an indelible link between the motif of participation in Christ's death and the expressions "with Christ" and "in Christ" (note 2 Cor 13:4 where the incorporative force of "with him" is shown by its being interchangeable with "in him"). The main accent of Paul's expression "to be crucified with Christ" lies, therefore, on incorporation into the Christ whose own path determines the destiny of those who are bound to him.

(3) The language of participation in Christ's cross points to a relationship that runs far deeper than that of disciple to teacher. Paul does not perceive himself to be charged to repeat Jesus' teaching, by standing in a line of tradition extending from rabbi Jesus to rabbi Peter to rabbi Paul (see Gal 1:12). On the contrary, Paul now exists (perfect tense, "I have been crucified with Christ"), not as disciple, but as one cocrucified.

(4) Finally, that perception of himself is as thoroughly apocalyptic as is his view of Christ's death itself. As we have seen, the crucifixion is *the* apocalyptic, cosmic event in which God confronts the powers that hold all of humanity in subjection, God's purpose being to bring all into the freedom that he bestows under his own hegemony. The apocalyptic nature of Paul's cocrucifixion with Christ is placed in relief when one notices who and what suffers crucifixion: In Gal 2:19 it is Christ and Paul who are crucified; in 3:1 it is Christ; in 5:24 it is

[188]Cf. Siber, *Christus.*

the cosmic power Paul calls "the Flesh"; and in 6:14 it is the cosmos itself and, once again, Paul.

In sum, Paul's participation in Christ's crucifixion is the form of the death Paul has already experienced as the paradigmatic eschatological *anthrôpos*. In this event Paul was torn away from the cosmos in which he had lived, and it was torn away from him. For in dying with Christ on Christ's cross, this zealous Pharisee suffered the loss of the Law, surely his earlier guide to the whole of the cosmos.

3:1–5 THE GALATIAN CHURCHES' BIRTH IDENTITY AND THEIR PRESENT LEANINGS

TRANSLATION

3:1. You foolish Galatians! Who has cast a spell on you, doing so in spite of the fact that in my sermons a picture of Jesus Christ marked by crucifixion was painted before your eyes? 2. Tell me just one thing! Did you receive the Spirit because you observed the Law, or as a result of the proclamation that has the power to elicit faith? 3. Are you really so foolish as to think that, having begun in the Spirit, you are now being perfected by means of the flesh? 4. Have you experienced such remarkable things in vain, if, indeed, that is conceivable? 5. When God even now supplies the Spirit to you, and when he works wonders in the midst of your communities, is he doing those things because you observe the Law, or is he doing them through the proclamation that elicits your faith?

LITERARY STRUCTURE AND SYNOPSIS

We have noted that Paul composed the climax of his revelatory history proper in the form of an evangelical argument addressed to the Teachers in the presence of the Galatian churches (2:15–21). Now he traces the march of the gospel into Galatia itself, thus continuing to some degree his account of the history created by the gospel. There are, however, several marks of disjuncture, indicating the beginning of a new section at 3:1.

Paul employs for a second time the epistolary rebuke (cf. 1:6), turning his attention back to the Galatians themselves in a sharp tone of voice. He then continues this acerbic note in the style of the diatribe, posing with some degree of sarcasm a series of rhetorical questions without counterpart in the preceding material.[1]

If the new section begins at 3:1, where does it end? With regard both to style

---

[1]Bultmann, *Stil*; Aune, *Literary Environment*, 200–201; Stowers, *Diatribe*.

and to substance there is a new turn at 3:6, where Paul begins to construct a scriptural exegesis that is tightly organized, however difficult it may be to trace every step in the line of exegetical argument. We see, then, that 3:1–5 is the letter's second rebuke paragraph. In it Paul contrasts the happy march of the gospel into Galatia with the odious defection occurring at the present time. For Gentiles the gospel message that had — and has — the power to evoke faith is the opposite of observance of the Law.

NOTES

3:1. *You foolish Galatians!* Immediately before he began the sketch of revelatory history (1:13–2:21), Paul addressed the Galatians engagingly as "my brothers and sisters" (1:11). Now, having sharpened his tongue by recalling his confrontation with Peter in Antioch, and by composing an emotional and combative speech directed to the seductive Teachers in Galatia, Paul stings the Galatians themselves with an emotional ejaculation and with a form of address that suggests they are distinctly lacking in wisdom.

Although comparing "the wise" to "the foolish" is a *topos* of letter writing, we would go astray were we to apply standard definitions to those terms.[2] As the following words make clear (and cf. 1 Cor 1:17–31), Paul sees only one true antidote to foolishness: the proclamation of the crucified Christ. With the genuine hearing of this proclamation wisdom begins, and with the departure from this proclamation foolishness sets in. The Galatians are foolish, therefore, because, by moving toward an observance of the Law which they think will be salvific, they are losing sight of the event that makes the world what it really is, Christ's atoning death and resurrection (6:14–15).[3]

Galatians. This identity marker is a strong reason for thinking that Paul founded the Galatian churches in the old ethnic kingdom centered in Ankyra and Pessinus. It is unlikely that he would have referred to citizens of the southern part of the Roman province by this name.[4]

cast a spell. Paul believes that in order fully to identify the Teachers' seductive wiles he must reach into the vocabulary of magic, for these people are not only frightening the Galatians; they are also leading them astray by casting a spell over them.[5] Given Gentile aversion to circumcision, the Teachers must indeed have

[2]Regarding the *topoi* of letter writing, see Introduction §10.
[3]Paul does not specify a group within the Galatian congregations. Presumably, his information has led him to think that a great many of those who have not yet succumbed to the Teachers' message are seriously considering the path of Law observance (see 5:2; 6:16; and cf. Jewett, "Agitators," 209).
[4]See Introduction §3.
[5]This is the only place in his letters at which Paul uses the verb *baskainô*, "to bewitch," "to put the evil eye upon," just as Galatians is the only letter in which he employs the verb *tarassô*, "to frighten" (1:7; 5:10). Both verbs are selected by Paul to refer to the Teachers' activity, indicating that they are damaging the minds of the Galatians; Delling, "*baskainô*," 595.

been virtual magicians to have made the Galatians long to come under the Law.[6] With his rhetorical question Paul thus suggests that by listening appreciatively to the Teachers' gospel, the Galatians are in fact leaving the realm of faith for that of superstition. When Gentiles take up observance of the Law as though that were salvific, they give themselves over to — or they return to (4:9) — a belief in magic.

in spite of the fact. In antiquity people were often thought to fall under magic spells.[7] As the sequence of Paul's clauses implies, however, it is to him astonishing that that should happen in the case of persons who have heard the true gospel.

a picture of Jesus Christ marked by crucifixion was painted. The verb *prographô* can have either of two major accents: to proclaim publicly, or to proclaim by providing a vivid portrait. Here we see a combination of the two. Paul told the Galatians the hideous story of Jesus' death by crucifixion, not, to be sure, so as to bring them to cheap tears, but so as to bring them face-to-face with three facts: (a) Jesus died as a condemned criminal. (b) His death is the event in which God has begun to free the whole of the cosmos from bondage to the powers of evil (1:4). (c) The Galatians were grasped by God in the realistic message of this death, and their being so grasped was signified in the baptism by which they participated in the death of that condemned criminal (3:13, 26–29).[8] "The kerygmatic proclamation [would become] the proclamation of an idea only, [were it not] narration as well."[9] Yet this narrative is more punctiliar than linear. Paul told the Galatians neither some of Jesus' parables nor a story of his life. He vividly narrated the essentially punctiliar event of Jesus' betrayal (cf. 1 Cor 11:23–26), condemnation, crucifixion, and resurrection. Now, referring to that original proclamation, Paul prepares to develop still further the climactic antinomy of the historical sketch in 1:13–2:21: the Law versus the crucifixion of Christ.

before your eyes. Like other ancient storytellers, Paul was able to speak "so vividly and so impressively that his hearers imagined the matter to have happened right before their eyes."[10] As we will learn, however, in the next verse, there is more to the gospel story than vividness. Paul recalls that the Galatians' eyes were made perceptive by the power of the message itself.

2. *Tell me just one thing!* With a rhetorical question Paul will now compel the Galatians to enter into the argument he is making against the false gospel of the Teachers.

receive the Spirit. Less immediately clear than the rhetorical nature of Paul's question is his reason for selecting the subject on which he will compel the Galatians to speak: the Spirit. Up to this point he has had no difficulty formulating his thoughts without such a reference. He has begun the present paragraph, moreover, not by speaking of the Spirit, but by recalling with great emphasis his proclamation of Christ. Why does he turn now to speak of the Spirit?

[6]Regarding Gentile aversion to circumcision, see, for example, Josephus *Ant.* 20.139; idem *J. W.* 2.454.
[7]See Neusner et al., *Magic.*
[8]Cf. Siegert, *Argumentation,* 254.
[9]Käsemann, *Questions,* 97; see also Hays, *Faith,* passim.
[10]H. D. Betz 131.

The reason is that he knows the Spirit to be one of the chief topics by which the Teachers are currently leading the Galatians from true faith into the realm of superstition and magic. Specifically, from v 5 we can draw an important conclusion about the worship services presided over by the Teachers. In those services they are showing the Galatians that Law-observant exegesis of the scriptures is the means by which one can be assured of a steady supply of the Spirit and of its wonder-working power.

To combat this virus, Paul takes the Galatians back to their birth as churches of Christ. Using a locution widely employed among early Christians to refer to the inception of Christian life ("to receive the Holy Spirit," e.g., Acts 2:38; John 20:22), Paul speaks of something that happens to human beings.[11] God causes the Spirit of his Son to invade their hearts (4:6). In the lives of the Galatians things began to be the way they really are when Paul preached Christ crucified to them and when the Spirit of Christ came upon them (cf. 3:14).

Did you receive the Spirit because you observed the Law, or as a result of the proclamation that has the power to elicit faith? Paul's rhetorical question finds its point, not surprisingly, in an antinomy:

Did you receive the Spirit
  by observing the Law or
  by *akoê pisteôs?*

For the Old Age side of the antinomy Paul uses a phrase he has employed three times in 2:16 — "by observing the Law" (= "by observance of the Law"). But the phrase on the New Age side — *ex akoês pisteôs* — appears here for the first time, and the precise force of it is not immediately apparent, as one can see from the various readings that have been proposed by interpreters.[12] The two nouns, *akoê* and *pistis,* form an abbreviation that poses two major translation problems: the meaning of *akoê* and the force of the expression *akoê pisteôs.* The best rendering is "the proclamation that has the power to elicit faith" (Comment #31).

3. *having begun in the Spirit, you are now being perfected by means of the flesh?* The image projected by these two clauses is that of a line with a starting point and an ending point, and along which there is movement. Paul accents the two ends of the line, thus employing the ancient eschatological pattern in which the end-time corresponds to the primal-time (e.g., Isaiah 43; cf. Heb 13:2). In a sarcastic tone of voice — certainly not missed by the Galatians — Paul portrays a development in which end does not at all correspond to the salvific beginning.[13]

Paul accents the lack of correspondence by identifying the primal-time as that of the Spirit and the end-time as that of the flesh, these two nouns being presented here for the first time in the letter as a pair of opposites. He puts them in

[11] See Lull, *Spirit.*
[12] Well summarized by Hays, *Faith,* 143–146.
[13] In Phil 1:6 Paul uses the verbs "begin" and "perfect" to refer without sarcasm to God's work in the Philippian church (Gnilka, *Philipperbrief,* 46). In that passage what is begun is the path along which God calls his church, destining it for wholesome perfection (Phil 3:12–14).

the dative case, thinking here of the Spirit and the flesh primarily as means that enable the human being to accomplish something. The Galatians' life as Christian congregations was begun by the powerful advent of the Spirit of God's Son (4:6). Now they are claiming to find a final perfection by means of the flesh, and that claim elicits Paul's derisive question.

Precisely what does Paul have in mind in his use here of the terms "perfection" and "flesh"? See Comment #32. With considerable sarcasm Paul refers to an important aspect of the Teachers' message: Is one really put on the road to perfection by removing the foreskin of the penis?

4. *Have you experienced such remarkable things . . . ?* Although the verb *paschô* can mean "to suffer," Paul uses it here to mean simply "to experience." And with the correlative adjective *tosauta*, "such remarkable things," he refers again to the Galatians' initial experience of the Spirit.

in vain. Paul momentarily entertains the thought that the Galatians will persist in linking their experience of the Spirit to their observance of the Law. If they do this, they will cause the beginning of their life as Christian communities to have no lasting result.

if, indeed, that is conceivable. In the next breath Paul recoils from that awesome thought, writing literally "if indeed it should be in vain." The Galatians are genuinely in danger (cf. 4:11, 20; 5:4; 6:8), but Paul can scarcely bring himself to consider the possibility of miscarriage: "Surely it is inconceivable!"

Why does miscarriage scarcely lie within the realm of possibility? Certainly not because of a steadfast character on the part of the Galatians. The steadfast one is the God who does not commence his liberating work in order to carry it partway through (Phil 1:6; Gal 5:10). It is God's faithfulness, then, that provides the foundation of Paul's confidence.

5. *When God even now supplies the Spirit to you, and when he works wonders in the midst of your communities, is he doing those things because you observe the Law, or is he doing them through the proclamation that elicits your faith?* Repeating to a large extent the rhetorical question of v 2, Paul makes two changes, both of them signaled by his use of substantive participles in the present tense:

he who is supplying the Spirit to you (*ho epichorêgôn*), and
he who is working wonders in your midst ([*ho*] *energôn*).

The first change is the matter of tense. Whereas in v 2 Paul asked about a past event, the genesis of the Galatian churches, he now inquires about the fabric of their present life, using present participles to refer to the continuous action of God.[14] That is to say, having spoken of the punctiliar past in vv 1–2 and of the relation of the past to the present in vv 3–4, Paul now completes the transition from past to continuous present by speaking solely of the latter in v 5: "When God even now supplies the Spirit."[15]

[14]See MT 150–151; ZBG §§371–372.
[15]Cf. the participle in 1 Thess 4:8 (*didonta*) and the prepositional phrase in Phil 1:19 (*epichorêgia tou pneumatos Iêsou Christou*, where it is debated whether the genitive is objective or subjective). One notes similarly Paul's use of the present participle in Gal 4:6

The second change is the shift from a verb of which the Galatians are the subject ("Did *you* receive the Spirit?") to the substantive participles by which Paul refers to God and his action.[16] That is not a subject on which the Galatians would have been slow to speak. One can easily imagine their saying:

Paul, God is steadily supplying the Spirit to us; but, truly instructed by the Teachers, we see now that God is doing that because we have begun to be observant of the Law.

Given this state of affairs, Paul reformulates the question of v 2 so as to speak of God's present activity:

In reality is God doing that because of your incipient Law observance or because your church life continues to be marked by the power of God's own message, the gospel that has the power to elicit faith?

By putting the question in this way, Paul presupposes two things that prove to be of importance in the reading of the letter.

First, the worship services presided over by the Teachers are focused not only on the observance of the Law but also and concretely on exegesis of the Law as the faithful activity to which God responds by continuing to give the Spirit. A number of Jewish Christians of Paul's time were convinced of that link.[17]

Second, the leadership of the Galatian churches has not fallen altogether into the hands of the Teachers. At least some of the persons to whom Paul entrusted catechetical responsibility when he departed are still active, and they continue to proclaim the Pauline gospel (6:6; Introduction §12). In their work God is even now continuing to supply the wondrous Spirit.

COMMENT #31
A BASIC PAULINE ANTINOMY: HUMAN OBSERVANCE OF THE LAW VERSUS THE DIVINE MESSAGE THAT ELICITS FAITH

With the rhetorical question of 3:2, Paul asks the Galatians to recall the juncture at which they received the Spirit, thus becoming children of God (cf. 4:6).

Did you receive the Spirit
by observing the Law or
by *akoê pisteôs*?

(*krazon*) to refer to the Spirit's present action in causing the Galatians to cry out "Abba, Father."

[16]Cf. "the God who called you" in 1:6.

[17]The pseudo-apostles who invaded Paul's Corinthian church drew a causative connection between exegesis and the supply of the Spirit; see Georgi, *Opponents*, 258–264; idem, "Corinthians, Second Letter to the," 185. See also *Jub.* 1:22–25; *Mek.*, Beshallach 7, lines 133–138; Schäfer, *Geist*, 114, 132–133 ("Study of the Torah makes possible the gift of the Holy Spirit"); Barclay, *Obeying*, 84. The thought that Law observance is connected with the coming of a new spirit is at least as old as Ezek 11:19–20.

In the Note on this verse, we saw that the final phrase, *ex akoês pisteôs*, poses two major translation problems: the meaning of *akoê* and the force of the expression *akoê pisteôs*. As these problems cannot be solved simply on linguistic grounds, they are best approached in the present Comment, even though that will involve us in a few linguistic observations.

WITH THE NOUN AKOÊ, DOES PAUL REFER TO THE ACT OF HEARING OR TO THAT WHICH IS HEARD?

The noun *akoê* can refer to the faculty of hearing (thus also the organ with which one hears, the ear), and in some instances the active use of that faculty, the act of hearing. Alternatively, *akoê* can have a passive meaning, referring to that which is heard, such as a report or message. In the context of 3:2 neither meaning can be excluded on linguistic grounds.

(1) *The active sense* — a reference to the act of hearing — has been elected by a number of commentators, the underlying assumption being that Paul intends to refer to alternatives that lie in the human sphere, one human act being contrasted with another human act:

Did you receive the Spirit
by your act of being Law-observant or
by your act of hearing?[18]

But that assumption begs the question that has to be faced: Does Paul intend to refer to human alternatives — to be observant of the Law or to listen — or does he speak in the first line of a human act and in the second line of an act of God, thus referring in the proper sense to an antinomy that has arisen in the dawn of the new creation (cf. 1:1, and see Comment #51)? Until that question is considered, there is no good reason to assume that *akoê* should be rendered "act of hearing."[19]

(2) *The passive sense* — a reference to the message that is heard — is suggested strongly by two factors, the first being internal to Galatians, the second being found in Romans. First, we can be confident that Paul expects the Galatians to interpret the contrast between Law observance and *akoê* in the light of the antinomies of 1:1; 1:11–12; and 2:16, each of which has placed opposite one another,

the acts of human beings   the apocalyptic act of God in Christ.

The rhetorical question would thus seem to be

Did you receive the Spirit
by *your* act of being Law-observant or
by the message enacted by *God?*

[18]An exegetical argument for this sense has been advanced by Barrett, *Romans*, 205, but it has been correctly refuted by Hays, *Faith*, 146–148.
[19]*Pace* Murphy-O'Connor, Review of H. D. Betz, 260.

Second, we can see that Paul clearly intends the passive sense of *akoê* in Rom 10:16–17, where he speaks emphatically — as he does in the present passage — about persons coming to be followers of Christ. To be sure, interpreters have debated the construal of the term *akoê* in Romans 10 also, but the case for taking it as a reference to the gospel message is so weighty as to be almost certain. In Rom 10:16 Paul quotes Isa 53:1 (LXX),

"Lord, who has believed our *akoê*?"

Here *akoê* renders the Hebrew word *šĕmû'â*, a noun that had become, by the time of Second Isaiah, a technical term for Yahweh's message, indeed for Yahweh's revelation. Thus, "Lord, who has believed what we have heard (that is to say, your message)?" After quoting this unambiguous text, Paul provides his exegesis in Rom 10:17, "Thus, faith comes from *akoê* . . ." In this exegesis of Isa 53:1 Paul gives the Romans no hint that he intends the term *akoê* to bear a meaning other than the one it clearly bears in the text of Isaiah. It follows that in this instance he uses the word *akoê* to refer to the gospel message uttered by God through the apostle.

The same is surely his intention in Gal 3:2. Paul is not asking the Galatians which of two human acts served as the generative locus in which they received the Spirit, a decision on their part to keep the Law or a decision on their part to hear with faith. On the contrary, he is asking rhetorically whether that generative locus was

> their act in becoming observant of the Law or
> God's message (*akoê*).

Paul knows the answer; the Galatians know the answer; Paul now compels them to recall it.

THE EXPRESSION AKOÊ PISTEÔS: THE MESSAGE THAT IS FAITH OR THE MESSAGE THAT ELICITS FAITH?

Given that conclusion, we ask about the meaning of the expression *akoê pisteôs*, lit. "the message of faith." Here again there are two major possibilities: (1) Paul may use the two nouns in apposition to one another, saying, that is, that faith is the message.[20] In Galatians itself Paul twice employs the term "faith" to refer to the gospel that is believed (1:23 and 6:10). Thus, the question of 3:2 may be "Did you receive the Spirit by your act of becoming Law-observant or by the message that consists of the gospel of faith?"

(2) Far more probable is the reading in which the noun "faith" identifies the goal of the message.[21] That, as we have seen, is the thrust of Paul's exegetical

---

[20] On the epexegetical genitive, see BDF §167.

[21] On the genitive of direction or purpose, see BDF §166, where *anastasis zoês* (John 5:29) is cited as the equivalent of *anastasis eis zoên* (2 Macc 7:14). Cf. further Bultmann, "*pisteuô*," 213; Schlier 122; Bonnard 63; Grässer, *Bund*, 88 n365.

argument in Rom 10:16–17, where he identifies the origin of faith. Faith is awakened by the gospel; the gospel has as its goal the awakening of faith. So in Gal 3:2 Paul's rhetorical question is whether the Galatians received the Spirit as the result of their observance of the Law or as the result of God's message (*akoê*), the gospel that has the power to elicit, to ignite, to kindle faith (*pistis*).[22] And in 3:5 he repeats that rhetorical question in the present tense. Recognizing that God is even now supplying the Spirit to the Galatians and thus working miracles in their communities, he asks whether God is doing that as a result of their commencing observance of the Law or as a result of the continued proclamation among them of the faith-eliciting gospel.

This conclusion is crucial to the interpretation of the entire letter, for it confirms the reading of 2:16 suggested earlier: Paul does not at all focus his attention — and thus his theology — on alternative lines of human action, such as

being observant of the Law   believing in Christ.

His focus lies on the apocalyptic event of God's action in Christ and — to say the same thing in other words — on the faith-eliciting message in which Christ is proclaimed.[23] In the rhetorical question of 3:2, then, Paul voices one of the apocalyptic antinomies that have arisen in the dawning of the new creation (Comment #51). The generative context in which the Spirit fell upon the Galatians was not their act of commencing observance of the Law; it was God's act in the revelatory proclamation of Jesus Christ suffering crucifixion, the act by which God kindled their faith.[24]

COMMENT #32
BEGINNING IN THE SPIRIT AND BEING PERFECTED IN THE FLESH

In the third of the rhetorical questions of 3:2–3 Paul asks the Galatians about the extent of their lethal foolishness: Does it reach so far as to include the conviction that, having begun their Christian lives seized by the power of the Spirit, they are now being perfected in the flesh? In formulating this sarcastic question Paul doubtless has in mind the Galatians' tendency to credit the proclamation of the Teachers. But what role is played in the Teachers' message by the idea that one can be perfected in the flesh? That is a question we can best approach by asking about the Galatians' linguistic experience with the terms "flesh" and "perfection."

---

[22] Bonnard suggestively speaks of the preaching "which produces faith" (63), a rendering that leans in the right direction, but goes a bit too far in its determination to avoid thinking of faith as a human deed. The mystery of faith's genesis is better represented by Schlier's translation: "the gift of the Spirit . . . from the revelation that kindles faith" (122); cf. Eckstein, *Verheissung*, 86–88.

[23] Cf. Keck, *Paul and His Letters*, 85.

[24] Cf. Käsemann, *Perspectives*, 84.

THE WORD "FLESH" IN THE GALATIANS' VOCABULARY PRIOR TO THE ARRIVAL OF THE TEACHERS

Although we cannot be certain, we may presume that the Galatians were acquainted to some degree with strains of medical and philosophical thought in which the term "flesh" played a role. They may have known in a rudimentary form, for example, the Pythagorean polarity in which flesh and bones form a contrast with the soul and sense perception.[25] Flesh is the corruptible part of the human being. Moreover, given the wide influence of the ideas of Epicurus (sometimes misunderstood by the ancients themselves), the Galatians may have been acquainted with the view that the flesh is the seat of desire.[26]

Prior to hearing the Teachers' message they will have had no distinctly Jewish or Christian instruction in which the term "flesh" played a role. There is no indication in any of Paul's letters that he mentioned flesh in his initial, evangelistic preaching.[27] It is true that in Gal 5:21 Paul gives the Galatians what he identifies as a second warning against various kinds of hedonistic activity. There is no good reason to think, however, that he issued the earlier warning under the banner of the term "flesh." One notes that that term plays no role in the similar warning of 1 Thess 4:1–8.

FROM THE TEACHERS THE GALATIANS LEARN SOME NEW THINGS ABOUT THE FLESH AND ABOUT PERFECTION

The Term "flesh"

It was the Teachers who first extended the Galatians' understanding of "flesh," using the term in two ways.

(1) *Flesh as the piece of skin cut from the end of the penis in circumcision.* The letter's final reference to "flesh" is revealing.

> Those who wish to put on a good show in the flesh, they are the ones who are trying to compel you to undergo circumcision . . . Their insistence on circumcising you springs, then, from their desire to boast in regard to your flesh (*en tê hymetera sarki*; Gal 6:12–13).

Paul's sarcasm warns us not to draw from this passage a simple and direct quotation from the Teachers' sermons or even from their daily conversation. One supposes that the Teachers actually said something like, "We are proud of the fruit of our mission; many of you Galatians are entering the blessed family of Abraham by commencing your observance of the Law in the rite of circumcision. God be praised!"

Certain that such euphoric language obscures the truth, Paul uses the term "flesh" here in a quite literal sense, referring to the *akrobystia*, the foreskin that,

---

[25]DK 1.450.4; Schweizer, "*sarx*," 102.

[26]Epicurus *Sent.* 4 and 18; Schweizer, "*sarx*," 103.

[27]The word is absent from 1 Thessalonians, the letter probably written before Galatians. See the observations made by Jewett, *Terms*, 108–111.

at the birth of a male, covers the end of the penis.[28] "The Teachers take pride in cutting off your foreskins!"

But does Paul reflect in his sarcasm the Teachers' own use of the term "flesh"? Quite probably he does. When we consider the second exegetical section of Galatians (4:21–5:1), we will see grounds for thinking that the Teachers spoke to the Galatians at length about God's covenant (Comment #45). Specifically, they took as one of their major themes the necessity for Gentiles to find their place in God's people Israel, by entering the covenant God made with Abraham. In developing this theme the Teachers doubtless drew in some way on the story in Genesis 17 (or on some retelling of it, such as we find in *Jubilees*). There God explicitly defines the covenant he makes with Abraham, linking it to the term "flesh":

This is my covenant, which you shall keep, between me and you and your offspring after you: Every male among you shall be circumcised. You shall circumcise the flesh of your foreskins (*tên sarka tês akrobystias hymôn*), and it shall be a sign of the covenant between me and you . . . So shall my covenant be in your flesh (*epi tês sarkos hymôn*) an everlasting covenant (Gen 17:10–13; NRSV).[29]

It was in the Teachers' expositions of such texts as this that the Galatians first developed a longing to enter the Abrahamic covenant, and it was in these expositions that the Galatian Gentiles sensed for the first time the ancient Hebraic connection between "covenant" and "flesh." They were convinced that, by removing the flesh of the *akrobystia*, as Abraham himself did, they entered into the covenant people, thus inheriting the blessing spoken long ago to Abraham by God.

In confidently overseeing this rite, then, the Teachers probably specified the connection between "covenant" and "circumcision" by referring to the covenant literally as "God's covenant *in your flesh*" (*epi tês sarkos hymôn*). And it is against this background that one senses the sharpness of Paul's comment in 6:12–13. Using the term "flesh" in this literal way, he says with effective sarcasm, "The Teachers boast in regard to your flesh. That is to say, they take pride in the large number of your foreskins they have cut off!"

(2) *The Flesh as a fearsome power.* From another of Paul's statements we can see that the Teachers used the term "flesh" in a second way. In 5:16 Paul gives the Galatians a solemn promise:

---

[28]The expression "your flesh" makes this reading certain. "When 'flesh' is qualified with the possessive pronoun 'your,' it is clearly . . . the flesh which was cut [off] in circumcision!" (Jewett, *Terms*, 96). As Jewett points out, Schweizer had noted that in a context dealing with circumcision the LXX twice adds *sarx* where the Hebrew text does not demand it (Gen 34:24; Jer 9:26).

[29]Later traditions continued and embroidered the connection between "covenant" and "flesh." Abraham, for example, was said to have "established the covenant in his flesh" (Sir 44:20). According to passages cited by Barclay, the rabbis sometimes referred to "the covenant of flesh" (*Obeying*, 180 n4).

In contradistinction to the Teachers, I, Paul, say to you: Lead your daily life guided by the Spirit, and, in this way, you will not end up carrying out the Impulsive Desire of the Flesh.

As this translation indicates, there are grounds for thinking that Paul words his promise by changing fundamentally a promise the Galatians are already hearing from the Teachers:

We say to you: Lead your daily life guided by the Law, and, doing so, you will not carry out the Impulsive Desire of the Flesh.

In the Note on 5:16 (see also Comment #49) we will see that the final two words — *epithymia sarkos* — form a Greek rendering of the Hebrew expression *yēṣer bāśār*, thus referring to a basically malignant power known in Jewish and Jewish-Christian traditions as "the Evil Impulse or Inclination."[30] Both Jews and Jewish Christians of Paul's time spoke at length about this monster — occasionally balancing it with something like a Good Inclination (*T. Asher* 1:5) — and with considerable consistency they identified the Law as the God-given antidote to it.[31] We can thus be confident that the Teachers spoke to the Galatians at some length about the Evil Inclination, referring to it by the Greek expression *hê epithymia sarkos*, "the Impulsive Desire of the Flesh."

Did the Teachers also draw a connection between their use of the term "flesh" to refer to the foreskin and their use of the same word to refer to the Impulsive Desire of the *Flesh*? That question takes us back to Gal 3:3, and specifically to Paul's sarcastic question: "Do you really think that you are now being *perfected* in the flesh?"

The Term "perfection"
(1) *Perfection as victory over the Impulsive Desire of the Flesh via the nomistic circumcision of the flesh.* In the Qumran sect, victory over the Impulsive Desire of the Flesh was connected with the motif of perfection:

Hear now, my sons, and I will uncover your eyes so that you may see and understand the works of God . . . so that you may walk *perfectly* in all his ways and not be drawn *by the thoughts of the Guilty Impulse* (*běmaḥšěbôt yēṣer 'ašmâ*) and by lustful eyes . . . (CD 2:14–16; Vermes, altered).

And a similar passage in the *Rule of the Community* speaks of circumcising the Impulse!

[30]The literature on the Evil Impulse/Evil Inclination/Impulsive Desire of the Flesh is extensive. See especially Porter, "Yecer hara"; Davies, *Paul*, 20–25; Urbach, *Sages*, 471–483; Flusser, "Dead Sea Sect," 255; Jewett, *Terms*, 93; Marcus, "James"; idem, "Paul." An important theological analysis of desire is now given in Hamerton-Kelly, *Violence*; see index there.

[31]The major texts are well considered in the two studies of Marcus mentioned in the preceding footnote. See also Comment #49.

[No member of the community] shall walk in the stubbornness of his heart so that he strays after his heart, after his eyes, and after the thought of his Impulse (*maḥăšebet yiṣrô*). On the contrary, they shall circumcise in the community the foreskin of the Impulse (*'ôrlat yēṣer*) . . . (1QS 5:5; Vermes, altered).

Connections of this sort were also made in Jewish-Christian circles, such as those reflected in James.[32]

Paul's sarcastic reference in 3:3 to the Galatians' "being perfected in the flesh" suggests that the Teachers belonged to one of those Jewish-Christian circles. Encountering the Pauline churches in Galatia, the Teachers found the members to be typical Gentiles, far from perfect (5:15). And in the Teachers' estimation, the reason for the Galatians' imperfection was not difficult to find: They were subject to the power of the Impulsive Desire of the Flesh, because Paul had failed to provide them with the needed instruction about the divinely provided antidote, the Law. The Teachers therefore told the Galatians not only of God's demand of perfection in the form of victory over the Impulsive Desire of the *Flesh* but also of the route to this perfecting victory, the circumcision of the *flesh* as the commencement of Law observance.[33]

(2) *The paradigm of Abraham, the one who achieved perfect victory over the Impulsive Desire of the Flesh by circumcising the flesh.* It is possible that the Teachers specified this part of their instruction by citing Abraham as the paradigm. We know that in other regards they gave a very large role to the patriarch, to the blessed covenant God made with him, to God's assurance that Abraham would have innumerable descendants through Sarah, and so on (see Comments #33 and #45). Jewish traditions, and traditions proper to Jewish Christians as well, also spoke of Abraham as the paradigmatic proselyte who achieved perfect victory over the Impulsive Flesh by observing the Law, and specifically by circumcising himself:

Abraham did not walk in it [the Impulse] . . . he kept the commandments of God and did not choose the will of his own spirit (CD 3:2–3; Vermes, altered).[34]

[Abraham's] faith was brought to perfection by his works (Jas 2:22; cf. Gen 17:1), specifically by his circumcising himself.[35]

[32]See quotations from James below, and Marcus, "James."
[33]On circumcision as perfection, see also such rabbinic traditions as *Gen. Rab.* 11:6; 46:4–5. Cf. the reference to circumcision as empowerment in *Tg. Cant.* 3:8.
[34]As the Teachers were engaged in evangelistic activity among Gentiles, it may be important to note that CD 3:2–3 falls in the passage identified by Murphy-O'Connor as possibly being a missionary document ("Missionary").
[35]For this last motif, two rabbinic references are worth citing: (a) *m. Ned.* 3:11: "Great is circumcision, for in spite of all the virtues that Abraham our father fulfilled, he was not called perfect, until he was circumcised, as it is said, 'Walk before me, and be thou perfect' (Gen 17:1)." (b) *Gen. Rab.* 46:4; circumcision removed Abraham's only blemish; thereafter he was perfect. See further *Jub.* 19:26–31; God's blessing of Abraham is linked with the overcoming of the Impulse (the spirit of Mastema).

We cannot say with confidence that the Teachers included such affirmations in their discourses on Abraham. We can be confident that they spoke about the need for perfection in the form of victory over the Impulsive Desire of the *Flesh*, and about circumcision of the *flesh* as the initial point in the line leading to that perfection.[36] In the present Comment it will suffice to return to Gal 3:3.

PAUL'S REFERENCE TO FLESH IN GAL 3:3

By placing the term "flesh" opposite the term "Spirit," Paul intends in the first instance to refer literally to the foreskin of the penis.[37] Given his knowledge of the Teachers' discourses, he phrases his rhetorical question in a way that conveys biting sarcasm:

Are you Galatians really so foolish as to think that, having begun your life in Christ by the power of his Spirit, you can now move on to perfection by means of a severed piece of flesh?

3:6–9 DESCENT FROM FAITHFUL ABRAHAM

TRANSLATION

3:6. Things were the same with Abraham: "He trusted God, and, as the final act in the drama by which God set Abraham fully right, God recognized Abraham's faithful trust." 7. You know, therefore, that those whose identity is derived from faith, these are the children of Abraham. 8. And the scripture, foreseeing what is now happening — namely that God is rectifying the Gentiles on the basis of faith — preached the gospel ahead of time to Abraham, saying, "In you all the Gentiles will be blessed." 9. So then, it is those whose identity is derived from faith who are blessed with faithful Abraham.

LITERARY STRUCTURE AND SYNOPSIS

Knowing that the Teachers have persuaded many of the Galatians that they can have an assured supply of the Spirit if they order their communal life by obser-

---

[36] It is also possible that, as part of their somewhat exotic instructions about the relationship between holy times and the movement of the cosmic elements (Note on 4:10 and Comment #41), the Teachers spoke of annual perfection. See *telesphoreô* in Philo *de Op. Mundi* 59.

[37] Paul has already used the term *sarx*, "flesh," three times, referring to human beings (1:16 and 2:16) and to the worldly sphere in which human beings necessarily live (2:20; cf. 1 Cor 5:10). In none of these cases does he pair the term with *pneuma*, "spirit."

vant exegesis of scripture, Paul allows the question of v 5 to lead into the first of his own exegetical sections. Both the basic character and the outer limits of this section are clear.[38] The series of OT texts quoted and interpreted in 3:6–16 shows that Paul is composing a unit that is fundamentally exegetical. And, although the series of quotations ends in 3:16, thematic considerations indicate that the unit continues until the opening reference to descent from Abraham (3:6–7) has found its modulated reprise in the reference to descent from God in 4:7. Indeed, careful attention to the latter part of the section shows that even there Paul continues to function as an exegete, quoting and interpreting early Christian baptismal, christological, and pneumatological formulas, so that, whereas the opening reference to descent from Abraham takes the form of scriptural exegesis, the closing references to descent from God (3:26; 4:7) are formulated by interpreting Christian tradition (Comment #40). An exegetical section, then, Gal 3:6–4:7 is focused primarily on the related themes of descent and inheritance.

With regard to structure, before Paul crafts the final climax in 4:7, he forms intermediate conclusions at 3:18, 3:25, and 3:29, in effect marking off four subsections:

3:6–18. In this first subsection Paul constructs a lengthy catena of scriptural texts accompanied by exegetical comments in which he addresses several matters in three distinct paragraphs. First he speaks of descent from Abraham (vv 6–9). Then he passes to the motif of universal slavery under the curse of the Law, formulating an intermediate climax by the announcement of liberation from that slavery in the cross of Christ, the person he will later identify as the promised seed of Abraham (vv 10–14; cf. vv 16, 19). Finally, in vv 15–18 he develops an antinomy that is implied in the first two paragraphs, namely the antinomy between God's covenantal promise to Abraham (vv 6–9) and the later-arriving Law with its universal curse (vv 10–14). Here he reveals the gulf between God's promise and the Law, showing that the former can be neither effected nor affected by the latter.

3:19–25. Compelled by his own argument to ask why the Law should have come into the picture at all, Paul devotes a subsection to the genesis of the Law, to the linked advents of faith and of Christ, and to the resulting antinomy between the Law and the faith of Christ.

3:26–29. Here Paul provides another intermediate climax through an exegesis not of scripture, but of an early Christian baptismal formula, as we have noted. The Galatians are heirs of Abraham (lit. "seed of Abraham") by virtue of their baptismal incorporation into Christ.

4:1–7. The final subsection spans three paragraphs, vv 1–2, vv 3–5a, vv 5b–7. Beginning with an illustration drawn from everyday life, Paul moves the exegetical section to its true and final climax, announcing the Galatians' liberation by Christ from slavery and affirming their adoption by the Spirit into the family of God. By Christ and by his Spirit the Galatians are heirs of God himself.

A second exegetical section lies ahead at 4:21–5:1, and its theme also concerns descent from Abraham. What do we find, then, in the intervening material,

---

[38]Cf. Smiga, "Language."

4:8–20? Here, as in 3:1–5, Paul deals with the birth of the Galatian churches, issuing, as in that earlier section, a call that they return to the contours of life established at their birth. Clearly, both of the letter's exegetical sections (3:6–4:7 and 4:21–5:1) are directed to the genetic identity of the Galatian churches. A pattern thus emerges:

A. *3:1–5.* The identity of the Galatian churches is known from their birth. Paul raises questions, then, about the relationship between that birth identity and disastrous developments under the tutelage of the Teachers.

B. *3:6–4:7.* The identity of the Galatian churches is known from what Abrahamic passages in scripture and baptismal traditions say about their descent: They are heirs of Abraham because they have been incorporated into Abraham's seed, Christ. From christological and pneumatological traditions it is clear, furthermore, that they are liberated slaves, indeed sons and heirs of God himself.

A'. *4:8–20.* The identity of the Galatian churches is known from their birth. Paul raises questions, then, about the relationship between that birth identity and disastrous developments under the tutelage of the Teachers.

B'. *4:21–5:1.* The identity of the Galatian churches is known from the true interpretation of Abrahamic passages in scripture and from Isaiah. In fact, they are children not of the slave girl, but of the free woman.

Returning to 3:6–4:7, we note, finally, that, although there is no part of the letter more revealing of Paul's grand intention, there is also no section in which the apostle places a heavier interpretive burden on his Galatian audience. In the Notes, and in Comments #33–#42, we will find three major keys: (1) Paul composes this exegetical piece because the Teachers have thrown down the exegetical gauntlet with their own detailed interpretation of the Law. (2) He can and does accept for discussion a number of the Teachers' texts, terms, and motifs, knowing that, by means of these, they have been very successful in capturing the Galatians' attention and allegiance. He can thus take for granted that the Galatians will recognize some similarities between his exegesis and that of the Teachers. (3) At several points, however, and especially at the end, Paul weaves an exegetical tapestry that reveals a basic frame of reference radically different from that of the Teachers. It is in noting both the connections and this difference in frame of reference that we can begin to hear this complex section as Paul intended the Galatians to hear it.

NOTES

3:6. *Things were the same with Abraham.* Paul employs the adverb *kathôs* in order to connect what he has just said to what he will now say.[39] In effect he says that

---

[39]The term *kathôs* can be combined with the verb *gegraptai*, "it stands written," to mean "just as it stands written in scripture" (e.g., Rom 1:17). Since in the present verse Paul

the rhetorical question of v 5 is one the Galatians can answer not only by recalling the early days in which they were apprehended by God in the gospel (the
akoê of vv 2 and 5) but also by turning to the witness of scripture. Specifically,
God's dependable granting of the Spirit via the proclamation that elicits faith
(v 5) can be further explicated if one will pay attention to the way things were in
the faithful relationship God established with Abraham. For in the case of the
patriarch — about whom the Galatians have already heard a great deal from the
Teachers — it was God's promise that had the power to elicit faith.

*"He trusted God, and, as the final act in the drama by which God set Abraham
fully right, God recognized Abraham's faithful trust."* We will see reasons to think
that several of the later texts in this exegetical section are ones Paul knows the
Teachers to be interpreting in their own way. The text with which he begins,
however, Gen 15:6, is his own selection. It is a text by which he can make connection with the Galatians' intense interest in Abraham. It is also one by which
he can bring into even tighter relationship with one another the motifs of trust
and of God's deed of rectification (2:16). Deleting the word "Abraham," because
he has already used it in his first clause, Paul draws the quotation from the Septuagint, which reads literally, "And Abraham trusted God, and it was accounted to
him as rectification."[40] The need for the embroidered, paraphrastic translation
given above becomes clear when we consider each element of the quotation in
relationship to Paul's interpretation of it.

He trusted God. Following the text of Gen 15:6, Paul allows Abraham to be
the subject of the verb *pisteuô* (with the dative), meaning in this construction "to
place one's trust in," "to have confidence in," "to rely on," and in the sense indicated by these renderings "to have faith in."[41] It is one of the points at which Paul
speaks clearly of an act taken by a human being (see Comment #29). The order
of the two clauses in the scripture quotation opens, however, the possibility of a
serious misunderstanding.

On the face of it the two clauses can be read to mean that Abraham took the
first step by trusting God. Then, as a second step, God responded to Abraham's
act of faith by declaring him right. For three reasons we can be confident that
that is not Paul's reading of Gen 15:6.

(a) There is first the little word *kathôs*, "things were the same (with Abraham),"
by which Paul links v 6 to v 5. In that earlier verse (in v 2 as well) Paul has

---

quotes Gen 15:6, a number of interpreters have considered the absence of *gegraptai* to be
insignificant, thus translating, "Just as it stands written in scripture that Abraham had faith
in God . . ." See, however, Meyer, Review of H. D. Betz, 319; Klumbies, "Zwischen," 117;
Stanley, *Scripture*, 235.

[40]Cf. Verhoef, *Geschreven*, 45–52.

[41]Whether in Paul's usage there is a significant difference between (a) *pisteuô* with the
simple dative of the noun and (b) *pisteuô* with a preposition before the noun (*eis* + accusative and *epi* + dative) is an issue waiting for a thoroughly convincing discussion. In the
genuine letters there are only four instances of the simpler construction, Gal 3:6 and Rom
4:3 (quotations from Gen 15:6), Rom 10:16 (a quotation from Isa 53:1), and Rom 4:17
(on this see BDF §294.2 and .5). Three of these have to do with Abraham. Did Paul think
that Abraham trusted God in the sense of believing God's promise to be true? That seems
to be suggested by Rom 4:21, on which see (c) below.

emphasized that the Galatians' faith was and is incited by the power of God's good news. In a carefully defined way, that faith can be said to be their act; but it is secondary to and caused by God's prior word. If, now, Paul understands Abraham's trust in God to be analogous to the trust enacted by the Galatians, he must presuppose that Abraham's trust, too, was kindled by a prior act of God.

(b) In its context Gen 15:6 demands this reading, specifying that prior act of God as his promise. That is to say, the Abraham stories are consistent in showing God to be the first and causative actor. Thus, the faith of Abraham in Genesis 15 is well encapsulated by a comment of Speiser: "God's reaffirmed promise of a son . . . sets Abraham's mind at rest."[42] In Galatians Paul's own later references to God's promise (3:16, 17, 18) reflect his certainty that Abraham's faith, far from being the first step, was itself elicited by the power of God's prior promise. Moreover, Paul elsewhere shows that God's promise to Abraham was in no way responsive to some act on the part of the patriarch. God's promise was predicated on nothing other than God's gracious will to create life, calling into existence the things that do not exist (Gal 3:21; cf. Rom 4:17).[43] It is precisely in this regard that Abraham's faith is analogous to the faith that was kindled — and that continues to be kindled — among the Galatians by the power of the gospel. The God who is now acting with priority is the God who has always done that.

(c) Finally, this point is made explicit by Paul in Rom 4:21, where he refers to Abraham's faithful trust as his being fully convinced (*plêrophorêtheis*) that what God had promised he was also able to do and would do. It is in the sense of believing God to be entirely faithful to his promise that Abraham trusted God alone.

God recognized. The Septuagint's passive verb (*elogisthai;* "it was accounted to him as rectification"; divine passive) is a reference to God's action; the Hebrew text has the active, "and he (God) judged it (Abraham's faith) to be right." Thus, both the primary action (the promise) and the final action (rectifying recognition) were deeds of God. God promised. That promise set Abraham's mind at rest, eliciting Abraham's trusting faith in God. As the final act in God's rectifying drama, God put his seal of recognition on Abraham's promise-kindled faith.[44]

fully right. The final word of Gen 15:6 (*sĕdāqâ*, "right") was rendered by the Septuagint translator with the prepositional phrase *eis dikaiosynên*, "as rectification." To Paul, as noted above, it is entirely clear that rectification is — both at its

---

[42] Speiser, *Genesis*, 115.

[43] To have faith is to have confidence and to trust, precisely in a situation which is so threatening as to leave room, according to all appearances, for nothing other than failure. For Paul, as for the ancient author of Genesis 15, faith has its genesis, therefore, neither in the threatening situation nor in the threatened human being, but rather in the God who promises.

[44] When Paul reworked the exegetical argument of Galatians 3 in order to use it in Romans 4, he gave more detailed attention to God's act of recognition (Rom 4:3, 8, 9, 12). He also explicated Gal 3:2 and 3:5, showing very clearly that the fundamental antinomy is not human faith versus human observance of the Law. In Romans 4 that fundamental antinomy is God's act of presuppositionless grace versus an act one might imagine God to have taken because he recognized himself to be indebted to human beings for something they had done.

inception and at its end — an act of God. Hence, in citing Gen 15:6 Paul doubtless finds in the closing phrase "as rectification" a reference to God's act. In Abraham's faith God sees and recognizes the true effect of his own promise, and that recognition is the climax of the integrated event in which God set Abraham fully right.

7. *You know, therefore.* In the present case the verb *ginôskete* is probably an epistolary disclosure formula in the indicative mood. By the little inferential particle *ara*, "therefore," Paul indicates that he is now functioning as an exegete, drawing out the meaning of Gen 15:6. He says, namely, that that verse of scripture enables one to know the identity of Abraham's children, a matter to which he returns when he next uses the same inferential particle (3:29).

those whose identity is derived from faith. Lit. "those of (or from) faith" (*hoi ek pisteôs*). The expression is apparently coined by Paul for use in the present argument. In commenting on 2:12 we noted that the expression "those of (or from) circumcision" (*hoi ek peritomês*) seems to have been employed in the Jerusalem church to refer to members of that church (and thus a party within it) who derived the essence of their identity from circumcision as the crucial sign of Law observance, accompanied by the food laws. Paul uses a similar expression in 3:10, "those of (or from) observance of the Law," that is those who derive their identity from observance of the Law (cf. *hoi ek nomou* in Rom 4:14). In the present verse, employing the same syntax, he devises the antinomous expression: those whose identity is derived from faith, meaning both the faith that is elicited by the message of Christ's death in our behalf (vv 2, 5) and the faith of Christ enacted in his death (2:16, 20–21).

these are the children of Abraham. Paul begins this clause with the demonstrative pronoun *houtoi*, placing it in the emphatic position because he is formulating a polemic regarding the identity of Abraham's descendants. The expression *huioi Abraam*, "children of Abraham," occurs nowhere else in Paul's letters, a fact suggesting that he is taking it from the vocabulary of the Teachers, in order to construct his own polemical definition (Comment #33). And that definition is not an antiquarian concern (note *eisin*, "are"). The Teachers have already spoken of the children of Abraham, identifying them, in a reasonable way, as those who follow Abraham in faithful observance of the Law, beginning with circumcision.

On grounds already displayed in 2:16–21 and 3:1–5 Paul finds even in Abraham the striking antinomy between the Law that demands observance and the promise that elicits faith; and he senses that antinomy in Gen 15:6. Who, then, are the children of Abraham? They are not the Law-people, but rather the faith-people.[45]

Taken somewhat "in its own right," the text of Gen 15:6 says nothing about Abraham's descendants. It is because of the work of the Teachers that Paul (a) places his exegetical emphasis on an expression not found in the text, "the de-

---

[45] In drawing this exegetical conclusion from Gen 15:6, Paul may be using, consciously or unconsciously, an interpretive rule that allows a general category (the identity of Abraham's descendants) to be set up on the basis of a particular instance (Abraham himself); see *binyan ab* as a rule of Rabbi Ishmael, "Hermeneutics," *EJ* 8.366–372.

scendants of Abraham," and (b) answers a question not posed in that text: "Who is it who can truly be said to be the children of Abraham?"

8. *And the scripture, foreseeing what is now happening — namely that God is rectifying the Gentiles on the basis of faith — preached the gospel ahead of time to Abraham, saying, "In you all the Gentiles will be blessed."* Here Paul gives his exegesis before citing the text.[46] But, whether text is followed by exegesis or exegesis is followed by text, Paul consistently takes captive some aspect of the Teachers' message:

3:6–7

(a) Paul selects the first text in order to establish rectification by faith as the point of departure for the exegetical section (Gen 15:6).

(b) He then offers an exegesis of that text designed to take captive the Teachers' terms (children of Abraham) and their issue as well (who are the children of Abraham?)

3:8

(a) Paul begins with the terms and issues arising from the true activity of the gospel at the present time: God's rectification of the Gentiles is now happening on the basis of faith.

(b) He can then cite one of the Teachers' major texts (Gen 12:3), showing that it is a witness to the gospel.

the scripture. For the first time in the letter Paul uses this term, doing so in an arresting manner, indicating that scripture is not a passive text to be quoted and interpreted by human beings as they will. On the contrary, it is alive, having, as it were, eyes and intelligence and a mouth.[47] So equipped already in Abraham's time, scripture foresaw that God would one day rectify the Gentiles by faith. And gifted with such foresight, it did nothing less than preach the gospel itself ahead of time to the patriarch, telling him that in him, the man of faith, all the Gentiles would one day be blessed.

Having noted that every one of Paul's preceding references to the Law is negative (2:16, 19, 21; 3:2, 5), the Galatians will surely have been doubly impressed to hear Paul suddenly say that the scripture is so fully in tune with God's will as to speak on his behalf, preaching the gospel itself. And when they had heard the entire letter several times, they may have pondered the question of how, exactly, the Law and scripture are related to one another. See Notes on 3:22 and 4:21, and Comments #35, #41, #48, and #50.[48]

[46]Cf. Halivni, *Midrash*, 34–35.
[47]It is possible that the Teachers have already done something similar; affirmations that scripture sees and knows are found in Philo and in rabbinic traditions (Philo *Leg. Alleg.* 3.118; Billerbeck 3.538). The Teachers may even have employed the word *proeuaggelizomai*, "to preach the gospel ahead of time," referring to an angelic proclamation of the Law to Abraham (Comment #7).
[48]On Paul as exegete, see Koch, *Schrift*; Hays, *Echoes*; Stanley, *Scripture*; J. L. Martyn, *Issues*, 209–227.

the scripture, foreseeing . . . preached the gospel ahead of time. Paul uses the personifying reference to scripture in a way peculiar to him, presupposing a simple syllogism. The major premise is provided by an event witnessed by Paul almost every day: God is now making things right in the Gentile world by the rectifying faith of Jesus Christ (2:16).[49] The minor premise is Paul's certainty that the God who is doing this new deed is the same God who dealt with Abraham. Conclusion: Read in light of this new deed, the promise spoken to Abraham by scripture (in God's behalf) was the word of this same God, indeed the gospel of Christ.

Paul could even add, were it necessary, that that backward reading can be seen as a demand of scripture itself. On what basis could scripture preach the gospel to Abraham ahead of time? It could do that, says Paul, because it looked ahead, thus seeing what God is doing in the present time. Scripture itself thus recognized the interpretive point of departure: God's present deed in Christ!

saying, "In you all the Gentiles will be blessed." Having prefixed his gospel exegesis, Paul can now cite the text thus interpreted, Gen 12:3 (with echoes of Gen 18:18 or 22:18), God's assurance to Abraham that in him all the Gentiles (*ethnê*) will one day be blessed.[50] For four reasons we can be confident that this text played an important role in the Teachers' sermons and that Paul takes it up because of that fact.

(a) Paul uses it nowhere else in the letters we have from him. (b) In writing to the Christians in Rome Paul reformulates his exegetical treatment of the Abrahamic traditions (Romans 4). Having in that instance no need to respond to the Teachers, however, he drops all reference to this text and to the issues raised by it. (c) As Paul's prefixed exegesis makes clear, his attention is focused on God's present deed of *rectifying* the Gentiles. The text, however, speaks of *blessing.* If Paul were freely selecting a text, it is likely that he would have chosen one that refers literally to God's act of rectification. (d) To consider the whole of Paul's argument in Gal 3:6–29 is to find, as we will see in the next Note, that Paul is concerned to correct a prior, simple reading of the prepositional phrase "in you"; the prior reading is almost certainly that of the Teachers.

In you. In their exegesis the Teachers may very well have emphasized this prepositional phrase:

> God's scriptural assurance to Abraham reads, "*In you,* Abraham, all the Gentiles will be blessed." It is by incorporation into Abraham, then, that you Gentiles can share in the Abrahamic blessing.

[49]That God is in this same way rectifying Jews as well as Gentiles Paul takes for granted (so 2:7, 9; and "the human being" in 2:16). In the whole of Galatians, however, the argument is tightly focused on the rectification of Gentiles, that being both the issue at stake and the focus of the Teachers' interpretation of the Abraham traditions. Cf. Boers, *Gentiles.*

[50]See Verhoef, *Geschreven,* 58–59; Stanley, *Scripture,* 236–237. In Genesis God's assurance to Abraham includes the promise of innumerable progeny, meaning the people of Israel (Gen 15:5). The Teachers are likely to have mentioned this motif *before* quoting Gen 12:3 (+ 18:18) with its reference to Gentiles: First, the elective founding of the corporate people of Israel; then the inclusion of the Gentiles in this blessed people. See

At this point in his own exegesis Paul is satisfied to stay with this simple reading of Gen 12:3 — the Gentiles are blessed in Abraham — for he has already defined Abraham's children as those who derive their identity from faith, not from Law observance. In 3:16, however, Paul will take a further step that qualifies the Teacher's reading of Gen 12:3 even more fundamentally. There, drawing on Gen 17:8, he says plainly that the promise of Gen 12:3 was spoken by God not only to Abraham but also to Abraham's seed. And when Paul identifies this seed as Christ, he interprets Gen 12:3 in a way that has the effect of significantly changing the Teacher's reading of "in you." In the later part of this exegetical section, that is to say, Paul argues as though the text read, "In you, Abraham, and in your seed, Christ, all the Gentiles will be blessed."

9. *So then, it is those whose identity is derived from faith who are blessed with faithful Abraham.* In this sentence Paul gives a conclusion to his interpretations of both Gen 15:6 and Gen 12:3, drawing from the former the expression "those whose identity is derived from faith" and from the latter the verb "are blessed." Since the force of this conclusion depends (as does that of v 7) on the argument that blessing (in v 7 descent) comes to a specified group of people by virtue of their association with Abraham, the portrait one draws of the patriarch becomes a crucial matter.

faithful Abraham. This may be another of the expressions Paul draws from the Teachers. It is at home in Jewish traditions in which Abraham is portrayed as the one who, hearing God's nomistic commands, faithfully observed them (*Jub.* 17:15; 1 Macc 2:52; etc.).[51] In any case, we can be confident that the Teachers interpreted Gen 12:3 to mean:

> Those who faithfully observe the Law are blessed with faithfully observant Abraham.

By quoting Gen 12:3 only after he has cited and interpreted Gen 15:6, Paul has given a radically different portrait of the patriarch. He says nothing of Abraham's having faithfully obeyed God's command that he circumcise himself and his sons (cf. Comment #45). The Abraham portrayed by Paul is faithful in only one sense: His mind was set at rest by the power of God's promissory word.

COMMENT #33
THE TEACHERS' SERMON ON DESCENT FROM ABRAHAM, AND PAUL'S MODULATION OF THAT THEME INTO DESCENT FROM GOD

THE TEACHERS' SERMON

From 1:6–9 we know that the Teachers are identifying their message as "the gospel." We also know that their gospel is somewhat complex, comprehending a

---

Comment #37. The Teachers made no mention of the Land of Canaan (Gen 12:7), and Paul also was silent about it. See Davies, *Land.* For a recent interpretation of Paul's understanding of the term *ethnê,* see Scott, *Nations.*

[51]Every Jewish tradition that speaks of Abraham's faith understands it to be of one piece with his obedient observance of God's commandments, notably the commandment of circumcision. When the Teachers spoke of "faithful Abraham" (cf. 3:9), they surely meant

number of motifs, several of which have to do with the patriarch Abraham (Comment #6). Now, by coordinating data in the letter with comparable data in the traditions of Christian Judaism and of some strains of Judaism itself, we can reconstruct with a reasonable degree of probability a sermon on descent from Abraham that the Teachers would have included in the proclamation of their gospel to the Galatians:[52]

Listen, now![53] It all began with Abraham. Looking beyond the fascinating movements of the heavenly bodies, he was the first to discern that there is but one God. Because of that perception, he turned from the service of dumb idols to the worship of that true God.[54] Therefore, God made him the father of our great nation Israel. But that was only the beginning, for God blessed Abraham in a way that is coming to its fulfillment only now in the messianic age. Speaking through a glorious angel, God said to Abraham:

> In you shall all nations of the world be blessed, for I shall multiply your descendants as the stars of heaven. Come outside, and look toward heaven, and number the stars, if you are able. So shall your descendants be, for I speak this blessing to you and to your descendants (cf. Gen 12:3; 15:5; 17:4; 18:18).

What is the meaning of this blessing which God gave to Abraham? Pay attention to these things: Abraham was the first proselyte. As we have said, he discerned the one true God and turned to him. God's blessing took the form, therefore, of an unshakable covenant with Abraham, and God defined the covenant as the commandment of circumcision.[55] He also revealed to Abraham the heavenly calendar, so that in his own lifetime our father was obedient to the Law, not only keeping the commandment of circumcision but also observing the holy feasts on the correct days.[56] Later, when God handed down the Law on tablets of stone at Sinai, he spoke once again by the mouths of his glorious angels, for they passed the Law through the hand of the mediator, Moses (Gal 3:19).[57] And now the Messiah has come, confirming for eternity God's blessed Law, revealed to Abraham and spoken through Moses.[58]

---

that he was faithfully observant, and they thought of his children in the same way. No one prior to Paul saw in the patriarch an antinomy between faith and observance of the Law. See Billerbeck 3.186–202; Lührmann, *Glaube*, 31–45.

[52]On the role of Abraham in the Teachers' theology, see Barrett, "Allegory"; J. L. Martyn, *Issues*, 7–24; Brinsmead, *Dialogical Response*; Hansen, *Abraham*; Walter, "Gegner." Rabbinic references are given for some of the motifs included in the following sermon, but usually in addition to references of early date. Regarding the scheme for referring to passages in the *Ascents of James*, see footnote 108 in Comment #6.

[53]At numerous points in the letter (mentioned here in parentheses) Paul's words reflect the message of the Teachers.

[54]Philo *de Abr.* 69–70; Josephus *Ant.* 1.155–156; *Jub.* 11:16–17; *Hebrew Testament of Naphtali* 9; Comment #41.

[55]Gen 17:10.

[56]*Jub.* 16:12–28; Sir 44:19–20.

[57]Deut 33:12 (LXX); *Jub.* 1:29; Acts 7:38, 53; Davies, "Josephus."

[58]Matt 5:17–18; *Ep. Pet. Jas.* 2:5 (HS 2.112).

And what does this mean for you Gentiles? Listen again to the scripture we have just quoted. When God said to Abraham that in him all nations of the world would be blessed, God spoke explicitly of blessing you Gentiles in Abraham. But this blessing will come to you only if you are included in the people of Israel via your legitimate incorporation into our father Abraham. For, in addition to being himself the first proselyte, Abraham was the great maker of proselytes.[59] You must become, therefore, Abraham's true descendants, his true seed, along with us.[60]

Listen yet again to scripture. It is written that Abraham had two sons: Isaac and Ishmael (Gal 4:22). On the day of the feast of the first fruits, Isaac was born of Sarah the free woman, and through him have come we Jews, true descendants of Abraham.[61] Earlier, Ishmael was born of Hagar the slave girl, and through him have come you Gentiles. You are descendants of the patriarch! We are in fact brothers![62]

Offspring through Ishmael, however, you are descended through the son who was begotten by Abraham while, lacking in trust, he was yet ignorant of God.[63] Most important of all, you have come through the slave girl, and, failing to observe God's covenantal Law, you are enslaved to the power of the Impulsive Desire of the Flesh (Gal 5:16). In a word, you Gentiles are not yet *true* descendants of Abraham. You have not been incorporated into Israel. In order to participate in God's blessing of Abraham, therefore, you are to make your descent legitimate.

Who are the genuine and therefore blessed descendants of Abraham, Abraham's true seed (Gal 3:7, 29)? Again the answer is given in scripture, for the Law makes clear that God has set Two Ways before human beings, the Way of death and the Way of life.[64] You can see this in the case of our father Abraham. He chose the Way of life. Turning from idols to the observance of the Law, he circumcised himself, thus avoiding walking in the deadly power of the Impulsive Desire of the Flesh.[65] It follows that Abraham's true descendants are those who choose the path of virtue, becoming faithfully obedient to the virtue-creating Law, along with faithful Abraham (Gal 3:6-9). And transference to the path of true descent is precisely what we now offer to you. For, fulfilling the ancient blessing he pronounced over Abraham, God is pleased at the present holy time to extend this line of true descent to the Gentiles. To be specific, God is creating descendants of Abraham through the Law-observant mission to Gentiles approved by his church in Jerusalem, the community that lives by the Law con-

---

[59]CD 16:4-6; *Tanh.* Lekh Lekha 32a; 'Abot. Nat. 12:27a (Goldin, *Rabbi Nathan*, 68); *Midr. Pss.* 110:1; *Gen. Rab.* 43:7.

[60]In both Jewish and Christian-Jewish tradition it was held that proselytes enter corpus Israel as descendants of Abraham; see for example, *Tanh.* Lekh Lekha 32a; *p. Bik.* 64a (on *m. Bik.* 1:4); *Ascents of James* 1.42.1 (Van Voorst, *Ascents*, 57; F. S. Jones, *Source*, 72).

[61]*Jub.* 16:13.

[62]*Jub.* 16:17; 1 Macc 12:21; *Ascents of James* 1.33.3; 1.34.1 (Van Voorst, *Ascents*, 48-49; F. S. Jones, *Source*, 60-61); *b. Sanh.* 59b.

[63]*Ascents of James* as in preceding footnote.

[64]For example, Deut 30:19; Jer 21:8.

[65]Gen 6:5; CD 3:1-3; 16:4-6; Jas 1:2-4, 12-15; 4:5-6. For the motif of turning from idols, cf. *JosAs*. On the Impulsive Desire of the Flesh, see Comment #49.

firmed to eternity by the Christ.[66] In our Lawful preaching to the Gentiles, we represent that church, the community of James, Cephas, and John (Gal 2:1–10).

What are you to do, therefore, as Abraham's descendants through Ishmael, the child of Hagar the slave girl? The gate of conversion stands open (Gal 4:9, 17)![67] You are to cast off your enslavement to the Flesh by turning in repentance and conversion to God's righteous Law, as it is confirmed by his Christ.[68] Follow Abraham in the holy, liberating, and perfecting rite of circumcision (Gal 3:3; 6:13).[69] Observe the feasts at their appointed times (Gal 4:10). Keep the sacred dietary requirements (Gal 2:11–14). And abstain from idolatry and from the passions of the Impulsive Flesh (Gal 5:19–21). Then you will be perfected as true descendants of Abraham, members of the covenant people of Israel, heirs of salvation according to the blessing which God solemnly uttered to Abraham and to his descendants (Gal 3:7, 8, 16).[70] Indeed, by entering the people of Israel, you will fill up the vast number of descendants God promised to Abraham.[71]

You say that you have already been converted by Paul? We say that you are still in a darkness similar to the darkness in which not long ago you were serving the elements of the cosmos, supposing them, as Abraham once did, to be gods that rule the world (Comment #41). In fact, the fights and contentions in your communities show that you have not really been converted, that Paul did not give you the divinely ordained antidote to the Impulsive Desire of the Flesh, the guidance of God's holy Law, the perfecting observance of which is commenced in the circumcision of the flesh (Gal 5:15). Being an unfaithful student of the Law-observant apostles in the mother church of Jerusalem, Paul failed to give you the

---

[66]*Ascents of James* 1.33.3–1.43.3 (Van Voorst, *Ascents*, 48–59; F. S. Jones, *Source*, 60–74); *Ep. Pet. Jas.* 2:5 (HS 2.112).

[67]Cf. Joseph's prayer for Asenath in *JosAs* 8:9.

[68]Cf. *JosAs* 15:7.

[69]Holding Gentiles to be Ishmaelite descendants of Abraham, in spite of their being uncircumcised, the Teachers may simply have ignored — or interpreted symbolically — the scriptural tradition according to which Abraham circumcised Ishmael (Gen 17:23). For, being yet ignorant of God's true power, Abraham did not carry out that act on Ishmael's eighth day. We can be confident that the Teachers' invitation to membership in God's covenant people was in some fashion addressed to the women in the Pauline churches along with the men. Precisely how the Teachers included the women, however, we cannot say with certainty. Presumably, the Teachers invited them to make the transition with the male members of their patriarchally structured families, as was often the case with female proselytes to Judaism. Paul nowhere hints that the Teachers were bringing in the women via a ritual bath (see Gal 5:3). For a discussion of some of the pertinent data in Philo, Justin Martyr, and rabbinic traditions, see now Lieu, "Circumcision," and the literature in her footnotes, notably the studies by S. J. D. Cohen.

[70]As the Teachers offered the Galatians a religious process that leads to perfection (Gal 3:3), one may note the motif of recreation in *JosAs*. In praying for Asenath's conversion Joseph links the image of God the creator to that of God the new creator: "Lord God . . . who gave life to all things and called them from the darkness to the light, and from the error to the truth, and from the death to the life, you, Lord, bless this virgin, and renew her by your spirit, and form her anew by your hidden hand, and make her alive again by your life . . ." (8:9; cf. Stuhlmacher, "Erwägungen"). See also *JosAs* 15:5 ("renewed and formed anew and made alive again"); cf. 16:16; 18:9.

[71]*Ascents of James* 1.42.1 (Van Voorst, *Ascents*, 57; F. S. Jones, *Source*, 72).

Law, thus allowing you to remain a group of sailors on the treacherous high seas in nothing more than a small and poorly equipped boat. He gave you no provisions for the trip, no map, no rudder, and no anchor. In a word, he failed to pass on to you God's greatest gift, the Law.[72] But that is exactly the mission to which God has called us. Through our work, the good news of God's Law is invading the world of Gentile sin (Comment #7).

We adjure you, therefore, to claim the inheritance of the blessing of Abraham, and thus to escape the curse of the Impulsive Desire of the Flesh and sin (Gal 1:4a; 3:18; 5:16). For, be assured, those who follow the path of the Flesh and sin will not inherit the Kingdom of God, lacking the perfection of virtue given by the Law (Gal 3:3). It is entirely possible for you to be shut out (Gal 4:17). You will do well to consider this possibility and to tremble with fear.[73] For you will certainly be shut out unless you are truly incorporated into Abraham by observing God's glorious and angelic Law. Turn therefore in true repentance, and come under the wings of the Divine Presence, so that with us you shall be saved as true descendants of father Abraham.

PAUL'S MODULATION OF THE THEME OF ABRAHAMIC DESCENT INTO THE THEME OF DESCENT FROM GOD

From 3:7 and 3:29 we can see that Paul takes pains to connect his exegetical argument in 3:6–4:7 with the Teachers' theme of descent from Abraham. Finding that they have enticed his Galatian churches with that theme, he gladly accepts it, affirming without ambivalence that "children of Abraham" is one of the ways of naming the church of God (3:29). Earlier, to be sure, Paul had sounded a note of discontinuity between the patriarchal traditions and the event of God's apocalypse in Christ (1:13–15). That note has no echo in regard to the patriarch himself.

Attention to 3:16 and 3:29 shows, however, that in the final analysis Paul marches clean off the Abrahamic map, as that map is drafted by the Teachers. The Gentile Galatians do not become descendants of Abraham by being incorporated into the Law-observant patriarch or into the line of his plural descendants (Comment #37). They became Abraham's children by being incorporated into Abraham's singular seed, Christ. And that means that their descent from Abraham is secondary to the descent from God that had its genesis in their baptism into Christ (3:26–27). Descent from God is the picture with which Paul ends his exegetical exercise (4:7), and it is the picture he draws not from scripture, but rather from the early Christian baptismal formula of 3:26–28, suggesting once again that his exegetical point of departure is the gospel, not scripture as such.[74]

---

[72]*Ep. Pet. Jas.* 2:3 (HS 2.112).
[73]Cf. *JosAs* 10:1–3.
[74]See J. L. Martyn, *Issues*, 209–229.

3:10–14 THE LAW'S CURSE AND THE END OF THAT CURSE

TRANSLATION

3:10. For those whose identity is derived from observance of the Law are under the power of a curse, because it stands written: "Cursed is everyone who is not steadfast in observing all of the things written in the book of the Law, so as to do them." 11. That before God no one is being rectified by the Law is clear from the fact that, "The one who is rectified by faith will live." 12. Moreover, the Law does not have its origin in faith; if it did have its origin there, it would not say, "The one who does the commandments will live by them."

13. Christ redeemed us from the Law's curse, becoming a curse in our behalf; for it stands written: "Cursed is everyone who is hanged on a tree." 14. He did this in order that the blessing of Abraham might come to the Gentiles in Jesus Christ; in order, that is, that we might receive the promise, which is the Spirit, through faith.

LITERARY STRUCTURE AND SYNOPSIS

The opening movement in Paul's exegetical symphony (3:6–9) was played out in bright tones, with a dual focus on God's life-giving blessing and the identification of the blessed as those whose faith has been awakened by the pronouncement of that blessing. Now Paul takes two further exegetical steps.

First, in 3:10–12 he turns from blessing to the somber and threatening note of an enslaving curse pronounced by the Law on all human beings, and to the contrast between the true promise spoken by God (v 11b) and the false promise uttered by that cursing Law (v 12). The results are emphatically negative: no one is being rectified by the Law; the Law does not have its origin in faith.

Second, in 3:13–15 Paul paints a picture of the only juncture at which God's blessing and the Law's curse met one another, the crucifixion of Christ. And in announcing the result of that meeting, he returns to the bright notes of 3:6–9: defeat for the enslaving curse spoken by the Law and victory for the liberating, promissory blessing spoken by God (cf. Comment #48).

NOTES

3:10. *For those whose identity is derived from observance of the Law are under the power of a curse, because it stands written: "Cursed is everyone who is not steadfast in observing all of the things written in the book of the Law, so as to do them."* In Comment #34 we will see grounds for thinking that the Teachers influenced the Galatians by speaking of a miniature Table of Opposites, referring in this connection to blessing and curse:

Those who observe the Law	Those who do not observe the Law
blessing	curse (Deut 27:23).

In making his own transition from v 9 to v 10, that is from the subject of blessing to that of curse, Paul also thinks of a miniature Table of Opposites, but it is radically different from that of the Teachers:

Those whose identity is derived from faith	Those whose identity is derived from observance of the Law
blessing	curse.[75]

those whose identity is derived from observance of the Law. Drawing perhaps on the expression *hoi ek peritomês*, "the circumcision party" (2:12), Paul coins an expression designed to refer, in the first instance, to the Teachers (see Note on 3:6). If it is the Teachers who have frightened the Galatians, speaking as much about curse as about blessing, then Paul is concerned to say that the Law with which they frighten the Galatians applies its curse to these persons themselves.[76]

are under the power of a curse. This is the first of ten junctures at which Paul employs the expressions *hypo tina einai* and *hypo tina genesthai*, "to be under the power of . . ." (Comment #39). Reaching back to his apocalyptic interpretation of the Jewish-Christian atonement formula in 1:4a, Paul strikes a note that subsequently permeates the whole of the exegetical section of 3:6–4:7: the human dilemma consists at its base, not of guilt, but of enslavement to powers lying beyond the human being's control.

As the quotation from Deut 27:26 will show, the first such power specified by Paul is a curse pronounced by the Law. Paul does not explicitly say of what this curse consists, but he does give a dynamic picture of it (Comment #34).[77]

because it stands written. Having provided his exegesis, Paul quotes Deut

---

[75] At first glance Paul's Table of Opposites would seem to exemplify the doctrine of the Two Ways as neatly as does that of the Teachers, those who choose to have faith being placed opposite those who choose to observe the Law. But, because Paul understands faith to be, in the first and determinative instance, the faithful death of Christ in our behalf, his Table of Opposites begins with the difference between an act of God and an act of the human being. See Comment #34.

[76] At a deep level Paul understands "those whose identity is derived from observance of the Law" to be, in a paradoxical way, an expression referring alike to Jew and Gentile, as we will see in considering Paul's exegesis of Deut 27:26 (and note *oudeis*, "no one," in v 11). Because both Jew and Gentile acknowledge the archaic pair of opposites — Law/Not-Law — both orient their lives to the Law, acknowledging it as the marker that differentiates them from one another. In that sense both are observers of the Law. In the present sentence, however, Paul refers primarily to the Teachers and to those under their influence, for the immediate issue is raised by those who consider the Law to be salvific for Gentiles. Cf. the Note on 6:14.

[77] Alongside the Law's curse, other enslaving powers are Sin (v 22), the Law itself (v 23), the pedagogue (v 25), guardians and overseers (4:2), the elements of the cosmos (4:3), and again the Law (4:4, 5; cf. 4:21; 5:18). See Comments #39 and #41.

27:26, hearing in that text the voice of the Law as it declares what it itself does: it pronounces a curse.[78]

"Cursed is everyone who is not steadfast in observing all of the things written in the book of the Law, so as to do them." There are at least five reasons to think that Paul cites here, as in v 8, one of the Teachers' own texts (Deut 27:26), hearing in it a witness to the truth of the gospel:[79]

(a) Paul does not elsewhere cite Deut 27:26.

(b) Aside from Gal 3:10 and 13 Paul uses the terms *katara*, "curse," and *epikataratos*, "cursed," nowhere else in his letters.[80]

(c) In his exegetical treatment of Abraham traditions in Romans 4, he does refer to "those who derive their identity from the Law" (Rom 4:14; cf. Gal 3:10), but, not facing the threat posed by the Teachers, he leaves aside both blessing and curse.

(d) The threatened curse of Deut 27:26 fits the Teachers' theology hand in glove. One supposes that it was with such scriptural passages that they threatened and frightened the Galatians (see 1:7; 4:17; 5:10).

(e) In the present verse Paul interprets Deut 27:26 in a way that is the precise opposite of its literal meaning, as we will see below. He might have selected this text in order to stand it on its head, but it seems probable that his concern is to turn one of the Teachers' texts against them.

The wording of Paul's quotation of Deut 27:26 has been extensively discussed. In essential regards it corresponds to the LXX, but it remains to some degree different from all texts known to us.[81] More important, partly because it is far more puzzling, is the fact just mentioned that, read plainly, the text says exactly the opposite of what Paul takes it to say. The result is a sentence that is, by the simple canons of logic, incoherent:

> Those whose identity is derived from *observance* of the Law are under the power of a curse, because it stands written, "Cursed is everyone who is *not observant* of the Law."

Faced with this incoherence, most interpreters have elected one of three readings.[82]

(a) One can assume that Paul has lost his way and is giving an exegesis that will have made as little sense to the Galatians as it has to many later readers. But elsewhere in this exegetical section — not to mention exegetical passages in others of his letters — Paul shows that he is an extraordinarily precise and subtle exe-

---

[78]As E. P. Sanders points out, Deut 27:26 is the only passage in the OT that explicitly links the terms "the Law" and "curse" (*Law*, 21).

[79]See also Barrett, "Allegory," 6–7.

[80]The use of the verb *kataraomai* in Rom 12:14 is of no pertinence to the interpretation of the noun and the adjective in Galatians.

[81]In addition to the commentaries, see Verhoef, *Geschreven*, 60–69; Koch, *Schrift*, 120; Stanley, *Scripture*, 238–243.

[82]See especially Stanley, "Curse"; also Scott, "Deuteronomic Tradition"; Boyarin, *Politics*, 136–157.

gete. As E. P. Sanders has noted, by citing Gen 15:6 in Gal 3:6 and Hab 2:4 in Gal 3:11, Paul brings into one catena the only two texts in the whole of the OT that explicitly link to one another the terms "rectification" and "faith."[83] There is no Pauline precedent for an exegetical blunder of the magnitude required by this first interpretation.

(b) A second reading is based on the recognition that Deut 27:26 can be taken to imply a curse on those who suppose themselves to be observant, while in actuality falling short of full observance. If, in reading this text, one accents the expression "all of the things," and if one posits that Paul assumes complete Law observance to be impossible, then his exegetical reasoning can be seen: Those who base their lives on Law observance stand under a curse, for none of them is truly and completely observant (that being impossible), and the Law pronounces a curse on everyone who fails to be observant in even the smallest detail (cf. Jas 2:10–11). This second reading has been adopted by a large number of exegetes. It has, however, two major weaknesses.

First, nowhere in the context, or in the letter taken as a whole, or even in the corpus of his other letters, does Paul refer to the assumption necessitated by this interpretation: that complete observance of the Law is impossible.[84] Repeatedly, he speaks of an antinomy consisting of Christ's faith versus our observance of the Law, not of Christ's faith versus our incomplete observance (2:16; 3:2; 3:5). When he strikes the note of impotence, he refers not to human inability to keep the whole of the Law, but rather to the Law's inability to bring about rectification and life (3:21; cf. Rom 8:3). Moreover, Paul speaks in Phil 3:4–6 about fulfilling the entire Law, certain that, as a Pharisee, he was completely observant, being as a result blameless (cf. 2 *Apoc. Bar.* 54:5, where spotlessness is connected with faithful subjection to God and to God's Law).[85]

Second, not only does Paul fail to mention the required assumption; he consistently fails to use it where it would clearly assist him. Had he assumed complete observance of the Law to be unattainable, he could have said in Gal 3:11:

That before God no one is being rectified by the Law is clear from the fact that no one completely observes the Law.

Instead, he says,

That before God no one is being rectified by the Law is clear from the fact that, "The one who is rectified by faith will live" (Hab 2:4).

---

[83] E. P. Sanders, *Palestinian Judaism*, 483–484.

[84] The solution offered by Wright is ingenious but unconvincing (*Covenant*, 144–151). That of Stanley falls finally into the category of this second reading, without escaping its weaknesses ("Curse"). Scott pursues a line of interpretation that tends to substitute history-of-religions comparisons for exegesis of Gal 3:10 in its context ("curse").

[85] On the Law that has been brought to completion (Gal 5:14), and on the Galatians' bringing to completion the Law of Christ (6:2), see Comment #48.

What is wrong with seeking rectification through Law observance is not that observance is impossible, but that the Law one is observing does not spring from faith (v 12).[86]

Finally, we note that in v 12 Paul continues the argument that he has based on Hab 2:4 by interpreting and then citing Lev 18:5:

> Moreover, the Law does not have its origin in faith; if it did have its origin there, it would not say, "The one who does the commandments will live by them."

The one spoken of in Lev 18:5 is explicitly the one who is observant, not one who attempts and fails, Law observance being impossible. The second interpretive route, widely favored, is almost certainly wrong.

(c) A far better clue is given in the recognition that Paul is formulating the whole of his exegetical train of thought over against the exegetical sermons of the Teachers. He takes Deut 27:26 (as well as Gen 12:3) from their exegetical arsenal, but he interprets it in light of his gospel. As we have noted, the Teachers will have cited Deut 27:26 as a threat to their Gentile hearers: "If you do not observe the Law, you stand under its curse." Paul accepts the text as it stands, that is as a reference to those who are not observant, but by referring in his exegesis to those who are observant, Paul removes the distinction between the two, thus displaying an understanding of the Law's curse that is worlds away from that of the Teachers. In a word, for Paul the curse of the Law falls on both observer and nonobserver.[87]

Noting also that the Law of v 10 (and of v 12b) is emphatically plural rather than singular,[88] we can summarize Paul's interpretation of Deut 27:26:

> The Law does not have the power to bless. It is the Law's business to pronounce a curse, and, by attending both to one of the Teachers' major texts and to my exegesis of it, you will see that the Law's curse falls both on those who are observant and on those who are not. By pronouncing a curse, the Law establishes a sphere of inimical power that is universal.

11. *That before God no one is being rectified by the Law is clear from the fact that, "The one who is rectified by faith will live."* Again, as he has already done in

---

[86] Is there a significant change or a reinterpretation in Rom 9:31–32, Paul implying there that Israel could have attained to the Law had she done so *ek pisteôs*, "by faith"? See Meyer, "Romans."

[87] Support for this reading comes from 3:12a. Because the Law does not have its origin in faith, all of those who have to do with it — by observing it and by not observing it — are under its curse.

[88] To note that the Law of 3:10, 12b is plural is not at all to revert to the thesis that complete observance of the Law is impossible. The pertinence of its being plural emerges only in connection with 5:3 and 5:14. See Comment #48.

vv 8 and 10, Paul introduces a citation from scripture only after he has said what it means.[89]

no one. With the little word *oudeis* Paul emphatically carries over a major motif of v 10: there are no significant distinguishing marks in the human family (cf. also 2:16, where Paul speaks of *anthrôpos*, "the human being").

is being rectified by the Law. Having deepened the gulf between the Law and God, speaking of what one might term "the blessing God" and "the cursing Law" (vv 8–10), Paul now returns to the subject of rectification, denying once again that it is being accomplished by the Law (cf. 2:21). With this denial Paul begins to speak in highly significant and concentrated ways not of Law observance, but of the Law itself (3:10 is the last of his references to Law observance). By the power of its universal curse, the Law has established its own realm, and in that cursed realm no one is being set right. Why not? Doubtless because the Law has as its business to pronounce a curse (v 10); but also because the source of rectification lies elsewhere.

"The one who is rectified by faith will live." Paul began his exegetical exercise with a text of his own selection (v 6; Gen 15:6). He then cited and interpreted two of the Teachers' texts (vv 8 and 10; Gen 12:3 and Deut 27:26). Now, as a fourth text, he again cites one of his own selection, thus making certain that the Teachers' texts, thus enclosed, are read in such a way as to serve the truth of the gospel. Moreover, Hab 2:4 makes the perfect companion to Gen 15:6: As we have noted, following E. P. Sanders, it is the only other passage in the OT to refer both to rectification and to faith. It also corresponds to Gen 12:3 in that both are promises which God spoke and which he is now enacting. Specifically, in Gen 12:3 Paul hears God assuring Abraham that in him God will one day rectify the Gentiles, and God is now doing that. In Hab 2:4 Paul hears God promising the prophet that in the good news of Christ, the good news that has the power to elicit faith, God will one day make things right by creating eschatological life. That one day is the now of the Galatians.

The verse from Habakkuk had had a rich history prior to Paul's quoting it. Originally, it was a salvation oracle (a vision of the way things will in fact be) in which God makes an indelible promise. To Habakkuk's contemporaries the unjust Babylonians seemed always to triumph, thus creating doubt that God was himself consistently powerful and consistently just. The prophet's message, however, runs counter to appearances: the Israelite who is rightly related to God will live through the trying times by being consistently faithful to God.[90] For Habakkuk, faith is life lived in accordance with the life-giving commandments of God; faith is thus a reflection of God's powerful faithfulness.[91] All of this is given in the Hebrew text:

The rectified one will remain alive by his faithfulness (to God, i.e. to God's life-giving commandments).

---

[89] On the force of the word *dêlon*, "it is clear," in 3:11, see Meyer, Review of H. D. Betz, 319.
[90] Wildberger, " 'Glauben' im Alten Testament," 139.
[91] Lührmann, "*Pistis*," 35.

The LXX translator made a significant linguistic change; emphasizing what was already implicit in the Hebrew text, he spoke of the faithfulness of God:[92]

The rectified one will remain alive by my (God's) faithfulness.

And the Essene author of the Habakkuk Commentary at Qumran, working with the Hebrew text, interpreted the promise in yet another way, saying that those who observe the Law will be delivered by God

> because of their suffering and because of their faith in the Teacher of Righteousness [i.e., because of their faithful concurrence with his interpretation of the Law] (1QpHab 8:1–3a; Vermes).

In his own interpretation — drawn with one modification from the LXX text — Paul pays attention to all three motifs: rectification, faith, and eschatological life.

The one who is rectified.[93] When, by this quotation, Paul reintroduces the subject of rectification, his first concern is to restate the question of Gal 2:16, "What means has God selected for making human beings right?" In his prefixed exegetical assertion (v 11a), as we have noted above, Paul denies that the Law is that means:

No one — no human being — is being rectified by the Law.

He then turns to scripture, saying that his negative assertion about the means of rectification for the human being is clear (*dêlon*) because in fact

"The one rectified by faith is the one who will live."

By combining his exegesis with his cited text, Paul thus draws a stark contrast between *oudeis*, "no one," and *ho dikaios*, "the one rectified," and in this way he contrasts, as he did earlier in 2:16, two means by which one might say the human being is rectified. It seems unlikely that Paul speaks here of the rectification of Christ himself.

by faith. Here there are two questions: (a) In Paul's reading, to whose faith does

---

[92] Did the translator himself understand "the rectified one" to be a reference to the messiah? See the discussion below and A. Strobel, *Untersuchungen*, 47–56; Koch, "Hab 2.4b," 73 n25.

[93] Hays has recently argued that, following a strain of Jewish-Christian tradition, Paul found in Habakkuk's figure of the rectified one a reference to Christ, the eschatological deliverer ("Righteous One"). In a word, Christ is the righteous one to whom God speaks the promise of Hab 2:4. As Hays formulates it, this is an impressive argument, certainly illuminating strands of Jewish and Jewish-Christian interpretation of Hab 2:4, presenting an interesting comparison of 1QpHab 8:1–3a with Heb 10:35–39, and perhaps telling us that Paul employed a double entendre in Rom 1:17, a reference both to Christ and to the Christian believer. It is, however, improbable that in writing Gal 3:11 Paul thought of the rectified one as Christ himself. See below.

the text of Habakkuk refer? (b) Does Paul understand the prepositional phrase "by faith" to modify the noun "the one who is rectified" or the verb "will live"?

(a) It is apparently Paul himself, rather than his source, who omits the possessive pronoun from Hab 2:4 (both in Gal 3:11 and in Rom 1:17), thus giving no linguistic guide as to whose faith he has in mind.[94] By doing that, he causes the phrase "by faith" to be interpreted from the context set by his own argument. From Gal 3:7, 8, and 9 one sees, then, that in the first instance Paul hears in Hab 2:4 a reference to faith on the part of the human being whom God has rectified in Christ. As we have seen repeatedly, however, that faith is far from being an autonomous deed of the human being. Just as the faith of which Habakkuk speaks is a reflection of God's faithfulness, so the faith to which Paul refers is elicited, kindled, incited by the faith of Christ, enacted in his atoning death. For that reason Paul can use the single word "faith" to speak simultaneously of Christ's faith and of the faith it kindles, referring in fact to the coming of this faith into the world as the eschatological event that is also the coming of Christ (3:23–25). In the promise of Hab 2:4 he hears, then, a reference to this hypostatized faith.[95] This is a point that must be consistently borne in mind when one uses the expression "rectification by faith."

(b) Is the promise as Paul hears it "The one who is rectified by faith will live," or is it "The one who is rectified will live by faith"? The second reading can be supported if one thinks that Paul quotes Lev 18:5 in the next verse, in order in some fashion to draw a contrast between *living* by faith and *living* by observing the commandments.[96] The first reading is suggested, however, by a contrast that can be seen internal to Gal 3:11 itself. Is the human being *rectified* "by the Law" or "by faith"? A decision between these two readings proves to be difficult, as one can see by surveying the commentaries.

But, in fact, Gal 3:21 suggests that the two readings would mean the same thing to Paul, for in that verse he equates rectification with making alive.

If a Law had been given that was strong enough to make people alive, then things would have been made right by the Law.

Being made alive by God and being rectified by God are the same event (cf. Rom 4:17 in its context). Paul's own reading of Hab 2:4 leads us, then, to paraphrase Gal 3:11 by taking the prepositional phrase both with the noun and with the verb:

Who is the one who is being rectified by God? Not the one who seeks rectification by the Law. That is clear from the fact that, "The one who is rectified by faith will find faith to be the wellspring of true life."

will live." The major clue to Paul's understanding of this future-tense verb lies in an expression he employs in 3:21b (see above): "strong enough to make alive."

[94] See Verhoef, *Geschreven*, 74.
[95] Cf. Haussleiter, *Glaube*; Howard, "Notes"; Hays, *Faith*.
[96] A strong argument for the adverbial reading of the prepositional phrase is given by Smith, "*Ho de dikaios ek pisteôs zêsetai.*"

God's deed of setting things right is not a mere matter of improving the scene of human existence. In Christ, God is engaged in new creation (6:15), in setting things right by making alive those threatened with certain death. To Paul's ears, then, Habakkuk's text does not speak of continued life, but of the new life God is now creating in the one who is rectified by faith.

Given the powerful climax provided by this quotation from Habakkuk, one might think that Paul would feel no more need for negative statements about the Law. Before he comes in v 13 to his climactic affirmation of redemption from the Law's curse, however, he adds one more exegetical attack, displaying in further detail what is wrong with the Law itself.

12. *Moreover, the Law does not have its origin in faith; if it did have its origin there, it would not say, "The one who does the commandments will live by them."* The reason for Paul's continued attack, and specifically for his citation of Lev 18:5 — "The one who does the commandments will live by them" — lies almost certainly in his anticipation that the Teachers will cite this very text in their exegetical rebuttal of his letter.[97] He is sure, that is, that, just as in the present passage he is meeting the Teachers' scriptural argument with a scriptural argument of his own, so the Teachers will do the same after hearing his letter. Noting Paul's use of Hab 2:4, they will almost certainly meet scripture with scripture, quoting Lev 18:5 or a similar text in order to demonstrate to the Galatians, once again, that Law observance is the divinely ordained path to life.[98] And in doing that, they will employ a well-fixed form, that of the Textual Contradiction. In composing vv 11–12 Paul himself employs that form as a sort of preemptive strike, in order to show that the promise of Lev 18:5 is a falsification of the gospel (Comment #35).

does not have its origin in faith. With this assertion Paul disqualifies the Law on the basis of its origin, a matter to which he will return in 3:19–20. Just as blessing and curse met one another for the first time in the event of Christ's crucifixion (v 13), so the Law and faith, having distinct origins, met there for the first time also (cf. vv 23–25).

if it did have its origin there, it would not say. With the little word *alla*, "but rather," Paul turns to Lev 18:5, indicating what the Law actually says as a result of its not having its genesis in faith. Translating *alla* more literally, we could render v 12, "Moreover, the Law does not have its origin in faith; *but rather*, failing to have its origin there, it says, 'The one who does the commandments will live by them.' "

"The one who does the commandments. Paul speaks simply of "the one," whereas the LXX version available to him probably spoke of "the man" (*an-*

---

[97]It is possible, of course, that in doing that the Teachers would have repeated themselves.
[98]Various Jewish interpretations of Lev 18:5 can be cited to illuminate the Teachers' probable reading of it as God's gracious provision of the path of life (cf. Ezek 20:11; Neh 9:29). Note that the quotation of Lev 18:5 in CD 3:15–16 lies in a context that emphasizes the power of the Law to overcome the death-dealing power of the Impulsive Desire of the Flesh, a theme of the Teachers (Comments #32 and #49). Cf. also 1QH 5:6. Without the antidote of God's Law (the healing plaster for the wound; *b. Qidd.* 30b) there is no effective resistance to the lethal Impulse. By keeping God's commandments, however, one will gain deliverance from the Impulse and thus life (cf. Sir 15:14–17; *Gen. Rab.* 89:1).

thrôpos). Did the Teachers adhere to the reading of the LXX, applying the term "man" to the Gentiles? Note the rabbinic tradition: "Whence can you know that a Gentile who practices the Law is equal to the High Priest? Because it says, 'Which if a *man* do, he shall live through them.' "[99]

will live by them." In v 21a Paul says categorically that the Law is impotent to grant life. Taken together with Paul's use of the form of the Textual Contradiction (Comment #35), that bald assertion seals the case against Lev 18:5. To Paul it is a false promise; in his daily work among the Gentiles he sees that it does not prove true (cf. Deut 18:22).[100] That this shocking reading of Lev 18:5 is the one intended by Paul is also suggested by his interpretation of that same text in Rom 10:5.[101] There, having drawn a strict distinction between two rectifications — the one that comes from God (vv 3, 6) and the one that comes from the Law (v 5a) — Paul cites Lev 18:5 as the voice of the latter (cf. Phil 3:9).[102] The wording Paul uses for Lev 18:5 in Rom 10:5 is somewhat uncertain; there are textual variants. It may well be, however, that in this case he changes the final phrase of that text from "will live by them" to "will live by *it*," thus referring to the nomistic rectification that he has just distinguished from the rectification that comes from God.[103]

13. *Christ redeemed us from the Law's curse, becoming a curse in our behalf; for it stands written: "Cursed is everyone who is hanged on a tree." 14. He did this in order that the blessing of Abraham might come to the Gentiles in Jesus Christ; in order, that is, that we might receive the promise, which is the Spirit, through faith.* Verses 13 and 14 constitute a single sentence in which Paul reaches back to vv 8–10, showing finally how and with what result the Law's curse and God's blessing have met one another.

[99]*Sipra*, Achrei Mot, Perek 13:12; see also *b. B. Qam.* 38a, where Lev 18:5 is taken as a promise to Gentiles. Stanley suggests that Paul may have omitted the word *anthrôpos* in order to make Lev 18:5 correspond in form to Hab 2:4 (*Scripture*, 245).

[100]Cf. Lindemann, "Gerechtigkeit"; Hays, *Faith*, 207, 219–221. Paul's reading of Lev 18:5 thus runs exactly counter to the targumic traditions in which that text is said to speak of everlasting life (see *Tg. Onq.* and *Tg. Ps.-J.*). Hübner, *Law*; Ridderbos, *Paul*; Wilckens, *Römer*; and others think that Paul considered Lev 18:5 to pronounce a promise that is *theoretically* true: if one could observe all the commandments, one would live. See the trenchant critique by E. P. Sanders, *Law*, 54 n20. There is, to be sure, some tension between Galatians and Romans in regard to the relationship between the Law and life. In Rom 7:10 (cf. 9:30–31) Paul identifies life as the goal of the commandment. Neither there nor elsewhere, however, does he say that the cause of failure to reach this goal was inadequate observance. See the comments of Meyer on Israel's unattained goal, "Romans," 1156–1157.

[101]In Rom 10:5 Paul credits the false promise of Lev 18:5 to Moses; that reading raises questions that cannot be pursued here. For example, does he mean to identify Moses as a false prophet, one who pronounced in the name of the Lord something that has not come true (cf. Deut 18:21–22)?

[102]In Rom 10:5 Paul hears the voice of the rectification that originates with God in Deut 30:12–14 rather than in Hab 2:4.

[103]See, for example, Wilckens, *Römer*, 2.224. The argument of Vos is partly correct: in Rom 10:5 Paul cites Lev 18:5 because his opponents have already done that ("Antinomie," 268). That in Romans 10, as in Galatians 3, Paul means to affirm the divine authority of Lev 18:5 is, however, altogether unlikely.

Christ redeemed us from the Law's curse. Having spoken (negatively) of the Law's genesis, Paul refers here to the termination of its curse. That universal curse would have had no terminus except for the appearance of a greater power, for standing on the scene presented in v 10 are only the cursing Law and human beings, the latter in a state of hopeless enslavement. The greater power arrived then in the person of Christ, who embodied the faith Paul has just contrasted with the Law (v 12). And to speak of what Christ did vis-à-vis the Law's curse, Paul now employs, in the past tense, the verb *exagorazô*, which refers to the action of one person redeeming another by delivering him from slavery.[104] That meaning is clear from Paul's use of the same verb in 4:5, where he speaks explicitly of redemption from enslavement (4:1, 3).[105]

With the meaning "to deliver from slavery," the verb *exagorazô* becomes, then, a synonym for the verb "to rectify," "to make right," supplying the definition that was lacking in 2:16 (Comment #28). By employing this verb Paul thus reinforces the picture of the human scene that he presupposes throughout the letter. To be a human being—whether Jew or Gentile—is to be a slave under the authority of malignant powers (2:4; 4:7; 4:24; 5:1; cf. Phil 2:7). In the present context the enslaving power is the Law's curse, and rectification consists of Christ's having freed us from the grip of that curse (cf. 1:4).

us. There are several grounds for being confident that Paul refers here to the whole of the human race.[106] (a) As we have seen in the Note on v 10, he considers the Law's curse to be universal, falling both on those who observe it and on those who do not (see also Comment #36). (b) In the second clause of the present verse Paul says that Christ's liberating act was carried out by him *hyper hêmôn,* "in our behalf," a phrase that refers in Paul's mouth to the redemptive act Christ has performed for *all* human beings (see 1:4, and cf. Rom 8:32). (c) As we have noted above, enslavement under the Law's curse is for Paul the major mark of the fact that, prior to Christ, all human beings stood under the power of the world's elements (Comments #39 and #41). (d) Liberated from this enslavement, "we" receive the Spirit (final clause of v 14), a reference by which Paul certainly does not intend to speak only of a Jewish sector within the church. For in early Christian parlance receipt of the Spirit is a fundamental characteristic of all members of the church of God.

In short, then, the pronouns of vv 13–14 point to one of the central facets of Paul's thought in Galatians: In essence the human race was a monolith prior to

---

[104]Cf. Diodorus Siculus 15.7.1. If one says that the deliverance involves the paying of a price, then to ask for the identity of the person or power to whom the price is paid is, as regards Paul's intentions, to press the image too far.

[105]A number of exegetes have seen in parts of 3:13–14 a pre-Pauline formula of some sort, perhaps a Jewish-Christian midrash on the Binding of Isaac (Genesis 22). See notably Dahl, "Atonement." Dahl's suggestion may have some pertinence to the interpretation of Rom 8:32, but it is probably irrelevant to Gal 3:13. It is for the Galatian situation that Paul turns to the words *katara* and *exagorazô*; and in any case, as we will see below, Paul is far from thinking that it was Jews only whom Christ redeemed from the Law's curse.

[106]The identity of this "us" continues to be debated. In addition to the commentaries, see Eckert, *Streit*, 78 n3; Hays, *Faith*, 128 n18; Wright, *Covenant*, 143.

Christ's advent, and it is the human race as a whole that Christ has liberated. True enough, Paul's own commission is focused on the preaching of the gospel to the Gentiles (1:16; 2:7, 9), and he is more than willing to emphasize that fact. He will not accept, however, the Teachers' insistence on a basic difference between Jews and Gentiles.

becoming a curse in our behalf. We expect something like "bearing the weight of the curse in our behalf." Instead, Paul strikingly says that Christ became a curse for us. Elsewhere he uses similar language:

[God] is the source of your life in Christ Jesus, who, by God's action, *has become* for us wisdom, and rectification, and sanctification, and redemption . . . (1 Cor 1:30).

The one who was free of sin God *made into* sin in our behalf, in order that in him we might become God's rectification (2 Cor 5:21).

The second of these is particularly instructive, for, almost certainly an early Jewish-Christian confession, it clearly reflects sacrificial language that was employed in ancient Israel.[107] By laying his hands on an animal that was to be sacrificed a man transmitted his sin to it, the result being that the animal, having become sin, was itself called "sin" (*ḥēṭ*, often translated as "sin-offering").[108] By using this linguistic pattern the early Christian who formulated the confession quoted in 2 Cor 5:21 expressed two convictions: (a) sin is something that can be transferred from one person to another; (b) God transferred our sin to Christ, thus freeing us from its effect.

By analogy it seems that in Gal 3:13 Paul does not intend to say that Christ fell under the Law's curse because he committed discrete transgressions.[109] On the contrary, just as Christ embodied (and elicited) the faith spoken of by Habakkuk (Gal 3:12), so he embodied the Law's curse. When one looked at him, as he was being crucified (3:1), one saw the only juncture at which that embodied faith met that embodied curse in all of its power.[110]

---

[107] See Furnish, *II Corinthians*, 340.

[108] See Jer 24:9; Zech 8:13; cf. Thyen, *Südenvergebung*.

[109] Contrast Philo's portrait of Cain, who suffered the curses of the cosmic elements because of his sin (*Quest. Gen.* 1.71–74).

[110] Gal 3:13 involves, therefore, more than the standard formulation of the doctrine of substitutionary atonement. To be sure, Christ became the Law's curse *in our behalf.* But he did that not simply by taking onto himself a punishment due us but by embodying the curse, in such a way as to be, in his crucifixion, *victorious* over its enslaving power. Paul places the thought of apocalyptic warfare in the foreground. There are not three actors — the guilty human being, Christ as the substitutionary sacrifice for that person's guilt, and God, who, accepting that sacrifice, forgives the guilty human being. There are four actors: the powerful, enslaving curse of the Law, human beings enslaved under the power of that curse, Christ, who comes to embody the enslaving curse, and God, who in this Christ powerfully defeats the Law's curse, thus liberating human beings from their state of enslavement. Central to the action in this apocalyptic struggle is, therefore, not forgiveness, but rather victory, God's victory in Christ and the resultant emancipation of human beings (Comment #28).

for it stands written: "Cursed is everyone who is hanged on a tree." Having prefixed his exegesis, as in v 10, Paul quotes the climactic text by which he addresses the subject of the Law's curse, Deut 21:23. We can be confident that it is not a text employed by the Teachers. On the contrary, it is a scriptural citation of Paul's own choosing, the only scriptural text, in fact, by which Paul ever interprets Christ's death.[111]

In ancient Israel this text had to do with instances in which criminals were guilty of particularly odious offenses. After the offender was stoned to death, a second step was taken: his dead body was hanged up on a tree, in order, by exposing it to public view, to provide a deterrent to crime. There was, however, a strict limit to the length of time the body could be left on the tree. It had to be taken down and buried before nightfall, because a corpse hanged up on a tree is that of a person cursed by God, and to leave such a corpse indefinitely exposed to view is to pollute the land given to Israel by God:

> . . . his body shall not remain all night upon the tree, but you shall bury him the same day, for everyone who has been hanged up on a tree is cursed by

[111]Early Christian understandings of the relationship between the scripture/Law and Christ's death form a very complex subject. See now R. E. Brown, *Death*. Fundamentally, there were three possibilities: (a) As Jesus was crucified by the Roman military establishment occupying Palestine, his death could have been interpreted as that of a Jewish martyr *who gave his all in behalf of the Law*. An analogy could have been drawn between Jesus and the Maccabean martyrs who, at the cost of their lives, upheld the Law in the face of a godless occupying power. But the traditions recounting Jesus' death included indications that the Jewish authorities had conveyed him to the Romans, and this element in the picture scarcely suggested in its simple form a positive relationship between Jesus' death and the Law. And since Paul knew of traditions linking Jesus' death to the Jewish authorities (1 Thess 2:15), he is unlikely ever to have interpreted Jesus as a martyr of the Maccabean stripe. (b) The second possibility would also affirm — in a sense to be explicated — a positive relationship between the Law and Jesus' death, finding in that event a fulfillment of the Law as scripture. From the formula quoted by Paul in 1 Cor 15:3 ("Christ died in behalf of our sins in accordance with the scriptures") we know that early Christians did indeed interpret Christ's death as a fulfillment of *scriptural prophecy*, and each of the four evangelists develops this motif in his own way, emphasizing the word "scripture" rather than the word "Law." Yet one would have to issue here a strong caveat, not least because of that terminological differentiation. In Mark's passion narrative, for example, Jesus is crucified by the Romans for *maiestas*, but with equal clarity he is under the Jewish Law a blasphemer, worthy of death, a criminal by the standard of the Law, and thus very probably one who was denied an honorable burial (R. E. Brown, "Burial"). 1 Cor 15:3 notwithstanding, then, we cannot find in any early Christian tradition a simple and positive relationship between Jesus' death and the Law. There is always the essential qualification that the Law played some kind of negative role in his death. (c) That observation leads us to the third possibility. Jesus, although crucified by the Romans for their own reasons, died in conflict with the Jewish Law. As we have noted, this understanding underlies Mark's passion narrative, where the Sanhedrin finds Jesus to have run afoul of the Law by committing blasphemy, and where a member of the Sanhedrin fulfills the Law by seeing to it that this condemned criminal is buried before sundown, yet in a way that is "scarcely honorable" (R. E. Brown, "Burial," 243). As we will see below, in Gal 3:13 Paul explores the view that Jesus died in *conflict* with the Law insofar as it had the power to pronounce a curse.

God; and you shall not defile the land which the Lord your God gave you as an inheritance (Deut 21:23; LXX).

Paul's citation deviates from the LXX in three important regards.[112]

(a) Whereas the LXX of Deut 21:22 follows the Hebrew in saying that the criminal is first put to death (by stoning), and only subsequently hanged up for public display, Paul limits his citation to Deut 21:23b, thus making it possible to read the expression "who is hanged on a tree" as a reference not to the elevation of a dead body, but rather to the act of executing a man by crucifixion, that is by nailing him alive to a cross. In short, for Paul "tree" means "cross."

This reading of Deut 21:23 as a reference to crucifixion is not unique to Paul. We find it in Qumran.[113] We also find it in sources that may reflect Jewish polemic against the early church's confession of Jesus as God's Messiah.[114] Indeed, a scriptural argument based on Deut 21:23 may have played an important role in the passion with which Paul the Pharisee rejected the church's confession: a crucified criminal, necessarily enduring the curse of God, cannot possibly have been God's Messiah.[115]

(b) Now, however, while retaining the view that in the crucifixion there was a head-on collision between the Law and Christ, Paul the apostle reverses the polemical use of Deut 21:23 by a second textual change. Both in the LXX and in the Hebrew the criminal guilty of a capital offense is said to be cursed by God. In a highly significant move Paul omits the phrase "by God," thus dissociating the curse from God, linking it solely to the Law, and causing the quoted text to

---

[112]Wilcox, to be sure, argues that Paul is drawing on a reading of Deut 21:23 other than that of the LXX ("Tree," 86–90). See also Verhoef, *Geschreven*, 81–86; Stanley, *Scripture*, 245–248.

[113]The Qumran Essenes knew of crucifixion as practiced by the Romans and others. They seem even to have adopted crucifixion as a form of punishment in their own community; and they saw in Deut 21:23 a reference in the Law to the punishment by *crucifixion* of treasonous *Israelites* (see footnotes 185 and 187 in chapter 2 above). Precisely on the basis of Deut 21:23, then, the Qumran Essenes would certainly not have accepted as God's Messiah a man crucified as a criminal.

[114]The use of Deut 21:23 in Jewish polemic against the confession of Jesus as God's Messiah is almost certainly reflected in the fourth-century *Syriac Didascalia* (see Connolly, *Didascalia*, pp. 222 line 25, 230 line 18). And two passages in Justin *Dial.* (89:1; 90:1) push that Jewish polemic back to the middle of the second century (cf. *Gospel of Nicodemus* 16). See G. Jeremias, *Lehrer*, 134–135; Roloff, "Anfänge," 40 n3; Hultgren, "Persecutions," 103; Stuhlmacher, *Criticism*, 24. It is impossible to be sure that this polemic was formulated as early as Paul's time, but, as noted above, we know from Qumran that by means of Deut 21:23 a connection had already been drawn between crucifixion and God's curse. The thesis that prior to Paul Deut 21:23 was employed in a positive way by Jewish Christians becomes unlikely when one notes that the arguments advanced in its favor draw on positive motifs in Gal 3:13–14 almost certainly coined by Paul himself. See Dahl, "Atonement"; Wilcox, "Tree."

[115]Hultgren, "Persecutions," 102–104. As we will see, even in his Christian interpretation of Deut 21:23 Paul retains the view of a head-on collision between the Law and the crucified Christ. As one crucified, Jesus did stand under the curse of the Law. Now, however, Paul sees that in that event God stood on the side of his Christ, not on the side of the cursing voice of the Law.

conform to his prefixed exegesis. The voice of God and the voice of the Law are by no means the same. It was the Law, not God, that pronounced a curse on the crucified one.

(c) Where the LXX speaks of the curse by using the perfect participle *kekatêra-menos*, Paul uses the adjective *epikataratos*, thus finding in the text itself a link between the curse pronounced by the Law on the crucified Christ and the curse pronounced by the Law on all human beings (*epikataratos* in Deut 27:26 quoted in v 10 above). The drama of the cross was not a private affair between God's Christ and the Law. On the contrary, as Paul says in his prefixed exegesis (v 13a), Christ's embodiment of the Law's curse was the act in which the Law was robbed of its universal power to curse. And what does the ensuing emancipation mean for the human race? Paul answers that question in two parallel clauses.

14. *in order that . . . in order, that is, that.* The two purpose clauses are linguistically parallel to one another, and taken together they complete the initial clause of v 13. By his atoning death Christ redeemed us from the Law's curse, not only in order to liberate us from that curse but also, that curse being laid aside,

> in order that
> a. The blessing of Abraham
>   b. might come
>   c. to the Gentiles
>   d. in Jesus Christ,
> in order, that is, that
>   c. we
>   b. might receive
> a. the promise, which is the Spirit
>   d. through faith.

To a degree Paul stays with the vocabulary of the Teachers, speaking initially of the blessing of Abraham and of the Gentiles. He makes, however, significant changes, especially in the second clause, where he replaces "the blessing" with "the promise" (remaining with that word for the remainder of the letter), and where he equates the promise with the Spirit the Galatians received when he preached the gospel to them.[116] Again, then, he takes the Teachers' vocabulary captive to the truth of the gospel.

the blessing of Abraham. The expression is drawn from Gen 28:3–4, where Isaac, Abraham's son, blesses his own son, Jacob, saying:

> May God Almighty bless you and make you fruitful and numerous, that you may become a company of peoples. May he give to you the blessing of Abraham, to you and to your offspring with you, so that you may take possession of the land . . . that God gave to Abraham (NRSV).

Aside from Galatians there is no indication of Paul's interest in the phrase "the blessing of Abraham." It seems likely, then, that just as it is the Teachers who

---

[116] See Lull, *Spirit*, 153–154.

have employed Gen 12:3, with its reference to the coming of the Abrahamic blessing to the Gentiles (Gal 3:8), so it is also the Teachers who have first introduced the Galatians to the pithy phrase "the blessing of Abraham."

might come. Whereas the Teachers referred to a movement on the part of the Gentiles — they can acquire the blessing of Abraham by *entering* the community of his true, Law-observant descendants — Paul refers to the advent of the Abrahamic blessing as it *comes to* the Gentiles (*ginomai eis*), now that the cursing voice of the Law has been silenced. Even an expected reference to the *fulfillment* of God's promise to Abraham is overshadowed by what might be termed Paul's "advent language" (Comment #37).

to the Gentiles. In the Notes on vv 10 and 11 we have seen that with his reading of Deut 27:26 and with the expression "no one" Paul took leave of all distinguishing marks in the human race. The statement that rectification is not found in the realm of the Law is true of every human being, not merely of the Jew. Does Paul now reintroduce the Jew/Gentile distinction, holding that, whereas the Jews always had the blessing of Abraham via the Law, that blessing comes to the Gentiles only in Christ?[117]

Not at all. Because the Galatians are Gentiles, because the Teachers are speaking exclusively of the redemption of the Gentiles, and because his own mission is directed to Gentiles, Paul speaks exclusively to the issue of Gentile redemption, as we have noted above. We have also seen, however, that, by referring to the receipt of the Spirit, Paul includes all members of the church, both former Jews, such as himself, and former Gentiles, such as the Galatians. Apart from Christ, neither Jew nor Gentile had received the Abrahamic blessing, that is to say the promised Spirit.

in Jesus Christ. With this phrase Paul reflects on a fact well known to the Galatian Gentiles, but about which the Teachers have confused them. The Spirit came to them not via the Law, but rather in Jesus Christ. In the present sentence that means specifically and emphatically in the Christ who was crucified and in whose crucifixion the Galatians themselves participated at their baptism (2:19; 3:27). In 3:14 Paul thus pens a reprise of 3:2 (a second reprise comes in 4:6): the Spirit came and comes from the proclamation of Christ's atoning death, not from the Law.[118]

in order, that is, that we might receive the promise, which is the Spirit.

---

[117]See Gager, *Origins*, 238, with references to the work of Gaston; cf. M. Barth, *Ephesians*, 242–252.
[118]Given Paul's extensive development of the Law/faith antinomy (2:16, 3:2, 5, 6–12), we should not have been surprised to hear him say that the blessing of Abraham passed to the Gentiles not via the Law, but rather by faith (cf. v 11). Instead, he says that this passage takes place in Jesus Christ, that is to say in his atoning death, and thus neither in the Law nor by something that human beings do, such as decide to have faith. We see once again that the primary and generative antinomy is the Law versus the death of Christ (N.B. 2:21). And from the last phrase of the present verse we see that the Law/faith antinomy is secondary to and derived from that primary one. If the Teachers are offering the Galatians the Abrahamic blessing via their incorporation into Law-observant Abraham (note *en soi*, "in you," in v 8, and cf. Gen 22:18), Paul will speak immediately not about faith, but rather about the figure of the dying Christ, presupposing the motif of incorporation into

we. This is another of those points at which Paul undermines ethnic and religious distinctions in the church by including himself, a person of Jewish lineage, with the Galatians, persons of Gentile descent. See Comment #36.

the promise. We have seen above that Paul takes over from the Teachers not only the text in which God says that he will bless the Gentiles in Abraham (v 8) but also the pithy expression "the blessing of Abraham." Having used that expression for the sake of contact with the Galatians' current interest, he now introduces the term "promise," henceforth putting that term in the place of the Teachers' word "blessing." He does not draw this new term from scripture (it does not stand in any of the texts he has quoted; indeed, it scarcely occurs at all in the LXX).[119] The word "promise" may very well have been linked with the gift of the Spirit in Christian tradition prior to Paul (Luke 24:49; Acts 1:4–5; 2:33; Eph 1:13). In any case, having now replaced the Teachers' word "blessing" with a term of his own selection, "promise," Paul stays with that term, giving it a key role in the next subsection of his exegesis as the entity that stands in sharp contrast to the Law (vv 16, 17; twice in v 18; [the verb in v 19]; vv 21, 22, 29), and returning to it in 4:23, 28.[120]

which is the Spirit. Substituting "promise" (without modifier) for "blessing of Abraham," and equating the promise with the Spirit, Paul assures the Galatians that they have been recipients of that promise for some time, having received the Spirit when they were grasped by the gospel of the crucified Christ (3:2).[121] Coming as the Spirit, God's promise institutes and constitutes a new state of affairs. As Paul makes clear elsewhere, however, this state of affairs is itself promissory of yet more (5:5).[122]

through faith. Having made doubly clear that it is Christ's death in conflict with the Law that has brought both liberation from the Law's curse and the gift of the Spirit, Paul can add, importantly, that this gift is received not through observance of the Law, but rather through the faith that is elicited by Christ's faithful death in our behalf (3:1–2).

With the two purpose clauses of 3:14 Paul has now summarized the argument of 3:1–5 and 3:6–13 in reverse order:

> . . . in order that the blessing of Abraham might come to the Gentiles in Jesus Christ (3:6–13)

> in order, that is, that we might receive the promise, which is the Spirit, through faith (3:1–5)

---

him (3:16 and 3:26–29). Cf. Dahl, *Studies*, 130–134; Hays, *Faith*, 157–176; Wilcox, "Tree," 96–99.

[119]The term "promise" appears in connection with Abraham, Isaac, and Jacob in *Ezekiel the Tragedian* 104–107, but that is very unlikely to have been the source from which Paul took it.

[120]This point was missed by an early scribe who continued to use the word "blessing" in v 14 (p46 etc.).

[121]Note Isa 44:3, "I will pour my spirit upon your descendants, and my blessing on your offspring."

[122]See Morse, *Logic*; Lehmann, *Transfiguration*, 234–235.

By reversing the order Paul indicates the relative weights of the two matters. He is willing, as we have seen, to make contact with the Galatians by taking up the Teachers' theme of the inclusion of the Gentiles in the Abrahamic blessing. For him, however, that theme can play its true role only by leading the discussion back to the coming of the Spirit to all members of the church. Verse 14 thus marks the end of the first section of the exegesis.

COMMENT #34
THE BLESSING GOD, THE CURSING LAW, AND THE CROSS

THE TEACHERS: THE ABRAHAMIC BLESSING, THE THREAT OF THE CURSE, AND THE DOCTRINE OF THE TWO WAYS

In their instruction of the Galatians the Teachers are certain to have balanced their comments about God's blessing of Abraham with references to the threat of God's curse.

(1) *Blessing and curse.* Just as it was surely in the Teachers' interpretation of Gen 12:3 that the Galatians first heard of the connection between Law observance and what they came to see as the much desired Abrahamic blessing (Gal 3:8), so it must have been from the Teachers that they first learned of the connection between failure to observe the Law and curse.[123] Because the Teachers found both blessing and curse in the Law, it is easy to imagine that they referred explicitly to the paired blessings and curses in Deuteronomy 27 and 28. In any case, they probably quoted the summary of the curses in Deut 27:26. For, as we have seen in the Note on 3:10, there are sound reasons to think that, when Paul cites that verse himself, he is taking captive one of the Teachers' own texts. Presumably, drawing both on Gen 12:3 and on Deut 27:26, the Teachers said something like the following:

As we have pointed out, it is imperative for you Galatian Gentiles to know what the Law tells us about the Abrahamic blessing. But in the same Law, God also speaks of curse: "Cursed is everyone who is not steadfast in observing all of the things written in the book of the Law, so as to do them." Take heed, then! God's blessing passes only to those Gentiles who escape God's curse by commencing observance of the Law. For blessing and curse are both pronounced by God in his Law.

In some such way the Teachers presented to the Galatians a miniature Table of Opposites in which they displayed two human alternatives, both of which are declared by the Law:

those who observe the Law	those who do not observe the Law
blessing (Gen 12:3)	curse (Deut 27:26).

---

[123]The threat Paul issued to the Galatians when he was with them had no connection with failure to observe the Law (5:21).

(2) *The curse of the Law in the framework of the doctrine of the Two Ways.* We can be confident, moreover, that the Teachers presented these alternatives as a form of the ancient doctrine of the Two Ways:[124]

> Walk in the way of Law observance, and, as the Law declares, God will bless you within the corpus of Abraham's descendants. Walk in the way of nonobservance, and, as the Law also declares, God will place his curse on you, excluding you from his people. God's holy Law speaks of these two ways, blessing and curse.

Thus, for the Teachers (a) both blessing and curse, having their origin in God, are stated in God's Law. (b) Blessing and curse are of equal age, both having been placed before ancient Israel throughout its history. (c) Now, with the advent of God's Messiah, both blessing and curse are spoken also to the Gentile nations, offering to Law-observant Gentiles the blessing of Abraham, and threatening with a curse those Gentiles who remain nonobservant (see 4:17).[125]

PAUL: THE BLESSING GOD, THE CURSING LAW, THE CROSS, AND THE SPIRIT

In his use of the terms "blessing" and "curse" Paul presents a fundamentally different picture.[126]

(1) *God blesses; the Law curses.* Whereas the Teachers find both blessing and curse in God's Law, Paul sees that the blessing and the curse do not come from the same source. Having begun in 2:19 to display a gulf between the Law and God, Paul dramatically widens that gulf in 3:8–20. He attributes the blessing to God. And he attributes the curse to the Law (a) that is plural in nature, consisting of many commandments (3:10, 12b), (b) that was instituted by angels in God's absence (3:19), and (c) that, linked with its opposite, the Not-Law, constituted one of the enslaving elements of the cosmos (4:3; Comment #41).[127] This same

---

[124]Various strands of Jewish and Jewish-Christian thought in the first century preserved that ancient doctrine, according to which Israel was constituted as God's people when God placed before them "the Way of life and the Way of death." To obey God's commandments is to live; to disobey them is to die (Jer 21:8; cf. Deut 27:12–13; Sir 2:12; 15:16; Matt 7:13–14; *m.* '*Abot* 2:1; Jas 2:8–13). Within this frame of reference, the Teachers used the terms "blessing" and "curse" to name the two actions of God that are dependent on the path chosen by the Gentiles to whom they brought their message.

[125]If, in relation to this aspect of the Teachers' message, one asks about the impact of the advent of Christ, then the third of these points gives the answer: According to the Teachers, Christ's coming involves extending both blessing and curse to the Gentiles.

[126]That Paul's picture is drawn from a Deuteronomic view of history is the thesis of Scott, "Deuteronomic Tradition." For reasons that will become clear in the present Comment, I find this thesis unconvincing. See also Comments #35 and #37.

[127]That God is the author of the blessing is a point Paul emphasizes repeatedly, by equating the blessing with the promise and then by equating both with the Spirit. The promise was spoken to Abraham by God (implied by the passive verb in v 16). It was freely given to Abraham by God (v 18). It has now been given to believers by God (passive verb in v 22). The curse, however, is the work of the Law that entered the picture 430 years after God had pronounced his blessing. Moreover, in its power to curse, the Law collided with God's Christ at the cross. It is clear, then, that in Galatians 2–4 (except for 4:21b), Paul is

bifurcation emerges in another form in 3:11–12, where Paul finds in Hab 2:4 and Lev 18:5 God's true promise of life and the Law's false promise of life respectively (Comment #35). Numerous interpreters have seen in Paul's denial that the Law is opposed to the (blessed) promises of God proof that both are to be credited to God (3:21a). But to read the denial of 3:21a in the light of 3:15 and 3:17 is to see that the major focus of that denial reflects a quite different intention on Paul's part: The angelic Law is not opposed to God's promissory blessing in the sense of being potent enough to annul it. In reading Gal 3:6–4:7 we are left, then, with Paul's startling attribution of the blessing to God and of the curse to the Law.

(2) *God's blessing antedated the Law's curse; yet it did that in a way that involves more than chronological anteriority.* Blessing and curse are not of equal age. God's blessing of Abraham antedated the Law and thus the curse of the Law (v 17). Yet that blessing was a point, not the beginning of a line (v 16). Thus, although God's promissory blessing antedated the Law's curse, these two entities did not run alongside one another throughout the period of the Law.[128] On the contrary, during that period the promise waited in the wings, so to speak (Comment #37).

(3) *God's blessing, the Law's curse, the cross, and the Spirit.*[129] The promissory blessing of God that had been waiting in the wings met the curse of the Law for the first time at the cross. As Paul hears Deut 21:23 (Gal 3:13), it was the Law, not God, that pronounced its curse on the crucified one, and the one thus cursed by the Law was in fact God's Christ. It was in the cross that Paul came to see a momentous fact about the Law: its cursing voice is not the voice of God.[130] But he saw also that that voice was robbed of its power when, approved by God in his Law-cursed death, Christ embodied the Law's curse, for in that embodiment Christ vanquished that curse, freeing the whole of humanity from its power.

One scarcely needs to say that the resulting picture is highly paradoxical, especially since, although Paul presupposes the resurrection, he does not allow it to divert his gaze from the cross. The victory of God's promissory blessing over the Law's curse was enacted, that is to say, in the apparent defeat of the crucifixion itself, suggesting that in that event God fundamentally redefined both strength and weakness, causing them from one point of view to exchange places (see espe-

---

very far from referring to "the Law of God" (contrast Rom 7:22, 25; 8:7). On the contrary, he speaks in Galatians 2–4 of the Law in its paired existence with the Not-Law, and, in that mode of existence, the Law is a cursing power, active at a considerable remove from God. Nowhere in Galatians is the Law a merely passive instrument that has fallen into the active hands of Sin (contrast Rom 7:11; 8:2–3). That, even in Galatians, Paul can also speak of the Law loosed from its cursing, paired existence, and thus functioning as a witness to God's redemptive action in the circumcision-free mission — even as a witness to the pattern of daily life in the church — is a matter taken up in Comments #45 and #48.

[128]The thought that God's promise ran through Israel's history *in hidden form* can be sensed in Romans 9–11 (cf. Käsemann, *Perspectives*, 68 line 11, where the German should be rendered "Measured by human criteria, salvation is fundamentally hidden in disaster"). This thought cannot be found in Galatians.

[129]Cf. Cosgrove, *Cross*; Cousar, *Cross*.

[130]In his poem "Jerusalem," William Blake grasps part of Paul's point: "When Satan first the black bow bent, And the Moral Law from the Gospel rent, He forg'd the Law into a sword, And spill'd the blood of Mercy's Lord." See also Comment #48.

cially 2 Corinthians 10–13 and Rom 8:36). For precisely when the Law exerted the ultimate power of its curse — doing its worst to Christ in the weakness of his death — Christ robbed the Law of its power to curse others. In this paradoxical cross, then, the way was opened for the Abrahamic blessing to come to the Gentiles. Or, putting the same thing in other words, the way was opened for the promised Spirit to come to all members of God's church, Jew and Gentile alike.

We see, then, that Paul's view of blessing and curse arises from the role played by the cursing Law in the crucifixion of Christ.[131] It is indeed typical of Paul's theology that the true nature of things emerges only in the light of God's act in Christ. Precisely how does the Law's curse look when it is viewed in light of its role in the crucifixion of Christ? Paul's answer has several parts:

(a) Knowing now that the Law's cursing role reached its climax when the Law pronounced its curse on none other than God's Christ, Paul also knows that the Teachers are completely mistaken in their way of identifying the curse. That curse does not apply merely to those who fail to observe the Law, excluding them from the gift of life. (b) True enough, in the period of the Law the curse set itself in opposition to the Abrahamic blessing, successfully blocking the coming of the blessing to the Gentiles prior to Christ (v 14) by uttering a false and misleading promise (v 12). (c) Even in that period, however, the Law did not in reality differentiate the observant from the nonobservant, cursing only the latter. On the contrary, the curse of the Law was universal, falling on every human being, observant and nonobservant, Jew and Gentile (v 10). (d) One is not altogether surprised, then, to see that, for Paul, Christ's act of redemption involves liberating human beings both from enslavement to the Law and from enslavement to the Not-Law (6:15), that pair forming one of the enslaving elements of the old cosmos (4:3–5).

(e) All of these points show, then, that the universal power of the Law's curse consists precisely of its act in differentiating and separating observant from nonobservant, the pious from the godless, Jew from Gentile. And the universal power of Christ is revealed in his lifting of that differentiating curse, so that the Abrahamic blessing might come to the Gentiles, so that God's one church might be created by the universal gift of the Spirit, so that in the church those who had been differentiated and separated from one another might be united (3:14, 28).

Paul's way of relating blessing and curse to the drama of the crucifixion and to the advent of the Spirit also reveals the apostle's decisive departure from the traditional form of the doctrine of the Two Ways. In a word, blessing and curse are not for Paul two alternative paths between which the human being can make a choice. If, after reading Gal 3:13, we were to speak at all of two ways, then we would have to say that one of these ways proves to be the way of the blessing God and the other the way of the cursing Law. For that reason the basic issue un-

---

[131]We see also the consequent role of Christ's Spirit. For God's blessing of Abraham (v 8) is the promise God uttered to Abraham (v 16), and that promise is none other than the Spirit now given by God to all members of his church (v 14). Noting that Paul equates the Abrahamic blessing/promise with the Spirit, we begin to understand why he portrays that promissory blessing as an act of God that waited in a kind of docetic state throughout the period of the Law. Only in the cross did God accomplish the defeat of the Law's curse, thus actualizing the blessed promise, the gift of the Spirit.

folding in Paul's exegetical argument regarding blessing and curse marches clean off the Teachers' map. The issue is not whether a human being observes the Law or fails to do so. The issue is whether the voice with which God pronounces his blessing has proved to be stronger than the voice with which the Law pronounces its curse (3:17, 21a). And the gospel is the good news that in the cross the blessing voice of God's promise has proved to be victorious over the cursing voice of the Law.

From later passages in the letter we can see that even in Galatians Paul's view of the Law is more complex — and richer — than one would think from these conclusions, drawn as they are from a close reading of only one passage, the exegetical argument of Gal 3:6–4:7. In due course we learn, for example, that the Law's cursing voice is more than balanced by the voice with which the Law itself bears its gospel witness when it has fallen into the hands of Christ (Comments #45, #48, and #50). Paul does not come to that matter, however, until he has first made clear that, in the event of Christ's crucifixion, God's ancient promissory blessing of Abraham triumphed over the enslaving curse of the Law.

COMMENT #35
THE TEXTUAL CONTRADICTION BETWEEN HABAKKUK 2:4 AND LEVITICUS 18:5

Signal aspects of the difference between Paul's exegetical logic and that of the Teachers have emerged in the preceding Comment. We have seen that Paul is far from following the Teachers in the way he reads the texts from what he calls sometimes scripture and sometimes the Law.[132] Another indication of the hermeneutical gulf between Paul and the Teachers emerges in 3:11–12, where Paul quotes Hab 2:4 and Lev 18:5.

These two texts do not at all say the same thing. Both speak of future life (*zēsetai*), but whereas Hab 2:4 says that faith leads to life, Lev 18:5 says that the route to life is observance of the Law. We will call the form displayed in Gal 3:11–12 a Textual Contradiction.

THE TEXTUAL CONTRADICTION

Ancient instances of the Textual Contradiction fall into two broad types. The first of these consists of traditions that display abstract rules developed in scholastic

---

[132]Comprehensive attempts to identify the logic followed by Paul in 3:6–4:7 have produced several major suggestions prior to the study of Vos, "Antinomie." Paul is said to have followed a juristic logic (G. Taylor), a rabbinic logic (N. A. Dahl), a rhetorical logic (H. D. Betz), and a narrative logic (R. B. Hays). The first three suggestions are well presented and perceptively criticized by Hays, *Faith*, 213–223; and in the pages that follow, Hays offers his own narrative analysis. This last has the virtue of emphasizing the role of an early Christian tradition on which Paul calls in 3:26–29. In light of those verses there is a sense in which one can refer to the narration of the Christ story. Nothing in Gal 3:6–4:7 suggests, however, that Paul is reflecting on the "location [of the Law] *within* the Christ story" (Hays, *Faith*, 228; emphasis added). The analysis presented below will sug-

discussions lacking a genuine polemical cast. This type of Textual Contradiction is of limited help in illuminating the line of thought in Gal 3:11–12, for Paul does not compose those verses in order to put himself at ease, by showing how a mind-troubling contradiction between two scripture texts can be resolved.[133] On the contrary, these verses fit well into the section begun at 3:6 by continuing the polemic in which Paul pits his own exegetical argument quite specifically against that of the Teachers.

Truly significant parallels are found, therefore, in a second type of Textual Contradiction, one that reflects actual conflict between two parties — often in the setting of a courtroom — the first of whom finds support for his position in one of the law's statements, whereas the second supports his position by citing a contradictory statement from the law. It is the strength of a recent study by J. S. Vos to have provided this truly comparable material, drawing it both from the rhetorical recommendations made by Cicero, Quintilian, and other rhetoricians and from Jewish sources.[134] Two factors are of particular importance, and they lead to a reasonably well defined form.

First, although we will continue to call the form a Textual Contradiction, we also note that *the point of departure* from which it is constructed is not the contradiction between two laws or texts, but rather, as noted above, the substantive conflict between assertions made by two parties who are in actual disagreement with one another.[135] The parties' citation of contradictory texts is secondary to their voicing of contradictory assertions.

Second, because both parties take for granted that the law (or scripture) cannot ultimately be in conflict with itself (Quintilian *Inst. Orat.* 7.7.2), one or the other of the parties must be able to find a resolution that affirms both texts.

The resulting form shows five steps:

(1) An assertion (in Jewish traditions a *halakah*) is made by party A.
(2) Party A cites an authoritative text in support of that assertion.
(3) A contradictory assertion (in Judaism a *halakah*) is made by party B.
(4) Party B cites an authoritative and contradictory text in support of that assertion.
(5) One of the parties wins the debate by giving a new interpretation to his opponent's text, being thereby able not only to honor both texts as aspects of the indivisible law but also to show that, correctly read, both texts support his own assertion.

---

gest the contrary. Note also, however, the thesis that Paul saw in Christ's death the crucial event in the history of the Law (Comment #48).

[133] The materials collected in the classic essay of Dahl, "Contradictions," provide needed assistance, but they are largely of the abstract type, suggesting in effect that the contradiction between Hab 2:4 and Lev 18:5 may have kept a lonely Paul awake at night until he "solved" it. See also Kennedy, *Interpretation,* 149. On the Textual Contradictions in Mark 9:11–13 and 12:35–37, see Marcus, *Way,* 94–110, 152.

[134] Vos, "Antinomie."

[135] Cicero *Top.* 26.96 (from Vos, "Antinomie," 260).

Philo's treatise on the unchangeableness of God provides an excellent example, for as Vos points out, the pertinent discussion there reflects an actual conflict.[136] One can represent it in the form given above:

(1) Philo asserts that God is not like a human being.

(2) In support of that assertion he cites Num 23:19, "God is not like a human being."

(3) Some persons known to Philo make a contradictory assertion: God is like a human being (note "some persons," *tines*, in *Quod Deus Imm.* 52).

(4) These persons support (or Philo knows that they can support) their assertion by citing Deut 8:5, "Like a human being he [God] shall train his son."

(5) Philo then victoriously solves the Textual Contradiction by showing that, at the level of intention, both Num 23:19 and Deut 8:5 support his assertion. Deut 8:5 speaks not of God's own nature, but rather of God's concern to provide instruction, something definitely needed by the masses who think that God is like a human being (the "body lovers").

PAUL ANTICIPATES THE TEACHERS' USE OF THE TEXTUAL CONTRADICTION

It is no long step from this example to Gal 3:11–12, provided we begin with a likely hypothesis: As Paul composes these two verses, he anticipates the Teachers' reaction to his assertion in 3:11a — "Before God no one is being rectified by the Law" — and to his citing Hab 2:4 in support of it (3:11b). In a word, given the relatively fixed tradition of the Textual Contradiction, Paul can be confident that, upon hearing his letter, the *Teachers* will employ that tradition, in order to say something like this:[137]

(1) As Paul's messenger read his letter aloud, we noted his lethally misleading assertion: Before God no one is being rectified by the Law.

(2) To undergird that assertion, he cites a text from the Law itself, specifically from the prophet Habakkuk: "The one who is rectified by faith will live."

(3) We assert, on the contrary, that one is indeed rectified by observing the Law.

(4) And we find clear support for our assertion in the same divinely given Law from which Paul draws his text, for in the book of Leviticus it says: "The one who does the commandments will live by them."

(5) We can say in conclusion, then, that, being the word of the one God, the Law does not really contradict itself. At the level of intention the text quoted by Paul and the text quoted by us actually say the same thing. Ha-

---

[136] *Quod Deus Imm.* 51–73. Together with related ones, this passage was cited and discussed by Dahl in "Contradictions" (166–168), but without the insight into its polemical cast that is now added by Vos.

[137] Can we assume both the Teachers and Paul to have known this form as a relatively fixed tradition? An affirmative answer is suggested by the breadth of the comparative material collected by Dahl, "Contradictions," and Vos, "Antinomie," and by the fact that in its five-step form the Textual Contradiction is both simple and reflective of common sense.

bakkuk's reference to life by faith is God's assurance of life to the one who faithfully observes God's commandments, as stated in Leviticus.[138]

PAUL'S USE OF THE TEXTUAL CONTRADICTION

Paul's line of thought now emerges, when we see that, anticipating the Teachers' use of the tradition of the Textual Contradiction, he alters that form quite significantly:

(1) On the basis of the truth of the gospel I make a fundamental assertion: Before God no one is being rectified by the Law.

(2) I then undergird that assertion with a quotation from scripture: "The one who is rectified by faith will live."

(3) In light of the way in which the Teachers quote — and will continue to quote — from the Law, I must add a second assertion: The Law does not have its origin in faith.

(4) Finally, given that second assertion, I cite a text from the Law that does not have its origin in faith — I think it is one of the Teachers' favorite texts — "The one who does the commandments will live by them."

Here three factors are revealing: line 4 (Paul's citation of the text from Leviticus), line 3 (Paul's second assertion), and the absence of line 5.

Line 4. As suggested earlier, Paul's citation of Lev 18:5 is a preemptive strike. Confident that the Teachers will cite it if he does not do so first, he adheres to the form of the Textual Contradiction by allowing his opponents' text to make up line 4.

Line 3. It is important to note that Paul could have followed the standard form in this line as well, reproducing the assertion he knows the Teachers to be making. In line 3, that is, he could have said, "Those who are troubling your minds are saying, to be sure, that one is rectified by observing the Law" (note line 3 in the example from Philo). And given the mental agility we know Paul to have possessed, we can be sure that, after stating the Teachers' assertion in line 3, and after citing their text in line 4, he could have completed the form of the Textual Contradiction with a fifth line in which he showed that Hab 2:4 and Lev 18:5 are to be harmonized in favor of his own assertion in the first line.[139]

---

[138]Cf. the interpretation of Hab 2:4 in 1QpHab 8: "Interpreted, this [text] concerns all those who *observe the Law* in the House of Judah, whom God will deliver from the House of Judgment because of their suffering and because of *their faith* in the Teacher of Righteousness" (Vermes, *Scrolls*; emphasis added).

[139]Neither Dahl nor Vos argues in precisely this way. But, assuming that Paul means to affirm both Hab 2:4 and Lev 18:5, these interpreters manage to find the essence of line 5 in the later verses of Galatians 3. Dahl credits Paul with demonstrating the validity of Lev 18:5 by arguing in Gal 3:19–25 that "the entire law of Moses itself [was] . . . a provisional, interim arrangement, valid only for pre-messianic times" ("Contradictions," 172–173). But, as Hays points out, Paul gives no indication in 3:19–25 that he is explaining how Lev 18:5 can be affirmed (*Faith*, 221). Crediting the apostle, in effect, with Quintilian's dictum that the law cannot finally stand in contradiction with itself, Vos assumes that Paul found both Hab 2:4 and Lev 18:5 in the substantively indivisible Law of God ("Antinomie," 265). For Vos, therefore, the tension between Paul and the Teachers is a "conflict between two

That is not at all Paul's way of using the tradition of the Textual Contradiction. In line 3 he formulates a second assertion of his own: The Law extolled and quoted by the Teachers does not have its origin in the faith about which Habakkuk speaks, the faith elicited in Abraham by God's promise, and the faith that has now arrived with the advent of Christ (Gal 3:6, 25).[140] Paul thus speaks of the origin of the Law to which the Teachers appeal, preparing the way for his assertion in Gal 3:19–20 that angels instituted that Law in God's absence (cf. Comments #38 and #48). By taking over line 3 for a second assertion of his own, Paul accomplishes several things.

(a) Addressing the issue of origin only for the Law represented in Lev 18:5 and not for the scriptural promise represented in Hab 2:4, Paul distinguishes the two from one another, but he also does more. He creates an imbalance in which it is only the Law that is placed in question, the divine origin of the promise being taken for granted. (b) Paul's assertion that the Law does not have its origin in the faith of which Habakkuk speaks does not suggest merely that Paul considers the Law of Lev 18:5 to be inferior. It shows that Paul does not adhere to a major presupposition of the Textual Contradiction, the assumption that the two texts, Hab 2:4 and Lev 18:5, have their origin in a monolith that is larger and more fundamental than either of them. (c) The foundational place of such a comprehensive monolith is given by Paul to the faith that is elicited by God's promise, as one sees it in Hab 2:4. Thus, the benchmark from which all else must be judged is not a harmony that can be discerned between two texts drawn from the same source. That benchmark is quite simply the faith elicited by God's promise. (d) Far from thinking, then, that Hab 2:4 is itself drawn from the Law, Paul uses it to disqualify the Law before he quotes from the Law. The result: Not having its origin in the benchmark of faith, the Law speaks a false promise when it says, "The one who does the commandments will live by them."[141]

Line 5. The absence of this line cannot now come as a surprise. The fundamental premise of the Textual Contradiction, that the law (or scripture) cannot ultimately be in conflict with itself, has for Paul no pertinence to the contradic-

---

parties each of whom calls on a different passage *in the same scripture*" (ibid.; emphasis added). In short, in Vos's view Paul argues as follows: True enough, the promise (Hab 2:4) and the Law (Lev 18:5) seem to contradict one another, the first supporting my gospel, the second supporting the gospel of the Teachers. In fact, however, when one considers both the letter of the Law and the intention of the Law-giver, God, one sees that there is no contradiction. For although Lev 18:5 says literally that the observer of the Law will live, one finds that God had something else in mind when he gave it: the Law should serve the cause of life in a quite indirect way. Placing the whole of humanity under the power of Sin (3:22), the Law paved the way for the fulfillment of the Abrahamic promise. Although gladly indebted to Vos for the comparative material mentioned earlier, I am compelled for reasons that will emerge in the following analysis to disagree with his conclusions.

[140]In making this fundamental change, Paul employs, to be sure, a motif at home in the tradition of the Textual Contradiction. As Vos points out, the rhetoricians recommend that under certain conditions one should ask about the origin of a given law (Hermogenes, *Peri staseôn* [ed. H. Rabe; Leipzig: Teubner, 1913] 87).

[141]Arguing on the basis of Gal 3:21b and Rom 8:3, Hays also concludes that Paul considered Lev 18:5 to be "unconditionally false" (*Faith*, 221).

tion between his text from Habakkuk and the Teachers' text from Leviticus. As we have seen in Comment #34, from the time of Paul's own participation in the crucifixion of Christ (2:19), he has been unable to assume in a simple way the integrity of a Law that contains both the blessing uttered by God and the curse spoken by the Law (see further Comment #48). Or, as noted above, although Paul continues to believe that there is a benchmark from which all else is to be judged, he can no longer identify that benchmark as a Law in which one can find both his text and the text of the Teachers. The benchmark is God's own blessing, the promising gospel spoken to Abraham ahead of time (Gal 3:8) and thus the faith elicited by that gospel.[142] In Hab 2:4 Paul hears nothing other than that blessing promise and that elicited faith. In Lev 18:5, however, he hears nothing other than the voice of the Law that, failing to have its origin in faith, can utter only a false promise, doubtless one means by which it enacts its universal curse.[143]

It follows that Paul is not at all concerned to "solve" the contradiction between two texts he considers to have been drawn from the same Law, showing thereby that they can be harmonized in favor of his original assertion (line 1). On the contrary, he is concerned to emphasize the contradiction between the two texts. He sees that God's promise in Hab 2:4 — rectifying faith will lead to life — is the truth of the gospel. And given the work of the Teachers in his Galatian churches, he also sees that the Law's promise in Lev 18:5 — observance of the Law will lead to life — is the falsification of the gospel.[144]

The contradiction between these two texts is altogether essential. For it is the result of the gulf between the voice of the cursing Law and the voice of the blessing God, and that gulf is not to be hidden. It is to be emphasized, until one sees that, in the cross, gulf became contradiction, and contradiction became collision, and collision became defeat for the Law's curse and victory for God's blessing (3:13).[145] Finally, then, Paul's use of the tradition of the Textual Contradiction in

[142]This gospel promise (Gal 3:8) was spoken to Abraham by scripture, that is to say by the *promissory, scriptural Law* functioning in God's behalf. There is here, then, a hint of Paul's view that the Law has two distinguishable voices, indeed two modes of existence. Prior to 4:21; 5:3, 14; 6:2, however, one finds at most a hint of this view (Comment #48).

[143]In Comments #48 and #50 we will consider in detail the three passages in Galatians in which Paul speaks of the Law in a decisively positive way, hearing in it God's own promise (4:21b; 5:14; 6:2). It is striking that in the second of these Paul quotes from Lev 19:18, "You shall love your neighbor as yourself." The fact that Paul should find in Leviticus both a false promise (Lev 18:5) and the positive statement of the Law of Christ (Lev 19:18) is clear indication of his conviction that, with the coming of Christ, the two voices of the Law have been brought out into the open.

[144]Regarding Paul's citation of Lev 18:5 in Rom 10:5, see Note on Gal 3:12.

[145]Paul's concern to portray a *conflict* that issues in defeat for the Law's curse and victory for God's blessing could remind one that Quintilian asks which of two conflicting laws is the stronger (*Inst. Orat.* 7.7.7). That is indeed a question fundamental to the argument Paul formulates in 3:15, 17, and 21a, where, far from saying that the Law's impotence to grant life merely puts it "at a disadvantage" (Vos, "Antinomie," 266), Paul says that the Law is doubly impotent: It cannot grant life, and it is unable effectively to oppose God's promise in the sense of being strong enough to annul that promise. It is, then, the contradiction between a true and potent promise and a false and impotent one that lends a

Gal 3:11–12 reflects his concern to distinguish one spirit from another.[146] We might even credit Paul with an emended form of 1 John 4:1:

> Beloved [Galatians, in light of the Teachers' work in your midst], do not believe every spirit [or every text], but test the spirits [and the texts] to see whether they are from God.

As at the close of Comment #34, so here we must remind ourselves that in Galatians 4, 5, and 6 Paul has other very important things to say of the Law, some of them seeming to involve more than a change in vocabulary. For example, in 4:21 Paul no longer speaks of the blessing God and the cursing Law. On the contrary, in composing the letter's second exegetical section (4:21–5:1), he presupposes that *the Law itself* has two voices. One is the cursing voice of Lev 18:5, whereas the other is the promissory voice that — speaking in God's behalf — can be heard in Hab 2:4, Genesis 16–21, and Isa 54:1 (Comments #35, #45, #48, and #50). Important as these changes will prove to be, however, none of them negates what Paul says in Gal 3:11–12.[147]

COMMENT #36
THEOLOGICAL PRONOUNS

At numerous junctures in 3:6–4:7 Paul speaks in the first person plural — "we," "us," "our." Also, and sometimes in the same sentence, he refers to "you" (plural); and at still other junctures he uses the pronoun "they" and the expression "those people." A chart arranged in three columns would show that the result is somewhat complex. Indeed, the pronominal alternations in Paul's text have often been thought to be a puzzle calling for a solution, and the solution offered has usually been to assign some references to Jews, some to Gentiles, and some to all Christians, whether of Jewish or of Gentile birth.[148]

To read the entire passage straight through is to see, however, that the pronominal alternations constitute a rhetorical, psychological, and fundamentally theological language game Paul is playing with the Galatians. At first hearing, to be sure, some of the Galatians may have thought that Paul intended his references to be neatly assigned to ethnically and religiously distinct groups. When he refers, for example, to "those whose identity is derived from observance of the Law"

---

striking note of discontinuity to Paul's exegetical argument, whereas we can be confident that the Teachers found a redemptive continuity in the integrity of the scriptural witness.

[146] Note the perceptive remark of Käsemann: "The apostle is not afraid to apply *to scripture* ... the distinguishing of spirits demanded of the prophets in 1 Cor 12:10" (*Romans*, 286; emphasis added). Cf. Beker, *Paul*, 54.

[147] Perhaps one should compare the movement between Gal 3:11–12 and Gal 4:21; 5:3, 14; 6:2 to the movement internal to Romans 9–11. In this regard see Walter, "Römer 9–11."

[148] Most of the exegetical debate pertinent to this matter up to 1983 is well presented in Hays, *Faith*. See also Robinson, "Distinction"; Cousar, *Cross*, 115–117; Longenecker 164; N. T. Wright, *Covenant*; Belleville, "Under Law." Belleville's reading of 3:23–25 ("Under Law," 69) can represent a number of unconvincing interpretations.

(3:10), he seems to be speaking of Jews and/or strictly observant Jewish Christians. And his statement that these people are under the power of the Law's curse would then be taken as an assertion limited to Jews and/or Jewish Christians. Following that reading of 3:10 and leaving aside the text quoted there, one could make definite ethnic assignments in 3:13–14, assuming it to be in part a soteriological formula worded by a Jewish Christian:

> Christ redeemed us (Jews) from the Law's curse, becoming a curse in our behalf; for it stands written: "Cursed is everyone who is hanged on a tree." He did this in order that the blessing of Abraham might pass to the Gentiles in Jesus Christ; in order, that is, that we (both Jews and Gentiles) might receive the promise, which is the Spirit, through faith.[149]

Similar assignments are often made in reading 4:4–6, taking it to be in part a formula drafted by a Gentile Christian:

> But when the fullness of time came, God sent his Son, born of a woman, born under the power of the Law, in order that he might redeem those held under the power of the Law (Jews), in order, that is, that we (Gentiles) might receive adoption as sons. And because you are sons, God sent the Spirit of his Son into our (both Jews and Gentiles) hearts, crying, "Abba, Father!"[150]

None of the solutions of this type is convincing. First, no genuine confidence can be placed in the thesis that in 3:13–14 and 4:4–6 Paul is quoting from pre-Pauline traditions of Jewish and Gentile origin respectively. Both 3:14 and 4:5 contain two purpose clauses, and in each case both clauses show signs of having been composed by Paul for the Galatian situation. Second, the expression "in our behalf" (3:13) always has for Paul the universal dimension of Christ's atoning death, just as the gift of the Spirit is universal for all Christians (3:14). Third, the point at which Paul introduces the expressions "those whose identity is derived from observance of the Law" and "to be under the power of [the Law's] curse" (3:10) is the juncture at which he combines text (Deut 27:26) and exegesis in such a way as to erase the distinction between Jew and Gentile (see Note on 3:10). Both the observant and the nonobservant live under the Law's curse. Fourth, as we will see in Comment #41, Paul views the Law as one of the enslaving elements of the cosmos by seeing it in its paired existence with the Not-Law. Thus, in its paired existence, the cosmic Law pronounced its curse on the whole of humanity, Gentile and Jew alike.

It follows that 4:3–6 is the point at which Paul brings his language game to a

---

[149]This reading is adopted by numerous interpreters; see Hays, *Faith*, 113. See especially Dahl, *Studies*, 132; the commentaries by H. D. Betz, Longenecker, and Lührmann; and the study of Belleville, "Under Law." Others agree in seeing an ethnic distinction but find it in precisely the reverse way. Gaston, for example, thinks that with the expression "under the Law's power" Paul refers only to Gentiles ("Enemies," 405–407). His argument founders on Paul's use of the plural pronoun and plural verbs in 4:3–5.

[150]Hays, *Faith*, 110.

climax, unmasking all purported distinctions in the human race, and thus leading the Galatians to sense the folly of the Teachers' distinction of Jew from Gentile. The Teachers' use of pronouns may very well have been simple: "*You* Gentiles were indeed in a state of slavery under the power of the dumb elements of the cosmos." If so, Paul's statement stands in sharp contrast:

When we were children — and I mean all of us whether Jews or Gentiles — we were held in a state of slavery under the power of the elements of the cosmos. But when the fullness of time came, God sent his Son, born of a woman, born under the power of the Law, in order that he might redeem those held under the power of the Law (all human beings), in order, that is, that we might receive adoption as sons. And because you are sons, God sent the Spirit of his Son into our hearts, crying, "Abba, Father!" (4:3–6).

In the period before the advent of Christ, the distinction of Jew from Gentile had as little correspondence to basic reality as that distinction now has in Christ (3:28).[151] When, then, Paul exhorts the Galatians to become as he is (4:12), he means two things. First, just as he is now a former Jew, so they are former Gentiles. Second, just as he now knows that his former identity as a Jew provided no genuine distinction even in its own time, so they are to know that their former identity as Gentiles provided no genuine distinction even in its own time. Before the advent of Christ humanity was an enslaved monolith; in Christ humanity is becoming a liberated unity.[152]

3:15–18 THE PROMISSORY COVENANT AND THE SINAITIC LAW

TRANSLATION

3:15. Brothers and sisters, drawing an illustration from everyday life among human beings, let me say that once a person has ratified his will, no one annuls it or adds a codicil to it. 16. Now the promises were spoken to Abraham "and to his seed." The text does not say, "and to the seeds," as though it were speaking about many people, but rather, speaking about one, it reads, "and to your seed," and that seed is Christ. 17. What I am saying is

---

[151]The interpretation of Blank (*Paulus und Jesus*) is well presented and evaluated in Hays, *Faith*, 87–89. In the midst of his argument Hays himself perceptively speaks of a reading he does not in the end espouse, but which is adopted in the present volume: ". . . we might equally well suppose that Paul for rhetorical purposes alternately identifies himself with [Gentile Christians and Jewish Christians]" (*Faith*, 117).

[152]See Boyarin, *Politics*, passim, and cf. Introduction §17.

this: The covenant, validated by God when he gave it, is something that the Law, coming into the picture 430 years later, does not invalidate, as though the Law were designed to nullify the promise. 18. For if the inheritance came from the Law, then it would not spring from the promise. And we know that is not the case, for God graciously gave the inheritance to Abraham by the promise.

LITERARY STRUCTURE AND SYNOPSIS

With the word *adelphoi*, "brothers and sisters," in v 15 Paul opens the third paragraph in the first subsection of his exegetical argument (see Literary Structure and Synopsis of 3:6–9). Paul accents two motifs: the precise nature of the covenantal promise made by God to Abraham, and the sharp differentiation of that promise from the Law. In v 18 Paul draws his conclusion, and in v 19 he raises a new question, the genesis of the Law. The paragraph consists, then, of vv 15–18.

No element in the paragraph is as important as Paul's interpretation of God's promise in v 16 (Gen 17:8). The tone, however, and the guidance for the interpretation of that text are set by v 15. There Paul introduces an illustration from everyday life, in order to dissociate the word *diathêkê* (in the Teachers' mouths "covenant") from the Sinaitic Law, thus preparing to link that term exclusively with the Abrahamic promise. After that, he develops at some length the antinomy between God's promise and the later-arriving Law. Why does he do this?

The Teachers are saying that the promissory blessing spoken by God to Abraham is specified in God's covenantal Law, the two forming an indivisible whole: As God is the author both of the Abrahamic blessing and of the covenantal Law, observance of the Law is the demand God has set for the imparting of that blessing. By contrast Paul sees that covenant and Law are quite distinct from one another. The covenant is the promise spoken by God himself to Abraham (and to Abraham's singular seed, Christ), whereas the Law is an entity that merely happened many years later. Moreover, were the Law really the specification of God's covenantal promise to Abraham, as the Teachers say, it would change that promise into something other than what it actually is. In fact, however, the Law lacks the power to specify and thus to alter the promise; it can no more do that than a codicil added to a person's will by a second party can become a genuine part of that will, effectively altering it. The inheritance graciously given by God to Abraham came by the promise; it did not come from the Law.

NOTES

3:15. *Brothers and sisters, drawing an illustration from everyday life among human beings.* In contrast to the stinging form of address employed in 3:1 ("You foolish Galatians"), Paul reverts to the endearing and familiar "brothers and sisters" of 1:11, thus beginning a new paragraph of his exegetical section by bringing the Galatians to his side.[153]

---

[153]Cf. Malherbe, "Family."

once a person has ratified his will, no one annuls it or adds a codicil to it. Before Paul returns to explicit exegesis, however, he draws an illustration from everyday life in order to insist that the specific words of God's promise cannot be altered (v 16).[154] The verbs in this illustration show that Paul uses the noun *diathêkê* here to refer to nothing other than a person's last will: "ratify a will" (*kyroô diathêkên*), "annul a will" (*atheteô*), "add a codicil" (*epidiatassomai*).[155] For the moment Paul thus dissociates the term *diathêkê* from its use in the vocabulary of Hebraic theology, where it means "covenant" (Comment #37).

no one. The illustration has two frames. In the first a person makes a valid will. In the second frame someone other than the testator is prevented from altering the will (in the Greek sentence *oudeis* is someone other than *anthrôpos*).[156] In considering vv 17–21 we will see that Paul intends to preclude the thought that the *angels* responsible for the Law can have changed the covenant *God* made with Abraham.

adds a codicil. An attempt to add a codicil would come at a point later than the will, just as the arrival of the Law came 430 years after the covenantal promise God made to Abraham (v 17). That analogy itself suffices to show that the sequential dimension to this picture in v 17 is far from being an instance of redemptive history (Comment #37).[157]

16. *Now the promises were spoken to Abraham "and to his seed." The text does not say, "and to the seeds," as though it were speaking about many people, but rather, speaking about one, it reads, "and to your seed," and that seed is Christ.* In wording this sentence Paul follows a midrashic form in which one reading of a

---

[154]On the word *homôs* in Paul, see BAGD.

[155]Regarding the legal picture of a will, see, on the Greek side, Egee, "Rechtswörter"; on the Jewish side, Bammel, "Gottes DIATHEKE." See also Grässer, *Bund*, 2–3. Räisänen thinks neither the Greek nor the Jewish data are illuminating (*Law*, 129). In any case, Paul crafts the illustration in light of the use he intends to make of it. Cf. in this regard 4:1–2.

[156]*Pace* Cosgrove, "Arguing," 536. The conclusions reached in Cosgrove's article, however, are helpful.

[157]In 3:15–4:7 there are indeed several locutions by which Paul expresses the thought of temporality: "adds a codicil," 3:15; "validated by God when he gave it," v 17; "the Law, coming into the picture 430 years later," v 17; "the Law . . . was added," v 19; "until the seed should come to whom the promise had been made," v 19; "before faith came," v 23; "imprisoned during the period that lasted until, as God intended, faith was invasively revealed," v 23; "until the advent of Christ," v 24; "now that faith has come, we are no longer under the power of that confining custodian," v 25; "so long as the heir is a child," 4:1; "until the arrival of the time set by the father," v 2; "but when the fullness of time came," v 4; "you are no longer a slave," v 7. Given these markers, one could be tempted to see here a redemptive-historical line. The matter of sequence, however, has here two forms, neither reflecting the perspective of redemptive history: (a) Looking back to v 14, we see that the promise antedates the coming of the Spirit. We see also, however, that the promise *is* the Spirit. And in v 16 the seed *is* Christ (see Comment #37). It follows that, between the promise and its fulfillment, the Law is a parenthesis, not an event on a line that extends from the promise through the Law to the advent of Christ and his Spirit. (b) Nor is the sequence of promise and Law an indication of redemptive history, unless one will so identify a sequence of potency and impotence. See Notes on v 15 and v 21.

text from scripture is negated in favor of another.[158] Following this form, Paul composes a sentence with three parts:

(a) Now the promises were spoken to Abraham "and to his seed."
(b) The text does not say, "and to the seeds," as though it were speaking about many people, but rather, speaking about one, it reads, "and to your seed,"
(c) and that seed is Christ.

the promises. It is curious that Paul should use the plural in a passage in which he is intent on emphasizing the covenantal promise as a punctiliar event (Abraham) that refers to a singular and punctiliar seed (Christ). The plural may reflect the fact that God repeated his promise to Abraham several times (note the plural in Gal 3:21). In any case, after the plural in v 16, Paul returns to the singular in vv 17–18, showing that he has no intention of referring to the linear history of the promises in the patriarchal generations and thence into the history of Israel (contrast Rom 9:9–13).

"and to his seed." Changing only the possessive pronoun from "your" to "his," Paul now quotes these words from v 8 of Genesis 17, a chapter focused on the covenantal promise God made to Abraham.[159] Two of the chapter's major motifs are left completely aside by Paul: God's assurance that Abraham and his descendants will possess the land of Canaan, and the definition of God's covenant as the rite of circumcision to be observed in every generation (Comment #45). For Paul God's covenantal promise to Abraham consists of only one thing, God's assurance that he will one day bless the Gentiles in Abraham (Gal 3:8). Thus, the analogy Paul has just laid out in v 15 — one must stay with the original linguistic precision of a text, not altering it at a later time — is a matter he applies only to one motif of Genesis 17, a move certain to have elicited sharp comment from the Teachers. Heedless of such criticism, Paul focuses his exegetical attention on the text of Gen 17:8: Providing Abraham with an assurance for the future, God

---

[158] Philo, for example, gives what he believes to be the correct (one could also say bizarre!) reading of the scriptural reference to Cain's murder of Abel: "So the words that follow, 'Cain rose up against Abel his brother and killed him' (Gen. 4:8), suggest, as far as superficial appearance goes, that Abel has been done away with; but when examined more carefully, they show that Cain has been killed by himself. It must be read in this way, 'Cain rose up and killed himself,' not someone else" (*Quod Det.* 47). Philo uses the midrashic form to probe for what he considers to be a deeper and timeless meaning in the text. Paul employs it in a highly situational polemic with the Teachers. Parallels can also be cited from rabbinic tradition; for example, "Man did eat the bread of strong horses (Ps 78:25). Do not read 'of strong horses' (*'byrym*), but rather 'of the limbs' (*'ybrym*), that is bread that is absorbed by the limbs" (*Mek.*, Beshallach, Vayissa 3 [Ex 16:15]; Hor. p. 167). Cf. Borgen, *Bread*, 63; and see *m. Sanh.* 4:5.

[159] Verhoef confesses himself to be somewhat uncertain (*Geschreven*, 88–89). The case for Gen 17:8 is, however, very strong, although there may be some influence from Gen 13:15. See Stanley, *Scripture*, 248.

spoke his covenantal promise not only to the patriarch but also to his seed, and the word "seed" is literally singular.[160]

The text does not say, "and to the seeds," as though it were speaking about many people, but rather, speaking about one, it reads, "and to your seed." Even in focusing his attention on this single verse, Paul ignores two factors: (a) the plain meaning of the word "seed" in Genesis 17, where it is clearly a collective referring to the people of Israel as the descendants of Abraham, generation after generation; (b) his own earlier willingness to discuss the issue of the identity of Abraham's plural children (v 7; cf. v 29; Rom 4:13–16).[161] Thus, bold move follows bold move, for the Galatians are sure to have learned of the expression "seed of Abraham" from the Teachers, and the Teachers will have used it in its collective sense, insisting that the Abrahamic blessing, having come long ago to the plural people of Israel, is now flowing to Gentiles who join that people by observance of the Law.[162] Moreover, the collective sense can be proved from Genesis 17, a fact of which the Teachers may very well have taken advantage in offering the Galatians their own interpretation of Paul's letter (Introduction §11).

Given developments in his Galatian churches, however, the singular is what Paul actually hears in Gen 17:8, and he is sure that that reading honors the true voice of God's scripture (cf. 3:8). Equating promise and covenant, Paul insists that God spoke his covenantal promise to only *two* persons: Abraham and his singular seed. What concerns him, then, is the identity of that seed to whom, in addition to Abraham, the convenantal promise was made.

and that seed is Christ. Paul continues the polemic of the preceding clause. The seed, and thus the God-given future of Abraham, is not the patriarch's plural, ethnically distinct descendants. It is the singular person, Christ. Paul hears in Gen 17:8 a messianic prophecy, showing that the point of departure for his exegesis is the advent of Christ.[163] It follows, as Paul will say in vv 26–29, that plural offspring of Abraham come into existence only when human beings are incorporated into Abraham's singular seed, Christ. Were one to judge solely from the present verse, one would conclude that for Paul there were, prior to Christ, no *sperma*, no children of Abraham (Comment #37).

17. *What I am saying is this: The covenant, validated by God when he gave it,*

---

[160]The singular form of the term "seed" in Gen 3:15 led some Jewish exegetes to find a reference to the messiah. See the next footnote.

[161]Paul might have been ready to defend his reading of Gen 17:8 by referring to 2 Sam 7:12–14, a text that could be read with Gen 17:8 — by *gĕzērâ šāwâ* — to support a singular and messianic reading of "seed" in other texts. See also 4QFlor 1:10–11 (Martinez, *Scrolls*, 136), where God promises a singular seed to David. See further Dahl, *Studies*, 130; Duling, "Promises"; Juel, *Exegesis*, 59–88; Hays, *Echoes*, 85. For rabbinic analogies in which Isaac is sometimes an individual and sometimes a collective, see Daube, *New Testament*, 438–444. The suggestion, however, that Paul is working with a typology based on Abraham's sacrifice of Isaac is not convincing (Dahl, *Crucified Messiah*, 146–166).

[162]Thinking of the Teachers' understanding of the term "covenant," one may recall Ps 105:8–10, "He is mindful of his covenant forever, of the word that he commanded, for a thousand generations, the covenant that he made with Abraham . . . to Israel for an everlasting covenant."

[163]Cf. Hays, "Righteous One," 210; J. L. Martyn, *Issues*, 209–229.

is something that the Law, coming into the picture 430 years later, does not invalidate, as though the Law were designed to nullify the promise.

What I am saying is this. From v 16, Paul could easily have passed immediately to the conclusion of 3:27 and 3:29,

> Seeing, therefore, that, as Abraham's singular seed, Christ is the recipient to whom God gave his promise, and seeing that, having been baptized into Christ, you are Christ's, it follows that you are yourselves Abraham's seed, heirs by virtue of the promise.

The Teachers' work in Galatia has made the Law so attractive, however, that Paul must supply further comment on the promise/Law antinomy before this conclusion can be drawn. To formulate additional comment, Paul returns to the word *diathêkê*.

covenant. In the Note on v 15 we have observed that, using the term *diathêkê* to refer to a human being's last will, Paul began to loosen the connection the Teachers have drawn between that term and the sacred Law of Sinai (an instance of rhetorical dissociation).[164] Now we see his next step. Paul retheologizes the word *diathêkê*, using it to refer to God's promissory covenant mentioned in scripture. Ignoring, however, the definition of the covenant in Genesis 17 and elsewhere as the sacred rite of circumcision, the primary mark of Law observance, Paul insists that the covenant is to be equated solely with God's promise to Abraham and thus sharply divorced from the Law.[165] The result is a polemic directed at the Teachers' assumption of the covenant-Law complex. What the Teachers see as a monolith Paul sees as an antinomy, for the advent of Christ has removed the term "covenant" from the Law and has attached it solely to the Abrahamic promise.[166]

validated by God when he gave it. To the verb *kyroô*, "to validate," Paul prefixes the preposition *pro*, "before," indicating that God's covenantal act antedated the Law, just as a will antedates an attempted codicil. Both here and in the final clause of v 18 Paul uses colorful verbs to emphasize that the promissory covenant had its origin in an act of God himself.

the Law, coming into the picture. In stark contrast Paul speaks of the Law's

---

[164]On rhetorical dissociation, see Comment #37, footnote 178.

[165]Divorcing the covenant from the Law is a move with profound implications for the view of Israel as God's corporate people. For poetically, one could summarize an element of classic Hebraic thought by saying that Law-observant Israel *was* the covenant (Lohmeyer, *Diatheke*, 75–77; Grässer, *Bund*, 128). It is the covenantal Law that shows God to be Israel's God and Israel to be God's people (in addition to Genesis 17, note, e.g., Deut 26:16–18; Wis 9:8–11). See Introduction §17 and Comment #52.

[166]For Paul's polemic there is no precedent in Jewish tradition. Even those Israelite theologians who spoke of a new covenant thought of it as involving renewed and perfected observance of the covenantal Law (e.g., Jer 31:31–34 and 1QS 1:7–8; Grässer, *Bund*, 67 n284). Regarding the indissoluble linking of "covenant" and "Law," see Jaubert, *La notion d'alliance*: "The Law . . . is inseparable in all of its parts from the covenant . . ." (457). The two-covenant picture in Gal 4:21–5:1 is somewhat different (Comment #45).

origin by using in a colorless way the word *ginomai*, "to come into being," "to happen."

430 years later. Holding Abraham to have been observant of the Law in his own time (cf. Sir 44:20), the Teachers will probably have considered the Law to be eternal.[167] Paul, however, locates the Law at a definite point in history, identifying it as an event considerably later than God's covenant.[168]

In light of vv 19-20 we can see, then, that the Law and its curse constitute an angelic parenthesis lodged between and differentiated from two punctiliar acts of God himself, the uttering of the promise to Abraham and to Abraham's singular seed, and the sending of that seed, Christ. This again indicates that the Law does not stand in a redemptive-historical line between the promise and the coming of the seed. Precisely the opposite (Comment #37).

(the Law) does not invalidate (the covenant), as though the Law were designed to nullify the promise. When Paul thinks both of the covenant and of the Law, the chief issue that arises in his mind is one of power. Is the later-arriving Law sufficiently powerful to invalidate (*akyroô*) or nullify (*katargeô*) the covenantal promise God had earlier made to Abraham? And if so, how would it do that? The answer to the second question can be inferred from v 16. In Paul's argument, were the Law to absorb the promise into itself, as the Teachers imply, it would rob the promise of its true reference: Christ as the singular seed of Abraham. And the answer to the first question is given already in the analogy of v 15. Just as a codicil added by someone other than the testator is impotent to falsify the testator's will, so the Law is impotent to invalidate God's promissory covenant with Abraham and Abraham's seed.[169]

The purpose clause with which Paul ends v 17 will prove helpful in the interpretation of vv 19-20.[170] Although the Law forms a genuine antinomy with the promise (v 18), even the angels who decreed the Law (v 19) did not intend thereby to nullify the Abrahamic promise.

18. *For if the inheritance came from the Law, then it would not spring from the promise. And we know that is not the case, for God graciously gave the inheritance to Abraham by the promise.* The initial clause is contrary to fact.[171] Because the inheritance was something God gave to Abraham by speaking a promise to him, the source of that inheritance cannot be the later-arriving Law. And what is the

---

[167]See Sir 24:9; Wis 18:4; Josephus *Ap.* 2.277; *Mek.*, Beshallach, Shirah 7 (Hor. p. 139; on Exod 15:9): "there is no before and after in the Torah."

[168]On the number 430, see Lührmann. Gen 15:13 (cf. Acts 7:6) and Exod 12:40 preserve different traditions about the length of Israel's stay in Egypt and thus about the span of time (roughly) from Abraham to the events on Mount Sinai.

[169]With the image of a potent will and an impotent codicil, Paul avoids the thought of an older law that can be surpassed by a younger one (Quintilian *Inst. Orat.* 7.7.8; from Vos, "Antinomie," 261).

[170]On *eis to* with the infinitive, see BDF §391.3, §402.2.

[171]Winger perceptively lists Gal 3:18 under his rubric: "Conditions that someone other than Paul apparently claims are fulfilled" ("Unreal Conditions," 111). Paul uses the term "inheritance" and its cognates in relation to Abraham and the Abrahamic promise only in Galatians — *klêronomeô*, 4:30; 5:21; *klêronomia*, 3:18; *klêronomos*, 3:29; 4:1, 7 — and in his reworking of the Abraham materials in Romans; see notably Rom 4:13.

inheritance now being given by God? It is the innumerable Abrahamic progeny among the uncircumcised Gentiles (Gen 12:3 in Gal 3:8), and it is the gift of the promised Spirit to all who are heirs of Abraham because they are heirs of God in Christ (3:14, 29; 4:7). In a word, the inheritance is the church-creating Spirit of Christ.

COMMENT #37
COVENANT, CHRIST, CHURCH, AND ISRAEL

We have already noted both the Teachers' concentration on the theme of Abrahamic descent and Paul's modulation of that theme into his own discourse on descent from God (Comment #33). Continuing to ponder the problems arising in 3:6–4:7, we can see another matter that calls for attention: the way in which both the Teachers and Paul connect Abrahamic descent to God's covenant, and the resultant ramifications for their respective pictures of the church and of Israel.[172]

COVENANT AND SEED OF ABRAHAM IN THE THEOLOGY OF THE TEACHERS
Like the theme of Abrahamic descent, the subject of God's covenant is one of the Teachers' topics, not a topic Paul has introduced on his own. Pondering the Teachers' use of the term "covenant" (*diathêkê*), and their use also of the expression "seed of Abraham" (*sperma Abraam*), we can bring into yet clearer focus some of the major elements in their theology:

(1) *Covenantal nomism.* In our reading of Galatians we may employ E. P. Sanders's neologism "covenantal nomism," but, as Sanders correctly sees, not in order fundamentally to characterize the theology of Paul.[173] It is the Teachers who hold to the traditional Jewish marriage of covenant and Law, tracing the covenant-Law complex back to Abraham. It is also they who identify Abraham as the primal parent of the holy seed. Part of their theology is well encapsulated in a passage in *Jubilees:*

> And all the seed of his [Abraham's] sons would become nations. And they would be counted with the nations [they would be, that is, Gentiles]. But from the sons of Isaac one would become a holy seed, and he [the people of Israel] would not be counted among the nations, because he would become the portion of the Most High . . .[174]

(2) *Redemptive history.* As noted in Comment #33, the expression "seed of Abraham" is important to the Teachers because it refers to the redemptive-

---

[172] In 4:21–5:1 Paul again weaves Abraham, covenant, Christ, and church into a colorful, exegetical tapestry. See J. L. Martyn, *Issues*, 191–208, and Comment #45; cf. Hansen, *Abraham*. On the subject of covenant, see especially Grässer, *Bund*; on the material in Qumran and rabbinic traditions, see Lichtenberger, "Bund."

[173] See E. P. Sanders, *Palestinian Judaism*, 511–515.

[174] *Jub.* 16:17 (cf. Gen 21:13). In 1 Macc 12:21 the Spartans and the Jews are said to be brothers, both being of the family of Abraham; cf. *Ascents of James* 1.33.3, 1.34.1 (Van Voorst, *Ascents*, 48; F. S. Jones, *Source*, 60).

historical line, the line that began with Abraham, that extended through the generations of the corporate people of Israel, that has now become explicitly messianic in the nomistic gospel of the Jerusalem church, and that is being climactically extended to the whole of the world through the Teachers' own mission to the Gentiles.

(3) *Transference into the people of God.* For the Teachers it is thus a crucial aspect of the arrival of the Messiah that the Gentiles now have the opportunity of transferring from their present existence as *ethnê/gôyīm* into the line of the Abrahamic, nomistic covenant.[175] In a word, God has now placed the Two Ways before Gentiles, offering them the Way of life as the alternative to the Way of death (Comments #34 and #49). By following Abraham in the rite of circumcision, Gentiles themselves can enter the already-existent people of God, the seed of Abraham, Israel.

COVENANT AND SEED OF ABRAHAM IN PAUL'S THEOLOGY

Paul's references to the terms *diathêkê* and *sperma Abraam* reveal a different picture.

(1) *Diathêkê* ("last will"; "covenant"). As we have seen in the Notes, Paul's first use of the word *diathêkê* comes in Gal 3:15:

> Brothers and sisters, drawing an illustration from everyday life among human beings, let me say that once a person has ratified his will (*diathêkê*), no one annuls it or adds a codicil to it.

As is frequently the case in our reading of Galatians, we can efficiently come to the heart of the matter by asking about the linguistic history of the term *diathêkê* in the Galatians' own vocabulary:

(a) In the Hellenistic period, as in the classic one, *diathêkê* refers consistently to a person's "last will." The Galatians will certainly have known the term with that meaning.

(b) We can be confident that in founding churches — no less in Galatia than elsewhere — Paul conveyed to his Gentile converts some form of the tradition of "the Lord's Supper" (1 Cor 11:20); and in giving the cup-word he may have consistently included the expression "new covenant" (*kainê diathêkê*; so 1 Cor 11:25; cf. Luke 22:20). If he did that in Galatia, it will have been from him that the Galatians first sensed that the word *diathêkê* could carry a meaning quite different from the one with which they were already familiar: the riches of the thought of the covenant made by God in Christ, as distinguished from a last will drawn up by a human being.[176]

---

[175]Viewed in the perspective of the history of religions, the Teachers are first cousins of Jews who — even apart from a messianic impetus — were concerned to convert Gentiles to Judaism itself. Cf. Klijn, "Opponents"; Walter, "Gegner"; Comment #6.

[176]Distinguished also from the "old covenant." To suggest that, in communicating a form of the eucharistic tradition to the Galatians, Paul may have introduced them to the use of *diathêkê* as covenant is quite different, however, from suggesting that he regularly instructed his Gentile churches on the grand subject of covenant.

(c) As we have seen, it is from the Teachers that the Galatians will have learned to use the term *diathêkê* in a way significantly related both to Abraham and to the Law of Sinai. Expanding somewhat on what we have earlier suggested about the Teachers' instructive sermons, we can imagine a paragraph in which they spoke explicitly of the covenant:

> The covenant God made with the first proselyte Abraham is the same as the covenant God reaffirmed through Moses at Sinai, thus establishing in all its generations the ancient and venerable people of Israel, a people set apart from all the other peoples of the earth by being the people of the covenantal Law. What are you Gentiles to do, then? You are to follow in the steps of Abraham, the first proselyte. By undergoing circumcision, you are to make your way into the covenant people, the seed of Abraham, the true Israel, the church of God that has as its mother the congregation of the apostles in Jerusalem.[177]

(d) It is especially against the background of the Teachers' covenantal instruction, then, that the Galatians will have sensed two significant changes that characterize Paul's argument in 3:15–18. First, in his initial use of the word *diathêkê* the apostle returns it to its distinctly secular meaning, dissociating it from its connection with the Law of Sinai, and thus — for the moment — pointedly detheologizing it.[178]

Second, the argument of 3:15–18 shows that, in declaring a divorce between God's covenant and the Law, Paul prepares the way for a retheologizing move of his own. Paul attaches the covenant exclusively to the promise God made to Abraham. And he uses the illustration of v 15 to show in what way God's covenantal promise is different from the Law. That is to say, the example of a person's last will precludes the thought that someone can alter it, but that picture also suggests that someone might make the attempt. And who might that be? In the illustration Paul has offered it is clearly a person other than the testator, for the latter could easily change his will at any time prior to his death.

That illustration has to do, then, with the distinction between the God who spoke the covenantal promise to Abraham and the angels who instituted the later-arriving Law in God's absence (vv 19–20). With the illustration of v 15, in short, Paul means absolutely to preclude the thought that the *angels* who are responsible for the Law (as though it were an attempted codicil, "added," v 19) can have changed the promissory covenant (the unalterable will) *God* made with Abraham. It is the certainty with which Paul speaks of the Law's impotence to

---

[177] On the Jerusalem church as "mother," see Comment #46.

[178] On the rhetorical *topos* of dissociation in Paul's letters, see Vos, "*Legem statuimus*." See also Perelman and Olbrechts-Tyteca: "By processes of *dissociation*, we mean techniques of separation which have the purpose of dissociating, separating, disuniting elements which are regarded as forming a whole or at least a unified group within some system of thought: dissociation modifies such a system by modifying certain concepts which make up its essential parts. It is in this way that these processes of dissociation are characteristic of all original philosophical thought" (*Rhetoric*, 190). See further Siegert, *Argumentation*, 182–185.

alter the promise — and in Galatians 3–4 it is only this certainty — that makes possible Paul's denial of a nomistically potent conflict between the Law and God's promise (v 21).[179]

(2) *Sperma Abraam* ("seed of Abraham"). In retheologizing the term *diathêkê* — in divorcing it from the Law and equating it with the promise — Paul gives a crucial role to his own interpretation of the expression "seed of Abraham." As we have seen in the Notes, the key sentence, Gal 3:16, has three parts:

(a) Now the [covenantal] promises were spoken to Abraham "and to his seed."
(b) The text does not say, "and to the seeds," as though it were speaking about many people, but rather, speaking about one, it reads, "and to your seed,"
(c) and that seed is Christ.[180]

Paul uses the negative — *ou legei* ("the text does not say") — to deny one reading of a text from scripture, so that, with the clause introduced by *alla* ("but rather"), he can provide the correct reading. The correct reading is what, given developments in Galatia, Paul actually hears in Gen 17:8. Able to foresee what God is now doing, scripture speaks directly to the present situation (Gal 3:8; 4:30; cf. Philo *Leg. Alleg.* 3.118).

Note, however, that Paul could have communicated the correct reading of the text in a nonpolemical manner. Omitting the second part of the verse, he could have dictated simply

(a) Now the promises were spoken to Abraham "and to his seed,"
(c) and the seed is Christ.

Why does he include the second, clearly polemical part? The context shows that he is concerned specifically to deny the Teachers' covenantal nomism, their redemptive-historical interpretation of the "seed of Abraham," their notion of

---

[179]The interpretation of Gal 3:21 is a matter of great importance. From Paul's denial that the Law is "against" (*kata*) God's promises, numerous interpreters have drawn three conclusions: (a) Both promise and Law have their origin in God. (b) There can be no insoluble contradiction between the Abrahamic promise and the Law (cf. the discussion of Gal 3:12 in Comment #35). (c) Given the temporal notes in vv 17, 19, and 23–25, the promise and the Law constitute a divinely ordained *sequence* of a redemptive-historical sort, even though they are not to be put on exactly the same level. Carefully related to its context, v 21 seems to me to say something quite different: (a) With the assertion of v 19 and with the partial syllogism of v 20, Paul attributes the genesis of the Law to angels acting in God's absence (Comment #38). (b) There is indeed a sequence: first the promise, then the Law. But the thrust of that sequence is determined by the illustration of v 15 and by the denial of v 17: it is a sequence marked by the inability of its second member to invalidate the first member. Thus, the sequence is not at all marked by a redemptive-historical continuity. In a word, it is the Law's *impotence* vis-à-vis the promise that makes possible Paul's pointed denial in v 21: "Having pictured the promise and the Law as an antinomy, I must pose an important question: Is the Law, then, opposed to the promise *in the sense that it has overpowered it*? Absolutely not!" (see again v 17, and cf. Eckstein, *Verheissung*, 205–206).

[180]On the singular "seed," see the Note on 3:16.

Gentile transference into the already-existent, covenantal people of God, and hence their view of the relationship between covenant and church.

COVENANTAL NOMISM, REDEMPTIVE HISTORY, AND TRANSFERENCE

These observations remind us that at numerous junctures in the history of Pauline interpretation, Paul has been credited with perspectives proper to theologians against whom he waged a life-and-death battle.[181] The history of the interpretation of Galatians offers a particularly clear case.

(1) *Covenantal nomism.* It has been suggested that in Galatians Paul himself argued for a modified form of covenantal nomism: faith in Christ accompanied by observance of the Law relieved of what are called its restrictive and nationalistic aspects.[182] But, while it is true that even the Paul of Galatians can clearly hear the Law when it testifies to and indeed expresses the gospel (4:21; cf. 5:14; 6:2), it is altogether beside the mark to attribute to him a modified form of covenantal nomism. As we have noted, he declares with polemical emphasis a divorce between the covenant and the *nomos*.[183]

(2) *Redemptive history.* At the present time a number of Pauline interpreters are reviving the view of Paul as a redemptive-historical theologian.[184] But, considering again Gal 3:16, we can see that Paul's interpretation of the seed to whom God made the covenantal promise is as polemically *punctiliar* as it is polemically *singular*. As U. Luz has put it, the covenantal promise uttered by God seems to

---

[181] See J. L. Martyn, *Issues*, 209–229.

[182] Two articles by Dunn are of direct pertinence: "Works" and "Theology"; consult now his commentary and his volume on the theology of Galatians. For four critiques, see Räisänen, "Galatians 2.16"; J. L. Martyn, "Events"; N. T. Wright, "Curse and Covenant: Galatians 3.10–14" in his *Covenant*; and Cranfield, "Works." In some regards, Wright and Dunn are in agreement. See now also Dunn, *Partings*; Neusner, "Really 'Ethnic'?"; and — on observance of the Law in the church — Comment #48.

[183] Following a pattern of "covenantal nomism" proposed by Hooker, Hansen suggests a reading of Galatians similar to Dunn's: Hooker's pattern of covenantal nomism "not only represents the structure of the OT covenants, it can also be seen in Paul's use of the Abrahamic promise in his letter to the Galatians" (*Abraham*, 162).

[184] To some extent, this revival is evident in the work of Beker, *Paul*, a matter discussed in my review (*Issues*, 176–181). See also the essays by Wright, Lull, and Scroggs in Bassler, *Pauline Theology*. Particularly in the work of Wright (*Covenant*), one finds a fascinating synthesis of a *biblical* theology, in some regards reminiscent of the nineteenth-century works of J. C. K. von Hofmann and J. Tobias Beck. It is true that Paul's argument contains what appear to be marks of a developmental sequence (see footnote 179 above). Noting these temporal expressions, one could indeed suggest a redemptive-historical sequence from which two conclusions can be drawn: (a) Both promise and Law have their true origin in God. (b) They thus form a divine sequence in a scheme of redemptive history, even though they are not to be put on exactly the same level (cf. Barclay, *Obeying*, 99–100). In fact, however, Paul's distinction between the cursing voice of the Law and the blessing voice of God makes this reading impossible. There is indeed a sequence: first God's promise to Abraham, then the advent of the cursing Law. What Paul finds in this sequence, however, is sure proof of the impotence of the later-arriving Law to alter the earlier and potent promise (3:15, 21a). The sequence, then, is that of promissory potency and nomistic impotence, not that of a redemptive continuity. See now the weighty essay of Cousar, "Romans 5–8."

have remained in a docetic state until the advent of the singular seed.[185] That covenantal promise did not create its own epoch, calling into existence a corporate *sperma Abraam* that would extend generation after generation — in a linear fashion — through the centuries. The distinction between linear and punctiliar is thus a distinction drawn by Paul himself. In Gal 3:16 he denies the Teachers' linear, redemptive-historical picture of a covenantal people, affirming instead the punctiliar portrait of the covenantal person, Christ.[186]

(3) *Transference into the people of God.* Here, too, in some recent strains of interpretation a theological motif is being given to Paul, whereas in fact it belongs to the Teachers. When one identifies as the subject of Galatians "the condition on which Gentiles *enter* the people of God," one presupposes that Paul is concerned with the specific line of movement along which it is now possible for Gentiles to transfer from their sinful state to the blessedness of those who are descendants of Abraham.[187] This possible movement is their own,[188] and the goal of their movement is that of getting into the people of God. The question is how they can get in.[189]

To a large extent, as we have seen earlier, this formulation describes the theology of the Teachers, the theology against which Paul wrote the letter to the Gala-

---

[185]Luz, " . . . the promise . . . does not found an epoch . . . On the contrary, in Galatians 3, with an almost docetic shyness, Paul is careful not to make the promise available to an historical demonstration" ("Bund," 322). Contrast Eckstein, *Verheissung,* 113.

[186]Is the result anti-Judaic, in the sense that in Gal 3:16 Paul denies the existence of corporate Israel as God's people? No, for Paul focuses his attention tightly on the difference between the falsity of the Teachers' *Gentile mission* and the divine authorization of his own *Gentile mission.* What Paul affirms is that Gentiles become sons of God by being incorporated into Christ, God's Son — in whom there is neither Jew nor Gentile (3:26–29) — not by being taken into an already-existent people of God. In a word, Gentiles are baptized into Christ, not into the Jewish people. See the final section of the present Comment and J. L. Martyn, *Issues,* 171–175.

[187]E. P. Sanders, *Law,* 18 (emphasis added). See especially the chart on page 7, where Sanders lays out the matter of transference, a subject more fully discussed in J. L. Martyn, *Issues,* 161–175.

[188]The caveat offered by E. P. Sanders (*Law,* 14 n23) was written in response to my friendly critique of the typescript, and it is intended as a partial qualification of the diagram mentioned on page 7: "[The diagram] shows what happens, which Paul, of course, thought of as being 'by grace,' but which also involves human commitment." It is true that Sanders (like Karl Barth before him) repeatedly emphasizes the priority of "solution" over "plight." With consistency, however, Sanders considers God's grace to have opened up the *possibility* of human movement from condemnation to salvation. Thus, in a quasi-Bultmannian fashion he sees human possibility as a category fundamental to the analysis of Paul's theology (something that cannot be supported even by Col 1:13, where God is the subject of *metestēsen*). On this matter, see further J. L. Martyn, *Issues,* 217–221, especially note 23 there. At its root, does Paul's good news belong to the category of human possibility or to that of divine power that is invasive not only of the cosmos but also of the human will? See Käsemann's comments on the translation of *dynamis* in Rom 1:16: *Questions,* 173 n4.

[189]"Getting in," "entering," and "being included" are three of the expressions that run through the Pauline work of E. P. Sanders, Dunn, and N. T. Wright, to name only a few. What one might call "entry language" is indeed characteristic of Qumran (e.g., 1QS 5:20). In the Galatian setting it reflects the theology of the Teachers, not that of Paul.

tians! In Paul's theology the fundamental and determining line of movement is God's, as we can see in part from a study of Paul's prepositions and verbs. In Gal 3:14, for example, Paul says that the blessing of Abraham has *come to* the Gentiles (*genêtai eis*), not that the Gentiles have been granted the possibility of entering the blessed family of Abraham. Similarly, Paul's frame of reference emerges in the verbs *erchomai* ("to come," 3:23, 25), *exapostellô* ("to send," 4:4, 6), and *exagorazô* ("to redeem," 3:13; 4:5). He speaks, that is, not of the *possibility* of human movement into the family of Abraham, but rather of the *power* of God's already-executed movement into the cosmos in the singular seed of Abraham, Christ.[190] In a word, Galatians is a particularly clear witness to one of Paul's basic convictions: the gospel is about the divine invasion of the cosmos (theology), not about human movement into blessedness (religion). The difference between the two is the major reason for Paul's writing the letter at all.

ISRAEL[191]

A word is necessary, in conclusion, regarding two further questions: In his battle with the Teachers over the matter of covenant and church, does Paul mean to deny God's elective creation of ancient Israel? And if so, does he later rescind that denial in writing his letter to the Christians in Rome? First, in Galatians itself three matters demand attention.

Galatians

Paul's Use of the Verb kaleô, *"to call into existence by election."* Every instance of this verb in Galatians refers to the genesis of the church (Gal 1:6, 15; 5:8, 13). Does Paul nevertheless understand that elective act to have its precedent in God's election of ancient Israel by the Abrahamic promise? Or, if Israel's election was not carried out in the promise, did it happen in the giving of the Law at Sinai?

The Promise. We have already noted the thrust of Gal 3:16, 26–29. There Paul asserts that God is now creating the church by his elective word, incorporating human beings into the one seed of Abraham, Christ. That is also an assertion the apostle makes only after painting a picture in which God's promise to Abraham remained in a docetic, unembodied state until the advent of the singular seed, Christ. And that picture is reinforced in 3:19. There, saying that the Law was added *until* the coming of the seed to whom — along with Abraham himself — God had spoken his promise, Paul implies that in the period of the Law there was no seed of Abraham.

The Law. The implications are shocking, for the resultant picture portrays God's election of ancient Israel neither in the Abrahamic promise nor in the

---

[190]See again J. L. Martyn, *Issues*, 217–221. The motif of inclusion is in fact used by Paul, for example in Romans 11. But one notes that Paul applies that motif both to Gentiles and to Jews who do not now believe in Christ (11:12, 17, 23–25).

[191]The bibliography here is immense. See notably Davies, "People"; E. P. Sanders, *Law* (and bibliography there); Walter, "Römer 9–11"; Von der Osten-Sacken, *Dialogue*; M. Barth, *Israel*; idem, *People*; Koenig, *Dialogue*; Brocke and Seim, *Augapfel*; Grässer, *Bund*; Baarda et al., *Paulus*; Hofius, "All Israel"; Haacker, "Geschichtstheologie"; Comment #52.

giving of the Sinaitic Law.[192] For if God was absent at the genesis of the Law (3:19–20), a divine, nomistic election of Israel seems excluded. Moreover, there is Paul's certainty that prior to the coming of Christ the human race was essentially an enslaved monolith, one of the enslavers being none other than the curse pronounced by the Law on both the observant and the nonobservant (3:10; Comment #34).

In Galatians, then, election is God's enactment of his promise in Christ, Abraham's only seed. It is the act by which God is now creating his church (the new creation; 6:15), not a deed carried out by God either in the time of Abraham or in the time of Moses. If, then, we had only Paul's letter to the Galatians, we would have no reason to credit the apostle with a belief in the divine election of the ancient people of Israel. Indeed, precisely the opposite.

Romans

Things are dramatically different in Romans, not to mention other letters of Paul.[193] Being a subject in its own right, that difference cannot be pursued in detail here, but a few hints are possible (see also Introduction §13). Two passages in Romans are crucial, chapters 9–11 and chapter 4.

Romans 9–11. In addition to using the verb "to call into existence by election" (*kaleô*) in order to speak of God's acts in each patriarchal generation (Rom 9:7, 12), Paul several times refers to Israel as God's people, the people whom God foreknew (Rom 9:4–5; 11:2). Indeed, the whole of the argument in Romans 9–11 presupposes God's election of ancient Israel. To be sure, the view of Israel's election presented there is dialectically complex. Shortly after listing God's special gifts to an apparently ethnic Israel, Paul relates God's elective grace to the distinction between

all Israelites	and	Israel
seed of Abraham	and	children [of Abraham]
children of the flesh	and	children of the promise (cf. Gal 4:23)
		= children of God (Rom 9:6–8).

And this distinction is related to another, that between God's hatred and God's love (Rom 9:13; quoting Mal 1:2–3)! Those turns in Paul's argument raise the question whether the distinction within Israel between children of the flesh and children of the promise may not play in Romans 9–11 a role similar to the one played in Galatians by the polemic of Gal 3:16. That is to say, even where Paul affirms the election of ancient Israel, as he does in Romans 9–11, that affirmation requires in Paul's mind a corresponding denial: God's election, being free of all presuppositions, cannot be traced through the generations of Israel on any basis other than the act of God himself, the one who issues the promise *newly* in each

---

[192]Whether this picture is correctly characterized as anti-Judaic depends on one's assessment of the letter's primary polarity. See the Introduction §17.
[193]See, as examples, Phil 3:5; 1 Cor 10:1–5. The analysis offered here will show why I cannot fully agree with the unqualified statement of E. P. Sanders that Paul "denies . . . the election of Irael" (*Law*, 208).

generation and solely on the basis of his own faithful perdurance; so that his purpose might *remain* without exception a matter of his election (Rom 9:11). An hypothesis follows: Perhaps both in Galatians and in Romans — although in different ways — Paul means emphatically to deny that God's elective grace was enacted in an ethnic, anthropological sense, either in the Abrahamic promise or in the giving of the Law.[194]

Romans 4. In the course of reworking Galatians 3 in order to form a new exegetical argument on the subject of Abraham, Paul refers in Romans 4 to Jewish Christians as the *plural* seed of Abraham who are inheritors of the promise *not only* on the basis of the Law *but also*, and fundamentally, on the basis of the faith of Abraham (Rom 4:16; cf. 4:12). It is true that the final clauses of Rom 4:16 are less than perfectly transparent.[195] Taking our guidance, however, from vv 12 and 14, we can see Paul's concern to say, first, that the heirs of Abraham are not simply those who are defined as such by *the Law* (v 14) and, second, that the competence to determine the identity of the heirs is indicated by *the promise* God spoke to Abraham before he was circumcised (v 12). For "that is the only way in which the legacy can remain a matter of God's undeserved graciousness."[196] Thus, even when Paul thinks of Jewish Christians — something he does not do in formulating the exegetical argument of Galatians 3 — the elective point of departure proves to be the Abrahamic promise, not the Sinaitic Law. Yet, for these Jewish Christians, the elective force of the Law is affirmed in a secondary way ("but also").

We are left, then, with a significant divergence between Galatians and Romans as regards the divine election of ancient Israel. In writing Romans Paul certainly did rescind his earlier denial of Israel's ancient election. Are we to say, then, that he changed his mind? At the minimum we can be sure that Paul gave the subject further thought, especially if he was aware, when he wrote Romans, that parts of his Galatian letter had been communicated to the Jerusalem church by the Teachers (perhaps through the False Brothers), accompanied by their own sharply critical interpretation.[197]

But that possibility simply emphasizes the fact that Galatians and Romans were written in quite different settings. To a considerable degree, therefore, the divergence is related to differences in those settings. When Paul wrote to the Romans, events required that he consider in depth both the anomaly presented by the Jewish people's massive rejection of the gospel of Christ, and the charge

---

[194]Cf. Matt 3:9: "Do not presume to say to yourselves, 'We have Abraham as our ancestor'; for I tell you, God is able from these stones to raise up children to Abraham" (NRSV).

[195]See especially Käsemann, *Romans*; Wilckens, *Römer*; Meyer, "Romans"; Dunn, *Romans.*

[196]Meyer, "Romans," 1142.

[197]Here, as elsewhere in the present volume, I take for granted that Romans reflects (a) Paul's concern to establish in the Roman church a base of operations for his forthcoming Spanish mission *and* (b) his anxiety as to whether the funds he has collected from his Gentile churches will be accepted by the church in Jerusalem, as a sign of the unity of God's church, drawn both from Jews and from Gentiles (without the demand of circumcision). See Introduction §13.

that he himself was largely indifferent to that development, if not in fact partially responsible for it (Rom 9:1–3). Moreover, in his consideration of that mysterious anomaly and in his answer to the charge of personal indifference, he found the existence of Jewish Christians to be of great significance.[198]

In Galatians, by contrast, neither Israel's massive "no" nor the existence of Jewish Christians as such enters Paul's mind as an issue (the former had not yet occurred). The battle of this letter is fought altogether on the frontier of the Gentile mission (Introduction §17). Active on that frontier, the Teachers are saying that God is now creating his church by adding Gentiles to Israel, the already-existent, ethnically and religiously distinct people of God. Given this development, Paul is driven to say that neither God's promise to Abraham nor the Sinaitic Law was a divine act of ethnic election. That is, then, a denial that Paul hurls specifically at the Teachers who are working among the Gentiles in Galatia. It is addressed neither to the Jerusalem church, whose members are active in the mission to the Jews, nor to the Jewish nation.

One fact is crucial. The denial in Galatians is crafted in a way that is thoroughly christological. What negates the Teachers' portrait of the election of ancient Israel is the nonethnic character of Christ, Abraham's singular seed (Gal 3:28). It is therefore Christ who reveals the nonethnic character of God's promise both at its inception and in its fulfillment. Paradoxically the nonethnic character of God's elective grace means two things. First, that the God who elected newly in each patriarchal generation is precisely the God who thereby *defined* enduring dependability (Rom 9:11). Second, that it is in the church drawn both from Jews and from Gentiles that this God is now enacting his covenant with Abraham, doing so in such a way as to create a corporate people in Christ, the singular seed of Abraham.

3:19–25 THE GENESIS OF THE SINAITIC LAW AND THE ADVENT OF CHRIST

TRANSLATION

3:19. Why, then, the Law at all? It was added in order to provoke transgressions, until the seed should come to whom the promise had been made. The Law was instituted by angels through a mediator. 20. Now a mediator does not represent one person (a singular party), but God is the one. 21. Is the Law, then, effectively opposed to the promises [of God]? Absolutely not! For if a Law had been given that was strong enough to make people alive, then things would have been made right by the Law. 22. But in actuality, the scripture imprisoned everything under the power of Sin, in

---

[198]See not only Rom 4:16 but also the "remnant" in Rom 9:27–28 (Isa 10:22); and the "elect" in Rom 11:7.

order that the promise might be given via the faith of Jesus Christ to those who believe. 23. Before faith came, we were confined under the Law's power, imprisoned during the period that lasted until, as God intended, faith was invasively revealed. 24. So then, the Law was our confining custodian until the advent of Christ, in order that we should be rectified by faith. 25. But now that faith has come, we are no longer under the power of that confining custodian.

LITERARY STRUCTURE AND SYNOPSIS

In the final sentences of the preceding paragraph Paul has drawn a sharp contrast between God's promise to Abraham and the later-arriving Law. He has suggested that, to some degree, God's covenantal promise is comparable to a person's last will, while the Law is comparable to a codicil added in vain, in that such a codicil is impotent to alter the previously established will. Now he faces an obvious question. Given this astonishing picture of the Law, why should it have come into existence at all?

Addressing this question by speaking of the genesis of the Law, Paul explores further the antinomy between God's promise and the Law, and he allows that antinomy to introduce another, the Law versus the faith that has arrived in and with Christ (cf. 3:11–12). In the resulting picture the Law proves to be an enslaving parenthesis that was lodged between God's promise to Abraham (and to Abraham's seed) and God's sending of the singular seed, Christ. Paul has worded the final sentence of the preceding paragraph in such a way as to emphasize the word "God" (v 18), attributing to this God both the promise and the inheritance. In stark contrast, God is not to be found among the actors associated with the origin of the Law. One is not altogether surprised, then, to see that Paul says nothing about the Law's being God's Law, or about its being holy, righteous, and good (contrast Rom 7:12, 14, 22).

After Paul has painted his startling portrait of the Law's genesis, and after he has reemphasized the universal power of the Law to enslave, he turns to speak of the dual advent of Christ, the seed of Abraham, and of faith. In this way he preaches again the good news of God's redeeming invasion of the sphere of slavery: "We are no longer under the power of the confining custodian, the Law."

NOTES

3:19. *Why, then, the Law at all?* The question is elliptical, lacking a verb in Greek as in English. Paul sometimes uses the neuter of the interrogative pronoun *tis* to mean "what?" (1 Cor 3:5; Rom 3:1), sometimes to mean "why?" (1 Cor 4:7; 15:29c; 15:30). Here the Galatians will have understood the word to mean "why?" and that is surely Paul's intention, for it is a question that inevitably follows from a number of things Paul has already said about the Law:

> It is the Law's business to pronounce a curse on both the observant and the nonobservant (3:10 and 13). It follows that no one is being rectified by the Law (v 11), that the Law does not have its origin in faith (v 12), and that the Law does not provide the Abrahamic inheritance (v 18).

To the question "Why, then, the Law at all?" Paul gives an answer in four parts, the third and fourth of which go beyond the question strictly interpreted:

(1) The Law was added
(2) in order to provoke transgressions
(3) until the seed should come to whom God made his promise.
(4) The Law was instituted
    (a) by angels
    (b) through a mediator.

It was added. Although never used in the LXX to refer to the Law's genesis, this verb (*prostithêmi*) could be understood as a divine passive, a circumlocution used to avoid direct reference to God. That is a linguistic construction Paul has already employed several times in the letter, the most recent being 3:16 ("the promises were spoken [by God] to Abraham"). Does he not mean, then, that it is God who added the Law to his promise, allowing it, to be sure, an inferior role?[199] We will shortly see strong reasons for thinking, on the contrary, that in the present passage Paul presents a picture of the Law's genesis from which God is absent (Comment #38). And noting the link between "add a codicil" (*epidiatassomai*) in v 15 and both "add" (*prostithêmi*) and "institute" (*diatassô*) in v 19, we can draw a conclusion that is simple, even if shocking: Angels added the Law to a scene which, until their act, consisted of the promise spoken by God himself.[200] Their act changed the scene, placing all of humanity under the Law's curse (v 10), but in the end that curse did not overcome the power of the promise (v 21). Concerning the verbs Paul uses to refer to the genesis of the Law, see Comment #38.

in order to provoke transgressions. The term *charin* (the accusative of *charis*, used as a preposition) can indicate either a cause (thus "because of transgressions") or a goal ("in order to produce or provoke transgressions"). Because the basic meaning of transgression is the breaking of an established and recognized command, Paul surely thinks of the Law as antedating these transgressions and, indeed, very probably as producing them.[201] If the gospel is now eliciting faith

[199] So, for example, Dahl, *Studies*, 173; Longenecker 138; Vos, "Antinomie," 266. In Comment #38 we will see that in Galatians 3 Paul's rhetoric does not provide a comparison in which he holds the Law to be a gift of God inferior to that of God's promise. In fact, the radicality of Paul's promise/Law antinomy is probably what caused domesticating copyists to change his "the Law was added" to "the Law was laid down" (D, G, Irenaeus). On the basis of Tertullian one could surmise that Marcion deleted 3:15–25 from his text of Galatians (so Harnack, *Marcion*, 73*), although from Irenaeus one could suggest the opposite (so Hoffmann, *Marcion*). In any case, some of the domesticating copyists may have feared that the bolder reading ("the Law was added") could lend support to the Marcionite view of the Law as the product of the Demiurge.

[200] In the opinion of Callan, "Midrash," Paul, working with midrashic traditions (surely correct), uses the verb "add" because he intends to refer to the incident of the golden calf and the necessity of God's giving a second (additional) set of tablets (cf. Stendahl, *Paul*, 29). Something like this line of thought is present in the much later *Syriac Didascalia* (Connolly, *Didascalia*, p. 222 line 21), but there is nothing in Paul's text that will have given the Galatians even a hint of such an idea.

[201] Cf. J. Schneider, "*parabasis*," 740.

(3:2, 5), the Law entered the picture, in its own time, in order to elicit transgressions (so also Rom 5:20). That is a view of the Law for which there is no proper parallel in Jewish traditions, where the Law is thought to increase resistance to transgressions.[202]

until the seed should come. The word "until" does not suggest the perspective of redemptive history. On the contrary, it indicates, as we have seen in Comment #37, that the Law was a parenthesis lying between two acts of God, his promise to Abraham and his sending of Christ. That parenthesis has now been closed (so also 3:23; 3:25). As Paul presents it in Galatians, the idea of the terminus of the Law's curse arises from the reversal of his earlier, Pharisaic interpretation of Deut 21:23 (v 13 above) and from his extraordinary reading of Gen 17:8 (v 16 above).[203]

In light of those interpretations, Paul now says something truly shocking about the period of the Law: Not only did that period come to an end in Christ. It also contained no seed of Abraham, for that seed first came on the scene in Christ himself.

to whom the promise had been made. In v 16, quoting Gen 17:8, Paul has shown that God uttered his promise (the future rectification of the Gentiles) not only to Abraham but also to Abraham's seed, Christ. It is as the recipient of God's promise that Christ arrived on the scene, and it is by incorporation into him that the Galatians have become the rectified and Spirit-endowed children of Abraham, indeed children of God (vv 14, 26–29). Looking back to Gal 3:8, then, one may suggest that, although Paul hears in Gen 12:3 a promise God spoke to Abraham, his fundamental sense is given in the certainty that God's promise was spoken also and crucially to Christ: "In *you*, Christ, all the Gentiles will be blessed."

The Law was instituted. Using for the second time a passive verb, Paul expands his view of the genesis of the Law: it was instituted (a participial form of the verb *diatassô*). Scarcely any clause in the letter has elicited a more heated interpretive debate, and thus at no point is it more important for us to ask how the Galatians are likely to have understood what they heard, before we ask what Paul intended them to hear.

Two linguistic observations are important. First, Paul's use of the verb *diatassô*

---

[202]Schoeps, *Paul*, 194–195. Does Paul think that provoking transgressions was a goal had in mind by the angels, or does he think ahead to vv 22 and 24, where he says that God caused the Law to serve his own purposes? The latter seems probable, but one cannot be certain.

[203]There have been attempts to show that Paul drew the motif of the Law's temporary existence from tradition later preserved among the rabbis (e.g., *b. Sanh.* 97a: 2,000 years of chaos, 2,000 years of law, 2,000 years of the time of the Messiah), or from a messianic interpretation of the Judah oracle in Genesis 49, or from traditions similar to ones found in Qumran (1QS 9:11; CD 6:10–11; 12:23–13:1; 20:1). Cf. Davies, *Torah*; Dahl, *Studies*; H. D. Betz 168 n52. The rabbinic data, however, are of very limited pertinence to an understanding of Paul. His assertion in Rom 10:4 — "Christ is the end (*telos*) of the Law" — has elicited, and will continue to elicit, endless discussion. It is worth noting that, in his attempt to show that Paul intends to refer to the completion of the Law rather than to its termination, Badenas (*Romans 10:4*) does not discuss Gal 3:19. See Comment #37 and Meyer, "Romans 10:4."

will not have taken the Galatians into linguistically foreign territory. They will have employed the word *diataxis* to refer to an "arrangement" (of troops, for example) that is the result of someone's issuing an order or an edict (*diatassô*). The verb's passive participle was used substantively to refer to the content of the edict (e.g., a bequest) or verbally to speak of an edict's being issued, as in Gal 3:19. The Galatians will have known, then, that Paul is speaking of an enactment, specifically an enactment of a law. Indeed, some of them may already have known the combination of the verb *diatassô*, "to institute," and the noun *nomos*, "law." Plato uses it to refer to the instituting of a law (*Laws* 932a). And with Hesiod we have an interesting reference to the *divine* enactment of a law:

> ... for the son of Cronos [Zeus]
> *has decreed* this *law* ... (*Works and Days* 276).

Second, doubly interesting is the fact that, whereas the verb *diatassô* occurs about two dozen times in the LXX, it is there never linked with the word "Law" (*nomos*).[204] That is not a combination, then, that the Galatians are likely to have encountered in the Teachers' exegesis. Thus, just as in his initial reference to the word *diathêkê* Paul took the Galatians back to a linguistic pattern with which they grew up ("last will" rather than "holy covenant"; v 15), so in referring to the genesis of the Law, Paul uses nonscriptural linguistic constructions. Neither the verb "add," that is to say, nor the verb "institute" is a scriptural way of speaking of the genesis of the Law.[205]

But, noting that the Galatians will have heard Paul's reference to the instituting of the Law against the background of the common use of the verb *diatassô*, we have to ask here, as in the case of the expression "was added," whether they will have heard a divine passive, taking Paul to imply that God is the actor who instituted the Law (cf. again Hesiod).

by angels.[206] Here Paul's prepositional phrase *di' aggelôn* can be either causal ("by angels" in the sense that angels instituted the Law) or instrumental ("through angels," meaning that the Law was instituted by God through the agency of angels). We can best come to Paul's intention after considering the possibility that it was from the Teachers that the Galatians first heard of a connection between the Law and angels.

We recall that early in the letter Paul refers to the Teachers' Law-observant

---

[204]Even in the case of the sharply negative statement about the Law that Ezekiel attributes to God, the verb is the expected one, "give": "I gave them statutes that were not good . . ." (Ezek 20:25).

[205]In the speech of Stephen in Acts 7:53, *diatagas*, "commands" or "ordinances," is linked with angelic activity at the genesis of the Law: "You are the ones that received the law as ordained by angels, and you have not kept it" (NRSV). Did both Paul and Luke draw on Hellenistic Jewish tradition in which the terms *diatassô* and *diatagê* were used to say that the Law was "instituted"? Even if that should be true, there is no scriptural basis for the locution; and Acts 7:53 may be best rendered, " . . . you received the Law by means of commands issued by angels" (BDF §206.1).

[206]Cf. Schlier; Gaston, *Torah*, 35–44; Räisänen, *Law*, 18–20.

message as a false gospel preached by an angel (1:8). In certain Jewish traditions angels are said to have played a role in the giving of the Law. In the Hebrew text of Deut 33:2 the Sinai event is recounted as follows:

> The Lord came from Sinai, and rose up from Seir upon them;
> he shone forth from Mount Paran;
> he came from the myriads of holy ones,
> at his right hand *ešdat* to them.

The word *ešdat* may have been as opaque to the LXX translators as it is to modern scholars.[207] In any case, these translators rendered the final line

> from his right hand angels with him.

Subsequently, one finds a complex tradition in which the incomparable glory of the Law was thought to be attested by angelic participation in its genesis.[208] The result is a motif one would expect the Teachers to emphasize, and Paul's sudden reference to an angel in Gal 1:8 suggests that they did exactly that, telling the Galatians that the glory of the Law is shown by the fact that God gave it at Sinai "through angels."

Paul, by contrast, stands that tradition on its head, speaking of the angels as the active party who themselves instituted the Law, and saying that they did that in God's absence![209] See Comment #38.

through a mediator. Paul uses a prepositional phrase that literally renders the Hebrew construction "by the hand of," thus pointing explicitly to agency (cf. Acts 5:12; 14:3; 19:11; Mark 6:2). He speaks, therefore, of a single mediator, Moses, who functioned between the angels and the Israelites.[210]

20. *Now a mediator does not represent one person (a singular party), but God is the one.* This rather cryptic sentence has been interpreted in many different ways.[211] Three factors, however, are clear. Paul ties it to the preceding sentence by means of the term "mediator." He words it as an interpretation of the *Shema*,

---

[207] See, for example, Mayes, *Deuteronomy*, 398–399.

[208] Pertinent texts include Josephus *Ant.* 15.136; *Jub.* 1:29; *T. Dan.* 6:2; Philo *de Somn.* 1.140–144; Acts 7:38, 53; Heb 2:2; *Apoc. Mos.* 1; *Pesiq. R.* 21:7–10. See Billerbeck 3.554–556; Callan, "Midrash"; Davies, "Josephus."

[209] Some interpreters feel that, if Paul had intended to speak of the angels as the active and thus as the causative party, he would have used the preposition *hypo* rather than *dia* (e.g., Berger, "Abraham," 56). But, as we have seen in the Note on 1:1, the evidence both from the papyri (Mayser, *Grammatik*, 2.2.421–423) and from early Christian literature (BDF §223) shows that in the Hellenistic period *dia* with the genitive and with a passive verb can mean either "through" (mediating agent) or "by" (originating actor). The analysis presented in Comment #38 strongly suggests that Paul thinks of the angels as the originating actors.

[210] Oepke, "*mesitês*," 615, mentions *Exod. Rab.* 6 etc., where Moses is the *sarsôr*; cf. Bloch, "la Figure de Moïse," especially 139–141.

[211] Cf. Burton, who mentions a nineteenth-century study in which about three hundred interpretations had been counted; Winger, *Law*, 99.

in which the oneness of God is affirmed (hence "God is the one").[212] And he presents in its two clauses two-thirds of a syllogism without stating the conclusion. Pondering these factors, one finds a highly probable reading: Taking the Galatians by the hand and coaxing them to draw the unstated conclusion, Paul leads them to the edge of an abyss and compels them to gaze down into its cavernous depth. There, without fully accepting it — and without Paul's intending them fully to accept it — they have to look at the vision of a godless Law. For the syllogism yields the conclusion that Moses, the mediator of the Sinaitic Law, did not speak for God (Comment #38).

21. *Is the Law, then, effectively opposed to the promises [of God]? Absolutely not!*[213] The fact that Paul must pose and emphatically negate this possibility is yet another sign that he sees in the promise and the Law a genuine antinomy. He is far indeed from merely comparing these two, concluding that the Law is inferior to the promise.[214] His need to pose this question shows, in fact, that his antinomous thinking has taken him right to the edge of the abyss mentioned above, where a warning sign poses a significant question: "As the promise was spoken directly by God himself, and as the Law is the product of angels acting in God's absence, is not the Law a power opposed to God's promise?" Indeed, Paul knows that the Teachers will charge him with plunging headlong into the abyss thus signified, by propounding an absolute *antithesis* between the God-given promise and the angel-generated Law.[215] He issues a sharp denial, therefore, thus preparing the way for vv 22 and 24, where he speaks of God's use of the Law.

Equally important is the observation that his denial exceeds the Teachers' prospective charge. Maintaining the *antinomy* — not an antithesis — between God's promise and the angel-generated Law, Paul denies not only that the Law is mono-

---

[212]On the *Shema*, see Reif, *Hebrew Prayer*; Hurtado, *One God*.

[213]On the expression *Mê genoito*, see Malherbe, "*Mê genoito*." It is an ejaculation Paul employs almost exclusively in Galatians (three times) and in Romans (nine times), usually indicating that he has been charged — or anticipates being charged — with holding a view he actually finds obscene. If the original text of v 21 asks whether the Law is opposed to the promises *of God*, certainly a good possibility (Metzger 594), then in the very defining of the limit to the promise/Law antinomy, Paul maintains the antinomy by linking the promise explicitly to God, while failing to do the same for the Sinaitic Law. He could have said, "Is the Law of God opposed, then, to the promises of God? By no means!" This he does not do. Moreover, he could have emphasized the limit of the antinomy by denying opposition in both directions: "Is the Law opposed to the promise; is the promise opposed to the Law? By no means!" He does not do this either, and indeed he cannot do it. For the promise, he has said, is the Spirit, and the promised seed is Christ. And the twin advent of Christ and of Christ's Spirit is the invasive event in which God has declared a liberating war against the curse of the Law. Thus, while Paul can limit the antinomy by saying that the Law is not effectively opposed to the promise, he does not and cannot deny that the promise is effectively opposed to the Law's curse (cf. 4:21–5:1; 5:17–18).

[214]The Law lacks the power to do two things: to invalidate the promise (v 21a) and to make alive (v 21b). The first of these deficiencies shows that Paul's thought goes well beyond a mere comparison of Law and promise, *pace*, among many others, Vos, "Antinomie," 266; Sandmel, *Genius*, 60.

[215]Regarding the crucial distinction between Paul's antinomies and Marcion's antitheses, see Introduction §15, Comment #51, and the Glossary.

lithically opposed to the promise but also that it is *effectively* opposed to the promise, in the sense that the Law has annulled the promise (the meaning of the preposition *kata* in v 21a is set by the argument of vv 15 and 17 and by the motif of potency that is continued in v 21b; cf. Rom 4:14).

For. The sentence begun with this word in the middle of v 21 extends through v 22. One can know that the Law is not univocally and effectively opposed to God's promise by noting (a) that, being unable to give life, it does not compete with the promise; (b) that, in one of its roles, it had a function quite different from that of the promise: it shut up everything under Sin's power; and (c) that, having the function of closing every door by which the human being would ascend to God, it served God's determination to give the promise not on the basis of the Law, but rather on the basis of Christ's faith.

For if a Law had been given. Composing a conditional sentence, Paul invites the Galatians to consider momentarily the case in which the Law had been other than it in fact is, namely so potent as to make alive.[216] The condition is contrary to fact, as the apodosis demonstrates by referring to the impotence of the Mosaic Law: ". . . then rectification would have come from the Law" (cf. 2:21). It is striking that, in the only sentence in which Paul follows tradition in joining the noun "Law" to the verb "give," he speaks of a state of affairs that does not exist—that never did exist—namely, that the Mosaic Law was God's gift for making things right.[217]

strong enough. Sufficiently powerful to pronounce a universal curse on humanity (3:10), the Law is impotent to make alive. In 4:3 and 4:9 Paul speaks similarly of the elements of the cosmos: they are sufficiently strong to enslave, but they are also weak and impotent (Comment #41).

to make people alive. When Paul says that the Law lacked—and lacks—the power to make people alive, that is to make things right (cf. Phil 3:9; Rom 8:3), he finds himself contradicting not only the theology of the Teachers but also one of the sustaining pillars of classic Hebraic thought.[218] For nothing is more characteristic of the Jewish picture of the Law than the assertion that it is God's chosen instrument for the giving of life.[219]

In Paul's mouth the verb "to make alive" refers to the active power to make

---

[216]See Winger, "the possibility [Paul] raises is . . . that the Jewish *nomos* . . . might have been different" (*Law*, 75 n47).

[217]Did Paul think when he wrote Romans that God originally intended the Law to make alive (Rom 7:10), and that the problem arose not from the Law's impotence, but rather from the Flesh (Rom 8:3) and/or from the fact that Israel oriented itself to the Law *hôs ex ergôn* rather than *ek pisteôs*? That is a question one can pursue in connection with Rom 9:31–32; see Meyer, "Romans 10:4."

[218]Klein, "Sündenverständnis," 273.

[219]Continuing a view powerfully expressed, for example, in Ps 119:93, Sirach speaks of "the Law of life," meaning that life is the goal which the Law in fact accomplishes, having been given directly by God for that purpose (45:5). One thinks also of a saying attributed to Hillel: "The more study of the Law the more life" (*m. 'Abot* 2:7). Even in apocalyptic strains of thought, where malignant powers are said to fight against God and to assail Israel, threatening her with death, the Law is celebrated as the potent counterforce, the soteriological means to life (e.g., 4 Ezra 7:17, 21; "the Law of life" in 14:30; cf. 8:56).

alive *by conquering death* (Rom 8:11; 1 Cor 15:22).[220] What human beings need is not continuance of existence, but rather the discontinuous event of being called to life as though from the grave. The power to defeat death, to make alive, lies, then, with God, and God has not invested that power in the Law.[221]

22. *But in actuality, the scripture imprisoned everything under the power of Sin.* Hearing the word *alla*, "but rather," one initially thinks that Paul will immediately turn from the impotence of the Law to the potency of God's promise. Instead, he first draws a contrast between an unreal expectation of the Law — that it will grant life — and the role of the Law *as scripture.*

the scripture imprisoned everything. Having mentioned the Law three times in v 21, Paul now speaks of the scripture. We have earlier noted that he draws no consistently neat distinction between the Law and the scripture, although, as we will see later, he does distinguish the cursing voice of the Law from its scriptural and promissory voice (Comments #48 and #50). He does tend, that is, to see scripture as God's ally, one could even say as God's positive, right hand. Thus, in 3:8 Paul has already said that, foreseeing God's future act of rectifying the Gentiles, scripture spoke the promise of Gen 12:3, thus preaching the gospel ahead of time to Abraham. Moreover, "what stands written in scripture" unmasks the Law, revealing it to be the power that curses (Gal 3:10). The true promise written in Hab 2:4 shows the Law's promise of life to be false (Gal 3:11–12). And "what stands written" also testifies to Christ's victory over the Law's curse (3:13). Now, in 3:22, Paul adds a new note. Acting as God's negative, left hand, so to speak, scripture also imprisoned the whole of creation.[222] Only in Gal 3:22–23 and Rom 11:32 does Paul use the verb *sygkleiô*, "to lock up"; a comparison of these two passages is instructive (Comment #39).

under the power of Sin. To speak of this imprisonment, Paul employs the striking expression "to be under the power of" (usually *hypo tina einai*, *hypo tina genesthai*), one that emerges eight times in Gal 3:10–4:5, setting much of the tone of this section. Only in the present verse, however, does Paul use this expression to speak of two active powers. One of these, the scripture, does not itself

---

On Ezek 20:25, see Greenberg, *Ezekiel 1–20*, 368–370; and note especially the repeated references in Ezekiel 20 to "my laws and my rules . . . by observing which man shall live."
[220] See de Boer, *Defeat*; and cf. the Amidah.
[221] There are two major ways in which Paul could have softened the blow of Gal 3:21b: (a) He could have indicated that life was the true goal of the Law (cf. Rom 7:10), but imperfect observance produced the effect of the Law's impotence. In the Note on 3:10, following E. P. Sanders, we have suggested that Paul never formulates an argument based on imperfect observance. In any case, nowhere *in Galatians* does Paul even hint that God intended to use the Law as the path by which he would grant life. And Rom 9:31–10:3 says nothing about imperfect observance (see again Meyer, "Romans 10:4"). (b) Paul could have limited the impotence to Gentiles, saying only that the Law was not able to make *them* alive. Nowhere does he draw such a distinction among human beings.
[222] *In Galatians* Paul consistently holds to the apocalyptic view that creation as a whole has fallen out of God's hands, being therefore in a state of imprisonment under the power of "the present evil age" (1:4; cf. 6:15). It is not surprising, then, that in this letter Paul does not mix together creational and new-creational arguments (Comment #40).

enslave, but merely conveys everything to the slave master, Sin. See again Comment #39.

in order that the promise might be given. The purpose clauses in vv 22 and 24 (*hina*) are both like and unlike the prepositional phrase of v 19 (*tôn parabaseôn charin*). All three state a reason for the Law's existence. But, whereas the phrase of v 19 implies a verb of which the Law itself is the subject,

the Law was added in order that *it* might provoke transgressions,

the corresponding clauses of vv 22 and 24 relate the scriptural Law to a verb of which God is the implied subject, thus speaking of God's purpose vis-à-vis the Law:[223]

The scripture imprisoned everything under Sin's power, in order that *God* might give the promise via the faith of Jesus Christ to those who believe (v 22).

The Law was our confining custodian until Christ came, in order that *God* might rectify us by faith (v 24).

In short, when the Law seemed to be in collusion with Sin, imprisoning the whole of creation under Sin's power, it actually served the purpose of God. It did that, however, only by its role as a jailer. It shut every door that might seem to lead from the human orb to the possession of God's promise, and in *that* way it played its part in God's plan to make his own entry into the human orb. And the intention behind both imprisonment and divine entry was God's determination to give the promise — thus making things right — by the faith of Christ.

via the faith of Jesus Christ. Paul has just emphasized Sin's enslavement of the whole world, including human beings. That state of enslavement has now been broken, not by an act on the part of some of the slaves, but rather by God's invasive act of liberation. All other doors being closed, God acted via "Christ's faith," an expression by which Paul refers to Christ's trustful obedience to God in the giving up of his own life for us (Comment #28). Paul says exactly the same thing when, in Rom 5:19, he names the act by which Adamic Sin has been vanquished: Christ's obedience.

to those who believe. The faith enacted by Christ in his death kindles trusting faith in him on the part of human beings, just as God's promise to Abraham incited the patriarch's trust in God (2:16; 3:1–2, 6; Comment #29).

23. *Before faith came, we were confined under the Law's power, imprisoned during the period that lasted until, as God intended, faith was invasively revealed.* Paul continues to speak of the era of the Law, saying three things about it: (a) It was the period in which "we" existed under the Law's power; (b) it had a definite terminus, the arrival of faith (vv 23, 25; cf. the advent of the promised seed in

[223]That *dothê* in v 22 and *dikaiôthômen* in v 24 are instances of the divine passive needs no argument.

v 19 and Christ's coming in v 24); (c) even in the era of the Law's dominion, God was on the verge of executing his ultimate purpose, thinking ahead (*mellô*) to the faith by which he would terminate it.

we were confined under the Law's power. Between vv 14 and 23 Paul has spoken consistently of actors other than himself and the Galatians: God, Abraham, the promise, the promised seed (Christ), the Law, the angelic givers of the Law, the mediator of the Law (Moses), the scripture, Sin. Now in vv 23–25, as in v 14, he broadens his attention to include a certain "we." We have seen reasons for thinking that with this pronoun Paul refers to the Galatians as well as to himself (Comment #36). All human beings were caught under the Law's power.

imprisoned. Using the verb *sygkleiô* a second time, Paul says about the Law what he has already said in v 22 about the act of scripture in conveying the creation to the prison ruled over by Sin. Like Sin, the Law was the universal prison warden.

during the period that lasted until. In vv 23 and 24 Paul employs the preposition *eis* with its temporal force, "until" (cf. *achris*, "until," in v 19). God had intentions, to be sure, during the Law's era, but they were focused altogether beyond that era, as God thought ahead to the faith he would one day reveal (*mellô* with aorist passive infinitive).

faith was invasively revealed. Paul's use of the passive verb "was revealed" shows his intention to speak here of God's eschatological act, and thus his concern to refer to the faith that is God's deed in Christ (so also "the faith" in vv 25 and 26). From 2:16, 3:22–25, and 4:4–6, we see that Paul is referring interchangeably to the coming of Christ, to the coming of Christ's Spirit, and to the coming both of Christ's faith and of the faith kindled by Christ's faith. It is that multifaceted advent that has brought to a close the parenthetical era of the Law, thus radically changing the world in which human beings live.

The present verse also attributes that change to a divine invasion. For Paul uses interchangeably the verbs *erchomai* ("before faith *came*") and *apokalyptô* ("until . . . faith *was revealed*"). Elsewhere the apostle can employ the verb *apokalyptô* to speak of the unveiling of something long ago prepared by God (1 Cor 2:9–10; cf. 1 Enoch 103:3; 4 Ezra 8:52). On the whole, however, his apocalyptic language refers not to an *unveiling* of some *thing*, but rather to an *invasion* carried out by some *one* who has moved into the world from outside it (Comment #3).[224]

24. *So then.* With a single sentence, vv 24 and 25, Paul now draws a summarizing conclusion to the paragraph he had begun at v 19 (cf. "so then" in 4:7), repeating all of its major motifs, but employing a new metaphor for the Law.

the Law was our confining custodian. Referring to the era that is now past, both for Jews and for Gentiles, Paul speaks of the Law as our *paidagôgos*. Partly because the Greek term is the root from which the word "pedagogue" is derived, and partly because of the indications, in the purpose clauses of vv 22 and 24, that

---

[224]The apocalyptic motif of divine invasion is lost when one credits Paul with recommending faith as a human alternative superior to observance of the Law, *pace* Wuellner, "Toposforschung."

Paul understands the Law to have served God's intention, a number of interpreters, from Clement of Alexandria onward, have seen here a reference to the Law as a teacher who, by training us, has prepared us for Christ.[225]

For two reasons one must judge this "pedagogical interpretation" unacceptable. (a) The statement that the Law was our *paidagôgos* is Paul's explication of the middle clause of v 23: "we were confined under the Law's power, imprisoned during [its] period." The Law of v 23, that is to say, is not a pedagogical guide, but rather an imprisoning warden. To be sure, one might consider the possibility that the explication in v 24 exceeds its foundation in v 23, were one not confronted with a second factor. (b) As we will see in Comment #39, in six of the ten times Paul refers to humans being "under the power of," he identifies that enslaving power as the Law. When he says in v 25, therefore, that since the coming of faith we are no longer "under the power of" the *paidagôgos*, he shows clearly that in that verse, as in 24, he is using the term *paidagôgos* in the sense of a distinctly unfriendly and confining custodian, different in no significant way from an imprisoning jailer.[226] On Paul's metaphors, see further Comments #9 and #43.

until the advent of Christ. As in v 23, the basic force of the preposition *eis* is temporal, "until." There is also, however, a minor note of purpose, in the strictly limited sense that Paul speaks not of the goal of the Law itself — as though it had been a friendly teacher — but rather of the goal God had in mind even during the period of the Law. As we have noted, that is, the Law was compelled to serve God's intention simply by holding all human beings in a bondage that precluded every route of deliverance except that of Christ.

in order that we should be rectified by faith. With a purpose clause parallel to that of v 22, Paul further explicates the intention God had in mind during the period of the Law, that of rectifying human beings by Christ's faith and by the faith that Christ's faith awakens.

25. *now that faith has come.* Just as Abraham's faith in God was kindled by God's promise — that is, by the scripture's preaching the gospel to him ahead of time (3:6, 8) — so the Christian's faith is now awakened by the gospel of Christ (3:1–2). Between these two occurrences of the faith-inciting gospel there was only the world characterized by the Law's curse. Paul envisions, then, a world that has been changed from without by God's incursion into it, and he perceives that incursion to be the event that has brought faith into existence.

[225] Note the comment of Fitzmyer, "The Law schooled and disciplined humanity in preparation for Christ" ("Law," 191); and cf. similar statements in Cranfield, "Law," 52. It is one of the strengths of the learned article of Lull, "Pedagogue," to emphasize that the modern Western world has no social institution that truly corresponds to that of the *paidagôgos* in ancient Greece. But the context of Gal 3:24–25 suffices to show that Paul's picture of the pedagogue is that of a man who confines and even imprisons his charge. Cf. Gale, *Analogy.* For these same reasons there is no hint here — or elsewhere in Paul's letters — of a pedagogical use of the Law (*usus legis didacticus*). See Comment #48.

[226] Cf. Rom 6:6; Brandenburger, *Fleisch*, 56; Käsemann, *Romans*, 190, 232; idem, *Perspectives*, 147.

we are no longer under the power of that confining custodian. "The time after the advent of faith" is one way of encapsulating the message of Galatians, and that time is the joyous time of liberation.

COMMENT #38
THE GENESIS OF THE SINAITIC LAW[227]

THE VERBS USED BY PAUL TO SPEAK OF THE SINAITIC LAW'S GENESIS[228]

Sir 45:5 can serve to represent countless instances in which Jewish tradition speaks of the genesis of the Law by using the verb "give" (*nātan*; *didômi*) and by specifying God as the verb's subject: "God gave the Law." Paul doubtless grew up with this traditional expression, a fact that has caused numerous exegetes to allow it a significant role in their interpretation of his letters.[229] If, however, we study the verbs the apostle actually employs when he speaks of the genesis of the Law, we may be surprised:

Gal 3:16–17   Whereas the promissory covenant was "spoken" and "validated" by God himself, the Law merely "*happened*" (*ginomai*).

Gal 3:18–19   Whereas God himself "graciously gave" the inheritance to Abraham by the promise, the Law was only "*added*" (*prostithêmi*).

Gal 3:19   The Law was "*decreed*" (*diatassô*) by angels who acted through a mediator.

To these three references in Galatians one may add three from Romans.

Rom 5:20   Into the scene characterized by war between Sin and grace the Law merely *entered by a side door* (*pareiserchomai*).

Rom 7:9   The commandment *came* (*erchomai*).

Rom 9:4   In a list of special marks granted to Israel by God, there is the *establishing of the Law* (*nomothesia*, often overtranslated "giving of the Law").[230]

---

[227]The major subject here is the genesis of the Sinaitic Law in its paired existence with the Not-Law (see also Comment #41). Concerning the original, promissory Law — the Law in the time of Abraham — and the closely related matter of the genesis of the Law of Christ, see the last part of this Comment, and especially Comments #48 and #50. For general bibliographies on the Law in Paul's letters, consult Räisänen, *Law*; E. P. Sanders, *Law*; Westerholm, *Law*; Thielman, *Law*. See further the articles on Law in *ABD* by Greengus, Sonsino, and E. P. Sanders; Dunn, *Paul and the Mosaic Law*.

[228]The textual basis for employing the expression "the Sinaitic Law" is Paul's references to Sinai in 4:24–25, the only instances in his letters (and two of the four in the NT; Acts 7:30, 38).

[229]For example, Beker, *Paul*, 235, 244.

[230]In writing Rom 9:4 (cf. 7:22, 25; 8:7), does Paul think of the original, promissory, Abrahamic Law, and thus not of the Law of Sinai? See Comment #48.

Even in writing to the Romans, Paul does not link the noun "Law" to the verb "give." The last of these references does represent, however, a strain of thought quite important in Romans, where Paul clearly speaks of the Law as "the Law of God" (Rom 7:22, 25; 8:7).

Galatians is another matter. For whereas the Teachers are likely to have spoken of God's giving the Law, Paul does not do so. Using strong "speaking" and "giving" verbs to attribute the Abrahamic promise directly and clearly to God, Paul refers to the Law's genesis either by employing colorless verbs or by referring to the genesis of the Law as the act of angels.[231] At one point he does link the word "Law" to the verb "give," but there he speaks of a state of affairs that never existed and that never could exist: the giving of a Law potent to make alive (Gal 3:20). On the basis of these linguistic observations alone, one could ask whether in writing Galatians Paul anticipates Marcion by suggesting that the Law did not come from the Father of Jesus Christ.

THE SYLLOGISM OF GAL 3:20

Having posed the rhetorical question of 3:19a,

Why, then, the Law at all?

Paul provides explicit references to the genesis of the Law in three sentences:

3:19b. It was added in order to provoke transgressions, until the seed should come to whom the promise had been made.
3:19c. The Law was instituted by angels through a mediator.
3:20. Now a mediator does not represent one person (a singular party), but God is the one.

The third of these sentences (v 20) is far from transparent, as one can see from the huge number of interpretations given to it. In the Note, however, we have observed three linguistic factors that provide guidance: (1) Tying this sentence to the preceding one (v 19c) by the term "mediator," Paul indicates that these two sentences are to be interpreted together. (2) Allowing God's oneness to be the final and climactic element in the sentence, Paul says in effect that he is drawing on the *Shema*, taking it, formally speaking, as his chief axiom. (3) That final and axiomatic element cannot be the end of the matter, however. For, read together, the two clauses of v 20 constitute only the first two-thirds of a syllogism that Paul expects the Galatians themselves to complete by drawing a conclusion. Presupposing the affirmation of v 19c (angels instituted the Law through a mediator), the syllogism is based on a commonsense understanding of the circumstances in which a mediator is needed:

Major premise (v 20a). When either party to some transaction is an individual, there is no mediator, for the individual acts in his own behalf.

---

[231]Nothing in Paul's text suggests that these angels are demonic (a later gnostic reading). The apostle does distinguish them, however, from God.

Minor premise (v 20b). God is an individual, being the *one* of whom the *Shema* speaks.

What conclusion, then, does Paul expect the Galatians to draw?[232] There are two major possibilities.

Conclusion 1. In the case of the Law's genesis, a mediator, Moses, was necessary because neither party to the transaction was an individual. There had to be a mediator, that is to say, between the plurality of angels on the one side and the plurality of Israelites on the other. How, then, is the *Shema*, the oneness of God, to be interpreted? Since, at the genesis of the Law, neither party to the transaction was an individual, and since God is one, the conclusion is clear: Moses, the mediator, did not speak for God, but rather for the angels. God had no role of any kind in the genesis of the Law.

Conclusion 2. Moses did not speak for God; God was not himself present at Sinai; there was from the Law's genesis, therefore, a great distance between God and the Law. In short, having found in the crucifixion clear evidence of a wide gulf between God and the Law (2:19; 3:13), Paul projects that gulf back to the Law's genesis, and he expects a similar projection on the part of the Galatians. When the Law came into being, God played no direct role, but he may have stood somewhere in the far-distant background.[233]

We can ponder these alternative readings with a simple confidence in the point shared by them: Paul expects the Galatians to see that, as Moses did not speak for God, God was absent at the genesis of the Sinaitic Law. More can be said, however, for four further observations have the cumulative effect of supporting the shocking, first reading: God played no part at all in the genesis of the Sinaitic Law.

(1) It is true that, in vv 22 and 24, Paul uses purpose clauses in order to say that the scripture/Law played an active part in God's grand plan for humanity: It blocked every route of effective dealings between human beings and God, except the route elected by God when he sent Christ into the world. But this motif may indicate only that God was able to use to his purposes *even* the Law in whose genesis he played no role.

(2) In v 21 Paul denies that the Law stands against God's promise, and from that denial one could argue that God must have had some role in the Law's genesis. As we have seen, however, vv 15, 17, and 19 suggest a quite different reading of v 21: the *angels* responsible for the later-arriving Law cannot have changed the promissory covenant *God* made with Abraham (vv 17 and 19). In v 21, then, Paul does not at all imply that the Sinaitic Law had its origin in God. Quite the contrary. He asserts that the Law has not stood and cannot stand *effectively* against the power of God's promise, any more than a codicil added by someone *other*

[232] Cf. Schweitzer, *Mysticism*, 70.
[233] Cf. Mussner; Räisänen, *Law*, 130–131.

than the testator can annul or change the testator's will. Thus, God himself spoke the promise to Abraham (v 17). The angels — not God — instituted the Sinaitic Law through the hand of Moses (v 19).

(3) In constructing the grand argument of 3:6–29 Paul portrays the contrast between the blessing/promising voice of God and the cursing/enslaving voice of the Law (Comment #34). Rereading that argument in the light of 4:21, however, we see that Paul can also hear both of these voices *in* the Law:

> Tell me, you who wish to live under the power of the Law! Do you really hear what the Law says?

On the one hand, there is the Law of Sinai, the Law that forms one of the enslaving elements of the old cosmos by being paired with the Not-Law (4:3; 6:15; 3:28; Comment #41). On the other hand, however, prior to the Sinaitic genesis of the Law/the Not-Law, there was the promissory *Law* that preached the gospel ahead of time to Abraham. Paul does not consider the Law to be a monolith (Comments #35 and #48). For God is the author of the Law's promissory, Abrahamic voice (3:8, 11; 4:21b), while not being the author of the Law's cursing, Sinaitic voice (3:17, 19–20; 4:24–25).

(4) Final confirmation of Paul's intention to say that God played no part in the genesis of the Sinaitic Law comes in his use of the rhetorical stratagem of dissociation in 3:15–18 (Comment #37, footnote 178). We have suggested (Comment #37) that the Teachers are speaking to the Galatians at some length about the term "covenant":

> The covenant God made with the first proselyte Abraham is the same as the covenant he reaffirmed through Moses at Sinai, thus establishing in all its generations the ancient and venerable people of Israel, a people set apart from all the other peoples of the earth by being the people of the *covenantal Law.* What are you Gentiles to do, then? You are to follow in the steps of Abraham. By undergoing circumcision, you are to make your way into the covenant people, the seed of Abraham, the true Israel, the church of God that has Jerusalem as its mother.

In Galatians 3, however, Paul attaches the term "covenant" exclusively to the promise God made to Abraham, dissociating it from the Sinaitic Law (3:17). If the Teachers are causing the Galatians to be highly interested in God's covenant, then Paul tells them that God's covenant is the Abrahamic promise and not the Sinaitic Law, an indication that the covenantal God played no role in the genesis of that Law.

The Unthinkable but Necessary Abyss
This picture will certainly have been identified by the Teachers and their steady followers among the Galatians as altogether outrageous, proof that Paul is the great falsifier of the genuine, Lawful gospel of the Jerusalem church. These first interpreters of Paul's letter will not have made one of the mistakes made by the

modern exegetes who suggest that in Gal 3:19–20 Paul intends merely to establish the inferiority of the Sinaitic Law.[234] They will have seen, on the contrary, that his rhetoric is not that of comparison (*synkrisis*) for the sake of an *a fortiori* argument showing that something else is *better* than the Law (contrast Heb 2:2–4).[235] To speak of comparative inferiority is in this case to domesticate a radical picture. One has again to note Paul's refusal to say that the Sinaitic Law was given by God and his boldness in saying that angels instituted it, acting in God's absence.

As though peering deeply into the abyss that would be constituted by totally separating the word "Law" from God, however, Paul draws back, emphatically binding the word "Law" to God via the Abrahamic promise. Drawing on his first reference to the Abrahamic promise (3:8), he speaks with care of the promissory *Law* (4:21b), of the *Law* that helps to guide the church in its daily life (5:14), and climactically of the *Law* of Christ (6:2). In due course, we will return to an analysis of these later passages (Comments #48 and #50). Here, however, we must also note that, in their own way, they reinforce the clarity with which Paul attributes two voices to the Law, the promissory voice of the original, Abrahamic Law that speaks for God, and the cursing and enslaving voice of the later-arriving Sinaitic Law that does not speak for God. We cannot avoid posing, then, a question of considerable import: Are we to identify as anti-Judaic Paul's picture of the genesis of the Sinaitic Law in Gal 3:19–20?

Pondering that question, we can scarcely avoid thinking of rabbinic tradition in which a share in the age to come is denied to one who says the Law is not from heaven, that is to say not from God (*m. Sanh.* 10:1).[236] Four simple observations suffice to show, however, that in Paul's case the expression "anti-Judaic" is inappropriate.

First, there is the crucial matter of the identity of Paul's addressees. As he formulates the arguments of Galatians 4 and 5, he is not at all thinking of Jews, and not even of the Christian Jews who make up the churches of Judea (Gal 1:22). If one can imagine Paul speaking in a synagogue or in one of those Judean churches, one can also imagine his constructing a sermon quite different from the arguments of Galatians 3 and 4. We know that he had no objection to the

---

[234]Callan, "Midrash," 555, and many other interpreters, such as, recently, Boyarin: "The Law is . . . demoted in importance vis-à-vis the promise" (*Politics*, 147).

[235]The passage in Hebrews is worth quoting because it clearly states an argument that is based on the comparison of two deeds, both considered deeds of God, and one being superior to the other. I give a paraphrase crafted by Meeks: "If the revelation at Sinai was confirmed by God and every disobedience to it punished, although it was delivered merely by angels and by Moses, 'a servant in God's house,' and administered by mortal priests in an earthly sanctuary, how shall we escape if we neglect a salvation so much greater that it was delivered by the Lord, the Son over all God's house, who made the final sacrifice and opened the way into the heavenly sanctuary?" (Review of R. E. Brown and J. P. Meier, 457). The argument in Hebrews is an interesting use of the comparative. It is not the argument of Paul in Galatians, *pace* Wuellner, "Toposforschung"; Eckstein, *Verheissung*, 200.

[236]See J. Maier, *Auseinandersetzung*, 151 nn468–469; Segal, *Powers*; and cf. *Ep. Pet. Jas.* 2:3 (HS 2.112).

continuance of Law observance among both Jews and Christian Jews (1 Cor 9:19–23), so long as it was not viewed as a salvific requirement that should be imposed on Christians of Gentile background (Gal 2:11–21).

Second, the word "continuance" is to be emphasized. In writing to the Galatians Paul is thinking in a highly concentrated way of Gentile Christians who are being tempted to *commence* observance of the Law, under the conviction that their incorporation into Christ and their receipt of his Spirit are insufficient to their salvation. The Galatians are being told, that is, that without observance of the Sinaitic Law, they are in mortal danger. The whole of Paul's complex picture of the Law in Galatians is drawn for that setting. And in that setting Paul sees that, *when Gentiles take up observance of the Law, after having been baptized into Christ,* they return to the slavery that characterizes all *religion* as such (4:8–11). For Gentiles Law observance is a religion, and nothing other than that.

Third, addressing *only* his Galatian churches, and speaking to them *only* in the context of these developments, Paul finds in the original, Abrahamic Law an utterance of God, convinced only that God had no role in the genesis of the Sinaitic Law. He does not deny, therefore, that "the Law" is from heaven, from God. He has been compelled only to distinguish from one another the two voices of the Law, and to emphasize that distinction in a shocking way to his Galatian churches.

Fourth, although in writing to the Roman Christians Paul speaks quite differently of the Law, holding Sin responsible for *using* the Law in Sin's nefarious plans (Rom 7:8–13), he maintains the picture in which the Law has two voices (Rom 3:21, e.g., is a restatement of Gal 4:21). Climactically, he refers to these two voices by speaking of "the Law of the Spirit of life in Christ Jesus" and "the Law of Sin and of death" (Rom 8:2).[237]

Finally, in anticipation of Comment #48, three caveats can be added.

(1) Paul does not think of the distinguishing of these two voices from one another as a wise and insightful move on his own part. On the contrary, the distinguishing of the Law's two voices (one could also say the distinguishing from one another of the two Laws!) is for Paul the act of Christ. It is in fact the crucial event in the history of the Law (Comment #48).

(2) This distinguishing act is also not related to a simple textual differentiation, as though Paul were hearing the promissory voice of the Law only in Genesis (Gal 3:8; 4:21–24, 30), and the cursing voice only in Leviticus (Gal 3:12) and Deuteronomy (Gal 3:10, 13). For Paul hears the promissory voice not only in the Abrahamic texts of Genesis 12–21 but also in the prophets — Hab 2:4 (Gal 3:11), Isa 54:1 (Gal 4:27) — and even in Lev 19:18 (Gal 5:14)! Thus, he hears both voices in Leviticus itself (Gal 3:12; 5:14). Rather than being a textual matter, the

---

[237] See Lührmann: "The new teachers in Galatia may have used the expression 'the Law of Christ' to indicate that the Law of Sinai is still valid in the Christian church . . . [Paul, however, sees] a splitting of the Law into the Law of Sinai and the Law of Christ, a view that is later completed in the opposition between 'the Law of the Spirit of life' and 'the Law of Sin and death' in Rom 8:2. The 'Law of Christ' is possible only through liberation from the Law that was given on Sinai" (96–97 of the German commentary; author's translation).

distinguishing of the Law's voices is for Paul a distinctly christological event.[238] Käsemann is right to say that Paul "is not afraid to apply *to scripture* . . . the distinguishing of spirits demanded of the prophets in 1 Cor 12:10."[239] We must add only that Paul's lack of fear is, in the apostle's own view, the product of *Christ's* deed of distinguishing the promising voice of the Law from the cursing and enslaving voice that — in God's absence — had its origin at Sinai.

(3) Paul's quotation of the *Shema* is a high paradox, for in the sentences of Gal 3:19–20 that ancient confession of the oneness of God becomes the climactic proof of the great distance between God and the Sinaitic Law. In Paul's mouth the *Shema* also functions, however, as an emphatic denial of a split internal to God, as though one god spoke the promise to Abraham and acted in Christ, whereas a second god instituted the Sinaitic Law (cf. Marcion).[240] Even in the context of the Gentile mission, Paul is far from thinking that the promissory and enslaving voices of the Law come from two gods. They come respectively from God and from a group of angels who acted in God's absence. If we were to ignore the crucial distinction between Paul's apocalyptic antinomies and Marcion's logical antitheses (Comments #3 and #51; Glossary), we would have to agree with M. Simon that — even with his anti-Judaism — Marcion "did little more than push to their logical conclusion the results which [Paul] barely managed to avoid."[241]

Considering that crucial difference between Paul and Marcion, however, we see that even Paul's shocking account of the genesis of the Sinaitic Law is not anti-Judaic. His concern is tightly focused. If his Gentile converts are considering commencing observance of the Sinaitic Law, he will compel them to ponder that move squarely in the light of Christ's deed in distinguishing that Law from the original and promissory Law, the latter being the Law spoken by *Christ's Father* to Abraham. In short, Paul compels the Galatians — in *their* setting — to gaze for a moment into the abyss of a Law that is for them godless, the Law of Sinai.

COMMENT #39
THE OLD ORB OF POWER AS SLAVE MASTER AND AS GOD'S SERVANT

In Galatians 3–5 Paul employs the expression "to be under the power of . . . " (usually *hypo tina einai*) a total of ten times, with some variations, in order to

---

[238]In the second and third centuries the drawing of distinctions within the Law became an important motif among Christian Jews, gnostics, and orthodox. See footnote 107 in Comment #48.

[239]Käsemann, *Romans*, 286, emphasis added.

[240]In what remains a classic study, Harnack concluded that Marcion had deleted Gal 3:15–25 from his text, identifying it as a post-Pauline insertion in which (v 21) opposition between the Law and the promise was denied (*Marcion*, 73*). See, however, Hoffmann, *Marcion*. Schweitzer can serve to represent those who have found in Gal 3:19–20 the view that the Law was given by angelic powers rather than by God (*Mysticism*, 70–71). Cf. also the antinomianism of the *Testim. Truth* 9 and its way of relating the anathema of Gal 1:8 to Gal 3:19; Koschorke, "Paulus," 182–183.

[241]Simon, *Israel* (French), 98; unfortunately, the English translation deletes the final clause: *Israel* (English), 74.

speak of a complex state of affairs that cannot be grasped by a single picture. The concerted series of images begins in 3:22, but there is an important precursor in 3:10:[242]

3:10	Those whose identity is derived from observance of the Law are *under the power of a curse.* (Cf. 3:13, where Paul presupposes that, prior to being redemptively liberated by Christ, "we" existed under the power of the Law's curse.)
3:22	The scripture imprisoned (*synekleisen*) everything *under the power of Sin,* in order that the promise might be given via the faith of Jesus Christ to those who believe.
3:23	We were confined (*ephrouroumetha*) *under the Law's power,* imprisoned during the period that lasted until, as God intended, faith was invasively revealed.
3:24–25	So then, the Law was our confining custodian until the advent of Christ, in order that we should be rectified by faith. But now that faith has come, we are no longer *under the power of that confining custodian.*
4:2	[The minor heir] is *under the power of guardians and overseers.*
4:3	We were held in a state of slavery *under the power of the elements of the cosmos.*
4:4	[God's Son] was born *under the power of the Law.*
4:5	Being *under the power of the Law,* we stood in need of redemptive liberation.
4:21a	You Galatians wish to be *under the power of the Law,* the result of which would be birth into the state of slavery.
5:18	If you Galatians are led by the Spirit, then in fact you are not *under the power of the Law.*

When we note that in the whole of Romans (sixteen chapters) Paul employs this striking expression only four times, whereas in Galatians (six chapters) he uses it ten times, we can see that he is greatly concerned to alert the Galatians to a signal fact of life: Apart from the advent of Christ, all human beings exist in a state of enslavement to powers other than God (see Comment #36).[243] And who are these powers?

THE LAW

Chief among the enslavers is the Law with its power to curse (seven of the ten Galatians passages). Given the remarkable success of the Teachers, Paul can re-preach the gospel to the Galatians only by speaking of the Law as the major enslaving power from which Christ has liberated us. Two observations can serve

---

[242] Some of the images are given by quotation; others by summary.
[243] The four instances in Romans show that in that letter itself Paul intends to qualify forensic apocalyptic by cosmological apocalyptic (see the Glossary). See Rom 3:9 and de Boer, "Apocalyptic Eschatology," 182–184.

to emphasize the shocking character of this affirmation. (1) We have already noted that Paul's insistence on the Law's impotence to make alive is without parallel in Jewish thought. How much more so is his view of the Law as enslaver! There is nothing truly like it in ancient Hebraic thought, in Judaism, and in Christian Judaism. (2) The shock is also underlined when we note that later, writing to the Roman church, Paul softens the motif of enslavement under the Law's power (Rom 6:14–15). It is as though the different setting, or something that happened in the interim between the writing of the two letters, or some new concern on Paul's part, or a combination of these factors led Paul to avoid referring in Romans 7 to the Law itself as an enslaver, speaking rather of Sin's *use* of the Law (Rom 7:11).

SIN (3:22) AND THE ELEMENTS OF THE COSMOS (4:3)
Gal 3:22 is the only point in the letter at which Paul speaks of Sin as a cosmic power, but the essence of that view is reflected in 1:4b. And it is a motif Paul will later develop at some length in writing to the Roman Christians, as we have just noted. Regarding the enslaving power of the elements of the cosmos, see Comment #41.

THE SCRIPTURE (3:22)
Is it Paul's intention to say that human beings were held in bondage by the Law, by Sin, by the world's elements, and also by the scripture? The picture is not that simple. Only in 3:22 does Paul use the motif of enslavement in such a way as to speak of two active powers, one of which, the scripture, does not itself enslave, but merely conveys everything to the slave master, Sin. The statement of 3:22 becomes yet clearer when we note that in writing to the Romans Paul rewords it, retaining a final purpose clause and using the same major verb, *sygkleiô*, "to lock up," but identifying the subject of that verb as God rather than as the scripture:

Gal 3:22	Rom 11:32
But in actuality the scripture *locked up everything* in the *prison ruled over by Sin,*	For God *locked up all people* into the state of *disobedience,*
in order that the promise might be given [by God] via the faith of Jesus Christ to those who believe.[244]	*in order that* he might have mercy on all people.

From this parallel one returns to Galatians better equipped to grasp Paul's meaning. For one can now see the significance of Paul's shift from speaking of the Law (Gal 3:21) to formulating a statement about scripture (v 22). Nothing in the preceding part of his argument would suggest that the Law as such was God's

[244]Only in Gal 3:22, 23 and Rom 11:32 does Paul use the verb *sygkleiô*, "to lock up," "to imprison."

ally. Greatly distanced from God, it seemed to have as its sole business the pronouncing of a curse. In 3:22, however, Paul speaks of scripture, and, unlike the Law, this scripture acts in God's behalf. As God's right hand the scripture preached the gospel ahead of time to Abraham (v 8); as God's left hand it then locked up the entire world until the gospel itself should occur in God's giving of the promised Spirit (see also the purpose clause of v 24).[245] If the Law could not block the power of God's promise (v 21a), scripture could and did block every door except that of the promise.

The resulting picture shows the complexity of the apocalyptic pattern in which there are genuine powers arrayed against God, yet ultimately subject to God's sovereignty (Comment #3).[246] On the one hand, as is demonstrated by the series of passages quoted above, Paul speaks repeatedly and emphatically of the universal and terrifying state of enslavement under the might of anti-God powers, the curse of the Law, Sin, and the elements of the cosmos.[247] The stark reality of that enslavement is shown in the fact that its power has been broken only by the atoning death of God's Christ (note *exagorazô*, "to redeem from slavery," in 3:13; 4:5). On the other hand, even that state of enslavement served God's purpose, for it precluded all thought that there might be some redemptive route other than that of Christ's atoning death. Both in 3:26–29 and in 4:4–7, therefore, the pattern of subjection to malignant powers gives way to the greater power of God's liberating deed in Christ.

3:26–29 BAPTISM INTO THE CHRIST WHO IS NEITHER JEW NOR GENTILE

TRANSLATION

3:26. For you are — all of you — sons of God through the faith that is in Christ Jesus. 27. For when all of you were baptized into Christ, you put on Christ as though he were your clothing. 28. There is neither Jew nor Greek; there is neither slave nor free; there is no "male and female"; for all of you are One in Christ Jesus. 29. And, if you are Christ's, then as a result of that, you are seed of Abraham, heirs in accordance with the promise.

---

[245] The fact that one purpose clause relates to an act of scripture (v 22) whereas the other relates to the function of the Law (v 24) shows, once again, that Paul presupposes a complex scripture-Law entity, within which there is a highly significant tension between promise and curse (Comments #34, #35, and #48).

[246] In 5:13–24 Paul will add to the list of anti-God powers the Impulsive Desire of the Flesh. See Comment #49.

[247] Cf. Wink, *Naming, Unmasking,* and *Engaging.*

LITERARY STRUCTURE AND SYNOPSIS

Continuing the exegetical section he began at 3:6, Paul composes a new paragraph (vv 26–29), addressing the theme of descent in a radically new way by immediately referring to the Galatians as sons of God. This turn in the argument anticipates the final climax of 4:7 (son and heir of God) without entirely preempting it, for 3:29 proves to be only the third of the intermediate conclusions. That vv 26–29 constitute a new paragraph is obvious from both style and vocabulary.

Style. In the immediately preceding verses Paul has used the "we" style (taking it from 3:14), gathering the Galatians together with himself, as those who, with the coming of faith, have been liberated from bondage to the Law. Now, returning to the plural "you" (from 3:1–5), he draws a conclusion that is tightly focused on the Galatians, taking them back to the moment of their baptism (v 27).

Vocabulary. Comparison with 1 Cor 12:13 and Col 3:9–11 shows that in this paragraph Paul quotes and interprets for the Galatian setting an early Christian liturgical tradition formulated for use in baptism (Comment #40). He thus continues to function as an exegete, but now he interprets Christian tradition. Frequent references to the Law are replaced by reference to baptism and especially by concentrated references to Christ (five references in four verses). Paul thus reminds the Galatians that in their baptism the Law played no role at all, either positive or negative (cf. 3:2). Standing in the waters of death (Rom 6:3–4) and stripped of their old identity, they became God's own sons, putting on Christ, God's Son (2:20), as though he were their clothing, thus acquiring a new identity that lies beyond ethnic, social, and sexual distinctions. In a word, the Galatians became one new person by being united in Christ himself. It is unlikely that Paul mentioned descent from Abraham at the time of their baptism, but that does not preclude his doing so now. For he can tell them the facts: When they were baptized, being incorporated into Abraham's seed (v 16), they became true descendants of Abraham quite apart from the Law, thus inheriting the Abrahamic promise, the Spirit.

NOTES

3:26. *For you are — all of you —.* Analysis of the baptismal tradition behind vv 26–28 (Comment #40) suggests that Paul has moved the word *pantes*, "all," to the emphatic position at the beginning of the sentence (as also in v 28b). Those members of the Galatian communities fully persuaded by the Teachers' message have probably begun in some way to separate themselves from their nonobservant brothers and sisters (at the eucharist?), sure that they alone have found the true route to sonship as Abraham's Law-observant descendants (5:15; 6:6). Perceiving that development to be based on an ethnic interpretation of Abraham, Paul takes all of the Galatians back to their origin as children not of Abraham, but of God.

sons of God. Thus shifting the ground abruptly and fundamentally by speaking of descent from God through Christ, Paul lays the foundation for putting descent from Abraham into second place (v 29), indeed for eventually eclipsing it in favor of descent from God (4:5–7). The point of Christian initiation is descent from God, not descent from Abraham, although the latter is secondarily included in the former.

It is probably from the baptismal liturgy that Paul takes the motif "sons of God." In formulating the liturgy Jewish Christians before him had apparently claimed for themselves the fulfillment of God's promise to reestablish Israel as his sons.[248] If this identification was already part of the baptismal formula, and if Paul had used that formula in his evangelistic work in Galatia, then he now knows that the Galatians will recall having been addressed at their own baptism as "sons of God," an address to which they presumably responded by the exclamation: "Abba, Father" (see 4:6 below). Affirming the corporate existence already given the Galatians, therefore, Paul can boldly say, "You *are* sons of God."

through the faith that is in Christ Jesus. Containing the second of these prepositional phrases — "in Christ Jesus" — the formula signified to the baptizands the realm of redemptive power into which they were now taken by God. They became sons of God by being incorporated into God's Son. Without displacing that motif, Paul prefaces it with a reference to faith, the first prepositional phrase being one of his insertions into the baptismal formula (Comment #40). The dual advent of Christ and of faith has been a major concern of Paul in the preceding sentences (vv 22–25). He reminds the Galatians, therefore, that in their baptism they were taken into the realm of the Christ whose faith had elicited their own faith.

27. *For when all of you.* Paul uses *hosoi* as the equivalent of *hapantes hosoi*, thus speaking to all of the Galatians.[249]

were baptized into Christ, you put on Christ as though he were your clothing. The liturgy presupposes the removal of clothing as one enters the water, an act signifying separation from "the old man and his [evil] deeds" (Col 3:9).[250] The

---

[248] In early Israelite theology Israel was said corporately — all of them — to be God's first-born son (Exod 4:22; Jer 31:9) whom he called out of Egypt (Hos 11:1). Over the centuries God's bitter disappointment that children elected by him should turn their backs on him (Isa 1:2–3; Hos 1:2) led to severe judgment, extending even to his giving Israel a new name: "Not my people" (Hos 1:9). Beyond that judgment, however, God made a renewed promise of sonship: ". . . in the place where it was said to them, 'You are not my people,' it *shall* be said to them, 'Sons of the living God'" (Hos 1:10). The promissory nature of this declaration, and others like it, was then taken up in Jewish thought, where Israel's future sonship was again linked with faithful obedience to God: "And they will do my commandments. And I shall be a father to them, and they will be sons to me. And they will all be called 'sons of the living God'" (*Jub.* 1:24–25). Some dimensions of this tradition may already have been taken into the early Christian baptismal liturgy Paul is citing, Christians intending by it to say that the prophetic promise of a reestablished divine sonship had now been fulfilled in the church, the community made up of the baptized sons of God at the end of time.

[249] Cf. Josephus *Ant.* 12.399; Acts 10:45.

[250] Cf. the putting away of evil desire and, as a protective covering, the putting on of its antidote, the good desire in *Herm. Man.* 12. In Col 3:5–15 (cf. Eph 4:20–32; 1 Pet 2:1) the baptismal images of the removal of clothing and the putting on of clothing are com-

new robe, put on as one comes out of the water, signifies Christ himself. For he is the "place" in which the baptized now find their corporate life. The sons are made sons by being conformed to the image of the Son (Rom 8:29; cf. Gal 4:19). Paul can affirm the Jewish-Christian image of baptism as a cleansing bath (1 Cor 6:11), but for him the image of new clothing has less to do with cleansing than with equipping the baptizand for participation in apocalyptic warfare. Recognizing the danger of its being understood as a cultic act that merely replaces circumcision as the rite of entry (1 Cor 1:11–17), Paul sees in baptism the juncture at which the person both participates in the death of Christ (Rom 6:4) and is equipped with the armor for apocalyptic battle (1 Thess 5:8–10; 1 Cor 15:53–54; Rom 13:12). These are motifs he can easily find reflected in the baptismal liturgy's reference to the end of the old cosmos with its taken-for-granted pairs of opposites.[251]

28. *There is neither Jew nor Greek; there is neither slave nor free; there is no* "male and female." Both at their baptism and now in hearing the liturgy again, the Galatians will have noted that in form the text presents what numerous thinkers of their day termed a table in which certain pairs of opposites were named and identified as the elements that give to the cosmos its dependable structure. To pronounce the nonexistence of these opposites is to announce nothing less than the end of the cosmos (Comments #40, #41, and #51). Paul names three of these elemental opposites because he is quoting the formula. In writing to the Galatians, however, he is interested only in the first pair. Not only for Jews of Paul's day but also for numerous Gentiles, one of the basic elements providing structure to the world in which one lived consisted of the religious distinction — to use Jewish terminology — between the Jew, the person of the Law, and the Gentile, the person of the Not-Law. Now baptism into Christ involves the recognition that that distinction does not any longer exist, and its nonexistence is what causes one to participate in Christ's death (cf. 2:19).[252]

neither slave nor free . . . no "male and female." Regarding Paul's view of the termination of the social distinction between slaves and free persons, see 1 Cor 7:20–24 and Philemon.[253] The variation in the wording of the last clause suggests that the author of the formula drew on Gen 1:27, thereby saying that in baptism the structure of the original creation had been set aside.[254] One senses in the

---

bined with traditional lists of vices and virtues. Contrast Gal 5:19–23, where Paul transforms such lists into marks of a community under the power of the Flesh and marks of a community under the power of the Spirit (Comment #49).

[251]Did the Teachers seek to discontinue the practice of baptism among the Galatians, substituting circumcision for it? That is highly unlikely. They presented circumcision as a route that was both supplementary and necessary, the route to the perfection required by God (3:3). Cf. Georgi, "Anmerkungen," 111.

[252]The word *eni* is here almost certainly the contracted form of *enesti*, not the strengthened form of *en*. Thus, "There does not exist either Jew or Greek . . ."

[253]Cf. Meeks, "Androgyne." In his review of H. D. Betz's commentary on Galatians, Aune remarks that social distinctions were abolished during some feasts, for example the hecatombaia (Review of H. D. Betz, 328). On Philemon, see Barclay, "Philemon."

[254]Cf. Aristotle *Metaphysics* 986a, where the Pythagorean Table of Opposites includes the pair "male and female," *arren* [*arsen*] *thêly*.

formula itself, then, an implied reference to new creation, a motif Paul will use in crafting a dramatic conclusion to the entire letter (6:15; cf. 2 Cor 5:17).

for all of you are One in Christ Jesus. Religious, social, and sexual pairs of opposites are not replaced by equality, but rather by a newly created unity. In Christ (in what Paul will later call "the body of Christ," 1 Cor 12:13, 27) persons who were Jews and persons who were Gentiles have been made into a new unity that is so fundamentally and irreducibly identified with Christ himself as to cause Paul to use the masculine form of the word "one."[255] Members of the church are not one *thing*; they are one *person*, having been taken into the corpus of the One New Man.

From reading others of Paul's letters, we know that the apostle was aware of the fact that even in the church, the beachhead of God's new creation, there were as yet some marks of sexual and social differentiation (e.g., 1 Corinthians 7; Philemon).[256] He had later, therefore, to think very seriously about the tension between the affirmation of real unity in Christ and the disconcerting continuation of the distinguishing marks of the old creation. In writing to the Galatians he does not pause over that matter.

29. *And, if you are Christ's, then as a result of that, you are seed of Abraham, heirs in accordance with the promise.*

if you are Christ's. With a factual condition Paul now brings together his identification of Christ as the singular seed of Abraham (vv 16, 19) and his citation of the baptismal motif of incorporation into Christ. For the Galatians there are no outstanding conditions to be met, and especially none having to do with observance of the Law. Their redemption consists of their already belonging to Christ.

as a result. Enticed by the Teachers, the Galatians have developed a longing to be counted Abraham's true descendants. As we have seen, that is a desire Paul can affirm (3:7). The crucial point is the order of events. Members of the church are not related to Christ via Abraham; they are related to Abraham via their incorporation into Christ.

Does Paul consider this order of events to be true for all members of the church, including those who were Jews by birth? Strictly speaking, this question lies outside the area Paul is considering as he writes Galatians. It is in one's reading of Romans that the question can be taken up. See the analysis of Rom 4:16 near the end of Comment #37.

seed of Abraham. Maintaining linguistic contact with his Galatian churches, Paul employs the Teachers' term "seed" in his conclusion. Apart, that is, from the Galatians' fascination with the Teachers' references to the *sperma* of Abraham, Paul would presumably have remained with the expression he used in v 7, "sons of Abraham" (cf. "sons of God" in v 26).

heirs. In Comment #33 we noted that five interrelated expressions form a significant part of the Teachers' vocabulary: "the blessing of Abraham," "the seed of Abraham," "the covenant," "the Law," and, finally, "the inheritance." In order to repreach the gospel in a way that is effectively related to the Galatians' current

---

[255] Cf. the syntactically anomalous pronoun *hou* in Col 2:19.
[256] Stuhlmacher, *Philemon*, 67.

interests, Paul is willing to employ all of these expressions himself. Thus, in v 18 he is satisfied to follow the Teachers in connecting the words "Abraham" and "inheritance." Here he does essentially the same, connecting the Galatians' descent from Abraham with their being heirs by virtue of the promise. He can do that, however, because he has already established two points: (a) the priority of their relationship with Christ, the seed to whom God spoke his Abrahamic promise, and (b) their being God's sons in Christ. At a later juncture Paul will emphasize this last image, returning to it in order to say that the Galatians' inheritance has come to them by their being adopted into God's family, being thus made into God's sons and heirs (4:5, 7).

the promise. Were Paul drawing simply and literally on the Abraham traditions in Genesis, he would probably say that the Galatians are heirs in accordance with the covenant God made with Abraham. In vv 14–22, however, Paul has allowed the early Christian term "promise" to take the place of the scriptural words "blessing" and "covenant," for promise emphasizes both God's immediate utterance and the effectuating of that utterance in the advent of the Spirit that is itself the promised inheritance.

COMMENT #40
NOT JEW AND GENTILE, BUT ONE IN CHRIST

In considering the literary structure of 3:26–29 we noted that throughout this paragraph Paul speaks directly to the Galatians as "you (plural)," closing by apprising them of their identity:

> And, if you are Christ's, then as a result of that, you are seed of Abraham, heirs in accordance with the promise (v 29).

Following the first two intermediate conclusions internal to the exegetical section of 3:6–4:7 (3:18, 25), this is the third, and, like the others, it is the result of exegetical labor. Here, however, the text Paul interprets for the Galatians is not drawn from scripture, but rather from early Christian tradition. It is in fact part of a baptismal liturgy.[257] We cannot identify the citation with precision, placing quotation marks around it, but comparison with similar citations in 1 Cor 12:13 and Col 3:9–11 leads us to reasonable confidence that the formula is confined to vv 26–28. With some degree of probability we can also place Paul's additions in brackets:

A BAPTISMAL FORMULA

Gal 3:26–28	1 Cor 12:13	Col 3:9–11
[For] you are [all] sons of God [through the faith that is] in Christ Jesus;	[For] in one Spirit	. . . having put off the old man with his deeds, and

[257]Cf. Eph 6:8 and Ign. *Smyr.* 1:2. See Braumann, *Taufverkündigung*; Meeks, "Androgyne," especially 180–183.

for when all of you were baptized into Christ, you put on Christ, as though he were your clothing.	we were all baptized into one body	having put on the new man where
There is neither Jew nor Greek; there is neither slave nor free; there is no "male and female" (Gen 1:27);	whether Jews or Greeks whether slaves or free, and	there is no Jew and Greek . . .
(cf. Gal 5:6; 6:15)		circumcision and uncircumcision
for all of you are One in Christ Jesus.	we were all made to drink one Spirit.	but Christ is all in all.

In some regards the Galatians passage may conform more closely than the others to an actual liturgy. It is in form an address directed to a group of baptizands, announcing to them — and to the attending witnesses — the facts of their new existence.

You are newly incorporated into the realm of Christ, having put off the old clothing of sin and having put on Christ as your new man. Having lost distinctions that formerly separated you from one another, you are now one in Christ.

There are three major possibilities as regards the conceptual background of the baptismal formula: (1) It can be seen as a development of a Stoic and Neoplatonic tradition that speaks of a spiritual and mental freedom from distinctions, and that even looks forward, in a sort of liberal state of mind, to the possibility that the marks of ethnic differentiation will one day disappear.[258] (2) It might have been built on the basis of the proto-gnostic thought that humanity was originally androgynous, thus declaring that baptism returns one to that lost state of undifferentiation.[259] (3) Finally, it might have been drawn from apocalyptic conceptions in which sexual differentiation is expected to be terminated at the resurrection. The possibility of apocalyptic derivation is increased if the formula was crafted in one of Paul's own churches, or even in one of the daughter churches of the church in Antioch. Moreover, comparison with *2 Enoch* 65:8–10, *2 Apoc. Bar.* 51:7–16, and especially Mark 12:25 suggests that the author of the baptismal liturgy was indeed influenced by forms of apocalyptic thought ("When they rise

[258]Wolfson, *Philo* 2.418; drawing partly on the work of A. J. Malherbe, G. F. Downing mentions comparable Cynic formulations: "A Cynic Preparation for Paul's Gospel for Jew and Greek, Slave and Free, Male and Female," *NTS* 42 (1996) 454–462.
[259]Meeks, "Androgyne," 189–197.

from the dead, they neither marry nor are given in marriage; Mark 12:25). One would be slow, however, to exclude altogether any one of the three possibilities.

PAUL'S INTERPRETATION OF THE FORMULA

Whatever forms of thought the author may have drawn on, neither in writing to the Galatians nor in composing 1 Corinthians does Paul think of a mere state of mind internal to the individual baptizand. For him, as for other early Christians, the baptizand is a person being taken into the corporate entity of God's church, not one who is merely given new patterns of thought pertinent to the private life of an individual (a state of being that Paul never contemplates in any case). And nothing in either Galatians or 1 Corinthians hints that Paul himself saw in the formula the affirmation that in baptism a state of unity was being regained after having been lost. For Paul the accent clearly lies on the eschatological *novum*, as we will see more clearly below.

Regarding Paul's interpretation of the formula for the Galatian setting, there are two major clues, and they lead to a single conclusion. First, one notes the marks of Paul's redaction. In v 26 he integrates the formula into the immediate context by using the word "for." Probability lies with the thesis that he is also responsible for tying the Galatians' baptismal identity ("sons of God") not only to Christ but also to the Galatians' faith, as it was elicited by Christ. For there is no mention of faith in the parallel passages in 1 Corinthians and Colossians, whereas the dual advent of Christ and of faith is the event Paul has celebrated in the preceding verses (3:22–25). He also adds the word "all," thus emphasizing the formula's motif of comprehensive unity in Christ: "For you are — *all of you* — sons of God through the faith that is in Christ Jesus." If the Teachers have sown seeds of discord, blessing those Galatians who are accepting circumcision and threatening the others with cursed damnation, Paul will bring them all back to the unity already given them in their baptism into Christ.

Second, there is the manner in which Paul argues. The whole of the letter shows that in writing to the Galatians Paul has no genuine interest in either the second pair of opposites, slave/free (on the social level), or the third, male/female.[260] By attending briefly to the third, however, we can bring into sharp focus the nature of Paul's argument in this passage, thus discerning its full impact on the pair of opposites that is of concern to him, Jew/Greek.

Pondering the matters of sexual differentiation and family, one recalls that the Jesus traditions in the synoptic gospels show a remarkable tension. On the one hand, when asked about divorce, Jesus uses the ancient and widespread argument based on the structure of creation. Drawing on the book of Genesis, he says:

> From the beginning of creation [there was no divorce] God made them male and female. For this reason a man shall leave his father and mother and be joined to his wife . . . (Mark 10:6–7; NRSV; Gen 1:27; 2:24).

---

[260] Did the Teachers' demand of circumcision and their scriptural equation of circumcision with the covenant (Genesis 17; Comment #45) function to imply that they were bringing the female members of Paul's churches into God's covenantal people on an inferior level? It is doubtful that anyone would have thought so at that time; in any case, Paul

On the other hand, when told that his biological mother and brothers are outside the crowded house in which he is teaching, Jesus is far from presupposing the creational basis of sexuality and marriage. On the contrary, he refers to what one might call the new-creational family:

> And he replied "Who are my mother and my brothers?" And looking at those who sat around him, he said, "Here are my mother and my brothers! Whoever does the will of God is my brother and sister and mother" (Mark 3:33–35; NRSV).

The traditions about Jesus find him arguing both on the basis of creation and on the basis of the gospel's power to bring about a new creation — the eschatological family — and between these two kinds of arguments there is a discernible tension.

One can sense a similar tension in Paul's letters, *if* one takes them as a whole. In Rom 1:18–32 Paul uses an argument explicitly based on creation, drawing certain conclusions from "the things [God] has made" in "the creation of the cosmos" (Rom 1:20).[261] In effect, Paul says in this passage that God's identity and the true sexual identity of human beings as male and female can both be inferred from creation.

What a different argument lies before us in Gal 3:26–29; 6:14–15! Here the basis is explicitly not creation, but rather the new creation in which the building blocks of the old creation are declared to be nonexistent. If one were to recall the affirmation "It is not good that the man should be alone" (Gen 2:18), one would also remember that the creational response to loneliness is married fidelity between man and woman (Gen 2:24; Mark 10:6–7). But in its announcement of the new creation, the apocalyptic baptismal formula declares the erasure of the distinction of male from female. Now the answer to loneliness is not marriage, but rather the new-creational community that God is calling into being in Christ, the church marked by mutual love, as it is led by the Spirit of Christ (Gal 3:28b; 5:6, 13, 22; 6:15).[262]

A tension between new-creational argument and creational argument is not to be found, however, within Galatians itself. In writing to his church in Corinth, for example, Paul will negotiate the relation between new creation and creation by advising married people to be married as though not being married (1 Cor 7:29).[263] For the Galatians he provides no such finesse. Indeed, in writing to the Galatians Paul avoids two things. He does not demonstrate the tension that can be seen between a creational argument and a new-creational one. And, correspondingly, he does not provide a way of relating the one to the other, as though in some manner new creation could be added to creation. Here he argues uncompromisingly on the basis of God's new creation.

---

nowhere gives even a hint about this matter. See the Note on 5:19b; Lieu, "Circumcision," and the literature in her footnotes, notably the studies by S. J. D. Cohen.

[261] See Tobin, "Romans 1:18–3:20," 304–305.

[262] Cf. Morse, *Not Every Spirit*, 273–287.

[263] Cf. Schrage, *Ethics*, 202–204.

The result of such a radical vision and of its radical argumentation is the new-creational view of the people of God harmonious with the one we have seen in Comment #37.[264] Just as, in Galatians 5:13–14, the need to surmount loneliness is now met not by marriage, but rather by the loving mutuality enacted in the new creation, the church of God, so the corresponding need to belong to a coherent community is not met by the making of a people ethnically and religiously differentiated from other peoples, but rather by the community of that new creation that God is calling into existence in Christ throughout the whole of the world. Thus, this corporate people is determined to no degree at all by the religious and ethnic factors that characterized the old creation (5:6; 6:15). This people is determined solely by incorporation into the Christ in whom those factors have no real existence.

The church, in short, is a family made up of former Jews and former Gentiles, not an enlarged version of a family that already exists.[265] Thus, neither in Paul's mouth nor in the mouth of the formula's author is the baptismal liturgy a rallying cry in favor of a new religion, Christianity, and against an older one, Judaism. What is new is not another subset in the category of religion, and thus a new religion in competition with an older one. What is new is the new corporate person, as the final clause of the formula shows (v 28b). It is Christ and the community of those incorporated into him who lie beyond religious distinctions.

Given the widespread and comforting view that true religion provides the dependable map to the world and to one's place in the world, it can be no surprise that the nonreligious, unified life in Christ involves a real death, and specifically the baptizand's participation in Christ's death (Gal 2:19–20; 5:24; Rom 6:3–4). The motif of invasion (Comment #37) is death-dealing in order to be life-giving. To draw a metaphor from 1944, God's redemptive act in Christ must first be compared to the cross-channel invasion as that event was experienced by the Germans.[266] Only as a second step can one compare God's redemptive act to the cross-channel invasion of 1944 as it was experienced by the Germans' captives.

For the old pairs of opposites are not discrete sins to be washed away or simply renounced. They are the basic building blocks of a cosmos from which one is now painfully separated by death. In this way, baptism is a participation both in Christ's death and in Christ's life; for genuine, eschatological life commences

---

[264]The apocalyptic baptismal formula is addressed explicitly to those who are "in Christ Jesus." It is not a program of cultural criticism — and emphatically not the genuine parent of any imperialistic, coercive politico-cultural system — declaring the end of the Jewish people (see, e.g., Rom 9:4–5). Boyarin's occasional deletion of the crucial prepositional phrase "in Christ Jesus" inevitably leads to some of the problems that emerge in his fascinating book *Politics* (e.g., 228). See the Introduction §17, and cf. Mamood and Armstrong, "Ethnic Groups."

[265]That Paul understood himself in a significant sense to be a former Jew is reflected in the wording of Rom 9:4. Even though he refers to the Jews as "my kindred according to the flesh" (9:3), he continues not by saying "to *us* belong the adoption, the glory . . . ," but rather "to *them* . . . " On the members of his churches as former Gentiles, see 1 Cor 12:2.

[266]Cf. Cullmann, *Christ and Time*.

when one is taken into the community of the new creation in which unity in God's Christ has replaced religious-ethnic differentiation. In a word, religious and ethnic differentiations and that which underlies them — the Law — are identified in effect as "the old things" that have now "passed away," giving place to the new creation (2 Cor 5:17).

4:1–7 ENSLAVEMENT AND LIBERATION

TRANSLATION

4:1. What I mean can be made yet clearer by a picture: So long as the heir is a child, he is no different from a slave, even though, in prospect, he is lord of the entire household. 2. He is under the authority of guardians and managers until the arrival of the time set by the father for his passage to the status of an adult.

3. Something very like this is true of us. When we were children, we were held in a state of slavery under the power of the elements of the cosmos. 4. But when the fullness of time came, God sent his Son, born of a woman, born under the power of the Law, 5. in order that he might redeem those held under the power of the Law, in order, that is, that we might receive adoption as sons. 6. And because you are sons, God sent the Spirit of his Son into our hearts, crying, "Abba, Father!"

7. So then, you are no longer a slave, but rather a son; and if you are a son, you are also an heir by God's act of adoption.

LITERARY STRUCTURE AND SYNOPSIS

Composing Gal 4:1–7 as the final subdivision of the letter's first exegetical section (3:6–4:7), Paul carefully binds it to the previous parts of that section. He begins by linking the word "heir" (4:1) to the word "heirs" (3:29). He explicates the motif of redemptive invasion he has already emphasized (3:13–14; 3:23–25) by speaking of God's sending both his Son and the Spirit of his Son (4:4, 6). And, reaching back to his earlier affirmation of the Galatians' sonship from God (3:26), Paul uses that motif to formulate the final climax to the exegetical section (4:7). In that way he brings to a closure the theme with which he began, descent from Abraham (3:6–7), but in this denouement he no longer refers to the identity of those who are descended from Abraham. He asserts that the Galatians are descended from God.

The internal structure involves three discrete steps.

(a) Paul first presents a picture drawn from legal custom regarding the period of guardianship for a son who is the heir of his father (vv 1–2). Although potentially the head of the household, the son, Paul says, is no different from a slave, being held under the power of guardians until the time set by his father for his majority.

(b) Paul then offers an analogy, using the formula "So also we . . . ," rendered above "Something very like this is true of us" (vv 3–5a). Here there are two scenes. *Scene 1:* Skillfully using sometimes the first person plural — "we" — and sometimes the second person plural — "you" (with the addition once of "they") — Paul paints a doleful picture of the whole of humanity (v 3; Comment #36).[1] All are enslaved under the power of the elements of the cosmos. The pronominal alternation also supports the hypothesis that Paul thinks of the Law as a cosmic power that affected all human beings; indeed, the Law proves to be one of the enslaving elements of the cosmos (cf. 3:10; Comment #41). *Scene 2:* Having thus portrayed the human condition, Paul speaks of a climactic event that has changed that scene fundamentally: the arrival of the time selected by God for accomplishing deliverance from slavery by the sending of his Son (vv 4–5a).

(c) Finally, Paul develops the analogy beyond the legal picture of vv 1–2. First, he speaks of adoption (v 5b). Our deliverance from the Law's tyranny does not set us free into a world of unrelatedness; the deliverance is God's deed for the purpose of adopting us into his family as sons.[2] We are delivered both from and into. Next, Paul refers to Christ's Spirit: God has sent the Spirit of his Son into the hearts of his newly adopted sons, and from within their hearts the Spirit then cries out to God as Father (v 6). In closing, Paul addresses the Galatians directly, conveying to them the result of God's timely action: Because they live in a world that God has graciously invaded via his Son and the Son's Spirit, they are no longer slaves, but rather sons and heirs by God's act (v 7). The resulting structure can be laid out in a chart:

Picture	Analogy
the heir in a household	we human beings
(v 1) as a *child*	(v 3) as *children*
(v 1) the heir is a virtual *slave*	(v 3) we were *enslaved*
(v 2) until the *time* set by the father	(v 4) but when the fullness of *time* came
	(v 4) God sent his Son
(vv 1–2) for his *transition* out of virtual slavery into active lordship.	(v 5) to bring about our *transition*, by delivering us from slavery.

[1] "We" v 3; "they" v 5; "we" v 5; "you" v 6; "we" v 6; "you" v 7.

[2] All of the Galatians, both men and women, will have understood Paul to be referring to them when he speaks of *huioi*, "sons" (3:7, 26; 4:6, 7 [twice, singular]), but the term cannot be consistently rendered "children" because of the substantive dimensions of the linguistic connection Paul draws in 4:6, "And because you are *sons*, God sent the Spirit of his *Son* into our hearts, crying, 'Abba, Father!'"

Further Development

(v 1) *heir*

(v 5) we receive adoption as sons
(v 6) and, as you are sons, God also sent into our hearts the Spirit of his Son, crying out "Abba, Father."
(v 7) Thus, you are a son; and if a son, then also an *heir* by God's act of redemptive adoption.

Paul paints the picture solely for the sake of the use he will make of it, thus allowing himself both freedom in shaping the picture itself and freedom to close with a development that goes beyond it.

FREEDOM IN PAINTING THE PICTURE

"No different from a slave." The son in the household is in fact different from a slave, if for no other reason than the fact that he knows — as do his guardians also — that he will one day be lord of the estate. Thus, when Paul says that, during his minority, the son does not at all differ from a slave, he is altering the picture somewhat, in order to make it altogether serviceable to his application. Focusing solely on the son's similarity to a slave, Paul is preparing to say that human beings are slaves.

"The time set by the father." The Roman imperial legal traditions indicate that the time at which the boy is "of age" is set by state law, not by the individual father.[3] To be sure, there are a few examples from provincial practice in which the father stipulates the age of majority. Paul could be drawing on a provincial arrangement.[4] In any case, rather than concentrating on the fine points of legal practice, he is thinking of God's timely and sovereign act in redeeming human beings from their slavery.

FREEDOM TO GO BEYOND THE PICTURE

". . . in order . . . that we might receive adoption as sons." The legal custom portrayed by Paul in vv 1–2 leaves no place for the motif of adoption, since that custom presupposes a child who has been from birth the son and heir. In his analogy, however, Paul has no intention of implying that human beings have been God's sons all along, only waiting for the day of their majority. On the contrary, they have been actual slaves, and have therefore to be made into sons. Consequently, Paul freely reaches beyond the legal picture of vv 1–2, making adoption a chief motif of vv 5–7.

"And because you are sons . . ." Paul uses adoption into sonship to define liberation. In sending Christ, God frees the slaves, but, as noted above, they are not thereby people who are "on their own." God frees them by making them his

[3] See H. D. Betz 202 n6, and especially 204 n21; also Longenecker.
[4] See Moore-Crispin, who cites papyrus evidence in order to argue that Paul's picture reflects Hellenistic law in Asia Minor ("Galatians 4:1–9," 209).

sons. And making them his sons, he equips them with the Spirit of his Son, the Spirit then proving their sonship by crying out through their mouths to God as "Abba, Father."

". . . and if you are a son, you are also an heir by God's act of adoption." Only in this way is Paul willing in v 7 to return to the motif of inheritance. Because the Galatians have been adopted as God's sons, they are also his heirs by his own deed.

Paul's freedom both in painting the picture and in going beyond it provides an important index to his understanding of language, and specifically of the metaphors of "slave," "sons," "adoption as sons," and "Father." The way in which Paul employs these images shows the apocalyptic character of his metaphors. For, in each case, Paul thinks that the true impact of the this-worldly image has been determined by God's act in Christ. For that reason a useful metaphor is not an image projected from the (human) known into the (divine) unknown. Things are the other way around. A metaphor true to the gospel is produced by the incursion of the unknown into the orb of what is presumed to be the known (Comment #9).

For Paul the meaning of the word "Father," for example, is not determined by the biological father one happens to have had. In the corporate worship of God's new family (Gal 6:10) the Spirit uses the word "Father" to call out to God through the worshipers' mouths. But in the context of this new family the word "Father" is thereby redefined on the basis of *God's* identity (1:1). In short, in Paul's letters the true source of analogical thought is the revelation that has come with *this* Father's redemptive and liberating incursion into the world in the advent of *his Son*. On this matter, see Comment #43.[5]

NOTES

4:1. *What I mean can be made yet clearer by a picture.* Literally, Paul writes merely "I say," expressing himself very nearly as he did in 3:15. At each of these junctures he makes a transition from a formally exegetical section to a figure drawn from common social arrangements, thus further clarifying the results of an exegetical argument.

he is no different from a slave, even though, in prospect, he is lord of the entire household. As the second clause shows, everyone in the household knows very well that the son and heir is quite different from a slave by reason of his future. Focusing his attention on the motif of slavery, Paul overdraws the picture because he anticipates the way in which he will use it.

2. *guardians and managers.* Without linguistic precedent Paul links to one another the widely attested Greek terms *epitropos*, "guardian," and *oikonomos*, "manager of a household," putting both words in the plural, in order to make

---

[5] See also K. Barth on the distinction of the *analogia fidei* from the *analogia entis* (*Church Dogmatics*, 2.1, 75–85 and 2.1, 223–243).

his picture fit the analogy he will draw in vv 3–5.[6] The guardians and managers correspond, then, to the plural elements of the cosmos.

until the arrival of the time set by the father. In the picture painted by Paul the first period is replaced by a second, in which the heir is no longer under the control of others. The boy experiences a profound change: having been a virtual slave, he is now the heir who has come into his inheritance. Regarding the cause of the radical change, the figure itself presents two factors. In the initial clause (v 1a) the first period is said to last so long as he is a child, the change in the son's world apparently happening as a result of maturation. In the final clause (v 2b), however, that change is said to occur with the arrival of a point in time set by the father (*prothesmia* [*hêmera*] *tou patros*), and thus to happen as a result of the father's act. The tension between v 1a and v 2b raises an important question. How much of the picture does Paul intend to draw across to the analogy? When he says, "Something very like this is true of us," does he mean to attribute a dramatic change in our lives both to a process of human maturation and to God's fixing the time of redemption? See below on v 4.

3. *Something very like this is true of us.* Paul has presented the picture solely in order to draw an analogy, and, as we have seen, the analogy pertains to the situation of all human beings (Comment #36). And what an analogy it proves to be! The sentence comprising vv 3–5 is nothing less than the theological center of the entire letter. It contains nearly all of the letter's major motifs, and it relates them to one another in such a way as to state what we may call the good news of Paul's letter to the Galatians:

> Like all other human beings, we were held in a state of *slavery* by the very *building blocks of the cosmos*, the cosmos having fallen to a significant degree out of God's control. But God did not leave us in that state of slavery. At a time selected by him, God *invaded* the partially foreign territory of the cosmos, *sending* his own Son into it, born, as all human beings are born, and *subject to the enslaving power of the Law*, as all human beings are subject to that power. The mission God gave to his Son was to *redeem from slavery* those who were thus caught under the Law's power, so that we who are incorporated into the Son might *receive adoption* at the hands of God himself.

(a) A clear presupposition of all that Paul has said about God's making right what has gone wrong (2:16; Comment #28) lies in the conviction that the universal human condition is a state of slavery. In 3:13 Paul has already shown that the most revealing synonym of "rectify/make right" (*dikaioô*) is "redeem from slavery" (*exagorazô*). (b) That the term "apocalypse" refers centrally to God's timely and redeeming invasion of the cosmos in Christ is a note Paul has struck dramatically in 3:23–25. Redemption is a cosmic event. (c) Finally, by identifying God's promise to Abraham with the Spirit of Christ (3:14), Paul has prepared the way for saying that those who have received the Spirit are not only redeemed but also

---

[6]The term *epitropos*, referring to the guardian of a minor, made its way into Hebrew as a loanword. See Krauss, *Lehnwörter*; R. Taubenschlag, *Greco-Roman Egypt*, 123–124.

caused to be God's adopted children. One can read the whole of the letter as lines of thought radiating out from 4:3–5 in such a way as to explicate the theme stated in 1:6–9.

we were held in a state of slavery. From the picture he has painted in vv 1–2 Paul draws into his analogy the motif of enslavement, leaving aside that of immaturity. And, using the imperfect tense, he describes the long-existing state of affairs prior to the advent of God's Son.

under the power of. See the discussion of the expression *hypo tina einai* in Comment #39.

the elements of the cosmos. Paul means the religious pairs of opposites, circumcision/uncircumcision, Jew/Gentile, Law/Not-Law (Comment #41).

4. *But when the fullness of time came.* Just as the picture of vv 1–2 identifies a turning point in the life of the child, so in his analogy Paul speaks of the coming of a definite point in time. Does Paul intend to refer, then, to a point that lies at the end of a line? Two observations could lead to that conclusion.

In Paul's world "the fulfilling of the time" could refer to the temporal aspect of a contractual arrangement.[7] When the contract had extended over an agreed-upon amount of time (the end of a line), one could say that the time was fulfilled, meaning that the point had arrived at which the contract was ended.

The image of a point at the end of a line could also come to mind when one thinks of locutions in the gospel traditions, such as the encapsulation of Jesus' preaching in Mark 1:15, "The time is fulfilled, and the kingdom of God has come near . . ." These two observations could suggest, then, that, after rejecting the Teachers' view of redemptive history in Gal 3:16 (Comment #37), Paul finally embraces in 4:4 his own way of affirming that view.

Three counterobservations, however, preclude this reading. (a) The figure of the pedagogue in 3:25 is not that of an instructor, but rather that of an imprisoning custodian. (b) Using some such expression as *hêlikian echein* ("to be of age"; John 9:21, 23), Paul could have concluded the picture of Gal 4:1–2 by striking the note of immaturity/maturity: ". . . until the arrival of maturity on the part of the heir." Instead, he refers to a sovereign act on the part of the father. (c) In drawing the analogy in vv 3–7 Paul could have employed again the contrast between immaturity and maturity, saying, "Something very like this is true of us. When we were children, we were immature." Instead, he says, "we were held in a state of slavery," a condition one does not outgrow. Furthermore, when Paul speaks of the past life of the Galatian Gentiles in vv 8–9, he refers to enslavement, not to immaturity. The conclusion is clear. Throughout this passage Paul does not think of a gradual maturation, but rather of a punctiliar liberation, enacted by God in his own sovereign time. Stepping on the scene, that is to say, God has closed the enslaving parenthesis of the Law at the time chosen by him alone.

God sent his Son. With this clause — drawn from an early Christian formula — Paul reiterates with added emphasis a point he has stated earlier in 3:23–25. Redemption has occurred in the human orb via an invasion that had its origin outside that orb (Comment #42).

[7]MM cite several papyri to show that the expression *plêroô ton chronon* is not a Hebraism.

born of a woman. The expression means to be born as a human being (Job 14:1; Matt 11:11).

born under the power of the Law. One could be tempted to offer the paraphrase "born a Jew," for Paul knows that Jesus was a Jew, and he takes that fact seriously. Later, for example, in writing to the Roman church, Paul quotes a formula in which Christ is identified as a descendant of David, "as regards the flesh" (Rom 1:3; cf. 9:5). Paul also believes, however, that everyone is enslaved by the cosmic elements, the Law being one of them (Comments #39 and #41). This clause is altogether parallel, therefore, to the preceding one. In it Paul does not say that God sent his Son into the salvific history of Israel (or even into the unsalvific history of Israel), but rather into the malignant orb in which all human beings have fallen prey to powers inimical to God and to themselves (see v 5 below, and cf. Phil 2:7).[8]

5. *in order that he might redeem those held under the power of the Law, in order, that is, that we might receive adoption as sons.* The early Christian formula from which Paul drew the clause "God sent his Son" ends with a clause in which the purpose (and result) of the sending is stated, this final clause being the element that a given author shapes to the context. So here Paul brings the sentence, begun in v 3, to its conclusion with two purpose/result clauses, worded by himself for the Galatian setting, and similar to those with which he ended the sentence in 3:13–14.

might redeem. Having spoken of universal enslavement in v 3, Paul identifies the purpose for which God sent the Son: it is that of redeeming the whole human race from slavery (on the verb *exagorazô*, see 3:13, the only other place in the NT at which the verb is connected to God's action in Christ).

those held under the power of the Law. Given the fact that in v 3 Paul has identified the slave masters as the elements of the cosmos, one should expect him to say that God sent the Son "in order to redeem those held under the power of the cosmic elements." In this letter, however, Paul is concerned to specify the element that presents the clear and present danger for the Galatians, the Law.

in order, that is, that we might receive. Paul returns to the "we" of v 3, linking himself with the Galatians, and indeed with all those who have been incorporated into Christ (3:26–29). This second purpose/result clause is thus to be read as an enriching explication of the first. Those whom Christ has set free from the power of the Law are the same as those whom he has caused to receive his Spirit (Comment #36).

adoption as sons. This phrase renders the word *huiothesia*, a term consistently used in Paul's time to refer to the event of adoption as a son (not the abstraction "sonship").[9] We have noted that adoption is a motif foreign to the picture of

---

[8] We have here one of the roots of the later affirmations that Christ was fully divine and fully human. For in Paul's view Christ was the Son of God whom God sent into the world, but that sending involved his being born fully under the malignant power of the cosmic elements, just as is every other human being.

[9] Scott, *Adoption.*

vv 1–2. But that only shows that Paul uses that picture for what it is worth, a portrait of liberation from slavery. There is more. We are not liberated to live on our own, that being in fact an impossibility. We are taken by God into his own family. Thus, the cosmic change enacted by God in his sovereign act of timely redemption involves also the sovereign act of adoption by which he creates the new family of his church (1:13; 5:10). "The adoptee is taken out of his previous state and is placed in a new relationship with his new *pater familias*. . . . In effect he starts a new life."[10]

6. *And because you are sons, God sent the Spirit of his Son into our hearts, crying, "Abba, Father!"* Drawing on baptismal traditions, Paul again takes the Galatians back to the moment of their baptism (3:26–29). It was there that they heard the performative words announcing their incorporation into Christ, God's Son (3:27), their adoption into God's family as God's sons (3:26), and their receipt of the Spirit of the Son.[11] From their baptism onward the identity of the Spirit has been clear to them. It is not a natural part of themselves, a spirit with which they were born, corresponding to the body they were given at birth. Nor is it one of the amorphous spirits abroad in the world. It is the Spirit of the Son, drawing its characteristics from him.[12]

sons. Does Paul here rescind the formula of 3:28 with its affirmation of the erasure of sexual distinctions in Christ? No. He uses the word "sons" inclusively in order to draw the link between God's Son and God's family, the members of which are sons by being incorporated into the Son. See Comment #43.

into our hearts. There is some manuscript evidence for "into your hearts," but it is almost certainly a secondary reading introduced in order to provide syntactical consistency to the sentence.[13] The grammatical roughness — "because *you* are sons . . . into *our* hearts" — is probably the result of Paul's drawing the second part of the sentence (excepting "of his Son") from baptismal tradition: "God sent the Spirit into our hearts, crying, Abba, Father!" In any case, the mixture of persons, "you" and "our," serves what we have seen to be one of Paul's intentions: to affirm the monolithic state of humanity prior to Christ's advent, and to demonstrate the erasure of distinctions within the church of God born in that advent. He, the former Jew, and the Galatians, former Gentiles, are one in Christ, and because they are one, common affirmations can and must be made about them.

In referring to the invasion of the heart, Paul embraces — via the baptismal formula — a motif established by the Hebrew prophets. Both Jeremiah and Ezekiel contrast obdurate and immutable stone with the malleable and permeable human heart (the will, the passion, the intellect),[14] using this contrast to envision a renewal of Israel by God's effective invasion of the human being:

[10]Lyall, "Adoption," 466.
[11]For Paul there is no chronological order between adoption into God's family and receipt of the Spirit.
[12]Schweizer, "*pneuma*"; Vos, *Pneumatologie*; Meyer, "Holy Spirit."
[13]"Into our hearts" is "strongly supported by early and diversified witnesses" (Metzger 595).
[14]Cf. Jewett, *Terms*, 322–323.

A new heart I will give you, and a new spirit I will put within you: and I will remove from your body the heart of stone and give you a heart of flesh. I will put my spirit within you, and make you follow my statutes and be careful to observe my ordinances (Ezek 36:26–27; NRSV; cf. Jer 31:31–34).[15]

Paul, however, speaks of something that has already happened both to him and to the Galatians. Moreover, the Spirit God has sent into the baptizands' hearts is now that of the crucified and resurrected Christ.

Has this divine invasion obliterated freedom of the will? Not at all. As Jeremiah and Ezekiel foresaw, by invading the human heart, God has freed the will to be obedient to himself.[16] The baptizands have become Spirit-impulsive children who cry out to their Father.[17]

crying, "Abba, Father!" Paul's syntax indicates that it is the Spirit that cries out "Abba! Father!" Equally clear is Paul's reference to a cry issued by the baptizands as they rise from the water. One sees, then, the folly of asking whether this vocal cry is an act of the Spirit or of the baptizands. It is the act of the Spirit just sent into their hearts, and in this way it is their act. The Spirit of God's Son is a suprahuman actor in its own right, but it has taken up residence in the Galatian churches as communities, affecting them so fundamentally as to be to some extent indistinguishable from them (Comment #49).

Even in Greek-speaking churches the baptizands arose from the water crying out to their new God with the Aramaic word for "Father," accompanied by the Greek translation *patêr* (cf. Rom 8:15–17; Mark 14:36). It is a confession encompassing a twofold acknowledgment: God is the absolute — and thus absolutely liberating — master, and God is the one whose care is without limit.

7. an heir by God's act of adoption. In the Note on 3:18 we have seen good reason to think that the Galatians were introduced to the motif of inheritance by the Teachers, who spoke of it as a highly desirable thing the Galatians could acquire — along with the blessing of Abraham — by following the patriarch in observance of the Law. One suspects that inheritance is not a figure Paul would have developed with great enthusiasm on his own, but given the valence it now has in the minds of the Galatians, he does not ignore it. In 3:18 and 3:29, then, and especially in 4:1–7 Paul makes his own use of the motif, finally insisting that, having inherited the church-creating Spirit of Christ, the Galatians have become heirs not through Abraham, but through God himself (cf. 4:30; 5:21).

[15] See Greenberg, "Conceptions," 375.

[16] On this subject, crucial similarities and differences between Paul and Augustine are instructively explored in Meyer, "Letter."

[17] On the connection between receipt of the Spirit and the status of sonship, compare Gal 4:6 with *Jub.* 1:22–25.

COMMENT #41
CHRIST AND THE ELEMENTS OF THE COSMOS[18]

THE DATA

In Gal 4:3 and 4:9 Paul mentions *ta stoicheia tou kosmou*, "the elements of the cosmos."[19] In both cases he speaks of two contrasting periods, distinguished from one another by a radical change in the relationship human beings have to these elements. The earlier of these periods is that prior to the advent of Christ; the second is the one since that event.

Four striking motifs are dominant in 4:3–15: (a) The elements of the cosmos had the power to enslave, and they exercised that power. (b) God has terminated that enslavement by sending his Son. (c) In their enslaving activity the elements had some kind of connection or relationship with the Law. At the minimum the elements and the Law were functionally parallel entities: both enslaved, and God's sending of Christ has effected liberation from both. (d) The elements enslaved "us," that is to say all human beings (Comment #36).

In the second reference, 4:8–11, three of the motifs mentioned above are repeated: (a) enslavement to the elements; (b) the termination of that enslavement by something God has done (he has known the Galatians); (c) the close connection drawn between enslavement to the elements and observance of the Law. Moreover, the third motif is clarified: Gentiles who have been known by God, and who now *turn* to the Law by following its holy calendar, are not thereby confirming the end of their veneration of the elements. On the contrary, they are *returning* to that veneration.[20] The elements and the Law are therefore more than functionally parallel entities, both having the power to enslave. If veneration of the Law is one form in which human beings venerate the cosmic elements, it is highly probable that in some fashion or other the Law *is* one of those elements. Thus, the universal "we," who were held under the power of the elements (4:3), are almost certainly the same persons as "those" who were held under the power of the Law (4:5).[21]

[18]Cf. J. L. Martyn, *Issues*, 125–140.
[19]It is important to read Galatians in its own right before making comparisons. Thus, the references to cosmic elements in Colossians, Hebrews, and 2 Peter (cf. *Herm. Vis.* 3.13.3) will be mentioned only in passing.
[20]That the holy times mentioned by Paul have to do with the Galatians' incipient acceptance of the Law is clear from the context. See also Lührmann, "Tage."
[21]See Comment #36, and cf. Reicke, "Law," 259–260. Other interpreters have argued that the "we" of 4:3 are Gentiles, whereas the "those" of 4:5 are Jews, supporting their reading in part by referring to 1 Cor 9:20–21. It is indeed clear that in this passage Paul differentiates Gentiles from Jews, identifying the former as persons "not under the Law" (*hoi anomoi*) and the latter as persons "under the Law" (*hoi hypo nomon*). But those very expressions show that in 1 Cor 9:20–21 Paul is following the tradition according to which all persons are identified by their relation to the Law. Jews (and the circumcision party in the Jerusalem church) are indeed *those of the Law*. But in the same terms Gentiles also derive their identity from the Law by being *those of the Not-Law*. Different from both, Paul declares himself to be "in the Law of Christ" (*ennomos Christou*), an affirmation that sounds the note struck in Gal 6:2. That is to say, to be in the Law of Christ is to be altogether beyond the distinction between the Law and the Not-Law.

There are also three new accents: (d) By addressing the Galatians directly, Paul now specifies their former enslavement as their worship of the elements. (e) He denies that the elements are deities, implying that in the Galatians' original religious life, they worshiped the elements as gods. (f) He insists that the elements are, on the contrary, weak and impotent.

These two references to the elements pose one of the more interesting and also one of the more important issues of Galatians, especially if one asks how these two references may be related to Paul's christology and to his view of the Law.[22] Why should Paul speak to the Galatians about the elements of the cosmos, and how does he intend them to construe his references? What, precisely, are these elements, how did they enslave, and how is it that their universally enslaving power has been broken by the advent of Christ? Was it not sufficient in Paul's mind to characterize the period prior to Christ as one of imprisonment under the Law (3:23, 25)? Why speak also of imprisonment under the elements, somehow identifying the Law as one of them?

These are exceedingly thorny questions, as one can see from the extraordinary number of studies given to them, and from the striking absence of a consensus.[23] As to the identity of the elements, we may begin with the four major possibilities listed by W. Bauer (BAGD):[24]

(1) "Elements (of learning), fundamental principles." As this is almost certainly the meaning of *stoicheia* in Heb 5:12, numerous exegetes, noting the motif of immaturity in Gal 4:1–2, have proposed it for the references in Galatians as well: Human beings were formerly given to the elementary forms of religion, Jewish and Gentile; these have now been surpassed by the new revelation in Christ.[25] But such a reading is precluded by observations made above in the Note on 4:4.[26]

(2) "Elemental substances, the basic elements from which everything in the natural world is made and of which it is composed," presumably the traditional four: earth, water, air, fire. The lexicographical labors of Blinzler and Rusam have shown this to be the most common meaning of the term *stoicheia*, and the

---

[22]The author of Colossians considers the relationships among the elements, the Law, and Christ to pose issues requiring explicit discussion. Regarding corresponding issues in Galatians, see the conclusion below.

[23]The basic bibliography is given in the commentaries of H. D. Betz, Borse, and Longenecker. See especially Blinzler, "Lexikalisches"; Hawkins, "Opponents," 181–250. Several studies of Schweizer are specially helpful for the role of the elements in the Colossian heresy, but one must take care not to allow the study of the elements in Colossians to set the agenda for the investigation of their role in Galatians; see most recently Schweizer, "Elements"; see also the constructive critique by DeMaris, *Controversy.*

[24]For additional possibilities, see Blinzler, "Lexikalisches," and Hawkins, "Opponents."

[25]See, for example, Burton 518. Recently, Longenecker finds Paul to be "building on the view of *ta stoicheia* as being 'first principles' or 'elemental teachings.'" Gal 4:3 is thus a reference to "the Mosaic law . . . [as the] 'basic principles' given by God in preparation for the coming of Christ," while Gal 4:9 is a reference to the "veneration of nature and cultic rituals that made up the Gentiles' 'basic principles' of religion" (165–166).

[26]Cf. also Hawkins, "Opponents," 183–185, 210–212.

only meaning attested for the expression *stoicheia tou kosmou*. One should accept it for any text of Paul's time, unless there is good reason not to do so.[27]

(3) "Elementary spirits which the syncretistic religious tendencies of later antiquity associated with the physical elements." This is the meaning favored by Bauer, H. D. Betz, and others, but the sources for it are mostly later than Paul.[28]

(4) "Heavenly bodies." A number of interpreters link this meaning with the preceding one; H. D. Betz, for example, speaks of "demonic entities of cosmic proportions and astral powers which are hostile towards man."[29] It is a reading that honors Paul's insistence that the elements held humanity in a state of slavery, clearly viewing them as inimical powers of some sort. Again, however, the thought that the astral elements are demonic and hostile to human beings is difficult to show by drawing on early sources.[30]

We can already draw an initial and tentative conclusion: Lexicographical observations strongly favor the second meaning listed by Bauer, the four traditional cosmic elements: earth, water, air, fire. As we have already noted, one must have a strong reason to read *ta stoicheia tou kosmou* in some other way.[31]

Interpretive disarray remains widespread, however, and, in any case, lexicography cannot settle an issue of such exegetical complexity. Would progress be made, perhaps, by inquiring into the history of the Galatians' linguistic experience, as we have done with the expressions "gospel" and "covenant" (Comments #7 and #37)? Paul employs the expression "the elements of the cosmos" without explanation; he may very well be using the expression in his own way, but he seems able to assume that it already has some meaning in the Galatians' vocabulary. What can we say, first of all, then, about the Galatians' experience with the expression prior to their hearing Paul's use of it in his letter?

THE GALATIANS' LINGUISTIC EXPERIENCE WITH THE EXPRESSION "THE ELEMENTS OF THE WORLD" PRIOR TO HEARING PAUL'S LETTER

Before the Coming of the Teachers

In the Introduction we followed H. D. Betz in admitting that we can know relatively little about the religion of the Galatians before they were seized by the

---

[27]Blinzler, "Lexikalisches," 439–441; Rusam, "Belege." Examples include Philo *Heres* 134; Wis 7:17; 19:18; 4 Macc 12:13; and, among Christian texts, 2 Pet 3:10 and 3:12, where the author refers to the dissolution of the world's elements in a final cosmic conflagration, a Stoic motif.

[28]Cf. Moore-Crispin, "Galatians 4:1–9," 211.

[29]H. D. Betz 205.

[30]Cf. Longenecker 165. Astutely leaving aside the motif of demonic hostility, Hawkins opts at the end of his investigation for "the heavenly bodies which determine the sequence of calendrical observances" ("Opponents," 249). As we will see, that may very well be the major meaning the term had for the Teachers; it is not, however, central to Paul's view.

[31]It is worth mentioning that over a period of some years Schweizer has written several pieces to show that both in Colossians and in Galatians the reference is to the traditional four elements. That is surely the reading with which to begin one's work, but as we will see below, the study of Galatians cannot come to rest there.

Pauline gospel. Living in the somewhat rustic Anatolian cities of Ankyra and Pessinus (perhaps also in the trading center of Tavium), some of the Galatians may have been adherents of an old Celtic religion. Pessinus, however, was the site of a major sanctuary dedicated to Cybele, the Great Mother of Life and the lover of Attis.[32]

Equally important is the fact that Paul can formulate an argument in the letter that presupposes a certain amount of intellectual sophistication. He can assume the Galatians' acquaintance with certain rhetorical conventions and with some expressions and terms that had acquired a degree of technical denotation, such as the verb *systoicheô* (Gal 4:25). Thus, whatever the form of their native religion(s), they were probably in command of some of the common philosophical theories about the structure of the cosmos. Specifically, they had almost certainly heard some form of the ubiquitous speculation about the elements that constitute the world's foundation. If, as noted above, one of Paul's Galatian churches was in Pessinus, it may be of some importance that Apuleius mentions the temple of Cybele there as the place in which the Phrygians reverence Isis under the name of "the Pessinuntine Mother of the Gods." For in the same passage Apuleius identifies Isis as *elementorum omnium domina*, "mistress of all the elements" (*Metamorphoses* 11.5; cf. 11.25).

These observations direct one's attention to the second of Paul's references to the elements. There he confidently says that in their past life the Galatians worshiped the elements as though they were gods. To be sure, the Galatians will almost certainly have referred to their gods — at least the major ones — by proper names. A newcomer to their cities will not have found them worshiping earth, air, fire, and water.[33] Yet, looking back on that earlier period, they may have concluded (especially under the tutelage of the Teachers; see below) that in their cults they were somehow reverencing the elements, at least as subordinate deities. That would represent nothing more than the insight of Philo, for example, who, continuing a tradition evident in Homer and Empedocles, speaks of persons who revere the elements as gods. They

call fire Hephaestus . . . air Hera . . . water Poseidon . . . and earth Demeter (*de Vita Cont.* 3).[34]

In Paul's time it is the common *Jewish* view that when Gentiles worship idols, they are in fact worshiping the elements. Thus, the Galatians may have held, for example, to some form of the common belief that changes in the elements, including the movements of the stars, cause the turning of the seasons, and so

---

[32]Cf. Nock, *Essays*, 2.893; Vermaseren, *Cybele*, 13–31; H. Koester, *Hellenistic Age*, 191.
[33]In this sense Vielhauer is right to follow Delling ("*stoicheô*") in saying: "There is not a trace of a stoicheia-cult in Galatia," *Geschichte*, 117; cf. idem, "Stoicheiadienst."
[34]Homer *Iliad* 20.67 (from Delling, "*stoicheô*," 675); Empedocles Frag. 6; DK 1.311; Freeman, *Ancilla*, 52. The Greek text of the fragment of Empedocles is given also in Kirk and Raven, *Presocratic*, 323.

affect the growing of the food necessary for the sustenance of life.[35] If they were adherents of the cult of the Great Mother, they may have engaged in orgiastic rites designed to assure the fertility of the earth.[36] However this may be, the Galatians are almost certain to have known the expression "the elements of the cosmos" — very probably as earth, air, fire, water — long before they laid eyes on either Paul or the Teachers, and Paul is able to assume some retrospective comprehension on their part when he links these elements with gods they worshiped before his arrival.

The Teachers May Have Commented on "the elements"

None of the letter's explicit references to the Teachers and to their message indicates that they spoke to the Galatians about the elements of the world. As we have seen in Comment #33, however, reconstructing the major motifs of the Teachers' message requires casting a net that reaches beyond the explicit references. Passages in which Paul makes no direct reference to the Teachers suggest strongly, for example, that they tied their instruction about the Law to affirmations they made about Abraham. Might they have spoken about the elements, even though Paul does not mention their having done so? Two factors suggest that they did:[37]

(1) We know that comments about the elements played a role not only in some Jewish portraits of Gentiles but also in corresponding forms of Jewish apologetic directed to Gentiles. One thinks, for example, of Wisdom 13, a text strangely overlooked in most of the attempts to understand Paul's references to the cosmic elements:

> For all men who were ignorant of God were foolish by nature; and they . . . did not recognize the craftsman, while paying heed to his works; but they supposed that either fire or wind or swift air, or the circle of the stars, or turbulent water, or the luminaries of heaven were the gods that rule the world. If through delight in the beauty of these things, men assumed them to be gods, let them know how much better than these is their Lord, for the author of beauty created them. And if men were amazed at their power and working, let them perceive from them how much more powerful is he who formed them. For

---

[35] Schweizer, "Elements," 457–458, cites and translates an interesting text from Alexander Polyhistor (DK 1.449). For the most part I follow Schweizer's translation: "among the sensible bodies are the four elements, fire, water, earth, air, which throughout undergo changes and are altered. And from them there came into being the animate, intellectual world . . . Light and darkness, warm and cold, dry and wet have equal shares in the world (*isomoira . . . en tô kosmô*); [but there are variations in their strength]. By a predominance of warm, summer comes, by a predominance of cold, winter . . ." On this text, see now the comments of DeMaris, *Controversy*.

[36] On the different forms of the Magna Mater/Cybele cult and their developments, see Gasparro, *Cybele*.

[37] See also Lührmann.

from the greatness and beauty of created things comes a corresponding perception of their Creator (Wis 13:1–5; RSV).[38]

This text forms a helpful background for Paul's charge that in their native religious life the Galatians worshiped the elements as gods (Gal 4:8). Three further
motifs are also important: (a) The author of Wisdom lists not only fire, wind, air,
and water but also the stars, perhaps reflecting the widespread linking of the
activity of the elements with the turning of the seasons and thus with the demar-
cation of sacred times.[39] (b) As a Jew of the Diaspora, he is concerned to bring
the Gentiles to the true knowledge of God (note the imperative verbs — "let them
know" and "let them perceive").[40] And (c) he is convinced that the elements do
indeed provide the route to God: Gentiles can ascend the ladder of perception
from contemplation of the world's elements *to* the knowledge of God. There is
ample evidence that this proselytizing reference to the world's elements was characteristic of numerous Diaspora Jews of Paul's time. And the following observation leads to the same conclusion regarding the Christian-Jewish missionaries
who made their way into Paul's Galatian churches:

(2) Some Jewish apologists formulated this teleological argument by referring
to Abraham's understanding of the elements. Two examples will suffice.

Philo, recalling that Abraham was reared in the religion of the Chaldeans,
speaks of the patriarch's ladder-like journey to the perception of the true God,
doing so in a way quite similar to that portrayed in Wisdom 13:

> The Chaldeans were especially active in the elaboration of astrology and as-
> cribed everything to the movements of the stars . . . Thus they glorified visible
> existence, leaving out of consideration the intelligible and invisible . . . They
> concluded that the world itself was God, thus profanely likening the created
> to the Creator. In this creed Abraham had been reared, and for a long time
> remained a Chaldean. Then opening the soul's eye as though after profound
> sleep, and beginning to see the pure beam instead of the deep darkness, he
> followed the ray and discerned what he had not beheld before, a charioteer

---

[38] See also Wis 7:17; 19:18; 4 Macc 12:13; *1 Enoch* 80:7. Disdain of those who revere the
elements as quasi-deities is not an exclusively Jewish motif. Delling mentions as an example Menander's mocking of those who divinize the elements ("*stoicheô*," 677).

[39] The claim that no pre-Pauline text includes the stars among the elements can be literally
maintained even in the face of Wisdom 13, for the term *stoicheia* does not occur there. It
seems clear, however, that in this text the author expands his other references to the elements (7:17; 19:18) to include the stars and, more broadly speaking, the luminaries of
heaven. That the heavenly bodies created on the fourth day mark the holy times is said,
for example, in *Jub.* 2:8–10 (cf. *1 Enoch* 82:9). One notes also that Philo speaks of the four
physical elements as the material out of which God created both *kosmos* and *ouranos*,
four also being the number of the seasons determined by the stars (*de Op. Mundi* 52). See
also Ben Sira, who relates the distinguishing of holy times to the elemental polarity set in
the cosmos by God (Sir 33:7–9, 14–15). On the great spring festival of Attis, March 15–27,
see Vermaseren, *Cybele*, 113–123, and H. Koester, *Hellenistic Age*, 192–194.

[40] Cf. Georgi, "Weisheit Salomos."

and pilot presiding over the world and directing in safety his own work . . . (*de Abr.* 69–70).[41]

And Josephus speaks in a similar way of Abraham's teleological journey from polytheism to monotheism:

> . . . he [Abraham] began to have more lofty conceptions of virtue than the rest of mankind, and determined to reform and change the ideas universally current concerning God. He was thus the first boldly to declare that God, the creator of the universe, is one, and that, if any other being contributed aught to man's welfare, each did so by His command and not by virtue of its own inherent power. This he inferred from the changes to which earth and sea are subject, from the course of sun and moon, and from all the celestial phenomena; for, he argued, were these bodies endowed with power, they would have provided for their own regularity, but since they lacked this last, it was manifest that even those services in which they cooperate for our greater benefit they render not in virtue of their own authority, but through the might of their commanding sovereign, to whom alone it is right to render our homage and thanksgiving (*Ant.* 1.155–156).[42]

Bearing in mind the weighty role played by Abraham in the Teachers' Gentile mission, we may make several suggestions with some degree of plausibility:

The Teachers are almost certain to have shared the Jewish view of Gentiles as people who ignorantly worship the visible parts of creation, and they may have spoken in this connection of the Gentile tendency to confuse the elements with God (cf. Wisdom 13 and Gal 4:8). It is not difficult to imagine their saying to the Galatians themselves:

> The presence of idols in the temples of your former religion shows that you Gentiles ignorantly reverenced the elements as though they were gods. More tragic still, Paul did nothing really to terminate your ill-informed relation to the elements. It is true that, like other peoples, you were always aware of the role of the astral elements in signaling the seasons you celebrated as holy. You did not know, however, the true calendar established by God, and Paul did not convey it to you. In truth the stars are nothing other than servants of the God of Israel who made them and who gave them a role in relation to his holy Law. As servants of this God, the elements shift the seasons in order to fix the correct times for the true feasts, those ordained by him.

The Teachers will not have spoken in this vein, however, simply in order to charge their Gentile hearers with ignorance. If they referred to the elements, they will probably have spoken of them in an evangelistic way:

[41] Cf. Goodenough, *Light*, 137 n87; W. L. Knox, "Abraham."
[42] Cf. Feldman, "Abraham."

You are to ascend from the foolish and idolatrous worship of the elements themselves to the knowledge of the true God who created them, celebrating the holy times ordained by him in his Law, and doing so at the junctures fixed by the activity of his servants, the astral elements.

Will they have offered the Gentiles a paradigm of this crucial ascent? We have already noted grounds for thinking that the Teachers made extensive use of traditions that present Abraham as the first Gentile to come to the true knowledge of God, being thus the paradigmatic proselyte (Comment #33). What can now be added is the possibility that, in presenting this picture of Abraham, they will not have overlooked the traditions in which the patriarch is said to have made the journey to the knowledge of God by an astrological contemplation of the elements, being the first to observe the holy feasts at the correct times (e.g., *Jubilees* 16).

Thus, it may have been as part of the Galatians' new understanding of the season-causing elements that they took up the calendrical observances laid out by the Teachers. That is one reading of the connection Paul draws between two of his charges: the Galatians, he says, are (re-)turning to the worship of the elements (4:9), and they are taking up from the Teachers the observance of holy times (4:10). One might hazard an imaginary encapsulation of yet another paragraph in the Teachers' message:

> In making the ascent from the pagan contemplation of the elements to the true knowledge of God, you follow in the steps of Abraham, for he did the same. You become, indeed, Abraham's true, Law-observant descendants, knowing for the first time why the constantly changing elements cause the turning of the seasons. As servants of God, they do that to enable us to observe at the correct time the holy feasts ordained by God (Gal 4:10).[43]

THE GALATIANS LISTEN TO PAUL'S LETTER

If the suggestions offered above are cogent, then in two regards Paul and the Teachers are in agreement: Both say — at least in effect — that in their former life the Galatians worshiped the elements as divinities. And both identify that worship as altogether foolish.

When, however, we take into account the whole of Paul's second reference to the elements, and when we combine it with the first, we see that Paul clearly parts ways with the Teachers. He does not for a moment entertain a form of ladder theology, encouraging Gentiles to acquire true knowledge of God by lifting their gaze from the elements to their maker.[44] More dramatically still, he refuses to speak of the elements from the Jewish point of view, finding in element worship a characteristic of *Gentiles*. On the contrary, he says that prior to Christ's

---

[43]The Galatians' attraction to the ladder theology basic to the journey from contemplation of the elements to knowledge of God may be reflected in Gal 4:9.
[44]Contrast Rom 1:19–20.

advent all human beings revered the elements.[45] As we noted early in this Comment, Paul considers the elements of the cosmos somehow to include both the falsely deified idols of Gentile religion and the Law. Thus, the formerly Jewish members of the church (in Jerusalem, in Antioch, etc.) — no less than the formerly Gentile ones (in Galatia) — were once enslaved to those elements. It follows, as we have seen, that, if formerly Gentile members *turn* to the Law, they in fact *return* to the worship of the falsely deified elements (4:9–10). One hardly needs to say that vis-à-vis the theology of the Teachers these statements of Paul constitute strong and explicitly polemical medicine.

It is clear, to be sure, that Paul cannot intend to refer to Jewish Christians (and by implication to Jews) as persons who in the past literally worshiped idols, images they held incorrectly to be gods (note again the change to "you [Galatians]" in 4:8–9; cf. Rom 2:22). Nor can he mean that Gentile Christians, in their former life, literally observed and were enslaved by the Law (cf. Rom 2:14–16, 26–27).[46] That he speaks of universal enslavement is, however, unmistakable; and this point will have been in itself enough to incite outrage on the part of the Teachers and their followers in the Galatian churches. Joining one of the Galatian congregations again, we can imagine hearing the Teachers' retort:

> Paul is suggesting that prior to the advent of God's Messiah the world was a monolith of enslavement to the elements; he is saying that Jews no less than Gentiles were held in bondage to them, indeed that the holy and just and good Law of God *is* one of these enslaving elements! Such talk is outrageous. We have never considered the elements to be gods; we know that the Law of God is not one of them; and being Abraham's seed, we ourselves have never been enslaved to anyone (cf. John 8:33).

We can also imagine that Paul anticipated such outrage. Not at all easy to understand is his expectation that his inclusion of the Law among the enslaving elements of the cosmos would prove even momentarily worthy of consideration when his letter was read aloud to the Galatians. This expectation is, in fact, one of the persistent puzzles of the letter.[47] Can it be made less puzzling?

An answer may lie in our noting again that Paul does not speak merely of the elements, but specifically in Gal 4:3 of the elements *of the cosmos*. It is, to be sure, a traditional way of referring to the elements of nature.[48] This expression

---

[45]As we have seen above, this point has been sensed by many interpreters, although most admit that it is difficult to explain. It is one of the major aspects of the *stoicheia* puzzle; see below.

[46]Correctly recognizing this point, Blinzler unfortunately flees from Galatians to Romans, concluding that by the elements of the cosmos Paul meant flesh, sin, and death ("Lexikalisches," 442–443).

[47]Vielhauer is more right than wrong to say that Paul includes the Law among the enslaving elements "in order to place the non-Jew and the Jew on the same level" ("Stoicheiadienst," 553). We are left, however, with the puzzle mentioned in the text.

[48]Aristotle, for example, can use as an equivalent the expression *stoicheia tês physeôs* (*Metaphysics* 986b), and Philo follows suit (*de Vita Mos.* 2.251). Cf. Blinzler, "Lexikalisches," 440–441.

may provide, however, a clue to the character of Paul's startling universalism, provided we allow it to pose a simple question: *Of what cosmos*, specifically, were these enslaving elements the fundamental parts?

The Cosmos of Which Paul Speaks

We note first that Paul employs the word "cosmos" at only one other point in the letter:

> . . . the cross of our Lord Jesus Christ, by which the cosmos has been crucified to me and I to the cosmos. For neither is circumcision anything nor is uncircumcision anything. What is something is the new creation (6:14–15).[49]

In Comment #51 we will ask about the implications of Paul's assertion that the cosmos from which Christ's cross has separated him consisted of pairs of opposites.[50] What is gone with the crucifixion of the cosmos is not simply circumcision, but rather both circumcision and uncircumcision, and thus the distinction of Jew from Gentile. Or, to take the matter to its root, what has suffered eclipse is not simply the Law, but rather the cosmos that had at its foundation both the Law and the Not-Law.

Equally important for our present concern is the background of this affirmation: In form it is a traditional way of referring to the totality of the cosmos, evident, for example, in Sirach:

> . . . all the works of the Most High are in pairs, one the opposite of the other (33:15).

In this tradition the word "cosmos" or its equivalent is intimately linked with pairs of opposites. It is obvious that in Gal 6:14–15 Paul shapes this tradition to his own theological concern, speaking of a *religious* pair of opposites so fundamental to life as to be called "cosmos." Given the identity of this pair, it is not difficult to see that its erasure brought about loss of cosmos for Paul, the Pharisee. But one sees also that Paul considers the erased cosmos to have been the cosmos of all human beings (Gal 3:26–28).

Do we have here, then, a clue to the puzzle posed by Gal 4:3, 8–9: what cosmos was it whose elements enslaved human beings and whose hegemony has been terminated in Christ? Was it a cosmos composed of elements that were

---

[49]Comparison with Col 2:20 is revealing: "If you died with Christ, parting from (*apo*) the elements of the world, why do you submit to rules as though you were living in (*en*) the world." As DeMaris observes, this text connects the *stoicheia tou kosmou* with *cosmos*: ". . . both terms seem to denote a sphere of existence . . . that one can part *from* or live *in*" (*Controversy*, 59).

[50]In considering the expression "elements of the cosmos" Burton felt strangely compelled to look outside the letter to ascertain the meaning of the prepositional phrase "of the cosmos," thus concluding that it refers "most naturally . . . to the world of humanity" (518).

themselves pairs of opposites? Is there precedent for linking pairs of opposites not only to the word "cosmos" (so Gal 6:14–15) but also to the term "elements" (Gal 4:3, 8–9), and thus to "the elements of the cosmos"? These prove to be significant questions, because they point to an area in which we do in fact have information.

The Elements of That Cosmos

Among the widely varied speculations about the elements of the cosmos, a significant number compare the traditional four elements with one another; and, being compared, the elements are then arranged in pairs of opposites (in Greek often called *t'anantia*). This is, in fact, an ancient way of speaking not only of the cosmos but also explicitly of its elements, not least when one wishes to refer to the elements' effects on (and in) human beings.[51] In Paul's own time Philo draws on Pythagorean tradition in order to develop the pattern at some length. Dealing with God's act of creation, he speaks of the division of the elements of the cosmos into equal parts, referring to the elements themselves as pairs of opposites.[52] Philo arranges the columns of element opposites in various ways, each involving the traditional four elements:

the rare		*the dense*
air	versus	earth
fire	versus	water

[51] The notion of opposition among the elements (sometimes *stoicheia*, sometimes *archai*) can be seen as early as Anaximander, Heraclitus, and Empedocles. A particularly clear exposition is given by Aristotle; see, for example, *Metaphysics* 986b, where, having cited the Pythagorean tradition of the opposites, he continues his account by the summarizing remark *t'anantia archai tôn ontôn*, an affirmation in which, as is often the case, *ta stoicheia* are represented by a synonym, *archai* (cf. also *merê*). Aristotle is a clear witness, therefore, for the continuation of the ancient tradition in which the elements are the opposites (*ta stoicheia = t'anantia*); cf. also 1005a, *panta gar e enantia e ex enantiôn*.

[52] "First he [God] made two sections, heavy and light, thus distinguishing the element of dense from that of rare particles. Then again he divided each of these two, the rare into air and fire, the dense into water and land, and these four He laid down as first foundations, to be the sensible elements of the sensible world (*stoicheia aisthêta aisthêtou kosmou*). Again He made a second division of heavy and light on different principles. He divided the light into cold and hot, giving to the cold the name of air and to the naturally hot the name of fire. The heavy He divided into wet and dry, and He called the dry 'land' and the wet 'water' ... observe how God in 'dividing in the middle,' actually did divide equally ... First, as to equality of number, he made the light parts equal in number to the heavy parts, earth and water which are heavy being two, and fire and air which are naturally light being two also ... In the same way we have one and one in darkness and light, in day and night, in winter and summer, in spring and autumn ..." (*Heres* 134–135, 146). Cf. 207: "Having taught us the lesson of equal division, the Scripture leads us on to the knowledge of opposites (*tên tôn enantiôn epistêmên*), by telling us that 'He placed the sections facing opposite each other' (Gen xv.10). For in truth we may take it that everything in the world is by nature opposite to something else" (cf. the citations from Aristotle given above). Cf. also Philo *de Deo* 107–149 (Siegert, *Philon*, 29–31).

the light			*the heavy*		
cold	versus	hot	wet	versus	dry
air	versus	fire	water	versus	earth[53]

Thus, from Philo — and from other authors as well — we see the tradition in which the elements *are* the pairs of opposites that constitute the foundation of the cosmos (*ta stoicheia = t'anantia*). A number of thinkers close to Paul's time, including both Ben Sira and the author of Wisdom, would have readily agreed with the traditional statement: The elements of the cosmos *are* pairs of opposites.

When, now, we bring together two points in Galatians at which Paul speaks of the old cosmos — 6:14–15 and 3:28 — we can see that, in his own way, he has in mind precisely this tradition. In writing Gal 6:14–15 Paul expects the Galatians to understand his testimony: the cross of Christ separated him from a *cosmos* that consisted of a pair of opposites, circumcision and uncircumcision. This declaration of the end of a cosmos leads us back to 3:28, where the same pair — Jew and Greek (Gentile) — introduces the baptismal tradition focused on pairs of opposites that have disappeared. For those who are incorporated into Christ, there is no Jew and Gentile. Moreover, the baptismal formula is broader than the affirmation of 6:14–15, including the social pair of slave and free and the creational pair of male and female.[54] Thus, a Christian baptizand acquainted with a traditional list of oppositional pairs — in whatever form — would have recognized in the baptizer's words a list of the oppositional *elements* that have now found their terminus in Christ, and thus a declaration of the end of the cosmos that was constituted by those elements.

Moreover, the formula of Gal 3:28 — with its announcement of liberation from enslaving pairs of element opposites — constitutes a key part of the context in which, in 4:3–5, Paul explicitly speaks of liberation from the enslaving elements of the cosmos. It is, then, a reasonable hypothesis that, when he speaks in 4:3 and 9 of the elements of that cosmos, Paul himself has in mind not earth, air, fire, and water, but rather the elemental pairs of opposites listed in 3:28, emphatically the first pair, Jew and Gentile, and thus the Law and the Not-Law.

To be sure, I have suggested above that, prior to hearing Paul's letter, the Galatians will have connected the expression *ta stoicheia tou kosmou* with the traditional earth/air and fire/water, the stars being added. Can Paul expect them suddenly to make this shift with him, sensing a reference to the elements of religious polarity?[55] Here, as elsewhere in this extraordinarily dense letter, Paul apparently

[53] Philo speaks of three matters that are intimately interrelated and that are pertinent to our interpretation of Gal 4:3, 8–9: the elements, the pairs of opposites, and the seasons, and thus times of special celebration.

[54] Both of these additional pairs figure in the tradition ascribed variously to Thales, Socrates, Plato, and the later Rabbi Judah. More important is the fact that male and female stand both in the text of Gen 1:27 and in the Pythagorean list of the elemental pairs of opposites. See Aristotle *Metaphysics* 986a, where the fifth pair in the Pythagorean list is *arren* [*arsen*] *thêly*.

[55] The transferred reading I am suggesting for Gal 3:28; 4:3, 9; 6:15 can perhaps be distantly compared with motifs in a passage in which Philo takes the wings of Isaiah's seraphim to refer *symbolically* to the elements. I have in mind *de Deo* 127–134, according to

assumes that the Galatian congregations will listen to the whole of the epistle several times and with extreme care. He takes for granted, that is, not only great perspicacity but also considerable patience. In regard to what he calls the elements of the old cosmos, he seems to think that the baptismal reference to the termination of pairs of opposites (3:28), coupled with his climactic reference to the death of the cosmos made up of the first of those pairs (6:14–15), will alert the Galatians to his intention in 4:3, 9. From those other passages, then, one finds a reasonable reading of Paul's line of thought in 4:3, 9:

Having accented the baptismal confession of 3:28, with its reference to the dissolution in Christ of certain pairs of opposites,

Jew/Gentile,
slave/free,
male/female,

Paul takes for granted the widespread tradition in which pairs of opposites are themselves identified as "the elements of the cosmos." Thus, in 4:3 he uses that expression itself to refer to the pairs of opposites that are passé, noting indeed that these oppositional elements had in fact enslaved all human beings prior to Christ.[56] And just as he has said that the opposition of the Law to the Not-Law affected the whole of humanity, thus being a true element of the cosmos (4:3), so he can finally say that for the Not-Law Galatians to turn to the Law—distinguishing holy times from profane ones by careful observation of what they identify as the astral elements—is for them to return to the old cosmos of the Law/ the Not-Law (4:9–10).

Heard in this way, Gal 6:14–15, 3:28, and 4:3, 8–9 constitute a typical instance of Paul's transformation of language.[57] In a word, Paul employs the ancient equation of the world's elements with archaic pairs of opposites to interpret the *religious* impact of Christ's advent. Following the baptismal formula, he applies that tradition not to the sensible elements, but rather to the elements of religious

---

Siegert a fragment of Philo's allegorical commentary on Genesis, introduced by a reference to Abraham's being visited by the three men (Gen 18:1–15). I give a somewhat paraphrastic translation of Siegert's reconstructed Greek text, interpreted in accordance with his commentary (Siegert, *Philon*, 30–31, 129–132): "Some of my teachers who knew the doctrines of the nature philosophers have said that the (six) elements are earth and water, air and fire, love and hate. In the same manner, however, the prophet (Isaiah), when he speaks of the four lower wings of the seraphim—the ones that serve to cover the face and the feet—means symbolically to refer to the hidden powers of the (first) four elements. When he speaks of the two seraphim wings that fly up to the First Ruler, he means the powers of hate and love. For the First Ruler alone mediates between war and peace, otherwise called love and hate." Note also that this text is another instance in which Abraham is brought into connection with teaching about the elements (*de Deo* 145–146).

[56] By juxtaposing Gal 3:28 and 4:3 Paul instructs the Galatians as to the identity of the oppositional elements. Cf. Philo's concern that people be led to knowledge of the opposites: *tēn tōn enantiōn epistēmēn* (*Heres* 207; cf. Wis 7:17).

[57] Cf. Paul's eschatological interpretation of Stoic maxims in Gal 6:2–10.

distinction.[58] These are the cosmic elements that have found their termination in Christ. Specifically, the cosmos that was crucified on the cross is the cosmos that was founded on the distinction between Jew and Gentile, between sacred and profane, between the Law and the Not-Law.[59] When we contemplate the identity of this crucified cosmos, it is not difficult to see how its departure could lead a Pharisee to speak of his own death (Gal 6:14).

COMMENT #42
"GOD SENT HIS SON"

In the Notes we have seen that the sentence comprising Gal 4:3–5 is the theological center of the entire epistle, relating its major motifs to one another in such a way as to state what we may call the good news of Paul's letter to the Galatians. The center of this center is the news that God sent his Son. How does Paul intend the Galatians to understand this apparently simple affirmation?

Paul probably draws it from an early Christian formula that was rooted in Hebraic traditions about God's sending Moses and the prophets to Israel (Exod 3:10; Isa 6:8; etc.) and that was influenced by references to God's sending from heaven into the world his angel, his wisdom, his spirit (Gen 24:40; Wis 9:10, 17; etc.). Applied to Jesus as God's own Son, the early Christian formula shows him to be the climactic messenger sent by God, indeed the special messenger who is far closer to God than the others (Mark 9:37; Luke 10:16; Mark 12:1–12; Rom 8:3; John 3:16–17; 1 John 4:9).[60]

---

[58] As noted above, when Paul connects the Galatians' veneration of the elements with their observance of holy times (4:9–10), he may seem momentarily to follow the Teachers in assuming the elements to include the stars. In fact, he adheres here also to the view that the elements are the religious pairs of opposites. For to say that the elements play a role in distinguishing holy times from profane ones is simply to specify yet another way in which they are related to the religious pairs of opposites that belong to the cosmos terminated by Christ's advent. The termination of that *religious cosmos* is a key motif in Phil 3:8, where the one who was blameless under the Law refers dramatically to his having suffered the loss of "all things" (*ta panta*).

[59] I am instructed by Meyer's use of the expression "binary categorizations of religious human beings" in his perceptive study "Worm" (e.g., 69). Especially on the basis of Gal 3:28, one might suggest that in Galatians Paul intends to speak of nothing more than the nomistic separation of human beings into insiders and outsiders, thus referring to a curse *produced* by the Law rather than to the Law itself. It seems to me correct to say that that binary religious categorization of human beings is the fundamental identity of the curse pronounced by the Law (on the anthropological use of the terms "circumcision" and "uncircumcision," cf. Marcus, "The Circumcision"). But in Galatians there is also the issue of the relationship between anthropological categorization and cosmic antinomies, both those of the old cosmos and those of the dawning new creation. For Paul, as for the Teachers, the Law is a cosmic power to be reckoned with in its own being. Thus, Paul discusses not only its effects but also its genesis (3:19–20). Moreover, in the cosmic terms of 6:14–15 the Law (circumcision) produces anthropological effects *in its opposition to* the Not-Law (uncircumcision), and it is in that paired existence that the Law itself proves to be an element of the old *cosmos*.

[60] See especially Schweizer, "God Sent His Son."

In Paul's mouth the affirmation that God sent his Son is distinctly apocalyptic, recalling his reference to his own encounter with Christ:

> God had in fact singled me out even before I was born, and had called me in his grace. So when it pleased him apocalyptically to reveal his Son to me, in order that I might preach him among the Gentiles, I immediately kept to myself . . . (1:15–16; Comment #14).

We have seen that Paul uses interchangeably the verbs "to apocalypse" and "to [cause to] come" (3:23), and this linguistic fact establishes a major point: redemption has come from outside the human orb. For Paul, to say that God *sent* his Son is to say that God *invaded* the cosmos in the person of Christ (cf. 3:23, 25). The Son is unlike other human beings in that his becoming a human being was, in a significant sense, God's own advent.

Does Paul presuppose, then, that in the technical sense the Son existed with God before he was sent? One might think so on the basis of Paul's use of the verb *exapostellein*, "to send out" (in Paul's letters only in Gal 4:4 and 4:6), for the verb means that the Son was sent out *from* the Father *into* the world. In fact, however, that affirmation falls short of necessarily implying personal preexistence, even when the verb is accompanied by such an expression as "from on high."[61] Gal 4:4 can be read as entirely harmonious with the idea of personal preexistence, but it can also be read apart from that idea.

The more helpful form of the question, then, is whether Paul understands Christ to be a this-worldly figure or an other-worldly one.[62] As one would expect in an apocalyptic perspective, the answer is both (Cf. Comment #3).

Christ was "born of a woman," that is to say born in the human manner, just as Paul was (cf. 1:15).[63] Moreover, with all other human beings, Christ was born "under the power of the Law," finding himself, therefore, a slave in the cosmos whose very elements function as slave masters (cf. Phil 2:7).[64] Even his being sent by God has its parallel — a partial one, to be sure — in Paul's being sent by God (1:1; Comment #1). It is, moreover, as a distinctly this-worldly figure that Christ has died on the cross, suffering the curse of the Law in a way that is analogous to that experienced by all other human beings, even as it brings that curse to its end.

[61] The same verb is used of God's sending his wisdom, for example, a motif that does not consistently imply Wisdom's preexistence (Wis 9:10; cf. 9:17).

[62] Cf. Meyer, "This-Worldliness"; J. L. Martyn, *Issues*, 279–297.

[63] In the expression "born of a woman" there is no hint that Paul knew and drew upon the tradition that Jesus was born of a virgin (see Note on 4:4). The theological intention behind the tradition of Jesus' virgin birth is, however, harmonious with the intention of Gal 4:4–5. See R. E. Brown, *Birth*.

[64] See especially Käsemann, "Philippians 2:5–11." On the basis of the remarkable parallels between *Poimandres* and the Philippian hymn (which probably does affirm preexistence), one can identify as proto-gnostic the idea that to become a human being is to become a slave in the cosmic harmony. In Paul's theology, however, the idea serves the apocalyptic worldview mentioned above (cf. Comment #3). It is precisely the motif of universal enslavement that leads Paul to have little or no interest in the cultic or moral sinlessness of Jesus (2 Cor 5:21; cf. Heb 4:15). Paul "conceives of sin as a power, not as defilement or guilt" (Meyer, "Romans," 1151 column 2).

The Son's other-worldly character, however, is without true parallel, as one can see by drawing further comparisons with Paul himself. Paul is sent by God as a prophetic apostle, comparable to Isaiah and Jeremiah (1:15), not as God's Son. Indeed, as an apostle, Paul is clearly distinguished from the Son by being his slave (Gal 1:10; cf. John 17:18). Moreover, whereas Paul is sent to preach God's Son to the Gentiles (1:16), the Son himself is sent by God into the whole of the cosmos, in order to redeem from slavery all human beings ("those held under the power of the Law"; Comment #41). In short, the Son's sending is an invasion of cosmic scope, reflecting the apocalyptic certainty that redemption has come from outside, changing the very world in which human beings live, so that it can no longer be identified simply as "the present evil age" (1:4). In this sense the Son is a distinctly other-worldly figure who has his origin in God.

How, then, is the statement of Gal 4:4–5 related to the this-worldly, cross-centered statement of Gal 3:13–14? There are several impressive marks of similarity. Both statements attribute redemption to Christ; both speak of that redemption by employing the verb *exagorazô*, "to redeem from slavery" (the only christological instances of that verb in the NT); and both end with two parallel clauses that state the intended consequence of the main verb, the last of those clauses being "in order that we might receive . . ."

Christ redeemed us from the Law's curse, becoming a curse in our behalf; for it stands written: "Cursed is everyone who is hanged on a tree." He did this in order that the blessing of Abraham might come to the Gentiles in Jesus Christ; in order, that is, that we might receive the promise, which is the Spirit, through faith (3:13–14).	God sent his Son, born of a woman, born under the power of the Law, in order that he might redeem those held under the power of the Law, in order, that is, that we might receive adoption as sons (4:4–5).

The interpreter's responsibility to compare these two texts has produced a host of studies. After listening to these various analyses, Hays has correctly concluded that the texts, somewhat differently accented, are nevertheless "two tellings . . . of the same story."[65] Christ's being sent by God was his being born under the Law (4:4), specifically the event of his birth under the Law's power to pronounce its universal curse (3:10). Finally, in his case this state of "being under" found its redemptive climax in his being crucified under the Law's curse, the event in which he robbed it of its power (3:13). In short, Christ's being sent by God, his existence under the Law's power, his betrayal (1 Cor 11:23), his crucifixion as one cursed by the Law, and his resurrection at the hands of God — all of these form an integrated story to which Paul can refer by mentioning any part of it.[66]

[65] Hays, *Faith*, 116.
[66] In addition to Hays, see Cousar, *Cross*; A. R. Brown, *Cross*.

4:8–11 RETURNING TO SLAVERY

TRANSLATION

4:8. It is true that formerly, not knowing God, you were enslaved to things that in nature are not gods. 9. But now, knowing God — or rather, being known by God — how is it that you are turning back to the weak and impotent elements, wishing once again to be their slaves? 10. You observe days and months and seasons and years. 11. I am anxious about you, worrying that the labor I have spent on you might prove to be labor lost!

LITERARY STRUCTURE AND SYNOPSIS

In considering the literary structure of 3:6–9 we noted that the letter contains two grand exegetical sections, 3:6–4:7 and 4:21–5:1, both concerned with the true identity of the Galatian churches. We also saw that these two carefully constructed compositions are preceded by sections in which Paul deduces the churches' identity from their birth rather than from scripture. That analysis led us, in turn, to see a remarkable structural correspondence between 3:1–4:7 and 4:8–5:1, the entire expanse from 3:1 to 5:1 being focused on the subject of the Galatians' identity.

A. 3:1–5. The identity of the Galatian churches is known from their birth. Paul raises questions, then, about the relationship between that birth identity and disastrous developments under the tutelage of the Teachers.

B. 3:6–4:7. The identity of the Galatian churches is known from what Abrahamic passages in scripture and baptismal traditions say about their descent: They are heirs of Abraham because they have been incorporated into Abraham's seed, Christ. From christological and pneumatological traditions it is clear, furthermore, that they are liberated slaves, indeed sons and heirs of God himself.

A′. 4:8–20. The identity of the Galatian churches is known from their birth. Paul raises questions, then, about the relationship between that birth identity and disastrous developments under the tutelage of the Teachers.

B′. 4:21–5:1. The identity of the Galatian churches is known from the true interpretation of Abrahamic passages in scripture and from Isaiah. In fact, they are children not of the slave girl, but of the free woman.

Two observations clarify the internal structure of 4:8–20. First, in the sentence comprising vv 8–9 Paul includes an expression of distress — "how can you possibly turn back?"[67] In v 10 he specifies the cause of his distress: As part of their

---

[67] For epistolary instances of distress, see Introduction §10.

nascent observance of the Law, the Galatians are beginning to celebrate certain holy times, as though such celebration were salvific. That reference then leads Paul to express his distress a second time, speaking of his anxiety about the Galatians' future (v 11).

Second, in v 12 Paul changes his tone, modulating the note of anxious distress into a friendly, epistolary request — "Brothers and sisters, I beg you to become as I am." He then continues with an emphatically pleasant recollection of the days in which he and his gospel found an enthusiastic reception among the Galatians (vv 13–15). A reference to the Teachers, however (vv 16–17), brings Paul back to the note of exasperated distress and anxiety about the effects of their work on the future of the Galatian churches (v 20). Thus, each of the two paragraphs, vv 8–11 and vv 12–20, ends on the note of anxiety.

The initial paragraph, vv 8–11, is dominated by contrasts. First, building on v 7, Paul contrasts the Galatians' former slavery as Gentile pagans with the liberation they experienced when, grasped by God, they were born as members of God's church. Second, he contrasts their existence as liberated churches of God with what awaits them if they follow the path laid out for them by the Teachers. The striking result is Paul's certainty that conversion to the Teachers' gospel will only lead the Galatians back to the slavery under the elements, the condition in which they were living before they were called by God in the gospel of Christ. In short, Gentile observance of the Law is equivalent to Gentile ignorance of God. For observance of the Law as though that were salvific is simply one form of religious enslavement to the cosmic elements. Paul closes the paragraph, therefore, by wondering aloud whether his work among the Galatians might prove to be in vain.

NOTES

4:8–9. *formerly . . . But now.* Paul uses a formula well attested in early Christian tradition to express the stark contrast between the Galatians' former existence and their life in Christ.[68]

not knowing God. Ignorance of God and its consequences — worship of the creation rather than the creator — was a widespread Jewish characterization of Gentiles (Jer 10:25; Ps 79:6; Wisdom 13; cf. Rom 1:25), here employed by Paul to speak of the Galatians' state when they worshiped idols rather than God (cf. 1 Thess 4:5). The antidote to such ignorance is a matter Paul takes up in v 9.

things that in nature are not gods. Elsewhere Paul speaks of many gods and many lords (1 Cor 8:5), of the god of this age (2 Cor 4:4), of the rulers of this age (1 Cor 2:8), of Satan (e.g., 1 Cor 7:5), of demons (1 Cor 10:20–21), and of angels (cf. Rom 8:38–39). All of these figures have real existence as living beings. Idols, however, are mere things, not beings in their own right, for they have no power and cannot actually speak (1 Cor 12:2; Isa 46:7).

in nature. The Galatians' idols were nothing more than natural things. They

---

[68] See, for example, Tachau, *"Einst."* It is the order of the contrasting clauses that causes Paul to introduce v 8 with the adversative particle *alla*, here rendered "It is true."

belonged to the created realm that can be perceived by the human senses, what Philo called the "sensible world."

9. *But now, knowing God.* For a moment Paul accepts the view that knowing God is the opposite of not knowing God.

or rather, being known by God. With the expression *mallon de* Paul pens a rhetorical self-correction, thus actually correcting the Teachers' religious message. The opposite of not knowing God is being known *by* God (Comment #43).

how is it that you are turning back . . . ? The correction in the initial clause of v 9 now enables Paul to pose a question. With rhetorical sarcasm he uses the verb *epistrephô,* "to turn," "to convert," in a mocking way:

> Given the theological fact that you have been known by God in his redemptive act in Christ, are you seriously considering a conversion that takes you back to the state in which I found you when I came into your cities? That is a serious question, for conversion is nothing more than a move from one religion to another.

In short, for the Galatians *to convert* to observance of the Law would be for them *to turn back* to their earlier state, by retreating from the realm of Christ to the realm of religion (note that Paul emphasizes the motif of a *return* by twice using the term *palin,* "again," in v 9).[69] They would still worship the enslaving elements of the cosmos, simply bowing now to the Law rather than to the Not-Law (Comment #41).

the weak and impotent elements. With the adjectives *asthenês* and *ptôchos* Paul speaks of the elements' impotence (*ptôchos* in the sense of being dependent on others; hence impotent). It is a motif that recalls the Jewish portrait of the Lawless Gentile in Wisdom 13. Lacking the guidance of the Law, and thus worshiping the cosmic elements rather than their creator, the Gentile turns for help to things that are impotent:

> For health he appeals to a thing that is weak;
> for life he prays to a thing that is dead . . .
> he asks strength of a thing whose hands have no strength (Wis 13:18–19).

Shocking is the fact that Paul uses the motif of impotence to characterize observance of the Law on the part of Gentiles. Equally shocking is the twin fact that, whereas he had earlier referred to the cosmic elements' power to enslave the

---

[69]Writing to the Thessalonians, to be sure, Paul used the verb *epistrephô* in a positive sense (1 Thess 1:9; cf. 2 Cor 3:16). See Gaventa, *Darkness.* Here, however, the locution is distinctly ironic, as Georgi has suggested (*Anmerkungen,* 112). The verb *metanoeô,* "to repent," is a partial synonym for *epistrephô,* a linguistic observation that prepares one to note an important aspect of Paul's theology: Having no confidence in repentance, Paul is equally disdainful of conversion, for, as noted above, it is nothing more than the human act of a change of religion, and religion is incapable of being anything other than religion. Put in the terms of Gal 4:9, all religions are attempts to know God; none is the event of being known by God.

whole of humanity, Paul now says that the elements are devoid of power. One recalls, however, that he has spoken in the same way of the Law. Powerful enough to enslave every human being (3:10, 22; 4:5; Comments #36 and #39), the Law is impotent to grant life (3:21), being no more able to deal with the problems of human existence than is the Not-Law of Gentile religion. Fully analyzed, then, the elements of religious differentiation are both potent and impotent, potent to enslave, and impotent to redeem from the state of enslavement.

wishing once again to be their slaves. In the tradition of the diatribe the speaker presents his conversation partner's intention in a laughable fashion spiked with biting irony. Drawing on that tradition and speaking yet again of the motif of a mere return to slavery, Paul reinforces the sarcastic mockery of the preceding clause.[70]

10. *You observe.* Here the verb (*paratêreô*, middle) refers to scrupulous observance of stipulations appropriate to religion (cf. Josephus *Ant.* 3.91, 14.264, 11.294), but there may be a secondary reference to astrological observations by which holy times can be fixed.[71]

days and months and seasons and years. That the Galatians are following the Teachers in observing certain holy times is taken by Paul as a sure sign that they are in the process of returning to the veneration of the cosmic elements. The grounds on which he can draw that connection and the way in which he does that are matters taken up in Comment #43.

11. *I am anxious . . . labor lost!* Picturing in his mind a daytime nightmare, the conversion of all of the Galatians to the message of the Teachers, and knowing that that development would indicate the total ineffectiveness of his labor in Galatia, Paul is filled, for the moment, with anxiety.[72] Neither an idol (v 8) nor the Law (v 10) can deliver the Galatians from the threat of missing God's kingdom (5:21). Striking the note of anxiety, Paul closes the paragraph of vv 8–11 in a manner that looks forward to the close of the next paragraph in vv 19–20.

COMMENT #43
TO BE KNOWN BY GOD IS TO KNOW THAT THERE ARE NO HOLY TIMES

KNOWING GOD AND BEING KNOWN BY GOD
In the course of dictating the sentence that comprises Gal 4:9, Paul pauses in order to correct himself. First, employing an early Christian formula in which a stark contrast is drawn between life in the Old Age and redeemed life in Christ, Paul momentarily accepts the ancient view that knowing God is the opposite of not knowing God.

> . . . formerly, not knowing God, you were enslaved to things that in nature are not gods. But now, knowing God . . .

[70]Bultmann, *Stil*, 103.
[71]The possibility of a secondary astrological reference is well argued by Lührmann, "Tage," 431.
[72]The locution *phoboumai hymas ktl* is an instance in which Paul anticipates in the first clause the picture he paints in the second one (prolepsis of the object *hymas*; BDF §476).

The statement of this view proves to be, however, Paul's preparation for a significant correction.

or rather, being known by God . . .

The resulting sentence encapsulates much of the letter's thrust. Presumably, the Teachers are enticing the Galatians by speaking of a state of perfection that can be achieved by ascent to true knowledge of God in the life of Law observance (3:3). In a word, the Teachers are preaching a religion (*eusebeia*) that takes the metaphorical form of a ladder. Ascent to the knowledge of God is the antidote to the lowly state characteristic of Gentile ignorance of God (see Comment #41 for ancient Jewish depictions of Abraham's ascent to knowledge of God).

When Paul corrects himself in midsentence, then, he formulates a polemic against the Teachers' religious message. The antidote to ignorance of God does not lie in our acquiring knowledge of God (religion). It lies, rather, in God's act of knowing us (the foundation of theology; cf. Jer 30:21; Psalm 139). Briefly put, in Christ God has known us not as Jews and Gentiles, but rather apart from all religious distinctions. And, as hinted above, God's graceful election of us by his rectifying and nonreligious invasion of the cosmos in Christ is the subject of the whole letter (see Note on 4:3 and Comment #37; cf. Rom 8:29).

This midsentence correction thus reflects Paul's distinctly apocalyptic use of metaphor. His insistence that the foundation of theology is God's act in Christ, not an act of the human being, determines his use of figurative language. For him a useful metaphor is not an image projected from the known into the unknown. Things are the other way around. A metaphor true to the gospel is produced by the incursion of the unknown into the orb of what is presumed to be the known.

One considers, for example, Paul's use of the term *huiothesia*, "adoption as a son" (4:5), and his immediately following reference to the Galatians as "sons." Both of these images emerge in Paul's language after he has said that in Christ there is no male and female (4:6; 3:28). Is he then guilty of a blatant inconsistency? That is a question one can answer only after giving careful attention to the order of Paul's statements in 4:4–6:

> But when the fullness of time came, God sent his Son, born of a woman, born under the power of the Law, in order that he might redeem those held under the power of the Law, in order, that is, that we might receive adoption as sons. And because you are sons, God sent the Spirit of his Son into our hearts, crying, "Abba, Father!"

Here everything begins anew with the incursion of God's Son into the world. That incursion is redemptive, Paul says, because of the bond it produces between this Son and those who are incorporated into him; and Paul portrays that bond by drawing a line between the Son and the sons. Creating life where there was none (3:21), God has made sons by incorporating them into his Son and by sending into their hearts the Spirit of his Son. Or, to change the metaphor, God has adopted them as his sons (4:7).

Does Paul's use of these metaphors rescind the confession of 3:28? Hardly! The gender-specific dimension of these images is a matter Paul leaves completely to one side. For, to say it again, in Paul's language a metaphor is produced by the incursion of the unknown into the orb of the (presumed) known, not a projection of the known into the unknown. It is thus a linguistically creative event in the corporate life of the church.[73] The use of the image grants — to an extent — both a vision of the unknown and the true perception of what was previously considered the known (e.g., the gender-specific character of the word "son"). All of the images in 4:4–6, then, explicate the image of 3:28, pointing to the newly created family of God in which the task of the Spirit is to lead all members to cry out, "Abba, Father!"[74] And, in the ecstatic language of the church, this last image lies as far beyond gender specificity as do the others.

HOLY TIMES

In 4:9–10 Paul says that the Galatians' observance of holy times is incompatible with their having been known by God, being a sure index of their return to the worship of the cosmic elements. This new turn in his argument raises two questions. First, on what grounds precisely and with what results does Paul see in the Galatians' newfound calendar proof of their return to the enslaving veneration of the cosmic elements? Second, why does he refer to that calendar by saying that the Galatians have begun to observe "days and months and seasons and years," thus using none of the Jewish expressions one might expect, given the work of the Teachers, such as "sabbath," "new moon," "atonement," "Passover," "First Fruits"?

If we momentarily leave aside the motif of enslavement, we can see good reasons for thinking that, in drawing a connection between holy times and the cosmic elements, Paul is in fact reflecting an aspect of the Teachers' own message. In Comment #41 we noted the probability that, considering the elements to include the stars, the Teachers are saying something like this to the Galatians:

> The presence of idols in the temples of your former religion shows that you Gentiles ignorantly reverenced the elements as though they were gods. More tragic still, Paul did nothing really to terminate your ill-informed relation to the elements. It is true that, like other peoples, you were always aware of the role of the astral elements in signaling the seasons you celebrated as holy. You did not know, however, the true calendar established by God, and Paul did not convey it to you. In truth, the stars are nothing other than servants of the God of Israel who made them and who gave them a role in relation to his holy Law. As servants of this God, the elements shift the seasons in order to fix the correct times for the true feasts, those ordained by God. What are you to do, then?

---

[73] Precisely the same thing appears in Jesus' parables of the Kingdom of God. Jesus allows the imminent incursion of God's kingdom to preside over the selection and the use of metaphors. See, for example, Mark 3:22–27, where it is Jesus' power to cast out demons that leads him to speak of the binding of the strong man.

[74] Cf. Sturm, "Apocalyptic"; J. L. Martyn, Issues, 89–110.

You are to ascend from the foolish and idolatrous worship of the elements themselves to the knowledge of the true God who made them, thus celebrating the holy times ordained by him in his Law, and doing so at the junctures fixed by the activity of his servants, the astral elements.

Finding this message convincing, a number of the Galatians have begun to observe the Teachers' holy times, discerning the correct dates for those special times by watching the movements of the stars.[75]

There is reason to think, then, that Paul is accurately describing developments among his Galatian churches when he draws a connection between their observance of holy times and their veneration of the elements. In speaking of that connection, however, he makes three significant changes.

First, without directly contradicting the view that the elements are — or at least include — the stars, he maintains his earlier assertion that in their true identity they are the religious pairs of opposites that formed the foundation of the old cosmos. Second, far from agreeing that in their newfound calendar the Galatians are merely giving the elements their due as servants of God, he says that they are returning to the worship of the elements instead of God, thereby enslaving themselves to the elements no less than they did when they celebrated other holy times as heathens. Third, Paul characterizes the elements as weak and impotent. These three changes can be economically reflected in a free paraphrase of 4:9–10:

You Galatians may think that, in celebrating the Teachers' alleged holy times, you are taking your bearings from God's servants, the celestial bodies. Actually, in taking guidance from the stars, you are returning to the worship of the elements rather than of God. For when, following the Teachers, you observe certain so-called holy times on dates you fix by looking to the stars, you are in fact enslaving yourselves once more to the elemental, religious pairs of opposites. Finding in the movements of the stars the rhythmic alternation between holy times and profane ones, you are returning to the cosmos whose elements are impotent actually to change things, consisting, as they do, of nothing more than the Law/the Not-Law, circumcision/uncircumcision, Jew/Gentile, holy/profane.

Is Paul following the Teachers' nomenclature when he refers to the Galatians' newfound calendar by speaking of days, months, seasons, and years? That is possible, but everything else we know of the Teachers' message — notably their de-

---

[75]Numerous texts show the various ways in which Jewish traditions connect one's observance of God's holy times with one's attendance to a world order signaled by the movements of the heavenly bodies. See the helpful collection of texts and the perceptive interpretations in Lührmann, "Tage," and especially Wis 7:17–19: "For it is he who gave me unerring knowledge of what exists, to know the structure of the world and the activity of the elements; the beginning and end and middle of times, the alternations of the solstices and the changes of the seasons, the cycles of the year and the constellations of the stars" (RSV).

manding circumcision and the observance of the Jewish food laws — suggests that they are using cultic terms familiar in Judaism and in Jewish Christianity, referring to such times as sabbath, new moon, day of atonement, Passover, and First Fruits.[76] Indeed, First Fruits may have been of special interest to them. From Paul's references in 4:22, 23, 29 to the birth of Isaac, we can suppose that the Teachers considered that event to be a pivotal juncture in the sacred history of Israel. If to that supposition we add the Jewish tradition that Isaac was born on the Feast of the First Fruits, it is a short step to the hypothesis that the Teachers celebrated Isaac's birth as part of their observance of the feast of the First Fruits (cf. *Jub.* 16:13).

But if the Teachers are using specific cultic terms to speak of times that are holy to God, why does Paul speak in an apparently colorless way of the Galatians' observance of days, months, seasons, and years? In fact, this list is not at all colorless. Paul draws it from the account of God's creation in Genesis, the first three days of which recount God's work of separating the world into pairs of opposites, light/darkness, water above/water below, sea/land. The fourth day corresponds to the first, for on it God supplements the creation of sun and moon with that of the stars, producing not only day and night but also the passing of time, the historical dimension of the world, and thus the fixing of times extending even to years.[77]

> Let there be luminaries in the dome of the sky to separate the day from the night, and let them mark the fixed times of seasons, days, and years . . . (Gen 1:14).[78]

Moreover, as numerous Jewish interpretations of Gen 1:14 show, God's work on the fourth day was understood to be the point at which God gave to the heavenly luminaries the power to distinguish holy times from profane ones.[79] Two texts warrant special mention. The author of *Jubilees*, championing the solar calendar, attributes to the sun the power to determine sabbaths, feasts, and jubilees (*Jub.* 2:8–10; cf. Wis 7:17–19; 1 *Enoch* 82:9). And when Ben Sira speaks of holy times,

---

[76]Lührmann is right to warn against interpreting Gal 4:10 on the basis of Col 2:16, where, connecting holy times to the elements, the author speaks in distinctly Jewish terms of "festivals, new moons, sabbaths" ("Tage," 430; see also T. Martin, "Schemes," although Martin thinks the Galatians are simply returning to their pagan calendar). But the suggestion I have made above is based entirely on data in Galatians. Note also Fitzmyer, "Days like the sabbath and *yom hakkippurim* are meant; months like the 'new moon'; seasons like Passover and Pentecost; years like the sabbatical years (Lev 25:5)." Cf. further 1 *Enoch* 75:3; 79:2; *Jub.* 1:14; CD 3:12–15; Josephus *Ant.* 3.237.

[77]Lührmann, "Tage," 441.

[78]Translators have rendered the second clause in various ways. NRSV, for example, follows the woodenly literal rendering of RSV, "and let them be for signs and for seasons and for days and years." It is clear, however, that the noun *'ôt* (LXX, *sêmeia*) refers here to an "omen indicating future events" (KB; cf. Speiser, *Genesis*). That is to say, God gives to the stars (with the sun and moon) the power to fix the times specified by the words that follow, seasons, days, and years (LXX, *kairous, hêmeras, eniautous*). Philo understood the *sêmeia* of Gen 1:14 to be "timely signs of coming events" (*sêmeia mellontôn; de Op. Mundi* 58).

[79]Pertinent texts are cited in Lührmann, "Tage."

he relates that subject to the archaic pairs of opposites (good/evil, life/death, etc.), thus considering the distinction of holy times from profane ones to be an elemental polarity set in the cosmos by God (Sir 33:7–9, 14–15). One notes also that the list of times in Gen 1:14 was sometimes supplemented by the addition of "months," and that the times were sometimes put in order of length.[80] In his way of referring to the Teachers' holy times, then, Paul is employing a traditional interpretation of Gen 1:14, thus portraying the Galatians' newfound calendar by using the language of the created world order: days, months, seasons, and years. If Paul is substituting this *creational* list of holy times for one in which the Teachers are employing *cultic language specific to Jewish Christianity*, then two conclusions follow, and both shed light on the nature of the argument in Galatians as a whole.

In the first place, Paul is drawing an astonishing connection between creation and the realm ruled over by the enslaving elements, the realm he has earlier identified as "the present evil age" (1:4). In fact, by drawing this connection, Paul presents a picture of creation not altogether dissimilar to one later proposed by Marcion and the second-century gnostics. Moreover, a comparison of this gloomy picture of creation with the portrait of the Law's genesis given in 3:19–20 raises the question whether, in writing to the Galatians, Paul in effect denies the divine origin both of creation and of the Law (Comment #38). Careful attention to this question only serves, however, to emphasize the central role played in the letter by Paul's radically apocalyptic theology. And to see the role of apocalyptic is to note the gulf that separates the apostle from Marcion and the gnostics.[81]

For in Paul's view what is fundamentally wrong with both creation and the Law is that both have fallen into the company of anti-God powers, the Law in its tandem existence with the Not-Law — so as to constitute one of the world's enslaving elements — and creation itself by having — after the advent of the Law/the Not-Law — such elements as its base.[82] In a word, *God's* creation has fallen prey to anti-God powers that have turned it into "the present evil age," and that is the reason for God's having to act in Christ to terminate the elemental pairs of opposites that are anything but his servants (3:28; Comment #41; cf. Rom 8:19–22). The elemental pairs of opposites that threaded their way through the whole of the old creation included holy times/profane times.

The second conclusion follows from the first. If the distinction of holy times from profane ones is an element of the old creation, then it is basic to all peoples. Here we return to the way in which Paul characterizes the Galatians' renewed

---

[80] Philo *de Op. Mundi* 55 and 60 (from Lührmann, "Tage").

[81] See Introduction §15; J. L. Martyn, *Issues*, 224–226.

[82] In Galatians Paul seems clearly to presuppose *events* in the *history* of the Law. That history began when God established what might be termed the Abrahamic Law, God's own promise to bless the Gentiles in Abraham and in Abraham's seed (3:8; 4:21b). The Law became, however, an enslaving cosmic element when — instituted by angels — it was paired with the Not-Law at Sinai. Still later, when that complex Law was taken in hand by Christ, its blessing and promissory voice was distinguished from its cursing and enslaving voice. At the cross Christ overcame the Law's cursing voice while restoring its promissory voice to its original, nonreligious, Abrahamic form (5:14; 6:2; Comment #48).

enslavement to the elements. Had he said that the Galatians were observing sabbaths, Passover, First Fruits, etc., one would perhaps say that his argument is at least partially anti-Judaic. To attend carefully to the creational language of 4:9–10 is to see, however, that the negative side of the picture is occupied by the universally fallen creation, not by Judaism. Thus, just as God's new creation in Christ is the end of *both* circumcision *and* uncircumcision (6:15), so also that new creation is the end of the cosmos that had as one of its elemental pairs of opposites holy times/profane times. By adopting the Teachers' holy calendar in their quest for salvation, the Galatians are behaving as though Christ had not come, thereby showing that they do not know what time it is.

4:12–20 JOYOUS DAYS AND ANXIOUS DAYS

TRANSLATION

4:12. Brothers and sisters, I beg you to become as I am, because I have become as you are. You did not wrong me in any way. 13. You know that it was due to an illness of mine that I preached the gospel to you in the first place; 14. and, although you were tempted to be offended at my sickness, you neither despised me nor regarded me with contempt. On the contrary, you welcomed me as an angel of God, indeed as Christ Jesus. 15. What has happened to the intense elation you felt? For I can give you evidence of that earlier feeling: Had it been possible, you would have plucked out your eyes and given them to me! 16. So then, has it turned out that I am now your enemy, rather than your friend, for having spoken the truth to you? 17. The people who have come into your churches with their false gospel are courting you, saying that they are deeply concerned about you, but they do not really have in mind what is good for you. On the contrary, their threat that you will be excluded springs in truth from their desire that you will make them the object of your affection. 18. To be courted by someone who is concerned for your welfare is in every instance a good thing; and not only when I am present with you. 19. My children, I am going through the pain of giving birth to you all over again, until Christ is formed in your congregations. 20. Would that I could be there with you now, and that I could change my tone of voice; for I am quite uncertain about you.

LITERARY FORM AND SYNOPSIS

Two observations show that 4:12–20 constitutes the second paragraph within the section 4:8–20 (see Literary Form and Synopsis of 4:8–11). In v 20 Paul repeats the note of anxiety he has struck in v 11. And both in v 12 and in v 20 he speaks emphatically not only of the Galatians but also of himself ("I . . . you"), indicating that the major subject of the paragraph is the history of his relationship with them.

In the beginning the Galatians attached themselves to Paul's gospel (v 13) and indeed to Paul himself (v 14) with uncommon enthusiasm. He became, so to speak, their best friend, sent to them, as it were, from heaven. With the arrival of the Teachers, however (lit. "they" in v 17), things have greatly changed. Many of the Galatians — perhaps almost all of them (see 5:2, 4) — have become convinced that Paul is really not their friend, but rather their enemy, the one who knowingly withheld from them the truth, God's eternal Law.

Faced with this development, Paul is not concerned to be polite. If the Teachers question his motives, he will question theirs. When the Teachers tell the Galatians that they will be shut out of God's kingdom unless they are observant of the Law, that threat may appear to be a genuine warning, issued for the Galatians' sake. In reality, Paul insists, in making that threat the Teachers are thinking only of themselves, intent on causing the Galatians to put them on a pedestal, as though they were the trustworthy messengers of God. And in this sham the Teachers are having great success. When Paul should be celebrating the growth of healthy children in Galatia, he finds himself in the situation of a prospective mother who is still in labor. For, changing the image somewhat, he says that Christ has not yet been truly formed in the Galatian churches, and for that reason he is anxiously concerned about them. As we saw in the analysis of Gal 2:1–14, the history of the gospel is the history of struggle.

NOTES

4:12. *Brothers and sisters.* At the paragraph's beginning and again at its end ("children") Paul uses terms of endearment, reflecting the close and affectionate relationship characteristic of his initial time with the Galatians, and equally reflective, he believes, of the basic facts of the present.

become as I am, because I have become as you are. In the background lies the tradition that students of a truly upright philosopher-teacher are to take him not only as an intellectual instructor but also as a model whose life can guide them into mature patterns in their own life.[83] Thus, the Galatians are to imitate Paul. In 1 Thessalonians, Philippians, and 1 Corinthians we find something similar: passages in which Paul uses the motif of imitation to place himself as a sort of middle term between his churches and Christ:

> You became imitators of us (i.e., of me) and of the Lord (1 Thess 1:6). What you have learned and received and heard and seen in me, do; and the God of peace will be with you (Phil 4:9). I urge you, then, be imitators of me . . . I sent to you Timothy . . . to remind you of my ways in Christ (1 Cor 4:16–17). Be imitators of me, as I am of Christ (1 Cor 11:1).

In Gal 4:12, however, the motif of imitation is in one regard handled quite differently. By using the relative adverb *hôs*, "as," in both halves of the sentence,

---

[83] See, for example, Seneca *Epistolae* 6.5–6 (Malherbe, *the Thessalonians*, 52–53).

Paul speaks of a mutual friendship rather than of a unidirectional imitation.[84] True friends are altogether like one another because they share all their fortunes. Because he has become *as* they are, they are to become *as* he is. Fundamentally, then, Paul speaks not of an imitation, but of a shared existence, and it is the nature of that shared existence that thus acquires true significance. What specifically does Paul have in mind?

We have already found a clue in the plural pronouns of 3:13, 4:3, and 4:5–6 (Comment #36). In those instances Paul has underlined the absolute solidarity of himself with the Galatians. Moreover, this solidarity can be seen *ante Christum* as well as *post Christum*. Not observant of the Law when he was among them, Paul became like them in that he could think of himself as a former Gentile (4:3).[85] Now — given their temptation to credit the message of the Teachers — they are to become like him in regarding themselves as former Jews (4:5). But the basis of this common existence is thoroughly christological. When the Galatians received Paul as though he were Christ (v 14), they perceived the apostle to be as far beyond all religious differentiations as is Christ himself (3:28). Now they are to regrasp that earlier perception, by knowing that in Christ they are as far beyond such differentiations as is Paul (cf. 4:19b).

You did not wrong me. Paul refers to the period during which the mutual friendship in Christ was marked by the total absence of the sort of animosity toward him that the Teachers have now incited among the Galatians.

13. *You know.* As at 3:1–2, Paul refers to the Galatians' memory of things characteristic of the period when he was among them.

due to an illness. The Galatians' joy at being seized by the good news was attended by the confidence that, although Paul's own intention had been to pass through their region on his way to another, they had been included in God's redemptive deed because Paul, becoming ill, had had to pause in his journey (Comment #17).[86]

an illness. Lit. "a weakness of the flesh." The flesh is vulnerable to sickness and is thus connected with suffering (1QpHab 9:2; 1QSa 2:5; Rom 8:3). It is useless to speculate about the nature of Paul's sickness. We can know only that the Galatians attached themselves to him in spite of it, a development Paul cites as evidence of the intensity of the Galatians' affection for him and as a demonstration of the power of the gospel to overcome obstacles.

in the first place. The expression *to proteron*, "the first time," or "formerly" or "once," or "originally," used here as an adverb modifying *euêggelisamên*, "preached the gospel," does not in itself indicate whether Paul means to refer to the one and only time he visited Galatia, or to the first of two visits (on the grammar, see BDF §62). Were one to proceed on the basis of Acts, one could favor the second reading, finding here Paul's way of referring to the first of two visits to Galatia (Acts 16:6 and 18:23). All elements of the context, however, favor a reference to the only visit Paul has made to Galatia.

---

[84] H. D. Betz is right to emphasize the topic of friendship; see also Fitzgerald, *Friendship.*
[85] Cf. Paul's use of the relative adverb *hôs* in 1 Cor 7:7–8; Räisänen, *Law,* 75.
[86] Cf. Murphy-O'Connor, "Missions," 80.

Most important, the picture Paul paints in this paragraph is marked by a simple and striking contrast between the enthusiastic reception the Galatians gave to him and his gospel when he founded their churches and the cool and critical stance the Galatians have adopted due to the influence of the Teachers. Had there been a second visit, Paul would surely have said how things went on that occasion, adding something like, "And the second time I was with you, you were still my true and faithful children. How different things are now from the way they were during both of my visits!" Hence the translation "in the first place."

14. *tempted to be offended at my sickness.* Paul indicates that his sick body ("my flesh") did indeed present a temptation to the Galatians. They could have been offended by it, considering it an indication that he was a sinful and evil magician.[87]

nor regarded me with contempt. Paul's verb (omitted by p46) is colorful: *ekptuein,* "to spit out." Tempted to view the sick apostle as an evil magician momentarily overcome by the malignant powers he normally used to control others, the Galatians could have reacted by spitting, hoping to cleanse their mouths of the unclean odors they inhaled in his presence.

you welcomed me as an angel of God, indeed as Christ Jesus. The contrast between Paul's being viewed as a sick and evil magician and his being welcomed as an angel sent by God is a matter Paul can explicate only by referring to Christ. For only in Christ himself are people given the power to perceive strength in weakness.[88] As God's messenger, Paul preached Christ (1:16); and that preaching included the conviction that, as he had himself suffered crucifixion with Christ, so in his present life he bears in his body physical scars — and illnesses — that are marks of his association with Jesus (6:17; cf. 2 Cor 4:5, 10). It was then the crucified Jesus Christ who lived in him, paradoxically transforming his weakness into strength without removing it (3:1; 2:19–20).

The odiously sick, apparently demonic figure was seen, then, to be in fact an angel sent from God, just as the legally executed criminal was seen to be in fact God's own Son. That correspondence caused the Galatians to welcome Paul, and that correspondence caused their attachment to Paul to be an attachment to Christ.

15. *the intense elation you felt.* Uninhibited joy and thankfulness characterized the Galatians' reception of the gospel of Christ and thus of Paul.

I can give you evidence. Speaking as though he were an instructive witness giving testimony, Paul reminds the Galatians of those earlier days.[89]

you would have plucked out your eyes. Instead of indicating the nature of Paul's illness, this clause may be a fixed literary motif indicating the depth of the Galatians' affection for Paul (H. D. Betz).

16. *your enemy, rather than your friend.* No note in the paragraph is so poignant as this one. The Teachers have convinced a number of the Galatians that, far from being their friend, Paul is actually their enemy, having knowingly withheld

[87] Cf. Schweizer, "*sarx,*" 125.
[88] See 2 Corinthians 10–13; J. L. Martyn, *Issues,* 89–110.
[89] See *martyreô* in the index of Malherbe, *Cynic.*

from them the one message necessary for life, the Law. In 4:29–30 Paul will, in effect, reply in kind, identifying the Teachers as the Galatians' enemies.

Did the Teachers use the word "enemy" itself in referring to Paul? It is notable that that word is applied to Paul in a second-century Jewish-Christian document, the pseudepigraphic *Epistle of Peter to James*. There Peter refers to Paul when he speaks of Gentiles who

> have rejected my lawful preaching and have preferred a lawless and absurd doctrine of the man who is my enemy (*ho echthros anthrôpos*; 2:3; HS 2.112).

Is this picture the second-century author's literary creation, crafted by drawing both from Matt 13:28 ("the enemy man") and from Gal 2:11–14 (the bitter fight between Peter and Paul)? That is possible, but there may also be a line of tradition extending from the Teachers in the mid-first century to circles of Jewish Christians in the second.[90]

for having spoken the truth. See 2:5, 14 on "the truth of the gospel."

17. *The people who have come into your churches with their false gospel.* Paul writes simply "they." Because the Teachers are still active in the Galatian churches, references to them that appear to be cryptic will have been easily understood by the Galatians.

are courting you, saying that they are deeply concerned about you. The verb *zêloô* refers here to the strenuous courting of the object of one's affection.[91] The Teachers themselves could have used the verb to speak in a distinctly positive way of their courting the Galatians (cf. Paul's own use of the verb in this way in 2 Cor 11:2). For they doubtless see in themselves an analogy to the man who, in traditional courtship, shows the woman that he is deeply concerned about her needs, desires, and general welfare. The Teachers doubtless intend the dimension of *pathos* in their rhetoric to be a reflection of their concern to bring to the Galatians what these Gentiles actually need, God's holy Law.

Paul is sure, however, that their *pathos* is an instance of *mere* rhetoric, a hollow show of feigned affection. One might think of Plato's distinction between a rhetorician and a teacher, a distinction designed to reveal that enthusiastic courtship can be a hollow show, put on by one whose real concern is focused on himself (e.g., *Gorgias* 456). Thus the paraphrastic addition "saying that they are deeply concerned about you."

their threat that you will be excluded. Paul refers abruptly to another facet of the Teachers' message. Dictating only the words "they wish to exclude you," Paul does not say from whom or from what the Teachers wish to exclude the Galatians.[92] Presumably, he can be brief because he knows that in the word "exclude"

---

[90] Luedemann, *Paulus*, 251–252.

[91] On *zêloô* plus direct object, see BDF §163. Dunn finds in 4:17 a reference to the Teachers' zeal for the covenant by which they "hoped to spark off an equivalent zeal among the Galatians" ("Echoes," 475). This reading does not take seriously enough the syntax, namely, the transitive use of the verb *zêloô* with the Galatians as the direct object.

[92] Mussner's suggestion that the Teachers seek to exclude the Galatians from Paul's company is possible, but less probable than the reading proposed below.

the Galatians will hear an echo of the Teachers' message. Perhaps the Teachers are portraying themselves as gatekeepers, intent on the altogether positive task of guiding the Galatians through the gate of Law observance into the blessing of Abraham (3:14).[93] In order, however, to emphasize the serious nature of the matter, they apparently link their invitation to a threat that accents exclusion:

> Because we are deeply concerned about your welfare, we must add a solemn warning. Failure to pass through the gate by which Gentiles enter into the Law-observant people of God will entail absolute exclusion. As God says in his holy Law, "Any uncircumcised male who is not circumcised in the flesh of his foreskin shall be cut off . . . he has broken my covenant."[94] If you do not accept circumcision as the first move in your observance of the Law, you will be excluded from the blessed people of God, and, needless to say, from the eucharist over which we preside.[95]

springs in truth from their desire that you will make them the object of your affection. Again using the verb *zêloô* with the meaning "strenuously to court the object of one's affection," Paul further maligns the Teachers' motives. Far from truly loving the Galatians, they love, he says, only themselves, wishing to be adored as those who hold the key to the gate leading to salvation.

18. *To be courted by someone who is concerned for your welfare is in every instance a good thing.* Having just said that the Teachers' courting of the Galatians is ungenuine (*zêlousin hymas ou kalôs*), Paul uses a rhetorical aphorism in order to portray the opposite. What the Galatians experienced at his hands should remind them that persons can be courted in a way that is truly focused on what is good for them (*zêlousthai en kalô*).

and not only when I am present with you. Paul interprets the preceding aphorism in such a way as to exclude the thought that his maligning of the Teachers is a matter of mere jealousy. Had faithful ministers of the gospel followed his footsteps into Galatia, wooing his churches in order, in his absence, to deepen their attachment to Christ, he would have rejoiced (cf. 1 Cor 3:5–10; Phil 1:15–18).

19. *My children.* Paul began the paragraph (v 12) with a familial term of endearment, "brothers and sisters." He closes it no less tenderly, speaking to the Galatians as his children. It is an identification reflecting the conviction that churches come into existence when they are begotten by the one who first preaches the gospel to them (see, e.g., 1 Cor 4:14–15; Phlm 10). The basic motif can be found in numerous religious and philosophical traditions.[96]

[93] See, for example, *Sipra*, Achrei Mot, Perek 13:12: "And it does not say, 'Open the gates, and let the Priests and Levites and Israel enter,' but it says, 'Open the gates that a righteous Gentile may enter' (Isa 26:2)." Cf. Moore, *Judaism*, 1.529.
[94] Gen 17:14; cf. *Jub.* 16:26. As we will see in considering Gal 4:21–5:1, we can be confident that the Teachers made much of Genesis 17, emphasizing the definition of God's covenant as circumcision.
[95] Cf. Schlier.
[96] See Malherbe, *Philosophers*, passim.

I am going through the pain of giving birth to you all over again. Unlike the familiar address that precedes it, this statement is almost without parallel. It is a stunning announcement, the impact of which arises in large part from Paul's use of the verb *ôdinô*, a matter to be fully considered in Comment #44. In the present Note it will suffice to survey the ways in which that verb is used in Greek literature.

Two major constructions appear. Employed intransitively (without a direct object), *ôdinô* refers to the sudden and severe pain a woman experiences in giving birth, thus meaning "to have the pains of childbirth." In this construction the verb has a single major focus, the woman's anguish.[97]

Used in the transitive construction (with a direct object)—as it is in Gal 4:19—the verb acquires two foci, first the woman's pains and second the product of those pains, the specific child born in the process: "to have birth pains in the process of giving birth to A."

It is scarcely surprising that, in its figurative use, the verb is commonly intransitive, providing only a picture of intense suffering. To make clear the anguish of Agamemnon's battle wounds, for example, Homer finds a simile in the anguish of a woman in her birth pains (*Iliad* 11.269; cf. the Cyclops in *Odyssey* 9.415).[98] In Greek literature there are a few instances in which the verb is both metaphorical and transitive. Plato refers, for example, to the pain that is involved in giving birth to a thought.[99] But instances in Greek literature in which the verb is both metaphorical and transitive are of little help in sensing Paul's intention in Gal 4:19. For in those cases the specified offspring is as metaphorical as are the birth pains, whereas in Gal 4:19 the offspring is not at all metaphorical. It is the Galatians themselves. One passage in the LXX, however, offers true assistance, Isa 45:9–11; and the use of the verb in apocalyptic traditions is similarly helpful. See Comment #44.

until Christ is formed in your congregations. This is the only place in his letters at which Paul employs the verb *morphoô*, meaning in the passive "to take on form," "to be formed."[100] It is possible, as Burton suggested, that Paul has to some degree reversed the metaphor of v 19a, now speaking of the Galatians as the mother in whose womb Christ is to be formed. Galen uses the verb *morphoô* to refer to the formation of an embryo.[101] But, as there is no thought of the Galatians ever giving birth to Christ, it is better to see here only the image of Christ becoming the real ego of the Galatian communities, in the sense that he will live in them as he already lives in Paul (2:20). What will make the Galatians viable for life apart from Paul's presence among them (4:18, 20) is the formation of Christ in their communities.

This reading is confirmed by other passages in which Paul employs verbs that

---

[97]The intransitive use of the verb thus reflects the construction in which the noun *ôdines* is the direct object of the verb *echô*, "to have birth pangs." See Bertram, "*ôdin*."

[98]The figurative use of the verb seems, therefore, to have begun as a simile (*Iliad* 11.269), later becoming a metaphor.

[99]*Theages* 148e; cf. Sophocles *Trachiniae* 325 (*symphoras baros*).

[100]Indeed, the verb occurs only this once in the whole of the LXX and NT.

[101]Galen, vol. 19, p. 181, in the edition by C. G. Kühn.

are linguistically and conceptually related to *morphoô*, using those verbs to draw a connection with Christ.[102] In Phil 3:10 Paul refers to his own hope of being conformed (*symmorphizomenos*) to the death of Christ. He also speaks to the Corinthians about a process under way in the church:

> And all of us, with unveiled faces, seeing the glory of the Lord as though re-flected in a mirror, are being transformed (*metamorphoumetha*) into the same image [the image of Christ] (2 Cor 3:18).

Finally, commencing his detailed instruction of the Roman Christians, he ex-horts them not to be conformed (*mê syschêmatizesthe*) to the pattern of this pres-ent age, but to be transformed (*metamorphousthe*) by the renewal of their minds (Rom 12:2). Taking these passages together with pertinent ones in Galatians it-self, we will shortly ask about the identity of the Christ who is yet to be formed in the Galatian churches (Comment #44).

in your congregations. At an earlier juncture Paul could speak of Christ's being in him (2:20), but even there Paul views himself as a representative individual. In the present verse he places the accent emphatically on the church as such, not on the Galatians as individuals.[103] The formation of Christ is a communal event that occurs in the birth and maturation of a church. The reference is thus both communal and future. The Galatians' readiness to turn to the nomistic mes-sage of the Teachers shows that the exclusive image of Christ has not yet been firmly formed in their communal life. Thus, even in the letter in which the major accent lies on the radical change that has already occurred in Christ's advent (e.g., 3:23–25), Paul refers emphatically to the future of Jesus Christ in the Gala-tian congregations.[104]

20. *Would that I could be there with you now.* By the conative imperfect *êthelon* Paul speaks of a wish that cannot be fulfilled at the moment (BDF §326). This wish is a commonplace in letters, reflecting the fact that communication would be more nearly complete if it could be made in person and orally. Here, however, the wish is more than a mere convention. Paul knows that the Teachers, being still present with the Galatians, are able to communicate with tone of voice, facial expression, etc., and that circumstances deny him these means of communi-cation.

It is striking that Paul says nothing at all about plans for a future visit, one that would indeed provide the opportunity for face-to-face talks. This omission has been cited in favor of the thesis that Galatians was written relatively late in Paul's life, after the Corinthian correspondence, when he was greatly occupied with his plans to launch a mission in Spain.[105] We have seen grounds, however, for dating

---

[102]See especially Koenig, "Transformation." Cf. also the verbs *syschêmatizô* and *allassô* and the adjective *symmorphos*.
[103]The prepositional phrase *en hymin* is always to be rendered "among you" unless there is strong reason to translate it otherwise.
[104]Cf. Morse, *Logic*.
[105]See, for example, J. Knox, "Galatians," 343.

Galatians relatively early (Comment #24). Presumably, the intensity of Paul's labors in some of the cities around the Aegean Sea precludes a trip to Galatia.

change my tone of voice. It is possible that this clause (*allaxai tên phônên mou*) explicates the one preceding it: "Would that I could be with you now, and exchange for the written letter my (more effective) speaking voice." More probable is the reading that finds here Paul's wish that in place of the angry and accusatory letter (recall, e.g., "You foolish Galatians!" in 3:1) he could speak to the Galatians both in person and in a fundamentally joyous and affirmative manner. We have noted that he begins and closes the paragraph with terms of endearment ("brothers and sisters" . . . "children"). He wishes that these terms could set the tone for the whole of his communication with the Galatians.

I am quite uncertain about you. Again Paul uses a verb, *aporeô*, with an affective color, as though to say, "Your susceptibility to the Teachers' wooing makes my head swim! I am at a loss as to what I might say to you!" In his consternation Paul indicates that there are, in fact, questions about the Galatians to which he has no certain answers. Indeed, in the course of dictating the letter, Paul experiences several mood changes, being, on the one hand, depressed as he contemplates the possibility that all of the Galatians will attach themselves to the nongospel of the Teachers (cf. 1:6; 3:1; 4:11; 5:9), and, on the other hand, confident that they will not do that (5:10). In the Introduction (§11) we have noted that in the immediate political sense the letter may very well have failed as thoroughly as did Paul's speech to Peter in the Antioch church (2:11–14). As he dictates it, Paul is painfully aware of that possibility.

COMMENT #44
PAUL IN ANXIOUS LABOR PAINS
UNTIL CHRIST IS FORMED IN THE GALATIAN CHURCHES

A COMPLEX METAPHOR

Following the lead of Gaventa, we see that the metaphor with which Paul closes the paragraph of 4:12–20 is so stunning and puzzling as to warrant careful analysis:[106]

> My children, I am going through the pain of giving birth to you all over again, until Christ is formed in your congregations (4:19).

The figure gives pause for several reasons, not the least being its complexity. After addressing the Galatians as his children, Paul says paradoxically that they have not yet been born. He then intensifies the paradox by saying that they have in fact been born once before. As he has pointed out in vv 13–15, that earlier birth was attended by great joy, both on his part and on theirs. Now, however, when he should be continuing to rejoice over a healthy offspring, he, a male, is thrown back to the stage of being in labor, trying in the midst of sharp pain to give birth

---

[106]Gaventa, "Maternity"; idem, "Our Mother St. Paul." At several junctures in this Comment I have drawn on Gaventa's perceptive studies.

to them again. And finally, he identifies the cause of this unhappy state of affairs. His renewed labor pains spring from the fact that Christ has not yet been formed in the corporate life of the Galatian communities.

With a complexity that far exceeds what is commonly called a mixed metaphor, the sentence presents several images that can scarcely be brought simultaneously into focus. It is clear that Paul is referring to the genesis of the Galatian churches, but that proves to be a subject about which he can speak only by twice contradicting himself. He gave birth to the Galatian churches at a point in the past; yet he is even now in birth pains, trying to give birth to them again. At that earlier point they received Christ (4:14); yet Christ has not yet been formed in their communities.

In the midst of such complex contradictions some degree of clarity can be had by comparing Paul's use of the verb *ôdinô* with the use of the verb elsewhere.

THE VERB "TO BE IN THE PAIN OF GIVING BIRTH"

The General Use. In the Note on v 19 we saw two pertinent things about the employment of the verb *ôdinô* in Greek literature. First, in its metaphorical use the verb usually lacks the direct object, providing only a picture of suffering comparable to that of a woman in labor, and thus useful even to refer to anguish experienced by a man. Second, there are a few instances in which the verb is both metaphorical and provided with a direct object, but these are of little help in discerning Paul's intention in Gal 4:19. For an author to say that one can suffer pains in giving birth to a thought, for example, is hardly comparable to a man's saying that he is suffering pains in giving birth to a group of other human beings. Two observations about Gal 4:19 are noteworthy, then: Paul uses the verb of himself metaphorically, and he provides it with a concrete direct object, the Galatians.

Paul's Use in Gal 4:19.[107] Indeed, in Gal 4:19 four noteworthy motifs are combined in a striking manner.

(1) Paul employs the verb to construct a metaphor.
(2) He provides this metaphorical verb with a direct object, so that it refers to much more than an instance of anguish; it means "to be in the pains of giving birth to a specified offspring."
(3) Paul names himself as the subject of the verb, even though he is a male.
(4) And he specifies the offspring as a corporate people, the Galatian churches.

We have seen that Greek literature from Homer onward seems to provide no true parallel to the combining of these four motifs. The OT offers, however, a text containing all four, and we can be confident that Paul knew and pondered that text.

It is a passage in which Second Isaiah takes into account persons among his

---

[107]Paul employs the verb *ôdinô* in 1 Thess 5:3, in Gal 4:27 (quoted from Isa 54:1), and in Rom 8:22. The passages in 1 Thessalonians and Romans will claim our attention below.

own people who doubt that God's creation of Israel is altogether as clear and inextinguishable as is his creation of the world. Silencing these doubters, God says:

> I form light and create darkness, I make well-being and I create evil; I the Lord do all these things . . . Woe to you who strive with your maker, earthen vessels with the potter! Does the clay say to the one who fashions it, "What are you making"? or "Your work has no handles"? Woe to anyone who says to a father, "What are you begetting (*ti gennêseis; mah-tôlîd*)?" or to a woman (LXX, a mother), "What are you bearing (*ti ôdinêseis; mah-tĕḥîlîn*)?" Thus says the Lord, the Holy One of Israel and its Maker: Will you question me about my children, or command me concerning the work of my hands? (Isa 45:7–11).[108]

This passage is of considerable interest, for reading it on the heels of attending to Gal 4:19, one can make three observations.

First, Second Isaiah's use of the verb "to be in the pain of giving birth" shows the same four motifs we find in Gal 4:19, and it combines them in the same way.

(1) In its own sentence the verb "to be in the pain of giving birth" (*ôdinô; ḥûl/ḥîl*) has the literal meaning. In the context, however, it functions as a metaphor for a deed of God.[109]

(2) The verb is transitive, having a direct object (*ti; mah*).

(3) The subject who is in the pain of giving birth is literally a woman (LXX, a mother), but in its metaphorical use, as noted above, the verb has God as its subject, although elsewhere in the context God is masculine (Isa 45:1, for example).

(4) The child born in this act of God is a corporate people, Israel.

Second, to speak of God's act in creating this corporate people, Second Isaiah uses not only the feminine metaphor of giving birth but also the masculine metaphor of begetting. Israel is the children God has begotten as well as borne. One recalls, then, that speaking of his own role in the genesis of churches, Paul also uses both of these metaphors:

> I do not write this to make you ashamed, but to admonish you as my beloved children. For though you have countless guardians in Christ, you do not have many fathers. For I begot you (*gennaô*) in Christ Jesus through the gospel (1 Cor 4:14–15).[110]

> My children, I am going through the pain of giving birth (*ôdinô*) to you all over again . . . (Gal 4:19).[111]

---

[108]NRSV changed somewhat by attending to the Hebrew text and to the translation of McKenzie, *Second Isaiah*. The verb *ôdinô* is many times used in the LXX as a metaphor, but usually in the intransitive construction.

[109]Cf. Deut 32:18; Isa 42:14; Job 38:29; Trible, "God."

[110]Paul employs the masculine metaphor in similar ways in Phlm 10; 1 Thess 2:11.

[111]On the image of Paul as a nurturing nurse in 1 Thess 2:7, see Malherbe, "Gentle"; Gaventa, "Apostles."

Third, from 1 Cor 14:25, Rom 9:20, and Rom 14:11 we can be confident that Paul gave serious thought to the interpretation of Isaiah 45, quoting in Rom 9:20 the lines in Isa 45:9 about the clay questioning the potter. These three observations lead to a simple conclusion.

In using the masculine image to refer to his role in the genesis of churches, Paul may very well have been influenced by practice of his own time in which a moral teacher is father to his students.[112] But the masculine metaphor of begetting a corporate people also lay before him in Isa 45:10, and, as noted above, we know him to have had an interest in that text. Moreover, the high degree of correspondence between the feminine image of Isa 45:10 and the feminine image of Gal 4:19 suggests that — consciously or unconsciously — Paul drew on the text in Isaiah when he formulated the metaphor of Gal 4:19.

Paul's Reasons. But if, from reading Isaiah 45 and other scriptural texts, Paul had in the back of his mind both masculine and feminine metaphors for the creation of God's corporate people, and if, as 1 Cor 4:14–15 and Phlm 10 suggest, his tendency, being a man, was to employ the masculine metaphor, why in Gal 4:19 does he turn to the feminine image? There are two closely related reasons.

(1) When, at a later juncture, Paul writes 1 Corinthians, he is confident that he can look back on the birth of the Corinthian church as a *punctiliar* event comparable to the begetting of a child, as we have seen above (1 Cor 4:14–15). The members of that church may still be babes, not yet ready for solid food (1 Cor 3:1–2), but they have definitely been born, and at an identifiable point in time.

With the Galatians it is a different story. The work of the Teachers has been so successful as to preclude a simple reference to the Galatians' birth as a punctiliar event accomplished in the past. Indeed, the Teachers' influence has in effect reversed the birth process. It has put the birth of the Galatians in question, throwing Paul back into anxious labor. To picture this decidedly *linear* state of affairs, Paul uses the feminine image. Because of the Teachers' work, he is once again an anxious mother in the pangs of giving birth to the Galatians.

(2) As Gaventa has emphasized, further insight into the image of Gal 4:19 can be had when one recalls the "established connection between apocalyptic expectation and the anguish of childbirth."[113] Leaving aside the present passage and Gal 4:27 (a quotation from Isa 54:1), one notes that Paul's other uses of the verb *ôdinô* are drawn from that apocalyptic tradition. Speaking in 1 Thessalonians of the coming of the day of the Lord (the parousia), Paul warns against a false assessment of the world situation: "When they say, 'There is peace and security,' then sudden destruction will come upon them, as labor pains come upon a pregnant woman, and there will be no escape" (1 Thess 5:3). And in Romans Paul

---

[112] See Malherbe, *the Thessalonians*, 56. Epicurus was addressed by his communities as father (ibid., 40). Cf. also Epictetus *Diss.* 3.22.81: the Cynic makes all of humankind his children, the men among them sons, the women daughters.

[113] Gaventa, "Maternity," 193; cf. Käsemann, "When Rom 8.19ff takes up the Jewish idea of the birth pangs of the Messiah . . . it is not the notion of moral perfection that is under consideration; it is apocalyptic expectation. The same is true . . . in Gal 4:19" (*Perspectives*, 31).

links the sufferings of the present time to the state of affairs in the whole of creation, for the creation is in bondage to decay, "groaning in labor pains" (Rom 8:18–22).

Returning to Galatians, we see that, in composing the paragraph made up of 4:12–20, Paul is concerned not only to measure the odious effects of the Teachers' work but also to reflect on its true nature. And this latter task involves interpreting in apocalyptic perspective both the Teachers' work and his own suffering. The first step in this interpretation is Paul's certainty that his suffering birth pains over the Galatians is the result of what he identifies as the persecuting activity of the Teachers (4:28). Second, that persecution is far more than a matter of inconvenience to him personally. Paul understands his suffering by drawing on the apocalyptic image of birth pains. He therefore sees in the Teachers' persecuting activity an instance of the last-ditch effort by which God's enemies hope to thwart the eschatological redemption of the elect.[114]

THE FORMATION OF CHRIST IN THE GALATIAN CHURCHES

Vivid as the metaphor of v 19a is, Paul cannot be satisfied to say that the Galatians' birth is incomplete. He must state the fundamental reason for that unhappy state of affairs, and for this purpose he speaks of the formation of Christ in the Galatian churches. What will make the Galatians viable for life apart from Paul's presence among them (4:18, 20) is the formation of Christ in their communities, corresponding to the formation of Christ in Paul himself (2:20).

The theological weight of this point can be felt when one ponders the fact that Paul could have closed the paragraph on the simple polemical level: "I am going through the pain of giving birth to you all over again because of those interlopers who are teaching you to observe the Law." However angry he is with the Teachers, he will not speak for more than a moment on the level of "me" versus "them," for to do so would be to lose sight of the fact that *the* issue at stake in Galatia is thoroughly theological (1:6) and specifically christological.

The major question posed by the final clause of Gal 4:19, then, is the identity of the Christ who has not yet been formed in the Galatian churches, in spite of the fact that all members of those congregations have been baptized into him and have put him on as though he were their clothes (3:27). As we have seen in the Note on 4:19, there are places in others of Paul's letters at which the motif of formation is emphasized, and some of these can shed light on the impact of that motif in 4:19. First, in 2 Cor 3:18 Paul draws a tight connection between Christ's form and the corporate life of the church of God.[115] Second, in Phil 3:10 he specifies the form of Christ as his death. And finally, in Rom 12:2 he refers to a significant pair of opposites:

---

[114]Cf. Rom 8:22–23: "We know that the whole creation has been groaning in labor pains until now; and not only the creation, but we ourselves . . ." If the line of analysis pursued in this Comment is valid, then Gal 4:19 has nothing to do with the idea of rebirth (*pace* H. D. Betz). See again Gaventa, "Maternity."

[115]The motif of glory so important in 2 Cor 3:18 is a matter to which, in writing to the Galatians, Paul would certainly not have made reference.

Do not be *conformed* to the pattern of this age, but be *transformed* by the renewal of your minds (Rom 12:2).

Returning to Gal 4:19 with its image of the formation of Christ in the Galatian churches, we can easily see the pertinence of all three of these other passages, not least Rom 12:2 with its pair of opposites.

In their baptism the Galatians had indeed been conformed not to the pattern of this age, but rather to the image of Christ. They had suffered crucifixion with him (Gal 2:19). Participating in his death, they had been separated from the tyrannous form of the present evil age (1:4). In short, combining the language of Rom 12:2 with that of Gal 1:4 and 4:19, we could say that the Galatians had been delivered from conformity to the present evil age, being indeed transformed by having Christ formed in them.

Now the work of the Teachers has reversed the formative pattern. Accepting their message, the Galatians have returned to a pattern of life in which they are indeed being conformed to the structures of the old cosmos. They have returned, for example, to the distinction of holy times from profane ones, being thus separated from Christ by losing his form in the life of their communities (4:9; 5:4). As to the identity of this Christ whose form the Galatians are now losing, the structure of the paragraph 4:12–20 provides yet another significant clue.

The substantive conclusion in 4:19 corresponds to the opening in 4:12. In that opening Paul has said that the Galatians are to become as he is, because he has become as they are. In the Note on v 12 we have seen that this double use of the word "as" is christological. When the Galatians received Paul as though he were Christ (v 14), they perceived the apostle to be as far beyond all religious differentiations as is Christ himself (3:28). The final key to the reading of v 19b is provided, then, by v 12 with its motif of double likeness. For the Galatians to become like Paul will involve their being once again parted from conformity to their old cosmos, just as Paul has been parted from conformity to his (6:14). And that in turn means that the Christ who is to be (re-)formed in their congregations is the Christ in whom there is neither Jew nor Gentile (3:28), for the corporate formation of this nonreligious Christ is a large part of what it means for the Galatian communities to be set right by the faith of Christ (2:16).

4:21–5:1 TWO GENTILE MISSIONS

TRANSLATION

4:21. Tell me, you who wish to live under the power of the Law! Do you really hear what the Law says? 22. For, while it does stand written in scripture that Abraham had two sons, one from the slave girl and one from the free woman, 23. the crucial point is that the son from the slave girl was

431

begotten by the power of the flesh, whereas the son from the free woman was begotten by the power of the promise. 24. These are allegorical matters; for these women are two covenants. One of these covenants is from Mount Sinai; it is bearing children into the state of slavery; it is Hagar. 25. Now this Hagar represents Mount Sinai in Arabia. Hagar also stands in the same oppositional column with the present Jerusalem, for like Hagar the present Jerusalem is in slavery together with her children. 26. But the Jerusalem that is above is free; she is our mother. 27. For it stands written in scripture:

> Rejoice, you barren woman, you who are not giving birth to children! Scream and cry aloud, you who are not in birth pains! For the children of the woman who is in lonely desolation are more numerous than the children of the woman who has a husband.

28. And you, brothers and sisters, are children of the promise in the pattern of Isaac. 29. Moreover, just as, at that time, the son begotten by the power of the flesh persecuted the son begotten by the power of the Spirit, so the same thing is true today. 30. But what does the scripture say? It says:

> Throw out the slave girl and her son. For the son of the slave girl will certainly not come into the inheritance along with the son of the free woman.

31. Therefore, brothers and sisters, we are not children of the slave girl. On the contrary, we are children of the free woman. 5:1. It was to bring us into the realm of freedom that Christ set us free. Stand your ground, therefore, and do not ever again take up the yoke of slavery!

LITERARY STRUCTURE AND SYNOPSIS

Paul marks the opening of the paragraph by the imperative verb "Tell me, you who wish to live under the power of the Law! Do you really hear what the Law says?" (4:21); and he signals the opening of the next paragraph with the expression "Look here! I, Paul, say to you . . ." (5:2; cf. 3:15). In 4:21–5:1 we have, then, a literary section focused on the interpretation of scripture, the second unit of that sort in the letter, the first being 3:6–4:7. The function of this unit in its broader context is a matter we have already considered (see Literary Structure and Synopsis of 3:6–9 and of 4:8–11). In both of the letter's exegetical sections Paul deals with the genetic identity of the Galatian churches.

The internal structure — indeed, the fundamental character — of the paragraph arises from the fact that in his reading of the stories of the births of Ishmael and Isaac to Hagar and Sarah respectively (Genesis 16–21) Paul finds a series of polar opposites arranged in two parallel columns. There are two mothers, opposites of one another by being slave and free, and there are two sons, opposites because they are born to these two mothers, but also because opposite powers begot them, the flesh and the promise. Other pairs of opposites continue the columnar polarization, and it is from the resulting columns of opposites that Paul draws his final exegetical conclusions in 4:30–5:1.

The full exhibition of the columnar opposites will be provided in Comment #45. Here we need only recognize, in anticipation, that in giving his reading of the birth stories in Genesis 16–21, Paul is correcting the list of polar opposites proposed by the Teachers from their own reading of those stories. In the main, then, Paul designs the paragraph to say one thing:

> Churches of two kinds are presently being born in the Gentile world. On the one hand, there are churches — relatively few in number — resulting from the enslaving Law-observant mission to Gentiles that the Teachers are carrying out, a mission they are pursuing with the approval of a vocal and powerful part of the Jerusalem church (cf. "the circumcision party" in 2:12). Indeed, as they pursue their mission — begetting children by circumcising the flesh (vv 23, 29) — they themselves have as one of their slogans "Jerusalem is our mother." On the other hand, there are other Gentile churches, large in number, stemming from the liberating circumcision-free mission being pursued by me, a mission I am now carrying out without the active and official sponsorship of the church in Jerusalem. Since, by your own birth you Galatian churches belong to this second group, you are to recall your true identity (4:31), you are to live it out by expelling the Teachers from your midst (4:30), and you are to refuse to return to the form of slavery represented by the Teachers' false gospel (5:1).

NOTES

4:21. *wish to live under the power of the Law!* The Teachers have been remarkably successful, changing even the Galatians' desires.

Do you really hear what the Law says? The negative, *ouk akouete,* "Do you not hear?," reveals the current state of affairs. Paul knows that the Teachers have already recounted to the Galatians the stories of the births of Ishmael and Isaac (see Note below on v 22: "the slave girl" and "the free woman"). He is equally sure, however, that in the true sense of hearing God's own voice in the Law, evident in the *Shema* ("Hear, O Israel"), the Galatians are not presently hearing and obeying the Law.

Striking is Paul's dual reference to the Law in 4:21, once negative — "wish to live under the power of the Law" — and once positive — "really hear what the Law says" — the latter being the first positive note about "the Law" in the letter. This dual reference is an unmistakable reflection of Paul's conviction that with the advent of Christ the Law is revealed to be a complex entity (cf. Rom 3:21), having the voice with which it pronounces a curse (3:10), but having also the gospel voice with which it speaks God's promise (3:8, 11; 4:27; cf. 5:14; 6:2; Comment #48).

22. *it does stand written in scripture.* For the reason just stated, Paul is worlds away from handing the Law over to the Teachers.[116] In the stories of Genesis 16–21 Paul finds a witness to the truth of the gospel.

Abraham. We have noted both that the Teachers are giving a central role to Abraham in their message and that, by contrast, Paul's interest in the patriarch is quite limited (Comment #33). The present paragraph supports that finding. After this initial reference Paul causes Abraham to drop from sight, not even allowing him to make a final appearance in the conclusion (4:31–5:1). Paul's interest is focused tightly on pairs, the two mothers and the two sons to whom they give birth.

two sons. Neither the Teachers nor Paul is interested in the fact that Abraham had numerous sons.

the slave girl . . . the free woman. Paul knows that in the Teachers' sermons the Galatians are already hearing about Hagar and Sarah. As Barrett has put it, an uninitiated reader of Gal 4:22 would ask: Which slave girl and which free woman?[117] The contrast between slave and free plays a role in the Teachers' reading of the patriarchal stories in Genesis 16–21. They say, that is, that the Law-observant descendants of Abraham through Sarah — the Isaacs — are free people, whereas Law-less Gentiles, descendants through Hagar — the Ishmaels — are slaves.[118]

23. *the crucial point is.* Paul uses the adversative particle *alla* not to draw a contrast with what precedes, but in order to correct the Teachers' reading of the patriarchal stories.[119]

begotten. Here and in v 29 Paul uses the verb *gennaô* with its masculine reference "to beget a child." In v 24 he uses the same verb with its feminine reference "to bear a child." The Genesis stories Paul is interpreting are focused on the significant births of Ishmael and Isaac (Abraham's fatherhood being assumed in both cases), but in these stories the births are consistently referred to by the verb *tiktô*, the verb *gennaô* being absent.[120] It seems that Paul has a reason for this substitution. He wishes to speak of the begetting of churches (Comment #45).

begotten by the power of the flesh . . . begotten by the power of the promise. Taking his linguistic cue neither from the Genesis stories nor from the Teachers, Paul coins two highly significant expressions by which he begins his correction of the Teachers' reading of those stories. He modifies his missioning verb "begot-

---

[116]*Pace* F. Watson, "In 5:14, Paul does claim that the kernel of the law . . . is a Christian possession, but his characteristic view in Galatians is to concede possession of the law to the Jewish community . . ." (*Paul,* 71).

[117]Barrett, "Allegory," 9.

[118]Whereas the stories in Genesis provide (in the LXX) the term *paidiskê,* "slave girl," the contrasting word *eleuthera,* "free woman," is not found there. It may have been introduced by Paul, but it is equally possible that the Teachers are responsible for it. That the Law (the line of Sarah and Isaac according to the Teachers) bestows freedom is an ancient tradition; see, for example, *m. 'Abot* 6:2: ". . . no man is free but he who occupies himself with the study of the Law." That the Ishmaelites rejected the Law (and thus freedom) became traditional; see, for example, *Lam. Rab.* 3,1,1.

[119]See Bouwman, "Schriftbeweis."

[120]The one instance of *gennaô,* Gen 17:20, has no relevance to the births of Ishmael and Isaac.

ten" with two contrasting prepositional phrases, *kata sarka*, lit. "according to the flesh," and *dia tês epaggelias*, lit. "through the promise." In v 28, turning explicitly from the Genesis stories to the genetic identity of the Galatian churches, he tells the members of these churches that they are children "*of* the promise" (not of the flesh), just as Isaac was. And in v 29, returning to the preposition *kata*, he continues the pattern of two contrasting phrases, speaking both of the Genesis stories and of the Galatians themselves by placing opposite one another two children: the child begotten "according to the flesh" (*kata sarka*) and the child begotten "according to the Spirit" (*kata pneuma*).

But the English expression "according to" does not convey Paul's intention. In v 29 he employs the second of the prepositional phrases in order to refer to the Spirit as the *power* that produced the birth of Isaac. It is also clear that Paul equates the Spirit whom God has sent into the Galatians' hearts (4:6) with the powerful promise by which God caused Isaac to be born (vv 23 and 29; cf. 3:14). With the expression "begotten *kata pneuma*," then, Paul refers to the Galatians as children who have been begotten by the power of the promised Spirit. And fundamentally, he speaks in the same way of the flesh. That is to say, in coining the phrases *kata sarka* and *kata pneuma*, Paul uses the preposition *kata* to mean "as a result of the power of."[121] Both the flesh and the promise/Spirit are powers able to produce children (see also Rom 9:8). Hence the translation given above.[122]

It seems to have been in combating the Teachers in his Galatian churches that Paul first coined as a pair the phrases "by the power of the flesh" and "by the power of the Spirit" (there is no such pair in 1 Thessalonians).[123] If so, we do well to consider the motif of power when, in others of Paul's letters, we encounter these phrases, and similar pairs, such as "Spirit" and "letter" in 2 Cor 3:6.

the flesh. Given the Teachers' demand for the covenantal circumcision of "the flesh" as the antidote to the lethal power of "the Impulsive Desire of the Flesh" (Comment #32), Paul probably intends a double meaning with his own expression "begotten by the power of the flesh." (a) Abraham begot Ishmael by the natural power of procreation, that is by the power of the human flesh as distinguished from the power of the divine God (cf. Isa 31:3). (b) The Teachers and others active in the Law-observant mission to Gentiles are begetting churches by the (impotent) power of the flesh. Circumcising the flesh, that is to say, as though

---

[121] See BAGD "*kata*," II. 5. δ.; cf. *anebên de kata apokalypsin*, "And I went up *as a result of* apocalyptic revelation," in Gal 2:2. Note also Paul's use of the phrase *kata sarka* with the verbs *oida* and *ginôsko* in 2 Cor 5:16 — to know *by the power of (or thanks to) the flesh* — and cf. the question of Alexander Aphrodisiensis whether it is the flesh itself or something in it that has the power of sensitive perception (cited by Schweizer, "*sarx*," 103). Cf. J. L. Martyn, *Issues*, 89–110.

[122] To translate "by the power of the flesh" and "by the power of the promise" (v 23) is to suggest that in this case Paul uses interchangeably the prepositions *kata* with accusative and *dia* with genitive. Perhaps in dictating the second phrase, Paul uses the preposition *dia* simply because he thinks of the promise as the means by which God stepped powerfully on the scene causing Abraham to have a child by Sarah. But if so, the promise is no less the power by which God acted than is the Spirit (so v 29).

[123] See especially Jewett, *Terms*, 95–116.

435

that were the potent antidote to the power of the Flesh, they are engaged in a human, religious exercise that no more involves the power of God than did the arrangement (via Hagar) by which Abraham and Sarah got Ishmael.

the promise (in v 29 the Spirit). By contrast God was the central actor in the birth of Isaac, that event taking place by the power of God's promise.[124]

24. *These are allegorical matters.* Used of a written text, the verb *allêgoreô* means either that the text is saying one thing while signifying another or that the interpreter is reading one thing in the text while finding the true signification in something the text does not literally say.[125] The import of Paul's sentence, the only explicit reference in the NT to allegory, is clear from what follows (cf. 1 Cor 5:6–8; 9:8–10; 10:1–10). For Paul, as for Philo, the two women in the Genesis story point beyond themselves.[126] For Paul, however, the two women are not timeless figures signifying timeless human qualities (Sarah as self-taught virtue and Hagar as imperfect training). For him, as for the Teachers, they are figures standing in two oppositional columns that tell two stories (Comment #45). Moreover, these stories are real in the sense that they refer to actual and unique developments both in Abraham's time and in the present time (notice "so also now" in v 29). Allegory is here tempered fundamentally by typology.[127]

for these women are two covenants. Paul does not draw the thought of two covenants from a literal reading of Genesis 16–21. Nothing is clearer in those stories than the singularity of the covenant God made with Abraham and the passing down of that covenant through Isaac and not through Ishmael. There is, thus, no Hagar covenant.

It is the Teachers who have emphasized the term "covenant," using it in the singular to refer to the nomistic covenant of Sinai and inviting the Galatian Gentiles to enter it. Sure that extending the Sinai covenant to Gentiles leads to their enslavement, Paul boldly finds two covenants in the Genesis stories, polar opposites of one another, one of them having to do with the circumcision of the flesh, the other representing the power of God's promise. Paul's thought of two covenants is a *novum*, introduced by the apostle himself as he composed this letter.[128]

One of these covenants is from Mount Sinai. With the particle *men*, "on the one hand," Paul prepares the reader for two balanced comments, one about the Hagar covenant and a second about the covenant represented by Sarah. In fact, speaking at length of the Hagar covenant (vv 24b–25), he never turns to a formal comment about the Sarah covenant as such (see Note on v 26).

When Paul says that the Hagar covenant is from Mount Sinai, he shows that he is working out his interpretation *from* present developments *to* the Genesis stories. For there is no reference to Sinai in those stories, or indeed in any other

---

[124]The literal absence of the term "promise" in the Genesis stories (and generally in the OT) is not a problem for Paul. See Comment #45.

[125]Büchsel, "*allêgoreô.*"

[126]Philo *de Post. Caini* 130, *de Cong.* 23, *de Mut.* 255.

[127]See Grässer, *Bund*, 70–71; Whitman, "Textual."

[128]On the expression "the new covenant in my blood" (Luke 22:20), see Grässer, *Bund*, 119. See also Paul's later references to "new covenant" and "old covenant" in 2 Cor 3:6, 14. That Galatians antedates 2 Corinthians is argued in Comment #24.

part of Genesis, just as there is no Hagar covenant there.[129] Paul reads the stories of Genesis 16–21 in light of what the Teachers are presently saying about the Sinaitic, covenantal Law. Indeed, noting that Paul does not use the term "Sinai" in his other letters, we may suppose that, along with "seed of Abraham" and "our mother in Jerusalem," the word "Sinai" plays a significant role in the Teachers' vocabulary.

it is bearing children into the state of slavery. Paul's putting the participle in the present tense — "is bearing children" — proves to be one of the major keys to his reading of the Genesis stories.[130] By using his missioning verb *gennaô* with its feminine meaning "to bear a child," Paul indicates what the Hagar/Sinai covenant is doing at the present time. Far from being a force for liberation, that covenant is now producing slaves by bearing children — founding churches among the Gentiles — into the state of slavery.

25. *Now this Hagar represents Mount Sinai in Arabia. Hagar also stands in the same oppositional column with the present Jerusalem.* That the line of Paul's thought in this verse is difficult to grasp can be seen in the fact that early copyists produced numerous and divergent readings.[131] Among these variations the important question is whether Paul mentioned Hagar. He dictated either

Mount Sinai is in Arabia, and that mountain is in the same oppositional column with the present Jerusalem, for . . . [the short reading]

or

Now this Hagar[132] represents Mount Sinai in Arabia, and she (Hagar) is in the same oppositional column with the present Jerusalem, for . . . [the long reading].

[129]It is possible to draw a loose connection between Hagar and Sinai by noting (a) that Hagar was driven out of Abraham's household into the wilderness of Beersheba, an area under Abraham's control (Gen 21:10–21, 31), and (b) that, when she provided a wife for her son Ishmael, both of them had moved on to Paran, the site at which the Israelites later camped when they *left* Sinai (Gen 21:21; Num 10:11–12; 12:16). What Paul is saying here provides no hint, however, that he made this connection. Given the work of the Teachers, it may have been enough for Paul that Hagar and her offspring lived in a wilderness, that Sinai is in the wilderness of Arabia (v 25), and that Sinai is the locus of the genesis of the Law. Apart from Stephen's speech in Acts 7, the word "Sinai" (*Sina*) appears in the NT only in Gal 4:24–25. Paul may very well draw it from the Teachers' sermons.

[130]Although "participles originally had no temporal function, but denoted only the *Aktionsart*" (BDF §339), in Hellenistic Greek a temporal dimension is sometimes detectable, as in the two present participles in Gal 3:5.

[131]The basic data are well presented by Mussner.

[132]In the short reading the neuter article *to* goes with *oros*, "mountain." In the long reading it indicates that Paul is simply repeating his reference to Hagar; for, as Borgen helpfully suggests, Paul's use of the neuter article has the sense of placing the word "Hagar" in quotation marks: "Now this 'Hagar,' mentioned in my previous sentence, represents Mount Sinai in Arabia" ("Hagar and Ishmael," 157). Cf. Eph 4:8–9.

The choice is difficult.[133] But both transcriptional probability and a consideration of the third verb in v 25 argue strongly for the long reading.

(a) Superior attestation indicates that Paul began his sentence with *de* ("and" or "now" or simply left untranslated), not with *gar*.[134] Finding, then, little sense in the assertion "*And* the name Hagar represents Mount Sinai in Arabia," an early scribe probably turned the assertion into an explanation by replacing the colorless *de* with *gar*: "*For* (*gar*) the name Hagar (*hagar*) represents Mount Sinai in Arabia." One now had a text in which the words *gar* and *hagar* were juxtaposed, and that led sometimes to the omission of *gar*, sometimes to the omission of *hagar*.[135] "The name Hagar" was probably in the text as Paul dictated it.

(b) In the last clause — lit. "for she [the present Jerusalem] is in slavery together with her children" — Paul states the conclusion that is to be drawn from the two preceding clauses. But how would a conclusion involving slavery be drawn if there were not a preceding reference to the slave Hagar? In short, Paul connects Jerusalem with slavery by saying that this Jerusalem stands in the same oppositional column with the slave Hagar, thus being connected — via Hagar — with the enslaving covenant of Sinai. The text dictated by Paul included "the name Hagar."[136]

Hagar also stands in the same oppositional column with. With the verb *systoicheô*, "to stand in the same column with," Paul explicitly refers to one of two columns of polar opposites, similar to those Aristotle attributes to the Pythagoreans (see Comment #41):

hot	cold
left	right
male	female

[133]It cannot be made simply by saying that the short reading is "a bare piece of geographical information of little interest to the readers or relevance to the context" (Barrett, "Allegory," 12). Mussner, for example, has made a strong case for the short reading, thus arriving at the following quite reasonable paraphrase: "To be sure, Mount Sinai lies in Arabia, to put matters geographically. In actuality, however, for my allegorical understanding, Mount Sinai corresponds to the present Jerusalem."

[134]Metzger 596; to this extent, p46 is to be followed.

[135]Metzger 596. One can also argue that once *gar* came into the text, the presence of *hagar* in v 24 led to changing *gar* into *hagar* in v 25 (so Borse).

[136]The two readings mentioned above construe quite differently the phrase "in Arabia." In the short reading Paul formulates a concession — "One has to admit that Mount Sinai is in Arabia, far removed from Jerusalem, but allegorically it is linked with the present Jerusalem, for . . ." In the long reading Paul makes a biting assertion — "Now this Hagar represents Mount Sinai in Arabia, for Arabia is the locale of the Arabs, Ishmaelite descendants of Hagar the slave. The Teachers, violating the baptismal confession of 3:28 by failing really to confess themselves to be former Jews, may celebrate what they take to be their absolute separation from the children of Ishmael. In fact, however, their observance of the Law connects them with Arabian Sinai, with the slave Hagar, with her son Ishmael, and thus with slavery!" And how would the Teachers have responded to such biting sarcasm? Drawing on Philo's interpretation of Hagar as "an Egyptian by birth, but a Hebrew *by her choice/rule of life*" (*de Abr.* 251), Borgen suggests that, seen in this way, Hagar (and Ishmael as well) could function for the Teachers — and may have functioned for them

and so on. For the Pythagoreans left and male stand in the same oppositional column. Similarly, Paul says that Hagar — the slave girl who represents the nomistic covenant of Sinai — stands in the same column with:

the present Jerusalem. In Comment #46 we will see reason to think that just as the Teachers are giving a key role in their discourses to the expression "descendants of Abraham" — a matter Paul takes up in his first exegetical section, 3:6–4:7 (see especially Comment #33) — so they are very probably employing with equal emphasis the slogan "Jerusalem is our mother," an expression that now elicits Paul's second exegetical section (see "our mother" in v 26).[137] In the Teachers' mouths the word "Jerusalem" is a metonym for the Jerusalem church, and that is a locution Paul also uses, being concerned not only to expose as ungodly the Law-observant mission to the Gentiles but also to do that in an ecclesiastically specific way (Comment #46). Insofar as the Jerusalem church is at present allowing itself to serve as sponsor — or at least as an acquiescing ally — for the Law-observant Gentile mission, it stands in the slavery column. Adding the adjective "present," Paul prepares the way for speaking of two Jerusalems, introducing them into his columns of polar opposites.

for like Hagar the present Jerusalem is in slavery together with her children. Paul writes simply, ". . . for is in slavery together with her children," thus presenting his reader with a syntactical problem. The subject of the verb could be either Hagar or the present Jerusalem.[138] Two factors inform our decision. First, Paul's use of the word "for" indicates that he intends to draw a conclusion from what precedes, not to repeat it. But he has already identified *Hagar* as a slave (vv 22–23), and he has already said that her covenant — the Law of Sinai — is even now bearing children into slavery. It would be redundant to make those identifications again in v 25b. Second, the relation of v 26a to v 25b sets up a direct contrast between two Jerusalems, one in slavery and one free. It is, then, the present Jerusalem that is in slavery together with her children.

together with her children. These children are Gentile churches founded in the Law-observant mission (Comment #45).

26. *But.* As we have seen earlier, Paul has begun in v 24 a standard syntactical unit that consists of *men . . . de,* "On the one hand . . . but on the other hand." Thus, one expects him to say,

On the one hand, the first of these two covenants is from Mount Sinai, is bearing children into slavery, is Hagar, and stands in the same	*But on the other hand*, the second of these covenants is from . . . is bearing children into freedom, is Sarah, and stands in the same

---

prior to Paul's writing his letter — as a model of the pagan who becomes by choice a proselyte, a Law-abiding Jew ("Hagar and Ishmael," 160–163).

[137] Although thinking presumably of the city of Jerusalem, Holtzmann made a significant suggestion in 1886: "The position of the agitators is clear: Their catchwords are 'descendants of Abraham' (3:16) and 'Jerusalem is our mother' (4:26). Paul's polemical exegesis shows what the agitators mean: The Old Testament knows nothing of a termination of the Law" (*Einleitung*, 243).

[138] With other exegetes Longenecker takes Hagar to be the subject.

oppositional column with the present Jerusalem; for like Hagar the present Jerusalem is in slavery together with her children.

oppositional column with the Jerusalem above; for like Sarah the Jerusalem above is free together with her children.

Paul is not concerned to achieve such grammatical balance. Once he has dropped the bomb by saying that there are two covenants, he does not return to the word "covenant," and he does not explicitly link it to Sarah (he does not even name Sarah).[139]

The reason for this grammatical asymmetry is easily discerned. Paul's chief interest does not lie with the two covenants, but rather with the two contrasting Jerusalems. It is in connection with them, then, that he finally employs the particle *de*, using it with its adversative force.

the Jerusalem that is above is free. There is ancient tradition that the old city of Jerusalem, subject to the ravages of war and famine, would be replaced one day by a Jerusalem made of indestructible jewels (Isa 54:10–12; cf. *1 Enoch* 90:28–29). There is even the apocalyptic notion that God prepared a transcendent Jerusalem at the beginning of creation (*2 Apoc. Bar.* 4:2–6). At present invisible (4 Ezra 7:26; cf. 10:38–54), this transcendent Jerusalem is ready to descend from heaven at the end-time (Rev 3:12; 21:2, 10). Finally, the author of Daniel placed the elect people in heaven, although he knew that they were physically on earth (Dan 7:13, 18; cf. 1QM 12:1–5).[140]

Paul echoes traditions such as these, but just as, speaking of "the present Jerusalem," he means the Jerusalem church, so with "the Jerusalem that is above" he refers not to a heavenly city, but to a heavenly church that stands in contrast with the empirical church located in the earthly city of Jerusalem.[141] Paul may picture this church as the community that is both above and future, being ready to descend to earth at the parousia.[142]

In Gal 4:26, then, Paul envisions a distinctly apocalyptic contrast. On the earthly stage he sees the Jerusalem church, at present satisfied to house the False

---

[139]In 2 Corinthians 3 Paul gives a quite different picture of two covenants. See Furnish, *II Corinthians*; Grässer, *Bund*, 77–95.

[140]See Oepke, and cf. van Oort, *Jerusalem*.

[141]The contrast, then, is entirely inner-church, not spiritual church versus ethnic synagogue. Regarding the "supernatural conception of Israel put forth by rabbinic Judaism," see Neusner, "Really 'Ethnic'?" (303).

[142]If this is Paul's intention in Gal 4:26, there is a *partial* parallel in Phil 3:20: ". . . their minds [the minds of those who preach circumcision] are set on earthly things. But our true existence as a body of citizens [our *politeuma*] is located in heaven, and from heaven we await a Savior, the Lord Jesus Christ." "Citizenship" is too abstract to serve by itself as a translation of *politeuma* in this text. Paul means that the church's existence as a *group of citizens* is in heaven. On earth, therefore, they are away from the locale from which they derive their citizen identity. For the concrete reference to a "corporate body of citizens" resident in a city that is foreign to them, see epigraphic evidence cited in IV. under *politeuma* in LSJ. In Philippians the image is that of an identifiable group of persons who, being literally resident in a place that is foreign to them (earth), derive their identity from their existence as a body of citizens (*politeuma*) with another home (heaven). In Galatians the image is that of churches on earth that are descended from a church in heaven.

Brothers with their ungodly support of the enslaving Law-observant mission to Gentiles. On the heavenly stage, in stark contrast, he sees the heavenly Jerusalem, that is to say the true church of God.[143] The identity of the Galatian churches is not determined by a line of descent from any entity that is earthly and past. For the heavenly Jerusalem church, not the earthly church in Jerusalem, is the mother of the Galatian churches.

our mother.[144] The word "mother" is applied neither to Hagar nor to Sarah in the Genesis texts. As suggested in Comment #46, however, the Teachers have very probably employed it to refer to the church in Jerusalem, perhaps drawing on two strands of tradition. One of these speaks of Jerusalem as the mother of her inhabitants.[145] The other amalgamates the figure of mother Jerusalem with that of mother Sarah. According to this tradition, Sarah/Jerusalem will one day nourish with her milk not only her native children but also the Gentiles.[146] The Teachers apparently say, then, that the Jerusalem church, in sponsoring the Law-observant mission, is properly mothering the Gentiles in the end-time.

In contrast, Paul insists that the mother of the Galatians — and of himself — is the Sarah/Jerusalem church in heaven, thus virtually repeating the apocalyptic motif struck in the first sentence of his letter.[147] He is an apostle, that is to say a person sent out on a mission not by any earthly church, certainly not by the one in Jerusalem, but rather by Jesus Christ and God the Father. The Galatians' birth identity is analogous to Paul's apostolic identity, for their mother is God's promissory church in heaven — *she* is *our* mother — in the sense that they were born by the power of God's promise in the circumcision-free mission to the Gentiles.

27. *For it stands written in scripture.* As further proof of the identity of the Galatians' mother, Paul cites one of the Zion poems in Isaiah (of no service to the Teachers, it is surely a text of Paul's choice):[148]

Rejoice, you barren woman, you who are not giving birth to children! Scream and cry aloud, you who are not in birth pains! For the children of the woman who is in lonely desolation are more numerous than the children of the woman who has a husband (Isa 54:1).[149]

---

[143]As the partial parallel in Phil 3:20 suggests, Paul does not expect that the Galatians will ascend to the Jerusalem church that is in heaven (*pace* H. D. Betz 246). His attention is focused on the assertion that the Galatians' mother church is in God's hands in heaven, not in the hands of the False Brothers in Jerusalem.

[144]The word *hêtis*, the indefinite relative, is here used as the equivalent of the simple relative *hê*, "she."

[145]Isa 51:17–20; 54:1 (cf. Gal 4:27!); 2 *Apoc. Bar.* 3:1–3; 10:16; Matt 23:37; 4 Ezra 10:7; *Tg. Cant.* 8:5.

[146]On Sarah as the representative of Jerusalem, in that — at Abraham's request — she nourishes Gentiles with her milk, see *Pesiq. Rab Kah.* 22:1.

[147]On Paul's including himself among those mothered by the heavenly church of God, see Comment #36.

[148]One element in the connection of Isaiah's text to the stories of Gen 16–21 is the motif of sterility (*steira*, Gen 11:30; Isa 54:1).

[149]Paul follows a Greek text firmly in the Septuagintal tradition. See Stanley, *Scripture,* 248 n231.

His own interpretation of this text can be seen only after we have briefly considered it in its original setting.

After the destructive invasion by the Babylonians, those enemies of Israel were saying in effect:

> Look at Jerusalem! Her husband, the god who would be able to make her grow in size and power, has deserted her. She is like a lonely woman without a husband, desolate and incapable of multiplying the number of her inhabitants.

The prophet believes this taunt to be partly true. Given her sins, God has indeed momentarily abandoned Jerusalem. To all appearances she is like a woman whose husband has left her desolate, without children and thus without a future. Now, however, Isaiah hears God's comforting voice ("Rejoice, you barren woman . . ."). God's angry withdrawal is overcome by his unquenchable love. Jerusalem's fortunes will soon be reversed ("For the children . . . more numerous . . .").[150] She is presently to be visited by God, and will soon be a mother city compelled greatly to enlarge her borders in order to house an enormous number of offspring.

In Isaiah's prophecy four notes call for emphasis: (a) There are not two women and two cities. On the contrary, the woman of the poem represents a single city, Jerusalem; and the two contrasting pictures of this woman — first in desolation, then in fecund affluence and power — represent two sequential periods in the life of this city.[151] (b) The contrast between the two pictures is stated in terms reminiscent of Sarah, for, having experienced a period of barrenness, the woman of Isaiah 54 is promised that she will become a mother blessed with a multitude of children (see especially Isa 54:3). (c) The cause of the woman's barrenness was her having been without a husband, that is to say without God's sustaining presence. (d) Renewed by God's return, Sarah-like Jerusalem is pictured by Isaiah in supra-terrestrial glory. She is, as it were, a heavenly Jerusalem, for her expanded walls and gates will be constructed by God from precious stones (Isa 54:11–12).

Why does Paul turn from Genesis 16–21 to this prophetic text with its contrasting pictures? We cannot give an incontestable answer, but a suggestion can be made with some confidence. Paul turns to Isa 54:1 because its pictures supply him with pairs of opposites with which he can supplement those he has already found in the Genesis stories, thus continuing the contrast between the Jerusalem church's Law-observant mission to Gentiles and the circumcision-free mission in which God is himself active.

In Isaiah's poem there is, first, *barrenness versus fecundity*. Continuing from Gal 4:25–26 the picture in which both Jerusalem churches are mothers, both

---

[150]In the first two lines of Isaiah's poem God speaks directly to Jerusalem; in the third God speaks about that city.

[151]When the Targum to Isa 54:1 identifies the temporarily barren woman with Jerusalem, it only makes explicit what is already clear in the original poem.

having missions that are extensions of themselves, Paul now adds a new motif from Isa 54:1. To the False Brothers the circumcision-free mission is a Godless enterprise and, for that reason, barren. In reality, says Paul, the circumcision-free mission, enjoying the blessing of God, is vastly more fecund than the Law-observant mission that is an extension of the present and earthly Jerusalem church.[152]

Second, there is *having a husband versus having no husband*. With this motif Paul enriches his columns of opposites. The mission extending from the heavenly Jerusalem church is not only astonishingly fecund. It also has no husband, that is to say no official sponsor *on earth*. And the Gentile mission extending from the earthly Jerusalem church is not only relatively arid. It also has in that church its husband, its official and visible sponsor (Comment #46).

It is true that in combining the two images of Isa 54:1, Paul speaks of the earthly Jerusalem church in a way that is literally inconsistent. This Jerusalem church is the *mother* who in her Law-observant mission is bearing few children; this church is also the *husband* who sponsors and — on a human level — legitimizes that mission. Such inconsistency, however, is characteristic of allegorical interpretation. The point is that the earthly Jerusalem church extends nothing other than itself in the enslaving Law-observant mission (v 25), doing that both by mothering that mission and by serving as its husband-like sponsor.

With that Law-observant mission the Galatians have, properly speaking, nothing to do, having been born in the mission of the Jerusalem church that is above, free, and (in earthly terms) unsponsored. In Isa 54:1, then, Paul hears God speaking comforting words to the Galatians, and also to himself and his evangelizing coworkers, precisely at the expense of the earthly Jerusalem church in its support of the Law-observant mission.

28. *And you, brothers and sisters, are children of the promise in the pattern of Isaac.* In Isa 54:1 Paul has heard the comforting words God directs to the Pauline, circumcision-free mission and the words of judgment God speaks about the Law-observant mission. Now, returning to the terms of the stories of Genesis 16–21, Paul speaks directly to the Galatians, again referring to their genetic identity by naming the power that is active in the circumcision-free mission, God's gospel-promise.

you. A number of manuscripts have "we" rather than "you."[153] But that reading probably reflects the early interpretation in which Gal 4:21–5:1 was taken to speak of a contrast between Christians ("we") and Jews (Introduction §16 and §17). This reading is surely incorrect.[154]

in the pattern of Isaac. The way in which Paul here uses the phrase *kata Isaak*, lit. "according to Isaac," reflects his typological exegesis of the stories in Genesis 16–21. He does not say, "And you, brothers and sisters, are children in the line

---

[152]Did the False Brothers and the Teachers speak of Sarah/the Jerusalem church as a woman who is fecund? Cf. the picture of Asenath as a City of Refuge for all Gentiles who repent (*JosAs* 15:7; 16:16; 19:5).

[153]Metzger 597.

[154]See Comment #45 and J. L. Martyn, *Issues*, 191–208.

that extends from Abraham *through* Isaac," as though his intention were to tell the Galatians that they have been included in a line extending through the centuries from Abraham, Isaac, and Jacob. His exegesis is thoroughly *punctiliar,* in the sense that he sees a divine correspondence between two *points,* God's action in the birth of Isaac and God's action in the birth of the Galatian congregations (cf. Comment #37).

29. *Moreover, just as, at that time, the son begotten by the power of the flesh persecuted the son begotten by the power of the Spirit, so the same thing is true today.*

Moreover. Whereas v 28 was a positive reference to the Galatians' identity, v 29 is on its face a negative reference to persecution. For that reason Paul begins v 29 with the adversative *alla,* "but rather." At a deeper level Paul finds in the fact that the Galatians are being persecuted additional evidence of their identity. Hence the translation "Moreover."

just as, at that time . . . so the same thing is true today. See the Note above on "in the pattern of Isaac," and cf. 1 Cor 10:6–7; Rom 5:21.

the son begotten by the power of the flesh . . . the son begotten by the power of the Spirit. In Paul's typological interpretation the contemporary Ishmael (begotten by circumcising the flesh!) consists of the churches founded in the Law-observant mission to Gentiles, and the contemporary Isaac (begotten by the power of the promised Spirit) consists of the churches founded in Paul's own mission (v 28).

persecuted. Genesis 21 includes a picture in which Ishmael innocently "plays" or "jests" with his half brother Isaac (Gen 21:9; Hebrew text, *měṣaḥēq;* LXX, *paizonta*). In some Jewish traditions the verb was taken to indicate hostility and even maliciousness on Ishmael's part. It is said, for example, that, while pretending merely to play, Ishmael shot dangerous arrows in the direction of Isaac.[155] On the story level of his typology Paul presupposes one of these traditions.

Everything we have seen thus far suggests that on the contemporary level Paul thinks of representatives of the Law-observant mission persecuting representatives of his own mission. Can this be his intention?

One can argue against this reading by pointing to the fact that Paul uses the verb "persecute" in Gal 1:13 and 23 (cf. Phil 3:6; 1 Cor 15:9) to refer to his own activity when, as a Pharisee, he persecuted the young church. It would follow that Paul speaks here of *Jewish* persecution of the Jewish sect that came to be called *Christians.* Additional support can be found in Paul's reference to the motif of inheritance in v 30, where he cites Gen 21:10, ". . . for the son of the slave girl will certainly not come into the inheritance along with the son of the free woman." In Matt 21:33–44, for example, we can detect early Christian tradition

---

[155]*Gen. Rab.* 53:11; cf. *Tg. Ps.-J.* Gen 21:10; Ishmael "made war" on Isaac. See Le Déaut, "Traditions targumique," 28–48; Ginzberg, *Legends,* 5.246 n211. Callaway is right to say that "in all of these midrashic traditions both Hagar and Ishmael assume a villainy which they do not have in the biblical stories, and Isaac and Sarah appear as victims" ("Midrashic Traditions," 99).

in which the inheritance was said to be taken from the Jews and given to the Christians. Paul's line of thought, in short, could be that Jewish persecution of the church (v 29) is bringing God's judgment in the form of the Jews' being disinherited (v 30; cf. 1 Thess 2:15–16). This is, in fact, the interpretation followed by the vast majority of exegetes. It does not fit well, however, into the reading of Gal 4:21–27 suggested above. Moreover, on the basis of that reading, an alternative interpretation of the persecution motif almost suggests itself.

Paul may have assumed that the Galatians would be guided by his sequence of vignettes reflecting the history of the Jerusalem church's dealings with him and his work (Comment #46). It is easy to imagine that he understood the False Brothers to be persecutors of himself (2:4; cf. 2 Cor 11:26). The circumcision party in the Jerusalem church played a significant role in the persecution-like experience he had to endure in Antioch (2:12). The Teachers, the latest in the line of actors whose energies have been directed against his mission, claim the sponsorship of the Jerusalem church, and are so successful in his Galatian churches as to throw him back into labor pains (4:19). Moreover, one aspect of the Teachers' achievement probably lies in their success at persuading the Galatians to dismiss the catechetical instructors put in place by Paul before he departed (6:6), a move Paul could very well understand as persecution not only of himself but also of the Galatian churches, leaving them without faithful guidance in the truth of the gospel.[156]

Thus, Paul's attention may have been drawn to the Jewish tradition about Ishmael's persecution of Isaac because of the history of his relations with the False Brothers, the circumcision party in the Jerusalem church, and climactically the Teachers. All of these people and their converts are not only begotten by the circumcision of the flesh. As Paul sees it, they are also actively opposed to the work God is carrying out in Paul's mission. In their labors he sees an odious persecution of his churches, children begotten by the power of the Spirit.

30. *But what does the scripture say? It says "Throw out the slave girl and her son. For the son of the slave girl will certainly not come into the inheritance along with the son of the free woman."* We saw in 3:8 that Paul portrays scripture itself as an actor with a speaking part in the divine-human drama. He has begun the present exegetical paragraph with the same view, asking the Galatians whether they have really heard the voice of Law/scripture. Now, in a similar vein, he brings the paragraph to a close by asking the Galatians what scripture is saying directly to them in their present circumstances (cf. 1 Cor 10:11).

He then answers his own question by quoting Gen 21:10, the verse immedi-

---

[156]The linearity of the sequence of Jerusalem vignettes may be reflected in the fact that Paul puts the verb "persecute" in the imperfect tense. Note also Paul's reference to persecution in 5:11 (the next instance of the verb "persecute" after 4:29). Having referred to the ringleader of the Teachers who have invaded his Galatian churches (5:10), Paul seems then to say that the Teachers are persecuting him, and that they would cease doing that if he would circumcise the members of his Gentile churches. So Sieffert, Zahn, Lagrange, and in part Burton (266).

ately following the one he has just interpreted in Gal 4:29.[157] A text in which the most likely reading in the LXX follows the Hebrew, Gen 21:10 can be rendered into English as follows:

> . . . and she [Sarah] said to Abraham, "Throw out this slave girl and her son. For the son of this slave girl will not come into the inheritance along with my son Isaac."[158]

Paul makes two changes, both based on his certainty that the scripture speaks to the Galatians in their present setting. First, for him the words are not spoken by Sarah, but rather by scripture; hence, they refer to "the slave girl," not to "this slave girl." Second, because the scriptural command has to do primarily with "the slave girl" and "the free woman" about whom Paul has been speaking since v 22, he provides the words "the son of the free woman" in place of "my son Isaac."

the slave girl and her son . . . the son of the free woman. The slave girl is the Teachers, and her son is the members of the Galatian churches who have completely embraced the Teachers' theology (5:4), actively participating in their Law-observant mission, probably replacing the catechetical instructors left in the Galatian churches by Paul (6:6). The son of the free woman is the Galatians as children of the heavenly Jerusalem, churches born in the mission empowered by the promised Spirit.

Throw out. If for the sake of the truth of the gospel the apostle can and must pronounce a curse on the Teachers (1:8–9), then the Galatian churches' adherence to the truth of the gospel requires them to expel from their congregations the Teachers (presumably with their firmly committed followers; cf. 1 Cor 5:13).

will certainly not come into the inheritance along with the son of the free woman. For Paul scripture declares that Gentiles converted in the Law-observant mission will not share in the inheritance (that is, the Spirit; see Note on 3:18) along with those converted in his own mission.[159]

31. *Therefore, brothers and sisters, we are not children of the slave girl. On the contrary, we are children of the free woman.* Once more Paul speaks of the Galatians' identity—and of his as well—by referring to their mother. She is the church of God that is in heaven and that sponsors the mission on earth in which the powerful Spirit of God's Son is begetting liberated churches among the Gentiles.

5:1 *realm of freedom.* Paul emphatically begins the sentence with the noun

---

[157]Gen 21:10 is the only verse Paul actually quotes from the Genesis texts which he has been at pains to interpret from Gal 4:22 onward, suggesting that he places extraordinary weight on this command.

[158]Perhaps being too cautious, Verhoef says that we cannot determine whether the text Paul used was identical with the present LXX (*Geschreven*, 104); see also Stanley, *Scripture*, 248–251.

[159]*Pace* Broer, "Gal 4,21–31." In *Tg. Ps.-J.* Gen 22:1 there is a tradition in which Isaac and Ishmael are involved in a dispute over the inheritance from Abraham; cf. Gaston, "Enemies," 406.

"freedom" in the dative case, a locution which early scribes found less than clear, as the textual variants show.[160] The precise force Paul intends with this dative is difficult to determine, but an argument can be made for Smyth's dative "of place whither"; hence "to bring us into the realm of freedom."[161] For the best guide is that given by Paul himself in the numerous expressions by which he speaks of realms of power (see Comments #3 and #39). In 2:4 and 5:13, for example, Paul uses the noun "freedom" to characterize a space, the realm that is the result of God's act in Christ. God has created this realm by delivering human beings from slavery under the power of specific slave masters — the Law's curse, Sin, the Law itself, the elements of the cosmos, and, as Paul will show in 5:13–24, the Impulsive Desire of the Flesh. Freedom, then, is neither an abstraction nor a thing that an individual can possess as though it were a right. Freedom is the condition given by God in the realm of deliverance from slavery, the space God has created by calling the church into being (Comment #22).

Christ set us free. Everything said in 4:21–31 about the mission God has entrusted to Paul, about Paul's work in that mission, and about the birth of the Galatian churches presupposes that it is Christ who is active in that mission and thus in its effects. Because Christ's redemptive act is past (3:13), present (4:19), and future (5:5), the gospel of Christ is "news of victory that puts victory into effect."[162]

Stand your ground, therefore, and do not ever again take up. Prior to their receiving the liberating Spirit of Christ, it would have been futile to exhort the Galatians. Now exhortation is both possible and necessary, for in setting the Galatians free from their old slave masters God has turned them into addressable communities (4:30). In fact, Paul begins the hortatory section of his letter at 5:13, but as a foretaste, he closes his exegesis of Genesis 16–21 with a hortatory *oun* ("therefore") and two imperative verbs.

the yoke of slavery! With the image of a yoke Paul intensifies the motif of enslavement that he has repeatedly identified as the universal state of human affairs.[163] By the power of the gospel of Christ, the Galatians have been freed from this universally enslaving yoke, but they will return to it if they take up the observance of the Law as though that were salvific (4:3, 24–25; Comment #41).

COMMENT #45
THE COVENANTS OF HAGAR AND SARAH:
TWO COVENANTS AND TWO GENTILE MISSIONS

GAL 4:21–5:1 AND GENESIS 16–21

Gal 4:21–5:1, the letter's second exegetical argument (the first being 3:6–4:7), is framed by two questions: "Tell me, you who wish to live under the power of the

---

[160]The absence of a grammatical connective between 4:31 and 5:1 also played a role in the emergence of variants. See Burton; Metzger 597.

[161]Smyth, *Greek Grammar*, §1531.

[162]Keck, "Introduction," 360.

[163]Note Sir 40:1: "Much labor was created for every human being, and a heavy yoke lies upon the children of Adam" (cf. Jeremiah 27–28).

Law! Do you really hear what the Law says?" (v 21) and "But what does the scripture say?" (v 30). The vocabulary with which Paul constructs this argument shows that he is interpreting the texts of Genesis 16 and 21, while taking side glances at Genesis 15 and 17, and developing the motif of promise from Genesis 15 and 18.[164] To a considerable extent Paul stays close to the Genesis texts (adding in v 27 the quotation of Isa 54:1).[165]

In the stories of Genesis 16–21 there are, however, weighty matters to which Paul gives no attention at all. In Genesis 17, for example, God explicitly defines the covenant he is making with Abraham. It is the commandment of circumcision (Gen 17:10). In the Genesis stories that is a crucial matter, yet one to which, in constructing his exegesis, Paul makes no explicit reference (but see the discussion of "flesh" under "to beget a child" below). Like all other exegetes, he is selective.[166]

He is also creative. As surely as the texts of Genesis 15–21 include motifs he chooses to suppress, so they also fail to supply him with some of the terms and expressions that are central to his interpretation. He does not hesitate to provide them himself, and in every verse:

Gal 4:22 two (sons)
          the free woman
Gal 4:23 was begotten by the power of the flesh . . . (was begotten) by the
          power of the promise[167]
Gal 4:24 allegorical matters
          two covenants
          Sinai
          bearing children into the state of slavery

---

[164]On the vocabulary, see J. L. Martyn, "Hagar and Sarah," in Meyer Festschrift; Luz, Geschichtsverständnis (not convincing on Gal 4:29–30 but otherwise helpful).

[165]See Verhoef, Geschreven, 89–104, 167–168, 200–211; Koch, Schrift, 204–211; Hays, Echoes, 111–121.

[166]Paul's silence regarding the definition of the Abrahamic covenant as circumcision is only one facet of his apparently arbitrary exegesis of Gen 16–21. If one leaves aside Paul's interpretive point of departure, the two Gentile missions in his own time, one can see that Ben Chorin is justified in saying that in Gal 4:21–5:1 Paul turns the patriarchal stories completely upside down (Paulus, 132). Cf. Klein, "A more brutal paganizing of what professes to be redemptive history can scarcely be imagined" (Rekonstruktion, 168). In order to see what Paul is talking about and what he is not talking about, one considers not only his silence regarding weighty factors in the Genesis texts but also his silence regarding equally weighty factors in his own setting: He refers nowhere to the people he will later call, in Rom 9:3, "my kinsmen by race." He does not mention the gospel mission to this people (contrast Gal 2:7, 9). And he does not speak of those who pursue that mission, while gladly accepting as part of God's work the circumcision-free mission to Gentiles.

[167]The noun "promise" and the verb "to promise" do not occur in the Abraham stories Paul is interpreting; indeed, they are scarcely to be found in the OT. But when, speaking of Isaac, Paul coins the expression "begotten by the power of the promise," he is certainly developing a key theological motif of these stories. The birth of Isaac happens only as a result of God's assuring word and, indeed, because of God's advent: "I will surely return to you in the spring, and Sarah your wife will have a son" (Gen 18:10; cf. 18:14; 15:4–5).

Gal   (entire; note particularly the following:)
4:25–26 is located in the same oppositional column with the present
         Jerusalem;
         is in slavery
         children
         the Jerusalem above
         mother
Gal 4:27 (Isa 54:1 with its two contrasts, a woman who is barren versus a
         woman who is fecund, and a woman who has a husband versus a
         woman who has none)
Gal 4:28 children of the promise
Gal 4:29 the one begotten by the power of the flesh persecuted the one
         (begotten) by the power of the Spirit
Gal 4:30 of the free woman
Gal 4:31 children of the free woman.

Why does Paul suppress certain motifs in his texts, while creating others? The best guidance lies, first, in several of Paul's added verbs: "to stand in the same oppositional column with," "to beget a child," and "to bear a child." Paul's unprecedented expression "two covenants" and his two Jerusalems provide further clues. The last of these demands its own Comment (#46).

THE VERB "TO STAND IN THE SAME OPPOSITIONAL COLUMN WITH"

Using the technical term *systoicheô*, Paul says in v 25 that Hagar "stands in the same oppositional column with" the present Jerusalem (regarding columns of opposites, see Comment #41). In its context that sounds like a correction. Knowing that the Teachers are interpreting the Genesis stories by means of columnar pairs of opposites, Paul is concerned to put the columns in correct order. We might paraphrase v 25, then, as follows (with one clause from v 24):

> In their reading of the stories of Abraham, Sarah, Hagar, Isaac, and Ishmael, the Teachers carry out their interpretation by referring to columns of polar opposites. Well and good. They tell you, for example, that, standing opposite the free woman Sarah, Hagar is in the same column with slavery, and so she is. But they have not taught you to hear the Law fully and accurately (v 21). For they have hid from you the astonishing truth: Hagar, the slave girl, represents Mount Sinai, the locus of the genesis of the Law; *and* she stands in the same column with the present Jerusalem. One can see that because the present Jerusalem is like the slave Hagar in that she is even now in slavery, together with the children to whom she is giving birth.

Noting this correction, and drawing on exegetical observations made in the Notes and in Comment #46, we can display, with a reasonable degree of probability, the columns of opposites the Teachers are finding in Genesis 16–21 (the Teachers neither cite nor interpret Isa 54:1):

Hagar	Sarah
slave	free
Ishmael	Isaac
the son who is not the true descendant of Abraham, having come through the slave girl, Hagar	the true Law-observant descendant of Abraham, as one can see from the fact that he was born on the day of the Feast of the First Fruits
Abraham's illicit descendants via Hagar, the Ishmaels	Abraham's true descendants via Sarah, the Isaacs
those who, uncircumcised in their flesh, are strangers to the covenant of Sinai and thus subject to the Impulsive Desire of the Flesh (Comments #32 and #49)	those who constitute the people of God, circumcised in their flesh, observant of the covenant of Sinai, and thus free of the Impulsive Desire of the Flesh (see Note on 5:16)
Gentiles	Jews
the half-converted Gentile churches of the Pauline orb that are, properly speaking, divorced from the mother church in Jerusalem, having been denied by Paul God's greatest gift, the Law confirmed to eternity by the Messiah, Jesus	the true church of the circumcised — "our mother Jerusalem" — and the offspring to which she is giving birth in our Law-observant mission to Gentiles

When we have analyzed the major clues to Paul's own interpretation, we will be able to see the columns of opposites as he senses them.[168]

---

[168]No passage in the letter has had a more interesting — and a more misleading — history of interpretation than 4:21–5:1. Although there have been some variations and a few reservations, one reading has dominated through the centuries, and it can be summarized in six points: (a) The pattern of two oppositional columns is accented. (b) The prepositional phrases by which this polar opposition is largely expressed — "according to the flesh" versus "according to the Spirit" etc. — are taken to be adjectival identity markers, differentiating from one another two existent peoples. There *is* a people "according to the flesh," and there *is* a people "according to the Spirit." (c) These two existent peoples are understood to be respectively the Jews and the Christians; the polarity of the passage is thus focused specifically on Judaism and Christianity. (d) Judaism is consequently characterized as the religion of slavery and Christianity as the religion of freedom. (e) Verse 29 is taken to be a reference to the synagogue's mid-first-century persecution of the church. (f) Verse 30 is then read as an affirmation of the resulting supersession — according to God's will — of the synagogue by the church. Henceforth Christians are God's people; Jews are not. See J. L. Martyn, "Hagar and Sarah," in Meyer Festschrift.

THE VERBS "TO BEGET A CHILD" (4:23, 29) AND "TO BEAR A CHILD" (4:24)

In the Note on v 23 we saw that in his interpretation of the births of Ishmael and Isaac Paul avoids altogether the birthing verb used in Genesis 16–21, *tiktô*, putting in its place *gennaô* used with its masculine meaning "to beget" in vv 23 and 29, and with its feminine meaning "to bear" in v 24. Is this properly speaking a substitution, and if it is, why should Paul make it?

Leaving aside Gal 4:21–5:1 (and the different case in Rom 9:11), one notes that Paul employs the verb "to beget," linking it with the noun "child/children," only in speaking of the genesis of Christians and of Christian churches through the power of the gospel entrusted to him by God:

> I appeal to you for my child Onesimus, whom I *begot* in my imprisonment (Phlm 10).

> I do not write this to make you ashamed, but to admonish you as my beloved children. For though you have countless guardians in Christ [Apollos, for example], you do not have many fathers. For I *begot* you in Christ Jesus through the gospel (1 Cor 4:14–15).[169]

In light of these examples one notes the absence of the verb "to beget" in Gal 4:19, "My children, I am going through the pain of giving birth to you all over again, until Christ is formed in your congregations." There Paul calls the Galatian churches his children, but the work of the Teachers makes it impossible for him to say simply that at a point in the past he begot them (Comment #44).

Passing, however, from 4:19 to 4:21–5:1, we see that Paul suppresses his mission-oriented verb "to beget" only for a moment. When he turns to the exegesis of the birth stories in Genesis 16 and 21, he brings that verb to the fore, as we have noted, even though it is not found in the texts he is interpreting. Why? Clouded as it is, the real begetting and birth — and consequent identity — of the Galatian churches remains his subject in 4:21–5:1, as a paraphrase of v 28 demonstrates:

> Brothers and sisters, given the identity of your mother, the Sarah-like heavenly Jerusalem, your own identity is clear: you are children begotten by the power of God's promise, just as Isaac was (cf. v 31).

Even in speaking so positively of the Galatians' birth identity, however, Paul does not leave behind the dark and foreboding tones of 4:19, as we can see from the fact that he speaks of two begettings and of two births.

Two Begettings. Not only does Paul employ his missioning verb "to beget" in

---

[169]Birth was a metaphor employed very widely for conversion. See the passages about proselytizing in *b. Yebam.* 22a and *Cant. Rab.* 1,3,3; and note in the latter passage the use of the verb "to form," which may be compared with the use of the corresponding verb in Gal 4:19. See also Kuhn, "*prosêlytos*"; Nock, *Conversion*; Gaventa, *Darkness*; Malherbe, *the Thessalonians*.

the interpretation of texts that lack it. He also modifies it with two prepositional phrases, thus producing a pair of opposites that he introduces into his own oppositional columns: "(Ishmael) begotten by the power of the flesh" and "(Isaac) begotten by the power of the promise/the Spirit" (vv 23 and 29). On the contemporary level the Galatians are the Isaacs, begotten by God's powerful promise, the Spirit (cf. 4:29 with 4:6 and 3:3). Some other contemporaries are the Ishmaels, being begotten by the power of the flesh. Who are these other people?

Our first clue to the identity of this group is the term "flesh."[170] In the Genesis story Ishmael is the son produced by the physical union between Abraham and Hagar, a human act rather than a divine one, and thus a deed of the flesh rather than of the Spirit (cf. Isa 31:3). All of this lies in the ancient narrative. When Paul coins the expression "begotten by the power of the flesh," however, he reflects a contemporary reality, namely the Teachers' demand that Gentiles enter the Sinai covenant by circumcising the flesh (3:3 and Comment #32).

One may pause to note that "to beget by circumcision" could be a way of referring to the proselytizing strain in some Jewish traditions (Comment #6). But the activities reflected in those traditions were probably unknown to the Galatians.[171] Why should Paul speak to the Galatians about a matter regarding which they very probably know nothing? Moreover, Paul has referred in 4:19 to the missionary activity of the Teachers, not to that of Jewish proselytizers.

In coining the oppositional expressions having to do with the siring of a child, then, Paul employs the verb by which he elsewhere refers to missionary labors. He does not speak, therefore, of the begetting of individuals, but of the begetting of churches. In short, modifying the verb "to beget" with the polarized phrases "by the power of the flesh" and "by the power of the promise/the Spirit," Paul speaks of two different ways in which churches are being begotten among Gentiles at the present time, and thus of two different Gentile missions.[172] This interpretation is further supported when we note Paul's use of the feminine motif of a mother giving birth to a child.

Two Births. Begotten by the power of the promised Spirit (4:28–29), the Galatians are the contemporary Isaacs, born to the Sarah covenant, the Jerusalem that is above. True, however, to the patriarchal birth stories of Genesis 16–21 and to his reading of them in terms of polar opposites, Paul speaks also of another birth, and it, too, has a contemporary reference. In v 24, thinking of the birth of Ishmael, the son begotten by the power of the flesh, Paul uses the image of giving

---

[170] See Jewett, *Terms,* 95–116.

[171] As far as we can tell, there were no Jewish communities in the Galatian cities of Ankyra and Pessinus in the middle of the first century (Introduction §3). Thus, a polemic focused on Jewish proselytizing would have been irrelevant to the Galatian situation and would have been sensed as such by the Galatians. The history of the interpretation of Gal 4:21–5:1 would be basically different had interpreters consistently observed a hermeneutical rule attributed by oral tradition to Walter Bauer: *On the way* toward ascertaining the intention of an early Christian author, the interpreter is to ask how the author's document was understood by those who first read or heard it (Introduction §18).

[172] The double use of the verb "to beget" in v 29 is Paul's way of referring to the two Gentile missions.

birth in order to describe the Hagar/Sinai covenant. That covenant is bearing children into the state of slavery. A single observation suffices to indicate that on the contemporary level Paul refers here to the work of the Teachers in their Law-observant mission to Gentiles.

It is the matter of the time reference of the clause in which Paul says that the Sinai covenant is "bearing children into the state of slavery." We have seen that in v 22 Paul begins his exegetical section with the past tense, honoring the story line from his text: Abraham had two sons, one begotten from the slave girl, one begotten from the free woman. With the exegetical notice, however, that these things are to be interpreted allegorically (v 24), Paul shifts, not surprisingly, to the present tense, maintaining that tense in every subsequent verse. We can be sure, however, that we are not dealing with the timeless present generally characteristic of allegory.[173] In v 29 Paul refers typologically and emphatically to the real present ("so also now").

The same thing is true of the participial clause "bearing children into the state of slavery," for with this clause Paul refers to births that are even now taking place in a mission distinct from, but also concurrent with, the mission in which the Galatians themselves were born.[174] The Hagar/Sinai covenant is not the *old* covenant, now superseded by the *new* covenant. On the contrary, the Hagar/Sinai covenant is presently active, giving birth to children begotten by the power of the flesh — that is, by circumcision — bearing these children, as befits the *Hagar/Sinai* covenant, into the state of slavery.

The conclusion is as clear as it is important. Paul draws into his columns of polar opposites not only his missioning verb "to beget a child" but also the verb "to bear a child." As we suggested earlier, when Paul thinks of his initial contact with the Galatians (4:13–15), he is filled with joy. Indeed, he can recall those happy days when he reads Genesis 16–21, knowing that in Galatia, as elsewhere, the circumcision-free mission was God's instrument for producing Isaac-like churches, begetting them by the power of God's promised Spirit, and giving birth to them via Sarah, the free woman, the Jerusalem above. Thus, from his exegetical argument itself Paul draws a conclusion regarding the Galatians' identity: happily, they are the liberated children of the free woman (vv 28 and 31).

He comes to that matter, however, only by distinguishing the kind of begetting and birthing process that brought them into being from its polar opposite, an utterly different begetting and birthing process that is presently threatening to bring them into a different state of being, slavery.[175] Given that threat, Paul re-

---

[173] On the mixture of allegory and typology, see the Note on v 24.

[174] To be sure, Erasmus — representing many interpreters from Marcion onward — credited Paul with speaking in the past tense of Judaism: "the first [testament] *gave birth* to a people subject to servitude of the law . . ." (Sider, *Erasmus*, 119; emphasis added). Had Paul wished to say this, however, he would surely have used the finite form of the simple past tense (aorist).

[175] We have already noticed the present-tense force of the clause "bearing children into slavery." Now we can add another weighty point. The phrase "into slavery" is clearly adverbial, modifying "bearing children." The resulting clause, therefore, does not present a static characteristic of Hagar that could as well be expressed by the sentence "Hagar was

minds the Galatians of their true birth identity, and he instructs them to maintain that identity by expelling from their churches the representatives of the mission associated with Sinai and the present Jerusalem (v 30).

TWO COVENANTS

This conclusion is further reinforced when we consider the fact that Paul has even taken into his two columns of opposites the sacred words "covenant" and "Jerusalem," moves of his own that have, we can be sure, no correspondents in the Teachers' columns of opposites. Immediately after indicating that the Genesis stories are to be read allegorically/typologically — that is to say, by noting pairs of opposites in those stories that refer to specific pairs of opposites in the current scene — Paul identifies the two women as two covenants (v 24), and later he relates the two women to two Jerusalems (vv 25–26). As noted earlier, the doubling of Jerusalem is a matter to be considered in Comment #46. Here we attend to the two covenants.

The reference in v 24 is Paul's only use of the term "covenant" in Gal 4:21–5:1. The first observation to be made about it is that it does not correspond to the use of the term in the Genesis stories Paul is interpreting. Three points are clear about the term "covenant" in those stories:

(1) There is only one covenant, and it includes both the promise of progeny and the commandment of circumcision:[176]

On that day the Lord made a covenant with Abram, saying . . . I will establish my covenant between me and you, and your descendants after you throughout their generations, for an everlasting covenant, to be God to you and to your descendants after you (Gen 15:18; 17:7).

This is my covenant, which you shall keep, between me and you and your descendants after you: Every male among you shall be circumcised. You shall be circumcised in the flesh of your foreskins, and it shall be a sign of the covenant between me and you . . . So shall my covenant be in your flesh an everlasting covenant (Gen 17:10–13).

---

a slave." These two factors compel us to contest the standard interpretation sketched in footnote 168 above. From Lightfoot to H. D. Betz there is a steady tendency to interpret all of the prepositional phrases laid out above on the basis of the last of them, the one in v 29, and thus — in a way that is incorrect even for v 29 — to take them as fundamentally adjectival, rather than as adverbial. Explicating the columns of opposites, H. D. Betz speaks of "two kinds of people, those who are 'according to [the] flesh' . . . and those who are 'according to [the] Spirit'" (249). But in the text Paul consistently has the contrasting prepositional phrases modify the verb *gennaô* (in finite and in participial form). Consequently, he does not at all speak statically of persons who *are* according to the flesh and persons who *are* according to the Spirit. He uses the prepositional phrases to refer to two different birthing processes, two different modes of birth.

[176]God makes his covenant with Abraham and with his multiple descendants, but there is no thought that its being passed from generation to generation causes it to be several covenants. Regarding the term "covenants" in Rom 9:4, see Grässer, *Bund*, 18.

(2) Abraham observed God's covenant without exception. He circumcised himself, his sons, and every male in his household (Gen 17:23–27; 21:4).

(3) Although, responding to God's command, Abraham circumcised Ishmael, just as he circumcised every other male in his house, God established his covenant with Isaac and emphatically not with Ishmael, as the exchange concerning the birth of Isaac shows.

[God promises Abraham a son by Sarah; Abraham laughs in disbelief, and preferring the certainty of the son he already has via Hagar, he pleads with God:] "Oh that Ishmael might live in your sight!" God said, "No, but your wife Sarah shall bear you a son, and you shall name him Isaac. I will establish my covenant with him . . . As for Ishmael, I have heard you; I will bless him . . . But I will establish my covenant with Isaac" (Gen 17:18–21).

At all three of these points Paul departs from the text of Genesis. He announces two covenants. Separating promise and nomistic commandment, he defines one covenant as that of promise (and of the Spirit, v 29), the other as that of the Law of Sinai (and of the circumcision of the flesh). He then identifies the second of these covenants as the covenant of Hagar and her son, ignoring the pointed absence in Genesis of a covenant involving Hagar and Ishmael.

In one regard the way in which Paul uses the term "covenant" in Gal 4:21–5:1 departs even from his own earlier usage. In Gal 3:15, 17, having divorced the promise from the Law, much as he does in the present passage, he spoke of only one covenant, tying it exclusively to the promise, and thus issuing a divorce between the terms "covenant" and "Law." In Galatians 3 Paul nowhere refers to the Sinai *covenant*; nor does he even hint that there might be two covenants. What was it that drove Paul — surely against all of his Pharisaic training — to bring the term "covenant" into the frame of reference set by the two columns of polar opposites, thus speaking of two covenants?

Paul sees that the Teachers are enticing the Galatians to long for inclusion in the venerable covenant of Sinai via circumcision as the commencement of Law observance.[177] He sees also that the Teachers' reading of Genesis 16–21 plays an important role in this seduction. In light of these developments Paul is compelled to use the term "covenant" himself, but he is forced to conclude that the Teachers' work has split the covenant into two. In the Teachers' labors among *Gentiles* Paul sees the activity of the enslaving nomistic covenant of Hagar/Sinai. In his own work he sees the effects of the liberating, promissory covenant of Sarah/Jerusalem above. In short, Paul identifies the two women as two covenants, in order to speak of these two missions.[178] For that purpose the one-covenant picture of Galatians 3 will not suffice. Gal 4:21–5:1 is the passage in which Paul

[177]With respect to the way in which the Teachers' message addressed the female members of Paul's Galatian churches, see Meeks, *Urban*, 75–77; Cohen, "Crossing," 24; Lieu, "Circumcision."

[178]On Paul's later references to two covenants (2 Cor 3:6, 14), see notably Furnish, *II Corinthians*; Grässer, *Bund*, 77–95; Hafemann, *Moses*.

faces most openly and squarely and explicitly and analytically the existence of the Law-observant Gentile mission.[179]

CONCLUSION

With the help of Isa 54:1 (see Note on v 27) Paul finds that, when the columns of polar opposites are correctly arranged, the stories in Genesis tell a tale radically different from the one heard in those stories by the Teachers (for the Teachers' columns, see earlier display):

Hagar	Sarah
slave	free
Ishmael	Isaac
the son begotten by the power of the flesh, that is by circumcision	the son begotten by the power of God's promise/the Spirit
begetting father: circumcision of the flesh	begetting father: the promissory Spirit
bearing mother: the covenant from Mount Sinai	bearing mother: the covenant of God's promise

[179] It is important to see that Paul takes the unprecedented step of referring to two covenants only in order to establish the integrity of God's one church. When we recall Gal 2:7, 9, we remember Paul's passion regarding the unity of the church. By the mission to the Jews (presupposing their continued nonsalvific observance of the Law), and by the circumcision-free mission to the Gentiles, God is calling into existence this one church. But the Teachers — and the supporters they have in the Jerusalem church — wish to produce this unity under the banner of the Sinai covenant, demanding that Gentile members of the church enter that covenant. Sure that this Law-observant mission to Gentiles is not God's work, Paul says that it produces nothing other than a new form of Gentile enslavement (see Comment #41). If, then, Paul is sure that the Law-observant mission, the Hagar covenant, is *not* God's work, can he mean to imply that God is ultimately the author of both covenants? Does he think, for example, that God used the Hagar covenant to imprison humanity until, climactically, he should provide the liberating covenant of Sarah? There is tradition for the view that God can change his own covenantal promise (e.g., Deut 28:62–68), but that view has no pertinence to the two *simultaneously active* covenants of Galatians 4. Since the Hagar covenant *is* the Law-observant mission to Gentiles, Paul does not in any way suggest that it has its origin in God (*pace* Grässer, *Bund*, 95, among others). As we have seen, it stands under God's curse (Gal 1:8–9). One is not surprised, therefore, to note that, in speaking of the Hagar covenant, Paul employs no expressions corresponding to the *hina* clauses that function in Gal 3:22, 24 to indicate God's use of the Law to his own purpose. In the Hagar covenant, by contrast, the Law is being put to a use contrary to God's will, a fact showing clearly that the Hagar covenant is not the Law as such. At least in passing, we may also note in the Septuagintal form of Psalm 83 (LXX 82) the reference to a covenant that is dangerous to God's people (for Paul the church of God) and that is authored by God's enemies, specifically, among others, by the Ishmaelites and the Hagarites.

the nomistic covenant, represented by Hagar and by Sinai, is bearing children—that is to say, Gentile churches, small in number (v 27)—into the state of slavery via the Law-observant mission to the Gentiles

the promissory covenant, represented by Sarah, is mother to those who escape from slavery, being the churches, large in number (v 27), that are resulting from the circumcision-free mission to the Gentiles

COMMENT #46
THE PRESENT JERUSALEM AND THE JERUSALEM ABOVE: A TALE OF TWO CHURCHES

In the preceding Comment we have seen that virtually all of the elements in Paul's exegesis of Genesis 16–21 are pairs of opposites specifically focused on the two Gentile missions, the one pursued by him and the one conducted by the Teachers. Is the same true of his reference to two Jerusalems? That is a question of considerable importance, for in the dominant interpretation Paul's reference to the enslaved and enslaving Jerusalem in Gal 4:25, like that to the Sinai covenant in 4:24, is taken to mean "the political and religious institution of Judaism." The passage is then read as a polemic against Judaism as such.[180] A brief consideration of Paul's references to Jerusalem in his other letters will facilitate our analysis of the references in Galatians.

THE WORD "JERUSALEM" IN 1 CORINTHIANS AND ROMANS
Half of Paul's ten references to Jerusalem fall in these two letters, the other five being in Galatians.

1 Corinthians

16:3–4. And when I arrive in Corinth, I will send those whom you accredit by letter to carry your gift to *Jerusalem*. If it seems advisable that I should also go, they will accompany me.

Romans

15:19. . . . so that from *Jerusalem* and as far around as Illyricum I have fully preached the gospel of Christ.

15:24–26. I hope to see you in passing as I go to Spain . . . At present, however, I am going to *Jerusalem* with aid for the saints. For Macedonia and Achaia have been pleased to make some contributions for the poor among the saints in *Jerusalem*.

15:30–31. I appeal to you, brothers and sisters . . . to strive together with me in your prayers . . . that I may be delivered from the unbelievers in Judea, and that my service for *Jerusalem* may be acceptable to the saints.

[180]H. D. Betz 246. Betz's conclusion: "According to Galatians, Judaism is excluded from salvation altogether . . ." (251).

From these passages it is obvious that Paul can use the word "Jerusalem" as a geographical term, coordinate with the terms "Illyricum" and "Spain." It is equally clear, however, that Paul's interest in geography is thoroughly ecclesiological. Jerusalem is the place from which the gospel has commenced its march into the rest of the world, and that is in itself a strong hint that, when he uses the word "Jerusalem," Paul thinks in the first instance of the Jerusalem church, not of the city as such, and certainly not of the Jewish cultus with its temple, its priests, and its traditions.

This reading receives support, furthermore, from the fact that Paul employs other place-names as metonyms for the churches in those locales. It is not Macedonia and Achaia, but rather the churches in those areas, that have assembled funds for the Jerusalem church. And the service those churches are thus performing is being rendered not to the city of Jerusalem, but rather to the church there. Worth particular note is the fact that in Rom 15:31 Paul uses the word "Jerusalem" as a metonym for the Jerusalem church.

The same ecclesiological geography is evident in 1 Corinthians 16. The gift of the Corinthian church is to be carried to the city of Jerusalem in order to be handed over to the Jerusalem church. From Romans and 1 Corinthians, then, one sees Paul using the term "Jerusalem" both literally to refer to the city *as the locale of the Jerusalem church* and as a metonym to speak of *that church itself*. Is that pattern also characteristic of Galatians?

The Word "Jerusalem" in Galatians

1:17   Nor did I make a trip up to *Jerusalem* to see those who were already apostles before I became one.

1:18   Then, after three years had passed, I did go up to *Jerusalem* in order to visit Cephas.

2:1–2 Then, after fourteen years, I went up to *Jerusalem* again, accompanied by Barnabas; and I also took along Titus . . . And I communicated to them (the Jerusalem church) the gospel that I preach among the Gentiles.

4:25   Hagar . . . stands in the same oppositional column with *the present Jerusalem*, for like Hagar the present Jerusalem is in slavery together with her children.

4:26   But (in contrast) *the Jerusalem that is above* is free; she (not the present Jerusalem) is our mother.

In the first three of these references we find exactly what we found in 1 Corinthians and Romans. To put the matter negatively, in 1 Corinthians, Romans, and Gal 1:17–2:2, Paul never uses the word "Jerusalem" to refer to the Jewish religion. It is true that the two instances in the first chapter of Galatians are geographical, but Jerusalem is there nothing other than the locale of the Jerusalem church. And in Gal 2:1–2, as we have seen in the Note, Paul employs the term "Jerusalem" both to refer to the city and — emphatically — as a metonym for the

Jerusalem church (cf. Rom 15:31). When, then, the Galatians hear Paul's reference to Jerusalem in 4:25, their ears are already tuned to expect a metonym in which "Jerusalem" is the Jerusalem church, and Paul takes no step to discourage that interpretation.[181]

PAUL'S VIEW OF THE JERUSALEM CHURCH IN GALATIANS[182]

That Paul intends the Galatians to hear in 4:25 a reference to the Jerusalem church becomes highly probable when we note that he includes in his letter a series of four vignettes of that older congregation. Each of these is painted against the background of statements about the Jerusalem church being made to the Galatians by the Teachers. And each—from the second through the fourth—shows an increased level of tension and distrust between Paul and that church.

First Vignette: Paul's Respectful Distance from the Jerusalem Church (Gal 1:17–18). In his preaching to the Galatians, Paul may have mentioned Jerusalem as the site of the crucifixion of Jesus, but there is no compelling reason to think that, in any substantive way, he referred to the Jerusalem church.[183] The Teachers, however, are certainly speaking at length about the church in Jerusalem, very probably using the word "Jerusalem" metonymically, as we will see below.[184] Behind Paul's references in 1:17–18 lies the Teachers' depiction of themselves as the only true representatives of the Jerusalem gospel. They charge that, although Paul himself got his gospel from the Jerusalem apostles, he has now deviated from that instruction in fundamental regards.[185]

Given this charge, Paul is compelled to speak of the Jerusalem church, but in the earliest of his pictures (1:17–18) that church is barely visible in the distance. He got his gospel directly from God, not from the church in Jerusalem. Given his certainty of that fact, he is equally sure that his gospel cannot be measured by any ecclesiastical authority, including the one in Jerusalem.

Second Vignette: The Meeting in the Jerusalem Church (Gal 2:1–10). Marked

---

[181]Cf. Mussner: "One would first think of the city of Jerusalem as the spiritual center of Judaism . . . It is also possible, however—indeed probable—that in speaking of 'the present Jerusalem,' Paul refers not to the city as the spiritual center of Judaism, but rather to *the city of Jewish Christianity*, whose radical exponents speak of *Jerusalem* as the repository of the true gospel. For them, therefore, Jerusalem is the decisive base of Christianity that authorizes them to preach a message contrary to that of Paul. In this regard, they may even have employed the slogan 'Jerusalem is our mother,' as H. J. Holtzmann suggested" (325).

[182]Cf. now Vouga, "Der Galaterbrief," 248–250.

[183]Paul obviously spoke to the Galatians about the Jerusalem church when he told them of his collection and of the way in which they were to assemble funds in their own churches (1 Cor 16:1). He did that, however, after writing Galatians (Comment #24).

[184]Similar ecclesiological metonyms are easy to find in modern usage. In the Church of England one would hear references to "Canterbury," meaning the authority of the cathedral there. Among Roman Catholic clerics "Rome" often means the ecclesiastical authorities in that city.

[185]Comment #6. In addition to charging that Paul was an unfaithful student of the Jerusalem apostles, the Teachers may have told the Galatians that he had proved himself to be callous about the financial suffering in the Jerusalem church. See Note on 2:10 and Comment #24.

ambivalence toward the Jerusalem church emerges in Paul's account of the meeting that took place when the Antioch church sent messengers to confer with the older congregation. Referring to the Jerusalem church by the metonym "Jerusalem" (2:2), he indicates that that congregation housed at least two distinct groups. One consisted of the recognized leaders, James, Peter, and John. A second was made up of persons Paul calls the False Brothers, a circle intent on compelling the Gentile churches, daughters of the Antioch church, to observe the Law of circumcision. It is this group that causes Paul to exercise tactical care in his approach to the Jerusalem church (2:2b). Thus, the presence of the False Brothers in that community and the leeway apparently given them by the Jerusalem apostles lead Paul to have distinctly ambivalent feelings about the Jerusalem church itself.

On the one hand, he is able to end his account of the meeting with a reference to a victory for the truth of the gospel. The leaders perceived God's hand in his circumcision-free mission to the Gentiles no less than in Peter's mission to the Jews. Moreover, with Barnabas, Paul is more than ready to collect funds in the Antioch church for the poor in the Jerusalem church, thus reflecting his certainty that the apostolic gospel was active in and through that church no less than in and through the church in Antioch.

On the other hand, there is the simple, but significant, fact that Paul says nothing about the way in which the leaders of the Jerusalem church related themselves to the False Brothers. One wonders, for example, why he does not say that in a climactic confrontation, witnessed by the whole of the Jerusalem church, the leaders firmly withstood the False Brothers' attempt to require circumcision of Gentile converts. Why does he have to say, instead, that the task of withstanding the False Brothers fell to him and Barnabas (2:5)? Obviously, the leaders did not directly confront and ultimately vanquish their colleagues. Nor does Paul say that, after the leaders recognized his mission, they instructed the False Brothers henceforth to leave him in peace. Clearly, the acknowledged leaders in Jerusalem did no such thing.[186] Much to Paul's displeasure, then, the False Brothers remained after the meeting what they had been before it: respected and influential members of the Jerusalem church belonging to or constituting a party within that church that was — or in any case could prove to be — supportive of the Law-observant mission to Gentiles (note also Acts 21:20).

Third Vignette: Messengers from the Jerusalem Church Come to the Church in Antioch (Gal 2:11–14). The continued existence of that party within the Jerusalem church is a presupposition of Paul's account of what is usually termed "the incident in Antioch," a turn of events, however, as revealing of developments in Jerusalem as it is of developments in Antioch. After the Jerusalem meeting the False Brothers simply licked their wounds and waited for a better opportunity to assail the Antioch church's circumcision-free mission. That opportunity appar-

---

[186]One might ask speculatively whether the False Brothers may have repented of their circumcision attempt, thus agreeing to abandon their opposition to the Antioch church's circumcision-free work among Gentiles. As that would have been a magnificent victory for "the truth of the gospel," Paul would surely have reported it had it happened.

ently came with the departure of Peter from the Jerusalem church and with the increased authority of James.[187]

Forming the nucleus of "the circumcision party" (Comment #25), the False Brothers seem now to have approached James, astutely scaling down their appeal: "If for Gentile converts circumcision is to be left aside, let us require at least the observance of the food laws." It was a clever move. Given the fact that this group was known under the name "the circumcision party," they may have intended to leave aside the demand of circumcision only for the moment. In any case, persuading James to dispatch messengers to the Antioch church, the False Brothers may have entertained the hope of provoking a confrontation with the man who had successfully antagonized them at the conference, the man who was now standing in the forefront of the Antioch church's Gentile mission, Paul.

James's motives and expectations may have been less concerned with Paul and more tightly focused on the future of Peter's mission to the Jews (Comment #26). In any case, James agreed to send messengers to Antioch. Thus, having formed their own party in the Jerusalem church, the False Brothers had now acquired greater influence there, and, with the cooperation of James, their influence continued to radiate out from that church.

If the False Brothers, now leaders of the circumcision party, hoped that the sending of the delegation to the Antioch church would draw their old enemy into a confrontation in which he would suffer defeat, they shortly saw their hope fulfilled in dramatic fashion. For Paul suffered a painful breach with his co-worker Barnabas, with Peter, and indeed with what had been for some time his home church, the one in Antioch.[188] For our present concerns, the important point is that Paul must also have come away from this political defeat with heightened distrust of the Jerusalem church itself. Certainly, there is no indication that he considered returning to Jerusalem with James's messengers, hoping by direct argument to lead the Jerusalem church to recognize "the truth of the gospel" in the matter of the food laws.

His political defeat and the shaking of his confidence in the Jerusalem church was not the end of the matter. We can be sure that James's messengers carried back to the Jerusalem church a full report, and we can be confident that this report brought about at least five further developments of consequence. (1) The messengers' report must have pleased the False Brothers considerably, showing them that Paul was far from invincible, and encouraging them to look for further ways to put an absolute end to his work. (2) The report must have added yet more strength to the position of the False Brothers in the Jerusalem church, solidifying in the minds of other members their portrait of Paul as an intransigent maverick, caring more for his private views than for the unity and health of God's church. (3) The report probably enabled the False Brothers to portray Paul as utterly undependable. That is to say, they are likely to have pointed out that, by withdrawing from the Antioch church, Paul had also terminated his participation in that

[187]James is named first among the "pillars" (2:9). See R. E. Brown et al., *Peter*, 30.
[188]That the breach with Peter and Barnabas was not permanent is suggested by 1 Cor 1:12; 9:5–6.

461

church's collection for the relief of the church in Jerusalem (Comment #24). (4) The report will have pleased James himself, to the degree that it included an assurance of Peter's compliance with the request that he not enter into close association with persons failing to keep the food laws. James may very well have regretted the breach with Paul, but we may suppose that, like Peter and the Jewish members of the Antioch church, he held Paul responsible for it.

Again, moreover, there is no indication that James did anything to curb the False Brothers. On the contrary, having complied with their request that he send messengers to the Antioch church, he may have been open to further suggestions from them. (5) Finally, the report of the Antioch incident seems to have made its way in some form to the Teachers, whether by their being themselves resident in the Jerusalem church at that time, or by their being in communication with persons belonging to the circumcision party in that church, perhaps the False Brothers themselves. And, drawing on the report, the Teachers apparently gave to the Galatians their account of the Antioch incident, perhaps emphasizing both Paul's intransigence and the powerful role played in Antioch's future work by the elder church in Jerusalem.

In whatever form we are to think of them, these five developments must have influenced the way in which Paul subsequently thought of the Jerusalem church. He had now to take into account the ability of the False Brothers, via James, to reach out into the life of other churches, even changing the nature of the Antioch church's Gentile mission. And with the developments in Galatia he had to take into consideration some kind of positive connection between the Teachers and the Jerusalem church insofar as it had fallen under the influence of the False Brothers. We have to imagine in Paul the sort of distrust that can grow into theological fury.

Fourth Vignette: The Jerusalem Church Is Mother to the Teachers, and Is to That Degree Supporting a Mission That Is Giving Birth to Churches Enslaved to the Law (Gal 4:25). We have already seen that Paul's metonymic reference to the Jerusalem church in 2:1 will have tuned the Galatians' ears to hear the same reference in 4:25. When, now, two observations about 4:25 are added to the sequence of historical vignettes sketched above, we see that a metonymic reference to the Jerusalem church in 4:25 is indeed Paul's intention.

(1) There is, first, the polemical tone to Paul's assertion in v 26. As we have seen in the Note, between the final clause of v 25 and the sentence of v 26 Paul draws a sharp and emphatic contrast (adversative *de*), saying in effect,

It is not the present Jerusalem — the Jerusalem that is in slavery together with her children — that is our mother. On the contrary, our mother is the Jerusalem above, the Jerusalem that is free.

Paul's polemic suggests not only that the Teachers are employing the term "Jerusalem" as a metonym for the Jerusalem church but also that they are using the word "mother," claiming authorization from that church for their mission, when they say "Jerusalem is our mother."[189] It is striking that Paul does not dispute this claim. If he had had secure confidence that, under the leadership of James, the Jerusalem church would have disowned the Teachers, falsifying their claim to be mothered by that congregation, he could easily have said so. Using the word "Jerusalem" as a metonym for the Jerusalem church, the Teachers are apparently able, at least partially, to substantiate their claim.[190]

To assess the hypothesis that the Teachers were able to make such a claim, we need only to recall the first three vignettes sketched above. At the time of the

[189]As we have noted earlier, this hypothesis was advanced in a different form by Holtzmann in 1886 (*Einleitung*, 243; cf. Mussner; Lührmann). It is based on more than the contrast Paul draws between "the present Jerusalem" and "the Jerusalem above." Certain pieces of later tradition, both rabbinic and Jewish-Christian, lend support. The Teachers will have said not only that they have "Jerusalem" as their mother but also that the Gentile Galatians can come under the motherhood of Jerusalem/Sarah as well. Bearing that in mind, one notes the possible pertinence of rabbinic traditions about the motherhood of Jerusalem/Sarah. First, in the nationalistic tradition Jerusalem is said to be the eschatological mother of Israel. At the end-time, when the dead are raised, she will give birth to her children and will bring in those who are in exile (*Tg. Cant.* 8:5). Second, this motif is also developed in such a way as explicitly to speak of the Gentiles. In the time to come, Jerusalem will be the mother not only of those proper to her but also of the Gentiles (*Tanh.*, Debarim 2b). Third, in *Pesiq. Rab Kah.* 22:1 there is a tradition that recounts what God did to the Gentiles when they committed the outrage of saying that it was not Sarah who actually gave birth to Isaac, but rather Hagar: "God caused the nipples of the Gentile women to dry up; and these matrons came to Sarah, kissed the dust at her feet, and said to her, 'Be good to us . . . nurse our children!' Our father Abraham said to her, 'It is not the time for you to hide yourself. Go out to the street and nurse their children! Sanctified be the name of God!' Thus does it say in Gen 21:7, 'Sarah will nurse children.' It does not say *bēn*, 'a child,' but rather *bānîm*, she will nurse children. Now from matters of this kind can we not draw the following inference? If a mortal, to whom joy came, rejoiced and caused everyone else to rejoice, all the more reason to conclude that when the Holy One comes to bring joy to Jerusalem, Jerusalem will say, 'Rejoicing in the Lord, I will cause joy [to others, namely to the Gentiles]' (Isa 61:10)." Here, a typological link is drawn between Sarah and Jerusalem, and that link has to do with the eschatological mothering of Gentiles. As Sarah nursed Gentile children at the request of Abraham, so Jerusalem will do the same when God comes to her. These three traditions — later to be sure — mesh to some extent with the Teachers' reading of the stories in Genesis 16–21. In forming their Table of Opposites, they draw links between the nomistic covenant of Sinai, Sarah, and Jerusalem, and for them those links offer true salvation to the Gentiles. In speaking to Gentiles they may have referred to the Jerusalem church as "our — and potentially your — mother." There are also pertinent Jewish-Christian traditions, on the basis of which Dahl was able correctly to say, "In the view of later Jewish Christians, the church in Jerusalem was the central mother church (cf. Hegesippus in Eusebius, *HE*. II 23,4; III 32,6; IV 22,4 and Ps-Clem *Hom* 11,35; *Ep Petri*) and this view was held from the church's earliest days (cf. Acts 1:8: Rom 15:19)" (*Volk*, 183).

[190]On the basis of the four vignettes, we can even offer a suggestion regarding an important development in the Galatians' vocabulary. There is no strong reason to think that these ethnic Galatians ever used the term "Jerusalem" as a way of referring to the Jewish cultus focused on the temple. Considering the Teachers' metonymic use of the term, however, there are grounds for thinking (a) that, prior to receiving Paul's letter, the Galatians had learned to refer to the Jerusalem church simply as "Jerusalem," and (b) that Paul knew of that development in their vocabulary when he wrote the letter.

Jerusalem meeting, the False Brothers passionately favored giving the support of the Jerusalem church to a Law-observant mission to the Gentiles. We have seen no good reason to think that the final result of the meeting caused them to abandon that passion. On the contrary, the subsequent dispatching of messengers to Antioch is best understood — insofar as the False Brothers were concerned — as the first step in a renewed attempt to establish such a mission. And the work of the Teachers is exactly the Law-observant mission to the Gentiles desired by the False Brothers. The remarkable success the Teachers are having among the Galatians may itself testify to the connections they have in the mother church.[191] It follows that in 4:25 Paul himself adopts one of the Teachers' locutions, using the word "Jerusalem" as a metonym for the Jerusalem church.

(2) The metonymic reading of "Jerusalem" in 4:25 is further supported when we note that in 4:21–5:1 Paul coordinates three motifs: (a) "begetting by the power of the flesh" (begetting by circumcision), (b) "bearing children into slavery," and (c) "the present Jerusalem." For in his account of the meeting in the church of Jerusalem (second vignette above) Paul coordinated these same three motifs: (a) the False Brothers' demand that Gentile converts be circumcised, (b) Paul's assessment of this demand as an attempt at enslavement, and (c) the locus in which that demand was lodged, the Jerusalem church. It is indeed in his comment about the False Brothers' demand for the circumcision of Gentiles — a demand voiced *in* the Jerusalem church — that Paul first mentions freedom and enslavement as a pair of opposites (2:4). When, then, in 4:22–25 Paul says that "the present Jerusalem" is begetting children by circumcision, thus bearing them into the state of slavery, he is surely using the Teachers' metonym for the Jerusalem church, modifying that metonym by the limiting word *present*.

To the degree that it affords hospitality to the False Brothers and their circumcision party, thus in some manner mothering the Law-observant mission to the Gentiles pursued by the Teachers, the Jerusalem church is nothing more than an earthly entity, limited to the *present* time and even analogous to the *present* evil age, painful as it doubtless is for Paul to harbor such a thought.[192] In this fourth vignette, then, the ambivalence shown in the second and the distrust reflected in the third have ripened into theological fury. In that state of anger Paul is not at all concerned to provide a complete and balanced portrait of the church in Jerusalem. On the contrary, he refers in Gal 4:25 to *the Jerusalem church that is being made present in Galatia* by the Teachers' claims (and probably on the basis of their relationship with the False Brothers). Thus, *to the degree* that, under the sway of the False Brothers, the Jerusalem church is offering support to the

---

[191] We have already noted the pertinence to Galatians of Käsemann's remark: "Only the authority of the church in Jerusalem could shake the authority Paul had in his own churches . . ." ("Legitimität," 490).

[192] Did the idea of assembling his own collection for the Jerusalem church arise in Paul's mind partly as a result of his portraits of that community in Galatians? Did he see in his collection and in its delivery, that is to say, a way of differentiating the Jerusalem church — as a highly valued community with which God continued to bind the Gentile churches — from the False Brothers and their allies? See Introduction §13 and Comment #24.

Teachers' work — thus reaching into the life of his churches as it earlier reached into the life of the Antioch church — Paul is sure that the Jerusalem congregation is itself producing Gentile churches that are enslaved.[193] From 2 Corinthians and Romans we know that this was far from Paul's final portrait of the elder church.[194] It is, however, the climactic one in his extraordinarily angry letter to the Galatians.[195]

But by adding the word "present," thus anticipating the contrasting word "above," and in effect preparing the way for placing two Jerusalems in the columns of opposites, Paul continues to speak not only of the Law-observant mission but also of the mission God has entrusted to him.[196] Just as in the cross of Christ, God has provided a fully potent antidote to the present evil age (1:4), so over against the present misled and misleading church of Jerusalem God has provided the church in heaven, "the Jerusalem above." And this true mother, although lacking earthly authorization, is nevertheless producing far more children than those being born in the Law-observant mission (Paul's interpretation of Isa 54:1

[193] On the motif of persecution in 4:29 and its possible connection with the False Brothers, see the Note and 2 Cor 11:26.

[194] Further Jerusalem vignettes could be sketched, therefore, from those two later letters. Regarding the picture of the Jerusalem church that may be reflected in 2 Corinthians, see the exegetical arguments of Käsemann, "Legitimität," and Barrett, "Opponents." Note particularly the thesis (as early as F. C. Baur) that the "super-apostles" of 2 Cor 11:5 and 12:11 were the primal apostles in the Jerusalem church, being therefore distinct from the "pseudo-apostles" who actually invaded Paul's Corinthian church, the latter claiming to be sponsored by the former (2 Cor 11:13). In Käsemann's hands this thesis continues with the observation that Paul did not feel compelled to attack the Jerusalem apostles themselves. He says only that he is not inferior to them. And by giving them the ironic sobriquet "super-apostles," he recognizes their possession of a certain kind of priority, while at the same time suggesting that he himself does not stand in awe of them (cf. Gal 2:6). Käsemann's summary: In 2 Corinthians 10–13 Paul is concerned to deal ruthlessly with the invaders of his Corinthian church (the "pseudo-apostles"), without getting caught in a direct conflict with the Jerusalem apostles ("Legitimität," 493). This reading is not universally accepted (see, e.g., Furnish, *II Corinthians*, 49, 502–505; Luedemann, *Paulus*, 134). The series of vignettes in Galatians, however, not to mention the anxiety expressed in Rom 15:25–32, can be offered in secondary support of it.

[195] Cf. now Trobisch, *Letter Collection*, where the thesis is advanced that Paul himself assembled and edited Galatians, 1 and 2 Corinthians, and Romans, sending the result, with a cover letter (Romans 16), to the church in Ephesus, hoping that this epistolary collection would be of service in presenting his side in a long dispute with the authorities of the Jerusalem church. Trobisch thinks that, in this letter collection, Galatians, having the literary form not of a private letter, but rather of an authorized document comparable to an affidavit (Gal 6:11–18), "should be used by [Paul's] friends to prove his case against the saints in Jerusalem" (94). The thesis is illuminating with respect to ancient letter collections, and suggestive as regards the history of Paul's relationship with the Jerusalem church. In some other regards, however, the thesis creates more problems than it solves — especially in connection with Paul's collection of money (see Comment #24) — and the forensic analysis of Galatians itself is untenable (Introduction §10). See further Vouga, "Der Galaterbrief."

[196] For rabbinic patterns of contrasting "the Jerusalem of this world (or age)" with "the Jerusalem of the future world (or age)," see Billerbeck 1.573; Neusner, "Really 'Ethnic'?"

in Gal 4:27). For the heavenly Jerusalem guides the true church below, divorcing it, precisely in its expansion, from an earth that is closed in on itself.[197] In this way the heavenly Jerusalem is God's servant, calling the church into existence as the new creation, in which religious differentiations and ossifying traditions are obliterated (Comment #51). Certain that this Jerusalem above, not the time-bound church in Jerusalem, is the mother of the Galatians, Paul completes his columns of opposites (Comment #45) by referring to the two Jerusalems:

The Present Jerusalem	The Jerusalem Above
that is to say, the Jerusalem church insofar as it allows the False Brothers to sponsor the Law-observant mission to the Gentiles, while blocking official support for the circumcision-free Gentile mission	that is to say, the mother of the churches born in the circumcision-free mission to Gentiles, their lacking official support from the Jerusalem church
the child begotten by the power of the flesh, engaging in persecutory activity — that is, the Teachers and their totally loyal followers who oust the catechetical instructors left by Paul as leaders in the Galatian churches (Gal 6:6)	the child begotten by the power of the Spirit, suffering persecution at the hands of the child begotten by the power of the flesh — that is, the catechetical leaders who form the nucleus of the Galatian churches and who are being ousted by the circumcising Teachers and their totally loyal followers
the slave girl and her son who are to be thrown out — that is, the Teachers and their totally loyal colleagues who are to be expelled from the Galatian churches (4:30)	the Galatian churches as those addressed by God in the words of Gen 21:10 — "Throw out the slave girl and her son. For the son of the slave girl will certainly not come into the inheritance along with the son of the free woman."

---

[197]I have drawn elements of this sentence from Käsemann, "Leiblichkeit," 8.

5:2–12 A WARNING

TRANSLATION

5:2. Look here! I, Paul, say to you that if you undergo circumcision, Christ will be of no help to you. 3. I testify once more to everyone who gets himself circumcised, that he is obligated to observe the whole of the Law. 4. Speaking to those of you who think you are being rectified by the Law, I say: You have nothing more to do with Christ; you have fallen out of the realm of grace!

5. With us things are entirely different: having the Spirit in our hearts, and having the confidence that comes from faith, we eagerly await the hope of rectification. 6. For in Christ Jesus neither circumcision nor uncircumcision accomplishes anything at all. The real power is faith actively working through love.

7. For some time you ran a good footrace. Who has hindered you from staying on course, so that you are no longer obediently committed to the truth? 8. The persuasion that is proving effective among you is not coming from the God who calls you. 9. It is like a little bit of yeast working its leavening power throughout the whole lump of dough.

10. In the realm ruled over by the Lord, I have confidence in you, believing that, as the future unfolds, you will not really follow these alien paths of thought. The man who is disturbing your minds will suffer his judgment, no matter who he is. 11. As for me, brothers and sisters, if, on occasion, I am preaching, as part of the gospel message, that one should be circumcised — as some wrongly report to you — why am I being persecuted to this day? My preaching circumcision would amount to wiping out the scandalous character of the cross. 12. I wish that the people who are troubling your minds would castrate themselves!

LITERARY STRUCTURE AND SYNOPSIS

Noting that in Galatians 5 and 6 there are a number of imperative and hortatory verbs, almost all interpreters have agreed that, before he closes his letter with an autographic postscript (6:11–18), Paul composes an exhortation.[1] If that analysis is essentially correct, where precisely does the hortatory section of the letter begin? In the main, two answers have been given. It begins with the verbs "stand your ground" and "do not ever again take up (the yoke of slavery)" in 5:1, or with the implied verb "do not allow (freedom to be turned into a military base of operations for the Flesh)" in 5:13.[2] For three reasons 5:13 is the far more likely answer (although, as we will see, the section beginning at 5:13 is better termed "pastoral" than "hortatory").[3] (a) We have noted that 5:1 functions more as part of the conclusion to the exegetical section begun at 4:21 than as an introduction to what follows, its imperative verbs being linked with the imperative verb of 4:30. (b) The sharp expression "Look here! I, Paul, say to you" (5:2) signals a new turn in the argument (cf. 3:15). It is not the mere continuation of 5:1. (c) Most important, there are no imperative and hortatory verbs in 5:2–12, whereas a number of such verbs punctuate the latter part of 5:13–6:10.[4] If, then, we speak of a pastoral section of the letter — a section that is partly hortatory (see Literary Structure and Synopsis for 5:13–24) — it begins at 5:13.

If the paragraph comprising 5:2–12 is not hortatory, how is it to be characterized? The best guidance lies in the fact that, instead of issuing exhortations addressed to the Galatians' wills, Paul speaks repeatedly in the indicative mood of the future.[5] Confronting the Galatians with prospects that are part of the real, *post Christum* world, he refers twice to their own future and once to the future of the Teachers' leader:

If you undergo circumcision, Christ will be of no help to you (v 2).

In the realm ruled over by the Lord, I have confidence in you, believing that, as the future unfolds, you will not really follow these alien paths of thought (v 10).

---

[1]Stowers is of a different opinion: The common assumption that, instead of being parenetic throughout, Paul's letters include a discrete parenetic section before the conclusion is incorrect, not only for 1 Thessalonians (as shown by Malherbe) but also for others (*Letter Writing*, 23).

[2]The various opinions are well presented by Merk, "Beginn." See also Barclay, *Obeying*, 24 and especially 25 n68. In a number of analyses 5:13–6:10 is said to be, at least in part, an instance of parenesis, that is to say a series of general ethical admonitions strung together so as to be addressed to a single audience (cf. Dibelius, *James*, 3). Some of those who have reviewed H. D. Betz's commentary have given special attention to the parenetic issue (e.g., Aune, Review of H. D. Betz, 324–325, and Meeks, Review of H. D. Betz, 305). There is further discussion in Lyons, *Autobiography*; Kraftchick, "Ethos."

[3]I use the term "pastoral" in a way that is somewhat similar to that evident in Malherbe, *the Thessalonians*, 68–94. As we will see, however, it is important to emphasize that, in writing to the Galatians, Paul couches his pastoral care to a considerable extent in the indicative mood (Comment #49).

[4]One is puzzled to find Longenecker, for example, speaking of "the *exhortations* of 5:1–12" (221; emphasis added), asserting that 5:1 heads up "its own section of exhortation" as does 5:13 (224).

[5]A threat in regard to the future can be indirectly hortatory, being a form of advisory dissuasion (cf. Stowers, *Letter Writing*, 94, 107), but for reasons laid out in Comment #49 it

The man who is disturbing your minds will suffer his judgment, no matter who he is (v 10).

Paul intends the first of these to be a simple statement of fact, not an exhortation. It is a warning of how things will actually turn out if the Galatians flock to the Teachers' false gospel. With the second, again delaying his exhortations, Paul changes his tone, but he still speaks of the future, expressing his confidence in the power of Christ specifically to shape the future of the Galatians. And with the third, Paul states a fact about future judgment similar to that stated in 1:8–9. We may also note Paul's wish about the future of the Teachers (v 12) and his entirely different statement about his own future and that of his coworkers (v 5). In 5:2–12, then, including a series of impressive images — the dream-like experience of losing one's footing (v 4), the running of a footrace (v 7), the permeative effect of yeast as it leavens a lump of dough (v 9) — Paul portrays both the present and the future of the world in which the Galatians actually find themselves, the world over which God presides. He thus prepares the way for the pastoral section of 5:13–6:10 by means of realistic statements about the future.

NOTES

5:2. *I, Paul, say to you.* Paul compels the Galatians to turn their attention from the voice of scripture in 4:21–5:1 (emphatically in 4:30) to his own voice, that of an apostle.[6]

if you undergo circumcision. This brief paragraph is marked by no fewer than five references to circumcision, indicating that Paul is thinking very concretely of the situation in his Galatian churches. Furthermore, to some degree these references show him to be distinguishing two groups from one another for the first time (contrast 1:6; 3:1). Although a number of the Galatians are embracing the Teachers' theology, already submitting to circumcision, there are others who have not yet done so. In a future-conditional sentence Paul speaks to the latter: "You have not yet submitted to circumcision. Let me tell you plainly what will ensue if you do."

Christ will be of no help to you. Far from saying that it is "not necessary" for Gentiles to observe the Law (a common reading of Galatians), Paul says that if they do, they abandon the only one who can and will deliver them — note the future tense — from the powers that enslave (Comment #39). The stakes could not be higher.

3. *I testify.* Functioning as a pedagogical witness, Paul gives the Galatians instruction that has been denied them by the Teachers (cf. the verb *martyromai,* "I can give you evidence," in 4:15).

once more. With the instruction of v 3 Paul wishes to emphasize the warning of v 2.

---

is nevertheless important to note the fact — and to seek the cause for it — that, in 5:2–24, Paul stays almost exclusively with the indicative mood.

[6]Compare Gal 4:21 and 5:2 with *2 Apoc. Bar.* 84:5–6. Both show the form (a) Moses said/the Law says, (b) I say to you. See the antitheses in Matt 5:21–48.

to everyone who gets himself circumcised. Paul now instructs all members of the Galatian churches, having in mind not only those who are tempted to succumb to the Teachers' message (v 2) but also those who have already done so. For the most part such conversions took place in family units.[7] Thus, literally speaking, Paul addresses the male heads of the Galatian households. The circumcision of the husband/father and sons is understood as the event by which the household enters into the observance of the Law.

obligated to observe the whole of the Law. At a later point in the letter we see that the Teachers are like the Jewish Christians criticized in the epistle of James, who to some degree pick and choose among the commandments, deciding which ones they will observe (Gal 6:13; Jas 2:10; 4:11). Perhaps the Teachers are extending a similar indulgence to the Galatian Gentiles, failing to require that they observe every commandment.[8] Perhaps it is in order to be successful in their Gentile mission that the Teachers emphasize circumcision, food laws, and holy times, omitting — for the time being? — many other matters in the Law.[9]

In any case, in the present verse Paul is emphatically referring to what we may term "the plural Law," the Law made up of many commandments. This nomenclature recalls the plural expression in 3:10 — "all the *things* written in the book of the Law" (Deut 27:28). It is also to this plural Law that Paul refers when he cites the false promise of Lev 18:5 — "The one who does the commandments will live by *them*" (Gal 3:12). It is this plural Law that is paired with the Not-Law to form one of the enslaving elements of the old cosmos (Comment #41). And it is in referring to this plural Law that Paul speaks of the necessity of complete observance, by using the verb *poieô*, "to do," "to keep," "to observe."

To be sure, Paul argues neither here nor elsewhere that it is impossible to keep the whole of the Law (see the Note on 3:10). He does point out, however, that a Gentile who commences observance of the Law sets out on a path that has no terminus. The instruction in v 3 is thus a polemic tightly focused on the message

---

[7] See Meeks, *Urban*, 75–77; Cohen, "Crossing," 24. The Teachers' call for circumcision doubtless presupposed in the main the patriarchal structure of the family. In response to early Christian evangelization, however, there were doubtless cases in which a wife came without her husband, and vice versa (see 1 Cor 7:12–16). See Lieu, "Circumcision."

[8] Note the comment of Daube: "The inter-dependence of all precepts, their fundamental equality, the importance of even the minor ones . . . these were common themes among the Tannaites" (*New Testament*, 251). Is it possible, however, that the Galatians have no intention of taking up observance of the Law as such? In the view of Klumbies the Galatians have accepted the Teachers' demand for circumcision and planet-directed holy times, without as yet intending to embrace the view that observance of the Law itself is necessary for salvation. This is an interesting interpretation of the letter, but Klumbies's reading of 4:21 — and of 4:21–5:1 — is unconvincing ("Zwischen," 121).

[9] The possibility has often been mentioned that the Teachers were merely observing the tradition according to which Gentile proselytes are presented with the Law gradually, so as not to drive them away at the outset (Eckert, *Streit*, 41; Jewett, "Agitators," 207–208; E. P. Sanders, *Law*, 29). That tradition may be reflected in the polemic of *Sipra*, Kedoshim, Perek 8:3: "As the native born Jew takes upon him (to obey) all the words of the Law, so the proselyte takes on him all the words of the Law. The authorities say, if a proselyte takes upon himself all the words of the Law except one single commandment, he is not to be received" (see Moore, *Judaism*, 1.331).

the Teachers are preaching to Gentiles, not a polemic against Judaism.[10] A Gentile seeking rectification and life by commencing observance of the Law — Paul does not call the plural Law God's Law — needs to know that in this way he places himself under enduring obligation.[11] Face-to-face with the plural Law, he becomes a permanent debtor (*opheiletês*), whose bill is always due.

4. *Speaking to those of you who think you are being rectified by the Law, I say.* Having addressed the warning of v 2 to those Galatians who are thus far only tempted to embrace the Teachers' message, and having directed the instruction of v 3 to all, Paul now speaks to the majority, those who have already fallen under the spell of the Teachers.

think you are being rectified by the Law. Emphasizing a point he has made in 3:11, Paul puts the verb *dikaiousthe* in the present tense (conative), thus referring to "action attempted, but not accomplished" (Moule, *Idiom*, 8; cf. BDF §319).

You have nothing more to do with Christ. These Galatians have come to think that their salvation results from an allegiance to Christ only when that allegiance is enacted in observance of the Law (Comment #33). Paul is certain that such a dual attachment is impossible. We have noted, to be sure, that when he is thinking of the Jewish-Christian churches in Judea, he finds no problem in their *continuing* Law observance, for he is confident that they attribute their salvation to Christ, not to their being observant (1:22; Comment #28). Thus, in mixed churches, such as the one in Antioch, the formerly Jewish members can continue to keep the Law only when Law observance has become for them a matter of no consequence, a concern that they can lay aside at the eucharist (Comment #26). As soon as one attaches to Law observance some degree of salvific potency, one has violated the gospel of Christ, thus severing oneself from him (cf. Rom 7:2). Luther was right to use in this regard the expression *solus christus*.

have fallen out of the realm of grace! The verb *ekpiptô* has a range of meanings, most having somehow to do with separation (LSJ). With an image common to nightmares, Paul says that the Galatians who are looking to the Law for their redemption have lost their footing, and are falling from the firm place to which they have been brought by Christ (5:1).

---

[10]It follows that the interpreter of Paul must take into account the issue of the locus of election. Israel understood herself to have been *elected* in God's gift to her of the Law, an act of grace *emphasized* in the fact that Law observance knows no terminus! See Werblowsky, "Torah." In Paul's view the church — including both born Jew and born Gentile — is *elected* by God in the grace of Christ, not in the Law.

[11]One can appreciate the illuminating insights in Barrett, *Freedom and Obligation*, without applauding the use of the term "obligation" in the title. Similarly, Meeks speaks of the "moral life [that early Christians, including Paul] understood to be required of them," thus referring to what he calls "the language of obligation" (*Origins*, 14). As regards Galatians, however, the statement in 5:3 is the only point at which Paul speaks directly to the issue of obligation, and here he notes that it is the plural Law — the Law that has no pertinence to the daily life of the church — that creates obligation. Does the way in which — and the context in which — Paul uses imperative verbs in Galatians 6 require that followers of Paul learn to speak of behavior in the church without referring to obligation? One recalls Kierkegaard's reference to faith that is "a happy passion." See Comments #48 and #49; cf. also David Martyn, "Ethical Economies"; Baird, "One," 123.

5. *With us things are entirely different.* By means of the emphatic pronoun "we," Paul draws a stark contrast between those Galatians who, undergoing circumcision, are leaving the gracious realm of Christ (v 4), and those who, with himself, remain in Christ (vv 5–6), thus being linked with the Spirit, with faith, and with hope.[12]

having the Spirit in our hearts, and having the confidence that comes from faith, we eagerly await. In a kind of shorthand Paul allows the prepositional phrases "in (or with) the Spirit" and "from (or on the basis of) faith" to modify the verb "wait eagerly," both prepositional phrases being causal. In 4:6 Paul had noted that the indwelling Spirit of Christ causes God's newly adopted children to cry out to God as their Father. He now adds that that inspired cry to God includes a remarkable confidence, for the Spirit whispers in the believer's ear the assurance of God's sustaining care. Thus, the Spirit of Christ and the faith that is kindled into flame by the gospel of Christ (3:2) cause Paul and his comrades to wait with eager longing for the future that God holds out to them.

we eagerly await. The verb is consistently used by Paul to speak of a special kind of waiting, one that is directed to the final redemptive act of God, and that is as confident of that act as God is consistently trustworthy in promising it (1 Cor 1:7; Phil 3:20; Rom 8:19, 23, 25). In the midst of the agony he is experiencing over the Galatians' defection from the truth of the gospel (4:19), Paul sounds the note of eager and confident waiting, a note that prepares for and affects the nature of the pastoral section he will begin in 5:13.

the hope of rectification. The two nouns, "hope" and "rectification," are here used as synonyms, the second being an epexegetical genitive: "we eagerly await what we confidently hope for, rectification at God's hands." In a letter in which Paul has polemically and consistently said that the human scene — indeed, the cosmos itself — has already been changed by God's rectifying deed in Christ's advent and death, it is a surprise to hear him speak with emphasis of hope, the only instance of this term in the letter. And it is a double surprise to hear him refer to rectification as a future event.[13] See Comment #47.

6. *For in Christ Jesus.* Paul and his comrades live in the realm established by the coming of Christ.

neither circumcision nor uncircumcision accomplishes anything at all. The real power is faith actively working through love. In a paragraph with five references to circumcision one should expect Paul now to say simply that that rite is impotent to accomplish anything. Instead, he indicates the impotence of both circumcision and uncircumcision, thus signaling the termination of the cosmos that had at its foundation a religious pair of opposites (Comments #40 and #41), and announcing the dawn of the cosmos that consists of the realm of Christ, the realm that lies beyond religious differentiations (Comment #51). In short, much more is involved than the identification of circumcision and uncircumcision as

---

[12]Cf. the emphatic "we" in 2 Cor 5:16 (Jewett, *Terms*, 126 n3).
[13]Rectification as a future event is characteristic of much Jewish tradition. On pertinent texts in the Qumran scrolls, see Kertelge, "For the faithful in Qumran 'rectification' is always a matter of hope . . ." ("*Rechtfertigung*," 41).

matters of no true importance. Paul declares the nonexistence of one world — an enslaving one — and the newly arriving existence of another, characterized by faith active in mutual love (5:13).

To say all of this, the apostle employs a formula with three members, the first two being negated, the third affirmed. The formula may be his own creation; he uses it twice in Galatians and once in 1 Corinthians:

Gal 5:6	Gal 6:15	1 Cor 7:19
(a) Neither circumcision (b) nor uncircumcision accomplishes anything at all. (c) The real power is faith actively working through love.	(a) Neither circumcision (b) nor uncircumcision is anything at all. (c) What is something is the new creation.	(a) Circumcision is nothing (b) and uncircumcision is nothing. (c) What counts for something is keeping the commandments of God.

Striking is the fact that, both in Gal 5:6 and in Gal 6:15, the third member of the formula is a single entity — *faith* active in love, and the *new creation*, respectively. Similarly in 5:14, linking the whole of the Law to behavior in God's church, Paul says that the Law has been brought to completion not in many commandments, but rather in one sentence: "You shall love your neighbor as yourself!" And in 5:22 he indicates the integrity of behavior in the church by using the singular word "fruit" to speak of what the Spirit produces in the fabric of the church's daily life.

In Galatians 5 and 6, then, Paul is at pains to say that, at its base, daily life in God's church is not many things, but rather one thing: faithful and dynamic love. Moreover, by identifying love as the first mark of the fruit borne by the Spirit (5:22), Paul says that the singular behavior of love in the corporate life of the church is not something that can be identified simply as a human deed. Corporate life marked by love is the fruit of the Spirit of Christ, because that corporate life has its genesis in God's act of gracious rectification in Jesus Christ. Communally enacted love is God's gift in the Spirit (Comment #49).[14]

Gal 5:6 and 6:15 are entirely harmonious, then, in announcing the death of one cosmos and the dawn of another. As God's new creation, the church lives beyond all religious marks of differentiation that prescribe behavioral norms by speaking of many requirements (Comment #48). For in Christ Jesus religion has now been replaced by:

faith actively working through love. With a participle of the verb *energeô*, "to

[14]The result is an apparent tension between Paul's use of the three-membered formula in Gal 5:6 and 6:15 and his use of that formula in 1 Cor 7:19, where the third member is distinctly plural rather than singular, being the keeping of God's commandments. On 1 Cor 7:19, see Schrage, *Korinther* (cf. idem, *Einzelgebote*, 231–232); Lindemann, "Toragebote"; Appendix B to Comment #48.

be at work," Paul indicates the relation between faith and love in the church of God. The participle can be either passive, "faith that is activated by love," or middle, "faith that is actively expressing itself through love." The question is extensively discussed.[15] Mussner (*ad loc.*) has made a convincing argument for the middle reading.

As 5:13–14 and 6:2 show, we should go wrong to think of this faith-energized love as a romantic feeling. It is the concrete pattern of life, established and incited by Christ's faithful, dying love for us. Under the sign of the cross (5:24) this loving pattern of life is continued in the community in which each member is the servant of the other, bearing the other's burdens.[16] We should also go wrong to say that this love adds something to faith. On the contrary, faith is itself a "happy passion" (Kierkegaard) active in love through the power of the Spirit (cf. 1 Corinthians 13).[17] What has taken the place of religion is the community of the new creation in which gospel-elicited faith expresses itself in love of the neighbor.[18]

Together with the motif of eager and confident waiting (v 5), this crucial linkage between faith and love plays its own role in preparing the way for the pastoral section of the letter (5:13–6:10). For in that next section love emerges as a central theme. It is the first fruit borne by the Spirit in the life of the community (5:22). It is evident in the pattern of mutual service (5:13). In that love the whole of the Law has been brought to completion precisely as the Law of Christ (5:14; 6:2). Thus, the action to which Paul will exhort the Galatians in 5:14, 16 "does not stand under the slogan 'I must and I shall,' but under the quite different one, 'I may and I can.'"[19] In short, because it is the fruit of the Spirit and a constituent part of faith, love in the Christian community is a response neither to some categorical imperative nor even to the Law.[20] On the contrary, "the voice of childlike freedom and rejoicing is heard in it," because it is the love elicited by Christ's love for us (2:20).[21]

7. *For some time you ran a good footrace.* In the period of time between his departure and the arrival of the Teachers, Paul had had reports indicating that the Galatian congregations were remaining steadfast (imperfect tense) to the gospel he had preached to them.

Who has hindered you from staying on course, so that you are no longer obediently committed to the truth? In order directly to refer to the Teachers without using their proper names, Paul explicates the rhetorical question of 3:1, "Who has cast a spell on you?"[22] The liberation Christ has accomplished for the Gala-

---

[15]The passive reading is defended by Clark, "Meaning."
[16]Cf. Hays, "The Law of Christ."
[17]See Käsemann, "Liebe."
[18]*Pace* H. D. Betz, who says that Paul is here establishing Christianity as a new religion (263).
[19]The quotation is from E. Käsemann.
[20]Lindemann, "Toragebote," 264.
[21]The quotation is from E. Käsemann.
[22]Harmonizing the two questions, an early scribe introduced the last clause of 5:7 into 3:1; Metzger 593.

tians (5:1) is nothing other than God's act of freeing the will for obedience to himself (Comment #29). Without now making distinctions among the Galatians, Paul tells them that, as communities made addressable by God's sending the Spirit into their hearts, they are as responsible for their apostasy (1:6) as were Peter and Barnabas at the time of the incident in the Antioch church (2:11–14). What they have lost is obedience to God's truth, a word Paul has used with emphasis in 2:5 and 2:14 as a synonym for "the gospel."

8. *persuasion.* In Paul's view the Teachers are mere rhetoricians, persuading the Galatians by flattery and threats (4:17; contrast 1:10). And as Paul has said in 1:6, when the Galatians give in to the Teachers' persuasion, they abandon—in the first instance—not himself, but rather:

the God who calls you. See 1:6.

9. *yeast.* With a proverb, quoted by him also in 1 Cor 5:6, Paul reflects on the possibility that all members of the Galatian churches may succumb to the Teachers' false gospel.[23]

10. *In the realm ruled over by the Lord, I have confidence in you.* Having contemplated the possibility that all of the Galatians will eventually defect from God, Paul quickly changes his tone, professing confidence in them.[24] This confidence has not arisen, however, because he has received encouraging reports about the Galatians. It has its genesis in the Lord Christ, for it is the confidence of an apocalyptic theologian who, equipped with bifocal lenses, sees that the power of Christ is "much more" than the power of the Teachers' false gospel (cf. Rom 5:12–21 and the future dimension of Gal 5:5).[25]

The man who is disturbing your minds. With the same verb he had earlier used to characterize all of the Teachers (1:7, *tarassô,* "to disturb," "to frighten," "to intimidate") Paul refers to the leader of the group.

will suffer his judgment. In 1:8–9 Paul has already delivered the Teachers to God's judgment. Now, in a clear reference to God's future judgment, Paul repeats that earlier motif, focusing his attention on the Teachers' leader (cf. the motif of future judgment in 5:2, 5, 21; 6:5, 7–9).[26]

11. (a) *As for me, brothers and sisters,* (b) *if, on occasion, I am preaching, as part of the gospel message, that one should be circumcised—as some wrongly report to you—* (c) *why am I being persecuted to this day?* (d) *My preaching circumcision would amount to wiping out the scandalous character of the cross.* Clauses (a), (b), and (c) make up a conditional sentence, the third clause being a rhetorical question that shows the condition to be contrary to fact. A final sentence (d) then confirms that the condition is untrue.[27] Paul wants the Galatians to respond as follows:

---

[23] In early Christian tradition, as in Jewish thought, yeast is often a negative image: see, for example, Mark 8:15.
[24] Paul may use here an epistolary convention (H. D. Betz), making "an ethos appeal" in order to cause the Galatians to see themselves as people he trusts. Cf. Kraftchick, "Ethos," 245; Olson, "Confidence."
[25] Regarding "much more" and bifocal lenses, see J. L. Martyn, *Issues,* 279–297.
[26] See Kuck, "Apocalyptic Motif," 296.
[27] Cf. Mussner 358 n106; Winger, "Unreal Conditions," 111.

The fact that you are being persecuted, Paul, confirms what we know very well, namely that the scandalous character of the cross is the center of your preaching. It cannot be, then, that you ever demand circumcision of your hearers.

The letter as a whole is characterized by the antinomy between God's act in the cross of Christ and the human act of circumcising the flesh (2:21; Comment #31).[28] But why does Paul explicitly interject that matter at this point? There are three major clues. Paul suddenly and emphatically refers to himself; he speaks to the Galatians with the endearing form of address; and, both in the preceding sentence and in the following one, he refers to the Teachers.

As for me, brothers and sisters. By addressing the Galatians affectionately (4:31), Paul leaves behind the warnings of 5:2–9, now differentiating all of the Galatians from the Teachers and openly inviting them to stand at his side rather than at the side of the Teachers.

if, on occasion, I am preaching, as part of the gospel message, that one should be circumcised — as some wrongly report to you. Paul coins the expression "preach circumcision" as the polar opposite of "preach Christ crucified," another expression of his own coinage (cf. 3:1; 1 Cor 1:23). He is concerned to encapsulate and to refute a charge being presently leveled against him by the Teachers. What exactly are the Teachers saying about him?

on occasion . . . as part of the gospel message. Literally, clause (b) reads simply "if I preach circumcision *eti.*" This little Greek adverb can have any one of several meanings. In the main, *eti* conveys either temporal force, "still," or an additive meaning, "in addition."[29] Most exegetes take it to be temporal in the present instance: "If I am still proclaiming the necessity of circumcision . . ." One must admit that this interpretation is supported by the fact that the same adverb emerges in clause (c), probably with its temporal meaning: "Why am I still persecuted?"

But — in addition to the difficulty of explaining what the Teachers could mean by implying that Paul preached circumcision in the past — everything in Galatians, not to mention Paul's other letters, indicates that he is not currently advocating the circumcision of Gentiles.[30] With Mussner it is best to take the first *eti*

[28]Cf. Gaventa, "Purpose."
[29]Mussner, citing Mayser, *Grammatik,* mentions and correctly excludes a third possibility, *eti* having a comparative force.
[30]Dunn helpfully lists six readings, clear evidence that the reference is opaque. Taking circumcision in a nonliteral sense, P. Borgen has argued that the Teachers could have credited Paul with preaching its necessity ("Paul Preaches Circumcision"): In his original preaching to the Galatians Paul had spoken of overcoming the desires of the flesh (5:21). Some Jews of Paul's time (Philo, for example) held victory over the desires of the flesh to be the real meaning of circumcision. Hence, Borgen argues, the Teachers may have said to the Galatians: "Look here! In his own way — not literally, to be sure — Paul himself preaches what might be called the spiritual essence of circumcision, insisting that you overcome the desires of the flesh. We tell you that it is crucial for you to press ahead with the rite itself." Barclay, *Obeying,* 50, is right, however, to be skeptical of this line of interpretation, as is Dunn. See further Howard, *Crisis,* 7–11; Linton, "Aspect."

in v 11 to mean "in addition to." The Teachers seem to be saying that *from time to time* Paul *adds* as part of his gospel message the demand of circumcision. But how could they have hoped to persuade the Galatians that such a charge is justified?

We do not know. They may have received a report, however, that on at least one occasion Paul circumcised a Gentile member of the church. We know that a tradition of this sort made its way to the author of Acts (the story of Paul's circumcision of Timothy after the latter had already become a Christian; Acts 16:1–3).[31] This tradition, or one like it, may have come to the Teachers, and they may have passed it on to the Galatians, saying that, under certain circumstances, Paul has been rumored to give circumcision a supplementary role in his preaching.

Whatever the precise nature of the charge, Paul answers it by stating yet again the core of his preaching, the scandalous story of Christ's crucifixion, to which there can be no salvific supplement of any sort.

as some wrongly report to you. For reasons stated above this clause is added in the translation.[32]

why am I being persecuted to this day? There is no good reason to think that Paul ever told the Galatians of his being persecuted and disciplined in various locales by numerous authorities, both Jewish and Gentile (1 Thess 2:16; 1 Cor 4:8–13; 2 Cor 11:23–29). The persecutors to whom he refers in the present verse are the Teachers (and, behind them, the False Brothers in the Jerusalem church). In 4:29 he has used the word "persecute" to refer to their activity, understanding it to be an attempt to destroy his churches. See the sequence of vignettes of the Jerusalem church presented in Comment #46.

The logic of the rhetorical question is thus clear: "If I were on occasion advocating circumcision of Gentile converts, the persecution of me that was commenced by the False Brothers at the Jerusalem meeting—and that continues to this day in the activity of the Teachers—would cease. In fact, as you yourselves know very well, that persecution has by no means come to an end. Consequently, you can see the falsity of the rumor that on occasion I am an advocate of the demand that Gentiles be circumcised."

wiping out the scandalous character of the cross. Were Paul to advocate the circumcision of Gentile converts, he would become a propagator of an acceptable religion, and the persecutory opposition to his work would cease. That move on his part would also terminate his proclamation of God's gracious—and scandalous—invasion of the world in the hideous event of Christ's crucifixion (2:21; 3:1; 1 Cor 1:23). For, to add religion to that redemptive, apocalyptic act of God is to be separated from that act (v 4).

12. *wish.* Paul begins the last sentence of the paragraph with a particle (*ophelon*) that introduces a wish, and the character of Paul's wish shows the depth of his feelings about the Teachers' seduction of his Galatian churches.[33]

---

[31] In addition to commentaries on Acts, cf. Cohen, "Timothy"; Linton, "Aspect."

[32] Winger lists Gal 5:11 under his rubric: "Conditions that someone other than Paul apparently claims are fulfilled" ("Unreal Conditions," 111).

[33] With the future *apokopsontai* the particle *ophelon* can express an attainable wish (BDF §384).

castrate themselves! Saying that, in the case of the Teachers, castration is the true conclusion of the rite of circumcision, Paul paints a rude, obscene, and literally bloody picture at their expense.[34] He may be thinking of the practice of castration among the priests in the cult of Cybele (one of that cult's major temples was located in Pessinus, very probably a city in which one of his Galatian churches was located; Introduction §3 and Comment #41). If so, Paul may mean that circumcision belongs together with castration in the sense that both are signs of a trust in the redemptive power of religion. He would then say, in effect: "I wish the Teachers would join the priests in the cult of Cybele by castrating themselves, thus showing what they really are, nothing more than men who place their trust in religion rather than in the God of the crucified Christ."

COMMENT #47
EAGERLY WAITING FOR THE HOPE OF RECTIFICATION

Prior to 5:5 Paul has made God's already-accomplished rectification one of the letter's chief themes. Denying that the Law has the power to make things right, Paul has told the Galatians that, as persons grasped by the gospel of Christ's atoning death, they have already been rectified (2:16, 20–21; 3:13, 24; 5:1). In 5:5, however, he says,

> having the Spirit in our hearts, and having the confidence that comes from faith, we eagerly await the hope of rectification.

Why does he seem here to abandon his earlier affirmations, referring to God's deed of setting things right as a future event?[35]

The broad context provides an answer. In the warning with which Paul opens the paragraph of 5:2–12 he declares to the Galatians the consequences for their future if they follow the Teachers' bankrupt theology (v 2). They will be separated from Christ and from his Spirit. Moreover, that separation will deprive them of the future Paul promises in 5:16, the Spirit's deliverance from the Impulsive Desire of the Flesh. Falling prey to that monster, they will have to bear divine judgment in the future (5:21; 6:5, 8), whereas those whose minds are led by the Spirit will in the future reap eternal life (6:8), as the Spirit continues to bear in that future the communal fruit of love, joy, and peace (5:22–23).

From Galatians itself, then, two things are clear: God's deed of rectification in Christ is accomplished, and that deed of God also remains under attack by the powers that enslave human beings, not least the Flesh (Comment #49). God's rectification is therefore consistently to be lived out in the communal life of God's church. In short, God's deed of rectification — accomplished in Christ —

---

[34] Numerous Gentiles saw in circumcision a symbol of castration. In the second century Hadrian explicitly equated the two, and forbade both (Barnard, "Hadrian").

[35] As we have seen in the Note on 5:5, holding rectification to be a future event is characteristic of much Jewish tradition.

is still finding its concrete form in the daily life of the church, as the church expands into the whole of the world.[36]

Thus, on the one hand, Paul issues in 5:2–12 several stern indications of the possible outcome of the attack mounted by anti-God powers in the Teachers' message. On the other hand, he speaks confidently of the future that will surely unfold under God's sovereignty. In vv 4–6, sharply differentiating himself from the Galatians who have succumbed to the Teachers' message, Paul clearly implies that the latter have lost their footing in the rectifying grace of Christ. They have separated themselves from the Spirit of Christ, from the faith that is incited by the gospel of Christ — the faith that is actively engaged in loving the neighbor — and from the confidence that eagerly awaits the future presided over by God.

Even in writing to the Galatians, then, Paul knows that rectification is "to be had on earth only as a pledged gift, always subject to attack, always to be authenticated in practice — a matter of promise and expectation."[37] The fecundity of the Spirit and of faith can be seen in the church that, in the pattern of mutual love, eagerly awaits the hope of God's climactic and irreversible rectification.

5:13–24 PASTORAL GUIDANCE, PART 1: DAILY LIFE IN WARTIME

TRANSLATION

5:13. For you were called to freedom, brothers and sisters; only do not allow freedom to be turned into a military base of operations for the Flesh, active as a cosmic power. On the contrary, through love be genuine servants of one another. 14. For the whole of the Law has been brought to completion in one sentence: "You shall love your neighbor as yourself!" 15. But if you snap at one another, each threatening to devour the other, take care that you are not eaten up by one another!

16. In contradistinction to the Teachers, I, Paul, say to you: Lead your daily life guided by the Spirit, and, in this way, you will not end up carrying out the Impulsive Desire of the Flesh. 17. For the Flesh is actively inclined against the Spirit, and the Spirit against the Flesh. Indeed these two powers constitute a pair of opposites at war with one another, the result being that you do not actually do the very things you wish to do. 18. If, however, in the daily life of your communities you are being consistently led by the Spirit, then you are not under the authority of the Law.

---

[36]Thus, rectification cannot be separated from sanctification (cf. Käsemann, *Questions*, 171).
[37]Käsemann, *Questions*, 170.

19. The effects of the Flesh are clear, and those effects are: fornication, vicious immorality, uncontrolled debauchery, 20. the worship of idols, belief in magic, instances of irreconcilable hatred, strife, resentment, outbursts of rage, mercenary ambition, dissensions, separation into divisive cliques, 21. grudging envy of the neighbor's success, bouts of drunkenness, nights of carousing, and other things of the same sort. In this regard, I warn you now, just as I warned you before: those who practice things of this sort will not inherit the Kingdom of God.

22. By contrast, the fruit borne by the Spirit is love, joy, peace, patience, kindness, generosity, faith, 23. gentleness, self-control. The Law does not forbid things of this kind! 24. And those who belong to Christ Jesus have crucified the Flesh, together with its passions and desires.

LITERARY STRUCTURE AND SYNOPSIS

Looking back for a moment to 5:1, we can imagine Paul composing his Galatian letter without including any of the elements that now make up 5:2–6:10.[38] Could he not easily have passed from the ringing conclusion of 5:1 to the epistolary postscript of 6:11–18? The statement of 5:1a summarizes, after all, not only the exegetical argument commenced at 4:21 but also the major motifs of chapters 1–4:

It was to bring us into the realm of freedom that Christ set us free.

And the exhortation of 5:1b specifically applies that statement to the situation in the Galatian churches:

Stand your ground, therefore, and do not ever again take up the yoke of slavery!

To that summarizing statement and hortatory application, then, Paul could have added the epistolary postscript of 6:11–18:

Notice the large letters I am using, as I now seize the pen to write to you with my own hand . . . neither is circumcision anything nor is uncircumcision anything. What is something is the new creation . . . Brothers and sisters, the grace of our Lord Jesus Christ be with your spirit. Amen!

For in that postscript, Paul adds a final attack on the Teachers (6:12–13), and he closes with a declaration of the new creation in which—as he has said repeatedly—all enslaving religious distinctions have been obliterated (6:14–18). What precisely would the letter lack if it did not include 5:2–6:10?

---

[38] In the view of O'Neill this is very nearly what Paul actually did, a later editor being responsible for what we have in 5:13–6:10 (*Recovery*, 71; cf. Smit, "Speech," 25). For reasons given below, O'Neill's analysis must be judged fascinating but procrustean.

In the main it would lack four elements: (a) The letter would not contain the warning predictions of 5:2–12. (b) It would have no explicit answer to the Teachers' charge that Paul fails to include in his own instruction guidance in everyday life (see Comment #33). (c) Although the letter would contain two passages focused on the subject of rectification (2:16–21 and 3:6–25) — the second passage defining it as deliverance from enslaving powers — Paul would have closed his epistle without giving a portrait that shows in detail what God's rectifying deed looks like in the daily life of the church. (d) The letter would lack an explicitly pastoral section in which Paul summons the Galatians to their place in a world marked by the polarity between the Spirit and the Flesh (on the use of the term "pastoral," see below). All four of these matters are closely related to one another, and (b), (c), and (d) are of such importance as to demand the apostle's extended attention. Thus, they coalesce to form Paul's agenda in 5:13–6:10.

For obvious reasons the two paragraphs of this section, 5:13–24 and 5:25–6:10, have often been joined and called the hortatory part of the letter.[39] There are three imperative verbs right at the beginning:

"*Do not allow* freedom to be turned into a military base of operations for the Flesh" (5:13).
"On the contrary, *be genuine servants* of one another" (5:13).
"*You shall love* your neighbor" (5:14).

The first of these verbs is implied, and the third is the imperative use of the future (Lev 19:18). That fact, however, does not lessen the hortatory tone. For these verbs are followed at length by eleven others that are either imperative or hortatory subjunctive:

In the first paragraph (5:13–24):
5:15 *blepete*, "take care"
5:16 *peripateite*, "lead your daily life"
In the second paragraph (5:25–6:10):
5:25 *stoichômen*, "let us carry out our daily lives"
5:26 *mê ginômetha kenodoxoi*, "do not think of yourself as better"
6:1 *katartizete*, "restore"
6:2 *bastazete*, "bear (one another's burdens)"
6:4 *dokimazetô*, "consider"
6:6 *koinôneitô*, "share goods"
6:7 *mê planasthe*, "do not be deceived"
6:9 *mê egkakômen*, "do not become weary (in doing the right thing)"
6:10 *ergazômetha*, "let us work."[40]

---

[39] Regarding 5:25 as the opening of a new paragraph, see Literary Structure and Synopsis for 5:25–6:10. Being the best comprehensive guide to 5:13–6:10, the work of Barclay, *Obeying*, is one to which we will refer at numerous points.
[40] Note also that in 6:2 *anaplêrôsete* begins a line of seven verbs that describe the future, the final verb being *therisomen*, "we will reap a harvest," in 6:9.

Were we, however, to list all of the verbs in the first paragraph, we would see that in tone that paragraph is to be distinguished from the second. Only in the second paragraph does Paul speak in a way that is truly and consistently hortatory. We have just seen, to be sure, that at the outset of the first paragraph, Paul turns his attention as a pastor to the very practical matter of the daily pattern of life in the Galatian communities, even focusing part of his attention on the relationship between behavior and the Law (5:14; Comment #48). Everyday life in the church is indeed the subject from 5:13 to 6:10.

In 5:13–24, however, Paul addresses that subject in a fundamentally descriptive way. Even 5:14 is not an exhortation. Having called on the Galatians to serve one another (5:13), Paul is concerned to make a statement about the present state of affairs. Communal life marked by mutual and loving service is related to a signal fact about the Law: The whole of the Law has now been brought to completion in the sentence "You shall love your neighbor as yourself!" Verse 15 is more a taunt than an exhortation: "Watch out!" And v 16 is at its core a promise rather than an exhortation (Comment #49). Moreover, and most important, all of the verbs in the weighty sentences of vv 17–24 are in the indicative mood.

Here and subsequently, it is best to avoid a comprehensive use of the words "parenetic" and "hortatory," referring instead to 5:13–24 as the first part of the letter's pastoral section.[41] Knowing that the power of Christ's rectifying love is embodied in the daily life of the church—as the church is led by Christ's Spirit—Paul is intent on describing the real world, the world that has been made what it is by God's sending into it Christ and his Spirit. This real world is the world that dawned for the Galatians when they were baptized into Christ (3:26–28), the world into which they were summoned by God when he sent the Spirit into their hearts, the world to which Paul will shortly refer as "the new creation" (6:15).

That world has about it the character of a drama. On its stage, as we have

---

[41] In using the word "pastoral," I draw in part on the helpful analysis of 1 Thessalonians by Malherbe, *the Thessalonians*, 68–94. Appreciative of numerous epistolary parallels, Malherbe speaks nevertheless of Paul's creating in "the pastoral letter" (1 Thessalonians) a new, Christian literary genre (69; cf. Stowers, *Letter Writing*, 23). Harnisch's statement that, at the outset of Galatians 5, one senses a "passing over into a different genus" ("Einübung," 287) can well be applied to 5:13–24. In using the term "pastoral" to speak of this section, however, I must add a qualifying distinction between pastoral care that is basically hortatory and care that is basically descriptive. True enough, it was as clear in Paul's time as it is in ours that exhortation can be accomplished indirectly. One can offer a portrait of a virtuous life, for example, in such a way as to imply the wisdom of emulation (frequent in parenetic letters). Or one can issue a threat designed to dissuade the reader from a certain course of action (cf. Gal 5:2–12). As we will see, however, Paul's use of the indicative mood in Gal 5:13–24 is significant in a way not well represented when one refers to this paragraph as hortatory. Here, Paul's pastoral concern is focused on providing the Galatians with a map of the world in which they actually live. One might compare this concern, to be sure, with that of, for example, Epictetus (see, e.g., *Diss.* 3.22, especially 3.22.107). But the apocalyptic frame within which Paul thinks about daily life precludes his exhorting the Galatians—either directly or indirectly—to avoid vice and to cultivate virtue (Comment #49). Paul turns, therefore, to concentrated exhortation only in 5:25–6:10.

begun to see, a number of actors are playing their parts. Speaking, then, as a pastor, Paul feels that the Galatians need nothing so much as to come to perceive these actors for what they really are. For, seeing the real actors on the real cosmic stage, seeing how they are in fact interacting with one another, the Galatians will be able once again to discern their own part. And, discerning their own part, they will be able to respond to exhortation when they hear it in 5:25–6:10.

In 5:13 Paul begins by speaking of an actor of great importance, the Flesh, referring to this actor more fully in v 16 as "the Impulsive Desire of the Flesh," and describing its effects in some detail in vv 19–21a (Comment #49). This actor is not a mere component of the human being, a person's flesh as distinguished from his spirit. The Flesh is rather a supra-human power, indeed an inimical, martial power seeking to establish a military base of operations in the Galatian churches, with the intention of destroying them as genuine communities (5:13, 19–21). To live in the real world, therefore, the Galatians must deal with this powerful actor. But, as the paragraph unfolds, one sees that, in their dealings with this actor, the Galatians are not alone.

For in v 16 Paul speaks of another actor, again supra-human, the Spirit. Here, too, Paul does not refer to a component of the human being, a person's spirit as distinguished from his flesh or his body. Paul speaks of the Spirit God has sent into the Galatians' hearts, the Spirit, specifically, of God's Son (4:6). The result is Paul's portrait of two supra-human powers — the Spirit and the Flesh — as these actors are locked in combat with one another (v 17). In a word, he speaks of a genuine war, a war of liberation that has been commenced by the Spirit upon its arrival.[42] And in this war the Galatians are far more than mere spectators. Having the Spirit in their hearts, they are soldiers who have been called into military service by the Spirit. Placed in the front trenches of the Spirit's war against the Flesh, they need a reliable map of the landscape (Comment #49).

For specific clues to the topographic details of the war in which the Galatians are caught up, Paul refers them to the marks of the two antagonists, the Flesh and the Spirit. And in listing those marks (vv 19–21a and 22–23a) Paul draws not on scripture, but rather on a widely known Greco-Roman and Jewish tradition in which a catalogue of *vices* is contrasted to a catalogue of *virtues*.[43] The result is a portrait of daily life that is appropriate to a group of soldiers who are on a

---

[42]Cf. B. B. Hall, "Imagery."

[43]To mention a few examples, one finds this tradition in Aristotle and the Stoics, also in Philo and Qumran, and in early Christian strains of tradition as well: Aristotle *Rhetoric* 1.9.1366b; Diogenes Laertius *Lives* 7.110–116; Philo *de Sac.* 20–30; 1QS 3:13–4:26; Mark 7:21–22. The critical literature is extensive. See Fitzgerald, "Lists"; idem, "Catalogue." It is scarcely surprising to discover that the virtues and vices were sometimes arranged in pairs of opposites, as in the passage from Aristotle mentioned above. Moreover, in Jewish and Jewish-Christian traditions the pairing of virtues and vices was often brought into relation both to the doctrine of the Two Ways and to the doctrine of the Evil Impulse (e.g., *T. Asher* 1:1–5:4; *Barn.* 19:2; *Did.* 1:2). Given the list of vices in the Jewish-Christian document of James (and in Jewish-Christian tradition), one cannot rule out the possibility that the Teachers themselves included such a list in their instruction. See James 3:13–18; Clementine *Hom.* 11.26–28. In Gal 5:19–23a Paul is himself relating the vice-and-virtue tradition to the doctrine of the Evil Impulse, but, for reasons given below — and analyzed

field of apocalyptic battle, and who are led there not by a set of regulations, but rather by the power that is certain to be the victor on that battlefield, the Spirit of Christ.

The distance of 5:19–23a from scripture is shown in two important ways. Paul does not identify as infractions of the Law the odious behavioral characteristics he lists in vv 19–21a (contrast *T. 12 Patr.*, where vices are repeatedly said to be transgressions of God's Law). Fornication, idolatry, etc., are rather the effects of the power called the Flesh (vv 19–21a).[44] Nor, in referring to behavioral characteristics elsewhere known as virtues, does Paul employ the Jewish tradition in which the Law is held to have the power to produce virtue. He speaks rather of the effects of the power called the Spirit (vv 22–23a).

It is, then, a serious mistake to read Paul's descriptions of the activities of the Flesh and the Spirit in Gal 5:19–23 as an example of nomistic, moral discourse focused on "vices" and "virtues."[45] By concentrating on the matter of community life, and by speaking of the Flesh and the Spirit as supra-human, apocalyptic powers, Paul transforms what had traditionally been a form of moral discourse — vices and virtues attributable to individuals — into marks left on communities by these two apocalyptic powers (Comment #49).[46]

In sum, then, at its core, 5:13–24 is not a prescription of the way the Galatians ought to behave, a series of exhortations focused on the demands laid on human beings by the Law or by some other system of moral norms. On the contrary, this paragraph is fundamentally a description of the way things are, given the advent of the Spirit, its declaration of war against the Flesh, and its community-building power, already evident in the Galatian churches.

NOTES

5:13. *For you were called to freedom, brothers and sisters; only do not allow freedom to be turned into a military base of operations for the Flesh, active as a cosmic power.*

---

in Comment #49 — we should go wrong to suppose (a) that he himself thinks he is listing vices and virtues and (b) that he is himself using the framework of the Two Ways.

[44]The Galatians' first contact with a catalogue of vices in Christian dress occurred when Paul employed one as he held services of baptism among them (Gal 5:21b). The use of a catalogue of vices unaccompanied by a list of virtues became common in early Christian traditions, especially in connection with baptism (see Wibbing, *Tugend- und Lasterkataloge*; Kamlah, *Paränese*; Schweizer, "Lasterkataloge"; Meeks, *Origins*; Fitzgerald, "Lists").

[45]True enough, one can couch moral discourse in the indicative mood, indirectly exhorting another human being — say a misbehaving child — by saying, "We do not do that to other people" (Meeks, *Origins*, 4). In 5:19–23, however, Paul uses the indicative in an apocalyptically descriptive fashion.

[46]It is in this regard that the picture Paul paints in Gal 5:19–23a diverges most significantly from the picture in 1QS 3:13–4:26. The Qumran community speaks of warfare between the spirits of truth and falsehood, attributing real power to them (1QS 3:22–24) and noting ways in which their warfare affects the community. The Covenantors also focus considerable attention, however, on the general picture of humanity and thus on the individual within whom the spirits act. "The nature of *all the children of men* is ruled by these (two spirits), and during their life all the hosts of men have a portion in their divisions and walk

you (plural). Throughout 5:13–6:10 — as elsewhere in the letter — Paul speaks to the Galatian churches as congregations. He does not think of individuals except as they exist in the community of the church (see Notes on 6:1 and 6:3). Moreover, except for the rather opaque reference in 5:17 (cf. 5:2, 4), he does not differentiate one group in the Galatian churches from another.

called to freedom. God is the New Creator who has called the Galatians into existence as members of his church (1:6; cf. Rom 4:17). In that new-creative act God called them into the realm of Christ where, for the first time, they are set free from all the powers that formerly enslaved them, the cursing Law, Sin, the elements of the cosmos, and now the Impulsive Desire of the Flesh (3:22–4:5; 5:1; Comment #39).

only do not allow freedom to be turned into. The clause introduced by the adverb "only" has no verb, but from the context we can see that Paul implies a verb in the imperative mood. And given his use of the preposition "into" (*eis*), we can surmise that he thinks of the terrible development in which a community allows freedom to be turned *into* something other than freedom. That is to say, because there is no such thing as an autonomously free will, "freedom from" easily becomes nothing more than a transfer from one form of slavery to another. Specifically, the Galatians could shed the tyranny of the Law only to become subject to the tyranny of the Impulsive Desire of the Flesh (v 16). Freedom that is both true and sufficiently powerful to stand the test of daily life is also "freedom for," and specifically freedom for service of the neighbor (v 14).

a military base of operations. The context — see especially 5:17 — provides strong reasons for thinking that Paul uses the word *aphormê* as a metaphor referring not merely to an "opportunity" (NRSV) or "opening" (NJB), but rather to "a point from which a war can be waged," "a base well suited to the operations of an army" (cf. Thucydides 1.90, etc.).[47] In considering the literary structure of 5:13–24 we have noted several instances in which Paul employs the imagery of a struggle that can become a military battle.

the Flesh, active as a cosmic power. At this juncture Paul writes only the word *sarx*, "flesh," but this reference is the first of a series in which Paul uses that word in a new way. Up to this point Paul has followed the Teachers in employing the word to refer to the foreskin of the penis that is removed in the rite of circumcision (3:3; 4:23, 29). Now we can see that he borrows another element of their vocabulary, for behind 5:16 one senses that the Teachers are using the expression "the Impulsive Desire of the Flesh" to speak of an entity that, in Jewish and Jewish-Christian traditions, is called the Evil Impulse or Inclination. To an extent, Paul follows suit. In vv 13, 17 (twice), 19, 24, and partly in 6:8, Paul uses the expression "the Flesh" as an abbreviation for "the Impulsive Desire of the

---

in (both) their ways. And the whole reward for their deeds shall be . . . according to whether *each man's* portion in their two divisions is great or small" (1QS 4:15–16; Vermes). In Gal 5:18–24 Paul speaks consistently and exclusively of the community of those who belong to Christ, those who have received the Spirit of Christ.

[47] Paul's use of the word *aphormê* in Rom 7:8, 11 is equally instructive: Sin established its base of operations via the commandment, using the commandment to produce the very thing the commandment was supposed to prevent (cf. Gen 3:1–3). See Meyer, "Worm."

Flesh," an apocalyptic, cosmic, supra-human power (hence the capital *F* to distinguish this cosmic power from the foreskin).[48] See Comment #49 and cf. Comment #32.

On the contrary, through love be genuine servants of one another. Paul has commenced the pastoral section of his letter with the implied imperative verb of v 13b ("do not allow"). Now he continues with a second imperative, *dia tês agapês douleuete allêlois*, lit. "through love be slaves of one another." Paul could have said simply, "Control your tendencies toward libertine immorality." But that exhortation would have involved two serious mistakes. (a) It would have implied that the Flesh is nothing more than immorality, whereas, as Paul has just said, the Flesh is a menacing power, and as he will shortly say, the effect of this power is most clearly shown in the destruction of community life (vv 15, 19–21a).[49] (b) That simple form of exhortation would have credited human beings with the ability to control the Flesh. Paul is sure, however, that exhortation is significant only when directed to communities that have been made addressable by the activity of the Spirit (Comment #49).

14. *For.* Paul begins v 14 with the inferential conjunction *gar*, indicating one of the grounds for his exhortation in v 13. A major question, as we will see, is whether, in stating this ground, Paul refers to something done by someone other than the Galatians themselves.

the whole of the Law. In v 3 Paul has spoken of *holos ho nomos*, lit. "the whole Law," whereas in v 14 he now refers to *ho pas nomos*, lit. "all the Law." There is no linguistic reason to think that he intends to differentiate the one from the other. Either Greek expression can serve to translate the Hebrew *kōl hattôrâ kûllâ.* In Comment #48, however, we will see reasons for thinking that Paul refers in v 3 to the cursing and enslaving voice of the Law, whereas in v 14 he speaks of the Law's promissory and guiding voice. Nowhere in the present commentary is it more urgent for the reader to consider Notes and Comments together than in the instance of 5:14.

has been brought to completion. Three issues demand attention, even though in this Note they can be discussed only in a preliminary fashion, fuller treatment being a concern in Comments #48 and #50: First, there is Paul's use here of the

---

[48]In current research the fundamental analysis is that given in two articles of Marcus, "James" and "Paul." H. D. Betz represents a number of interpreters when he says that Gal 5:17 presents "one of the fundamental *anthropological* doctrines of Paul" (278), adding that "the flesh and its 'desiring' (*epithymeô*) are *human* agents of evil, while the Spirit is the divine agent of good" (279; emphasis added). Consequently, in interpreting 5:17, Betz hears Paul referring to the war between the Flesh and the Spirit as a struggle being waged within *the individual.* "The human 'I' wills, but it is prevented from carrying out its will . . . because it is paralyzed through these dualistic forces within." And, further, "*the human body* is a battlefield" (279–280; emphasis added). See Comment #49, where we will note grounds for finding that in Gal 5:13–24 Paul consistently thinks not of the individual (the "I" of Romans 7 is absent), but rather of the Galatian churches, the war between the Spirit and the Flesh taking place in these churches *as communities.*

[49]The destruction of community remains a major motif in 5:25–26, for, as Kuck correctly points out, thinking of oneself as better than others is the opposite of serving one another in love ("Apocalyptic Motif," 291).

verb *plêroô*, lit. "make full," "fulfill." How is it to be translated in this instance? Second, why does Paul put this verb in the perfect tense? Third, why does Paul use the passive rather than the active voice?

(1) Translating the verb *plêroô*. In its literal use the verb *plêroô*, "make full," frequently refers to the filling of a container that was previously altogether or partially empty, the result being that the container is full. Used as a trope, the verb has various shades of meaning, four of which could be suggested for the present instance where Paul employs the verb with reference to the Law.

(a) "is fulfilled." There is a long tradition in which the verb *plêroô* in Gal 5:14 is rendered "fulfill," meaning in effect "fully observe" (e.g., RSV). Thus: "the whole of the Law is *fulfilled* in the one commandment of neighbor love," in the sense that the person who loves the neighbor is considered to have *completely observed* the *essence* of the Law, thus fulfilling the Law's *real* requirement. If there were reason to think that, in using the Greek verb *plêroô*, Paul had in mind the verb *qûm* (piel "to fulfill"), then it could be pertinent to note that the rabbis sometimes used this verb to speak of the Law's being *completely observed*.[50] But the broad context given by Paul's references to the Law in Gal 2:16–5:4 precludes this interpretation, not least because, in wording 5:14, Paul uses the verb *plêroô* — in his own way — rather than repeating from 5:3 the verb *poieô* ("observe").[51] About this verbal change, H. D. Betz remarks,

> [In 5:14] the "whole Law" is not to be "done" (*poiein*), as individual laws have to be done (cf. 3:10, 12; 5:3), but is rather "fulfilled."[52]

[50]For example, *b. Yoma* 28b: "Abraham fulfilled the whole Law." Did the Teachers say that Abraham *fulfilled* (completely observed) *the whole Law*?

[51]Nowhere in the OT is the noun "Law" (*torah/nomos*) linked with the verb "fulfill" (*millē'/plêroô*); and the *Greek* expression "to fulfill the Law" seems to be absent from Jewish traditions of Paul's time as well (Barclay, *Obeying*, 138). Philo, however, speaks of Israel as the nation that has brought the Law's commandments out of darkness into the light, by fulfilling the divine exhortations with laudable deeds (*plêrôsai tous logous* [*scil. tas theias paraineseis*] *ergois epainetois; de Praem*. 79–83). Similarly, *T. Naph.* (8:7), noting that "the commandments of the Law are double," adds that they are to be fulfilled (*plêrountai*) without exception, apparently meaning that the observance of one of a pair of commandments cannot be a substitute for the observance of its mate. Other passages suggest that at least the equivalent of the expression "to fulfill the Law" may well have been known in Paul's time, and there are pertinent passages in Matthew, notably 5:17–20. There are even Jewish traditions in which the whole Law is said to be fulfilled in one commandment, but, as we will see in Appendix A to Comment #48, what is meant is that that commandment is either the "great principle" (*kĕlāl gādôl*) of the Law or that it is the point at which a non-Jew can enter into the Law, its being presupposed that the rest of the Law is also to be observed with undiminished rigor. The conclusion is that, if the expression "to fulfill the whole of the Law" was current in Paul's time, it meant to keep the Law completely, *observing the commandments without exception*. The expression would be precisely represented, then, in a Jewish-Christian reference to keeping the whole of the Law now found in James: "For whoever keeps the whole Law (*holon ton nomon têrêsê*) but fails in one point has become guilty of breaking all of it" (Jas 2:10). As we will see in Comment #48, in Gal 5:14 Paul does not speak in this vein. For him *ho pas nomos peplêrotai* does not refer to the observance of all the commandments.

[52]H. D. Betz 275; see also Moule, "Fulfillment Words."

This comment is helpful. Fully to honor the verbal change, however, is to see that, in translating 5:14, we cannot use the English word "fulfill." In common parlance this verb very often takes as its direct object the noun "requirements," and for that reason "fulfill" is frequently indistinguishable from "fully perform all required stipulations." But it is precisely Paul's shift to the verb *plêroô* that precludes in 5:14 the thought of Law observance in that sense. In short, Paul does not say here that one fulfills/performs the many requirements of the Law by fulfilling/performing the one requirement of neighbor love.

(b) "is summarized." There is a recent tendency to render *plêroô* in Gal 5:14 as "summarize" (NEB, NRSV, NJB). Thus: "the whole of the Law is *summed up* in the one commandment of neighbor love." In fact, however, this translation does not arise from a reading of Gal 5:14 in the context set by the rest of the letter. On the contrary, it is drawn from a partially parallel passage in Rom 13:8–10.[53] In Appendix B to Comment #48 we will see grounds for reading Rom 13:8–10 in light of Gal 5:14, rather than vice versa.

(c) "is brought to completion." The verb *plêroô* can also be used in connection with a promise or a prophecy. A promise, for example, can be thought of as partially empty, until it is fulfilled by being *brought to completion* (Matt 1:22; John 13:18; cf. Rom 15:19; BAGD, "*plêroô*," 3.; LSJ III.3.).[54]

(d) "is made perfect." Finally, in a similar manner, *plêroô* can have the connotation of bringing to perfection. Something can be thought imperfect, until it is *made perfect* by being "filled out," thus becoming what it was intended to be (so, e.g., "your joy" in John 15:11; cf. Phil 2:2). Something could also be made perfect by being *restored* to its original identity, after having suffered some kind of deterioration.[55]

We will shortly find that, in penning 5:14, Paul thinks of the Law primarily as a scriptural sentence (Lev 19:18) that has remained partially empty, incomplete, and imperfect, until, being brought to completion, it has been restored to its original identity (Comment #48). Seeing that this scriptural sentence articulates God's own mind (cf. 3:8), Paul leaves behind the language of Law observance (*poieô ton nomon*, etc.), turning instead to the verb *plêroô*, in order to speak of the Law's having been brought to perfect completion (the last two meanings listed above).

(2) Interpreting the perfect tense: *peplêrôtai*. Commentators universally take the verb to show the gnomic use of the perfect tense. Paul is thus said to be formulating a sort of maxim, in order, in effect, to continue to speak in v 14 of something the Galatians are to do. Having exhorted them to serve one another in love (v 13), Paul then gives an aphoristic explication of *their act* of loving service (v 14): "You are to serve one another in love (v 13), for it is always true —

---

[53]This practice seems to have been begun by an ancient scribe (365 *pc*).

[54]Note *b. Mak.* 24b, where the reflexive form of the root *qûm* is used to refer to the bringing of a prophecy to completion.

[55]Note the references in Thucydides and Aristotle from which LSJ arrive at a rendering of the passive of *anaplêroô*: "to be restored to its former size or state." Note also *anaplêrôsis* as "restoration," and cf. Gal 6:2.

and thus true in your case as well — that, when one loves the neighbor, one fulfills (the essence of) the Law."[56]

We may pause to ask, however, whether Paul may not have selected the perfect tense in order to refer to the present state of affairs that is the result of a past action (the simple and most frequent sense of the Greek perfect).[57] On this reading Paul intends in v 14 to speak of the present state of affairs with the Law itself, as that state of affairs is the result of something that has happened to the Law. The Law is now completed, as the result of its having been brought to completion. As we proceed — especially in Comment #48 — we will see reasons for reading the perfect tense in this way: "You are to serve one another in love, for the Law has now been brought to completion in one sentence: 'You shall love your neighbor as yourself!' "[58]

(3) Interpreting the passive voice: *peplêrôtai*. Had Paul put the verb in the active voice — "Someone has brought the Law to completion" — how would he have identified the subject of that verb? He would scarcely have referred to the Galatians, for his exhortation that they serve one another is certainly not based on something they have already done to the Law. A strong case can be made, then, for the thesis that in 5:14 Paul thinks of an act of Christ:

5:1. It was to bring us into the realm of freedom that *Christ set us free*. Stand your ground, therefore, and do not ever again take up the yoke of slavery! . . . 13. For you were called to freedom, brothers and sisters; only do not allow freedom to be turned into a military base of operations for the Flesh, active as a cosmic power. On the contrary, through love be genuine servants of one another. 14. For *Christ has brought the Law to completion* in one sentence: "You shall love your neighbor as yourself!"

[56]The interpretation of 5:14 as a reference to something the Galatians are to do could be supported by looking forward to 6:2, for there Paul speaks explicitly of their act: In bearing one another's burdens *they* will bring to completion (future tense) the Law of Christ. This way of reading 5:14 (note that DFG et al. have the present tense *plêroutai*) reflects the very old and widespread tendency to think that in Galatians Paul speaks mainly of alternative actions that can be taken by human beings. See, for example, H. D. Betz (275): "According to him [Paul], the Jew is obliged to *do* the Torah (cf. 3:10, 12; 5:3; also 6:13), while the Christian *fulfills* the Torah through the act of love, to which he has been freed by Christ (5:1, 13)."

[57]BDF §340, §342. Citing Acts 5:28, "You have filled Jerusalem with your teaching," BDF remarks, "a perfect like *peplêrôkate* . . . may be resolved into *eplêrôsate kai nun plêrês estin* ['you filled it, and it is now full']." See also Kühner, *Grammatik*, 147.

[58]Since this reading is the most obvious way of taking into account the perfect tense in 5:14, one is astonished to look for it in vain in the commentaries. Mussner may take a step in the direction of this reading: "Also in regard to ethics, Paul thinks in a 'redemptive-historical' manner: Love (*agapê*), that has been revealed in an exemplary way in Christ's sacrificial death, is the eschatological fulfillment and completion of the Law" (370). In a footnote, however, he abandons that modest step, taking Paul to be speaking of something the Galatians should do: "The perfect tense verb *peplêrôtai* is gnomic in this sense: the Law is always fulfilled when the love commandment is fulfilled." In general, commentators adopt the domesticated reading represented in the texts in which the verb has been changed into the present tense (DFG et al.).

To be sure, at first glance, this reading may seem rather wild. Neither in 5:13 nor in 5:14 does Paul speak of Christ directly. The freedom to which Paul refers at the outset of 5:13, however, is the freedom Christ has won for the Galatians, and this freedom is precisely liberation from the tyranny of the Law: Christ has done something that has affected the Law (5:1). Moreover, there is a clear link between 5:14, with its reference to the Law's having been "brought to completion" (*peplêrôtai*), and 6:2, with its reference to the future event of "bringing to completion" the Law *of Christ* (*anaplêrôsete ton nomon tou Christou*). One may very well wonder, then, whether "the Law of Christ" has found its genesis in an act of Christ vis-à-vis the Law (Comment #48). That reading is altogether harmonious with our earlier reading of the perfect tense of the verb "has been brought to completion": In 5:14 Paul refers to the result of a past event in the Law's history, that past event being an act in which Christ took the Law in hand (Comment #50).

We can prepare the way for Comments #48 and #50, therefore, by proposing in the form of an hypothesis a reading of 5:13–14 and 6:2:

(a) In Gal 5:3 Paul speaks for the twenty-fifth time of the enslaving Law.

(b) In 5:13 he exhorts the Galatians to serve one another in love. Then, in order to provide one of the grounds for this exhortation, he takes the crucial step of referring to a watershed event in the history of the Law (5:14). It has been brought to completion as the result of an act of Christ (perfect passive of *plêroô*), and for that reason the Law is no longer enslaving. Indeed, having been brought to completion by Christ in the one sentence that speaks about love of neighbor, the Law is now pertinent to the daily life of the liberated church, the new community that is made up of those who belong to Christ (Gal 5:1; Lev 19:18; Gal 5:24).

(c) Finally, having referred in 5:14 to the Law that has been brought to completion by an act of Christ, Paul can make the assertion of 6:2:

> In love, bear one another's burdens, and in this way you will bring to completion in the corporate life of your churches (future tense of *anaplêroô*) the Law that Christ himself has brought to completion. For Christ brought the Law to completion, when he made it his own Law, by loving us and giving his life for us. Indeed, he did that precisely in accordance with the will of God our Father, whose promise and whose guidance are spoken by the Law that is now the Law of Christ (1:4; 2:20; 3:8; 5:14; 6:2).[59]

[59]The relation between the passive of 5:14 ("the Law has been brought to completion [by Christ]") and the active of 6:2 ("you will bring the Law of Christ to completion") is well interpreted by recalling earlier passages in the letter. In 2:16, for example, Paul presents a line of thought in which a deed of Christ precedes and elicits a deed of the human being with respect to Christ. "(a) Even we ourselves know, however, that a person is not rectified by observance of the Law, but rather by the faith of Christ Jesus. (b) Thus, even we have placed our trust in Christ Jesus, in order that the source of our rectification might be the faith of Christ and not observance of the Law . . ." The assertion of 5:14 is related to that of 6:2 as (a) and (b) are related to one another in 2:16. Paul speaks in 5:14 of something that Christ has done: He has brought the Law to perfect completion in the single sentence of neighbor love (Lev 19:18). Then, having referred in 5:14 to this deed of Christ, Paul

As we will see in Comments #48 and #50, this hypothesis gains force when one reads 5:3 and 5:14 in light of statements Paul has earlier made about the Law in Galatians 3 and 4.

in one sentence. Lit. "in one logos." It is true that, like one of its Hebrew counterparts, *dābār*, the word *logos* occasionally serves in the LXX to mean "commandment." Had Paul intended to refer to Lev 19:18 as a commandment, however, he could have made that intention clear by writing *entolê* ("commandment"), a word with which he was well acquainted (in addition to Rom 13:9; 1 Cor 7:19; 14:37; Rom 7:8–13). Had he spoken of an *entolê*, however, the Galatians would have sensed a reference to an element of the *Sinaitic Law*. Especially in the Galatian setting, Paul has good reason to avoid speaking of Lev 19:18 as a commandment, saying instead that the whole of the Law is brought to completion in the single *sentence* that he then quotes from *scripture (en tô)*.[60] He thus refers to the original, singular Law that did not consist of commandments (Comment #48).

"You shall love your neighbor as yourself!" Following the wording of Lev 19:18 in the LXX,[61] Paul now specifies the sentence in which the promissory voice of the Law, in its guiding function — the voice now caused by Christ to be the whole of the Law (Comment #48) — has been brought to completion.[62] Regarding the *birth* of churches among the Gentiles, it is the Law of Hab 2:4, Genesis 16–21, and Isa 54:1 that is being brought to completion in the circumcision-free mission (Gal 3:11; 4:21–5:1; cf. Rom 10:15, 18). As regards *daily life* in those churches, what has been brought to completion is the Law of Lev 19:18.

15. *But if you snap at one another, each threatening to devour the other, take care that you are not eaten up by one another!* Using colorful terms descriptive of a vicious dogfight that ends in mutual destruction, Paul takes into account developments actually happening in the Galatian churches.[63] See Note on 6:6.

16. *In contradistinction to the Teachers, I, Paul, say to you: Lead your daily life guided by the Spirit, and, in this way, you will not end up carrying out the Impulsive Desire of the Flesh.*

---

takes that deed to be the empowering foundation, on the basis of which he can speak in 6:2 not only of the Law in Christ's hands but also of the pattern of life in which, by following in Christ's steps, the Galatians will bring to completion in their corporate life the Law that has already been brought to completion by Christ.

[60] On *logos* as "sentence," see LSJ, "*logos*," IX.3.b. Note also the movement from "commandment" to "sentence" in Rom 13:8–10. The widespread tendency to render *logos* as "commandment" in Gal 5:14 (NEB, NJB, NRSV) is unwarranted.

[61] Stanley, *Scripture*, 251.

[62] Pondering both Gal 3:12 and 5:14, one sees that for Paul the book of Leviticus contains both the false promise spoken by the cursing Law (Lev 18:5) and the sentence in which the original/promissory Law speaks of the behavior appropriate to the daily life of the church (Lev 19:18). Paul distinguishes spirits *within* the Law (Comments #35 and #48).

[63] The fact that the diatribe literature has instances in which human conduct is hyperbolically compared with the behavior of wild animals (H. D. Betz 277 n43) does not decide the question whether Paul means to describe actual developments in the Galatian congregations. The conditional sentence — *ei* with the present indicative — points, lacking other signals, to a state of affairs that is supposed by the author to exist. It seems probable, more-

In contradistinction to the Teachers, I, Paul, say to you. With the words *legô de,* "But I say," Paul emphasizes that the sentence thus introduced is spoken by him, not by the Teachers.[64] We can surmise, then, that he is rewording a promise issued to the Galatians by the Teachers, and from 3:21 we can easily guess what it was: "Lead your daily life guided by the Law, the gift by which God grants life, and we promise you that you will not fall under the power of the Impulsive Desire of the Flesh (the Evil Impulse)." See Comment #49.

the Spirit. Earlier in the letter Paul has used the term *pneuma* seven times, referring in each instance to the Spirit whom God has sent into the Galatians' hearts, the Spirit, specifically, of Christ (3:2, 3, 5, 14; 4:6, 29; 5:5). Here, too, he speaks not of a component of the human being, but rather of the Spirit of God's Son. Like Christ himself, the Spirit of Christ is in effect God coming on the scene in order to act here and now.

Lead your daily life. Employing the verb *peripateô,* "to walk," as the equivalent of the Hebrew *hālak,* Paul refers to daily conduct in the Galatian communities.

Lead your daily life guided by the Spirit. In order to speak of the relationship between the Spirit of Christ and daily conduct in the Galatian churches, Paul constructs a sentence with two clauses. In the first he uses an imperative verb with the dative noun "Spirit" — *pneumati peripateite,* "walk in the Spirit" — and in the second, using a verb preceded by the accented negative *ou mê,* he answers the first clause with an emphatic assurance that a certain thing will not happen: "you will by no means end up carrying out the dictates of the Impulsive Desire of the Flesh." In mentioning the Spirit, Paul presupposes yet again the letter's major motif, that of the redemptive invasion God has carried out by sending into the present evil age his Son and the Spirit of his Son. The way in which this motif of divine invasion affects Paul's use of the imperative verb "lead your daily life" is a crucial matter (Comment #49).

you will not end up carrying out the Impulsive Desire of the Flesh. Paul uses the verb *teleô,* "fully to carry out," "to perform," in a construction (aorist subjunctive following the emphatic negative *ou mê*) indicating something that definitely will not happen in the future (BDF §365).[65]

the Impulsive Desire of the Flesh. Literally, Paul writes *epithymia sarkos,* a Greek expression rendering the Hebrew *yēṣer bāśār,* "the desire of the flesh."[66] In Comment #32 and in the Note on 5:13 we have seen that Paul is almost certainly following a locution being used by the Teachers to refer to the Evil Impulse (hence the addition of the adjective "impulsive"). In Comment #49 we will also see that he is going beyond the Teachers, in that, instead of speaking of an entity

---

over, that the Teachers have seized the Galatians' attention partly by telling them that their tendency to contentiousness is the work of the Impulsive Flesh (Comment #49).

[64] See also 3:17; 4:1; 5:2, where, emphatically correcting the Teachers, Paul writes *legô de.*
[65] If the Teachers used this same construction in their form of the promise, they may have had in mind that the verb "to carry out" can take as its object *either* the Law (Acts 13:29) *or* one's desires (Artemidorus Daldianus 3.22; Achilles Tatius 2.13.3; see BAGD).
[66] See Porter, "Yecer hara"; Davies, *Paul,* 20–31; Flusser, "Dead Sea Sect." Crucial steps pertinent to the interpretation of the Inclination (= the Impulsive Desire of the Flesh) in James and in Paul are taken in Marcus, "James"; idem, "Paul."

that is merely internal to the individual human being, Paul refers to a cosmic power arrayed against God, standing, as it does, in the company of other anti-God powers, the cursing voice of the Law, Sin, and the elements of the cosmos. Using the abbreviation "the Flesh" in vv 13, 17 (twice), 19, 24, and partly in 6:8, Paul continues to speak of this malignant power, noting that it can take up residence in a human community, leading that community into patterns of behavior that destroy it as a corporate entity. Seeing the Evil Impulse in its apocalyptic frame, Paul considers it neither a dictator whose power is so great as to relieve the human being of all responsibility nor a mere inclination that can be easily resisted.

17. *For the Flesh is actively inclined against the Spirit, and the Spirit against the Flesh. Indeed these two powers constitute a pair of opposites at war with one another, the result being that you do not actually do the very things you wish to do.*

For. Concerning the sense in which Paul can offer v 17 as (part of) the ground of the promise in v 16, see the Appendix to Comment #49.

actively inclined against. The Flesh and the Spirit are mutually exclusive, but not as distinct orbs, as though Flesh were simply the human sphere, and Spirit the sphere of God (contrast Isa 31:3). We may indeed think of them as orbs of *power*, but we must then add that the orb of the Spirit has now invaded and thus penetrated the orb of the Flesh. More fully expressed, the two are *actors* engaged in combat with one another.[67] That point is clear, and it is essential. In making it, however, Paul composes a sentence whose syntax and word selection will probably have been surprising to the Galatians.

Aside from the present text, there is no instance known to us of the Greek expression *epithymeô kata* and the genitive, lit. "to desire against."[68] It is strange, therefore, that Paul should write *hê sarx epithymei kata tou pneumatos*, lit. "the Flesh *desires against* the Spirit." Paul's meaning was surely grasped, however, by Polycarp, when, drawing on Gal 5:17, he said *pasa epithymia kata tou pneumatos strateuetai*, "every (evil) desire *wars against* the Spirit" (*Phil.* 5:3). Polycarp, that is, understood Paul to be speaking of a *war* between (evil) desires and the Spirit. And, sensing the strangeness of Paul's apparently un-Greek expression, *epithymeô kata*, he changed it to the common locution *strateuomai kata*, "to make war against."[69]

But how is Paul's strange expression to be explained? Attention to Hebrew syntax may help. In the Talmud one notes, for example, *b. Ber.* 5a (cf. 61b): "A man should always *incite* the Good Inclination *against* the Evil Impulse."[70] It may

---

[67]Brandenburger, *Fleisch*, 45. Paul's picture is in some degree similar to Philo's portrait of the two contentious wives of the soul (*de Sac.* 20–30), but for Paul the combat between the Spirit and the Flesh takes place in the communal setting of the church, not internally in the individual.

[68]The verb *epithymeô*, "to desire," was used in various constructions: (a) with the genitive or accusative of the thing desired, (b) with the accusative of a person sexually desired, (c) with an infinitive, and (d) with an accusative and infinitive.

[69]See also 1 Pet 2:11; Marcus, "Paul," 19 n21.

[70]The construction is *rāgaz* (hiphil) *'al*, "cause to be excited against." Cf. Urbach, *Sages*, 475–476.

even be pertinent to note that Rashi (eleventh century) explains the passage in *b. Ber.* 5a in a way similar to that taken in Pol. *Phil.* 5:3: a man "should wage war against the evil inclination."[71]

In short, having accepted the expression *epithymia sarkos*, "Impulsive Desire of the Flesh," as a way of referring to an anti-God power, Paul moves from the noun *epithymia* to the verb *epithymeô*, and — consciously or unconsciously — he draws on Hebrew syntax in order to paint an emphatically dynamic picture: "The Flesh incites a community against the Spirit . . . " Both the Flesh, that is to say, and the Spirit awaken desires; both have their own plans for the human race; and their plans are so thoroughly at odds that they themselves are constantly at war with one another.[72]

constitute a pair of opposites. Using the verb *antikeimai* in one of its technical senses, "to constitute a pair of opposites (in the Table of Opposites)," Paul continues to speak of the way things really are. For, erroneously considering the Flesh to be opposed by the Law — whereas the two are in fact secret allies — the Teachers and their followers among the Galatians fail to see and to participate in the true war of liberation from the Flesh (cf. 1QS 4:17–18a, 23).[73] The fact is that, since the advent of the Spirit, it is the Spirit itself that is opposed to the Flesh (cf. v 16). It is with the Galatians' baptism, then, that the real war has begun. This war is not, therefore, a timeless anthropological rivalry, a struggle that has been raging in the heart of the human being since the dawn of time.[74] On the contrary, it is the apocalyptic battle of the end-time, the war that has been declared by the Spirit, not by the Flesh.

at war with one another. For reasons stated above, this clause is added to the translation, in order to assure that the bellicose dimension of Paul's picture is not overlooked. Note that elsewhere Paul uses the verb *antikeimai* to refer to adversaries and enemies (1 Cor 16:9; Phil 1:28; cf. also 2 Thess 2:4; 1 Tim 1:10; 5:14; Exod 23:22).

the result being that you do not actually do the very things you wish to do. The *hina* clause is consecutive (as it is in 1 Thess 5:4; 2 Cor 1:17; 7:9), stating the result, not the purpose.[75] The particle *mê* almost certainly negates *poiête* (so most exegetes except Borse).

Given the promise of v 16, one should have expected quite a different closure in this sentence:

For the Flesh is actively inclined against the Spirit, and the Spirit against the Flesh. These two powers constitute a pair of opposites at war with one another,

[71]Urbach, *Sages*, 476; cf. Flusser, "Dead Sea Sect," 255.
[72]As we will see in Comment #49, for Paul this war is distinctly apocalyptic in nature. The third mark of the Spirit's fruit — and thus one of its major weapons — is peace! Cf. Eph 6:10–20.
[73]See also Brandenburger, *Fleisch*, 46; Jewett, *Terms*, 81, citing K. G. Kuhn.
[74]Longenecker (245) speaks of this picture as "Paul's understanding of humanity before God since 'sin entered into the world' (cf. Rom 5:12)." As the parenthetical reference suggests, the interpretation is drawn from Romans, not from Galatians.
[75]See BDF §391.5; ZBG §351; Moule, *Idiom-Book*, 142.

and the result of this war, commenced by the Spirit, is that the Spirit is in the process of liberating you from the power of the Flesh.

Why does Paul portray instead a decidedly negative result to the Spirit's war of liberation, seeming to indicate that the result of that war is the inability of the Galatians to carry out their intentions? The picture, unusually difficult to understand, has led interpreters in various directions.[76] In the Appendix to Comment #49 we will see grounds for thinking that Paul refers specifically to an absence of active integrity that characterizes those Galatians who are embracing the message of the Teachers. The "you" to whom he speaks are the members of the Galatian churches who think they can seek rectification in observance of the Law, while remaining followers of Christ (5:4): "Having received the perfectly potent Spirit (4:6; 5:16), but being now led by the Law that is decisively impotent to curb the Flesh (cf. 3:3), you are swept up willy-nilly in the whirlwind of the battle between the Spirit and the Flesh. Lacking active integrity, you find that, when you want to end your dissensions, you succeed only in intensifying them."

18. *If, however, in the daily life of your communities you are being consistently led by the Spirit, then you are not under the authority of the Law.*

however. The particle *de* has here its strongly contrastive force. The portrait of behavioral failure (v 17) does not describe the church when it is led by the Spirit.

in the daily life of your communities you are being consistently led. The verb (present tense) points to a continuous state of affairs, and, being plural, it refers to the communal life of the Galatian churches, insofar as they continue in the truth of the gospel. The lack of integrity portrayed in the final clause of v 17 is overcome when the community of God's new creation is consistently led by the Spirit.

not under the authority of the Law. Repeating a linguistic pattern he has used extensively in Galatians 3 and 4 (on *hypo tina einai*, "to be under the power of," see Comment #39), Paul reminds the Galatians that they are free of the tyranny of the Sinaitic Law, the Law that is observed by some and not observed by others.[77] Given the work of the Teachers, however, the Galatians are constantly tempted to reenter the world of the Law/the Not-Law. What is startling, then, is

[76]As Barclay notes (*Obeying*, 113–114, with references), there have been three main readings of the final clause of v 17. Taking it to state consequence, commentators have said that the battle of the Flesh and the Spirit has as its result (a) that the Flesh often frustrates the Spirit-inspired wishes of the believer; (b) that the Flesh and the Spirit frustrate one another, producing a stalemate. Taking it to be a telic clause, others have thought that the purpose of the battle lies in (c) the Spirit's frustrating the desires of the Flesh. Barclay's own reading is based on the assumption that in 5:17 Paul intends to warn the Galatians against libertinism. Taking the relative pronoun *ha* to mean "whatever," Barclay finds just such a warning: the purpose of the Spirit's battle against the Flesh is to see to it that "the Galatians are not in the dangerous position of being *free* to 'do *whatever* you want' . . ." (*Obeying*, 115; emphasis added). But this reading imports the motif of dangerous freedom into 5:17. Together with virtually the whole of 5:13–24, the clause *hina mê poiete* is descriptive rather than hortatory. Paul *describes* the result of the warfare: because of it, the Galatians *are not doing* what they wish to do.

[77]Following the preposition *hypo*, the anarthrous noun *nomos* is definite.

the line of thought followed by Paul as he moves from v 18 to vv 19–21a. Because the Galatians are tempted to reenter the Law's world, and because the Law lacks the power to curb the Flesh, Paul will now speak of the effects of the Flesh, in order to portray the daily life of the community that looks to the Law for its guidance! We could paraphrase v 18: "If, however, in the daily life of your communities you are being consistently led by the Spirit, then you are not under the authority of the Law, the weakling that cannot deliver you from the power of the Flesh." Thus, Paul's portrait of the-Flesh-run-wild is fundamentally as characteristic of the nomistic community as it is of the pagan world!

19. *The effects of the Flesh.* Lit. "the works of the Flesh," an expression that may owe something to a locution preserved in *T. Levi* 19:1 — "the works of Beliar" (cf. *Herm. Man.* 6.2.4). With this verse Paul begins two lists, first what he calls typical "effects of the Flesh" (*erga tês sarkos;* vv 19–21a) and second what he terms "the fruit of the Spirit" (*karpos tou pneumatos;* vv 22–23a). Interpreters commonly refer to these lists as catalogues of vices and virtues. This identification seriously distorts Paul's understanding (Comment #49). For Paul speaks neither of vices nor of virtues attributable to individuals, but rather of marks of a community under the influence of the Flesh and marks of a community led by the Spirit.

are clear. In the indicative mood Paul *describes* the effects that the Flesh actually produces, just as in v 22 he will describe the fruit borne by Christ's Spirit (*estin* in both instances).[78]

and those effects are: fornication, vicious immorality, uncontrolled debauchery, 20. *the worship of idols, belief in magic, instances of irreconcilable hatred, strife, resentment, outbursts of rage, mercenary ambition, dissensions, separation into divisive cliques,* 21. *grudging envy of the neighbor's success, bouts of drunkenness, nights of carousing.*

fornication, vicious immorality, uncontrolled debauchery. Paul begins his list with three terms used in Jewish polemic against Gentiles. The first sometimes denotes sexual activity with a prostitute, but it can also refer more generally to sexual unfaithfulness in marriage.[79] The second can take its coloring from forms of violence in sexual activity. The third points to the prideful flaunting of debauchery. The terms are traditional, but, in using them here, Paul may imply that some of the Galatians are tempted to participate in the rites of "holy prostitution" practiced in such cults as that of Cybele.[80] In any case, he refers to the misuse of the God-given human capacity for engaging in sexual activity.

20. *the worship of idols, belief in magic, instances of irreconcilable hatred, strife, resentment, outbursts of rage, mercenary ambition, dissensions, separation into divisive cliques,* 21. *grudging envy of the neighbor's success.* The next group of words begins with what might be considered the source from which the others spring,

---

[78] See Duff, "Significance."

[79] With regard to sexual activity the list of the effects of the Flesh could raise the question of the meaning of the baptismal formula of 3:28. If in Christ there is "neither slave nor free," how is the Christian slave to respond to the master who instructs her or him to provide sexual favors to an overnight guest (e.g., Petronius *Satyricon* 75.11)? See Barclay, "Philemon."

[80] See Nock, *Essays,* 2.893; Vermaseren, *Cybele,* 13–31; H. Koester, *Hellenistic Age,* 191.

and thus the essence of which the others are specific instances: the worship of idols. Paul may think quite concretely of the Galatians' former religious practices as worshipers of the Great Mother etc. But he surely has in mind that there are many ways in which people can worship something other than God, and he explicates the effect of such idolatry by referring to developments that destroy community. As he indicates by the second term (*pharmakeia*), one can find a pseudo-peace and security in the black magic of drugs. Or one can deify one's own opinion and person, with the result that one harbors irreconcilable hatred, strife, rage, and jealousy toward persons of other opinions (*echthrai, eris, zêlos, thymos*). Or financial prowess and uncontrolled ambition (*eritheiai*) can become one's highest good, producing a condescending attitude toward others. Or several people can escalate differences of opinion into dissensions and divisive cliques (*dichostasiai, haireseis*). Or one can embody a form of envious narcissism that is able only grudgingly to enter into the celebration of a neighbor's good fortune (*phthonos*). This last matter is one to which Paul gives special attention, suggesting that he knows it to be a problem in the Galatian churches (*phthonos*, "grudging envy," in v 21 is a motif Paul specifies by the participial expression in v 26, *allêlous phthonountes*, "envying one another").[81]

bouts of drunkenness, nights of carousing. Having emphasized developments that are destructive of community, Paul reflects on the way in which the use of wine and liquor can lead one to withdraw into oneself, thus being absent to the neighbor who may be in genuine need. One sees again that Paul's major emphasis in speaking of the Flesh lies on the ways in which that power destroys community life.

and other things of the same sort. Paul takes care that his list not be read as a new kind of law, covering in detail every possibility.

I warn you now, just as I warned you before. Paul's use of the verb *prolegô* in 1 Thess 3:4 and 2 Cor 13:2 suggests the meaning "to warn ahead of time." He insists that, when he was with the Galatians, he issued a warning about future judgment essentially equivalent to that of v 21b (in Qumran an eschatological warning follows a list of vices: 1QS 4:12–14). Why does he do this? He knows that the Galatian communities are presently having severe behavioral problems (v 15). He also knows that the Teachers are blaming these disorders on the inadequacy of the moral instruction he gave the Galatians when he was with them (Comment #33). He therefore reminds the Galatians that, before he moved on from their cities — probably indeed in the course of baptizing them — he employed some such list as the one he has just given, warning the Galatians about the future of those who practice such things.

those who practice things of this sort. What Paul says in 6:2 suffices to show that he does not mean his list to refer to one or two isolated missteps. With the verb *prassô* he speaks of regular activity, hence "practice." The list of vv 19–21a points to the effects of the Flesh that are at the same time deeds practiced by human beings in community.

---

[81] On *phthonos* as the deformation of desire into envious rivalry, see Hamerton-Kelly, *Violence*, 113.

will not inherit the Kingdom of God. As H. D. Betz points out, v 21b may be a piece of a catechetical tradition that antedates Paul, Jewish-Christian in origin (cf. 1 Cor 6:9–10; Eph 5:3–5). Paul himself is concerned to speak of God's judgment in the church. God has not set the Galatians right, simply to have them enjoy that condition apart from his continuing presence. If some persons wish to have the gift while spitting into the face of the Giver, they incur his judgment. Nothing Paul has said about God's grace implies that God has removed himself from the seat of the absolute sovereign, whose gift of freedom is the gift to be obedient to him in his presence.

22. *By contrast, the fruit borne by the Spirit is love, joy, peace, patience, kindness, generosity, faith,* 23. *gentleness, self-control.*

By contrast. Using the particle *de* with its contrastive force, Paul indicates that the two lists are totally incompatible; a middle ground (*ana meson*) is excluded.

fruit. We have noted that the Spirit and the Flesh are like one another in that both are supra-human powers. Whereas, however, the Flesh is *somewhat* like the operator of a marionette, pulling certain strings to produce certain effects (*erga*), the Spirit is like a healthy tree or vine that continuously bears fruit, and this fruit forms a single unit (*karpos* is singular), even though several of its marks can be listed.[82]

If the list of the effects of the Flesh is somewhat disorganized, reflective of chaos, the list of the marks of the Spirit's fruit is carefully structured, though it, too, is not intended to be exhaustive. There are three groups, each composed of three words.

love, joy, peace. Continuing his emphasis on community life, Paul probably draws the terms for the first three marks of the Spirit's fruit more from Hebraic tradition (Deut 6:4–5; Lev 19:18) than from a traditional list of virtues an individual might seek to possess (note the inclusion of "love toward all the sons of truth" as a community characteristic in Qumran; 1QS 4:5; and cf. *Barn.* 19:2 and *Did.* 1:2). Paul does not speak of a romantic emotion between two persons, but rather of the kind of love that was defined by Christ when he gave his life "for us." Thus, the love that is now a communal characteristic of daily life in the church as community is the love that has its ultimate source and pattern in God (5:6, 13, 14; 2:20).

Few aspects of the picture Paul is drawing are as important as the fact that, in the warfare commenced by the Spirit against the Flesh, the violence that is a major characteristic of the Flesh (vv 19–21a) is not met by a greater violence, but rather by love, joy, and peace.[83]

One sees this kind of love when one encounters communal joy and peace (1:3; cf. 1 Cor 13:4–6; Rom 14:17). One sees it when one meets the kind of patience, kindness, and generosity that reflects God's:

patience, kindness, generosity. The first of these, *makrothymia,* is sometimes

---

[82]Cf. 2 Cor 6:6–10; Eph 4:2–3; Col 4:12–15; 2 Pet 1:5–7.
[83]See Hamerton-Kelly, *Violence.* The richness of this reversal (violence/peace) can be compared with the image of Paul the nursing mother as presented in Gaventa, "Mother's Milk."

understood to be a virtue along with such other virtues as gentleness (*epieikeia;* 1 *Clem.* 13:1) and kindness (*chrêstotês;* 2 Cor 6:6) and self-control (*egkrateia; Barn.* 2:2). For Paul all three of these terms are communal marks of the Spirit's fruit because they are characteristics of the God who sent the Spirit (Rom 2:4; cf. *Letter of Aristeas* 188).[84]

faith, 23. gentleness, self-control. One recalls that in 3:2, 5 Paul referred to the gospel of Christ as the power that kindled the Galatians' faith, bringing about their reception of the Spirit (Comment #31). In that instance one could refer both to faith and to the receipt of the Spirit as the fruit of the gospel. But the interrelationships among the gospel, faith, and the Spirit are complex and rich. The gospel link between faith and the Spirit is also characteristic of the continuing life of the Galatians' churches. For faith is more than a onetime occurrence. Like gentle humility, faith is a mark of the fruit that the Spirit is bearing in the daily life of the community of Christ.[85]

While several terms in the list of the effects of the Flesh indicate lack of control — uncontrolled debauchery, outbursts of rage, bouts of drunkenness — Paul fundamentally transforms the opposite motif of self-control by referring to it as a mark of the Spirit's fruit. In fact, that transformation is a key to the way in which Paul understands what he has listed in vv 19–21a as the effects of the Flesh. His mentioning uncontrolled debauchery, for example, does not function, in the first instance, as an exhortation for the individual to exercise greater self-control. For the strength to exercise self-control comes only in community, and specifically in the community in which the Spirit is bearing its fruit. Here again, at the climax of vv 19–23a, Paul transforms lists of vices and virtues into something fundamentally different — marks of a community under the sway of the Flesh contrasted with marks of a community under the leading of the Spirit. Self-control is known only in the latter community.

The Law does not forbid things of this kind! Following expected form, Paul has earlier closed his list of the effects of the Flesh with an eschatological threat (v 21b). Tradition would now suggest that he end the list of the Spirit's fruit with an eschatological promise, referring to the future of those who are led by the Spirit (cf. 1QS 4:6–8). Later, in Gal 6:7–8, Paul adheres to the expected form, linking Flesh to threat and Spirit to promise:

> For whatever a person sows is exactly what he will reap. One who sows to his own flesh will reap corruption from the Flesh; but one who sows to the Spirit will reap eternal life from the Spirit.

Why does Paul not follow this form in 5:23, closing the list of the Spirit's fruit with the promise that those led by the Spirit will reap a rich harvest in the future?

To some extent he does follow the traditional form, but he tailors his promising

---

[84]See K. Barth on God's ways of loving, as interpreted in Dorothy Martyn, *Yellow Hat*, 145–166.
[85]In 1 Cor 12:9, listing various manifestations of the Spirit in the life of the church, Paul refers to a faith that works miracles. Cf. the expression "wonders" in Gal 3:5.

assurance to the Galatians' need. Hearing Paul's letter, the Teachers will certainly threaten the Galatians: "Once again Paul is misleading you with his antinomian message! Following the guidance of the Spirit without observing the Law will lead to the disaster of Law-less patterns of life." Knowing that the Teachers will issue this threat, Paul is now concerned to put the Galatians' minds at ease:

> Let me assure you, dear Galatians, that the fruit-bearing Spirit will never lead your communities into patterns of behavior that are against the Law.

This assurance will scarcely have silenced the Teachers. They will have said, one supposes, that, although what Paul has listed as marks of the Spirit's fruit are not violations of the Law, his consistent polemic against circumcision shows that the Spirit of which he speaks *does* lead the church into marked infractions of the Law.

In his assurance, however, Paul presupposes what he has said about the whole of the Law in 5:14. Loosed from its paired mode of existence (circumcision/uncircumcision etc.), the promissory and guiding Law of love (the Law of Christ; 6:2) has *become* the whole of the Law. In light of that fact the Spirit that bears the fruit of love will never lead the church into patterns of behavior that are against the Law.

24. *those who belong to Christ.* In the broad context — see especially 5:5 and 5:17 — this expression has about it the note of exclusivity: "those who belong to Christ and to him alone" (cf. 3:27–29).

have crucified the Flesh, together with its passions and desires. The Flesh, as a cosmic power, reveals its strength by having its own passions and desires (vv 19–21a), and by using them to acquire a base of military operations in communities of human beings. It arouses not only desires (note *epithymia* in 5:16) but also passions that destroy community, both of these being amply exemplified in 5:19–21a. New is the picture in which those who belong to Christ are not being crucified (Comment #30), but are, rather, carrying out a crucifixion, thereby vanquishing the Flesh.[86] The resultant vista brings together three pictures that Paul has sketched in earlier parts of the letter.

First, there is the picture in which Paul presents Christ's cross not as defeat, but rather as victory over the curse of the Law (3:13). Second, there is the picture in which Paul portrays, in promissory form, the victory of the Spirit over the Flesh (5:16). And third, there is Paul's portrayal of the church's participation in the Spirit's victorious war against the Flesh (5:16–23). Bringing these pictures together, Paul now says that the superior power in that war can be identified not only as the Spirit but also as the cross. The church, that is to say, participates victoriously in the Spirit's apocalyptic war by participating in the victorious cross of Christ. Several dimensions of this new vista are striking.

In presenting it Paul emphasizes a point he has had in mind all along: The

---

[86] For rabbinic tradition about the destruction of the Evil Impulse, see *b. Sukk.* 52b; Porter, "Yecer hara," 128. Marcus finds an anticipation of this tradition in CD 6:32 ("Paul," 10).

Spirit that is locked in combat with the Flesh — and that achieves its victory by bearing the fruit of love, joy, and peace in the daily life of the church — is not an amorphous spirit running here and there in the world. It is the Spirit of Christ, and specifically the Spirit of the crucified Christ. Being the Spirit of Christ, it is permanently bound up with the real and earthly event of Christ's crucifixion.[87] In a word, the Spirit leads its column of soldiers to victory over the Flesh not via observance of the Law (the secret ally of the Flesh!), but rather via their corporate participation in the cross.

For this very reason, however, one is surprised to hear Paul say that it is the believers themselves who have crucified the Flesh. One might have expected him to say that it was in Christ's own crucifixion that the Flesh suffered its death (just as the curse of the Law suffered there its defeat; 3:13). Or Paul could have extended the picture of war painted in 5:13–23 by promising that at the end, with the arrival of God's kingdom (v 21), the Spirit will bring its work to completion in a total triumph over the Flesh. Instead, he says that the vanquishing of that enemy is a deed of the believers themselves.

Moreover, the victory of which Paul speaks does not lie in the future; it has already been accomplished — those who belong to Christ "have crucified the Flesh." This temporal note provides a key to Paul's affirmation. It was at some point in the past that, as Christ's own, the Galatians vanquished the Flesh, nailing it to the cross (to borrow an expression from Col 2:14). Precisely when did they do that?

We can answer the question by going back to the beginning of v 24. As we have noted above, Paul's use of the expression "those who belong to Christ" indicates that it was in their baptism that the Galatians crucified the Flesh. Just as their baptism into Christ gave them a new Lord, so it involved a decisive separation from the Flesh, a separation so radical as to amount to the death of the Flesh, whose effects are pictured in 5:19–21a.[88]

That victory was decisive, but it is paradoxically incomplete. To attend to the whole of 5:13–26 is to hear Paul speaking both of the past victory in baptism (the present verse) and of the constant reenacting of that victory in the daily life of the community (5:16 and 5:25). It is an instance of the famous Pauline "already" and "not yet." We return to the fact that Paul refers here to crucifixion. The cross is for Paul (a) a real and victorious event accomplished by Christ in the past, (b) an event in which believers have participated at their baptism, both by being themselves crucified (2:19–20) and by crucifying the Flesh, and (c) an event which they repeat every day, as — in their daily life as communities marked by mutual service — they are led by the Spirit of the crucified one to utter the "Abba! Father!" to God (cf. 2 Cor 4:10–12).

---

[87] See Vos, *Pneumatologie*; Cousar, *Cross*, passim; A. R. Brown, *Cross*.

[88] This picture is thus worlds away from the medieval Christian formulation in which one spoke of the mortification of the flesh, referring to an individual's killing his bodily desires. Paul speaks here, as earlier, of baptism as a *corporate* victory over a cosmic power. Cf., in a nonapocalyptic frame of reference, Justin *1 Apol.* 61:1–3, 14–17.

COMMENT #48
THE LAW AND DAILY LIFE IN THE CHURCH OF GOD[89]

In 5:13, having warned the Galatians not to allow their freedom to be turned into a military base of operations for the Flesh, active as a cosmic power, Paul issues an exhortation: "On the contrary, through love be genuine servants of one another." Then, using the indicative mood in v 14, he speaks in a descriptive and decisively affirmative way about the Law:

> For the whole of the Law has been brought to completion in one sentence: "You shall love your neighbor as yourself!"

Given the fact that Paul has previously painted for the Galatians a strongly negative and even malignant picture of the Law — regarding the term *nomos*, the sole formal exception in earlier parts of the letter is 4:21b — one is astonished to find him saying in 5:14 that the Law is positively related to the life of the church. How is this surprising assertion to be understood?

A simple observation brings that question into focus, even though it does not itself provide an answer. Paul's affirmative reference in 5:14 to "the whole of the Law" has its *literary* parallel in 5:3, where, speaking with equal clarity of "the whole of the Law," Paul continues the letter's malignant portrait of the Law. Is there a true paradox here, the whole of the Law in 5:14 being the same as the whole of the Law in 5:3, so that Paul both denies and affirms the Law's pertinence to the life of the church?[90] Or is there some sense in which Paul speaks in 5:3 and 5:14 of genuinely different aspects or voices of the Law?

[89]For reasons that will become clear by the close of Comment #49, "daily life," as I am using the expression, corresponds neither to what is often termed "ethics" nor to what is generally meant by the word "morals." Both of those terms, and the concerns and literary forms connected with them, were alive and well in Paul's time (see especially Furnish, *Ethics*; idem, *Moral Teaching*; Schrage, *Ethics*; Malherbe, *Moral Exhortation*; Meeks, *Moral World*; idem, *Origins*; Sampley, *Walking*; Hays, *Community*). It is easy to accept Meeks's definitions: "'Morality' . . . names a dimension of life, a pervasive and, often, only partly conscious set of value-laden dispositions, inclinations, attitudes, and habits." Ethics is "a reflective, second-order activity: it is morality rendered self-conscious; it asks about the logic of moral discourse and action, about the grounds for judgment, about the anatomy of duty or the roots and structure of virtue" (*Origins*, 4; cf. Keck, "Rethinking"). It is also easy to see, however, that the picture Paul presents in Gal 5:13–24 is so thoroughly permeated by apocalyptic motifs as to be seriously domesticated when it is pressed into the categories usually associated with morals and ethics. For Paul's picture, rather than being basically hortatory, is in the first instance a description of daily life in the real world, made what it is by the advent of Christ and his Spirit. See Literary Structure and Synopsis for 5:13–24; Comment #49; and Duff, "Significance"; idem, *Humanization*. Cf. Cousar's reference to "embodying the gospel" (*Letters*, 145–146). Some of the major points of Comment #48 are presented in compact form in J. L. Martyn, *Issues*, 235–249.

[90]Schrage, for example, finds in Paul an essentially paradoxical view of the Law. "Paul's battle against legalism is not against observance of the law, but against the perverse interpretation of such observance as a condition of salvation. God 'justifies without works of the law,' and the law has ceased to be a way of salvation, a 'yoke of slavery' (Gal 5:1) and a curse (Gal 3:10, 13); but this does not mean that Christians are dispensed from obeying the commandments (1 Cor 7:19). Therefore the Old Testament and its law are presup-

THE WHOLE OF THE LAW IN GAL 5:3

In the cautionary paragraph made up of 5:2–12 Paul focuses one of his warnings on both the obligation and the danger attached to observance of the Law, when (as in the case of Gentiles) that observance is thought to be salvific:

> I testify once more to everyone who gets himself circumcised, that he is obligated to observe the whole of the Law (*holon ton nomon poiêsai*). Speaking to those of you who think you are being rectified by the Law, I say: You have nothing more to do with Christ; you have fallen out of the realm of grace (Gal 5:3–4).

The identity of the Law in 5:3 is easily discerned. Continuing, as we have noted, the negative portrait he has drawn in virtually all of his previous references to the Law (*nomos*), Paul speaks in 5:3 of the Sinaitic Law that is inexorably linked with observance (*erga nomou, poieô ton nomon,* etc.), the Law that — in Galatians — pronounces a curse on all of humanity (3:10), the Law that speaks a false promise (3:12; Lev 18:5), the Law that pronounced its climactic curse on God's Christ (Gal 3:13), the Law that was instituted at Sinai by angels acting in God's absence (3:19–20), the Law that holds the whole of humanity under its power, being, together with the Not-Law, one of the enslaving elements of the cosmos (4:3, 5, 21a, 24; Comments #38, #39, and #41).

Two further observations will prove to be important. First, by its nature, the Sinaitic Law is plural: it consists of numerous commandments, each of which must be observed, once the life of observance is commenced in the rite of circumcision (note not only 5:3 but also the plural references to commandments in 3:10 and 3:12). Second, for the Galatians to seek their rectification by taking up the observance of these many commandments is for them to place themselves again under the enslaving power of this plural Law, thus being separated from Christ (5:4; cf. 4:9).[91]

THE WHOLE OF THE LAW IN GAL 5:14

The linguistic fact that in 5:14 Paul speaks again of "the whole of the Law" need not mean that he intends in 5:14 to paint a picture of the Law in all regards the same as the one he has painted in 5:3.[92] Indeed, there are unmistakable differences between these two pictures. How are these differences to be interpreted?

(1) *In Gal 5:3 and 5:14 Paul gives different, dialectically related portraits of the Sinaitic Law.* This is the dominant interpretation, and certainly the one with which to begin.[93] For, as we have seen, Paul refers in both verses to "the whole

---

posed and enforced as the criterion of Christian conduct" (*Ethics,* 205). Cf. Räisänen, *Law,* 69–83; E. P. Sanders, *Law,* 97.

[91] Nothing said here implies that it is impossible to keep the whole of this plural Law. On Paul's positive reference to the commandments of God (1 Cor 7:19), see Appendix B below.

[92] In the Notes we have observed that the linguistic difference between *holos ho nomos* (5:3) and *ho pas nomos* (5:14) is in itself inconsequential.

[93] See again, for example, Schrage, *Ethics,* 205; Räisänen, *Law,* 69–83; E. P. Sanders, *Law,* 97.

of the Law," giving the Galatians no hint by that expression itself that he intends to speak of two different Laws, or even of two distinguishable voices of one Law. Some interpreters have said, then, that the significant difference between 5:3 and 5:14 lies simply in the change of verbs: Whereas in 5:3 Paul speaks of *observing* (*poieô*) the whole of the Sinaitic Law (all of its many commandments), in 5:14 he says that one *fulfills* (*plêroô*) the whole of the Sinaitic Law by keeping the single commandment of neighbor love, Lev 19:18 being the Law's *essence*.[94] Following this route, interpreters commonly speak of Gal 5:14 as a "reduction" of the many into the one. Or, alternatively, drawing either on rabbinic data or on Rom 13:9, they say that Paul is here "summarizing" the plural Law in a single commandment.[95]

As we proceed, and especially in Appendices A and B, attached to the present Comment, we will see reasons for questioning this common reading. And, in any case, before turning from Galatians either to rabbinic materials or to Romans, would it not be wise to ask whether the differences between the portraits of the Law in 5:3 and 5:14 are well explained by passages in Galatians itself?

(2) *In Gal 5:14 Paul refers to a voice of the Law that is distinct from the voice of the Sinaitic Law to which he has referred in 5:3.* As we will see below, earlier passages in the letter strongly suggest that Paul considers the Law to have more than one voice (4:21; 3:8, 10–12, 15–18).[96] With regard to 5:3 and 5:14, then, one is led to propose an hypothesis that can be tested as to its heuristic power:

Whereas Paul refers in 5:3 to the voice of the Sinaitic Law that curses and enslaves (3:10, 13, 19; 4:3–5, 21a, 24–25), he speaks in 5:14 of the voice of the original, pre-Sinaitic Law that articulates God's own mind (3:8; 4:21b).[97]

Even at first glance, one sees four motifs in 5:14 that begin to provide support for this hypothesis.

(a) *Positive.* As we have noted, Paul's reference to the Law (*nomos*) in 5:14 is

---

[94]See H. D. Betz, who emphasizes the distinction between "doing" the Law (5:4) and "fulfilling" it (5:14). In the Note on 5:14 we have observed that in common English parlance the expression "to fulfill the Law" has come to mean nothing other than "to meet all of the Law's *requirements*." For that reason alone a different rendering of the verb *peplêrôtai* is called for. See further below.

[95]For example, Furnish, *Love Command*, 97; E. P. Sanders, *Law*, 95, 97.

[96]After pursuing the line of interpretation laid out below under "The Law Has Two Voices," I was glad to see the following comment in Lührmann (German edition, 97): "The new teachers in Galatia may have used the expression 'the Law of Christ' to indicate that the Law of Sinai is still valid in the Christian church . . . [Paul, however, sees a] splitting of the Law into the Law of Sinai and the Law of Christ, a view that is later completed in the opposition between 'the Law of the Spirit of life' and 'the Law of Sin and death' in Rom 8:2. The 'Law of Christ' is possible only through liberation from the Law that was given on Sinai" (my translation). See also the percipient remarks of Meyer about a cleavage in the Law in Romans 7 ("Worm," 78).

[97]This hypothesis is different both from the suggestion of Hübner that in Gal 5:14 Paul does not refer to the Torah and from the thesis of Stuhlmacher that Paul draws on a distinction between the "Zion-Torah" and the "Moses-Torah" (Stuhlmacher, "Gesetz," 273–275; cf. Gese, *Beiträge*, 49–62).

the first formally affirmative one in the whole of the letter, except for 4:21b.[98] The Law of 5:14 does not have a voice that curses, does not make a false promise, and does not separate one from Christ. On the contrary, this Law speaks in such a way as to be positively related to daily life in the church, a characteristic one would expect in Galatians of the original, Abrahamic Law that speaks God's own mind (3:8; 4:21b; cf. 3:11).

(b) *Brought to completion.* The change of verbs from *poieô,* "observe," to *peplêrôtai,* "has been brought to completion," involves much more than a substitution of "fulfill" for "observe." In the Note on 5:14 we have seen that, taking the perfect tense of the verb *peplêrôtai* at face value, one finds Paul referring in this verse to *an event in the history of the Law.* The whole of the Law *has been brought to completion,* and this event in its history has now caused the Law to be pertinent to the daily life of the church. After a close reading of 4:21–5:1, one can scarcely imagine Paul's saying this in Galatians of the enslaving voice of the Sinaitic Law (Comment #45). It is easy, however, to think that he says it of the voice of the Abrahamic Law that speaks in God's behalf (again 3:8; 4:21b).

(c) *Singular.* The reading thus suggested receives further support in Paul's use of the motif of singularity. One can say immediately that the Law of 5:14 is smaller than the Law of 5:3, lacking at least the commandments of circumcision, dietary laws, and regulations for holy times. Far more may be involved, however, than comparative difference in size. In 5:14 Paul speaks of a Law that has been brought to completion "*in one sentence*" (*en heni logô*). He thus connects this Law emphatically, not with a small number of commandments, but rather with the motif of singularity.

To be sure, as we have seen, numerous interpreters have credited Paul with "summarizing" the Sinaitic Law. But we have expressed doubts about this reading, noting Paul's reference to an *event* in the history of the Law. Could it be, then, that in 5:14 Paul thinks of a Law that was singular at its inception, its singularity being now revealed and/or climactically restored at the juncture at which it has been brought to completion?

Singularity is precisely a characteristic one would expect in Galatians of the Law that, in the time of Abraham, uttered God's own promise. In 3:8 Paul says specifically that what the scripture preached ahead of time to Abraham was not a series of commandments, but rather the word of the promissory gospel, "In you all the Gentiles will be blessed." And in 3:10–18 Paul speaks, on the one hand, of the plural commandments of the cursing, Sinaitic Law, and on the other hand, of the singular promise spoken by God 430 years earlier, both to Abraham and to Abraham's singular seed, Christ.[99]

---

[98] Contrast Romans, where 8:3 and 13:8–10 are far from being the first positive portraits of the Law (note, e.g., Rom 3:21, 31; 7:16, 22, 24). See Appendix B to the present Comment.

[99] In the six chapters of Galatians Paul uses the word "promise" ten times (compared with eight in the sixteen chapters of Romans), eight times in the singular — 3:14, 17, 18 (twice), 22, 29; 4:23, 28 — and twice in the plural, 3:16 and 3:21. In the Note on 3:16 we have suggested that the two instances of the plural may reflect nothing more than Paul's awareness that God repeated his promise (singular) to Abraham several times. In any case, after the plural in 3:16 and 3:21, Paul returns to the singular in 3:17–18 and in 3:22, 29 (and in 4:23,

(d) *Sentence rather than commandment.* When Paul says that the Law has been brought to completion in one "*sentence*," he apparently avoids the term "commandment" (*entolê*), thus connecting this Law with one sentence, rather than with many commandments. Noting this locution, one is yet more confident that, unlike the Sinaitic Law of 5:3, the Law of 5:14 does not consist of commandments at all.[100]

A convincing reading of Paul's reference to the Law in 5:14 will take into account all four of these motifs, and other factors as well. We return, then, to the testing of the hypothesis proposed above, noting especially the references to passages in Galatians 3 and 4:

> Whereas Paul refers in 5:3 to the voice of the Sinaitic Law that curses and enslaves (3:10, 13, 19; 4:3–5, 21a, 24–25), he speaks in 5:14 of the voice of the original, pre-Sinaitic Law that articulates God's own mind (3:8; 4:21b).[101]

Does a close reading of those earlier passages support this hypothesis?

THE LAW HAS TWO VOICES[102]

(1) *The Law in its paired existence with the Not-Law, that is to say the Sinaitic Law, consisting of numerous commandments.*[103] As we have seen, Paul's negative reference to the Law in 5:3 is no surprise. Before that point, he has twenty-five times spoken of the Law in its paired existence with the Not-Law, thus referring to the Sinaitic Law (4:24–25) that curses and enslaves (note especially the cumulative effect of analyses given in Comments #34, #38, #39, and #41).[104]

---

28), showing that he has no intention of referring to the linear history of the promises in the patriarchal generations and thence into the history of Israel (cf. Rom 9:9–13).

[100]On 1 Cor 7:19, Paul's reference to the keeping of the commandments of God, see Appendix B to the present Comment.

[101]In the process of further testing this hypothesis, we will find it convenient — without prejudging any of the issues involved — to adopt a tentative nomenclature. We will sometimes refer to the Law of 5:3 as the plural Law, recalling that it consists of many commandments. And we will sometimes speak of the Law of 5:14 as the singular Law, noting that, having been brought to completion, it articulates God's mind for the church in one sentence.

[102]Having been led to this bifurcated view of the Law in writing to the Galatians, Paul developed it in a modified form in Romans. See Meyer's analysis of Rom 7:7–25, and especially his reference to "*two* diametrically opposed laws" that constitute a "'cleavage' ... in the *law*." In Romans both, Meyer says, are the Mosaic Law, but one is that Law as the Law of God (Rom 7:22, 25b), while the other is that Law as it has been used by Sin to produce death (Rom 7:23a, 23c, 25c; 8:2b; "Worm," 78–79); cf. footnote 96 above.

[103]The textual basis for employing the expression "the Sinaitic Law" is Paul's references to Sinai in 4:24–25.

[104]Paul employs four linguistic markers in his references to the plural, Sinaitic Law: (a) *erga nomou*, "observance of the Law," (b) *poieô ton nomon*, "to keep the Law," (c) *poieô auta* (3:10, 12), "to keep the commandments," and (d) *hypo nomon einai*, "to be enslaved under the Law's power." Paul's use of the expression *poieô ton nomon* corresponds to expressions frequently employed in Jewish tradition, such as 'āśâ miṣwôt and šāmar miṣwôt.

(2) *The Law prior to — and, at a later time, loosed from — its paired existence with the Not-Law, that is to say the original, pre-Sinaitic Law, consisting of God's single, promising word.* Paul's positive reference to the Law in 5:14 is indeed surprising, but a close reading of Galatians 3 and 4 shows that, like the negative reference in 5:3, it has its precedent, even if less obvious.

In 4:21 Paul tells the Galatians, in effect, that the Law has two voices. The Galatians can come *under* the Law, thereby being enslaved by the power of its cursing voice (4:21a; cf. 3:10), or they can *hear* the voice with which the Law speaks of the birth of circumcision-free churches among the Gentiles, thereby sensing their own true identity (4:21b, 22, 27, 31).

Taking our bearings from 4:21b, we can also retrace certain aspects of the argument of Gal 3:6–4:7. We have seen that, in constructing that initial exegetical argument, Paul draws a sharp contrast between two voices, the blessing/promising voice of God and the cursing/enslaving voice of the Law (Comment #34). Equally important for the present inquiry is the observation that in 4:21 Paul finds precisely the same contrasting voices *in* the Law. Thus, he does not link the Law monolithically with the curse. On the contrary, he hears both the promising voice and the cursing voice in the large complex of the Law.[105] Not only in 4:21b but also in 3:8, Paul refers to what we have called the original, pre-Sinaitic Law as an entity with a voice that does not curse, uttering, as it does, God's promise to Abraham. Thus, prior to the Sinaitic genesis of the Law/the Not-Law as one of the enslaving cosmic elements (3:17, 19; 4:3), there was the promissory voice of the Law, the voice with which, speaking in God's behalf, the Law (as *hê graphê*) preached the gospel ahead of time to Abraham (and to Abraham's seed; 3:16) in the form not of commandments, but rather of the promise: "In you all the Gentiles *will be blessed*" (Gal 3:8; Gen 12:3; Gal 3:16–18).[106]

This original voice also pronounced the promise that is a statement of God's rectifying good news — "the one who is rectified by faith *will live*" (Gal 3:11; Hab 2:4) — proving itself thereby to be the singular, true promise that is altogether distinct from the false promise of the Law in its plural and paired existence (Gal 3:12; Lev 18:5). Moreover, the contradiction between Hab 2:4 and Lev 18:5 (Gal 3:11–12; Comment #35), taken together with the polarity between Gal 4:21a and 4:21b, shows conclusively that, in writing Galatians 3 and 4, Paul has in mind a Law with two quite distinct voices, one false and cursing, and one —

---

[105] Noting these two voices of *the Law*, we see that, *within* the Law complex, the Sinaitic Law is antinomously related to the Abrahamic promise. We are also reminded that the promise, not the Sinaitic Law, is God's uttering of *the gospel* to Abraham ahead of time. The simple polarization of gospel and Law, therefore, distorts the complexity of Paul's understanding of both.

[106] One would think it illogical to speak of a period prior to the existence of a cosmic element. As we have seen in Comment #41, however, for Paul it is the cosmos of religion that has as one of its elements the Law/the Not-Law. And there is clearly a sense in which Paul considers the cosmos of religion to be later than the cosmos created (in prospect) by God when he spoke his promise to Abraham (Gal 3:17; compare and contrast Rom 5:12–21).

representing God — true and promising. Thus, both from 3:11–12 and from 4:21, the attentive reader learns — before coming to 5:3 and 5:14 — that, after hearing the promissory voice of the Law testify successfully *against* the Law's cursing voice, Paul cannot consider the Law to be a monolith.[107]

Does the distinction between the Law's two voices in Galatians 3 and 4 illuminate Paul's negative and positive references to the Law in 5:3 and 5:14? That question can be profitably pursued by recalling the verb Paul uses in 5:14. As we have seen, he speaks there of an *event* in the Law's history, identifying the Law that is pertinent to the church's daily life as the Law that *has been brought to completion*. We may ask, then, whether this reference to an event in the Law's history may be closely related to the distinction between the voice of the Sinaitic, cursing Law (3:10, e.g.) and the voice of the original, Abrahamic, promising Law (3:8; 4:21b). And since, with its original voice, the Law spoke its promise both to Abraham and to Abraham's seed, Christ (3:16), we may also ask whether the distinction between these two voices may be related to the advent of Christ, his advent being the event that has enacted that distinction.

---

[107]In the second and third centuries the drawing of distinctions within the Law became an important motif among Christian Jews, gnostics, and orthodox. See especially the theory of false pericopes in the *Kerygmata Petrou* (HS 2.118–121 [Strecker]); the *Letter of Ptolemy to Flora* (Foerster, *Gnosis*, 154–161); Irenaeus *Haer.* 4.24–29; and the *Syriac Didascalia* (Connolly, *Didascalia*). In the five books of Moses Ptolemy found (a) the Law of God (itself composed of three subparts), (b) the additions of Moses, and (c) the traditions of the elders. Perhaps influenced both by Galatians itself and by Ptolemy, the author of the *Didascalia* spoke repeatedly of a clean distinction between the eternally valid first Law, which "consists of the Ten Words and the Judgments," and the *deuterosis*, the punitive Second Legislation with its cursing bonds of circumcision etc. Similarities and differences between these writings and those of Paul warrant more investigation than they have received. *Similarities:* Three motifs in the *Letter of Ptolemy to Flora* and the *Didascalia* can be compared with motifs in Galatians: (a) The distinction(s) internal to the Law have been *revealed by Christ*: "The words of the Saviour teach us that it [the Law] is divided into three parts" (Ptolemy 4:1); "He teaches what is the Law and what is the Second Legislation" (*Didascalia*, p. 218; cf. "If one accepts his [the true prophet's] doctrine, then will he learn which portions of the Scriptures answer to the truth and which are false," *Kerygmata Petrou* [HS 2.119]). (b) Christ came in order to destroy the second law, with its injustice, thus *setting us loose from its curse* (Ptolemy 5:7; *Didascalia*, p. 224). (c) In his act of making distinctions in the Law and of liberating us from the second Law, Christ fulfilled, *restored*, and *perfected* the Law of God (Ptolemy 5:3, 9; *Didascalia*, p. 224). Two *differences* are also noteworthy: (a) Over against the second Law, Ptolemy and the author of the *Didascalia* place not the singular, Abrahamic promise, but rather the plural Decalogue, as its commandments were perfected by Christ. (b) For the catholic author of the *Didascalia* God is expressly identified as the author both of the first Law and of the Second Legislation, whereas Ptolemy attributes the law of divorce, for example, to Moses and the law of corban to the elders. In writing Galatians does Paul come closer to preparing the way for Ptolemy? In any case, the apostle is very far from linking God to the genesis of the Sinaitic Law (Gal 2:19; 3:19–20; 4:24–25), and for that reason, as we have seen, he "is not afraid to apply *to scripture* . . . the distinguishing of spirits demanded of the prophets in 1 Cor 12:10" (Käsemann, *Romans*, 286; emphasis added).

CHRIST AND THE LAW'S TWO VOICES[108]

In Galatians the Law's relationship to Christ is a subject best approached by noting, first, that the Law has done something to Christ, as we have begun to sense above (see also Comment #34), and, second, that Christ has also done something to the Law.

(1) *What the Law did to Christ.* In its Old-Age, paired existence with the Not-Law, the plural, Sinaitic Law formed the inimical orb into which Christ came. Thus, like every other human being, Christ himself was born into the state of enslavement under the power of that Law (4:4; cf. Phil 2:7). Together with all others, Christ was subject to the curse of the Law in its plural mode of existence (Gal 3:10; 4:3). But in his case there was also a head-on and climactic collision with that curse. As Christ hung on the cross, dying for us (1:4), the Law pronounced a specific curse on him (3:13; Deut 21:23), doing that with the malignant power it possessed as one of the enslaving, paired elements of the old cosmos.

(2) *What Christ did to the Law.* Nothing in Galatians suggests that—unlike the very elements of the cosmos—the Law has escaped the influence of Christ. Quite the reverse. When, then, we turn the question around, asking what Christ did to the Law, we see three motifs that are both distinct from and closely related to one another.[109]

(a) *Christ has defeated the cursing voice of the Law.* In the collision between Christ and the cursing voice of the Sinaitic Law, Christ was distinctly the victor (3:13; 4:5; 5:1). In his crucifixion Christ bore the Law's curse for us, thus vanquishing the cursing voice of the Law, confining it—properly speaking—to the era before his arrival (3:17).[110] Christ's victory over the Law's cursing voice is, to

---

[108]The Law's relationship to Christ plays an explicit role both in 5:3 and in 5:14. On the negative side Paul follows the warning of 5:3 by insisting, as he has many times earlier, that rectification comes from Christ, not from the Law (cf. 2:21 etc.). On the positive side, by referring in 5:14 to the Law's being brought to completion, Paul points forward to 6:2, where he speaks of bringing to completion the Law of Christ, a subject to which we will return below in Comment #50.

[109]As we have just noted, Paul speaks of what the Law did to Christ by using a specific verb: the Law *cursed* Christ. With regard to verbs, Christ's doing something to the Law is a subject Paul treats in Galatians somewhat indirectly. For to speak of Christ's activity vis-à-vis the cursing and enslaving voice of the Law, Paul uses verbs that take as their direct object human beings rather than the Law itself: "Christ *redeemed us* from the Law's curse" (3:13); "God sent his Son . . . in order that he might *redeem those* held under the power of the Law" (4:5). One might interpret this picture, however, by supplying several verbs of which Christ is the subject and the Law the object: At the cross Christ *defeated* the Law in its cursing and enslaving mode of existence, thus setting us free. By the same token, when he came on the scene, Christ *unleashed* the Law's promising voice, thoroughly *differentiating* it from the cursing voice (4:21). To anticipate a bit, this act on Christ's part had the effect of *bringing* the scriptural voice of the Law *to completion*, causing it indeed to become (again) the whole of the Law (5:14). Thus *taking* the Law *in hand*, Christ made it his own Law by *restoring* it to the state it had in the time of Abraham (6:2).

[110]To be precise, the era of the Law in its paired existence began 430 years after Abraham and ended with the arrival of Abraham's singular seed (3:17, 19). It is a paradoxical truth

a large extent, the good news that permeates the whole of the letter (cf. Col 2:14–15).

(b) *Christ has enacted — and is enacting — the promise of the Law's original voice, being the seed to whom, along with Abraham, the promise was spoken.*

There was, first, the promise of the Law's original voice in the time of Abraham. The message that the Law (as *hê graphê*) preached ahead of time to Abraham did not consist of numerous commandments, or even of one commandment, such as covenantal circumcision.[111] In the time of Abraham the Law consisted solely of God's promise, and, for that reason, it preached nothing other than the singular gospel of Christ himself (3:8). For Christ is the singular seed of Abraham, and there is no gospel other than his (3:16; 1:6). From its Abrahamic inception, then, the original voice of the Law was positively and closely related to Christ, and, from its inception, this voice was the singular, evangelical promise, not a series of commandments. By the same token, the true promise pronounced in Hab 2:4 was and is the promise of the gospel of the Christ who is now making things right by his faith and by the faith that his faith elicits (3:11).[112]

There is, second, the promise of the Law's original voice in the present time. These indications themselves speak of the present connection between the promissory voice of the Law and Christ. One is not surprised to see, then, that the

---

that to some extent the Law's cursing voice survived its collision with Christ at the cross. Thus, even though greatly weaker than the promissory voice (3:17, 21), the cursing voice still poses a threat even to the baptized Galatians. For they can lose sight of what time it really is, thus becoming again slaves under the curse of the Law (4:10; 5:3).

[111]At no point in interpreting Galatians is it more important to avoid reading this document in the light of Romans. In Galatians — contrast Rom 4:9–12 — Paul totally and systematically ignores every aspect of God's dealing with Abraham, except the promise. Paul thus suppresses God's giving to Abraham the covenant of circumcision (Gen 17:10–14), and he eclipses Jewish traditions in which God is said to have given the Law itself to Abraham, thus enabling the patriarch to be fully observant prior to Sinai (*Jub.* 16:12–28; Sir 44:19–20). In this letter Abraham is the pre-Sinaitic — and thus pre-religious — figure. See Comment #33 and Introduction §17.

[112]In his own mind does Paul locate Habakkuk chronologically between Abraham and Christ, even putting him after the genesis of the Sinaitic Law? That is the sort of question to which Paul gives no attention in writing to the Galatians. A major concern in Gal 3:6–18 is the clean distinction between two voices, that of the cursing Law and that of the Abrahamic promise. In developing this distinction Paul hears the voice of God in the scripture of Hab 2:4, without naming or thinking of the individual through whom God spoke the rectifying gospel-word, and without thinking of that individual's date. The same thing is to be said, moreover, of Paul's reading of Leviticus. In Lev 18:5 (Gal 3:12) Paul hears the false promise of the cursing and plural Law ("The one who does the commandments will live by *them*"), whereas in Lev 19:18 (Gal 5:14) he hears the voice of the singular Law in its guiding function ("You shall love your neighbor as yourself"). Does Paul not know that the whole of Leviticus falls after Sinai, being in fact the major collection of the priestly laws? And if so, how can he hear in any part of Leviticus the voice that the Law had in the time of Abraham? Those are questions that can be answered only by noting that Paul's consistent point of departure for reading the Law is the advent of Christ. It is Christ who has distinguished from one another the promising and the cursing voices of the Law. His doing that is of fundamental significance, but the result is a matter that is not related to what we might call the fine points of chronology (beyond what Paul says in 3:17).

circumcision-free mission, promised in the original, covenantal Law of Genesis 16–21 and Isa 54:1, is the mission in which the gospel of Christ is presently marching into the Gentile world, giving birth to churches among the Gentiles and freeing them from the cursing voice of the Law/the Not-Law (Gal 4:21–5:1). In that mission the gospel of Christ has unleashed the promissory voice of the Law (4:21b), affirming and enacting its distinction from the Law's cursing voice (4:21a), and thus restoring it to the singularity it had in the time of Abraham.

(c) *Christ has brought to completion the imperative of the Law's original voice, the imperative that provides guidance for the everyday life of the church.* We can now return to 5:14, noting again Paul's use of the perfect-passive verb: "the whole of the Law *has been brought to completion.*" In light of indications earlier in the letter that Christ has done something to the Law—defeating its cursing voice and enacting its promissory voice—we may ask whether Paul words 5:14 as he does because he is still thinking of Christ's effect on the Law. Specifically, does Paul think that, in his loving death for us, Christ acted in a way that has had *two* positive effects on the Law? Does Paul think, first, that Christ enacted the *promise* of the Law's original voice, the promise that is now *giving birth* to circumcision-free churches among the Gentiles (3:8; 4:21b)? And does he think, second, that Christ has brought to completion the *imperative* of the Law's original voice, the imperative that provides guidance for the *everyday life* of those churches, precisely in the form of neighbor love (5:14)?[113]

The second of those questions is the important one for our understanding of 5:14. It is also a question to which we can attend by posing yet another. Precisely where is Lev 19:18 in Paul's view of the Law? We can be certain that for Paul Lev 19:18 is part of the original Law that speaks in God's behalf. It is therefore not one of the commandments that make up the plural and cursing Law of Sinai (5:3).[114] We can see that in form Lev 19:18 is a commandment (belonging literarily to the Sinaitic legislation), but *Paul* clearly does not consider it to be such, almost certainly avoiding the word "commandment" when he refers to it as a "sentence." We can also see, however, that in form Lev 19:18 is not a promise that can easily be equated with, or subsumed under, the Abrahamic promise, to which Paul refers in Galatians 3 and 4.[115] Three factors suggest, however, that, in his view, Lev 18:5—along with the Abrahamic promise—belongs to *the original—pre-Sinaitic—Law* that articulates God's mind:

> Like God's promise to Abraham (Gen 12:3; Gal 3:8; 4:21b), Lev 19:18 is a
> word of God pertaining to the circumcision-free churches made up of former

---

[113]It would almost certainly be incorrect to credit Paul, the fundamentally apocalyptic-antinomous thinker (Comments #3 and #51), with the view that the Law has *three* distinct voices, one cursing, one promising, and one guiding. As we will suggest below, in Paul's view the promissory voice and the guiding voice constitute the original Law that Christ has restored to its pre-Sinaitic state.

[114]On the *positive* references to the noncursing, plural commandments in Rom 13:9 and 1 Cor 7:19, see Appendix B below.

[115]Paul himself certainly knew that Lev 19:18 does not belong literally to the cycle of Abrahamic traditions in Genesis.

Gentiles. Those churches are to *hear* both the promise of Gen 12:3 and the guiding imperative of Lev 19:18.

Like God's promise, Lev 19:18 is a *singular sentence*, not a series of commandments.

Like God's promise, the singular sentence of Lev 19:18 is closely *related to Christ*. In restoring the Law—silencing its cursing voice and enacting its promissory voice—Christ has also brought to completion the power of the Law to speak again the *imperative* that proves now to be God's guidance for the daily life of the church, the imperative of Lev 19:18 being an echo of Christ's love.[116]

Thus, the harmonious relationship between the Law's promise and the Law's imperative is a matter Paul senses only after the advent of Christ. That is to say, in Christ Paul sees two things about the original Law. That pre-Sinaitic and thus pre-religious Law was both a *singular word of promise*—pointing to the *birth* of circumcision-free churches among the Gentiles—and a *singular word of imperative guidance*—pointing to the *daily life* of those churches. Regarding the latter, with the main clause of 5:14—"For the whole of the Law has been brought to completion"—Paul speaks of the deed of Christ that has *caused* the Law's imperative to be addressed to the church.

To recapitulate, then, in Galatians the promise of Gen 12:3 (Gal 3:8) and the imperative of Lev 19:18 (Gal 5:14) constitute the voice of the original Law of God. As accents of that voice, this promise and this imperative have waited, so to speak, for the time when Christ would decisively differentiate them from the accents of the cursing voice of the Sinaitic Law. And when Christ carried out that differentiation, he brought the Law to completion, restoring the promissory and guiding accents of the Law to their original singularity, indeed to their original unity.

The motif of unity requires emphasis. Following Paul's own manner of speech in 4:21, we have referred repeatedly to distinct voices of the Law. We have also said that the original voice of the Law is itself complex, being made up of two accents, promise (3:8) and imperative (5:14). Illuminating as we have found that way of speaking to be, however, it has limitations. For Paul himself does not follow it in 5:14. With emphasis he refers there to "the whole of the Law," not to one or more of its voices and accents. It must be, then, that, when Christ enacted the Law's promise (4:21b), and when he brought to completion the Law's imperative (5:14), he profoundly singularized the Law, thus restoring it to its original form. That is to say, not only did Christ silence the Law's cursing and plural voice. He also caused the Law's promise and the Law's singular imperative to

---

[116]As one studies two *texts*, the OT scriptures and Paul's letters, one sees that there is much value in Hays's *Echoes*. The image of an echo, however, may be used *first* to indicate that Paul hears echoes of Christ in scripture. See J. L. Martyn, *Issues*, 209–229; cf. Walter, "Problematik."

become — in their coalescence — the unified whole of the Law that speaks in God's behalf.[117] Nothing God promises and nothing God demands is absent from this whole Law. For Christ's complex effect on the Law is the crucial, restorative, and all-determining event in the history of the Law (5:14).

It is now clear that we are speaking, in fact, of the Law "in the hands of Christ." Even prior to our detailed consideration of that expression (Comment #50), we can add, then, one more word about the way in which this promissory and guiding Law is related to Christ.

This Law is permanently secondary to Christ. One recalls Paul's exhortation in 5:13b: "do not allow freedom to be turned into a military base of operations for the Flesh, active as a cosmic power." One also recalls that the primary ground of that exhortation is Christ's deed of liberation — "For [by Christ] you were called to freedom, brothers and sisters" (5:13a repeats 5:1). That loving and liberating deed of Christ, then, stands at the foundation of the loving pattern of mutual service in the church of God (2:20). In 5:14 Paul can *add* an assertion about the Law. Knowing, that is, that the Galatians are now concerned to be positively related to the Law, Paul can give them a word of needed assurance (cf. 5:23b): The pattern of mutual and loving service in daily life is positively related to the Law, *because* Christ himself has brought the whole of the Law to completion in the one imperative sentence of Lev 19:18: "You shall love your neighbor as yourself!"

Thus, the Law of love written in Lev 19:18 does not at all stand by itself. In the life of the church this Law is specified by its relation to Christ (6:2; Comment #50). It follows, then, that mutually loving behavior in the church is not a matter of *Law and order*, the former being the parent of the latter. It is a matter of *order and Law*, in the sense that the order of Christ's love proves to be the foundation for — indeed, proves to be — the Law of Christ (6:2).[118]

One question remains. If the reading presented above is what Paul intended when he wrote 5:14, why did he not make it easier for the Galatians to grasp it? In what we think of as a plain manner of speech, he could have avoided altogether a reference to the Law, speaking instead of Lev 19:18 as God's promissory guidance:

---

[117]One can ask whether there is a sense in which Paul sees Christ's singularizing effect on the Law to be comparable to the Platonic/Philonic movement from the Many to the One (cf. Goodenough, *Light*, 212). One can even point to the contrast between old (and inferior) multiplicity and new (and superior) unity in the exordium of Hebrews, and repeatedly thereafter (cf. Attridge, *Hebrews*, 209). Paul, however, uses the contrast between the Many and the One in quite a different way. For him Christ's singularizing effect on the Law is the liberating, and thus *noncomparative, restoration* of the Law to the state it had in the time of Abraham.

[118]For this formulation I draw on numerous conversations with Paul L. Lehmann. See now Duff, *Humanization*, 61; Lehmann, *Decalogue*. Note also that both in ancient Hebraic theology and in Judaism God's Law *is* God's gracious and founding election (Werblowsky, "Torah").

Through love be genuine servants of one another. For the whole of God's *promissory guidance* (*hê agôgê tês epaggelias tou theou*) has been brought to completion by Christ in the form of a single guiding sentence (*logos agôgos*), an imperative that reflects Christ's love for us: "You shall love your neighbor as yourself!" (Lev 19:18).[119]

We can scarcely doubt that such a statement would have made things much plainer to the Galatians.[120]

By referring to promissory guidance, and by thus avoiding a positive reference to the Law, however, Paul would have played into the hands of the Teachers. For in effect, he would have given them the right to say that his gospel cuts his Gentile churches altogether loose from the guidance of the Law. Paul takes pains, therefore, to preclude that reading of his gospel, even at the expense of simplicity. One recalls that in 4:21 Paul did not write,

> Tell me, you who wish to live under the power of the *Law*! Do you hear what the *promise* says?

Instead, presupposing that the *Law's* promising voice has now been distinguished from the *Law's* cursing voice, he wrote,

> Tell me, you who wish to live under the power of the Law! Do you really hear what the Law says?

Similarly, in 5:3 and 5:14, Paul speaks first of the plural and enslaving Law of Sinai and then of the singular and guiding Law that is God's own imperative. It is in this way that Paul is able to refer in 5:14 to *the Law* apart from which the church does not live its daily life. He insists only that that Law, far from consisting of many commandments, is the single, guiding word of God that — together with God's powerful promise — has now become the whole of the Law for the church.[121]

---

[119] I have provided hypothetical Greek expressions for illustrative purposes. On the term *agôgê* as the guidance of a law, see, for example, Plato *Laws* 645a. Cf. *agesthe* in Gal 5:18, where, explicating his earlier equation of the promise with the Spirit (3:14; 4:23, 29), Paul moves from the guidance of Lev 19:18 to the guidance of the Spirit.

[120] One may pose a similar issue with regard to the distinction between plural and singular. Given the interpretation advanced here — in Galatians 5 Paul intends to draw a contrast between a plural Law (5:3) and a singular one (5:14) — we may ask why Paul does not speak in these instances as explicitly of plural and singular as he did in referring to seeds and seed in 3:16? It may be impossible to give a full answer to this question, but one can at least say that numerous passages in Paul's letters attest to the apostle's assumption that clarity can be had without one's being fully explicit! And, in any case, in 5:14 Paul is quite emphatic in his expression *en heni logô*, "in one sentence."

[121] See Appendix B below.

APPENDIX A TO COMMENT #48:
GAL 5:14 AND TRADITIONS ABOUT SUMMARIZING THE LAW

Is Gal 5:14 illumined by Jewish and/or Jewish-Christian traditions relating the whole Law to a single commandment or principle?

A POINT OF ENTRY INTO THE LAW

Does Paul refer in Gal 5:14 to the singular Law in order to identify a point of entry into the Law of Moses? The tradition in which a scholar identifies a point of entry into the Law eventually made its way into rabbinic literature.[122] Among numerous rabbinic examples, one passage is especially revealing. In the famous story recounting a Gentile's visits to Shammai and Hillel (ca. the time of Jesus) there are significant references to "the whole Law":

> On another occasion it happened that a certain heathen came before Shammai and said to him, "Make me a proselyte, on condition that you teach me the whole Law (*kōl hattôrâ kûllâ*) while I stand on one foot." Thereupon Shammai repulsed him with the builder's cubit which was in his hand. When he went before Hillel, he said to him, "What is hateful to you, do not to your neighbor. That is the whole Law (*kōl hattôrâ kûllâ*), while everything else is commentary. Go and learn it" (*b. Shabb.* 31a).[123]

Here, Hillel uses the expression "the whole Law" in the course of identifying for a would-be proselyte the point of entry into the Law. He provides, that is, a pedagogically effective introduction to the Law in its entirety. For, as he explicitly says, "everything else" is to be learned and observed no less than that point of entry. Is it perhaps Paul's intention in Gal 5:14 to identify for the Galatians the door through which a Gentile can enter into the whole of the Mosaic Law?

The formal similarity between Paul's assertion and Hillel's comment could cause one momentarily to entertain that possibility, in spite of the differences between 5:14 and 5:3 noted earlier. In fact, however, that reading is altogether precluded by the context of Gal 5:14.[124] As we have seen, nothing is clearer from previous parts of the letter than Paul's sharp negation of circumcision, the food regulations, and the stipulations for holy times. He can scarcely be citing Lev

---

[122]That this tradition antedates the pertinent references in rabbinic literature is suggested (a) by the reference in the citation below to Hillel, a contemporary of Jesus, (b) by the tradition about Jesus also cited below, especially as it is preserved in Luke 10:25–28, and (c) by two passages in the *Testaments of the Twelve Patriarchs*, unlikely to be Christian interpolations. See *T. Iss.* 5:1–2: "Keep *the Law of God*, my children; achieve integrity: live without malice, not tinkering with God's commands or your neighbor's affairs. *Love the Lord and your neighbor* . . ."; and *T. Dan* 5:1–3: "Observe the Lord's commandments, then, my children, and keep *his Law*. Avoid wrath, and hate lying . . . Throughout all your life *love the Lord and one another* with a true heart" (OTP). Cf. Philo *de Spec. Leg.* 2.63 and Fitzmyer, *Luke*, 879.

[123]The attribution to Shammai and Hillel is a matter discussed by Neusner, *Pharisees*, 1:321–324. See also *Mek.*, Beshallach, Vayissa 1 (Hor. p. 157), and cf. *Tanh.* Sheftim 16b.

[124]So, correctly, Barclay, *Obeying*, 136.

19:18, then, as a point through which the Galatian Gentiles are to enter into the whole of the Law, thereafter observing all of its commandments.[125]

A GREAT PRINCIPLE IN THE LAW

Does Paul refer in Gal 5:14 to a (or the) great principle in the Law of Moses, identifying it as Lev 19:18?[126] It is again the form of Paul's assertion that might lead one to this interpretation, for he says that the *whole* of the Law has been brought to completion "in *one* sentence." We are reminded of the fact that, given the large number of commandments in the Law, some rabbis searched for one underlying principle or a few underlying principles, with a result somewhat similar to that reached in the quest for a point of entry into the Law.[127] One of the traditions about Rabbi Akiba (ca. 50–135 C.E.) calls for citation, not least because of its reference to Lev 19:18. About that verse in Leviticus, Akiba is said to have remarked,

That is a great principle in the Torah (*Gen. Rab.* 24:7).

Just as Hillel identifies a point of entry into the Law in order to lead a neophyte into the observance of all of it, so (with other rabbis) Akiba speaks of a "great principle *in* the Torah" (*kĕlāl gādôl battôrâ*) in order to facilitate the observance of all other parts of it.[128]

The same motif dominates the Jewish-Christian traditions in which Deut 6:4–5 is linked with Lev 19:18 to form a kind of double commandment that can

---

[125] It is Paul's negative comment in Gal 5:3 rather than the positive assertion of 5:14 that can be associated with the tradition about Hillel and the whole of the Law. For in 5:3 Paul does speak of circumcision as a point of entry into the whole of the Law, in the sense, as we have seen, that the circumcised entrant is afterward obligated to observe all of the other commandments without exception. Cf. Jas 2:10.

[126] This is the reading suggested by several commentators and by numerous interpreters who, without giving a detailed argument, credit Paul with speaking of the essence of the Law. H. D. Betz, for example, says that the issue posed by Gal 5:14 is "whether Paul has in mind the total number of prescriptions and prohibitions of the Jewish Torah, or whether he is thinking of a principle (the rabbinic *kll*) which sums up and contains the whole of the Torah" (274). For two reasons, then, Betz concludes that "Paul thinks of a principle rather than the sum-total of individual prescriptions and prohibitions: (1) he gives his explicit formulation in v 14b ['in one word']; (2) the 'whole Law' is not to be done (*poiein*), as individual laws have to be done (cf. 3:10, 12; 5:3), but is rather 'fulfilled.'"

[127] In addition to *Gen. Rab.* 24:7 cited below, see, for example, *Mek.*, Beshallach, Vayissa 1 (Hor. p. 157; on Exod 15:26); *p. Ned.* 9:4, 41c; and *Sipra*, Kedoshim, Perek 4:12. On the distinction of a principle from the narrower notions and detailed rules that can be arranged under it, see Daube, *New Testament*, 65; E. P. Sanders, *Palestinian Judaism*, 112–114 (with references to Moore); Longenecker 243; Schoeps, *Paul*, 208; Donaldson, "The Law That Hangs," 689–692.

[128] Donaldson is right to emphasize this point, as it has been made by numerous other scholars cited by him: "Nowhere in this [rabbinic] material is the 'fundamental principle' seen replacing or overriding the individual commandments which it sums up . . . The operating assumption was that the more detailed regulations could be *derived* from the general statements" ("The Law That Hangs," 692).

serve as the principle of the Law. The tradition in Luke 10:25–28 is particularly instructive:

> Just then a lawyer stood up to test Jesus. "Teacher," he said, "what must I do to inherit eternal life?" He said to him, "What is written in the law? What do you read there?" He answered, "You shall love the Lord your God with all your heart, and with all your soul, and with all your strength, and with all your mind; and your neighbor as yourself." And he (Jesus) said to him, "You have given the right answer; do this and you will live" (NRSV).

The form of this tradition suggests that the Jewish Christians who preserved it may have known the combination of Deut 6:4–5 and Lev 19:18 to be a Jewish formulation antedating Jesus.[129] In any case, for these Jewish Christians the issue was that of the comparative importance *among* the many commandments. There was no thought of deleting or negating some of them.[130] With the *Shema* and Lev 19:18 identified as a kind of basic principle, the other elements of the Law could be put in order of importance, its being assumed that all are to be observed (cf. the rabbinic "light" and "heavy" commandments, *each* of which is to be observed; e.g., *m. 'Abot* 2:1).[131]

Thus, both the rabbinic quest for a great principle underlying the whole of the Law and the similar Jewish-Christian tradition just cited are, in intention, worlds removed from Paul's assertion in Gal 5:14. Given Paul's pointed polemic against circumcision, the food laws, and stipulations for holy times, as noted above, it is clear that the apostle does not function in a rabbinic manner, citing Lev 19:18 as a broad principle, a *kĕlāl*, that is to be distinguished from a *pĕrāṭ*, an individual and specific rule. Nor does he think of reducing the numerous commandments to one commandment, thus providing in that sense a "summary" of the Law.[132] Indeed, in formulating the assertion of 5:14 Paul does not even think of a Law that contains commandments, as we have already noted.[133]

[129] See Fitzmyer, *Luke*, 879 (and cf. the somewhat different tradition preserved in Mark 12:28–34; Matt 22:34–40; Luke 20:39–40). That the linking of Deut 6:4 with Lev 19:18 is a Jewish tradition antedating Jesus is argued by Burchard, "Liebesgebot," 57; cf. Berger, *Gesetzesauslegung*, 229–230; Marcus, "Authority."

[130] The use of this Jewish-Christian tradition in the *mixed* communities reflected in the gospels is another matter. See Donaldson's recent analysis of Matt 22:40, as it pertains to the Matthean community that included Gentiles: "The Law That Hangs."

[131] A similar differentiation is made by Philo when he speaks both of particular laws and of heads summarizing the particular laws (*nomôn tôn en merei kephalaia; de Dec.* 19; cf. *de Spec. Leg.* 1.1.1). In Philo, too, there is not the slightest intention of using these distinctions to negate any part of the Law. Indeed, in summary, one can say that none of the traditions pertinent to the expression "the whole of the Law" reflects a pattern of thought that distinguishes essence from quantity, in the sense that part of the Law can be identified as the essence of all of the Law, that part thus serving as a substitute for the rest of the Law (cf. Jas 2:10).

[132] *Pace*, for example, Räisänen, *Law*, 23–28; E. P. Sanders, *Law*, 95.

[133] The point requires emphasis. Paul does not have in mind a reduced version of the Law, arrived at either (a) by subtracting circumcision, food laws, and holy times, thus arriving at a reduced remainder, or (b) by epitomizing the Law in one commandment (so Furnish, *Love Command*, 97, and many other interpreters). Paul's view is far more radical: After

We must conclude that Paul's intention in wording the assertion of 5:14 is foreign to the intentions reflected in the traditions displayed above. Indeed, a comparison of his assertion with those traditions is helpful precisely in showing us what Paul does not have in mind. The apostle is concerned to speak neither of a point of entry into the Law nor of a principle under which the detailed rules of the Law can be arranged as specific instances.[134]

APPENDIX B TO COMMENT #48: 1 COR 7:19 AND ROM 13:8–10

1 COR 7:19
In Gal 5:6 and 6:15 Paul employs a formula with three members, the first two being negated, the third affirmed. The formula may be his own creation; he uses it twice in Galatians and once in 1 Corinthians:

Gal 5:6	Gal 6:15	1 Cor 7:19
(a) Neither circumcision	(a) Neither circumcision	(a) Circumcision is nothing
(b) nor uncircumcision accomplishes anything at all.	(b) nor uncircumcision is anything at all.	(b) and uncircumcision is nothing.
(c) The real power is faith actively working through love.	(c) What is something is the new creation.	(c) What counts for something is keeping the commandments of God.

Striking is the fact that, both in Gal 5:6 and in Gal 6:15, the third member of the formula is a single entity — *faith* active in love, and the *new creation*, respectively. One is reminded of the motif of singularity in Gal 5:14: Christ has brought the whole of the Law to completion, not in many commandments, but rather in one sentence, "You shall love your neighbor as yourself!"

We are therefore astonished to find Paul using the three-membered formula to tell his church in Corinth that what counts for something is "keeping the commandments of God" (*têrêsis entolôn theou*). Using psychological terms, one can say that whereas the Galatian churches were "overcontrolled," the Corinthian church was somewhat "out of control." A better reading can be had, however, simply by attending closely to the text.

It is precisely the startling expression "the commandments of God" that is the major clue to Paul's intention. To be sure, this expression is traditional, being

---

the advent of Christ, one can no longer listen to the Law with the presupposition that it speaks nothing other than the word of God.

[134] Note Donaldson's suggestion that even Matthew (in his mixed community) uses "a rabbinic formulation in the service of an unrabbinic interpretation of the Torah" ("The Law That Hangs," 696).

found many times in the OT and in various pieces of Jewish literature. One may nevertheless ask whether in 1 Cor 7:19 Paul attaches a particular meaning to the qualifier "of God." Indeed, one may even ask whether he may know some form of the tradition, according to which Jesus set over against one another "the commandment of God" and "the tradition of human beings" (Mark 7:5–13; cf. Rom 14:14).[135] In any case, the wording of 1 Cor 7:19 itself suggests that Paul uses the expression "the commandments *of God*" because he presupposes something he does not explicitly state: Not all of the commandments come from God![136]

The verse itself shows that Paul does not consider circumcision to be one of the commandments of God.[137] It follows that here, as in Gal 3:11–12; 4:21, Paul does not at all assume the integrity of the Law as a homogeneous monolith (Comment #35). On the contrary, he takes for granted precisely the differentiation we have seen in our consideration of Gal 5:3 and 5:14. That is to say, in 1 Cor 7:19, as in Gal 5:14, Paul presupposes, in his own mind, Christ's act of differentiating the promising and guiding Law *of God* from the cursing and enslaving Law of Sinai.[138] The commandments mentioned in 1 Cor 7:19 do not include circumcision, food regulations, holy times, etc. The commandments *of God* are the whole of the Law to which Paul has referred in Gal 5:14. They are the commandments — as we will see below — that are brought to their completing sum total in love of neighbor (Rom 13:9), that sum total being the result of Christ's having brought the whole of the Law to its completion in love of neighbor (Gal 5:14). The commandments of God in 1 Cor 7:19 are thus the commandments that members of the church bring to completion *by* actively loving the neighbor (Gal 6:2; Rom 13:8–10).

Rom 13:8–10

We have already briefly noted that, when Gal 5:14 is rendered "For the whole law *is summed up* in one commandment . . ." (NRSV; NEB, "can be summed up"; JB, "is summarized"), it is not being translated on the basis of its own Greek text, but rather on the basis of Rom 13:9.[139] For it is only in the latter text that, using the verb *anakephalaioô*, "to bring certain things to their sum total," Paul identifies Lev 19:18 as the sum total of the commandments.[140] Gal 5:14 must be

---

[135]See Pesch, *Markusevangelium*, 1.372–373; Gnilka, *Markus*, 1.282–284.

[136]The genitive *theou*, "of God," answers the question "Which commandments?" Cf. Winger, *Law*, 44.

[137]Since he does not hold circumcision to be one of God's commandments, Paul can say to the mixed church in Corinth that one's circumcised or uncircumcised state at the time of one's becoming a Christian is a matter of indifference (1 Cor 7:18).

[138]For a quite different reading of 1 Cor 7:19, see Schrage, *Ethics*, 205; idem, *Korinther*; idem, "Probleme," 20–21, where there is a pointed reference to *schwärmerisch-spiritualistisch* misreading of Paul's assertion that the Spirit is the norm and criterion of Christian life.

[139]Of the variants in Gal 5:14, both *plêroutai* and *anakephalaioutai* are drawn from Rom 13:9.

[140]The importation of (a certain reading of) Rom 13:9 into Gal 5:14 is widespread in the critical literature. Two examples will suffice: At one point E. P. Sanders comments, "The *summary* [of the Law] which Paul twice gives, to love the neighbor (Gal 5:14; Rom 13:8–10) is . . . a quotation of Lev 19:18 and is a *summary* well-known in Judaism" (*Law*, 95;

translated, of course, on the basis of its own text. A brief comparison of Gal 5:14 (and 6:2) with Rom 13:9 (in the context of Rom 13:8–10) may prove helpful, however, in one's attempts to understand Paul's intention in speaking as he did in the latter text.

Writing to a church he did not found, the one in Rome, and looking over his shoulder at the church in Jerusalem (Rom 15:25–31), Paul speaks in Rom 13:8–10 of the fabric of daily life in the Christian community, as that life is related to the Law and its commandments.[141] We begin with the NRSV translation:

> (Rom 13:8) Owe no one anything, except to love one another; for the one who loves another has fulfilled (*peplêrôken*) the law. (9) The commandments, "You shall not commit adultery; You shall not murder; You shall not steal; You shall not covet"; and any other commandment, are summed up in this word (*logos*), "Love your neighbor as yourself" (Lev 19:18). (10) Love does no wrong to a neighbor; therefore, love is the fulfilling (*plêrôma*) of the law.

The similarities with Gal 5:14 and 6:2 are obvious. (1) In Romans, as in those earlier texts, Paul uses the verb *plêroô* (together with one of its nouns, *plêrôma*) to link the life of mutual love to the Law. (2) He again cites Lev 19:18. (3) He again identifies that text in Leviticus as a sentence (a *logos*), rather than as a commandment. And (4), even more clearly than in Gal 5:3, 14, Paul moves from plural commandments to the single sentence of Lev 19:18.[142] These similarities suffice to show that, in writing Rom 13:8–10, Paul will certainly have known that, to a large extent, he was repeating what he had said in the earlier letter, speaking in Rom 13:8 and 13:10 not of fulfilling the Law (NRSV; NEB margin; JB), but rather of *bringing it to completion*.[143]

The differences between Gal 5:14; 6:2 and Rom 13:8–10 are even more interesting than their similarities. Whereas in the whole of Galatians Paul does not use the term "commandment," in Rom 13:9 he quotes several commandments,

---

emphasis added). Similarly, Furnish renders Gal 5:14 "For the whole Law has been epitomized in just this one commandment, namely: 'You shall love your neighbor as yourself.'" He then remarks, "The . . . verb which I have translated 'has been epitomized' (literally, 'has been fulfilled,' cf. RSV) is equivalent to the verb 'summed up' which Paul uses in Rom 13:9 (this is quite properly recognized in both NEB and JB)" (*Love Command*, 97). See Appendix A to the present Comment.

[141] Cf. Meyer, "Romans," 1163–1164.

[142] One notes also that in Rom 8:1–4 Paul links the motif of the Law's being brought to completion with the motif of the singularity of God's absolute demand. There, as in Gal 4:4, Paul refers to God's sending of his Son as the redemptive event that has broken the power of the Law to condemn (Rom 8:1). The Law nevertheless retains — as it does in Galatians — a role after the advent of Christ. For, wresting the condemning and impotent Law out of the hands of its captor (Flesh/Sin), the Spirit of Christ lays hold of *God's holy and just commandment* (Meyer's translation of the singular *to dikaiôma tou nomou*, "Romans," 1151), transforming it into "the Law of the Spirit of life," and bringing it to completion (*plêroô*) in the community that orders its daily life under the leading of the Spirit.

[143] In the Notes on Gal 5:14 and 6:2 reasons are given for not rendering the verb *plêroô* in those texts with the English expression "to fulfill."

explicitly identifying them by the term *entolê*, "commandment."[144] And in referring to these commandments, he uses a verb he did not employ in Galatians, saying that in the sentence of Lev 19:18 the commandments are "brought to their sum total," their *kephalaion*.[145] The major issue posed by Rom 13:8–10 is the interpretation of this new verb. One asks specifically, how does Paul view the commandments, once he has been shown their sum total in the sentence of Lev 19:18? A single observation will enable us to answer that crucial question.

Noting the literary structure of Rom 13:8–10, we see that Paul does more than recall his references in Galatians to the bringing of the Law to completion in the love of neighbor (Lev 19:18). In Rom 13:8 and 10 he uses those references to frame, and thus to interpret, his new assertion in Rom 13:9 that *the commandments are brought to their sum total* in the love of neighbor (Lev 19:18). That is to say, in wording Rom 13:8–10, Paul not only presupposes what he had said earlier in Gal 5:14 and 6:2. He also takes for granted a sort of nimble movement back and forth between those two earlier affirmations, using them as the framework within which he will speak not only about the Law but also about the commandments:[146]

Galatians	Romans
6:2: Bear one another's burdens, and in this way you will bring to *completion* the Law of Christ.	13:8: The one who loves another has brought the Law to *completion*.[147]
5:14: For the whole of the Law has been brought to *completion* (by Christ) in one sentence: "You shall love your neighbor as yourself!"	13:9: For the commandments, "You shall not commit adultery; You shall not murder; You shall not steal; You shall not covet"; and any other commandment, are brought to their *sum total* in this sentence: "You shall love your neighbor as yourself."
6:2: Bear one another's burdens, and in this way you will bring to *completion* the Law of Christ.	13:10: Love does no wrong to the neighbor; love, then, is the *completion* of the Law.

To take seriously the reminiscence of Gal 5:14; 6:2 in Rom 13:8–10 is to see that in Romans — as in 1 Cor 7:19 — Paul is interpreting his Galatians assertions

---

[144]Since it is Paul's intention in Rom 13:8–10 to speak of the Law and its commandments as a guide for the daily life of the church, as in Gal 5:14, he cites commandments having to do with the violation of one's fellow human being, numbers 6, 7, 8, and 10 in the Decalogue.

[145]Schlier, *"kephalê,"* 681.

[146]In a word, knowing that Christ has brought *the Law* to completion in the love of neighbor (Gal 5:14), and that, in bearing one another's burdens, Christians themselves bring *the Law* to completion, as it has been thus taken in hand by Christ (Gal 6:2), Paul can turn in Romans to speak explicitly about the relationship Christians have to *the commandments.*

[147]Here the perfect tense is gnomic; Meyer, "Romans," 1164.

as they bear on the commandments of God. Just as the *whole of the Law* has been brought to its completion in love of neighbor (Gal 5:14; Rom 13:8, 10), so *all of God's commandments* are brought to their sum total in love of neighbor (Rom 13:9).

If we ask why Paul should introduce the verb "to bring certain things to their sum total" in Rom 13:9 — rather than using there, as in Rom 13:8, the verb "to bring something to its completion" — the answer is easily found. He is concerned to speak explicitly of the plural commandments (cf. again 1 Cor 7:19). *They* are brought to their sum total, just as the Law is brought to *its* completion. By the framework of Rom 13:8 and 10, then, Paul shows that the completion of the Law (*plêrôma nomou*) is the same as the sum total of God's commandments (*kephalaion entolôn*).[148] When he says, therefore, that all the commandments are brought to their completing sum total in love of neighbor, he means that — *post Christum* — love has *taken the place of the commandments*, being itself the comprehensive and indelible guard against violation of the neighbor.[149] Thus, Rom 13:8–10 is as far removed from the rabbinic and Jewish-Christian traditions analyzed in Appendix A as is Gal 5:14.

Moreover — and more important — Gal 5:14, 1 Cor 7:19, and Rom 13:8–10 show that Paul knows nothing of the use of the Sinaitic Law to guide the daily behavior of the church.[150] God's absolute demand of loving the neighbor stands in place of the commandments, because nothing contained in the commandments *of God* is absent from that single demand.[151] Paul can therefore prepare the way for his reference to the commandments themselves by saying with emphasis in his topic sentence: "Owe no one *anything at all*, except to love one another" (Rom 13:8).

In writing to the church in Rome does Paul abandon the view of Galatians that the Law has two voices? One has only to note the similarity of Gal 4:21 and Rom 3:21 to see that he does no such thing:

Gal 4:21	Rom 3:21
Tell me, you who wish to live under the power of the Law! Do you really hear what the Law says?	But now the rectifying action of God has been disclosed apart from the Law, although the Law and the prophets bear witness to it.

---

[148]The noun *plêrôma*, often, as its form suggests, a passive reference to "*that* which makes something full," can also be used as the equivalent to the active form, *plêrôsis*, thus referring to the *act* that fulfills (e.g., Philo *de Abr.* 268). Rom 13:10 may thus repeat 13:8, speaking of the act of bringing the Law to completion (so BAGD; NRSV).

[149]So rightly Lindemann, "Love does not somehow enable one to do the Torah commandments. On the contrary, love takes the place of the commandments" ("Toragebote," 262).

[150]The reference is to the so-called *usus legis didacticus*, the educational use of the Mosaic Law in the church. See, for example, E. W. Gritsch and R. W. Jenson, *Lutheranism* (Philadelphia: Fortress, 1976) 63. Cf. Hofius, "Paul knows nothing of a new, ethical use of the Mosaic Law for the Christian church" ("Gesetz Christi," 278); Barclay, "Romans 14.1–15.6." For a quite different analysis, see Hays, "Scripture."

[151]Cf. Käsemann, "Love."

In Romans, no less than in Galatians, Paul's portrait of the Law is complex.[152] The Law has a condemning voice (e.g., Rom 3:19–20), so that God must reveal his rectification in Christ apart from it (Rom 3:21; 8:1). And the Law has the voice with which it speaks of the gospel (e.g., Rom 4:3–25). In Romans the Law is far more passive than it is in Galatians, being taken in hand first by Sin, and then by the Spirit of Christ (Romans 7–8). But, as one passes from Galatians to Romans, one finds no substantive and fundamental change in Paul's view of the Law.

What one does find is a remarkable malleability in Paul's thinking about the Law. For, in wording Rom 13:8–10, Paul gives to all of God's commandments the role he earlier gave in Galatians to the original *pre*-Sinaitic Law, spoken by God to Abraham.[153] In Galatians it is that pre-Sinaitic Law that Christ has brought to its completion in the love of neighbor (Lev 19:18). In 1 Corinthians that same, original Law proves to be the commandments *of God*. And in Romans Paul closes the circle, returning to Lev 19:18 by saying that the commandments of God are brought to their sum total in the love of neighbor. Underlying 1 Corinthians and Romans, then, are the affirmations of Gal 5:14 and 6:2.[154]

Rather than translating Gal 5:14 on the basis of Rom 13:9, then, one does almost the reverse. The reminiscence of Gal 5:14; 6:2 in Rom 13:8–10 provides grounds for a new paraphrastic translation of the latter text:

> Owe no one anything at all, except to love one another. For the one who loves another has brought the Law to completion (*nomon peplêrôken*). What does one say, then, of the commandments, "You shall not commit adultery; You shall not murder; You shall not steal; You shall not covet"? Like the whole of the Law, these and all other commandments are brought to their completing sum total (*anakephalaioutai*) in this sentence: "You shall love your neighbor as yourself." Love does no wrong to a neighbor, such as the wrongs mentioned in the commandments. For that reason, taking the place of the commandments, love is the completion of the Law (*plêrôma nomou*).[155]

[152]On Romans 7, see especially Meyer, "Worm."

[153]Paul's interpretation of circumcision in Romans is a subject in itself. Here we note only that, in Rom 13:9, Paul ignores, as he did in Galatians, the testimony of Genesis 17, where, just as God blessed Abraham with an indelible promise, so God gave to Abraham the *commandment* of circumcision.

[154]From Galatians, Romans, and 1 Corinthians it is clear that Paul sees the practice of circumcision, the observance of food laws, and the keeping of holy times neither as interpretations of the sentence about mutual love (Lev 19:18) nor as concrete acts by which the Law of God and the commandments of God are brought to their sum total in that Levitical sentence.

[155]This reading — as the completion of the Law, love of neighbor has taken the place of the commandments — is strongly confirmed when one attends to Paul's line of argument in Romans 14 (cf. Lindemann, "Toragebote," 262). As we have seen, in Rom 13:8–10 Paul views that replacement in positive terms: Because love is the indelible guard against violation of the neighbor, it is the replacing sum total of the commandments. But, in effect, Paul can also view that replacement negatively. Specifically, once he has seen the sum total of the commandments, he does not revert to the Law in the making of what is often called ethical decisions. In regard to food, for example, one recalls the strictures of

COMMENT #49:
THE GALATIANS' ROLE IN THE SPIRIT'S WAR OF LIBERATION

THE PROBLEM OF PROVIDING SPECIFIC GUIDANCE
FOR THE CHURCH'S DAILY LIFE

In Comment #48 we have seen that, according to Gal 5:14, the whole of the Law *post Christum* is the Law that Christ has loosed from its paired and plural mode of existence, restoring it to the original singularity in which it spoke God's own word.[156] It is the singular Law of love, and nothing other than that. We have also seen that this is the Law that is positively related to daily life in the church, because it does nothing other than reflect the preeminence of Christ's love. For that reason it is the Law apart from which the church does not live. Turning from 5:14 to 5:15–24, one notes, however, that, when Paul takes up the matter of specific and detailed guidance for the church's everyday life, he repairs neither to the plural Law of Sinai nor to the singular Law of love. He could easily have done the one or the other.

He could have reverted to the Sinaitic Law, drawing on the Jewish traditions in which the Law is said to be the antidote to vice and the producer of virtue.[157] Thus, he could have said in effect that, although the plural, Sinaitic Law has nothing to do with the rectifying event that occurs at the point of one's entry into the church (so 2:16; 3:21; 4:24–25; 5:3–4), that Law nevertheless remains — with its commandments — the guide to the daily sustenance of Christian behavior, when circumcision, food laws, and regulations for holy times have been removed from it.[158] This seems to be the reading of Paul's ethics proposed by a number of interpreters.[159]

For two reasons it is also a reading that cannot be supported from Galatians. First, according to this letter, the daily life of the church *is* the scene of God's rectification, not an addition to it (Comments #47 and #48).[160] Second, Galatians

---

the dietary commandments. Reading Romans 14, then, one sees that Paul is very far indeed from taking his bearings from those commandments. On the contrary, the ground of his exhortation is nothing other than the mutual love that has taken the place of the commandments, having its origin in Christ's death for all. For a rather different reading of the role of scripture in Paul's "ethics," see Hays, "Scripture."

[156] "Loosed from" does not mean "reduced from."

[157] On the Law as the antidote to vice, see comments below under "The Guidance Provided by the Teachers." The Law as the producer of virtue is a common Jewish motif: for example, Josephus *Ap.* 2.170–171 (*eusebeia* and *aretê*), 291–296.

[158] This reading presupposes the venerable and untenable view that Paul drew a significant distinction between rectification and sanctification. See the following two footnotes.

[159] See, for example, Schrage, *Ethics*, 204–207. In current Pauline research one often encounters references to the similar differentiation E. P. Sanders makes between "getting in" and "staying in": One gets into the church by believing in Christ, and one stays in by keeping the commandments (*Palestinian Judaism*, passim). See, however, Lindemann, "Toragebote."

[160] Note Käsemann, "Neither can support be found . . . as has sometimes been thought, for distinguishing between the righteousness of the beginning and the righteousness of the end, between righteousness of faith and righteousness of life" (*Questions*, 171); cf. Way, *Lordship*, 259.

5 and 6 show that Paul is worlds away from finding the guide to Christian behavior in the Sinaitic Law. Immediately before giving the first of two lists by which he speaks of daily life, he emphatically repeats his assurance that the Galatians are not under the authority of the Law (5:18). Consequently, in composing the pastoral section of his letter, Paul does not seek to guide the daily life of the Galatian churches by drawing on the commandments that are found in the Sinaitic Law.[161]

Nor does Paul develop a detailed picture of Christian life by drawing on various commandments in the singular Law of love (5:14), not least because, as we have seen, that Law does not consist of commandments. Even so, however, Paul could have turned to it for specific guidance. Drawing, that is, on the Jewish tradition in which the Law is said to be the producer of virtues, being itself the epitome of virtue, Paul could have considered one after another the various aspects of love — patience, kindness, endurance, and so on. Developing each aspect, he could have arrived at a comprehensive and detailed picture of behavior in a community that is informed in the whole of its life by the Law of love. That is the route Paul will later elect in writing 1 Corinthians 13, and it is not altogether unlike the way by which he proceeds to compose the second of his behavioral lists in Galatians itself (5:22–23a: love, joy, peace, and so on). The first of those lists, however — the effects of the Flesh — is not drawn from the Law of love (even negatively) any more than it is composed on the basis of various commandments in the Sinaitic Law.

Where will Paul turn, then, in order to provide the Galatians with specific guidance for the daily life of their communities? In reading 5:16–24 one sees that Paul takes four major steps. First, he issues a promise explicitly focused on the Spirit, rather than on the Law (v 16). Second, referring to one of the presuppositions of that promise, he speaks of the Spirit and the Flesh as two combatants, engaged in a war with one another (v 17). Third, certain that that war is the determinative context for the Galatians' daily life — that war being the scene of the Spirit's victory and thus of the Galatians' real life (5:25) — Paul gives the Galatians a description of the war. He provides specific guidance, that is, by transforming the traditional lists of vices and virtues into community characteristics in the midst of the war. On the one hand, there are marks of a community under the influence of the Flesh and, on the other hand, there are marks of a community in which the Spirit is fruitfully active (vv 19–24). Fourth, centrally concerned with the Spirit's apocalyptic war against the Flesh, Paul employs the language of exhortation in the promise itself (v 16), thus giving to hortatory expressions a very peculiar stamp.

THE PROMISE IN 5:16, FOUNDATIONAL GUIDANCE

As we have seen in the Notes, one can begin fully to sense the impact of Paul's promise in 5:16 only by seeing first that, in wording it, he is keenly aware of

---

[161]The corresponding observation is made about Romans 14 by Lindemann, "Toragebote," 262. Note, for comparison, the role of the Law in James, and cf. the statement of L. T. Johnson: "For James the term *nomos* . . . finds its focus in the love of neighbor, but that love is explicated by specific attitudes and actions prescribed by Torah" (*James*, 32).

current developments in the Galatian churches. He knows, that is, that the Galatians will hear his promise as a rewording of a promise they are already hearing from the Teachers. It is, then, in the differences between the two promises — and not least in the differences between their presuppositions — that we can see yet further into the issue of daily life as Paul perceives it.

THE GUIDANCE PROVIDED BY THE TEACHERS

Identifying the Law as the God-given antidote to "the Impulsive Desire of the Flesh" (see definition below), the Teachers are providing the Galatians with what they consider to be comforting assurance:

> If you Galatians will *become* observant of the Law, we can promise you that you will not fall prey to the Impulsive Desire of the Flesh.

It is a conditional promise, holding good *if* the Galatians do what the Teachers exhort them to do, namely become observant of the Law. It is also a promise founded on a view of the Impulsive Flesh and the Law that is familiar to us from both Jewish and Jewish-Christian traditions.

(1) *The Flesh.*[162] Drawing on these traditions about the Impulsive Desire of the Flesh, we can suggest six motifs that the Teachers probably included in their own instruction:[163]

(a) Internal to the individual, the Impulsive Flesh has the individual as its major locus of operations.[164]

(b) The Impulsive Flesh is to some extent an entity with a life of its own, but it remains within the individual.[165]

---

[162]As we have seen in the Note on 5:16, the Teachers almost certainly speak of the *epithymia sarkos*, lit. "the desire of the flesh," that being their Greek rendering of the Hebrew *yēṣer bāśār*. Whether, like Paul, they also use the abbreviation "the Flesh" (Gal 5:13, 17 [twice], 19, 24) we cannot say. In any case, in speaking both of the Teachers and of Paul, I employ interchangeably the expressions "Impulsive Desire of the Flesh," "Impulsive Flesh," "Impulse," "Inclination," and "Flesh."

[163]In each case I give one or two illustrative citations. For the whole of these texts, for others like them, and for further interpretation, see Marcus, "James"; idem, "Paul."

[164]"For there are two ways of good and evil, and with these are the two inclinations *in our breasts*, distinguishing the one [way] from the other" (*T. Asher* 1:5). "[No member of the community] shall walk in the stubbornness of his heart, so that he strays after his heart, after his eyes, and after the thought of *his* Impulse (*maḥăšebet yiṣrô*). On the contrary, they shall circumcise in the community the foreskin of the Impulse ('*ôrlat yēṣer*)" (1QS 5:5). Similarly, referring to an unfortunate state of affairs (and using the word "spirit" to refer to the Inclination), the Jewish-Christian author of James speaks of "the spirit that he [God] has made to dwell *in us*" (Jas 4:5; cf. Sir 15:14-17).

[165]"Hear now, my sons, and I will uncover your eyes so that you may see and understand the works of God . . . so that you may walk perfectly in all his ways and not be drawn *by the thoughts of the guilty impulse* (*běmaḥšěbôt yēṣer 'ašmâ*) and by lustful eyes" (CD 2:14-16). See also 1QS 5:5 cited in preceding footnote. At Qumran the OT expression "the inclination of the thoughts" has become "the thoughts of the inclination," suggesting that, in some sense, the Inclination has its own existence (Marcus, "James," 612). Essentially, however, it remains internal to the individual.

(c) It is dangerous to the individual.[166]

(d) But the individual can master the Impulsive Flesh by choosing to observe the Law.[167]

(e) Viewed in the framework of the doctrine of the Two Ways, the Impulsive Flesh presents the individual with the necessity of making a choice; the individual is competent to make that choice and is responsible for the effects of that choice.[168]

(f) To choose to observe the Law is not only to master the Impulsive Flesh; it is also to achieve perfection of virtue.[169]

(2) *The antidote: observance of the Law.* Holding such views of the Flesh and of the Law, and concentrating their attention on human acts, the Teachers are exhorting the Galatians to make the right decision. By choosing to observe the Law, these Galatian Gentiles are to transfer from the path of the Flesh (an entity essentially internal to each of them as an individual) to the path of the Law, thus mastering the Flesh and achieving perfection of virtue (3:3).[170] For the human act of circumcising the flesh — as the commencement of Law

[166]"If a man does not set bounds to his impulses and bridle them like horses which defy the reins, he is the victim of a well-nigh fatal passion, and that defiance will cause him to be carried away before he knows it" (Philo *de Spec. Leg.* 4.79). "One is tempted by one's own desire (*epithymia*), being lured and enticed by it; then, when that desire has conceived, it gives birth to sin, and that sin, when it is fully grown, gives birth to death" (Jas 1:14–15). In Qumran the Inclination of an individual, if not resisted by strict observance of the Law, also presents a danger to the community (1QS 5:3–7).

[167]"For God created man from the beginning . . . and gave him into the hand of his inclination (*yēṣer*). If you choose, you may keep the commandments . . . Death and life are before a man; that which he shall choose shall be given him" (Sir 15:14–17). In the metaphorical language of Qumran the Inclination is a danger until it is circumcised (1QS 5:3–7).

[168]"And each one chose the stubbornness of his heart" (CD 19:20). Note also that the individual's freedom of choice is accented in the passage from Sirach cited in the preceding footnote. That freedom to choose is a gift of God. For, although God caused the Inclination to dwell in the human being, "he gives all the more grace" (Jas 4:5–6). Thus, the human being can yield to the Inclination, the result being sin and death. Or, by following God's commandments, he can choose to resist the Inclination, the result being life (Jas 1:2–4, 12–15). This point holds good in the framework of forensic apocalyptic as well as in that of the wisdom tradition of the Two Ways. See de Boer, "Apocalyptic Eschatology," and "forensic apocalyptic eschatology" in the Glossary.

[169]Note the motif of perfection in CD 2:14–16 and the reference to Abraham in CD 3:2–3: "Abraham did not walk in it [the Inclination] . . . he kept the commandments of God and did not choose the will of his own spirit" (cf. Murphy-O'Connor, "Missionary"). Regarding Abraham, see also *Gen. Rab.* 46:1, 4, where circumcision is said to have removed Abraham's only blemish; thereafter he was perfect (cf. *m. Ned.* 3:11). In Jewish-Christian tradition Abraham's faith was brought to perfection by his observance of the Law (Jas 2:22).

[170]In Comment #37 we have seen that this transfer has the corporate dimension of joining the people of Israel (truly represented in the church of Jerusalem); but, speaking to Gentiles, the Teachers focus their exhortation on the individual.

observance — is the antidote to the human act of following the dictates of the Flesh.[171]

THE GUIDANCE PROVIDED IN PAUL'S PROMISE

(1) *The Flesh.* In 5:13–24 Paul speaks for the first time in his letter of the Flesh as a distinctly assertive actor (hence the capital *F*), in all probability following the Teachers in doing so. Indeed, to some degree, he shows that he is in agreement with them. He believes, for example, that the Impulsive Desire of the Flesh exists, and that it is itself the major reason for the Galatians' need of guidance in daily life. Certain, however, that the opposite of the Flesh is not the Law, but rather the Spirit, Paul presents a picture of the Flesh that is different from that of the Teachers in regard to all six of the motifs mentioned above:

(a) As the Spirit is invading the present evil age by creating the new community in which it bears its fruit of love, joy, and peace, so the Flesh has its major locus of action in the community, not in the individual.

(b) As the Spirit is the Spirit of Christ, a power distinct from the Galatians, so the Flesh is an entity that has, to an important extent, a life of its own. It is not a mere part of the human being, less noble than other parts, "our lower nature" (so NEB in 5:13, 16, 17, 19). Both the Flesh and the Spirit are apocalyptic powers that do things not only *in* but also *to* the Galatians (5:13, 17, 19–21a, 22–23a).[172]

(c) As noted above, the Flesh is a danger to the Galatian communities, being intent on maintaining in communal form its own orb of power, the present evil age (1:4; 5:13).

---

[171] In their own "home" setting, that of Christian Judaism, the Teachers will doubtless have viewed Law observance as a path made possible by God's grace in establishing his covenant with Israel (cf. the references to Qumran texts in Comments #27 and #28). Similarly, they will have viewed their mission as the gracious, messianic extension of that covenant to the Gentiles. As far as we can see from Paul's letter, however — not least from the Teachers' threat (4:17) — the Galatian Gentiles will have heard in the Teachers' instruction the demand that they themselves *do* something, namely commence observance of the Law, however clearly the Teachers may have said that one can do this only with the help of God. See Comments #33 and #37.

[172] In the early Christian church it was Paul who brought the Impulsive Flesh fully into the apocalyptic worldview, by seeing it as the opposite of the Spirit of Christ. See again Marcus, "Paul." To be sure, the Qumran community speaks of warfare between the spirits of truth and falsehood, attributing real power to them and noting ways in which their warfare affects the community (1QS 3:22–24). The Covenantors also focus considerable attention, however, on the general picture of humanity, and thus on the individual within whom the spirits act. "The nature of *all the children of men* is ruled by these (two spirits), and during their life all the hosts of men have a portion in their divisions and walk in (both) their ways. And the whole reward for their deeds shall be . . . according to whether *each man's* portion in their two divisions is great or small" (1QS 4:15–16; Vermes). In Gal 5:18–24 Paul does not speak of humanity, but rather consistently and exclusively of the community of those who belong to Christ, those who have received the Spirit of Christ.

(d) Nothing is more foreign to Paul than the thought that the Flesh can be defeated by a course of human action.[173]

(e) As we will see in greater detail below, for Paul the Spirit and the Flesh are not related to one another in such a way as to call upon the Galatians to decide for the one or the other.

(f) In Paul's view there is no thought that human beings can achieve perfection.[174]

(2) *The antidote: the Spirit.* Returning to 5:16, we see that Paul considers the Teachers' promise to be lethally false, not least because it presupposes fundamental misunderstandings of the Flesh, the Law, and the Spirit. Because the Spirit is the Spirit of Christ (4:6), because this Spirit—rather than the Law—is the opposite of the Flesh, and because the Flesh is known on the basis of its opposite, it follows that the true character of the Flesh, and of the drama in which it is an actor, has only recently been revealed. In 5:16, then, Paul issues a comprehensive correction, thus providing in his own promise the foundation for the specific guidance he believes the Galatians to need:

> Even after the advent of Christ and his Spirit, the Flesh does in fact continue to exist, and, unrestrained, it will destroy your communities. It is clear, however, that the antidote to the Flesh does not lie in something you can do, namely commence Law observance. The God-given antidote to the Flesh is the Spirit of Christ. And, since the antidote to the Flesh is the Spirit rather than the Law, the solution to the problem of the Flesh lies in something God has already done. For God has already sent the Spirit into your hearts, calling you into existence as his church. Continue to lead your communal life guided by the Spirit, then, and I can promise you that you will not end up carrying out the Impulsive Desire of the Flesh (paraphrase of 5:16).

THE SPIRIT AND THE FLESH AS WARRIORS[175]

With the promise of v 16 Paul provides the foundation for daily guidance, but he does not yet give details. From that promise, therefore, he moves first to one of its major presuppositions: The Spirit and the Flesh are engaged in a dramatic conflict (v 17). Then he turns to the task of portraying the nature of that conflict, the basic character of its major actors, and the place of the Galatians in it (vv 18–24). Remarkable is the fact that in referring to this conflict, and in analyzing its actors, Paul speaks in a thoroughly descriptive fashion: all of the verbs in vv 17–24 are in the indicative mood. Paul does not initially move from his

---

[173] On Gal 5:24, see the Note. See also Marcus, "Paul," 15–16; de Boer, "Apocalyptic Eschatology," passim.

[174] On Phil 3:12–14, see Gnilka, *Philipperbrief.*

[175] See Comment #3. The picture of a cosmic, dualistic struggle between good and evil is ancient and widespread. As we will see below in discussing the so-called catalogues of virtues and vices, Iranian traditions included mythological lists in which personified spirits of good and evil oppose each other. See Kamlah, *Paränese*; Fitzgerald, "Lists"; idem, "Catalogue."

foundational promise to specific details by means of exhortation. On the contrary, he seems to think that he can develop the promise of v 16 into the particulars of daily guidance by first of all *describing* for the Galatians the world in which they actually live *post Christum*.

THE WAR (5:17)[176]

Paul is quick to state the obvious presupposition of the promise of v 16: The Spirit and the Flesh are at war with one another:

> For the Flesh is actively inclined against the Spirit, and the Spirit against the Flesh. Indeed these two powers constitute a pair of opposites at war with one another . . . (5:17a).

One recalls the weighty role Paul has given in prior sections of the letter to the motif of divine invasion (Comments #37 and #42). That motif is also central to 5:13-24. As we have noted, the Spirit to which Paul refers here is not an inherent component of the human being, comparable, let us say, to an individual's heart.[177] It is the Spirit of God's Son, the Spirit that God has sent invasively into the human orb (4:6).

In a significant sense, peace is a result of that invasion, for the Spirit bears its fruit of love, joy, and peace in the community of God's church (5:22; contrast 5:15). In another sense, however, the divine invasion has certainly not happened peacefully. Indeed, it has been necessitated by the fact that the human orb has been subject to an alien, occupying power, the Flesh. With the sending of the Spirit, then, God has invaded the territory of the Flesh (cf. 1:4), inaugurating a war against that monster.

It follows that the opposition between the Spirit and the Flesh cannot be grasped either in the image of an infection and a medicinal antidote or in the picture of the Two Ways that are set before the human being, in order to call for a decision.[178] On the contrary, that opposition is a genuine conflict, an apocalyptic war. It is also of recent vintage. For the Spirit's war against the Flesh is not an inherent part of creation (as in Qumran), a conflict that was inaugurated with the genesis of the Sinaitic Law, or the result of a human decision to attack the Flesh. This war was declared by God when he sent his Son and the Spirit of this

---

[176]On the relation between God's act of rectification and the motif of cosmic war, see Comment #28. The institution of the holy war is the deep soil in which cosmological apocalyptic took root in Israel, and it stands ultimately behind Paul's battle imagery. Cf. B. B. Hall, "Imagery"; de Boer, "Apocalyptic Eschatology."

[177]Thus, the antinomy between the Spirit and the Flesh is neither an anthropological dualism (H. D. Betz 278–280), focused on the inner psychic economy of the individual human being, nor an ethical dualism focused on alleged decisions made by the individual.

[178]Recognizing that Stowers is right to note the close relation between letters of exhortation and letters of advice (Stowers, *Letter Writing*, 91–152), Schrage nevertheless comments perceptively, "In letters focused on the giving of advice, the fundamental presupposition is the freedom to make decisions (Stowers 109). One can scarcely say that in the hortatory section of Galatians Paul only gives good advice" ("Probleme," 12).

Son into the territory of the Flesh. This war is, then, the new-creational struggle, the apocalyptic war of the end-time, the war in which God's forces are the ones on the march (regarding the line of movement, see Comment #37). The Spirit's weapons, however, are strange indeed. For example, the Spirit bears the fruit of communal *peace*, in order to overcome the *violence* engendered by the Flesh (vv 15, 22; cf. Eph 6:10–20).[179]

THE GALATIANS' PLACE IN THIS WAR

(1) *Distant observers?* If Paul identifies the major actors in this war as the active belligerents, the Spirit and the Flesh, does he then portray a drama in which the Galatians themselves are essentially inactive characters, persons who view the battlefield from afar? One might think so for a moment, for, as we have seen, the two warriors are distinct from human beings.

A further moment of reflection shows that, although distinguished from the Galatians, the Spirit and the Flesh are at war in such a way as vitally to affect the Galatian communities. Just as the Spirit is distinct from the Galatians, being the Spirit of God's Son, so the Spirit is also *in* the Galatians as communities, having been sent by God *into* their hearts (4:6). And, as noted above, the Flesh is actively seeking a military base of operations *in* the Galatian communities (5:13). Those communities are not at all distant observers of the apocalyptic war of the end-time. Somehow permeable both to the Flesh and to the Spirit, the Galatian churches are very much in the thick of the battle.

(2) *Passive puppets?* Are the Galatians caught up in this war, however, essentially as puppets, incapable of decisive action? One could think so in the course of reading the whole of 5:17:

> For the Flesh is actively inclined against the Spirit, and the Spirit against the Flesh. Indeed these two powers constitute a pair of opposites at war with one another, *the result being that you do not actually do the very things you wish to do.*

What is one to make of the final, surprising clause? Why should the war between the Spirit and the Flesh lead to a failure to do what one wishes to do?

In the Appendix to the present Comment we will find that, using a plural verb — "you (plural) do not actually do the very things you (plural) wish to do" — Paul speaks here to the Galatians who are trying to direct their allegiance both to Christ and to the Sinaitic Law. The result is that, although these converts of the Teachers earlier received the Spirit, they are now actually being led by the Flesh (cf. 3:3), thus being swept into a failure to avoid behavior they wish to avoid. In short the note of tragic failure in 5:17 is one that Paul directs only to the Galatians who are attempting the impossible, that is to follow both Christ and the Sinaitic Law. Elsewhere, notably in 5:13, Paul issues an exhortation that presupposes active engagement on the part of the Galatians.

(3) *Soldiers.* Indeed in 5:13, identifying the Flesh as a power seeking to estab-

---

[179]Cf. Hamerton-Kelly, *Violence.*

lish a base of military operations in the Galatian communities, Paul exhorts the Galatians to resist. They have then an active role in the war. It was given them at their baptism. Just as they are the new communities begotten by the power of the Spirit (4:29), so, given the Spirit's war against the Flesh, they find themselves to be serving in the Spirit's army, fully equipped and nourished for that service by the Spirit itself. Is there not the need, however, for yet greater specificity as regards their daily life?[180] In Galatians 5 that is a question Paul answers largely by the lists of 5:19–21a and 5:22–23a and by the statements of vv 21b and 24.

PAUL'S TRANSFORMATION OF THE TRADITIONAL LISTS OF VICES AND VIRTUES

At least a number of the Galatians will have sensed that Paul draws the lists of vv 19–21a and vv 22–23a from the widespread philosophic and religious tradition of compiling catalogues of vices and virtues (see Literary Form and Synopsis for 5:13–24). Momentarily, then, they may have thought that, having identified them as soldiers, Paul now lists in vv 19–23 the *vices* soldiers *should avoid* and the *virtues* they *should cultivate*. In fact, however, taking as his basic frame of reference the apocalyptic war between the Spirit and the Flesh, Paul paints a picture far removed from that given in the traditional catalogues. He does not introduce the list in vv 19–21a by identifying "fornication . . . the worship of idols . . . outbursts of rage," etc., as vices with which individuals can be charged, and from which, alternatively, they can abstain. On the contrary, for him this first list presents "*the effects of* the Flesh," deeds accomplished in a significant sense *by* the Flesh as an apocalyptic power. Similarly, for Paul, the list of vv 22–23a, love, joy, peace, etc., is not a catalogue of virtues, but rather "*the fruit borne by* the Spirit," communal evidence of the Spirit's own activity. Thus, none of the things in either list is an autonomous act of a human being that could be correctly called that individual's vice or virtue.[181] On the contrary, Paul lists actions that are without exception effected by the two warring powers, the Flesh and the Spirit. And all of the actions are communal in nature.

The effects of the Flesh are developments that destroy community — outbursts of rage etc. — and the fruit of the Spirit consists of characteristics that build and support community — love, joy, peace, etc. Thus, in the apocalyptic war of the end-time, vices and virtues attributable to individuals have lost both their individualistic nature and their character as vices and virtues. They have become marks

---

[180] Schrage is certainly correct to say that Paul is concerned with concrete specificity (*Einzelgebote*, 59–70; "Probleme," 23 n116). Similarly, commenting on Gal 6:10, Bonnard says correctly, "In the NT *ergazomai* never designates a general or interior activity; on the contrary, it refers to immediate acts in which faith applies itself to human situations quite concretely" (127). The question posed by Gal 5:13–24 is the means by which Paul achieves specificity.

[181] Cf. Käsemann, "the concept of virtue as used in our morality is fundamentally inapplicable to him [Paul]" (*Questions*, 194). But, just as the lists had originally to do with vices and virtues, so after Paul they lost the apostle's apocalyptic and corporate frame of reference, becoming again simply vices and virtues. Enjoying wide circulation and embroidering, they became in time "the Seven Virtues" and "the Seven Deadly Sins." See Meeks, *Origins*, 66–71; Fitzgerald, "Lists."

of community character, so that if one speaks of "character formation," one adds that it is the community's character that is being formed by the Spirit (cf. 4:19). In the framework of the apocalyptic war a community that has succumbed to the Flesh bears the marks of the Flesh. A community that is led by the Spirit shows in its common life the fruit borne by the Spirit. The profound radicality of Paul's apocalyptic picture is seriously domesticated when one credits him with speaking of vices and virtues.[182] We return, then, to our earlier question: in what sense are the Galatian soldiers persons who have an active role in the drama?

THE APOCALYPTIC WAR, THE TRANSFORMED LISTS, AND THE GALATIANS' ACTS

After listing communal developments that reflect the powerful effects of the Flesh, Paul does in fact warn the Galatians about *their* acts:

> Those who *practice* things of this sort will not inherit the Kingdom of God (5:21b).

And after listing the communal fruit of the Spirit, he adds,

> Those who belong to Christ Jesus *have crucified* the Flesh, together with its passions and desires (v 24).

As *combatants*, in whom and through whom the Flesh and the Spirit carry on their war, the Galatians are led into certain *acts* by the one belligerent power or

---

[182]Given the structure of the learned book of Meeks, *Origins*, there is an inevitable tendency to read Paul's letters through the lenses of second- and third-century sources, the latter being very well interpreted. But, to turn to such passages as Gal 5:19–23a, after quoting from the moral lists of Aristides and Pliny the Younger (both second-century)—not to mention certain parts of the *Didache*, the *Epistle of Barnabas*, and the *Doctrina XII Apostolorum*—is to run the risk of missing the major surprise of Gal 5:19–23a: the degree to which Paul's apocalyptic view has transformed the language of the catalogue tradition (*Origins*, 8–9, 15, 66–71). As we have seen, it is the Teachers, not Paul, who view the problem of the Impulsive Flesh in light of the doctrine of the Two Ways, and who therefore accept the ancient pattern in which vices and virtues exemplify precisely that doctrine. True enough, Meeks himself speaks of the Christian development in which "humility," for example, is transformed by being juxtaposed with "the metaphoric pattern" of Christ's crucifixion and resurrection (15; cf. 66, 84–90). But, on the whole, Meeks's willingness to analyze early Christian moral sensibilities as developments reflecting "socialization" and "resocialization" leaves largely out of account the degree to which apocalyptic frames of reference—notably the motif of cosmic warfare—led Paul to a radically new view of the cosmos itself, and thus to an apocalyptic transformation of the language of vices and virtues. Thus, if one were able to imagine a conversation in which one could teach Paul the modern usage of such inelegant terms as "resocialization," one would also be able to imagine his coining the still more inelegant term "recosmosization," in order to refer to the deed by which God is bringing about the death of the old and enslaving cosmos and the birth of a community so novel as to be called the new creation, a community in which language itself is transformed. After Paul, the kernel of his apocalyptic vision was mostly lost, and socializing attempts were indeed made to foster patterns of morality, without reference to the radical foundation of God's recosmosization. But these attempts cannot serve as the key to Paul's own views.

by the other. The Galatians themselves do things as communities. In a significant sense, then, they are responsible actors. And because they are responsible actors, Paul does more than give them a description of the apocalyptic war between the Spirit and the Flesh. He speaks to them in the imperative mood. Even in what we might call Paul's apocalyptic ethics there is a place for exhortation.

THE NATURE OF THE IMPERATIVE IN GAL 5:16

The nature of Paul's imperative is, however, a crucial matter. We return briefly to the imperative verb with which he begins the promise in 5:16:

> In contradistinction to the Teachers, I, Paul, say to you: *Lead your daily life guided by the Spirit,* and, in this way, you will not end up carrying out the Impulsive Desire of the Flesh.

Granting that Paul disagrees with the Teachers as to the identity of the Flesh's opposite — it is the Spirit rather than the Law — a number of commentators think that Paul nevertheless agrees with the Teachers on a truly significant point: Paul is said to see in the opposition between the Spirit and the Flesh a new edition of the doctrine of the Two Ways. Does not the promise of 5:16 show, after all, that Paul thinks of the Flesh and the Spirit as two alternatives placed before a human being who is competent to decide for the one or for the other? In fact, this interpretation reflects a failure to see the centrality of the metaphor of warfare, analyzed above, and for that reason it presents a false reading of Paul's imperative in Gal 5:16 (and a consequent misreading of the hortatory dimensions of 5:25–6:10).

That is to say, it is easy to misunderstand the thrust of the promissory sentence of 5:16, as though Paul intended it to be the equivalent of a simple condition, focused on the *inception* of a relationship with the Spirit: "*If* you will *commence* a life with the Spirit, then I can promise you that you will not carry out the Impulsive Desire of the Flesh." It is true that the promise of the second clause is predicated on the imperative given in the first. That imperative itself, however, is predicated on three major factors that *precede* it, reflecting Paul's awareness that, in formulating his promise, he is not speaking to humanity in general. On the contrary, he is addressing the Galatian churches that have been created as addressable communities by the invasive Spirit. In a word, the promise presupposes the history of the Galatians' relationship with the Spirit.

(1) Some time ago Paul preached the gospel of Christ to the Galatians. The power of that gospel elicited their faith, and the result of this faith-kindling gospel was that they received the Spirit (3:1–2). In short, the beginning of the Galatians' life as members of the church was not the result of a human act of deciding for the Spirit rather than for the Flesh. At that beginning lay God's act of sending the Spirit into their hearts, begetting them by the power of the Spirit (4:29), and freeing their enslaved wills for obedience to him in the Spirit (4:6). In their baptism the Galatians crucified the Flesh (5:24), but they did that under the direction of the Spirit, just as their cry to God as Father was in fact the deed of the Spirit.

(2) Because God continues to supply the Spirit to the Galatians (3:5), the Spirit itself remains active in their corporate life, continuing to cry out to God through their own mouths, and continuing to bear the fruit of love in the corporate life of their communities (5:22).

(3) Through the invasive Spirit, then, God has created and continues to create the Galatian churches as *addressable communities*, communities that are able to hear God's imperatives *because of* the indwelling Spirit.[183]

In light of this history, two readings of the imperative of 5:16a are excluded.

First, it is a mistake, as noted above, to treat that imperative as the equivalent of an inceptive conditional clause, as though Paul had said, "*If* you will *commence* a relationship with the Spirit, I can make you a promise." Knowing the history of the Spirit in the Galatian churches, Paul does not lay the Spirit before the Galatians as a new possibility, a mere alternative to the Flesh. He does not exhort them, therefore, to make a sovereign choice between the two, as though the Spirit and the Flesh were two paths, both of which lay equally open before them. On the contrary, with his imperative Paul calls on the Galatians steadily to be what they already are.[184] Metaphorically speaking, the Spirit is the general who has already affected the Galatians' will itself, inciting them to service in its war against the Flesh.

It is also a mistake to read the promise of 5:16 as though Paul were informing the Galatians of the availability of the Spirit, the Spirit being a *resource* on which they can call for help in *their* struggle against the Flesh. As we have seen, the war against the Flesh is in the first instance the Spirit's war (v 17), the war declared by the Spirit upon its advent, and carried out by the Spirit as it bears its fruit in the daily life of the church. Thus, the Spirit is and remains the primary actor in the military engagement. The Galatians are soldiers already enrolled in *the Spirit's* army, not contestants in a struggle that is theirs, and in which they are merely free to call on the Spirit for aid. Their deeds are first of all the acts of the Spirit (5:22; cf. 4:6), and secondly the acts of themselves as persons into whose hearts the Spirit has made its entrance (5:24).[185] The imperative element in 5:16 is conceptually equivalent, then, to the hortatory element in 5:25:

> If, then, we live in the Spirit — and it is certain that we already do — let us carry out our daily lives under the guidance of the Spirit (5:25).

Similarly, the promise of 5:16 can be fully rendered

> Stay consistently in line with the Spirit. For, as you are led by the Spirit — the victorious power already sent into your hearts by God — you will not fall victim to the Spirit's enemy, the Impulsive Desire of the Flesh.

[183] Cf. Schrage, "Probleme," 13–14.

[184] In this Bultmannian formulation one sees a crucial dimension of Paul's understanding of the will. Were the Galatians to fail to continue the life they are being given in the Spirit (5:22–23a), they would not be exercising freedom of will. On the contrary, they would find that they are again slaves of the Flesh, and thus in the state properly called bondage of the will. For there is only one form of free will, and that is obedience to the leading of the Spirit.

[185] See Duff, *Humanization*, 61.

CONCLUSION

In writing to the Galatians Paul is far from reducing daily life to a matter of morals vis-à-vis an ethical code, however conceived. At its root, behavior in the church of God is a subject Paul takes up in the first instance not by giving a hortatory prescription of "what ought to be," but rather by providing a description of "what is," now that, by sending the Son and the Spirit of the Son, God has commenced his invasive — and ultimately victorious — war against the Flesh. "What is" proves therefore to be the result of that invasive action of God, the war in which God is calling into existence his new creation, the church, with a view toward ultimately delivering the whole of humanity — indeed, the whole of the cosmos (Gal 3:22; Rom 8:21) — from the grip of the powers of the present evil age, the curse of the Law, Sin, the elements of the old cosmos, and not least the Flesh.

In this war the church is God's cosmic vanguard, the soldiers who receive their behavioral bearings in the midst of and from the contours of this war. It is therefore by describing the Spirit's victorious war against the Flesh, and by portraying the Galatians' place in this war, that Paul speaks with specificity in 5:13–24 of the behavior for which the church is fully inspired, to which it is summoned, and for which it is responsible.

It is both true and important that, pursuing the motif of responsibility, Paul turns from the essentially descriptive paragraph of 5:13–24 to a series of imperative and hortatory verbs in the next paragraph, 5:25–6:10. He is free to do that, however, only because in 5:13–24 he has descriptively portrayed the activity by which God has graciously created an addressable community, a church that, led by the Spirit, is able to hear the imperative and to be thankful to God for it.

APPENDIX TO COMMENT #49:
A FORMULA FOR COMMUNAL DISCORD

GAL 5:17

Interpreters have long been perplexed by the final clause of 5:17:

> For the Flesh is actively inclined against the Spirit, and the Spirit against the Flesh. Indeed these two powers constitute a pair of opposites at war with one another, *the result being that you do not actually do the very things you wish to do.*

What are we to make of this final, surprising clause? Why should the war between the Spirit and the Flesh lead to a failure to do what one wishes to do? Faced with this unexpected conclusion, one could initially think of looking for help in the seventh chapter of Romans, for there, too, Paul seems to speak of a failure to carry out one's intentions.

Gal 5:17	Rom 7:22–23; 15 (19)
17a. For the Flesh is actively inclined against the Spirit, and the	22. I delight in the Law of God in my inmost self, 23. but what I see is

536

Spirit against the Flesh. 17b. Indeed these two powers constitute a pair of opposites at war with one another,

a different Law, operative in my members. This different Law is in conflict with the Law of God to which I adhere in my intentions, and in this conflict the different Law keeps me imprisoned to itself, thus being the Law that controls me, the Law that has fallen into the hands of Sin.

17c. the result being that you do not actually do the very things you wish to do.

15. I do not recognize my own actions. For what I wish — the good — is not what I do; on the contrary, what I hate — the evil that I do not want — is what I actually do.[186]

The standard reading of Romans 7 credits Paul with centering his attention on two motifs, a split internal to the individual self and the resulting impotence of the self actually to carry out its own will.

From this reading of Romans 7 it would seem a short step back to the earlier passage in Gal 5:17. To be sure, as H. D. Betz points out, Paul does not speak in Galatians of a split in the self. Does he not refer, however, as Betz says, to the human body as a battlefield between two contesting forces (Betz 280)? And does he not identify the result of this state of affairs as the disabling of the human will to carry out its intentions?

Pondering this apparently Romanesque reading of Gal 5:17, we are faced with three questions. (1) In Rom 7:15 (19) Paul says that the self *does not* do what it wishes to do, and does what it does not wish. He could have spoken explicitly of an impotence of the will, saying that the self is *unable* to do what it wishes (*ou gar ho thelô touto dynamai poiêsai*)[187] — and is unable to avoid doing what it does not wish. Is it really Paul's intention in Romans 7 to refer to an impotence of the will? (2) Given the absence of an explicit reference to that motif, is the standard interpretation of Romans 7 in need of significant correction? (3) If so, would that corrected interpretation of Romans 7 play a role in leading us to a different reading of Gal 5:17?

A NEW INTERPRETATION OF ROMANS 7

A phenomenal advance in the interpretation of Romans 7 was made in 1990 by Paul W. Meyer.[188] Agreeing with the dominant view that in Romans 7 Paul describes the human situation apart from Christ, Meyer nevertheless offers an anal-

---

[186]Basically, this interpretive translation of Rom 7:22–23, 15 (19) is drawn from Meyer, "Worm."

[187]Both with the negative and without it, the locution *dynamai poiêsai* — and its equivalents — are, of course, very common. In early Christian usage see, for example, Matt 9:28, and in Paul's letters cf. 1 Cor 15:50.

[188]"Worm."

ysis in which both of the motifs that characterize the standard interpretation are laid aside, the supposed split internal to the individual self and the resulting impotence of the self actually to carry out its own will.

First, in Romans 7 "both 'inmost self' (v. 22) and 'members' (v. 23) are but two aspects of the same self that is 'sold under sin'" (Meyer, "Worm," 76). The tragic element in Romans 7 does not arise, then, from a divided self, but rather from the self's enslavement to the power of Sin, precisely as Sin has wrested the Law out of the hands of God. That is to say, rather than speaking of two parts to the self, Paul refers to *two Laws* (7:22–23, 25; 8:2), which prove to be the Mosaic Law functioning as the Law of God and the Mosaic Law as it has fallen into the hands of Sin.[189] The terrifying *fundamentum* to the whole of Paul's argument is the fact that the Mosaic Law is not only God's Law but also Sin's Law, a tool of Sin. One can see, then, that Romans 7 culminates in a cleavage, but that cleavage "is in the *Law* and not in the self" (Meyer, "Worm," 78).

Second (continuing with Meyer), the result of this terrifying cleavage in the Law — the result of the fact that God's Law has fallen into the hands of Sin — is far more serious than a mere impotence of the human will. In Rom 7:15 (19) Paul's major accent lies not on inaction, but rather on action and result. Indeed, in the first clause of 7:15 Paul speaks explicitly of the result of his actions, saying that it is a mystery to him; he himself does not recognize it. Clearly, something much more sinister is involved than an impotence of the will. A menacing actor other than the self is onstage, and that actor uses for its deadly purposes precisely God's holy and just and good Law. In short, Paul speaks of Sin's power to deceive him via the Law, the result being that he *accomplishes* the *opposite* of what he intended.

The subject of the discourse in Romans 7, then, "is not simple frustration of good intent, but good intention carried out and then surprised and dumbfounded by the evil it has produced" (Meyer, "Worm," 76). And the form in which this good intention is carried out is precisely that of observance of the Law. Thinking of the Law as God's Law, and of his own clearly willed, altogether admirable and blameless observance of it (Rom 7:12; Phil 3:6), Paul takes as his subject the power of Sin to corrupt the highest good. For in Christ he now looks back on the demonic power of Sin "to use the Mosaic Law to effect just the opposite of what its devoted adherents expect, even and especially when it is obeyed . . ." (Meyer, "Worm," 80). In short, Paul's argument attaches impotence

---

[189] In this reading Meyer takes *tês hamartias* to be a genitive of possession, an interpretation supported by Rom 7:8–11 (seizing *the* Law, Sin used it to kill me). For an alternative reading, see Winger, *Law*. There *tês hamartias* and its equivalents are taken as genitives of source, "identifying the power whose control is in turn identified by the term *nomos*" (195). This interpretation is related to Winger's finding in Rom 7:21 — with numerous other interpreters — a metaphorical use of *nomos* (force, rule, controlling power) that then sets the precedent for a metaphorical use of *nomos* in 7:22–23 (*Law*, 186 and 186 n138). Meyer, on the other hand, taking *ton nomon* in 7:21 to be an adverbial accusative of respect, arrives at a paraphrase in which Paul refers in that verse itself to the Mosaic Law: "So then, as far as the (Mosaic) law is concerned, the outcome (of the above experience) is that for me, the very one who wishes to do the good, evil is what I find at hand" ("Worm," 79).

not to the human will, but rather to the Law. The Law itself is the actor who proves to be disabled vis-à-vis the sinister power of Sin. Indeed, it is for that reason that God sent his own Son in behalf of all, "to deal with Sin as the Law could not (Rom 8:3–4)" (ibid.).

THE NEW INTERPRETATION OF ROMANS 7 AND A NEW READING OF GAL 5:17

Does Gal 5:17 read differently when taken in light of Meyer's interpretation of Romans 7?[190] That is a question we can consider by noting both similarities and differences between these two texts.

The picture of a bifurcated Law in Romans 7 has its earlier form in Galatians, where Paul considers the Law to have two distinct voices, as we have seen. Moreover, in Gal 5:17, as in Rom 7:15, Paul does not speak of an *inability* to do what one wishes to do (*hina mê ha ean thelête touta dynêthête poiêsai*), but rather of a *failure* to do those things. Rom 7:15 and Gal 5:17 are similar in that neither contains an explicit reference to an impotence of the will.

The form of the texts, however, shows them to be in one regard significantly different. Romans 7 is marked by Paul's repeatedly speaking *of* an "*I*," whereas in Gal 5:17 he speaks *to* a "*you (plural)*," the Galatians. In Galatians, then, Paul does not speak anthropologically *of* a general failure to act on one's intentions. He speaks specifically and pastorally *to* the Galatian Christians about their failing to do something they corporately wish to do. This simple observation suggests the possibility that Paul intends the Galatians to hear a reference to a development that is to some degree peculiar to *their* corporate life.

But what does Paul mean when he says that this failure to do what they wish is the result of the war between the Flesh and the Spirit? That is a question best approached by recalling Paul's practice of speaking to the Galatian churches as a whole, when in fact he is thinking of the numerous members who are in the process of accepting the nomistic theology of the Teachers (see 1:6; 3:1; etc.). In 5:17, that is to say, Paul is thinking of the fact that many of the Galatians are having themselves circumcised, confident that they can commence Law observance as the route to rectification without abandoning their allegiance to Christ (5:3–4). But how, exactly, does he think that a failure to act on their intentions is characteristic of the Galatians who are commencing observance of the Law? And how can he say that that failure is the result, for them, of the war between the Spirit and the Flesh? Two observations prove to be helpful.

On the one hand, throughout 5:13–26 Paul presupposes a war that has commenced only with the advent of the Spirit, as we have seen. Addressing the Galatians who have experienced the Spirit's advent in baptism, he portrays the situation of the Galatian churches *post Christum*.

On the other hand, the failure to avoid undesired acts, as it is portrayed in 5:17,

---

[190] Reading the earlier letter, Galatians, in light of the later — a common if usually unconscious procedure — can lead to serious misinterpretation. With caution, however, we can make comparisons, honoring the specifics of the Galatian setting (see below) and noting significant differences between the two letters.

can be characteristic neither of the Christian freedom Paul has so compellingly pictured in 5:1 and 13, nor of the loving communal life that is the fruit of the Spirit (5:22–23a). We return, then, to the hypothesis that in 5:17 Paul is speaking to the Galatians about the stance being taken on the battlefield by those among them who are trying to direct their allegiance both to Christ and to the Sinaitic Law. They are persons into whose hearts God has sent the Spirit of his Son (4:6). As a result they have indeed been placed on the battlefield on which the Spirit has commenced its war against the Flesh. Convinced by the Teachers, however, that they can be rectified only by observing the Law, they have, as Paul puts it, nothing more to do with Christ, having fallen out of the realm of grace (5:4)! As baptized persons standing in the midst of the battlefield, they are removing themselves from the victorious general, the Spirit of Christ! The result is that they are "double-minded." Claiming to have the Spirit, they are actually led by the Flesh. And the result of their double-mindedness is that the war between the Flesh and the Spirit is sweeping *them* into a radical failure consistently to avoid behavior they wish to avoid (5:15).

Read in this way, 5:17 (with its initial *gar*) offers part of the ground of the promise of 5:16, proving that promise negatively, so to speak. Indeed, with this reading we can now sense the line of thought that runs through the whole of 5:16–18, for in these verses Paul speaks to the confused and double-minded Galatians — and to others tempted to follow their lead into the same confusion:[191]

(v 16) But, in contradistinction to the Teachers, I, Paul, say to you: Lead your daily life guided by the Spirit, and, in this way, you will not end up carrying out the Impulsive Desire of the Flesh. (v 17) For on the negative side you can see the truth of this promise even in the moment in which you claim, while on the battlefield itself, to find rectification in the Law. That is to say, having received the perfectly potent Spirit (4:6; 5:16), but claiming now to be led by the Law that is impotent to curb the Flesh (cf. 3:3), you are swept up willy-nilly in the whirlwind of the battle. Lacking active integrity, you find that, when you want to end your dissensions, you succeed only in intensifying them. (v 18) If, however, in the daily life of your communities you are being consistently led by the Spirit, then you are not under the authority of the Law, the weakling that cannot deliver you from the power of the Flesh.[192]

---

[191] Formally, one may compare Epictetus *Diss.* 2.26.1–2, 4–5.
[192] In addition to the force of the contrasting *ei de* in 5:18 — "If, however . . ." — note that in 5:24 Paul refers to the victory over the Flesh that characterizes a community that belongs *exclusively* to Christ.

5:25–6:10 PASTORAL GUIDANCE, PART 2: EXHORTATION

TRANSLATION

5:25. If, then, we live in the Spirit — and we do — let us carry out our daily lives under the guidance of the Spirit.

26. Do not think of yourself as better than others, provoking one another, envying one another. 6:1. Brothers and sisters, if someone should be caught committing a transgression of some sort, you who are spiritual are to restore that person to his former condition in the community, doing so in a spirit of gentleness, taking care, lest you yourself be tempted. 2. Bear one another's burdens, and in this way you will bring to completion the Law of Christ. 3. For if someone thinks he is somebody, when in fact he is nothing of the sort, he deceives himself. 4. In place of such self-deception, let each one of you consider his own work; then you will keep your boasting to yourself, not directing it to your neighbor. 5. For each one will bear his own burden.

6. The one who is being taught the word is to share his goods with the teacher. 7. Do not be deceived, pretending that it is possible to thumb your nose at God. For whatever a person sows is exactly what he will reap. 8. One who sows to his own flesh will reap corruption from the Flesh; but one who sows to the Spirit will reap eternal life from the Spirit.

9. Do what is right, without growing weary of it; for at the appropriate time we will reap a harvest, if we do not give up. 10. Every time we have an opportunity, then, let us work for the good of all, and especially for the good of those who make up the household of faith.

LITERARY STRUCTURE AND SYNOPSIS[1]

What does daily life look like when God is making things right? In 5:13–24 Paul has begun to answer that question, speaking in a fundamentally descriptive way about the Spirit's liberating war against the enslaving Flesh, and about the Galatians' role in that war. Now, presupposing the Spirit's powerful presence in the Galatian churches, Paul uses nine hortatory/imperative verbs, one in almost every sentence, something he does nowhere else in the letter:

> 5:25 *stoichômen*, "let us carry out our daily lives"
> 5:26 *mê ginômetha kenodoxoi*, "do not think of yourself as better"

---

[1]Helpful lines of interpretation are given in Cosgrove, *Cross*; idem, "The Law and the Spirit"; Barclay, *Obeying*; Kuck, "Apocalyptic Motif."

6:1 *katartizete,* "restore"
6:2 *bastazete,* "bear (one another's burdens)"
6:4 *dokimazetô,* "consider"
6:6 *koinôneitô,* "share goods"
6:7 *mê planasthe,* "do not be deceived"
6:9 *mê egkakômen,* "do not become weary (in doing the right thing)"
6:10 *ergazômetha,* "let us work."

The beginning of the paragraph is signaled by the exhortation of 5:25, in which Paul repeats the major motif of 5:13–24, the role of the Spirit in the daily life of the Galatian communities.[2] The end of the paragraph is then marked by the autographic subscript (6:11–18). The material between these markers is not structured with great finesse, but in general terms we can see, after the introduction, three subunits:

Introduction — 5:25
Community responsibilities in light of the future judgment of the individual — 5:26–6:5
Catechetical instruction in the word of God, and the crucial matter of a church's maintaining that instruction, in light of God's ultimate judgment — 6:6–8
Conclusion — 6:9–10.

There are also three major motifs: Paul issues the exhortations in the power of the Spirit. He tailors them to the Galatian situation. And he focuses them on the real future over which God presides.

GENERAL MAXIMS BECOME EXHORTATIONS IN THE SPIRIT

Asking earlier about the character of the imperative verb in 5:16, we concluded that, in using the imperative mood, Paul presupposes the presence of the Spirit of Christ in the Galatian churches (Comment #49). Paul knows, that is, that by sending the Spirit into the Galatians' hearts (4:6), God created their churches as addressable communities, communities *able* to hear and heed the divine imperative. Paul holds the same presupposition throughout 5:25–6:10, making that point clear in his initial and comprehensive exhortation:

If, then, we live in the Spirit — *and we do* — let us carry out our daily lives under the guidance of the Spirit (5:25).

This introductory sentence casts its beneficent shadow over the whole of 5:25–6:10, indicating that all of the exhortations are intended by Paul to reflect the character of a community in which the Spirit is decisively active, bearing its

---

[2]That 5:25 begins a new paragraph is well argued, for example, by Schlier; H. D. Betz; Barclay, *Obeying.*

fruit of love, joy, and peace.[3] Just as it is the Spirit who — through the Galatians' mouths — cries out to God as Father (4:6), just as it is the Spirit who promises deliverance from the lethal effects of the Flesh (5:16), just as it is the Spirit who bears the fruit of mutual love and gentleness (5:22–23a), so it is the Spirit, active in their communities, who makes it possible for Paul effectively to exhort the Galatians to share each other's burdens, thus bringing to completion the Law of Christ (6:2).

One is not surprised, then, to note a degree of correspondence between the fruit of the Spirit (5:22–23a) and these exhortations:

The Fruit of the Spirit	Exhortation
gentleness (*prautês*)	restore . . . in a spirit of gentleness (*en pneumati prautêtas*, 6:1)
self-control (*egkrateia*)	Let each one of you consider his own work; then you will keep your boasting to yourself, not directing it to your neighbor. For each one will bear his own burden (6:4–5).
patience (*makrothymia*)	bear one another's burdens (6:2)
generosity (*agathôsyne*)	share goods (6:6; cf. 6:9–10).

Paul uses the maxims, that is, to explicate the list of the fruit of the Spirit into a series of exhortations that presuppose the Spirit's activity in the Galatian communities.

Maxims Addressed to Specific Developments in the Galatian Churches

Are not these exhortations, however, of a remarkably general sort, having little or nothing to do with the situation that is peculiar to the Galatian churches? This question is raised by the fact that 5:25–6:10 is largely made up of individual maxims taken from proverbial collections, that Paul (and the Galatians as well) would have heard on the street, in the workshop, and in the home (see H. D. Betz). Some of the material is Stoic in formulation; some can be compared with proverbs common in numerous cultures of the Hellenistic period, including Jewish wisdom.[4]

The result is a string of maxims that would seem to be valid not only in every place but also in every time. In 6:5, for example, drawing on an aphoristic maxim common in the diatribe literature, Paul says that each person will bear his own burden.[5] Reading the verb "will bear" as a gnomic future, equivalent to "must bear," one can find here a maxim true for all persons in every place and time.

---

[3] Cf. Harnisch, "Einübung."

[4] In addition to H. D. Betz, see notably Kraftchick, "Ethos," and Barclay, *Obeying*, 170–177. It is worth noting that, in composing 5:25–6:10, Paul continues to formulate his pastoral guidance without drawing on scripture.

[5] H. D. Betz mentions several instances of this motif.

At several points in the Notes, however, we will see that Paul transforms the general and timeless maxims into exhortations tailored to the situation that has developed in his Galatian churches since the arrival of the Teachers.[6] At the present juncture three examples will suffice.

Convinced that observance of the Law is bringing them to a higher plane of life, the Galatians who have accepted the Teachers' message are lording it over their fellows, thus exacerbating divisive tendencies (5:15). To them — and to their envious fellows — Paul says, "Do not think of yourself as better than others, provoking one another, envying one another" (5:26).

Second, there is the exhortation of 6:6, where Paul refers to the Teachers' attempt to terminate the work of the catechetical instructors left in place by him when he departed from the Galatian cities.

Third, as we will see in the Notes on 6:3, 4, and 5, Paul takes care to connect the maxims/exhortations to one another, in ways that underline their pertinence to the current life of the Galatian churches.[7]

MAXIMS THAT PROVIDE GUIDANCE BY GIVING APOCALYPTIC ASSURANCE OF GOD'S FUTURE JUDGMENT

Does Paul achieve specificity by leaving behind the apocalyptic perspective we found to be characteristic of the initial pastoral paragraph (5:13–24)? On the contrary, he specifies and transforms the general maxims by speaking in a distinctly apocalyptic manner, using verbs in the future tense to refer literally to the future.[8] This point is particularly clear in vv 7–9, where Paul speaks of God's future judgment. But, in vv 4 and 5 as well, Paul changes the gnomic future of a maxim into a literal future; and there is no reason to exempt the verb in v 2 from the same interpretation. The tone of the paragraph is thus set not only by the series of hortatory and imperative verbs (see above) but also by a string of verbs in the future tense:

v 2   you will bring to completion the Law of Christ
v 4   you will keep your boasting to yourself

[6]It is worth noting (a) that immediately before he commences the pastoral section of the letter in 5:13, Paul refers directly and emotionally to the Teachers (5:7–12); and (b) that immediately after closing his pastoral section in 6:10, he again refers to the Teachers with equal directness and affect (6:12–13). It seems unlikely that, as he composes the intervening material, he drives the Teachers from his mind. Cf. Eckert, *Streit*, 132; the commentaries of Longenecker and Matera; Matera, "Culmination"; Barclay, *Obeying*, 155–177.

[7]As maxims, a number of the sentences in 5:25–6:10 are indeed disconnected assertions. In Paul's hands, however, they are linked to one another in quite revealing ways. Having referred in v 3 to self-deception, for example, Paul introduces v 4 with an adversative particle (rendered above "In place of such self-deception") in order to speak of the antidote to one's deceiving oneself (see Kuck, "Apocalyptic Motif," 293). Then, rather than simply adding v 5 to the string (so H. D. Betz), Paul uses the conjunction "for" (*gar*) to link the exhortation of v 4 to its true ground, the future judgment of God. Even so, as Barclay points out, the level of Paul's specificity may have been disappointing to many of the Galatians, who were finding in the Mosaic Law — doubtless expansively interpreted by the Teachers — just the highly detailed guidance they felt they needed (*Obeying*, 170).

[8]See Kuck, "Apocalyptic Motif."

v 5   each one will bear his own burden

v 7   whatever a person sows is exactly what he will reap

v 8   . . . will reap corruption

         . . . will reap eternal life

v 9   at the appropriate time, we will reap a harvest.

Thus, Paul's transformation of maxims in 5:25–6:10 can serve as an excellent example of his determination to "take every thought captive to Christ" (2 Cor 10:5; Comments #8 and #9), doing so in a way that is focused both on the situation at hand and on the future that will be determined by God. Rectification now and in that future is the work of the fruit-bearing Spirit of Christ. And that rectification involves the individual's Spirit-led work in the community, in light of God's future judgment.

NOTES

5:25. If, then, we live in the Spirit — and we do — let us carry out our daily lives under the guidance of the Spirit. In the last clause of this sentence Paul uses the verb *stoicheô* ("be in line with," "follow the guidance of," "lead one's life by") in order to issue an exhortation, something he has not done since 5:16. The nature of this exhortation (and of the eight that follow through the whole of 5:25–6:10) is set by the first clause.[9] For in that clause (a real condition) Paul states the fact that serves as the foundation for all of his exhortations. He means:

> If it is in sending the Spirit into our hearts that God has made us alive (3:21; 4:6) — and it is — then let us celebrate that life-giving invasion by consistently following the guidance of the Spirit in our daily lives. For the Spirit produces the order of love, joy, and peace, not the chaos of mutual destruction (5:22, 15).

26. Do not think of yourself as better than others, provoking one another, envying one another. To a significant degree the image of a dogfight in 5:15 and the motif of envy in 5:26 provide the broad frame for the list of the effects of the Flesh (5:19–21a), strongly suggesting that the list is indeed pertinent to actual developments in the Galatian communities ("envying one another" in v 26 specifies the general reference in v 21 to "grudging envy of the neighbor's success"). Thus, in v 26 Paul reaches back to the pattern of life characteristic of a community under the influence of the Flesh, in order further to specify the everyday life that is excluded by the leading of the Spirit. Perhaps the followers of the Teachers are inclined to parade their observance of the Law as a clear indication that they are superior to the others. Some of those others, then, are provoked to envy, and the result of comparative pride and burning envy is the opposite of mutual service.[10]

---

[9] See Comment #49. The nine hortatory and imperative verbs in 5:25–6:10 are listed above under Literary Structure and Synopsis.

[10] Kuck, "Apocalyptic Motif," 291.

6:1. Brothers and sisters. Regarding the translation of *adelphoi*, see Note on 1:2.

should be caught. The verb *prolambanō* can have a slight temporal force. Paul may refer to an instance in which the person is detected before it is possible to escape notice, as in a shady business deal.

committing a transgression of some sort. Even though the reference is general—"of some sort"—one might wonder how Paul thinks the Galatians will identify a specific transgression, now that they are no longer "under the authority of the Law" (5:18; cf. Note on 2:18).[11] First, he has already specified for them a list of representative effects of the Flesh. Now he emphasizes elements of that list that destroy community, such as a tendency consistently to compare oneself with others. Moreover, Paul thinks that the Spirit that builds community will provide criteria for identifying transgressions that destroy community.

you who are spiritual. Paul probably intends to speak both with sharp irony and with absolute inclusiveness. The irony is directed to the Galatians who, fully under the influence of the Teachers, have drawn apart from the others, certain that they are the truly spiritual ones, by virtue of their exegetically mature observance of the Law (3:5; 5:3). Against that kind of exclusiveness, Paul says two things: "The spiritual ones" (*hoi pneumatikoi*) is a designation for the *whole* of the church, a community free of hierarchical distinctions. The Spirit leads members of the church to help one another, not to stand apart from one another in the feeling of superiority.

to restore that person to his former condition in the community . . . lest you yourself be tempted. Because Paul speaks of the way in which a tightly knit community deals with an erring member, one thinks of a passage in one of the Dead Sea Scrolls that pertains to a similar matter. Having referred to a person's entry into the Qumran community, and having noted the regulation that a yearly account be taken both of a member's understanding and of his offenses, the *Rule of the Community* continues by speaking of the instance in which a member of the community is reproved for having done something requiring correction:

> They shall rebuke one another in truth, humility, and charity. Let no one address his [erring] companion with anger . . . but let him rebuke him on the very same day lest he incur guilt because of him. And furthermore, let no man accuse his companion before the Congregation without having first admonished him in the presence of witnesses (1QS 5:24–6:1; Vermes; cf. CD 9:6–23).

The word that is here twice rendered "rebuke" and once "admonish" is *yākah*, a verb that conveys the thought of calling one to account, in order that things might be restored to their right state *in the community*, thus including the motif of communal rectification.[12] Paul has in mind something similar.

---

[11] See Schrage, *Einzelgebote.*

[12] Cf. Barclay, *Obeying*, 174. Both as regards the communal aspect in a tightly knit community and as regards the matter of communal rectification, the Qumran scrolls provide a closer parallel than do the texts H. D. Betz cites in Plutarch, Epictetus, Lucian, et al.

The restoration, then, is to be completely devoid of lasting stigma. It is to be carried out with the gentleness that is one of the marks of the Spirit-led community (*en pneumati prautêtos* looks back to *prautês* in 5:23); and also with circumspection. For, as the next clause indicates, all are subject to missteps. Indeed, because every member of the community (note the singular verbs at the end of 6:1) is on the battlefront pictured in 5:17a, everyone is subject to the tempting power of the Flesh.

2. *Bear one another's burdens.* In its context this injunction may imply that the transgressing brother or sister is a burdened person, a person who carries, for example, the load of some kind of addiction. In that case Paul seems to say in effect: "I know that, in his addiction, brother Dionysius has wronged several of you. Together with other members of the church, you are to restore him to his former condition in the community, doing so in full knowledge of the fact that you are as subject to missteps as he is. In this way all of you are to bear the burden of Dionysius as though it were your own, for, in the solidarity of the community, it is."

you will bring to completion. In 5:14 Paul has used the verb *plêroô* in the perfect passive, third person singular. Now he employs the complex form *anaplêroô* in the future active, first person plural, thus both binding 6:2 to 5:14 and differentiating the two from one another.[13] In the Note on 5:14 we have seen reason not to translate *plêroô* as "fulfill," rendering instead "the whole of the Law *has been brought to completion.*" And, in Comment #48, we have suggested that Paul means to refer in 5:14 to an event in the Law's *history*: Differentiating the guiding voice of the original Law from the cursing voice of the Sinaitic Law, Christ has brought the former to completion in the sentence about neighbor love, thus making it the whole of the Law for the daily life of the church.

Now, in 6:2, Paul speaks of something the Galatians themselves will do. In bearing one another's burdens they will bring to completion "the Law of Christ." How is their future deed related to the past deed of Christ? (a) Christ's having brought the Law to completion (5:14) is the deed in which he took possession of the Law, making it his own Law, the Law of Christ. (b) In bearing one another's burdens the Galatians will themselves repeat Christ's deed, following in his train, the major difference being that the Law they will bring to completion is the Law that is now the Law *of Christ*.

It is just possible, then, that in 6:2 Paul uses the complex form of the verb, with the prefix *ana*, in order to give a hint of the motif of repetition, as one sees that motif in such compounds as *anazaô*, "to repeat the event of coming to life" (Rom 7:9).[14] Thus, "Bear one another's burdens, and in this way you yourselves will repeat Christ's deed, bringing to completion in your communities the Law

---

[13] Although a number of manuscripts have in 6:2 the aorist imperative — "bring to completion!" — those that have the verb in the future tense very probably preserve the original reading (Metzger 598).

[14] LSJ, "*ana*," F.3.: *anablastanô, anabioô, anagennaô*. In twenty-six of seventy-one *ana* compounds in the NT, the *ana* means "again" or "back" (MH 295).

that Christ has already brought to completion in the sentence about loving the neighbor."

the Law of Christ. Unique to Gal 6:2, the expression is linguistically simple.[15] The articular noun *ho nomos*, "the Law," is followed by a second noun in the genitive case, *tou Christou*, "of Christ." Many commentators express surprise, noting that at numerous junctures in the letter — 2:21 is notable — Paul has seemed to speak of the Law and Christ as polar opposites that cannot be combined.[16] Interpretations then range across a remarkable spectrum, five major readings being offered. (a) The expression "the Law of Christ (the Messiah)" has been related to Jewish traditions about the role of the Law in the future, messianic age.[17] (b) The expression has been taken to refer to the teaching of Jesus.[18] (c) The Teachers have been credited with having originated the expression, 6:2 being read, then, as one of several junctures in the letter at which Paul seeks to capture his enemies' locutions for his own argument.[19] (d) Paul has been thought to speak of fulfilling the Mosaic Law in a way exemplified by Christ, that is fulfilling it by love.[20] (e) Finally, the expression has been taken as an instance in which the noun *ho nomos* refers to a principle. On this reading, Paul is not speaking of the Law at all, but rather of the principle of love, for which Christ is the paradigm.[21]

In all of these interpretations, attention is given to Gal 5:14, especially in light of the fact that the verb of 6:2 (*anaplêroô*) is forecast by the verb of 5:14 (*plêroô*). Some interpreters also refer to one or more of the instances in Romans in which Paul follows the noun *nomos* by another noun in the genitive case (Rom 3:27; 7:22, 23, 25; 8:2, 7). We will shortly see reason to think that Gal 5:14 and the passages in Romans do indeed provide guidance, leading to the conclusion that

---

[15]The *syntactical unit* is not unique. Josephus, for example, uses the noun *nomos*, "Law," followed by a noun in the genitive case, *theou*, "of God" (*Ant.* 11.121, 124, 130). Paul himself uses the same syntax several times in Romans, although the second noun is never "Christ" (Comment #50).

[16]For example, Hays, who speaks of "the absolute opposition between 'law' and 'Christ' that Paul has deliberately established in the letter (see especially 5:4) . . ." ("The Law of Christ," 276).

[17]See Davies, *Torah*; cf. Schäfer, "Torah"; Banks, "Role."

[18]For example, C. H. Dodd, "*ENNOMOS CHRISTOU.*" The relation between Gal 6:2 and 1 Cor 9:21 poses significant issues, for in 1 Cor 9:21 Paul characterizes himself by using an expression strikingly similar to that of Gal 6:2: "To those not under the Law I became as one not under the Law — though I am not free from God's law but am under Christ's law [*ennomos Christou*] — so that I might win those not under the Law." In the final analysis (see Comment #50) 1 Cor 9:19–23 is entirely harmonious with Gal 6:2: To be in the Law of Christ is to be beyond the distinction between the Law and the Not-Law. See also Comment #41.

[19]Georgi, "Anmerkungen"; followed by H. D. Betz and by Brinsmead, *Dialogical Response.* This reading can be neither proved nor disproved. In any case, it is likely that the Teachers thought of Christ's affirming and perhaps interpreting the Law (Comments #6 and #33).

[20]Barclay takes the expression *ho nomos tou Christou* to mean "the [Mosaic] law as redefined and fulfilled by Christ in love" (*Obeying*, 134). Note also the helpful summaries of other readings in *Obeying*, 127–131, and in Longenecker 275–276.

[21]Hays, "The Law of Christ." See the section "*Nomos* in Galatians" in Comment #50.

in Gal 6:2 Paul refers to the Law as it has been taken in hand by Christ himself (Comment #50).

3. *For if someone thinks he is somebody, when in fact he is nothing of the sort, he deceives himself.* In a letter that is consistently focused on matters of life and death, why should Paul include a truly trite maxim, offering it as a ground for the weighty exhortations of vv 1 and 2?[22] Three observations may prove helpful. First, we have already seen strong reason for thinking that members of the Galatian churches who have followed the Teachers are characterizing themselves as persons on the route to perfection and thus several levels above the others (3:3; 5:26; 6:1). Being themselves virtually immune to temptation, they are able to "help" their weaker and transgressing fellows, while needing no help themselves. Second, we can assume that these proud Galatians are being led into such an opinion of themselves by the Teachers. Third, we also recall that in Galatians Paul uses the expression *dokein einai ti(s)*, "to think (one or oneself) to be something," in his earlier references to the so-called pillars of the Jerusalem church (2:2, 6, 9).

In Paul's mind, then, the maxim of 6:3 may contain an echo of the critical stance he has already expressed toward the way in which the Jerusalem church thinks of its leaders, considering them to be "somebody," persons elevated above the other members of the church. For, presenting themselves as representatives of the Jerusalem church, the Teachers may be importing such hierarchical arrangements into the Galatian communities. On this reading, Paul's response is unequivocal. Hierarchical arrangements in the church obscure two facts: Apart from the power of Christ's grace, all stand under the enslaving power of the Law's curse (3:10; 5:4; cf. Rom 3:9); and in Christ all marks of differentiation having to do with superiority and inferiority are obliterated (Gal 3:28).

4. *In place of such self-deception, let each one of you consider his own work; then you will keep your boasting to yourself, not directing it to your neighbor.*

In place of such self-deception. In this instance Paul uses the particle *de* with its adversative force, thus drawing on the widespread tradition in which self-examination is said to be the antidote to self-deception (v 3).[23] As v 5 shows, however, he insists that self-examination is a valuable exercise only if carried out in light of God's eschatological judgment.

each one of you. As the nature of the exhortation shows, Paul must address it to the individual. We have seen repeatedly, however, that he presupposes the existence of the addressable individual only in the community of the church.

consider his own work. Paul qualifies the motif of self-examination (a) by the fact that the criterion for that examination is the Law of Christ (6:2), and (b) by the knowledge that ultimate examination is the prerogative of God (6:5, 8; cf. 2 Cor 10:18; 1 Cor 4:3–5). There is, however, nothing masochistic about Paul's view of the work that human beings do in the community led by the Spirit, as though one should deny the gifts one has been given for the common edification (1 Cor 12:4–11). The issue, as the following clauses show, is the precise identity

---

[22] Barrett, *Freedom*, 80.
[23] See, for example, Diogenes Laertius *Lives* 8.22; Kuck, "Apocalyptic Motif," 293.

of the "work" to which Paul refers, and the way in which one may think about one's work in the context of community life.

If we take our bearings from Paul's references elsewhere to "boasting" (see below), we can conclude that he refers here to the work that is involved in preaching and living out the gospel (cf. 2:14).[24] The question, then, is whether one constantly indulges in comparisons, boasting to others about the superiority of one's own gospel work.

then you will keep your boasting to yourself, not directing it to your neighbor. The prepositional phrases *eis heauton* (lit. "to oneself") and *eis ton heteron* (lit. "to the other") are difficult to interpret. They are often taken to indicate that, testing one's own accomplishments, one will find a ground for pride (*kauchēma*) in them, not in the accomplishments of one's neighbor (NRSV: "All must test their own work; then that work, rather than their neighbor's work, will become a cause for pride").

It seems better to take the preposition *eis* to indicate the direction of one's boasting, thus finding a contrast between boasting *to* oneself and boasting *to* others, the former being the joyous celebration of the Spirit's work through oneself, the latter a celebration of comparative superiority to a neighbor.[25] Again we may suppose that Paul has in mind developments in the Galatian churches. Like the pseudo-apostles who later invaded his Corinthian church, the Teachers are very probably boasting *to* the Galatians (and *to* the False Brothers in Jerusalem; 6:13), emphasizing their superiority to Paul in a self-congratulating tone of voice (cf. 2 Cor 10:13–18).[26] And, like the Teachers, their followers among the Galatians are congratulating themselves on their superiority to their fellows who are not observant of the Law.

5. *For each one will bear his own burden.* Here, completing the subunit of 5:26–6:5, Paul states the reason for considering one's own work, and thus for avoiding boasts that take the form of comparing oneself with others: Each one *will appear* before God at the future judgment. Having spoken, then, about the individual's "work" in preaching and living out the gospel (*to ergon* in v 4), Paul changes only the term itself, referring now to that gospel work as a "burden" or "load" (*phortion*), which the individual will present to God for God's evaluation.[27]

---

[24]Schrage is right to note the contrast between the plural *erga* in 5:19 and the singular *ergon* in 6:4, thus speaking in this connection of "a unitary basic intention that is to be distinguished from the atomizing of ethics" ("Probleme," 23).

[25]See Barclay, *Obeying*, 160.

[26]Boasting is a subject Paul takes up with particular emphasis in his Corinthian letters, and also in Romans. See Bultmann, "*kauchaomai*." Important comparative material is also given by H. D. Betz 302 n97. As he writes Galatians, Paul says that the ground of his own boasting is, paradoxically, the cross, rather than something pertaining to himself (6:14). Ultimately, his boast is a *confession* of his own cocrucifixion with Christ (2:19; cf. 1 Cor 1:31)!

[27]See the convincing arguments of Cosgrove, "The Law and the Spirit," 354; Kuck, "Apocalyptic Motif," 294–296. See especially the collection of futuristic texts in Kuck, 296, beginning with Gal 5:5, and note not only the future tenses in 6:7–9 but also the verb *bastasei* in 5:10 and in 6:5.

6. *The one who is being taught the word is to share his goods with the teacher.*
As a maxim, this exhortation has numerous parallels in the philosophical schools.
Of particular interest is a passage of the Hippocratic oath in which the initiate
swears:

> to hold him who taught me this art as equal to my parents and to live my life
> in partnership with him (*biou koinôsasthai*), and if he is in need of money, to
> give him a share of mine . . .[28]

In Paul's hands the maxim is taken to refer to an arrangement in the church:
There are those who teach the gospel, and there are those who are taught it
(1 Cor 12:28; cf. Eph 4:11).

Paul's intention may be quite specific. Since the substantive participles are
singular, referring to one who is taught and to one who is teaching, the most
obvious reference is the most simple: Knowing that there is a variety of gifts in
God's church (1 Cor 12:4–11, 28), Paul wishes to reinforce a practice that, far
from being a quid pro quo arrangement, is an instance of truly mutual service
(5:13): Let the one who is receiving catechetical instruction share in the support
of the one who is giving the instruction (cf. 1 Thess 5:12–13; 1 Cor 9:4–7; 2 Cor
11:7–9; Phil 4:10).[29] Paul may very well see this matter as a specification of the
term "generosity" in the list of the fruit of the Spirit (5:22). Why, however, should
he include this particular exhortation in *this* letter? That question can be answered only by imagining developments that Paul need not mention because
they are known both to him and to the Galatians. There are two significant possibilities:

(a) Gal 6:6–10 can be interpreted in connection with passages in other letters
in which Paul speaks of a collection of funds for transmission to the church in Jerusalem.[30]

Gal 6:6 can be seen as similar to Paul's reference to the collection in Rom
15:27:

> . . . if the Gentiles have come to share in their spiritual blessings [a reference
> to the debt of the Gentile churches to the church in Jerusalem], they ought
> also to be of service to them in material things (NRSV).

Gal 6:7–8 can then be read as striking a note comparable to the collection reference in 2 Cor 9:6:

[28]The oath is mentioned by Oepke; H. D. Betz cites it from L. Edelstein, *The Hippocratic
Oath: Text, Translation and Interpretation* (Baltimore: Johns Hopkins, 1943). I take
Edelstein's translation from Betz.
[29]Cf. H. W. Beyer, "*katêcheô*."
[30]Cf. Lightfoot 55; Lietzmann (relating Gal 6:7 to 2 Cor 9:6–10); Borse, *Standort*, 37–38,
145; Hurtado, "Collection"; Lührmann 39; H. D. Betz; Dahl, "Galatians," 72–74; Strelan,
"Burden-Bearing" (relating "burden" in 6:2 to the financial needs of the Jerusalem
church).

the one who sows sparingly will also reap sparingly, and the one who sows bountifully will also reap bountifully (NRSV).

Finally, the expression "the household of faith" (Gal 6:10) can be taken to refer to the brothers and sisters in the Jerusalem church. From these comparisons it is possible to suggest that, in Gal 6:6, Paul means to exhort the Galatians to proceed with their part in his collection of funds for the Jerusalem church.

Tempting as this reading may be, two observations render it very unlikely. First, it requires that we take the expression "the teacher" (*ho katêchôn*) — that is to say, the one who teaches "the word," *the gospel* — as a reference to the church in Jerusalem. In light of the increasingly dark portraits of the Jerusalem church painted by Paul in this letter (Comment #46), it is scarcely conceivable that, at the time he wrote Galatians, he would refer to that church as the trustworthy teacher of the gospel. Second, we have seen in Comment #24 that the matter of the collection(s) is best handled with a comprehensive hypothesis, according to which Paul had not yet commenced his collection when he wrote Galatians.

(b) Far more probable is a simple reading that Paul takes no step to avoid. He would certainly not have left the Galatian scene without seeing to it that the churches there were equipped with catechetical instructors, teaching the gospel in the Pauline form. One may assume, in fact, that these instructors are the people who sent (or carried) a message to Paul about the arrival and work of the incursive Teachers.

And what was the fate of these instructors once the Teachers began to wield significant influence in the Galatian churches? Those who remained steadfast to the Pauline gospel are certain to have been a primary target of the Teachers' hostility.[31] We can assume, then, that, as Paul writes his letter, the Teachers are intent on terminating these Pauline instructors, replacing them with ones loyal to themselves. Under these circumstances Paul would have good reason to reiterate the rule guaranteeing adequate support for the gospel instructor.[32]

7. *Do not be deceived, pretending that it is possible to thumb your nose at God. For whatever a person sows is exactly what he will reap.* 8. *One who sows to his own flesh will reap corruption from the Flesh; but one who sows to the Spirit will reap eternal life from the Spirit.* Verses 7 and 8 are to be taken together, for they consist of a maxim — "Whatever a person sows is exactly what he will reap" (v 7b) — preceded by a theological warning (v 7a) and followed by a second warning that is distinctly eschatological (v 8). The result is another example of Paul's concern to offer more than a mere collection of generally instructive maxims.

Do not be deceived . . . thumb your nose at God. The Galatians may very well think that, should they terminate their support of Paul's catechetical instructors (v 6), they would do something that involves only themselves, those instructors,

---

[31] Eckert, *Streit*, 147.

[32] In the Introduction (§12) we considered the possibility that, in the final analysis, the Pauline catechetical instructors had to move to some other locale, such as Ephesus, taking their much-loved letter with them, thus both preserving it and beginning its circulation in other churches.

and indirectly Paul. In fact, where the truth of the gospel is at stake, one is always dealing with God. To silence the preaching of the truth of the gospel is to defect from *God* (1:6).[33] And while such defection is possible, terminating one's relationship with God — thumbing one's nose and walking away — is not, as the following clauses make clear.

whatever a person sows is exactly what he will reap. The maxim employs a widely used metaphor drawn from the world of agriculture, and focused on the seed a farmer sows.[34] Different seeds produce different plants.

8. *One who sows to his own flesh will reap corruption from the Flesh.* Paul suddenly changes the picture, speaking now of different soils rather than of different seeds (cf. Mark 4:3–9; Matt 13:3–9; Luke 8:5–8). And, drawing on motifs he has used earlier (Comment #49), he paints portraits of two quite different persons, the first being the person who sows the seeds of the future into the soil of his own flesh.[35] In a rhetorically clever way Paul portrays this person by using terms he takes from the vocabulary of the Teachers.

He knows that the Teachers are speaking at length both about the flesh and about the Flesh (Comment #49). The latter, the Teachers say, is the Impulsive Desire of the Flesh, altogether evident in the life of Gentiles. Unchecked, it issues in death. Opposite the Flesh, however, God has provided an antidote, the circumcision of the flesh, as the commencement of Law observance.

Given the Teachers' double use of the terms "flesh" and "Flesh," Paul now employs these terms in a telling double entendre of his own. To sow to *one's own* flesh is to be circumcised, under the illusion that, as the commencement of Law observance, circumcision of one's flesh is the antidote to the enslaving power called Flesh. To sow to one's flesh is then also to fall victim to the Flesh, precisely because nomistic circumcision of the flesh is impotent to curb the Flesh. For this reason Law observance, when considered to be salvific, is fully as dangerous as libertine indulgence.[36]

but one who sows to the Spirit will reap eternal life from the Spirit. The second person portrayed by Paul does not focus his attention on himself (Paul does not speak of sowing to *one's own* spirit!). This person's attention is focused on the Spirit of Christ, the power that bears the fruit of love, joy, and peace in the community of Christ.[37] By *describing* a contrast between this person and the preceding one, Paul awakens those into whose hearts God has already sent the Spirit (4:6), reminding them both of the Flesh's genuine power and of the Spirit's ultimate power.

9. *Do what is right, without growing weary of it; for at the appropriate time we will reap a harvest, if we do not give up.* 10. *Every time we have an opportunity, then, let us work for the good of all, and especially for the good of those who make up the household of faith.* Paul closes the string of apocalyptically interpreted

---

[33] See Preisker, "*myktêrizô.*"
[34] Barclay, *Obeying,* 164 n63.
[35] On the significance of *heauton,* see Jewett, *Terms,* 96.
[36] Barclay, *Obeying,* 212.
[37] Cf. Schweizer, "*pneuma,*" 430–431; Barclay, *Obeying,* 165.

maxims with a couplet, the two exhortations being tied to one another by subject matter ("do what is right"; "work for the good") and by a catchword, *kairos* ("at the appropriate time," "every time"). Similarly, the first part of the couplet is linked to v 8 both by a catchword in the future tense ("reap a harvest") and by substance: those who direct their minds to the Spirit as it bears fruit in the community (v 8) are those who will reap a harvest of the Spirit, neither growing weary nor giving up (v 9).

And what exactly is that harvest? The context suggests that, as the Spirit is itself the dawning light of the new creation, so the fruit of the Spirit (5:22–23) is itself the beginning of the eschatological harvest. The first buds that embody the promise of the future are already found in the true community that is marked by the patient perseverance necessary for genuine service to others.

all . . . the household of failth. The words express a paradox. A major part of Paul's polemic in the letter has been directed against the Teachers' insistence on drawing distinctions within the human family, continuing the separation of Jew from Gentile, observant from nonobservant. Reaching back to a baptismal confession, Paul has reminded the Galatians that Christ is the end of such distinctions. In him there is neither Jew nor Gentile; there is, on the contrary, a new unity (*heis*, "One," in 3:28). And this new unity, this "household of faith," is God's new creation, as Paul will say in the next paragraph (6:15).

But God is not replacing the old and enslaving distinction — Jew and Gentile — with a new and equally enslaving one — a religious distinction between church and world. On the contrary, God is summoning his new creation onto the world scene by calling into existence the church that exists for the sake of "all."[38] For in Christ — through the preached gospel of Christ and through the pattern of living in which each one serves the neighbor (5:14) — God is regrasping the whole of the world for himself, by summoning the church into the service of *all.*[39]

COMMENT #50
THE LAW IN THE HANDS OF CHRIST

In 6:2 Paul issues an exhortation, grounding it in a remarkable assertion:

> Bear one another's burdens, and in this way you will bring to completion the Law of Christ (*ho nomos tou Christou*).

---

[38] In other letters Paul refers to the church as the saints (*hoi hagioi*) quite distinct from the unrighteous (*hoi adikoi*), indeed distinct from the *kosmos* (e.g., 1 Cor 6:1–2). But the distinction does not statically demarcate a holy people. On the contrary, it is thoroughly dynamic, for the apostle expects it steadily to diminish as "those who have never been told of him (Christ) shall see" (Rom 15:21, a quotation from Isa 52:15). As is suggested by Paul's quotation of Isa 52:15, a similar understanding of election — God called Israel into existence as his people, in order to make of her a light for all the nations — plays a prominent role in Second Isaiah (e.g., 42:6; 45:22; 49:6); note later traditions as well (Urbach, *Sages*, 541–554).

[39] Cf. Marcus, "Apocalypticism," 26.

We have observed that Paul's reference to "the Law of Christ" has received numerous and markedly divergent interpretations, five major readings being offered by commentators (see the Note on 6:2). A degree of order can be introduced into the resulting complexity, however, if we pose three simple questions.

First, assuming that the Galatians' understanding of this expression will have been affected by Paul's use of the term *nomos*, "the Law," in earlier parts of the letter—and that Paul himself will have taken that contextual force into account—we may ask about those prior instances. Up to this point in composing his letter, how has Paul used the noun *nomos*, "the Law"?

Second, knowing that Paul employs the syntactical unit "the Law *of A*" (the noun *nomos* followed by another noun in the genitive case) elsewhere in his letters—notably and significantly in Romans—we may ask about the force of that locution in those other instances.

Third, returning to Galatians, and specifically to Gal 5:14—the other juncture in the letter at which Paul speaks of the Law's being brought to completion—we may ask whether similarities appear between that verse and the way in which— in Romans—Paul uses the expression "the Law of A."

Nomos in Galatians

Gal 6:2 is the thirty-first of Paul's references in Galatians to *nomos*, and in all of the other significant instances the reference is to *the* Law.[40] In Comment #48 we have discussed Paul's certainty that the Law has two voices, even, one might say, two modes of existence. We have thus spoken analytically of the plural, cursing Law (having its origin at Sinai) and of the singular, promissory, and guiding Law (having its origin in God). At the end of the present Comment we will return to 5:14, concluding that the distinction between the Law's two voices is a major key to the meaning of the expression "the Law of Christ." No factor related to that distinction has led us, however, to think that with the word *nomos* Paul means anything other than *the* Law. And the same will have been true for the Galatians. In listening to the Teachers' discourses they are encountering numerous references to *nomos*, the Law. And, as they now listen to Paul's letter, all of the thirty previous instances of that term will have prepared them to hear in 6:2 the thirty-first juncture at which Paul refers to *the* Law.[41]

---

[40]Of a total of thirty-two instances, only eight are articular, but, as the contexts show, all are definite references to the Law, except for 3:21a, a condition contrary to fact.

[41]Arguing differently, a number of interpreters have suggested that in Gal 6:2 Paul uses the word *nomos* to mean "principle" or "structure of existence," rather than the Law. See notably Hays, "The Law of Christ," 275–276, and Räisänen ("*Nomos* is being used in a loose sense, almost metaphorically, much as it is used in Rom 3.27 and 8.2" [*Law*, 80]). The argument of Hays is definite and clear: "In view of the absolute opposition between 'law' and 'Christ' that Paul has deliberately established in the letter (see especially 5:4), the expression 'law of Christ' must fall upon his readers' ears as a breathtaking paradox. The sentence [Gal 6:2] is intelligible within the context of Galatians only if the word *nomos* is invested with a different meaning: not the torah of Moses, not a body of rules, but a regulative principle or structure of existence, in this case the structure of existence embodied paradigmatically in Jesus Christ" (276). Then, however, as none of the preceding thirty instances of *nomos* in Galatians suggests that meaning, Hays—with Schrage

"THE LAW OF . . ." IN ROMANS

In the Note on 6:2 we have seen that the expression "the Law of Christ" is unique. The syntactical unit, however — "the Law of A," *nomos* followed by another noun in the genitive case — is found in a number of other texts. Josephus, for example, refers interchangeably to *hoi nomoi Môuseôs* ("the laws of Moses") and *ho nomos tou theou* ("the law of God"; *Ant.* 11.121, 124, 130). For him, as for all Jews, the Mosaic laws constitute the Law *of God*, the Law of which God is the authenticating source.

More important, the expression "the Law of A" occurs thirteen times in Paul's own letters, inclusive of Gal 6:2.[42] Four passages in Romans call for special attention:

Rom 3:27. Then what becomes of boasting? It is excluded. By what Law? By the Law of observance ([*ho nomos*] *tôn ergôn*)? No, but by the Law of faith (*nomos pisteôs*).

Rom 7:22; 8:7. I delight in the Law of God (*ho nomos tou theou*) . . . the mind of the Flesh is hostile to God; it does not submit to the Law of God (*ho nomos tou theou*).

Rom 7:23, 25. . . . taking me captive to the Law of Sin (*ho nomos tês hamartias*) . . . with my Flesh I am a slave to the Law of Sin (*nomos tês hamartias*).

Rom 8:2. For the Law of the Spirit of life in Christ Jesus (*ho nomos tou pneumatos kai tês zoês en Christô Iêsou*) has set you free from the Law of Sin and Death (*ho nomos tês hamartias kai tou thanatou*).

In none of these passages are there grounds for finding in the term *nomos* anything other than "the Law." The question is the precise force of the second noun, the one in the genitive case. What does Paul intend when he refers to "the Law *of A*"? Winger is surely right to take "the Law of God" (Rom 7:22; 8:7) to indicate the Law of which God is the source (note citation of Josephus above).[43] But that reading also shades over into the sense of determination — "the Law of God" is the Law determined by the one who is its source — and possessive determination

---

(*Einzelgebote*, 99), Räisänen, and others — resorts to Romans, believing to find analogies in, for example, Rom 3:27 ("the *nomos* [principle] of faith") and 8:2 ("the *nomos* [principle] of the Spirit of life"). We will shortly see that certain passages in Romans can be of assistance in our quest to understand Gal 6:2. In none of these passages, however, can a convincing case be made for finding in the term *nomos* a reference to a principle or a structure of existence. On the contrary, notably in Romans 7 and 8, one finds that *nomos* means without exception "the Law." See especially Meyer, "Worm," 79. There is every reason, then, for taking Gal 6:2 to be the thirty-first juncture in this letter at which Paul refers to *the* Law (note that, although E. P. Sanders reads "principle" in Rom 3:27, he finds "Law" in Gal 6:2 [*Law*, 15 n26, 97–98]).

[42] Gal 6:2; 1 Cor 9:9; Rom 3:27 (twice); 7:2, 22, 23 (twice); 25 (twice); 8:2, 7; 9:31. See especially Winger, *Law*, 43–44, 159–196.

[43] Winger, *Law*, 44.

is not only a very frequent sense of the genitive but also the best reading of the genitive in Rom 3:27; 7:23, 25; 8:2. One does well to translate the syntactical unit as "the Law *in the possession of* A" or "the Law *as it has been taken in hand by* A" or "the Law *as it is determined by* A." Thus, in Rom 3:27, Paul's question seems clear: Is boasting excluded by the Law, as the Law is determined by its being observed? Or is boasting excluded by the Law, as the Law is under the determinative influence of faith?[44]

It is Paul's use of this locution in Romans 7 and 8 that proves to be particularly instructive. One notes a certain sequence in Paul's argument as it pertains to the relation between the Law and Sin. He first speaks at some length of Sin as an emphatically dynamic actor, able to seize and use the Law's commandments to its own ends.

> Sin, seizing a military base of operations in the commandment, produced in me all kinds of covetousness . . . For Sin, seizing a military base of operations in the commandment, deceived me and used the commandment to kill me (Rom 7:8, 11).

Developing this picture, then, Paul can refer in Rom 7:23, 25; 8:2 to "the Law of Sin," meaning the Law in the possession of Sin, the Law as it has been taken in hand by Sin, the Law that has been used by Sin to deceive, to produce covetousness, and to kill.[45]

From these observations it is a short step to the suggestion that, with the polar expression "the Law of the Spirit of life in Christ Jesus" (*ho nomos tou pneumatos kai tês zoês en Christô Iêsou*; Rom 8:2), Paul means the Law as it has been taken in hand by the life-giving Spirit of Christ. Placing Rom 8:2 alongside Gal 6:2, then, one asks a question by analogy: When Paul coins the expression "the Law of Christ" in writing to the Galatians, does he refer to the Law as it has been taken in hand by Christ himself?[46]

WHAT CHRIST HAS DONE TO THE LAW ACCORDING TO GALATIANS

If we retrace some of the steps we took in Comment #48 — note especially the section "What Christ did to the Law" in the section titled "Christ and the Law's Two Voices" — we see evidence that in Galatians itself (3:8, 11; 4:21b; 5:14) Paul does indeed refer to the Law as it has been affected by Christ. For in our analysis

---

[44] See Meyer, "Romans," 1141.

[45] See especially Meyer, "Worm."

[46] I have said that Paul coins the expression (modulating it later in 1 Cor 9:21). In the Note on Gal 6:2 I mentioned the different thesis of Georgi, that the Teachers originated the expression, a suggestion that, being subject neither to proof nor to disproof, remains an intriguing possibility ("Anmerkungen," 111). For the Teachers could very well have coined the expression in order to say that the Sinaitic Law remains altogether in force, being in fact confirmed to eternity by Christ (Comments #6 and #33). Whether the expression was coined by the Teachers or by Paul, however, the theological issue between the two is clear. For the Teachers primacy belongs to the Law. They therefore view God's Christ in light of God's Law, rather than the Law in light of Christ. For Paul primacy belongs to Christ, and the Law is seen altogether in the light of his powerful advent.

of 5:14 we saw that Paul thinks of the Law as having had a history, and that he considers Christ's effect on the Law to have been the decisive event in that history. Distinguishing the earlier, scriptural, and singular Law—God's Law (3:8, 11; 4:21b; 5:14)—from the later-arriving, cursing, and plural Law of Sinai (3:10, 19; 4:21a; 5:3), Christ has in fact brought the scriptural Law to completion, restoring it to its original singularity, and thus causing it to be the whole of the Law for the church.

CONCLUSION

We see, then, that in Gal 6:2 Paul coins the expression "the Law of Christ" in order to refer to the Law that Christ has brought to completion for the life of the church, the new creation (5:14), thus making that Law his own Law. We thus find confirmation of the hypothesis we earlier advanced for the reading of Gal 5:3, 5:13–14, and 6:2:

(1) In Gal 5:3 Paul speaks for the twenty-fifth time of the enslaving Law.

(2) In 5:13 he exhorts the Galatians to serve one another in love. Then, in order to provide one of the grounds for this exhortation, he takes the crucial step of referring to a watershed event in the history of the Law (5:14). It has been brought to completion as the result of an act of Christ (perfect passive of *plêroô*), and for that reason the Law is no longer enslaving. Indeed, having been brought to completion by Christ in the one sentence that speaks about love of neighbor, the Law is now pertinent to the daily life of the liberated church, the new community that is made up of those who belong to Christ (Gal 5:1; Lev 19:18; Gal 5:24).

(3) Finally, having referred in 5:14 to the Law that has been brought to completion by an act of Christ, Paul can make the assertion of 6:2:

> In love, bear one another's burdens, and in this way you will bring to completion in the corporate life of your churches (future tense of *anaplêroô*) the Law that Christ himself has brought to completion. For Christ brought the Law to completion, when he made it his own Law, by loving us and giving his life for us. Indeed, he did that precisely in accordance with the will of God our Father, whose promise and whose guidance are spoken by the scriptural Law that is now the Law in the hands of Christ (1:4; 2:20; 3:8; 5:14; 6:2).[47]

---

[47] See now Stanton, "Law of Christ."

6:11–18 Autographic Subscript

Translation

6:11. Notice the large letters I am using, as I now seize the pen to write to you with my own hand. 12. Those who wish to put on a good show in the flesh, they are the ones who are trying to compel you to undergo circumcision. Indeed, they are doing that only in order that they themselves might escape the persecution that awaits those who preach the cross of Christ. 13. For these circumcised people do not even keep the Law themselves! Their insistence on circumcising you springs, then, from their desire to boast in regard to your flesh.

14. As for me, God forbid that I should boast in anything except the cross of our Lord Jesus Christ, by which the cosmos has been crucified to me and I to the cosmos. 15. For neither is circumcision anything nor is uncircumcision anything. What is something is the new creation. 16. As to all those who will follow this standard in their lives, let peace and mercy be upon them, that is to say upon the Israel of God.

17. Let no one make trouble for me anymore. For I bear in my own body scars that are the marks of Jesus.

18. Brothers and sisters, the grace of our Lord Jesus Christ be with your spirit. Amen!

Literary Structure and Synopsis

To a significant extent Paul crafts the end of his letter to match its beginning. At that earlier point, knowing that his messenger would read the epistle aloud in a service of worship, in which God's name has been invoked and God's presence acknowledged, Paul formed the core of the letter's prescript into a prayer, made up of a blessing (1:3–4) and a doxology (1:5). In this way he invited the Galatians to join him in speaking the "Amen!" directly to God. Now, in closing, he brings the Galatians once again into the presence of God. With the blessings of 6:16 and 6:18 and with the final "Amen!" Paul makes clear to the Galatians that, in listening to his letter, they have been dealing not simply with him but also and fundamentally with God. It is from God that the Galatians are defecting (1:6), and it is to God and to "our Lord Jesus Christ" that Paul finally commits them (1:5; 6:18).

In order again to specify what is at stake in the Galatians' defection from God, Paul first returns to an explicit portrait of the Teachers and their message, forming his description so as to emphasize the contrast between the Teachers' preaching, focused as it is on circumcision (Law observance), and his own preaching, having as its focus the cross on which Christ was crucified (cf. 3:1–5). The recapitulating contrast is genuine, and it is sharp.[48]

---

[48] Cf. Weima, *Closings*.

Noting this contrast, however, a number of interpreters have missed the point, thus taking the letter to reflect in essence nothing more than a rivalry between two religious thinkers, Paul and the leading figure among the Teachers (5:10). In his part of the debate Paul is then said to exhort the Galatians to side with him, rather than with the Teachers, writing a letter that is a personal and polemical apology, a negation of circumcision and thus an attack on Judaism.

In 6:14a, however, Paul draws a *personal* contrast between the Teachers and himself, only in order to prepare the way for his descriptive reference to the *cosmic* event of the gospel. For in 6:14b–15, speaking in the indicative mood, Paul refers to the nonexistence of *both* circumcision *and* uncircumcision. The gospel of the cross announces the end of the *elemental* antinomy that formerly consisted of the Law/the Not-Law. What is gone, then, is the elemental pair of opposites that stood at the foundation of the entire cosmos of religion. And, far from trivializing this event, Paul says that it involves death, the lethal loss of cosmos and the lethal loss of one's own identity (Comment #51). In the moment in which—participating in Christ's crucifixion—Paul was separated from the foundational elements of religion, his cosmos suffered death, and Paul himself suffered a corresponding death.

To take one's bearings from the subscript, then, is to see that fundamentally the letter is not about what *should* not be (the Teachers' inferior preaching). Nor is it even about what *should* be (Paul's superior preaching). It is about what does not exist and about what does exist. No longer having real existence is the cosmos of religion, and taking its place is God's new creation, that is to say Christ and the church (the Israel of God) in which the Spirit is bearing the fruit of love.

NOTES

6:11. *Notice the large letters I am using, as I now . . . write to you with my own hand.*

large letters. Providing an autographic subscript that is far more than a polite farewell (1 Cor 16:21; cf. Phlm 19; Rom 16:22; Col 4:18), Paul writes with large letters in order emphatically to say to the Galatians: "I now summarize, indeed sharpen, the import of my entire letter. Pay attention!"[49]

12. *the ones who are trying to compel you to undergo circumcision.* In his final description of the Teachers' labors Paul echoes his earlier reference to the False Brothers in the Jerusalem church. Like those charlatans—as Paul sees them—the Teachers are *trying* to compel the Galatians to be circumcised (*anagkazousin* is conative present tense; BDF §319; cf. Gal 2:3). But the Teachers' lack of complete success does not cause Paul to speak politely. In his description he not only reduces their mission to the single act of circumcision. He also follows a practice common in debates of every age. He claims to be able to enter the Teachers'

---

[49]An example of an autographic subscript in a papyrus letter is given by Stowers, *Letter Writing*, 60–61. On the debate between Deissmann ("clumsy letters") and Clark ("large letters"), see BAGD; H. D. Betz. In legal documents the autographic subscript served as authorization (Trobisch, *Letter Collection*, 87).

minds, characterizing, in three clauses, what he takes to be their reprehensible motives.[50]

    (a) The Teachers are persons who *wish to put on a good show in the flesh* (v 12a).

    (b) They carry out their circumcising mission *in order that they themselves might escape the persecution that awaits those who preach the cross of Christ* (v 12c).

    (c) They have a *desire to boast in regard to your flesh* (v 13c).

[they] wish to put on a good show in the flesh . . . [they have a] desire to boast in regard to your flesh. The first and third of the motive clauses are virtual equivalents. The verbs in them are similar, *euprosôpeô* meaning "to put on a good show"[51] and *kauchaomai* meaning "to boast." And in both clauses Paul uses the term "flesh." In light of prior instances in which he has employed that term to refer to the foreskin of the penis — see notably 3:3 — one can sense that he is ridiculing the Teachers.[52]

The Teachers themselves believe they are called by God to the noble task of carrying the good news of the messianic and Spirit-supplying Law to the Gentiles (see Note on 3:5). Considering this "gospel" to be both false and enslaving, Paul employs barbed humor, inviting the Galatians to laugh at the Teachers, as though they were actors in one of Aristophanes' comedies. In actuality, the Teachers' attention, he says, is focused neither on the Spirit (6:12a) nor on the Law (6:13a), but rather on the penis, and specifically on their own reputation as its cultic surgeons (cf. 5:12)![53]

[they are concerned to] escape the persecution that awaits those who preach the cross of Christ. Were the Teachers to center their message in the cross, rather than in the demand for Law observance, they would speak — in some form — of the end of all religious differentiations, such as the differentiation of holy, circumcised people from profane and uncircumcised people. And were they thus to preach this message, they would incur the wrath of persons able, in some way, to persecute them. Who might these persons be? That is a question illuminated by several earlier passages in the letter.

---

[50] Important as motives may be to Paul, comparison with a passage in Philippians leads to the conclusion that he attacks the Teachers on motivational ground only because they preach a false gospel, focused on Law observance rather than on the redemptive death of Christ. In Phil 1:15–18 Paul mentions persons whose motive for preaching Christ is far from honorable; yet if it is really Christ whom they preach, Paul can rejoice in their work.

[51] See MM for a second-century-B.C. citation from the Tebtunis papyri.

[52] Regarding the expression "your flesh" in 6:13, note the comment of Jewett, "When 'flesh' is qualified with the possessive pronoun 'your,' it is clearly not a power which acts of its own accord. Nor is it a symbol for the material, sensual side of man. Rather it is the flesh which was cut [off] in circumcision!" (*Terms*, 96). See also the expression in 4:23, 29: "to beget by Law-observant circumcision."

[53] Cf. the sarcastically comic role given to the phallus by Aristophanes in *Lysistrata*; and note the fourth-century-B.C. clay figurine showing a comic actor in the characteristic, short padded dress with phallus attached: *OHCW*, 175.

(a) Gal 2:3–4. In describing the Jerusalem conference Paul has referred to the False Brothers in the Jerusalem church as persons intent on *compelling the circumcision* of Titus. In that attempt they did not succeed, but we have seen reason to think that, after the conference, they were able to increase their influence in the Jerusalem church, gaining the ear of James (Comments #25 and #46).

(b) Gal 2:12. Paul has portrayed Peter as an evangelist who, at one juncture, took a partly Law-observant stance in the Antioch church, because he was *afraid* of the circumcision party in the Jerusalem church, a group probably led by the False Brothers.

(c) Gal 4:29. At the present time the False Brothers and their circumcision party in the Jerusalem church are to some degree sponsoring—or at least applauding—the labors of the Teachers, and Paul sees in the Teachers' work a direct and immediate *persecution*, both of himself and of his circumcision-free Gentile churches in Galatia (cf. 4:19, 29; 6:6).

(d) Gal 5:11–12. Paul has indicated that, were he to *cease preaching the cross* (preaching circumcision instead), he would *escape such persecution.*[54]

Reading 6:12–13 in the context of these earlier references, we see that, just as the Teachers are persecuting Paul, so they themselves would be subjected to persecution were they to follow his example, preaching the cross in such a way as to forgo the demand that Gentiles be circumcised. Presumably, then, their persecutors would be the False Brothers and their cohorts in the circumcision party, persons now possessing considerable power in the church of Jerusalem (Comment #46). In fact, Paul says, intent on escaping that persecution, the Teachers are constructing a sheltered position by boasting to the False Brothers that they are succeeding in circumcising a large number of Gentile converts (6:13). In reporting to the False Brothers, the Teachers may be saying in essence:

> We are proud of the fruit of our mission, no less here in Galatia than elsewhere. Many of the Galatians, although previously misled by Paul, are now being circumcised, are keeping the food laws, and are observing the holy times, thus coming under the blessed wings of the Shekinah. God be praised!

Whatever the language, Paul sees in it a falsification of the truth of the gospel. He responds, therefore, with biting sarcasm, saying to the Galatians: "The Teachers are not really concerned with your welfare (4:17). They are actually interested only in currying favor with a powerful group in the Jerusalem church, thus avoiding the wrath of that group."[55]

---

[54]Paul's references to his own persecution of the nascent church (1:13, 23; cf. Phil 3:6) constitute a matter he does not link to the motifs of 6:12–13, circumcision, cross, fear of persecution, and the possibility of escaping it. The motifs he mentions in 2:3–4, 12; 4:19, 29; 5:11–12; 6:6, 12–13 are all inner-church developments.

[55]There is also the possibility that the False Brothers themselves are living under the threat of some kind of persecution from Palestinian zealots, were they freely to allow circumcision-free churches to be founded among the Gentiles. See the suggestive interpretation offered by Jewett, "Agitators," 206.

13. *these circumcised people.* Using a substantive participle, *hoi peritemno-menoi*, Paul continues to refer to the Teachers, again distinguishing them from the Galatians ("they . . . you . . .").[56] The form of the participle — present passive — has occasioned considerable comment.[57] As a way of referring to the Teachers, one should perhaps have expected Paul to use a perfect passive: "those who are circumcised as a result of having been circumcised"; and in fact, some manuscripts have that reading.[58] The present-passive participle probably preserves, however, what Paul wrote. Employed as a substantive, this participle has no temporal reference.[59] Linguistically, Paul simply refers to "the circumcised people." The context, and the syntax of vv 12–13, indicate that he speaks of the Teachers (v 12a = v 13c).

do not even keep the Law themselves! Two possible readings of this charge are worth mentioning. (a) Pursuing their mission in Gentile lands, the Teachers may find that they cannot keep every commandment.[60] Writing in the second century, Justin has the Jew Trypho (whom he places in Ephesus) say that it is impossible for him truly to sacrifice the paschal lamb, for that precept of the Law can be performed only in Jerusalem (Justin *Dial.* 46). (b) Alternatively, the Teachers may be like the Jewish Christians criticized in the epistle of James, who to some degree pick and choose among the commandments, deciding — for whatever reasons — which ones they will observe (Jas 2:10; 4:11). In the Note on Gal 5:3 we have already mentioned the possibility that the Teachers are extending to the Galatians a certain flexibility, requiring circumcision, food laws, and the observance of holy times, while leaving aside numerous other parts of the Law. Perhaps the Teachers are allowing themselves a similar flexibility, being nevertheless convinced in their own minds that they are fully observant of the Law.

14. *As for me, God forbid that I should boast in anything except the cross of our Lord Jesus Christ, by which the cosmos has been crucified to me and I to the cosmos.* In light of Paul's earlier admonition to keep one's boasting to oneself (6:4), the crucial point here is the paradoxical nature of Paul's own boast:

boast in . . . the cross of our Lord Jesus Christ. If, as suggested above, the Teachers are preening their feathers with the boast that their evangelistic labors put Paul's to shame, Paul takes as the ground of his own boast the cross of Christ. The result is a distinct paradox, in which Paul redefines the word "boast," so that, in his case, it does not mean what it means in the case of the Teachers. For the ground of Paul's boast is not some accomplishment of his own. That ground is rather an event that happened apart from him — Christ was crucified (3:1). To

[56]There is no convincing reason to think that between v 12 and v 13 Paul changes his frame of reference, suddenly using the participle *hoi peritemnomenoi* to speak of a group other than the Teachers.

[57]On the theory — from A. Neander (1831) onward — that Paul refers to Gentiles who have accepted circumcision and who demand the same of other Gentiles, see Hawkins, "Opponents," 21–31, 86–120; Barclay, *Obeying*, 42–43, and notes there.

[58]On the textual problem, see Hawkins, "Opponents," 87–89.

[59]On *Acta Petri et Pauli* 63, and on the impact of the fact that the Greek Fathers saw a reference to born Jews, see Hawkins, "Opponents," 92–93.

[60]See Hengel, *The Pre-Christian Paul*, 31–34.

be sure, he participated in that event, as he will emphasize in the final clause of the present verse (and see 2:19–20; 6:17). In no sense, however, did Paul *choose* to participate in Christ's crucifixion, thereafter looking back on that choice with pride. On the contrary, his being cocrucified with Christ was the event in which he was taken to his own death. Only in a very peculiar sense, then, does Paul say that he boasts in the event of the cross. He means that he preaches the cross as the foundation of his *confidence*. For he knows the cross to be the cosmic event in which God stepped on the scene, in order to make things right. In a word, Paul does not boast of himself. He confidently boasts "of the (crucified) Lord" (1 Cor 1:31).[61]

by which the cosmos has been crucified to me and I to the cosmos. Paul preaches the cross as the foundation of his confidence, because the cross — not the advent of the Law — is the watershed event for the whole of the cosmos, affecting everything after it (*estaurôtai*; perfect tense, "has been crucified"). Putting the matter in terms of his personal witness, he speaks of this watershed event by saying that it was by the cross (*di' hou*) that he himself suffered the loss of one cosmos, and saw the birth of another, God's new creation (v 15).

the cosmos has been crucified to me. The identity of the cosmos that met its death in the cross is revealed by the fact that that cosmos had as one of its foundational elements the pair of opposites we have called the Law/the Not-Law (Comment #41). When Paul lived by that pair of opposites (1:13–14), his nomistic cosmos remained undisturbed.

In the time of God's own choosing, however, God seized Paul, apocalyptically revealing his Son to him (1:15–16). As this event unfolded, Paul came to see that his precious Law — previously the lamp to his feet and the light to his path (Gal 2:19; Ps 119:105) — had pronounced a sentence on itself, by uttering a curse on the one who was in fact God's Christ (3:13)! Now, instead of retaining his view of the Law, Paul came to see God's view of the cross. And, in seeing that view, Paul suffered the loss of the nomistic cosmos in which he had been living, thus experiencing the anguish of genuine death. The crucifixion of Christ (no longer an event separate from himself) was now the crucifixion of Paul's cosmos, everything he had held sacred and dependable.

and I to the cosmos. By the same token, Paul says that Christ's cross brought about his own crucifixion to the cosmos. He thus uses the image of crucifixion to emphasize his own lethal separation from his previous, cherished and acknowledged identity. With this event, that is to say, Paul ceased to be known by others on the basis of his place in that old cosmos of the Law (1:13–16). He became as much a stranger to his previous comrades — and indeed to all people who live in the world of the Law/the Not-Law — as their world became a stranger to him (cf. 1 Cor 4:8–13).

15. *For neither is circumcision anything nor is uncircumcision anything. What is something is the new creation.* To speak of the death of the old cosmos, and to refer to its replacement by another, Paul employs a three-membered formula,

---

[61] See Bultmann, "*kauchaomai*," 649–650. The result, as H. D. Betz says, is a boast that can find its ultimate form only in a doxology or a hymn (318). See further Cousar, *Cross.*

one wording of which he has already used in 5:6 (see Note there and Appendix B to Comment #48). In the context set by 6:12 and 13 — Paul's furious references to the Teachers' attempt to compel the Galatians' circumcision — one could have expected him emphatically to focus his attack on the rite of circumcision, saying that it accomplishes nothing. Instead, he declares the nothingness of both circumcision and uncircumcision, thereby identifying the cosmos that met its death in the cross. The world that is now passé is not Judaism as such, but rather the world of *all* religious differentiation.[62]

The scope and the radical nature of this declaration are easily missed. Reading v 15 by itself, for example, a number of interpreters have failed to see that, with the conjunction "for" (*gar*), Paul carries over into v 15 the cosmic and therefore absolute dimensions of v 14. He does not speak in comparative terms.[63] His participation in Christ's crucifixion did not cause him to think of circumcision as *less important* than he had previously thought it to be, thus leading him to tell the Galatian Gentiles that circumcision is *not necessary* to their redemption (a frequently encountered reading of Galatians). On the contrary, the cross separated Paul totally from the whole of the religious *cosmos*, of which a fundamental element was the pair of opposites called circumcision and uncircumcision, the Law/the Not-Law (Comments #41 and #51).

new creation. This is an expression at home in apocalyptic writings, in which the accent lies on the motif of radical, uncompromising newness.[64] Following this radical tradition, Paul does not say that, in Christ, the old cosmos has been repaired by being propped up, or somewhat modified. Because the old cosmos had fallen into the hands of powers alien to God (see 1:4; Comments #3 and #39), God had to invade enemy territory, sending his Son and the Spirit of his Son, and thereby confronting those powers in an apocalyptic war (Comment #49). The result is that, far from repairing the old cosmos, God is in the process of replacing it. See further Comment #51.

16. *As to all those who will follow this standard in their lives, let peace and mercy be upon them, that is to say upon the Israel of God.* This apparently simple sentence poses a series of issues.

let peace and mercy be upon them. The kernel of the sentence is a blessing with which Paul invokes the peace that only God can give and the mercy that only God can show. As he was growing up in an observant home, and especially

---

[62]Cf. Käsemann, "God does not just want a new religiosity but a renewed creation under the cosmocrator Christ" (*Romans*, 242; German 234); Introduction §17.

[63]Unintentionally domesticating the radical nature of Paul's theology by using comparative expressions, Dunn, for example, reads Gal 6:14–15 as a text in which Paul formulates his polemic by speaking of an "over-evaluation of the significance of both circumcision and uncircumcision" (342).

[64]The major references to the expression "new creation" are *Jub.* 4:26; *1 Enoch* 72:1; 4 Ezra 7:75; *2 Apoc. Bar.* 32:6; 1QS 4:25; 1QH 11:10–14; 13:11–12. The roots of the motif lie in Isa 65:17–25. Whereas in Qumran, the new creation is expected in the future, being the *termination* of the struggle between the two spirits (Truth and Falsehood; 1QS 4:24–25), Paul uses the expression to announce and to identify what God has done in Christ, *inaugurating* the end-time struggle (Gal 6:15; 2 Cor 5:17). See Sjöberg, "Neuschöpfung"; Stuhlmacher, "Erwägungen"; G. Schneider, "Neuschöpfung."

as he was receiving intensive instruction in the Law (1:14; Phil 3:5–6), Paul must have heard various forms of a similar blessing, in which one asked God to bestow his peace and mercy on his people Israel. Examples are diverse, ranging from those contained in the scripture itself to at least one that may have been, in some form and in some locales, a part of a synagogue liturgy in Paul's time:

> *eirênê epi ton Israêl:* Peace be upon Israel (Pss 125:5; 128:6 [LXX 124:5; 127:6]).

> *tou kyriou to eleos epi ton Israêl eis ton aiôna kai eti:* May the mercy of the Lord be upon Israel forevermore (*Pss. Sol.* 11:9; cf. 9:11).

> *šālôm ... wĕhēsed ... 'alênû wĕ'al kōl yiśrā'ēl 'ammēk:* May peace ... and mercy ... be upon us and upon all Israel thy people (*Shemonê Esrê* 19 [Babylonian recension]).[65]

Thus, in Gal 6:16b — "let peace and mercy be upon them" — Paul has formed his sentence as a sort of quotation from such blessings, at the same time making several changes.

As to all those who will follow this standard in their lives. The traditional blessings are not pronounced on the populace of the world. As we see above, they are restrictive, invoking God's grace on Israel. At the end of his blessing, Paul himself will use the word "Israel" (although we will have to ask below about his intention in making that reference). First, however, Paul places a restrictive clause *before* his blessing.[66] In this way he gives to his blessing a threatening side. He does not hand over to God's curse the Galatians who have become thoroughgoing followers of the Teachers (contrast 1:8–9), but he will not conceal the fact that the future will bring God's judgment on those who do not follow the standard of the new creation (cf. 5:21b; 6:7–8).

those who will follow this standard. In 5:25 Paul has employed the verb *stoicheô* ("be in line with," "follow the guidance of," "lead one's life by") in order to exhort the Galatians consistently to carry out their daily lives under the guidance of the Spirit whom God had sent into their hearts. Now, using the same verb in the future tense, Paul invokes God's peace and mercy only on those who will consistently lead their daily lives under a certain standard.[67] If the Teachers are telling the Galatians that, together with his converts, Paul has cut himself loose from all stable and dependable norms (2:17), Paul will insist otherwise. He does not hesitate to specify the Spirit's guidance (5:16, 25) by speaking of a pattern of communal life lived under a definable standard.

this standard. With the expression *ho kanôn houtos* (lit. "this straight rod," "this

---

[65]The text is given in Richardson, *Israel*, 79.
[66]Paul uses an expression that is at once restrictive and inclusive, "all those who." Regarding *hosoi* as equivalent to *pantes hosoi*, see, for example, Josephus *Ant.* 12.399; BAGD.
[67]In writing 5:13–6:10 Paul is concerned to show the integrity of belief and communal, daily life in the church of God (Mussner).

chalk line," hence "this standard"), Paul refers to the new creation he has just announced in v 15. The standard, then, is not a nomistic rule, however novel. On the contrary, the standard is the *real world* that has now been made what it is by the *event* of God's gracious invasion via his Son and the Spirit of the Son. In short, the standard is not a "should" but rather an "is," a cosmic announcement couched in the indicative mood in order to *describe* the real world:

> Neither *is* circumcision anything nor *is* uncircumcision anything. What *is* something *is* the new creation (6:15).

The restriction Paul places on his blessing proves, therefore, to be inevitable. Given the *fact* of God's invasion of the human orb in the sending of his Son and the Spirit of his Son, Paul *can* pronounce his blessing only on those who will continue to follow in the train of that grand *fact*. In the restriction of his blessing, Paul simply continues to deal with the way things are in the real world.

that is to say upon the Israel of God. Having restricted his blessing to those who will consistently live in the real world, God's *new* creation, and having worded the blessing itself in a traditional way, Paul continues to follow tradition by ending his blessing with a reference to Israel (note the blessing citations above). Expected as it may seem, however, this final phrase poses three important questions. (a) What sense does Paul intend for the word *kai* ("and" or "that is to say") with which he introduces this phrase? (b) Precisely why does Paul refer to Israel at the close of his letter? (c) Why, in that reference, does he add the words "of God," thus speaking of the Israel *of God*? The first of these questions, being grammatical, can be stated and partially analyzed in the present Note. Answers to it and to the other two are then suggested in Comment #52.

Paul writes *kai epi ton Israel tou theou*. For this instance of the little word *kai*, there are two possible translations. Paul may use it as the simple copulative ("and"), meaning that his blessing is extended *both* to the restricted group of those who follow the standard of the new creation *and* to a second group, "the Israel of God." Alternatively, he may employ *kai* as an explicative ("that is to say"), thus identifying those who follow the standard of God's new creation *as* "the Israel of God."[68] Arguments have been advanced for each of these readings, but no satisfactory consensus has emerged.[69] However, by attending to the second and third of the questions mentioned above, we will be able to elect one of the readings with confidence, as our translation shows (Comment #52).

[68]BAGD "*kai*," I.3.; BDF §442 (9); Mayser, *Grammatik*, 2.3.141.
[69]The debate to 1968 is well reflected in Richardson, *Israel*, 74–84. For taking *kai* as the simple copulative "and," see especially Schrenk, "Israel Gottes"; idem, "Segenswunsch"; and Richardson himself. For the explicative/epexegetical reading, "that is to say," see Dahl, "Name." More recently, Luz has given a very strong argument for the epexegetical reading (*Geschichtsverständnis*, 269, 285). See also Davies, "People," 10 n2, who suggests in the final analysis that, if Luz's reading were correct, one would expect to find support for it in Romans 9–11, "where Paul deals extensively with 'Israel.'" But that section of Romans may have been written in part as Paul's attempt to deal with the difficulties that had arisen between himself and the Jerusalem church *as a result of* Gal 6:16, read as a reference to the church *as* God's Israel. See Introduction §13.

17. Let no one make trouble for me anymore. At several points in this profoundly angry letter, Paul has openly expressed his exasperation with the Teachers' counterfeit gospel, with the Teachers themselves, and with the Galatians' credulity (1:6; 3:1; 4:19; 5:12). Now, in what amounts to a peremptory and unilateral demand, he calls a halt to the Teachers' labors and to the Galatians' credulity, giving as the grounds for this imperious order his own physical state.

For I bear in my own body. Considering his physique to be a major form of communication, alongside the words of his letter, Paul points literally to his own body.[70] He can do this because his body tells the story of the forward march of the gospel, just as do his words (cf. Comment #11).

scars. Partly because Paul uses the verb *bastazô,* "to bear" (cf. 6:2), we can be confident that with the word *stigmata* he speaks of scars he has received at the hands of those who persecute him for preaching the gospel of the crucified Christ (5:11; 1 Cor 4:11; 2 Cor 6:4–5; 11:23–27; cf. Acts 16:22–24).[71] He does not see his apostolic sufferings as a matter of bad luck! On the contrary, as the powers of the present evil age (1:4) sense God's liberating invasion, they put up a bitter fight, wounding God's emissaries.[72] Scars Paul has received, therefore, from Gentile stones and from Jewish whips (2 Cor 11:24–26) reflect the wounds of a soldier sent into the front trenches of God's redemptive and liberating war (Comment #49).[73] Since God has inaugurated that war in the cross, and since Paul knows himself to suffer on the cross with Christ (2:19), he can now speak of his scars as:

the marks of Jesus. Paul bears in his body the Jesus scars (*tou Iêsou* is probably genitive of quality; BDF §165).[74] The painful wounds he has endured and continues to endure in his preaching are like those endured by Jesus, in the sense

---

[70]Note the thesis of Käsemann that in many passages Paul understands the body to be the possibility of communication (*Essays,* 133). See further Schweizer, *"sôma";* Jewett, *Terms,* 218.

[71]Paul's references to persecution in his Corinthian letters form our main guide. That he does not use the term *stigma* in those references is no more a problem than that *some* of the persecutions mentioned had not yet happened when Paul wrote to the Galatians. Paul's reference to scars is probably not significantly illuminated by either of two ancient practices that were connected with the term *stigma.* Some masters *branded* their slaves as well as their cattle (MM), and religious devotees sometimes had themselves *tattooed* (BAGD). For the various readings that have been drawn from such comparisons, see Güttgemanns, *Apostel,* 126–135. The later practice in which some Christians had the name of Christ tattooed on their wrists or arms is a matter significantly different from the apostle's speaking of apocalyptic battle wounds. See O. Betz, *"stigma,"* 664.

[72]On the whole, Paul drew no distinction between malevolent persecution at the hands of various authorities and such disasters as shipwrecks and floods. Both hindered his labors, and his labors in preaching Christ were the means by which God was furthering the march of the rectifying gospel into the world (Rom 15:18–19).

[73]As Antipater was said to bear on almost every part of his person the marks of wounds showing his loyalty to Caesar (Josephus J.W. 1.193), so Paul points to his body as it testifies to his belonging to the crucified Jesus. Perhaps it is this latter factor that causes Paul to use the name "Jesus" by itself (only this once in Galatians). The stigmata *Iêsou* are in fact a mark of the kind of apostle Paul is, a wandering evangelist whose life pattern is that of Jesus (2 Cor 4:10).

[74]See 2 Cor 11:22–28; Gallas, "Synagogalstrafen."

that Paul's own injuries are inflicted by the same powers that crucified Jesus (1 Cor 2:8; Gal 4:19; cf. Borse). For this reason his scars are nothing other than the present epiphany of the crucifixion of Jesus. Paul's physical body is thus a place in which one finds a sign of the present activity of the redeemer in the world.[75]

> We have this treasure [the gospel] in clay jars, so that it may be made clear that the extraordinary power belongs to God and does not come from us. We are afflicted in every way, but not crushed; perplexed, but not driven to despair; persecuted but not forsaken; struck down but not destroyed; always carrying in our body the putting to death of Jesus, so that the life of Jesus may also be made visible in our bodies (2 Cor 4:7–10).[76]

The glad tiding of Jesus' redemptive death is preached by the one who inevitably participates in that death, and whose apostolic sufferings are paradoxically the locus of God's gift of life, being the present form of Jesus' own death-life pattern.

With this reference to his own body, Paul can emphasize his order that the Teachers cease their activity. For the sign under which God is making things right in his new creation is not the physical mark one receives in the religious rite of circumcision, but rather the physical scars Paul has received because he preaches the gospel.

18. *Brothers and sisters.* Instead of greeting by name a few members of the Galatian churches (cf., e.g., 1 Cor 16:17; Phil 4:18) — perhaps thereby taking the risk of worsening the tensions within the communities — Paul returns to the word by which he identifies *all* of the Galatians as siblings in God's newly created family (on the translation of *adelphoi*, see 1:2).[77] As the Galatians have been included in that family, Paul is fundamentally confident that, in the final analysis, God will be victorious in liberating them from all forms of malignant enslavement (5:10; 1 Cor 15:20–28).

the grace of our Lord Jesus Christ. As Paul pronounced a gracious blessing on the Galatians in his prescript (1:3), so he closes in a similar manner, the word "grace" providing a summary of the way in which God is setting things right in Christ, without requiring a precondition of any sort on the part of human beings (cf. 1 Thess 5:28; 1 Cor 16:23; 2 Cor 13:14; Phil 4:23; Phlm 25; Rom 16:20).

be with your spirit. This clause has its parallel in two of Paul's other final blessings, Phil 4:23 and Phlm 25. Having repreached the gospel in the form of an epistolary argument, Paul makes his penultimate word the request that God pour his free grace into the Galatians' innermost parts, thoroughly affecting the whole of their beings.[78]

Amen! Finally, Paul hopes that, as they hear the letter read aloud, the Gala-

---

[75]Several of the preceding sentences are taken in part from Güttgemanns, *Apostel*, 132–135. See also Kay, *Praesens*.

[76]Following BAGD in rendering *hê nekrôsis* as "the putting to death."

[77]See Malherbe, "Family."

[78]This is the only instance in Galatians in which Paul employs the word *pneuma* to refer to the human spirit. Cf. Jewett, *Terms*, 183–184; Anderson, "The Use of 'ruah.'"

tians will themselves join in the "Amen," thus returning to the God who called their communities into existence in the first place (cf. the Notes on 1:5 and 1:6).

COMMENT #51
APOCALYPTIC ANTINOMIES AND THE NEW CREATION

THE DISAPPEARANCE OF THE OLD ANTINOMIES

In Comment #41 we have seen that, in writing to the Galatians, Paul draws on the widespread tradition in which the elements of the cosmos are found to be pairs of opposites, antinomies.[79] We have also noted that, bringing this tradition of antinomies into a thoroughly apocalyptic perspective, Paul makes in Galatians an astonishing — indeed, a frightening — announcement: The antinomies that lay at the foundation of the cosmos have now disappeared. Previously, there were such elemental pairs of opposites as Jew/Gentile, circumcision/uncircumcision, the Law/the Not-Law. With the advent of Christ, however, these antinomies, and thus their cosmos itself, have come to an end. It is true that Paul does not use images that are obviously apocalyptic — falling stars, a blood-red moon, an earthquake, etc. — but his language is as thoroughly cosmic and as fully apocalyptic as it would have been had he done so. Citing an early Christian baptismal tradition, Paul emphatically says that the cosmos, founded as it was on religious pairs of opposites, does not any longer exist:

> For when all of you were baptized into Christ, you put on Christ as though he were your clothing.
> There *is* neither Jew nor Greek;
> there *is* neither slave nor free;
> there *is* no "male and female";
> for all of you are One in Christ Jesus (3:27–28).

By citing this tradition, Paul takes the Galatians back to the moment of their own baptism, in order to remind them of the true nature of that event. The baptismal

---

[79]Throughout the present volume I use the term "antinomy" in an idiosyncratic way, namely to render the numerous expressions by which the ancients referred (in many languages) to a pair of opposites that inheres in the *cosmos* — in Greek an *enantion* — an oppositional pair so fundamental to the cosmos, being one of its elements, as to make the cosmos what it is. The most obvious of the ancient examples is the list of oppositional pairs that Aristotle attributed to the Pythagoreans: Limit and Unlimited; Odd and Even; Unity and Plurality; Right and Left; Male and Female; and so on (*Metaphysics* 986a). For examples from Persia, Egypt, and Palestine, not least Isa 45:7, see the texts and works cited in Lloyd, *Polarity*; J. L. Martyn, "Apocalyptic Antinomies," 422 n12. Note especially Sir 33:15: "All the works of the Most High are in pairs, one the opposite of the other." For Paul, as for the Pythagoreans, an antinomy is more than an antithesis, for an antinomy lies at the foundation of the cosmos, whereas in common usage an antithesis is a form of rhetoric, a product of human thought (see Comments #8 and #9; and note the difference between my idiosyncratic use of the term "antinomy" and that of the rhetoricians such as Quintilian: Comment #35). Moreover, in Paul's view, as we will see, the antinomies of God's new creation have their origin in the apocalypse of Christ and of his Spirit. For this reason they are fundamentally different from Marcion's ontological antitheses (Introduction §15).

scene was highly dramatic. As persons who were acquainted with some form of the tradition of elemental, oppositional pairs, the Galatians heard in the baptizer's words a list of the oppositional elements that had ceased to exist. In that declaration they suffered *the loss of the cosmos,* as though a fissure had opened up under their feet, hurling them into an abyss with no dimensions.

Throughout his letter, moreover, Paul repeatedly reinforces this matter of loss of cosmos. Using Jewish terms because of the nature of the Teachers' message, Paul presents a universal picture. That is to say, finding the Law to be an enslaving power precisely in its opposition to the Not-Law, Paul denies the existence of numerous pairs of opposites that, in one form or another, are identified by all people as the beacons from which one gains one's bearings:

to sin	to observe the Law (2:17–19)
to be wrong	to be set right by observing the Law (2:16, 21; 3:12)
to be dead	to be made alive by the Law (3:21).[80]

Paul can therefore summarize his own letter by speaking of the crucifixion of the cosmos:

> . . . the cross of our Lord Jesus Christ, by which the cosmos has been crucified to me and I to the cosmos. For neither is circumcision anything nor is uncircumcision anything. What is something is the new creation (6:14–15).

In this way Paul refers to the cosmic event experienced by every member of the Galatian churches. They were all crucified with Christ. They all suffered the consequent loss of the world of religious differentiation. For crucifixion with Christ means the death of the cosmos of religion, the cosmos in which all human beings live. Swept away are the basic guidelines which — in one form or another — all people had formerly considered permanently dependable.

THE EMERGENCE OF NEW ANTINOMIES

With equal emphasis, however, Paul also says that in its death the cosmos has been replaced by the new creation. Here two major pictures make their appearance, and both involve the relationship between cosmos and sets of antinomies.

(1) *New unity.* Interpreting the baptismal formula cited above (3:28), Paul says that *polarity* in the cosmos has been replaced by *unity* in Christ. The old cosmos had pairs of opposites. The new creation, marked by anthropological unity in Christ, does not have pairs of opposites, for with the eclipse of Jew/Gentile, slave/free, and male/female, "all of you are *One* in Christ Jesus" (3:28b).

---

[80]The emphasis Paul places in Galatians on the termination of such elemental pairs of opposites reflects, of course, the polemical character of the letter. Paul is concerned, that is, with the Teachers' failure to announce the termination of these oppositional pairs, and with the resultant falsity of the Teachers' message. Indeed, the Teachers not only presuppose the antinomies Paul knows to be gone. They also explicate these antinomies and their cosmos by developing a full-blown Table of Opposites — in Greek *t'anantia* — which they claim to find by reading the Law (4:21–5:1; 5:16; Comment #45).

(2) *New pairs of opposites.* Reading elsewhere in Galatians, however, we see that, important as this anthropological pattern may be, it presents only part of the picture. At numerous junctures Paul says quite clearly that in the horrifying crucifixion of the cosmos, God is bringing to birth not only anthropological unity in Christ but also a new set of antinomies. Two examples can be seen without difficulty.

There is, first, the Spirit and the Flesh. Paul speaks of these two powers as one would speak of a cosmic pair of opposites (5:17; Comment #49). The Spirit and the Flesh are an oppositional pair that cause the world to be what it *now* actually is.

Second, Paul speaks several times of a new-creation antinomy made up of the death of Christ versus the Law. Since God has elected to make things right via the death of his Christ, rather than via the Law (2:21), there is now — emphatically for the Galatian situation — a specific antinomy between the cross and circumcision, between the rectifying death of Christ and all religion (e.g., 5:11; 6:12–14; cf. 4:8–11). And since the Law (*scil.* religion) is in fact impotent to curb the Flesh, it is crucial to see that the true and potent opposite to that monster is the Spirit, rather than the Law (Comment #49).

Beyond unity in Christ, then, one notes in Galatians the antinomies of the new creation (see Paul's Table of Opposites in Comments #45 and #46). Like the Old-Age antinomies, those of the new creation are cosmic in scope. They are also thoroughly apocalyptic, in the sense that they are being born in the apocalypse of Christ. Six motifs play their roles in Paul's vision of the new creation, as it dawns with its new and dynamic pairs of opposites.

THE DAWN OF THE NEW CREATION

(1) The Spirit and its opposite, the Flesh, are not timeless first principles, called into being by God at the beginning (contrast not only Sir 33:15 but also 1QS 3:13–4:26).

(2) This pair of opposites owes its birth to God's *new*-creative act. It is born of the new event, God's sending both his Son and the Spirit of his Son into the present evil age.

(3) The advent of the Son and of his Spirit is thus the cosmic, apocalyptic event. There was a "before," and there is now an "after." And it is at the point at which the "after" invades the "before" that the Spirit and the Flesh have become a dynamic pair of opposites. They form an apocalyptic antinomy characteristic of the dawn of God's new creation.

(4) This apocalyptic antinomy receives its dynamism both from the event that gave it its birth and from the warfare begun with that event (Comment #49).[81] As noted in Comment #3, the motif of warfare between pairs of opposites could remind one of the philosophy of Heraclitus ("War [between the opposites] is the father of all things;" Frag. 53) or, nearer to Paul, of the theology of Qumran, in

---

[81] It is worth noting that Widengren identifies as the two main motifs of apocalyptic thought (a) cosmic changes and catastrophes and (b) the war-like final struggle in the cosmos (*Ideen*, 150; cf. B. B. Hall, "Imagery").

which there is strife (*rîb*) between the two Spirits. But in both of these views the struggle is thought to inhere in the cosmos. Indeed, in the perspective of Qumran the warring antinomy of the Spirit of Truth versus the Spirit of False-hood, stemming as it does from the original creation, will find in the new creation not its birth, but rather its termination (1QS 4:16, 25). In Paul's apocalyptic the picture is quite different. The Spirit and the Flesh constitute an apocalyptic antinomy, in the sense that they are two opposed orbs of power, actively at war with one another *since* the advent of the Spirit. The territory in which human beings now live is a newly invaded space, and that means that its structures cannot remain unchanged (including the fundamental structure of argument; Comments #8 and #9).

(5) It follows that when Christians live as though the effective opposite of the Flesh were the Law, they abandon life in the creation that has now been made what it is by the advent of Christ and of his Spirit. It is they who are not living in the real world. For the true war of liberation has been initiated not at Sinai, but rather in God's apocalypse of the crucified one.

(6) All of the preceding motifs come together in the central question of the Galatian letter: What time is it? One hardly needs to point out that the matter of discerning the time lies at the heart of apocalyptic; and in none of his other letters does Paul address that issue in terms more clearly apocalyptic. What time is it? It is the time after the apocalypse of the faith of Christ (3:23–25), the time of things being set right by that faith, the time of the presence of the Spirit, and thus the time of the war of liberation commenced by the Spirit. In a word, it is the time of the dawn of the new creation with its new antinomies. The result is a holistic vision, in scope categorically cosmic and emphatically apocalyptic.

THE EMBODIMENT OF THE NEW CREATION

Even in the face of this vision one may ask whether the new creation has an embodiment. In the common sense of the expression, can Paul point to it? In effect, the apostle gives three mutually illuminating answers. The new creation is embodied in Christ, in the church, and thus in the Israel of God.

Christ. Paul connects the christological note of 6:14a with the cosmic, new-creational note of 6:14b and 15. Just as it is in the cross of Christ that God has accomplished the new creation, so there is a significant sense in which Christ *is* the new creation (see again the word "seed" in 3:16 and the term "One" in 3:28, and cf. the expression "the one man, Jesus Christ" in Rom 5:17; cf. further 1 Cor 15:22, 45). Sent by God, Christ is the descendant whom God promised long ago to Abraham (3:16), the one who is, as it were, the seed of the new creation.

The Church. At numerous junctures Paul has spoken of the church's incorporation in this new-creation Christ. It is by being Christ's — by being baptized into him, by putting him on as though he were their clothes (3:27), by having his Spirit in their hearts (4:6), by having him determine the form of their communal life (4:19), by belonging utterly to him, the cosmocrator of the new creation (5:24) — that the Galatians (with all other members of God's church; 1:13) are Abraham's corporate seed and God's new creation in Christ (3:29).

The Israel of God. Finally, as Paul says at the close of 6:16, the new creation is also the Israel of God, the people (the *qāhal*) that God is now calling into existence in Christ, rather than in the Law (Comment #52). However furious he may be with the Teachers, Paul will not allow their view of the nomistic people of God to separate him either from the God of Israel or from Israel itself. God's new creation is not a romantic haven in which the individual can hug himself to sleep.[82] It is embodied in those who, re-created by Christ's love, serve one another in the new community of mutual concern (5:13), God's Israel.

COMMENT #52
THE ISRAEL OF GOD

At the end of the blessing in 6:16 Paul writes the apparently simple phrase *kai epi ton Israel tou theou*, intending to say either of two things. If he uses the word *kai* to mean "and," then he intends to pronounce his blessing both upon those who follow the standard of the new creation *and* upon a second group, "the Israel of God."[83] If, however, he uses this little word to mean "that is to say," then he intends to identify those who follow that standard *as* "the Israel of God." In the Note on 6:16 we have seen that it is unwise to choose either of these readings until we have addressed two other matters.

Israel. Why does Paul refer to Israel at all? One can answer that he merely follows tradition in doing so (see the blessing traditions of Ps 125:5 etc., cited in the Note on 6:16). There are good reasons to think, however, that, in addition to drawing on those traditions, Paul writes in a way that reflects references the Teachers are making to God's blessing of Israel.

We have already seen grounds for supposing that the Teachers are speaking at length about the "seed of Abraham," employing that expression to refer to the corporate people of God (Comment #33). We have also noted that the Teachers are inviting the Gentile Galatians to participate in the "*blessing* of Abraham," entering the company of those who are Abraham's seed via observance of the Law (see the Note on 3:14 and Comment #33). In speaking of the desirability of participating in God's blessing of Abraham, the Teachers may be tying that blessing not only to the expression "seed of Abraham" but also to the word "*Israel*," for Abraham is the father of Israel. Specifically, in their evangelistic invitation to the Gentile Galatians, the Teachers may very well be employing in their liturgy one of the traditional Israel blessings, sharpening the Galatians' desire for inclusion in God's people by invoking God's peace and mercy explicitly "upon Israel."

The Israel of God. On this reading, why does Paul coin his own expression, invoking peace and mercy upon "the Israel *of God*," a locution peculiar to this passage?[84] The numerous and extensive discussions of this question often reflect

---

[82] Cf. J. L. Martyn, *Issues,* 47–69.

[83] So Billerbeck 3.578.

[84] That the expression is Paul's coinage is strongly suggested by two other passages. In 1 Cor 10:18 Paul is surely responsible for the expression *ho Israel kata sarka* ("that part of Israel that had its identity as a result of the flesh"), by which he refers to ancient Israel, insofar as it oriented itself to idols rather than to God (Schrage, "Israel," 150). It is also Paul who says in Rom 9:6, *ou pantes hoi ex Israel houtoi Israel; oud' hoti eisin sperma*

the assumption that it is to be answered on the basis of data in several of Paul's letters, including especially Romans 9–11.[85] But we are again at a juncture at which it may be helpful to restrict our view for a moment to the Galatians' interpretation of Paul's text. Those original interpreters do not know that Paul will later refer to Israel and to Israelites in 1 Cor 10:18 ("Israel that had its identity as a result of the flesh"), in 2 Cor 3:7, 13 ("the people of Israel"), and in Romans 9–11 ("Israel" eleven times; "Israelite" twice). They do know, however, that in their own letter Paul has several times taken serious account of the Teachers' discourses, by referring in his own way to God's people as the blessed descendants of Abraham (3:6–29; 4:21–5:1). The Galatians will have sensed, then, that, with the locution "the Israel of God," Paul ends his letter by posing, in effect, two closely related questions that he considers crucial in light of the Teachers' labors: the question of God's identity and the question of the identity of Israel.[86]

Paul can consider the Galatians competent to answer these questions on the basis of his earlier references to God's promissory blessing of Abraham and his seed, notably the references in 3:15–29. For Paul has already shown that the identity of God and the identity of Abraham's descendants are issues of great consequence. He has also shown that everything depends on the order in which these two issues are approached. That is to say, the identity of Israel is determined by the identity of God. Thus, pronouncing the blessing of 6:16 on the Israel *of God*, Paul says in effect:

As the Teachers are correctly assuring you, the future of Israel includes the certainty of God's blessing. Peace and mercy will be upon them. But Israel is the Israel *of God*, and, as we have seen, God's identity is shown in the fact that, through the voice of scripture, he proclaimed the gospel ahead of time to Abraham, speaking his blessing to Abraham "and to Abraham's seed." I have already reminded you of the precise wording of the text from which we know of this promissory blessing. That text does not say that God spoke his promise to Abraham "and to Abraham's seeds," as though it were speaking about many people. On the contrary, speaking about one, the text reads, "and to your seed," and that singular seed of Abraham is Christ (3:16). Regarding God's identity, it follows that God is the promising God who sent his Son, precisely as the singular seed of Abraham. Regarding Israel's identity, it follows that Israel is the plural seed that God is now calling into existence by incorporating them into that singular seed (3:29). Therefore, because Israel is God's *new* creation in Christ, let the blessing of peace and mercy be upon this Israel of God, precisely as the company of those who will continue to live by the standard of

---

Abraam, pantes tekna, "not all who are from Israel are Israel; neither simply because they are descendants of Abraham are they all his children." Gal 6:16, 1 Cor 10:18, and Rom 9:6 are not to be put on a single level, but they do show Paul's creativity at coining arresting — and differentiating — expressions having to do with Israel.

[85] See, for example, von der Osten-Sacken, *Dialogue*, 146.

[86] Regarding the closely related matter of the Galatians' identity, see Literary Structure and Synopsis for both 3:6–4:7 and 4:21–5:1.

God's new creation, in which there *is* neither circumcision nor uncircumcision, neither Jew nor Gentile (3:28).

By attending to the argument of 3:15–29, then, we have before us, in the company of the Galatians, answers to all three of the questions posed by the blessing of 6:16. (1) Using the word *kai* to mean "that is to say," Paul equates the Israel of God with those who will follow the standard of God's *new* creation. (2) He refers to Israel because the Teachers are themselves doing that. (3) And he adds the phrase "of God" in order to correct the Teachers' references.

Since the Teachers are identifying Israel on the basis of Law observance, Paul will identify Israel on the basis of God, intending thereby to remind the Galatians that God has identified himself by his promise rather than by the Sinaitic Law (cf. 2:19, Comment #48, and Rom 4:11–17). Putting 3:15–29 together with 6:15–16, then, one can see Paul's intention. He is saying in effect that it is in the promise, rather than in the Law, that God has invested both the power to bring about the *new* creation and the power to provide the identity of his people Israel, the church. The God of Israel is first of all the God of Christ (3:16, 29), and it follows, for the author of Galatians, that the Israel of God is the people whom God is calling into existence in Christ (1:6, 13), the community of those who know themselves to be, in Christ, former Jews and former Gentiles.[87]

Unlike the Galatians, we know a number of Paul's other letters, and from them we can see that the apostle was profoundly hesitant to separate the name "Israel" from those who bore that name because of their religious and ethnic identity.[88] It would be a great mistake to attribute to Paul the simplistic view that the church has replaced the Jewish people as God's own.[89] When he penned Gal 6:16, he was not thinking of the Jewish people. And he was certainly not intending to distinguish a true Israel from a false one, in the sense that the church now supplanted the synagogue.[90] On the contrary, his attention was focused quite tightly on developments *within* the church. He was thinking, in all probability, of the way in which the Teachers were using the name "Israel" in their attempt to compel his Gentile churches in Galatia to commence observance of the Law. Given that theologically odious development, Paul could not preach the truth of the gospel without employing extreme formulations. Two of those extreme formulations are *Gal 3:15–29*—the denial of a promissory/ethnic line between

---

[87] The order of Paul's words in the last two phrases — *eirēnē ep' autous kai eleos kai epi ton Israel tou theou* — may seem a bit strange, but the import of the final *kai* is not set by that of the penultimate one. The syntax places in parallel the two phrases governed by the preposition *epi*. See Dahl, "Name," and Luz, "Geschichtsverständnis." That Paul's reference is to what he earlier called "the church of God" (1:13) has been effectively argued by D. Zeller, "Skandal," 265. See also Schrage, "Anstoss."

[88] So correctly Gutbrod, "*Israel*," 388. Paul employs the word "Israel" fifteen times and the word "Israelite" twice. In only one of seventeen instances, then — Gal 6:16 — does he clearly use that name to speak of the church.

[89] See especially Davies, "People"; Grässer, *Bund*, 19 n53.

[90] By speaking in 1 Cor 10:18 of an ancient Israel "that had its identity as a result of the flesh" (= the Israel that worshiped idols), Paul implied an Israel according to the Spirit (so 1 Cor 10:2–4) *in the same time frame*. See Schrage, "Israel."

Abraham and Christ (contrast Rom 1:3a) — and *Gal 6:15–16* — the announcement of a totally *new* creation in which all religious distinctions are obliterated, coupled with the pronouncement of a blessing on the church as the Israel *of God*. Paul thoroughly intended these formulations; but he intended them as a proclamation of the gospel *to the Galatians*.

On the one hand, then, addressed to former Gentiles who are tempted to commence Law observance in order to gain entrance into God's people, Galatians is the earliest document in which a Christian author identifies the church itself as Israel.[91] On the other hand, Romans is written against a different horizon. It is the letter in which Paul considers the issue of God's faithfulness to those who are the apostle's brothers and sisters by virtue of the flesh. It is no surprise, then, to see that Romans is punctuated — in chapters 9–11 — with numerous references to Israel.[92] Moreover, Paul composes the discourse of Romans 9–11 in light of two developments subsequent to his writing Galatians. First, by the time Paul writes Romans, he has reason to think that the Teachers have shared at least elements of his Galatian letter with their colleagues in the Jerusalem church, thus loosing that highly affective epistle from the precise setting to which it was directed (Introduction §13). Second, Paul knows that, when he travels to Jerusalem with his collection of funds, he will have to interpret for the Jerusalem church the way in which he has used the name "Israel" in writing to the Galatians (Rom 15:25–33). In Romans 9–11 Paul does not rescind the blessing of Gal 6:16, but he does interpret it in a new way.[93]

[91] *Pace* Richardson, *Israel.*
[92] In Rom 9:3 Paul begins by expressing his anguish concerning *tôn adelphôn mou tôn suggenôn mou kata sarka,* "my brothers and sisters, my kinsmen by virtue of the flesh."
[93] See Walter, "Römer 9–11"; Meyer, "Romans"; J. L. Martyn, *Issues,* 37–45; Meeks, "Trusting"; Introduction §13.

GALATIANS
(New Revised Standard Version)

◆

THE LETTER OF PAUL TO THE GALATIANS

1 Paul an apostle — sent neither by human commission nor from human authorities, but through Jesus Christ and God the Father, who raised him from the dead — 2and all the members of God's family*a* who are with me,

To the churches of Galatia:

3 Grace to you and peace from God our Father and the Lord Jesus Christ, 4who gave himself for our sins to set us free from the present evil age, according to the will of our God and Father, 5to whom be the glory forever and ever. Amen.

6 I am astonished that you are so quickly deserting the one who called you in the grace of Christ and are turning to a different gospel — 7not that there is another gospel, but there are some who are confusing you and want to pervert the gospel of Christ. 8But even if we or an angel*b* from heaven should proclaim to you a gospel contrary to what we proclaimed to you, let that one be accursed! 9As we have said before, so now I repeat, if anyone proclaims to you a gospel contrary to what you received, let that one be accursed!

10 Am I now seeking human approval, or God's approval? Or am I trying to please people? If I were still pleasing people, I would not be a servant*c* of Christ.

11 For I want you to know, brothers and sisters,*d* that the gospel that was proclaimed by me is not of human origin; 12for I did not receive it from a human source, nor was I taught it, but I received it through a revelation of Jesus Christ.

13 You have heard, no doubt, of my earlier life in Judaism. I was violently persecuting the church of God and was trying to destroy it. 14I advanced in Judaism beyond many among my people of the same age, for I was far more zealous for the traditions of my ancestors. 15But when God, who had set me apart before I was born and called me through his grace, was pleased 16to reveal his Son to me,*e* so that I might proclaim him among the Gentiles, I did not confer with any human being, 17nor did I go up to Jerusalem to those who were already apostles

a Gk *all the brothers*   *b* Or *a messenger*   *c* Gk *slave*   *d* Gk *brothers*   *e* Gk *in me*

before me, but I went away at once into Arabia, and afterwards I returned to Damascus.

18 Then after three years I did go up to Jerusalem to visit Cephas and stayed with him fifteen days; [19]but I did not see any other apostle except James the Lord's brother. [20]In what I am writing to you, before God, I do not lie! [21]Then I went into the regions of Syria and Cilicia, [22]and I was still unknown by sight to the churches of Judea that are in Christ; [23]they only heard it said, "The one who formerly was persecuting us is now proclaiming the faith he once tried to destroy." [24]And they glorified God because of me.

2 Then after fourteen years I went up again to Jerusalem with Barnabas, taking Titus along with me. [2]I went up in response to a revelation. Then I laid before them (though only in a private meeting with the acknowledged leaders) the gospel that I proclaim among the Gentiles, in order to make sure that I was not running, or had not run, in vain. [3]But even Titus, who was with me, was not compelled to be circumcised, though he was a Greek. [4]But because of false believers[f] secretly brought in, who slipped in to spy on the freedom we have in Christ Jesus, so that they might enslave us — [5]we did not submit to them even for a moment, so that the truth of the gospel might always remain with you. [6]And from those who were supposed to be acknowledged leaders (what they actually were makes no difference to me; God shows no partiality) — those leaders contributed nothing to me. [7]On the contrary, when they saw that I had been entrusted with the gospel for the uncircumcised, just as Peter had been entrusted with the gospel for the circumcised [8](for he who worked through Peter making him an apostle to the circumcised also worked through me in sending me to the Gentiles), [9]and when James and Cephas and John, who were acknowledged pillars, recognized the grace that had been given to me, they gave to Barnabas and me the right hand of fellowship, agreeing that we should go to the Gentiles and they to the circumcised. [10]They asked only one thing, that we remember the poor, which was actually what I was[g] eager to do.

11 But when Cephas came to Antioch, I opposed him to his face, because he stood self-condemned; [12]for until certain people came from James, he used to eat with the Gentiles. But after they came, he drew back and kept himself separate for fear of the circumcision faction. [13]And the other Jews joined him in this hypocrisy, so that even Barnabas was led astray by their hypocrisy. [14]But when I saw that they were not acting consistently with the truth of the gospel, I said to Cephas before them all, "If you, though a Jew, live like a Gentile and not like a Jew, how can you compel the Gentiles to live like Jews?"[h]

15 We ourselves are Jews by birth and not Gentile sinners; [16]yet we know that a person is justified[i] not by the works of the law but through faith in Jesus Christ.[j] And we have come to believe in Christ Jesus, so that we might be justified by faith in Christ,[k] and not by doing the works of the law, because no one will be

---

f Gk *false brothers*   g Or *had been*
extends into the following paragraph
where   j Or *the faith of Jesus Christ*

h Some interpreters hold that the quotation
i Or *reckoned as righteous;* and so else-
k Or *the faith of Christ*

justified by the works of the law. [17]But if, in our effort to be justified in Christ, we ourselves have been found to be sinners, is Christ then a servant of sin? Certainly not! [18]But if I build up again the very things that I once tore down, then I demonstrate that I am a transgressor. [19]For through the law I died to the law, so that I might live to God. I have been crucified with Christ; [20]and it is no longer I who live, but it is Christ who lives in me. And the life I now live in the flesh I live by faith in the Son of God,[l] who loved me and gave himself for me. [21]I do not nullify the grace of God; for if justification[m] comes through the law, then Christ died for nothing.

3 You foolish Galatians! Who has bewitched you? It was before your eyes that Jesus Christ was publicly exhibited as crucified! [2]The only thing I want to learn from you is this: Did you receive the Spirit by doing the works of the law or by believing what you heard? [3]Are you so foolish? Having started with the Spirit, are you now ending with the flesh? [4]Did you experience so much for nothing? — if it really was for nothing. [5]Well then, does God[n] supply you with the Spirit and work miracles among you by your doing the works of the law, or by your believing what you heard?

6 Just as Abraham "believed God, and it was reckoned to him as righteousness," [7]so, you see, those who believe are the descendants of Abraham. [8]And the scripture, foreseeing that God would justify the Gentiles by faith, declared the gospel beforehand to Abraham, saying, "All the Gentiles shall be blessed in you." [9]For this reason, those who believe are blessed with Abraham who believed.

10 For all who rely on the works of the law are under a curse; for it is written, "Cursed is everyone who does not observe and obey all the things written in the book of the law." [11]Now it is evident that no one is justified before God by the law; for "The one who is righteous will live by faith."[o] [12]But the law does not rest on faith; on the contrary, "Whoever does the works of the law[p] will live by them." [13]Christ redeemed us from the curse of the law by becoming a curse for us — for it is written, "Cursed is everyone who hangs on a tree" — [14]in order that in Christ Jesus the blessing of Abraham might come to the Gentiles, so that we might receive the promise of the Spirit through faith.

15 Brothers and sisters,[q] I give an example from daily life: once a person's will[r] has been ratified, no one adds to it or annuls it. [16]Now the promises were made to Abraham and to his offspring;[s] it does not say, "And to offsprings,"[t] as of many; but it says, "And to your offsprings,"[s] that is, to one person, who is Christ. [17]My point is this: the law, which came four hundred thirty years later, does not annul a covenant previously ratified by God, so as to nullify the promise. [18]For if the inheritance comes from the law, it no longer comes from the promise; but God granted it to Abraham through the promise.

19 Why then the law? It was added because of transgressions, until the offspring[s] would come to whom the promise had been made; and it was ordained

---

l Or *by the faith of the Son of God*   *m* Or *righteousness*   *n* Gk *he*   *o* Or *The one who is righteous through faith will live*   *p* Gk *does them*   *q* Gk *Brothers*
r Or *covenant* (as in verse 17)   *s* Gk *seed*   *t* Gk *seeds*

through angels by a mediator. [20]Now a mediator involves more than one party; but God is one.

21 Is the law then opposed to the promises of God? Certainly not! For if a law had been given that could make alive, then righteousness would indeed come through the law. [22]But the scripture has imprisoned all things under the power of sin, so that what was promised through faith in Jesus Christ[u] might be given to those who believe.

23 Now before faith came, we were imprisoned and guarded under the law until faith would be revealed. [24]Therefore the law was our disciplinarian until Christ came, so that we might be justified by faith. [25]But now that faith has come, we are no longer subject to a disciplinarian, [26]for in Christ Jesus you are all children of God through faith. [27]As many of you as were baptized into Christ have clothed yourselves with Christ. [28]There is no longer Jew or Greek, there is no longer slave or free, there is no longer male and female; for all of you are one in Christ Jesus. [29]And if you belong to Christ, then you are Abraham's offspring,[s] heirs according to the promise.

4 My point is this: heirs, as long as they are minors, are no better than slaves, though they are the owners of all the property; [2]but they remain under guardians and trustees until the date set by the father. [3]So with us; while we were minors, we were enslaved to the elemental spirits[v] of the world. [4]But when the fullness of time had come, God sent his Son, born of a woman, born under the law, [5]in order to redeem those who were under the law, so that we might receive adoption as children. [6]And because you are children, God has sent the Spirit of his Son into our[w] hearts, crying, "Abba![x] Father!" [7]So you are no longer a slave but a child, and if a child then also an heir, through God.[y]

8 Formerly, when you did not know God, you were enslaved to beings that by nature are not gods. [9]Now, however, that you have come to know God, or rather to be known by God, how can you turn back again to the weak and beggarly elemental spirits?[z] How can you want to be enslaved to them again? [10]You are observing special days, and months, and seasons, and years. [11]I am afraid that my work for you may have been wasted.

12 Friends,[a] I beg you, become as I am, for I also have become as you are. You have done me no wrong. [13]You know that it was because of a physical infirmity that I first announced the gospel to you; [14]though my condition put you to the test, you did not scorn or despise me, but welcomed me as an angel of God, as Christ Jesus. [15]What has become of the good will you felt? For I testify that, had it been possible, you would have torn out your eyes and given them to me. [16]Have I now become your enemy by telling you the truth? [17]They make much of you, but for no good purpose; they want to exclude you, so that you may make much of them. [18]It is good to be made much of for a good purpose at all times,

s Gk seed   u Or through the faith of Jesus Christ   v Or the rudiments   w Other ancient authorities read your   x Aramaic for Father   y Other ancient authorities read an heir of God through Christ   z Or beggarly rudiments   a Gk Brothers

and not only when I am present with you. ¹⁹My little children, for whom I am again in the pain of childbirth until Christ is formed in you, ²⁰I wish I were present with you now and could change my tone, for I am perplexed about you.

21 Tell me, you who desire to be subject to the law, will you not listen to the law? ²²For it is written that Abraham had two sons, one by a slave woman and the other by a free woman. ²³One, the child of the slave, was born according to the flesh; the other, the child of the free woman, was born through the promise. ²⁴Now this is an allegory: these women are two covenants. One woman, in fact, is Hagar, from Mount Sinai, bearing children for slavery. ²⁵Now Hagar is Mount Sinai in Arabia*b* and corresponds to the present Jerusalem, for she is in slavery with her children. ²⁶But the other woman corresponds to the Jerusalem above; she is free, and she is our mother. ²⁷For it is written,

"Rejoice, you childless one, you who bear no children,
   burst into song and shout, you who endure no birthpangs;
for the children of the desolate woman are more numerous
   than the children of the one who is married."

²⁸Now you,*c* my friends,*d* are children of the promise, like Isaac. ²⁹But just as at that time the child who was born according to the flesh persecuted the child who was born according to the Spirit, so it is now also. ³⁰But what does the scripture say? "Drive out the slave and her child; for the child of the slave will not share the inheritance with the child of the free woman." ³¹So then, friends,*d* we are 5 children, not of the slave but of the freewoman. ¹For freedom Christ has set us free. Stand firm, therefore, and do not submit again to a yoke of slavery.

2 Listen! I, Paul, am telling you that if you let yourselves be circumcised, Christ will be of no benefit to you. ³Once again I testify to every man who lets himself be circumcised that he is obliged to obey the entire law. ⁴You who want to be justified by the law have cut yourselves off from Christ; you have fallen away from grace. ⁵For through the Spirit, by faith, we eagerly wait for the hope of righteousness. ⁶For in Christ Jesus neither circumcision nor uncircumcision counts for anything; the only thing that counts is faith working*e* through love.

7 You were running well; who prevented you from obeying the truth? ⁸Such persuasion does not come from the one who calls you. ⁹A little yeast leavens the whole batch of dough. ¹⁰I am confident about you in the Lord that you will not think otherwise. But whoever it is that is confusing you will pay the penalty. ¹¹But my friends,*f* why am I still being persecuted if I am still preaching circumcision? In that case the offense of the cross has been removed. ¹²I wish those who unsettle you would castrate themselves!

13 For you were called to freedom, brothers and sisters;*f* only do not use your freedom as an opportunity for self-indulgence,*g* but through love become slaves to one another. ¹⁴For the whole law is summed up in a single commandment,

b Other ancient authorities read *For Sinai is a mountain in Arabia*   *c* Other ancient authorities read *we*   *d* Gk *brothers*   *e* Or *made effective*   *f* Gk *brothers*
g Gk *the flesh*

"You shall love your neighbor as yourself." [15]If, however, you bite and devour one another, take care that you are not consumed by one another.

16 Live by the Spirit, I say, and do not gratify the desires of the flesh. [17]For what the flesh desires is opposed to the Spirit, and what the Spirit desires is opposed to the flesh; for these are opposed to each other, to prevent you from doing what you want. [18]But if you are led by the Spirit, you are not subject to the law. [19]Now the works of the flesh are obvious: fornication, impurity, licentiousness, [20]idolatry, sorcery, enmities, strife, jealousy, anger, quarrels, dissensions, factions, [21]envy,[h] drunkenness, carousing, and things like these. I am warning you, as I warned you before: those who do such things will not inherit the kingdom of God.

22 By contrast, the fruit of the Spirit is love, joy, peace, patience, kindness, generosity, faithfulness, [23]gentleness, and self-control. There is no law against such things. [24]And those who belong to Christ Jesus have crucified the flesh with its passions and desires. [25]If we live by the Spirit, let us also be guided by the Spirit. [26]Let us not become conceited, competing against one another, envying one another.

6 My friends,[i] if anyone is detected in a transgression, you who have received the Spirit should restore such a one in a spirit of gentleness. Take care that you yourselves are not tempted. [2]Bear one another's burdens, and in this way you will fulfill[j] the law of Christ. [3]For if those who are nothing think they are something, they deceive themselves. [4]All must test their own work; then that work, rather than their neighbor's work, will become a cause for pride. [5]For all must carry their own loads.

6 Those who are taught the word must share in all good things with their teacher.

7 Do not be deceived; God is not mocked, for you reap whatever you sow. [8]If you sow to your own flesh, you will reap corruption from the flesh; but if you sow to the Spirit, you will reap eternal life from the Spirit. [9]So let us not grow weary in doing what is right, for we will reap at harvest-time, if we do not give up. [10]So then, whenever we have an opportunity, let us work for the good of all, and especially for those of the family of faith.

11 See what large letters I make when I am writing in my own hand! [12]It is those who want to make a good showing in the flesh that try to compel you to be circumcised—only that they may not be persecuted for the cross of Christ. [13]Even the circumcised do not themselves obey the law, but they want you to be circumcised so that they may boast about your flesh. [14]May I never boast of anything except the cross of our Lord Jesus Christ, by which[k] the world has been crucified to me, and I to the world. [15]For[l] neither circumcision nor uncircumci-

---

h Other ancient authorities add *murder*   i Gk *Brothers*   j Other ancient authorities read *in this way fulfill*   k Or *through whom*   l Other ancient authorities add *in Christ Jesus*

sion is anything; but a new creation is everything! [16]As for those who will follow this rule — peace be upon them, and mercy, and upon the Israel of God.

17 From now on, let no one make trouble for me; for I carry the marks of Jesus branded on my body.

18 May the grace of our Lord Jesus Christ be with your spirit, brothers and sisters.[m] Amen.

m Gk *brothers*

GLOSSARY

◆

Amidah: the major prayer at synagogue services, consisting of eighteen or nineteen benedictions. See Note on Galatians 1:1.

anacoluthon: a sentence that lacks the syntactical completion required by its beginning.

antinomy/antithesis: an antinomy is a pair of opposites discovered by human beings to be so fundamental to the cosmos as to constitute one of its elements. An antithesis consists of two contradictory statements or propositions formulated by a human being. See Comment #51.

cosmological apocalyptic eschatology: a specific understanding of what is wrong, and a view of the future: Anti-God powers have managed to commence their own rule over the world, leading human beings into idolatry and thus into slavery, producing a wrong situation that was not intended by God and that will not be long tolerated by him. For in his own time, God will inaugurate a victorious and liberating apocalyptic war against these evil powers, delivering his elect from their grasp and thus making right that which has gone wrong because of the powers' malignant machinations. This kind of apocalyptic eschatology is fundamental to Paul's Galatian letter. See de Boer, "Apocalyptic Eschatology," and Comment #3.

covenantal nomism: an expression coined by E. P. Sanders to refer to the symbiosis that consists of God's covenant and God's Law. See Comment #37.

Diaspora: the Jewish communities scattered throughout many parts of the world outside Palestine, but not evident in ethnic Galatia. See Introduction §3.

enthusiastic: emphasizing the present, already accomplished dimension of God's redemptive act in Christ (German: *schwärmerisch*).

forensic apocalyptic eschatology: a specific understanding of what is wrong, and a view of the future: Things have gone wrong because human beings have willfully rejected God, thereby bringing about death and the corruption and perversion of the world. Given this self-caused plight, God has graciously provided the cursing and blessing Law as the remedy, thus placing before human beings the Two Ways, the way of death and the way of life. Human beings are individually accountable before the bar of the Judge. But, by one's own decision, one can accept God's Law, repent of one's sins, receive nomistic forgiveness, and be assured of eternal life. For at the last judgment, the deserved sentence of death will be reversed for those who choose the path of Law observance, whereas that sentence will be permanently confirmed for those who do not. This kind of apocalyptic eschatology — focused on the religious doctrine of the Two Ways — is fundamental to the Teachers' message. See de Boer, "Apocalyptic Eschatology."

Impulsive Desire of the Flesh: For the Teachers, as for other Christian Jews, the Flesh is the tendency of the human being to rebel against God. For Paul it is one of the cosmic powers arrayed against God. See Comment #49.

Jewish-Christian and Christian-Jewish: adjectives referring to churches that remained to a significant degree happily linked to Jewish legal traditions. In the hyphenated expression (whether adjectival or nominal) the second term is the dominant one. Churches, for example, that were essentially Jewish sects would be groups of Christian Jews, rather than groups of Jewish Christians. See Comment #6.

midrash: an interpretation of scripture.

nomistic: legal in the sense of being derived from the Law of Sinai.

parenesis: "admonition," traditional exhortation designed to cultivate religious and moral life. Common in writings characterized by forensic apocalyptic eschatology.

religion: the various communal, cultic means — always involving the distinction of sacred from profane — by which human beings seek to know and to be happily related to the gods or God. Religion is thus a human enterprise that Paul sharply distinguishes from God's apocalyptic act in Christ.

Shema: Deuteronomy 6:4–9, the paragraph accenting the oneness of God, and beginning "Hear, O Israel: The Lord our God, the Lord is one."

targum: a translation of Hebrew scripture into Aramaic.

the Teachers: the Christian-Jewish evangelists who came into Paul's Galatian churches after his departure. See Introduction §6; Comments #6 and #33.

Two Ways: Various strands of Jewish and Jewish-Christian thought in the first century preserved and interpreted the ancient portrait of God's placing before Israel "the Way of life and the Way of death." To obey God's commandments is to live; to disobey them is to die (Jer 21:8; cf. Deut 27:12–13; Sir 2:12; 15:16; Matt 7:13–14; *m.* '*Abot* 2:1; Jas 2:8–13). Within this frame of reference, the Teachers used the terms "blessing" and "curse" to name the two actions of God they considered to be dependent on the path chosen by the Gentiles to whom they brought their message. Cf. "forensic apocalyptic theology" above.

INDEX OF BIBLICAL
AND OTHER
ANCIENT REFERENCES

◆

PSEUDEPIGRAPHA OF THE OLD TESTAMENT

PHILO AND JOSEPHUS

INDEX OF MAJOR SUBJECTS

◆

INDEX OF COMMENTATORS
AND MODERN AUTHORS

◆

605